Teaching Students with Learning and Behavior Problems

THIRD EDITION

W9-AGA-421

Diane Pedrotty Rivera
University of Texas at Austin

Deborah Deutsch Smith
University of New Mexico

ALLYN AND BACON

Boston • London • Toronto • Sydney • Tokyo • Singapore

Dedicated to Ryan Rivera and to the memory of Paul C. Pedrotty, Sr.;
and to Marion Meyer, whose continuing support is always appreciated

Senior Editor: Ray Short
Editorial Assistant: Christine Svitila
Marketing Manager: Kris Farnsworth
Production Administrator: Elaine Ober
Editorial-Production Service: Trinity Publishers Services
Cover Administrator: Linda Knowles
Composition Buyer: Linda Cox
Manufacturing Buyer: Megan Cochran

Copyright © 1997, 1989, 1981 by Allyn & Bacon
A Viacom Company
160 Gould Street
Needham Heights, Mass. 02194

Internet: www.abacon.com
America Online: keyword: College Online

Library of Congress Cataloging-in-Publication Data

Rivera, Diane Pedrotty.
    Teaching students with learning and behavior problems / Diane
Pedrotty Rivera, Deborah Deutsch Smith. — 3rd ed.
        p.   cm.
    2nd ed. names Deborah Deutsch Smith as sole author.
    Includes bibliographical references and indexes.
    ISBN 0-205-16448-X (pbk.)
        1. Learning disabled children—Education—United States.
    2. Special education—United States.   I. Smith, Deborah Deutsch.
    II. Title.
    LC4705.S63   1997
    371.9—dc20   96-26089
                                                         CIP

Printed in the United States of America

10   9   8   7   6   5   4   3   02   01   00

Photo Credits: Will Faller, pp. 22, 49, 73, 93 (middle, bottom), 115, 157, 220, 242, 310,
393, 414; Stephen Marks, p. 349; Jim Pickerell, pp. 1, 268; Brian Smith, pp. 93 (top), 188.

Contents

Preface

This is the third edition of a textbook that is intended to instruct practitioners about how to teach students with learning and behavior problems. Since the last edition of this book, the amount of research on better practices for instructing students with special needs has been staggering. We definitely know more today about promoting academic, social, and behavioral success in students with special needs.

The field of special education has made remarkable progress over the years in every way. Special education curricular options are extensive and diverse. More instructional methods, procedures, and interventions have been developed and verified through research. Teachers have improved ways to sequence instruction. Technology has emerged as an important component of instruction for all students, and collaborative partnerships between professionals and families have been strengthened. Each of these developments allows students' abilities and learning styles to be matched better with instructional programs.

Understanding one's philosophy about education is an important first step in teaching. Teachers must assess what instructional preferences they bring to the classroom (as a result of their own schooling experiences and preservice training), what they view education's role to be, how they think discipline should be established in the classroom, and how they feel about working with other professionals and families. It is also important for teachers to evaluate their personal attitudes, prejudices, and values about people and society. Thus, one of the first tasks of "teacher preparation" is self-reflection and values clarification. This is a useful exercise because teachers' attitudes, prejudices, and values often influence the way they interact with children and with the school community.

Purpose and Audience

The purpose of this textbook is to present information about the best practices in special education curriculum and instruction. We hope that this book will help teachers find their work more exciting and successful, and that students with learning and behavior difficulties will profit more from school. This book is intended for undergraduate students who are taking their first teacher preparation instructional methodology course and for graduate students who are returning to higher education to expand their repertoire of effective instructional and curricular options. The book focuses on school-age students who have mild to moderate learning and behavior problems; certainly, many of the interventions could also be applied to youngsters with severe learning difficulties.

New Features

We have incorporated several new features into this text. In a few chapters, "Scenarios" illustrate the application of interventions. "Spotlight on Diversity" offers suggestions for teaching youngsters with special needs who are from culturally and linguistically diverse backgrounds. "Tips for Teachers" provides suggestions and guidelines for applying some of the interventions discussed in the chapters. "Adapting Instruction in the General Education Setting" offers ideas for adapting instructional techniques to youngsters with special needs who receive some or most of their education in the general classroom. "Focus on Technology" provides suggestions for infusing instructional and assistive technology into educational settings. Instructional technology can be used to supplement teaching, and assistive technology can help students with special needs access the curriculum and instruction more equitably. Finally, key terms are boldfaced throughout the book. Definitions of these terms are in the Glossary.

New Content

We have also added new content in this edition. The reader will find "Objectives," "Making Connections," and "As you read" in each chapter. The "Objectives" are intended to help the reader master the content of each chapter; the reader should be sure to review the "Objectives" before moving to the next chapter. "Making Connections" reviews previous content that relates to the new content that the reader will be learning. The review can make the new content more relevant to the reader. "As you read" boxes are located before each major section in a chapter. The information taps lower- and higher-order thinking with activities to apply the content that will be covered.

Three new chapters have been added to this edition to reflect updated research on teaching and learning. Collaborative Partnerships (chapter 2), Designing Instruction (chapter 4), and Implementing Instruction (chapter 5) present new content about the instructional process.

The remaining chapters have been updated to include the most current research-based approaches to teaching students with learning and behavior problems. For example, chapter 1 contains an expanded section on effective teaching characteristics. The Individualized Education Program process (chapter 3) reflects best practice in identifying students who are in need of special education services. Alternative assessment techniques are discussed more fully in chapter 6.

Textbook Organization

The textbook has three parts. Part I introduces the reader to the fundamentals of teaching. It provides information about common characteristics of learners with special needs and lists skills that teachers should possess. Part I also covers the development of collaborative partnerships with other professionals, paraprofessionals, and families, along with techniques to foster successful collaborative endeavors. We discuss the process of developing Individualized Education Programs in detail, and explore the three phases of teaching (Designing, Implementing, and Evaluating Instruction) thoroughly.

Part II presents the newest information about social and behavioral instruction. In the beginning, there is a comprehensive section explaining techniques for managing disruptive behavior in a variety of settings. Next, we discuss techniques for teaching students a variety of social skills.

In Part III, we pay specific attention to improving academic skills. We cover reading, mathematics, and written communication in depth, presenting many instructional techniques in a practical manner. These methods have been verified through considerable research and are simple enough for teachers to implement in their classrooms. This section of the text also tells teachers how to teach their students study skills so that they might learn more from traditional content courses found in middle and high schools. Finally, we present the latest information about transitions across the school years and into adulthood. We hope you enjoy the book and find that this methodology helps your students.

Acknowledgments

Although two names appear on the cover of this book, many people contributed in important ways to its creation. First, we would like to thank the staff members of the Department of Special Education at The University of Texas and the Alliance 20 project at The University of New Mexico for their assistance in preparing this book. In particular, at The University of Texas, many thanks go to Dr. Steve Larsen for securing research assistance, to Maria Caldwell for typing the references, and to Carole Lattimer and Paulette Jackson for copying chapters and ensuring that those many overnight delivery packages did indeed go out on time! Special thanks go to Valerie Appert and Paula Lucero at The University of New Mexico for helping to develop figures and for dealing with many faxes!

We would like to thank those who contributed to and enhanced this book. Our deepest appreciation goes to Drs. Brian R. Bryant and Ginger Blalock, whose chapters about reading and transition strengthen and broaden this text. This book is clearly better because of their efforts, for their depth of knowledge in those areas immeasurably strengthened the material.

We would also like to acknowledge the reviewers of this book. Many thanks go to Dr. Delores M. John (University of Missouri–St. Louis), Dr. Scott Sparks (Ohio University), Dr. Brenda L. Townsend (University of South Florida), and Dr. John Vokurka (Western Kentucky University) for their thoughtful, informative, and invaluable critiques of the material in this book. Also, a special thanks goes to Dr. Chriss Walther-Thomas (College of William and Mary) for her excellent suggestions pertaining to chapter 2 and for her quick response in a tight time line. Their suggestions for improvement greatly improved this book, and we are grateful for their time, expertise, and commitment to this project.

Thanks also go to Ray Short, editor at Allyn and Bacon, and to his editorial assistant, Christine Svitila. We are very grateful for Ray's support of this third edition and for Christine's answering our questions and many requests for information. Thank you!

Finally, and certainly not least, we wish to thank our families. Thank you to Brian and Jim, and to Ryan and Steven, who offered endless support, understanding, and patience throughout this process. Our deepest thanks and appreciation go to our family members; their support was one of the major reasons that we accomplished this project.

The text you are about to read is truly the product of the combined efforts of many people. We wish you happy reading!

Chapter 1
An Introduction to Teaching and Learning

Today's educational system provides many instructional options for students with special needs. Depending on their abilities to profit from the general education curriculum, their academic and behavioral characteristics, and their ultimate goals, students are served in classes that can best meet their academic and social needs. The challenge for teachers is to implement and adapt methods that will help students meet their potential. Teachers must understand the learning characteristics of all their students and possess knowledge about both curricular content and instructional methodology. The purpose of this text is to assist teachers, and those who are preparing to teach, in gaining and refining the skills necessary to become effective instructors. This text encourages readers to develop positive learning environments in which all students acquire vital academic and social skills.

In this chapter, we provide an overview of educational trends that have influenced instructional delivery and curricular content evident in many of today's schools. We briefly discuss several key pieces of legislation that have resulted in effective educational practices for youngsters with learning and behavior problems. We review characteristics typical in students with special needs; this content is intended to be a refresher for readers who have had an introductory course on students with special needs. Finally, we discuss environmental and instructional characteristics that have proven effective with young people with learning and behavior problems; this content serves as a foundation for information in later chapters on curriculum and instruction.

Making Connections

Before you read, think about your own education. Identify a teacher who made a difference in your life and in whose classroom you learned a great deal. Think about the characteristics of that special teacher and the classroom environment that was structured to foster effective instruction. Consider any legislation you are aware of that has made a difference in the educational lives of students with disabilities. Reflect on school reform efforts and the instructional changes that may be occurring in classrooms. Consider how school reform makes it necessary for families and professionals to develop collaborative partnerships. Finally, think about the changing demographics in the United States and how professionals must respond to and interact with students from backgrounds that represent linguistic, cultural, racial, ethnic, and socioeconomic diversity.

1

Objectives
After studying this chapter, the reader will be able to

1. Discuss educational trends and their impact on curriculum and instruction.
2. Describe components of key legislation.
3. Identify learner, environmental, and teacher characteristics.
4. Describe effective teaching characteristics.

● ●

Educational Trends

As you read, think about . . .
1. Identifying criteria for judging the effectiveness of school reform trends in classrooms.
2. Connecting social and political events to school reform trends.
3. Designing classroom instruction that meets the diverse needs of all students in general and special education settings.
4. Interpreting position statements from professional organizations about school reform.

Educational trends often reflect society in general. Social and political factors can influence educational philosophy and practice. These factors must be examined and, as appropriate, may be infused into the decision-making processes within the educational framework to promote constructive, beneficial change for all students and teachers and the community.

Several educational trends are noteworthy and will continue to impact educational philosophy and practice into the twenty-first century. For example, the changing demographics of the United States affects instruction, curriculum, and teacher-preparation. A diverse student population with a rich cultural and linguistic heritage attends schools in the United States. It is estimated that by the twenty-first century, approximately one-third of all school-age children will be from culturally and linguistically diverse families, primarily of African American, Asian, and Hispanic descent (Smith & Luckasson, 1995; Williams, 1992). Some of these students will require special education or bilingual special education services to meet their individual needs. Educators must persevere in their efforts to incorporate multicultural education into the curriculum, including "diverse ethnic perspectives" (Banks, 1991) and techniques to accommodate students who are non-English-speaking or whose native language is not English. Spotlight on Diversity offers several guidelines for considering these issues.

Techniques for Accommodating Diversity in the Classroom
- Appreciate the presence of cultural and linguistic diversity in your school as an advantage for learning in the classroom.
- Learn about the various cultural groups represented in your class, and remember that people are individuals as well.
- Involve parents in your program by creating volunteer opportunities and by corresponding with them in their native language.
- Work with assessment professionals to distinguish between language differences and language impairments for students whose native language is not English.

- Recognize that for students acquiring English as a second language, communicative skills emerge sooner than the complex language proficiency necessary to learn academic skills.

- Incorporate culturally diverse materials into the curriculum. Avoid materials that misrepresent events and people, that neglect to include an ethnically diverse portrayal, and that stereotype groups of people.

- Recognize and include cultural diversity and heritage in the curriculum throughout the school year, and teach students about a variety of customs, traditions, and holidays representative of people around the world. ●

A second educational trend is school reform. Clearly, national and international social and political events influence how we educate and what we teach students. Historical events such as Sputnik (1957), Nation at Risk (1983), National Council of Teachers of Mathematics *Curriculum and Evaluation Standards* (1989), and Goals 2000 (1994) speak well to that point. All of these events spurred school reform efforts to better prepare youngsters for postsecondary education and adulthood. School reform initially targeted general education, and then restructured educational services for students with disabilities (a trend first known as the "Regular Education Initiative," then as "Full Inclusion"). This restructuring trend is based on the premise that students with disabilities can receive an appropriate education in the general education setting with the necessary support services and accommodations. The **"inclusion"** movement created great debate (Fuchs & Fuchs, 1994; Stainback & Stainback, 1991), spurred some research and model programs (e.g., Heller, Spooner, Spooner, & Algozzine, 1992; Semmel, Abernathy, Butera, & Lesar, 1991), and led major education organizations to develop position statements (e.g., Learning Disabilities Association of America, 1993; Council for Exceptional Children, 1993; Council for Exceptional Children—Division for Learning Disabilities, 1993; National Joint Committee on Learning Disabilities, 1993). The organizations emphasized that Individualized Education Programs (IEPs) must be tailored to specific needs of individual students, that the general education classroom is not an appropriate placement for all students with disabilities, that students with disabilities who are placed in general education classrooms require a range of services to meet their individual needs, and that parents and professionals should work together to achieve restructuring in each students best educational interest. In short, most of the special education organizations wanted to maintain a continuum of services for students' with disabilities, yet acknowledged the importance of including students with disabilities in mainstream settings as much as possible.

As a result of the "inclusion movement," more students with disabilities are educated for the majority of the school day in the general education setting, and the special education teacher's role has expanded to include collaborative consultation and team teaching with other professionals. Schools continue to focus on providing appropriate curricular and instructional adaptations, support services, and funding assistance to meet the diverse educational objectives of students with special needs. As these and other trends find their way into the educational arena, school systems and teacher-training programs continue to identify ways in which their practices can accommodate influential social and political factors.

● ●

Key Legislation

As you read, think about . . .

1. Analyzing the components of key pieces of school-related legislation.
2. Comparing and contrasting public school settings prior to the enactment of current legislation, as described in this section.
3. Explaining to parents their rights as guaranteed by the legislation described below.

The Education for All Handicapped Children Act (EHA; P.L. 94–142), which was passed in 1975, proved to be landmark legislation that protected the rights of children with disabilities and their families. The major components of P.L. 94–142 included (1) **free appropriate public education (FAPE)** for all students with disabilities, (2) notification and **procedural safeguards** for parents, (3) identification and services to all children, (4) appropriate and necessary related services, (5) individualized assessment administered in the child's primary language by a trained professional, (6) **Individualized Education Programs (IEPs),** and (7) education in the least restrictive environment. Since then, other important legislation has been enacted to protect the rights of individuals with disabilities. Although it is not the intent of this text to provide a thorough explanation of educational legislation, it is important for us to mention three other influential laws affecting schools and children.

In 1986, P.L. 99–457 (an amendment to P.L. 94–142) was enacted with mandates and incentives for public schools to provide services for infants, toddlers, and their families. In 1991, public schools were mandated to provide preschool special education services for children ages three to five, and many states provided programs for children up to age two. Public schools were also required to provide an **Individualized Family Service Plan (IFSP),** which specifies levels of functioning, strengths, outcomes, services, service manager, dates of services, and transitioning methods. The IFSP is reviewed every six months and is a family-oriented process.

P.L. 94–142 was amended and reauthorized in 1990, becoming the Individuals with Disabilities Education Act, or IDEA (P.L. 101–476; 1990). While retaining EHA's key components, IDEA included:

- changing the title of the law
- changing the word *handicapped* to *disabled* and emphasizing "people first" language (e.g., an individual with a disability)
- adding the categories of traumatic brain injury and autism
- mandating transition services and educational planning by no later than age sixteen
- calling for further study on incorporating "attention deficit disorder" into the law
- explaining federal court intervention against states in violation of the law.

In 1988, the Technology-Related Assistance for Individuals with Disabilities Act was passed, and in 1994 it was amended. This act tried to provide people with disabilities with access to **assistive technology devices** and **services.** The law's intent was to create statewide systems that would respond to consumer needs for assistive technology. The "Tech Act" applies to public schools and students with disabilities who may require assistive technology devices and services to promote integration and full participation in educational environments. The challenge for professionals and families is to determine specific students' needs and whether or not assistive technology is the appropriate vehicle for meeting those needs. Moreover, there are issues about funding these devices and preparing teachers to implement the devices with students (see chapter 5 for additional technology information).

Learner Characteristics

As you read, think about . . .

1. Reviewing the characteristics of students with learning and behavior problems that you studied in introductory courses.
2. Interpreting those learner characteristics within the context of academic and social settings. Consider potential problem areas for students with special needs.
3. Describing characteristics of individuals with effective social skills. Consider potential problem areas for students with deficit social skills.
4. Designing an activity to help students with learning and behavior problems become aware of their special needs and of their strengths. Identify ways to help these students develop self-confidence.

All children differ in temperament, cognitive abilities, personality, and experience. These factors, and many others (motivation, support at home, past education), contribute to success in school. Students with special needs, regardless of their categorical identification, present their teachers with difficulties in learning abilities and styles. These difficulties affect students' learning as well as their adjustment at school. In this section, a few characteristics commonly observed in individuals with special needs are discussed. These characteristics influence how individually tailored instructional programs need to be developed. It is important to remember that teaching styles can be changed to facilitate positive change in the learning behaviors of students.

Academic Learning

A primary characteristic of most students with special needs is that they are academically behind their typical counterparts (Mehring & Colson, 1990; Mercer, 1991). By high school and into adulthood, many of these students are significantly behind their classmates who have no disabilities in achievement (Cawley & Miller, 1989; Deshler & Schumaker, 1986; Hughes & Smith, 1990), and an alarming number (estimated between 27 and 44 percent) of students with disabilities never graduate from high school (U.S. Department of Education, 1994; Zigmond, 1990).

The tactics and strategies found in Parts II and III of this text will facilitate learning for many of these students. With careful, systematic, and direct instruction, most can perform or function at least at grade-level. However, recent research has shown that some of these students possess various characteristics that greatly hinder learning throughout their lives.These learning characteristics can be altered with substantial results. We briefly discuss some of these learning characteristics (attribution, learned helplessness, inactive learning, attention deficits, metacognitive deficits) here.

Attribution

Attribution is an internal justification that individuals devise to explain their success or failure at a task. School failure may result not only in academic deficits, but also in motivational deficits. After repeated experiences with failure, many students come to expect failure. This expectation becomes outwardly directed, viewed as something beyond one's control. Such individuals may be afraid to respond, take risks, or actively engage in learning. They come to believe that their failure is due to a lack of ability. In turn, this results in lowered expectations and a belief that they cannot succeed. Eventually, such individuals meet their own expectations. They do not believe in themselves and do not try to learn. This situation is frequently called **learned helplessness.** Such students expect to fail.

Students oriented toward mastery tend to find ways to overcome failure (using different strategies, asking for help, studying harder). Students who expect academic failure are more passive, and often attribute success to luck rather than to their abilities or effort. In some ways, special education teachers may contribute to students' learned helplessness through their educational planning (Kleinhammer-Tramill, Tramill, Schrepel, & Davis 1983). When teachers direct the entire school day, select students' rewards for achievement, make tasks too easy, and offer too much assistance, students do not become self-directed. They are less likely to persist on difficult tasks and follow them through to completion. Therefore, many do not learn that their efforts can achieve success.

To help conceptualize motivation and attribution, Grimes (1981) developed a useful schema that describes student motivation as it relates to success and attribution. Table 1.1 presents her comparison of high achievers with low achievers and describes their attribution on a number of factors.

On a more positive note, attribution can be changed (Borkowski, Weyhing, & Turner, 1986; Mehring & Colson, 1990). Students can come to recognize that their efforts do result in success, but for those who have experienced considerable school failure, this process is intensive and prolonged.

When attempting to change students' attributions, teachers should be task-specific, discussing actual performance and how it can be improved. Students need to be given good strategies and procedures to improve their performances and should be reinforced for using them. Aponik and Dembo (1983) suggested that students can be taught to break down problems and tasks into smaller units (by using task analysis techniques) so they are manageable and more easily solved. This increases the likelihood of success. Self-management procedures and strategy training (discussed later, in chapter 7) engage students more actively and help students to learn that they, and their efforts, are responsible for successful experiences. When students achieve success, teachers should discuss with them the factors that contributed to their accomplishment.

Mehring and Colson (1990) described another technique to engage students in their learning and to identify attributions that may impede the learning process. The teacher and student complete the Teacher-Student Motivation Planning Form during different phases of instruction, such as before and after teaching. They gather information about student behavior, teacher and student attributions, and previous, current, and revised intervention plans. The intent of the form is to provide a profile of student learning, to document important information that affects learning, and to generate more teacher-student interaction.

Type of achievement related to expectations of society and schools	Type of adult feedback Attribution made by child	Type of affect associated with internal evaluation of performance	Child's understanding of his/her role in cause-effect relationships	Expectations and probability of subsequent behavior
High Achiever Success is positively valued by our society. Success is defined by schools as desirable.	Positive feedback from adults. The child receives positive labels such as smart, gifted, etc. Child accepts and internalizes positive labels. The cause of success is attributed by the child to ability and effort.	The positive affects of pride, accomplishment, and competence are associated with successful performance. The child reinforces his/her performance with internal positive self-statements. The child's self-concept is enhanced.	The child perceives that his/her effort determines positive outcome. Energy is seen as a means of solving problems.	The child has expectancy of success for future performance. Increased probability of future success serves as an incentive to work harder.
Low Achiever Failure is negatively valued by our society. Failure is defined by schools as undesirable.	Negative feedback from adults. The child receives negative labels such as slow, learning problems, etc. Child accepts and internalizes negative labels. The cause of failure is attributed by the child to lack of ability.	The negative affects of frustration, shame, indifference, and incompetence are associated with failure. Internal statements of the child are primarily negative, reflecting his/her lack of ability. The child's self-concept is decreased.	The child perceives no causal relationship between effort and outcome. Therefore, the child considers effort a waste of energy. Energy is spent on avoiding the task.	The child expects failure in the future. Increased probability of failure leaves no incentive to expend effort.

Table 1.1
Student Motivation as Related to the Attributional Process

Source: From "Learned Helplessness and Attribution Theory: Redefining Children's Learning Problems," by L. Grimes, 1981, *Learning Disability Quarterly, 4*, p. 92. Copyright 1981 by the Council for Learning Disabilities. Reprinted with permission.

Inactive Learning

Inactive learning is an approach to learning that lacks planning and strategies to engage the learner in the task. Possibly due in part to attribution, many students with special needs are called "inactive learners" (Torgesen & Licht, 1983). Inactive learners are less engaged and organized in their approach to memory and other academic tasks, and they seldom plan for such tasks. They seem to have no useful strategies to help them remember or study. In this regard, many recent research studies are helpful, particularly in the area of strategy training (for more information see chapter 13 on study skills). It appears that students can engage in self-questioning strategies to become more actively involved in learning. Also, teachers can plan activities that require students' active, rather than passive, involvement. Instead of relying on lectures and teacher-directed activities, lessons and units can be planned where youngsters need to discover, think, solve problems, and develop a product. Students who participate in the development and implementation of their educational programs become more active learners. For instance, researchers (e.g., Van Reusen, Bos, Schumaker, & Deshler, 1987) found that teaching students how to become more involved in their educational planning or choosing their own teaching techniques resulted in more active learning and academic success.

Clearly, students need to become more actively involved in the curriculum and their school programs. When they take more interest in learning, learning becomes more meaningful. They find purpose for their learning, which might not have been as obvious as before.

Attention

Attention is the act of concentrating on a task or the features of a task for an appropriate amount of time. Many students with special needs have selective attention problems. These students cannot attend to the task to be learned or may pay attention to the wrong features of tasks they are asked to complete. Many of these students are also observed as being distractible. There is evidence that selective attention problems can be corrected or lessened through educational procedures.

For example, rewarding students for remembering particular features of assigned tasks can lead to improved attention and academic achievement. Using advance organizers to help students focus their energies and attention on the important information to be learned in content classes has proven beneficial. Providing students with strategies they can use and apply in academic situations (test taking, note taking) helps to focus attention. Actively involving students in their academic programs and procedures and providing more drill and practice activities that key students to relevant cues have proven effective. Some people now see selective attention problems as relating to task persistence, motivation, attribution, and passivity. As teachers select instructional interventions, they must consider and address each student's learning style.

Metacognition

Metacognition is the ability to think about the strategies needed to complete tasks that involve self-regulatory skills. Researchers (e.g., Wong & Jones, 1982; Ellis & Lenz, 1996) have suggested that many learning problems stem from students' inability to identify effective strategies for completing tasks. Metacognitive deficits may interfere with their ability to plan, monitor, and evaluate the efficiency and effectiveness of strategies that they have chosen in order to complete academic assignments or engage in social interactions. Metacognitive strategies, such as self-questioning, self-regulating, and self-evaluating, can provide learners with feedback about the activity in which they are engaged. The lack of effective metacognitive skills tends to impede the learning process and contribute to motivational and attributional difficulties associated with learning problems (see chapter 5 for additional information about metacognition and learning).

Social Skills

Many students with special needs do not exhibit good social skills. (Chapter 8 is devoted exclusively to this topic.) Either these youngsters do not possess the skills required for interpersonal interactions, or they do not use those skills. They are not socially competent. For many, this lack lowers their social status and can affect their lives while in school, at home, and on the job. Social skills training has not been a priority for students with special needs until recently. For those students deficient in social skills, education and training aimed at developing social competence must become a part of the curriculum.

Disruption

Students with special needs are often more disruptive than students with no special needs. Students who have special needs may disturb the learning environment for themselves and their peers. They follow the classroom and school rules less frequently. As discussed in detail in chapter 7, there are many reasons for this. These students might be frustrated with the academic content presented to them. They might not understand the explicit and implied rules at school. They might purposely seek to destroy the learning environment. Regardless of the reason, their disruptive behavior may cause them to have a lowered social status and lowered academic achievement.

If students do not spend time learning, they will not learn. This is particularly true for students with disabilities. Disruptive students spend a substantial amount of time not learning. As discussed in chapter 7, teachers can reduce or eliminate disruptions by systematically applying various intervention strategies.

The relationship between disruption and academic learning is well-documented. During the 1970s, considerable research was conducted and techniques were developed to reduce inappropriate or disruptive classroom behaviors. It was thought that if disruptions were eliminated, students' academic achievement would improve. This did not occur.

What, then, is the relationship between academic performance and the reduction of disruption? Reduction in disruption alone does not guarantee collateral increases in attention-to-task or academic improvement. However, when students are reinforced for increased academic output, disruption decreases (Ayllon & Roberts, 1974; Ferritor, Buckholdt, Hamblin, & Smith, 1972).

● ●

Characteristics of Learning Environments

As you read, think about . . .

1. Checking teacher expectations in different classroom environments. Identify the skills needed to meet those classroom environmental expectations.
2. Comparing and contrasting the characteristics of effective and ineffective learners.
3. Discerning how youngsters from diverse backgrounds adapt to classroom environmental expectations.

The characteristics of the learning environment and the expectations of teachers are referred to as the **setting demands.** These demands are critical variables in determining the success of students with special needs. Special and general educators must be sensitive to the environmental expectations placed on students to achieve academic and social success and the individual learning needs of students with disabilities. Over a decade of research in general and special education learning environments (i.e., instructional and curricular expectations) has documented the importance of understanding and considering the setting demands (Schumaker & Deshler, 1984) as students with special needs are prepared for and placed in general education classrooms and least restrictive environments for some or all of their school day.

Researchers (e.g., Schumm & Vaughn, 1991; Schumm & Vaughn, 1992; Ysseldyke, Thurlow, Wotruba, & Nania, 1990) have shown that general education teachers are interested in adapting instruction and curriculum to accommodate individual needs of students with disabilities. At the same time, teachers generally do not make these adjustments for a variety of reasons (e.g., they lack time, they lack the training to meet the needs of students with disabilities, they don't think making adaptations is appropriate). Therefore, students with disabilities in elementary and secondary general education settings are often expected to perform academically and socially within the realm of instructional and curricular expectations for all students. Typically, these setting demands include adhering to certain behavioral rules and codes (e.g., following directions, staying in seat, speaking when called upon, not displaying temper outbursts, listening, raising hand to speak, working independently) and demonstrating academic abilities and study skills. For example, reading textbooks, reading for meaning, understanding written directions, skimming reading passages, taking notes, completing written expression activities (such as worksheets, compositions, workbooks, and letters), computing and problem solving, and completing homework are considered specific academic and study skills that good students possess. Additionally, students with special needs must be able to function successfully in classrooms where instruction is usually given to the whole class with limited individualization and modification (McIntosh, Vaughn, Schumm, Haager, & Lee, 1994).

For students to meet the demands of their settings, they must possess specific **requisite abilities** (Bryant & Rivera, 1995). For example, a setting demand might be that a student takes notes during the lecture; analysis of this setting demand suggests that students must possess effective listening skills, the ability to identify important points, and the ability to record information quickly. These are requisite abilities for performing that task. Now, consider some of the characteristics of students with learning and behavior problems; they often have selective attention problems, disruptive behaviors, metacognitive deficits, and inactive approaches to learning. Clearly, the setting demands may be problematic for many students to achieve if they lack the requisite abilities.

Students with special needs often need to learn the skills just described, whether they receive instruction in special education or general education classes (see chapter 5 "Delivery of Instruction" for instructional steps when teaching new skills to students). Special education and general education teachers must continue to collaborate to identify ways to help students with special needs placed in general education classrooms meet the setting demands (see chapter 2 for additional information about developing collaborative partnerships). For those students with special needs who experience great difficulty adhering to the academic and social demands of general education, other least restrictive environments or educational support systems must be identified to better meet the needs and promote the success of individual students.

● ●

Teacher Characteristics

As you read, think about . . .

1. Describing characteristics of effective teachers.
2. Explaining how you currently deal with stress.
3. Designing a stress management program tailored to your individual needs.
4. Analyzing how you spend your time and possible ways to improve time management skills.
5. Designing a time management program for your students.

Teachers of students with special needs serve in a variety of roles. They teach youngsters who have great individual differences. Some may present social skills deficits; most possess academic skill deficiencies. Besides their teaching duties, these teachers often consult with parents and other teachers, assess students, write and manage individualized program plans (see chapter 3), and conduct in-service training activities. The numerous roles filled by special education teachers are important to students, their families, and the school district. But first and foremost, special education teachers' purpose is to educate students with special needs.

To fulfill all of these roles, teachers must possess certain competencies. They must have the knowledge necessary to teach content and be proficient in educational methods through which they can impart that content to their students. Special educators must possess effective collaboration and communication skills to work well with other teachers, parents, staff, and administrators. Especially they need effective techniques to manage stress.

Teacher Competencies

Experts have focused on the competencies that should be emphasized in teacher preparation programs so teachers can meet the challenging role expectations of their job. The competency areas and statements that Graves et al. (1992) formulated were prepared for teachers of students with learning disabilities, but are applicable to all special education teachers. This list shows the depth of knowledge and breadth of skills required of special educators. For example, they identified competencies in the areas of (1) the nature and needs of students; (2) academic support; (3) curriculum for support and modifications of school core curriculum; (4) assessment methods and interpretation; (5) classroom assessment, management, and motivation; (6) collaboration and consultation skills; (7) specialized instructional strategies, technologies, and materials; (8) historical and legal aspects; (9) nontraditional practices and procedures; and (10) clinical and field experiences.

Stress Management

Stress is a physiological experience that can affect a person in a variety of ways, including physical, emotional, social, and intellectual effects (DeShong, 1981). Stress can be triggered by a number of different personal scenarios (e.g., life changes, life stages, time constraints, role conflict, personality intolerance) and professional situations (e.g., organizational policies and procedures, role conflict or ambiguity, time constraints, career development and security, administrative support, paperwork responsibilities, discipline, pedagogy). Although some stress is viewed as healthy, stress left unchecked and unmanaged can lead to physiological problems (e.g., headaches, insomnia, stomach ailments, fatigue, high blood pressure) and psychological difficulties (passivity, aggressiveness, guilt, feeling of helplessness, irritability, burnout) (Chusmir & Durand, 1987).

Educators respond to many different role responsibilities during a school day. Not only are they responsible for providing effective instruction to a diverse student population, but they also must collaborate and communicate effectively with other professionals, parents, and administrators. Educators are confronted with a variety of social issues and problems that impact the educational system, such as homelessness, abuse and neglect, poverty, and disease. Very often, they are also confronted with the violence, gangs, and weapons found on many neighborhood streets.

It is no wonder that for many teachers, stress is a major factor that needs to be addressed productively. Special educators are paying attention to this issue (e.g., Billingsley & Cross, 1991; Cohen & Hart-Hester, 1987; Olson & Platt, 1996). Tips for Teachers offers a number of ideas for managing stress more effectively; naturally, the selection of stress management techniques is a personal choice and will vary considerably among individuals.

Tips for Teachers

Stress Management Techniques

1. Manage your time.
   - Audit your time, documenting how it is spent.
   - Avoid activities that waste time.
   - Establish and adhere to time lines. Be realistic about deadlines.
   - Monitor time spent in meetings. Use an agenda and stick to it.
   - Keep a calendar handy to record time commitments.
   - Designate a time each day to complete paperwork and make phone calls.
2. Develop an organization system.
   - Develop an "in" and "out" basket system to organize tasks that must be addressed and that are completed.
   - Handle paper information, then (1) recycle it, (2) file it, or (3) delegate it.
   - Put documents that you will need later in a labeled file that is part of a filing system. Avoid making piles that must be sifted through to find "missing" documents.
3. Delegate.
   - Use the skills of paraprofessionals and parents to help accomplish classroom routines, to develop materials, and to perform other instructional tasks as appropriate.
   - Involve students in classroom routines and in correcting their own schoolwork.
4. Develop effective coping strategies.
   - Learn to say "no."
   - Identify a positive non-work-related activity to do regularly.
   - Seek administrative and/or colleague support.
   - Establish a positive network.
   - Focus on what you can change.
   - Use a problem-solving approach to identify issues, barriers, and solutions.
   - Listen to your body and the physical signals that might be symptomatic of stress. ■

Effective Teaching

As you read, think about . . .

1. Identifying teacher behaviors that promote effective instruction.
2. Describing student behaviors during instruction and how teachers address these behaviors.
3. Designing a lesson that fosters active, engaged student learning.

Typically, students with disabilities must be taught specific strategies that enable them to learn. Unlike many of their counterparts, some of these students do not learn incidentally; their teachers must deliberately plan for their instruction. Throughout this text, we suggest ways to teach students directly and systematically. Here, several important points about effective instruction are highlighted and should be kept in mind when reading the rest of this book.

Critical Teaching Skills

Although we discuss specific procedures that remediate specific deficit areas later in this book, we will now mention some general teaching skills that are important for teachers to use throughout the school day, regardless of the topic of instruction. A number of different researchers and educational experts have attempted to identify key variables or behaviors that excellent teachers use. Many of the experts' lists of skills overlap, but it is useful to study each list.

Kea (1987) and Deshler and Schumaker (1986) identified teacher behaviors that they believe enhance the quality or intensity of classroom instruction, particularly at the secondary school level. They found that many middle and secondary special education teachers fail to use the following teaching actions, which the researchers believe to be critical to good instruction:

1. Provide positive and corrective feedback.
2. Use organizers throughout the instructional session.
3. Ensure high levels of responding during instruction.
4. Program youth involvement in discussions.
5. Provide regular reviews of key instructional points and checks of comprehension.
6. Monitor student performance.
7. Require mastery learning.
8. Communicate high expectations to students.
9. Communicate rationales for instructional activities.
10. Facilitate independence.

In another attempt to identify those variables that differentiate excellent teachers, Rosenshine (1983) listed the following behaviors on which elementary teachers rely:

1. Structure the learning.
2. Proceed in small steps but at a brisk pace.
3. Give detailed and redundant instructions and explanations.
4. Provide many examples.

5. Ask many questions and provide overt, active practice.
6. Provide feedback and corrections, particularly in the initial stages of learning.
7. Divide instructional assignments into smaller, more manageable assignments (pp. 336–37).

In a more recent review of instructional variables, Christenson, Ysseldyke, and Thurlow (1989) identified the following factors as essential for teaching students with mild disabilities:

- The degree to which classroom management is effective and efficient.
- The degree to which there is a sense of "positiveness" in the school environment.
- The degree to which there is an appropriate instructional match.
- The degree to which teaching goals and teacher expectations for student performance and success are stated clearly and are understood by students.
- The degree to which teachers present lessons clearly and follow specific instructional procedures.
- The degree to which instructional support is provided for the individual student.
- The degree to which sufficient time is allocated to academics and instructional time is used efficiently.
- The degree to which the student has an opportunity to respond to instructional tasks and questions.
- The degree to which the teacher actively monitors student progress and understanding.
- The degree to which student performance is evaluated appropriately and frequently (p. 22).

Teachers also need to use language that their students can understand. If the teacher's rate of speech is too fast, if vocabulary is beyond the students' comprehension, or if the syntax is too complex, students will not gain meaning from the educational experience. They will not be able to follow the teacher's directions if they do not comprehend what is being said to them. Matching students' cognitive comprehension skills with the language intended to deliver information is an important teacher skill (see chapter 5).

Beyond these skills, teachers must develop a style, a way to be comfortable with the students they teach. Teachers need to enjoy their working relationships with students. In turn, students should come to respect and enjoy their teachers. Learning does not have to be dull and routine. Teachers need to keep these critical teaching behaviors in mind, but they can also diversify educational experiences and add occasional elements of fun into the learning environment. This can be accomplished by allowing students to work on interesting topics, solve problems, or use technology as an enhancement to instruction.

Instructional Time

The more time students spend learning, the more they learn. A strong relationship exists between (1) the amount of time allocated to academics, (2) the amount of time students are actually engaged in instruction ("academic learning time"), and (3) the amount of time students are actively engaged in academic tasks (Berliner, 1984; Christenson, et al., 1989).

Allocated time refers to the amount of time scheduled during the school day or year for various content areas and types of instruction. Engaged instruction or **academic learning time** means the amount of time students are on-task in a learning situation; this may include listening to the teacher lecture, listening to a student read, or completing a worksheet. **Active engagement** is when students are involved (e.g., performing tasks, discussing topics, explaining how answers were reached) in academic tasks; here, students are viewed as participants in the learning process, rather than just recipients. There is a strong relationship between the amount of time students are actively engaged in instruction (as opposed to passive engagement, such as listening to a lecture) and high mastery levels (Bickel & Bickel, 1986). Therefore, students should be actively involved as much as possible and should attain high levels of accuracy before moving on to other skills.

How much instructional time do students receive at school? Rosenshine (1980) categorized classroom activities into three broad types: academic (reading, mathematics, science, social studies), nonacademic (music, art, physical education, story time, sharing), and noninstructional (transitions before and after breaks, housekeeping tasks, waiting). Although Rosenshine's study included only typical elementary students (bright and at-risk students were not included), the results presented in Table 1.2 reveal how much instruction does and does not occur in many general education classroom settings.

On the average, 58 percent of the school day is allocated to academic activities, 23 percent to nonacademic activities, and 19 percent to noninstructional activities. Allocating more time for academics does not make students spend less time engaged in tasks. Teachers who schedule more time for instruction did not see their students tire or become less interested in academic tasks. There does not seem to be a correlation between more work time and students' drop in attention. Rosenshine also found seatwork to be the predominant form of instruction (66 percent for reading and 75 percent for math). Students were less engaged in tasks for seatwork assignments than for teacher-led activities.

Other studies report less instructional time occurring in classrooms than Rosenshine found. For example, Rieth, Polsgrove, and Semmel (1979) discussed studies where academic responding time was extremely low. In one study, fifth-graders spent less than eight minutes responding orally or in writing to the teacher's questions. In

Table 1.2
Instructional Time in Elementary Schools

Category	Grade 2		Grade 5	
	Time allotted	Time engaged	Time allotted	Time engaged
Overall academics	2:15	1:30	2:50	1:55
Reading	1:30	1:04	1:50	1:20
Mathematics	36	26	44	35
Nonacademics	55		1:50	
Noninstructional	44		45	

Source: Adapted from "How Time Is Spent in Elementary Classrooms," by B. V. Rosenshine, 1980, in C. Denham and A. Lieberman (Eds.), *Time to Learn,* Washington, DC: National Institute of Education.

Table 1.3
Mean Percentages
for Time-Use
Variables

Daily activity	Estimated time used	Estimated time needed	Measured time used
Direct instruction	63.67	69.86	51.48
Consulting with staff	7.13	10.93	8.51
Consulting with parents	3.73	7.71	3.6
Conducting in-service training	1.25	4.08	0.6
Preparation for instruction	12.08	17.6	16.38
Staffings	5.05	6.45	2.8
Assessment and evaluation	7.68	13.83	8.82
Work with IEPs	5.92	9.15	1.38
Record keeping	5.38	7.72	3.77
General school duties	3.1	3.6	9.22

Source: From "Resource Teacher Time Utilization: An Observational Study," by L. R. Sargent, 1981, *Exceptional Children, 47*, p. 422. Copyright 1981 by the Council for Exceptional Children. Reprinted with permission.

contrast, students spent more than 50 percent of class time engaged in transitional activities. In another study they cited, inner-city students averaged no more than twenty seconds in directed reading per day. Thurlow, Graden, Greener, and Ysseldyke (1983) found that students spent about 45 minutes per day in academic responding. These findings are worrisome. If students are to learn academic material, they must respond to the material. How can students learn to read, if given neither the opportunity to do so, nor direct guided instruction aimed at improving reading skills?

Regarding special education instruction, Sargent (1981) conducted an interesting time-utilization study to determine how resource teachers spent their school day. The results are in Table 1.3.

It appears that the demands on resource room teachers extend beyond classroom instruction. If they spend only 51 percent of their time on instruction, and some of that time is lost to noninstructional and nonacademic activities, the amount of time their students engage in academic learning might be very small. Students with special needs require more direct instruction than their typical counterparts and might receive less because of their teachers' other duties and their own tendencies to disrupt more and pay less attention to academic tasks. Clearly, teachers must try to allocate more time for instruction and for students' engagement. This will require a restructuring of the school day.

In a more recent study, Pemberton and Smith (1994) analyzed teacher-time data across five public school settings: (1) a self-contained (SC) special education classroom where students with disabilities spent most of their school day with a special education teacher who modified curriculum and the environment, (2) a resource room pull-out program (RPO) in which students with disabilities received instruction in a special setting with modified curriculum, (3) a resource room pull-in (RPI) program for students to receive services involving modified curriculum in the general education setting, (4) a regular education (RE) classroom where the general education teacher was responsible for delivering services to students with disabilities for all or part of the school day, and (5) a full inclusion program (IRE and ISE) in which a general and special education teacher worked together to present curriculum and instruction to all students and in which students with disabilities spent their entire school day within the general education setting.

Several findings from the study are noteworthy. First, they concluded that on average across the five settings, 42 percent of the school day was spent on academic instruction, 21 percent of the time was devoted to nonacademic activities (e.g., arts and crafts, business management, other), 17 percent of the school day was spent on transition (e.g., changing classes and activities), 7.5 percent was devoted to morning and afternoon recess periods, and lunch occupied 12.5 percent of the school day. These results compared to Rosenshine's time-allocation data show that in some settings, not as much instruction occurs as in other settings; this finding is disconcerting, considering all students' needs to receive appropriate and intensive instruction to promote learning.

The second piece of the Pemberton and Smith (1994) study showed that 42 percent of the day was allocated to academics, while nonacademic activities took up 21 percent of the day. Based on this 63 percent of the school day time, Table 1.4 shows the number of minutes and percentage of time allocated to academic content areas. For instance, the data reveal that the percentage of reading time ranged from 8.19 percent in the RE to 33.76 percent in the RPO. In the full-inclusion setting where a special and general education teacher were present, the special education teacher spent 30.04 percent of the time on reading and the general education teacher spent 30.62 percent of the time. Even when two teachers were present, the time spent on reading was less than the time allocated to reading in the RPO. Additionally, the researchers examined student-teacher interactions for one school day in the full-inclusion setting. They found that special education teachers spent 29 percent of their time interacting with youngsters who had special needs and 71 percent of their time with typical students. General education teachers showed similar interaction patterns; 28.5 percent of time was spent with students with special needs and 71.5

	Regular education classroom (RE)		Resource room pull in (RPI)		Resource room pull out (RPO)		Self-contained special education classroom (SC)		Full inclusion special education (ISE)		Full inclusion regular education (IRE)	
	$\bar{X}$	%	$\bar{X}$	%	$\bar{X}$	%	$\bar{X}$	%	$\bar{X}$	%	$\bar{X}$	%
Total Academics	154.0	60.05	142.5	77.86	191.0	81.1	129.5	60.53	197.5	82.97	194.0	75.2
Reading	21.0	8.19	61.0	33.33	80.0	33.76	59.5	27.80	71.5	30.04	79.0	30.62
Mathematics	33.0	12.87	16.0	8.74	3.0	1.27	47.5	22.2	69.5	29.2	67.0	25.97
Spelling	1.5	0.58	18.0	9.84	13.5	5.7	7.0	3.27	0.0	0.0	2.0	0.78
Language	29.0	11.31	7.5	4.10	62.5	26.37	10.5	4.91	29.0	12.18	17.0	6.59
Science	24.0	9.36	39.5	21.58	21.0	8.86	0.0	0.0	27.0	11.34	26.0	10.08
Social studies	45.5	17.74	0.5	0.27	5.5	2.32	4.5	2.10	0.0	0.0	3.0	1.16

Table 1.4

Time Allocated to Activities for Students in Five Service Levels

Note: Entries are mean number of minutes per day and percentage per day.

percent of the time was spent with the rest of the students. There were eight students in the classroom who had disabilities and 28 students who did not have disabilities. What these data suggest is that students with disabilities receive considerably less interactive time from both instructors; this is disconcerting, considering that students with special needs require intensive instruction to master skills. Moreover, in this study, the instructor designated for youngsters with disabilities (i.e., the special education teacher) did not show any more interactive time with students who needed extra help. Overall, the data suggest that students with special needs in different instructional settings received varying degrees of learning opportunities. They did achieve equivalent amounts of interactions from both teachers in inclusive settings. The question is, if students with disabilities are receiving only equivalent amounts of interactive time, is this sufficient to meet their intensive, individual instruction needs? Clearly, special educators must carefully analyze individual students' needs, and the appropriate amount of services, instructional time, and teacher-interactions to allocate to meet these learning needs.

Summary

The educational system is legally required to provide an appropriate education to students with disabilities. The ultimate questions are: What constitutes an appropriate education for an individual? and Where can that education best be delivered? Today, professionals and parents with children in both special and general education are debating these issues. There can be no uniform answers. Students with special needs are different from each other. They possess varied learning styles, abilities, and characteristics.

Where students with special needs should receive their education is of great concern. This must be determined from data about where the student learns best. One factor to consider is whether the student can cope with the demands of the general education setting or whether the setting can be modified to suit his or her needs. Before placing students, teachers must determine whether students can meet the behavioral and academic expectations of the environment.

The teachers who provide special education must possess many special skills and competencies. They must be proficient in using the critical teaching skills discussed in this chapter. They must use their instructional time efficiently, and must match their language to the students' abilities to understand oral and written communication. Other skills, however, extend beyond teaching. Today, teachers must be able to work collaboratively with educators and professionals from other disciplines, and they must be able to form partnerships with parents. Special educators face many demands on their time and expertise, but their most important task is ensuring that each student with a disability receives the best education possible. The primary purpose of this text is to help teachers teach by suggesting a variety of methods that research and clinical practice have shown to be effective. Throughout this book, we present teaching strategies, procedures, and tactics to improve students' social and academic skills.

Study and Discussion Questions

1. Discuss educational trends and their impact on curriculum and instruction.
2. Describe components of key legislation.

3. Identify learner, environmental, and teacher characteristics.
4. Describe effective teaching characteristics.
5. Describe the relationship between disruption and academic learning.
6. Observe classrooms and compare teacher expectations across environments.
7. For each teacher competency area, decide which skills will help a teacher achieve competency in that area.
8. Design a stress management program for yourself and your students.
9. Identify and explain the three types of instructional time.
10. Describe classroom situations that detract from and promote active, engaged student learning.

● ●

References and Suggested Readings

Educational Trends

Banks, J. A. (1991). *Teaching strategies for ethnic studies.* Boston: Allyn & Bacon.

Council for Exceptional Children. (1993, April). *Statement on inclusive schools and communities.* Reston, VA: Author.

Council for Exceptional Children—Division for Learning Disabilities. (1993). *Inclusion: What does it mean for students with learning disabilities?* Reston, VA: Author.

Fuchs, D., & Fuchs, L. S. (1994). *Inclusive schools movement and the radicalization of special education reform. Exceptional Children, 60*(4), 294–309.

Heller, H. W., Spooner, M., Spooner, F., & Algozzine, B. (1992). Helping general educators accommodate students with disabilities. *Teacher Education and Special Education, 15*(4), 269–274.

Learning Disabilities Association of America. (1993, January). *Position paper on full inclusion of all students with learning disabilities in the regular education classroom.* Pittsburgh, PA: Author.

National Joint Committee on Learning Disabilities. (1993, January). *A reaction to "full inclusion": A reaffirmation of the right of students with learning disabilities to a continuum of services.* Author.

Semmel, M. I., Abernathy, T. V., Butera, G., & Lesar, S. (1991). Teacher perceptions of the regular education initiative. *Exceptional Children, 58*, 9–23.

Smith, D. D., & Luckasson, R. (1995). *Introduction to special education—Teaching in an age of challenge* (2nd ed.). Boston: Allyn & Bacon.

Stainback, W., & Stainback, S. (1991). Rationale for integration and restructuring: A synopsis. In J. W. Lloyd, N. N. Singh, & A. C. Repp (Eds.), *The regular education initiative* (pp. 225–239). Sycamore, IL: Sycamore.

Williams, B. F. (1992). Changing demographics: Challenges for educators. *Intervention in School and Clinic, 27*(3), 157–163.

Key Legislation

Education for All Handicapped Children Act (EHA), 20 U.S.C. sections 1400 et seq. and amendments.

Technology-Related Assistance for Individuals with Disabilities Act of 1988 and amendments (Catalogue No. 850, Senate Rep. No. 100–438). Washington, DC: U.S. Government Printing Office.

Learner Characteristics
Academic Learning

Cawley, J. F., & Miller, J. H. (1989). Cross-sectional comparisons of the mathematical performance of children with learning disabilities: Are we on the right track toward comprehensive programming? *Journal of Learning Disabilities, 23,* 250–254, 259.

Deshler, D. D., & Schumaker, J. B. (1986). Learning strategies: An instructional alternative for low-achieving adolescents. *Exceptional Children, 52,* 583–590.

Hughes, C. A., & Smith, J. O. (1990). Cognitive and academic performance of college students with learning disabilities: A synthesis of literature. *Learning Disability Quarterly, 13,* 66–79.

Keogh, B. K. (1983). Individual differences in temperament—A contribution to the personal, social, and education competence of learning disabled children. In J. D. McKinney & L. Feagans (Eds.), *Current topics in learning disabilities* (Vol. 1). Norwood, NJ: Ablex.

Mehring, T. A., & Colson, S. E. (1990). Motivation and mildly handicapped learners. *Focus on Exceptional Children, 22*(5), 1–14.

Mercer, C. D. (1991). *Students with learning disabilities* (4th ed.). Columbus, OH: Merrill.

U.S. Department of Education. (1994). *Sixteenth annual report to Congress on the Implementation of the Individuals with Disabilities Education Act.* Washington, DC: Author.

Zigmond, N. (1990). Rethinking secondary school programs for students with learning disabilities. *Focus on Exceptional Children, 23*(1), 1–12.

Attribution

Aponik, D. A., & Dembo, M. (1983). LD and normal adolescents' causal attributions of success and failure at different levels of task difficulty. *Learning Disability Quarterly, 6,* 31–39.

Borkowski, J. G., Weyhing, R. S., & Turner, L. A. (1986). Attributional retraining and the teaching of strategies. *Exceptional Children, 53,* 130–137.

Canino, F. J. (1981). Learned-helplessness theory: Implications for research in learning disabilities. *Journal of Special Education, 15,* 471–484.

Ellis, E. S. (1986). The role of motivation and pedagogy on the generalization of cognitive strategy training. *Journal of Learning Disabilities, 19,* 66–70.

Grimes, L. (1981). Learned helplessness and attribution theory: Redefining children's learning problems. *Learning Disability Quarterly, 4,* 92–100.

Kleinhammer-Tramill, P. J., Tramill, J. L., Schrepel, S. N., & Davis, S. F. (1983). Learned helplessness in learning disabled adolescents as a function of noncontingent rewards. *Learning Disability Quarterly, 6,* 61–66.

Mehring, T. A., & Colson, S. E. (1990). Motivation and mildly handicapped learners. *Focus on Exceptional Children, 22*(5), 1–14.

Pearl, R. (1982). LD children's attributions for success and failure: A replication with a labeled LD sample. *Learning Disability Quarterly, 5,* 173–176.

Pearl, R., Bryan, T., & Herzog, A. (1983). Learning disabled and nondisabled children's strategy analyses under high and low success conditions. *Learning Disability Quarterly, 6,* 67–74.

Pflaum, S. W., & Pascarella, E. T. (1982). Attribution retraining for learning disabled students: Some thoughts on the practical implications of the evidence. *Learning Disability Quarterly, 5,* 422–426.

Tollefson, N., Tracy, D. B., Johnsen, E. P., Buenning, M., Farmer, A., & Barke, C. R. (1982). Attribution patterns of learning disabled adolescents. *Learning Disability Quarterly, 5,* 14–20.

Inactive Learning

Lenz, B. K., Alley, G. R., & Schumaker, J. B. (1987). Activating the inactive learner: Advance organizers in the secondary content classroom. *Learning Disability Quarterly, 10,* 53–62.

Torgesen, J. K. (1982). The learning disabled child as an inactive learner: Educational implications. *Topics in Learning and Learning Disabilities, 2,* 45–52.

Torgesen, J. K., & Licht, B. G. (1983). The learning disabled child as an inactive learner: Retrospect and prospects. In J. D. McKinney & L. Feagans (Eds.), *Current topics in learning disabilities* (Vol. 1). Norwood, NJ: Ablex.

Van Reusen, T., Bos, C., Schumaker, J., & Deshler, D. (1987). *The education planning strategy.* Lawrence, KS: Edge Enterprises.

Wong, B. Y. L., & Jones, W. (1982). Increasing metacomprehension in learning disabled and normally achieving students through self-questioning training. *Learning Disability Quarterly, 5,* 228–240.

Attention

Torgesen, J. K. (1981). The relationship between memory and attention in learning disabilities. *Exceptional Education Quarterly, 2,* 51–59.

Walker, N. W. (1985). Impulsivity in learning disabled children: Past research findings and methodological inconsistencies. *Learning Disability Quarterly, 8,* 85–94.

Metacognition

Ellis, E. S., & Lenz, B. K. (1996). Perspectives on instruction in learning strategies. In D. D. Deshler, E. S. Ellis, & B. K. Lenz (Eds.), *Teaching adolescents with learning disabilities* (2nd ed., pp. 9–60). Denver, CO: Love.

Wong, B. Y. L., & Jones, W. (1982). Increasing metacomprehension in learning disabled and normally achieving students through self-questioning training. *Learning Disability Quarterly, 5,* 228–240.

Social Skills and Disruption (see also chapters 7 and 8)

Ayllon, T., & Roberts, M. D. (1974). Eliminating discipline problems by strengthening academic performance. *Journal of Applied Behavior Analysis, 7,* 71–76.

Epstein, M. H., & Cullinan, D. (1983). Academic performance of behaviorally disordered and learning disabled pupils. *The Journal of Special Education, 17,* 304–307.

Ferritor, D. E., Buckholdt, D., Hamblin, R. L., & Smith, L. (1972). The non-effects of contingent reinforcement for attending on work accomplished. *Journal of Applied Behavior Analysis, 5,* 7–17.

Smith, D. D., & Rivera, D. M. (1993). *Effective discipline* (2nd ed.), Austin, TX: PRO-ED.

Characteristics of Learning Environments

Bryant, B. R., & Rivera, D. P. (1995, November). *Cooperative learning: Teaching in an age of technology.* Paper presented at the meeting of the Learning Disabilities Association of Texas, Austin.

Mcintosh, R., Vaughn, S., Schumm, J. S., Haager, D., & Lee, O. (1994). Observations of students with learning disabilities in general education classrooms. *Exceptional Children, 60*(3), 249–261.

Robinson, S. M., Braxdale, C. T., & Colson, S. E. (1985). Preparing dysfunctional learners to enter junior high school: A transitional curriculum. *Focus on Exceptional Children, 18,* 1–12.

Schumaker, J. B., & Deshler, D. D. (1984). Setting demand variables: A major factor in program planning for LD adolescents. *Topics in Language Disorders, 4,* 22–44.

Schumaker, J. B., Deshler, D. D., Alley, G. R., & Warner, M. M. (1983). Toward the development of an intervention model for learning-disabled adolescents. *Exceptional Education Quarterly, 4,* 45–74.

Schumm, J. S., & Vaughn, S. (1991). Making adaptations for mainstreamed students: Regular classroom teachers' perspectives. *Remedial and Special Education, 12*(4), 18–27.

Schumm, J. S., & Vaughn, S. (1992). Planning for mainstreamed special education students: Perceptions of general education teachers. *Exceptionality, 3,* 81–90.

Ysseldyke, J. E., Thurlow, M. L., Wotruba, J. W., & Nania, P. A. (1990). Instructional arrangements: Perceptions from general education. *Teaching Exceptional Children, 22*(4), 4–8.

Teacher Characteristics

Billingsley, B. S., & Cross, L. H. (1991). Teachers' decisions to transfer from special to general education. *Journal of Special Education, 24,* 496–511.

Chusmir, L. H., & Durand, D. E. (1987, May). Stress and the working woman. *Personnel,* 38–43.

Cohen, S. B., & Hart-Hester, S. (1987). Time management strategies. *Teaching Exceptional Children, 20*(1), 56–57.

Deshler, D. D., & Schumaker, J. B. (1986). Learning strategies: An instructional alternative for low-achieving adolescents. *Exceptional Children, 52,* 583–590.

DeShong, B. R. (1981). *The special educator—Stress and survival.* Rockville, MD: Aspen.

Graves, A., Landers, M. R., Lokerson, J., Luchow, J., Horvath, M., & Garnett, K. (1992). *The DLD competencies for teachers of students with learning disabilities.* Reston, VA: Council for Exceptional Children—Division for Learning Disabilities.

Heller, H. W. (1983). Special education professional standards: Need, value, and use. *Exceptional Children, 50,* 199–228.

Hudson, P. J., Morsink, C. V., Branscum, G., & Boone, R. (1987). Competencies for teachers of students with learning disabilities. *Journal of Learning Disabilities, 20,* 232–236.

Kea, C. D. (1987). An analysis of critical teaching behaviors as applied by secondary special education teachers. Chicago: Presentation, Council for Exceptional Children's Annual Convention.

National Joint Committee on Learning Disabilities. (1987). Learning disabilities: Issues in the preparation of professional personnel. *Journal of Learning Disabilities, 20,* 229–231.

Newcomer, P. L. (1982). Competencies for professionals in learning disabilities. *Learning Disability Quarterly, 5,* 241–252.

Olson, J., & Platt, J. (1996). *Teaching children and adolescents with special needs* (2nd ed.). Columbus, OH: Merrill.

Rosenshine, B. V. (1979). Content, time, and direct instruction. In P. L. Peterson and H. J. Walberg, *Research on teaching: Concepts, findings, and implications.* Berkeley, CA: McCutchan.

Rosenshine, B. V. (1983). Teaching functions in instructional programs. *The Elementary School Journal, 83,* 335–351.

Teacher Education Division, Council for Exceptional Children. (1986). *The validation of quality practices in personnel preparation for special education.* Reston, VA: Council for Exceptional Children.

Effective Teaching
Critical Teaching Skills

Bickel, W. E., & Bickel, D. D. (1986). Effective schools, classrooms, and instruction: Implications for special education. *Exceptional Children, 52,* 489–500.

Christenson, S. L., Ysseldyke, J. E., & Thurlow, M. L. (1989). Critical instructional factors for students with mild handicaps: An integrative review. *Remedial and Special Education, 10*(5), 21–31.

Morsink, C. V., Soar, R. S., Soar, R. M., & Thomas, R. (1986). Research on teaching: Opening the door to special education classrooms. *Exceptional Children, 53,* 32–40.

Instructional Time

Berliner, D. C. (1984). The half-full glass: A review of research on teaching. In P. L. Hosford (Ed.), *Using what we know about teaching* (pp. 51–77). Alexandria, VA: Association for Supervision and Curriculum Development.

Bickel, W. E., & Bickel, D. D. (1986). Effective schools, classrooms, and instruction: Implications for special education, *Exceptional Children, 52,* 489–500.

Christenson, S. L., Ysseldyke, J. E., & Thurlow, M. L. (1989). Critical instructional factors for students with mild handicaps: An integrative review. *Remedial and Special Education, 10*(5), 21–31.

Kavale, K., & Forness, S. R. (1986). School learning, time, and learning disabilities: The disassociated learner. *Journal of Learning Disabilities, 19,* 130–138.

Pemberton, J. B., & Smith, D. D. (1994, July). *An analysis of teacher-time during the school day: A study comparing five special educative service delivery models available to students with disabilities.* Paper presented at the Symposium on Inclusive Education, Cambridge University, Institute of Education, Cambridge, England.

Rieth, H. J., Polsgrove, L., & Semmel, M. I. (1979). Relationship between instructional time and academic achievement: Implications for research and practice. *Education Unlimited, 1,* 53–56.

Rosenshine, B. V. (1979). Content, time, and direct instruction. In P. L. Peterson and H. J. Walberg, *Research on teaching: Concepts, findings and implications.* Berkeley, CA: McCutchan.

Rosenshine, B. V. (1980). How time is spent in elementary classrooms. In C. Denham and A. Lieberman (Eds.), *Time to learn.* Washington, DC: National Institute of Education.

Sargent, L. R. (1981). Resource teacher time utilization: An observational study. *Exceptional Children, 47,* 420–425.

Thurlow, M., Graden, J., Greener, J., & Ysseldyke, J. (1983). LD and non-LD students' opportunities to learn. *Learning Disability Quarterly, 6,* 172–183.

Chapter 2
Collaborative Partnerships

Making Connections

Before you read, consider the school reform trends discussed in chapter 1 and the effect of those trends on the roles of special education and general education teachers to meet the needs of students with learning and behavior difficulties. In particular, consider how the characteristics of students described in chapter 1 may contribute to learning difficulties in the general education setting, and how special education teachers can work more effectively with general education teachers to foster academic and social success. Finally, think about the importance of specific skills that professionals need in order to work more collaboratively with each other, paraprofessionals, and families.

As discussed in chapter 1, many youngsters with learning and behavior problems receive most of their education in the general education classroom, because of the school reform and "inclusion" movement. To ensure that all students receive appropriate educational services, it is critical to develop collaborative partnerships between professionals, paraprofessionals, and families. (We use the term families in this and other chapters to denote various family structures, such as extended families, children with guardians, single-parent families, and "blended" families.) Although the notion of having teachers and families build collaborative relationships is not new, **collaboration** has certainly become a major trend in schools because of attempts to educate students with disabilities in general education classrooms more frequently. The idea behind collaboration is that having several people identify and implement solutions is mutually beneficial (Idol, Nevin, & Paolucci-Whitcomb, 1994; Nevin, Thousand, Paolucci-Whitcomb, & Villa, 1990).

In this chapter, we discuss the development of collaborative partnerships between professionals, paraprofessionals, and families. We also provide information about specific collaborative skills that are necessary when establishing effective relationships. We have selected these topics for discussion because of the importance of collaboration in a variety of situations with many different individuals. However, it is beyond the scope of this chapter to discuss each topic fully; therefore, the reader may glean further information from the additional readings in the reference list.

1. Describe effective practices for collaborating with professionals.
2. Explain ways in which teachers and paraprofessionals can work together effectively.
3. Discuss practices that promote collaborative partnerships with families.
4. Describe skills needed for effective collaborative partnerships.

● ●

Collaborating with Professionals

As you read, think about . . .

1. Analyzing how the role of the special education teacher has evolved since the 1960s.
2. Comparing and contrasting collaborative consultation, cooperative consultation, and co-teaching.
3. Designing a collaborative consultation arrangement to work with students in the general education setting who have reading comprehension problems.
4. Designing a science lesson that will be co-taught with the science teacher.
5. Brainstorming ways that collaborative consultation, cooperative consultation, and teaming can be used for students who could benefit from part-time, pull-out special education services.
6. Analyzing the setting demands of your university class and designing a plan to help yourself become an even better student to meet these demands.

Many professionals, such as educators, psychologists, counselors, social workers, administrators, and therapists, are part of the school community that is responsible for working together to provide a high-quality education for all students. Because of the individual needs of youth with learning and behavior problems, special education teachers must often collaborate with different professionals to plan and implement the Individualized Education Program (IEP). Therefore, all educators must know techniques and skills that promote effective, collaborative partnerships. In this section, we explain the importance of collaborative partnerships and discuss their development.

The Need for Collaborative Partnerships

A collaborative partnership implies that individuals are working together toward common educational goals. Historically, special educators have been engaged in this practice for years. In the 1960s and 1970s, the practice of educating children with special needs solely in self-contained special education classrooms was greatly criticized (Dunn, 1968; Robinson, 1991) as limiting, restrictive, and unresponsive to individual educational needs. Consequently, resource rooms were established as an alternative service delivery option for some youngsters with special needs; this meant that these students spent a portion of their day in the general education classroom, creating a need for special educators to collaborate with general education teachers to monitor student progress.

In 1975, with the passage of P.L. 94–142, **mainstreaming** became a popular way to implement the legally required concept of the **least restrictive environment.** As a result, many students with special needs spent more time in general education settings; special education teachers had to maintain contact with classroom teachers and often assumed a consultative role, monitoring progress and problem-solving academic and behavioral concerns (Villa, Thousand, Paolucci-Whitcomb, & Nevin, 1990).

The special education teacher's role became multidimensional as teachers instructed youngsters in special education settings for at least a portion of the school day and consulted and collaborated with general education teachers at other times. General education teachers also faced new challenges, having some children with special needs in their classes after years of limited contact with these youngsters. Educators needed to collaborate and consult about best practices; however, the realities of school day routines and instructional demands restricted opportunities for collaboration (Robinson, 1991).

In the 1980s and into the 1990s, educators became concerned about the rising number of students referred for special education services and questioned the appropriateness of some children's qualifying for services when perhaps some of these students needed academic and behavioral accommodations in the general education setting rather than special education services. Prereferral interventions were sought where teams of educators problem-solved solutions for a specific student's academic difficulties, and general education teachers implemented the recommendations. In some instances, this practice reduced the number of inappropriate referrals to special education (West & Idol, 1990). Collaborative partnerships (e.g., Teacher Assistance Teams [Chalfant & Van Dusen Pysh, 1989], Consulting Teacher Model [Idol, 1988], Prereferral Intervention System [Graden, Casey, & Christenson, 1985]) were developed to assist teachers in accommodating students with learning and behavior problems.

With increasing numbers of students with learning and behavior problems spending more time in general education classes, various service delivery options have been developed. For example, more emphasis is now placed on "pull-in" programs rather than solely on "pull-out" programs. Special and general educators spend more time co-teaching or teaming lessons and providing joint services to all students in the general education classroom. The "class within a class" model developed by Dr. Floyd Hudson promotes more academic interventions in the general education setting for youngsters with academic problems. This model permits students with learning problems, including those students who qualify for special education services, to benefit from the expertise of special education intervention. Finally, the collaborative consultation process has become a prominent service delivery model for retaining students with learning and behavior problems in general education classes in which educators determine effective academic and behavioral interventions that general education teachers typically implement.

Developing Collaborative Partnerships

In this section, we explain ways to develop collaborative partnerships, which should help students with learning and behavior problems function more successfully in the general education setting. We describe the collaborative consultation process, the cooperative consultation model, and co-teaching.

Collaborative Consultation

Collaborative consultation is defined as "an interactive process that enables groups of people with diverse expertise to generate creative solutions to mutually defined problems. The outcome is enhanced and altered from original solutions that group members would produce independently" (Idol et al., 1994, p. 1). Collaborative consultation has two purposes. First, collaborative consultation can be viewed as a service delivery option for students who can benefit from general education class placement most or all of the school day. In this case, special education teachers consult with general education teachers about student progress and concerns. Specific intervention plans are developed that general education teachers implement. Second, collaborative consultation involves prereferral discussions to promote academic success and reduce excessive, inappropriate referrals for special education assessment.

Collaborative consultation rests on the assumptions of promoting educational alternatives for all students, enhancing all educators' opportunities to learn new techniques, promoting parity among participants, and acknowledging that all educators are responsible for all students (Friend & Bursuck, 1996; Robinson, 1991). Collaborative consultation is based on the notion that all participants will contribute their expertise. The contributors identify problems together and seek creative solutions.

Idol et al. (1994) identify six stages of the collaborative consultation process, as explained here:

Stage 1. **Gaining entry and establishing team goals**
Participants establish rapport and specifically identify each member's goals, agendas, and desired outcomes for the collaborative process. In this stage, it is important to ensure that each participant is clear about what he or she would like to have occur during the collaborative process and what each member is capable of contributing to the partnership in terms of time, expertise, and commitment.

Stage 2. **Problem identification**
Participants engage in assessment practices (see chapter 6 for information about assessment techniques) to determine the student's current level of academic performance, behavioral considerations, and affective or emotional status. Participants can derive assessment data from previously administered instruments and behavioral rating scales, teacher observation, and current informal assessment measures. Using available data, the participants develop a profile of the student's strengths and weaknesses and identify specific problems that may account for academic or behavioral problems.

Stage 3. **Intervention recommendations**
Specific interventions are recommended based on any problems identified in stage 2. An important consideration during this stage is the identification of interventions that teachers can implement easily yet accommodate the special needs of the student. During this stage, participants could also identify other students for whom the same interventions may be appropriate and effective.

Stage 4. **Implementation of recommendations**
The intervention for the specific targeted problem is implemented. The special education teacher may be asked to model the intervention or provide feedback to the classroom teacher about the implementation process. The general education teacher may model an intervention for the special education teacher to learn, or both teachers could work together to implement a

behavior management plan. In other words, teachers could implement interventions and work together in one of several ways.

Stage 5. **Evaluation**

Monitoring student progress to determine the effectiveness of the interventions is extremely important. Classroom teachers can use evaluation techniques to determine whether or not the intervention is effective.

Stage 6. **Follow-up**

Participants must meet regularly to determine if the intervention is effective and to identify additional potential problem areas that could be addressed during the collaborative process. During stage 1, participants could designate a time schedule that is mutually convenient for discussions about student progress. Participants will need to adhere to the schedule or find alternative meeting times to ensure that communication is maintained.

Figure 2.1 shows an example of a form that can be used to document decisions and procedures during the collaborative process.

Cooperative Consultation

Cooperative consultation is a collaborative process between special and general education teachers that involves examining instructional expectations, identifying problems, generating alternative interventions, and monitoring progress (Riegel, 1988). Cooperative consultation assists general education teachers in providing appropriate accommodations for elementary and secondary level youngsters with learning and behavior problems who may receive most of their instruction in the general education classroom.

There are many similarities between collaborative consultation and cooperative consultation. For example, both are based on the premise that together, special education and general education teachers can identify appropriate assistance structures

Figure 2.1
Example of plan for documenting collaborative decisions

Collaboration plan

Special education teacher

_____

Student

_____

General education teacher

_____

Grade

_____

What the special education teacher will do:

What the general education teacher will do:

What the student will do:

Follow-up conference date[a]: _____

Successes:

Problems:

Ideas to Solve Problems:

[a]Schedule conferences at least once a week at first.

for students with learning and behavior problems. Both models also emphasize identifying problems, recommending interventions, and monitoring students. However, cooperative consultation places a heavy emphasis on comparing teachers' expectations to students' strengths and weaknesses, and making instructional recommendations to accommodate individual differences in learning. The cooperative consultation model systematizes this analysis, producing specific recommendations to promote a better match between the learner and the learning environment.

Cooperative consultation is based on the belief that collaboration between professionals with diverse expertise is mutually beneficial. This process also recognizes the demands placed on youngsters with special needs to equal the success of their peers in the general education setting. If teachers identify these demands and plan appropriate accommodations, some students with special needs may be capable of meeting the instructional demands of the general education setting. Some students may not; for them, other accommodations and service delivery options must be explored.

The cooperative consultation process consists of six steps. Step 1 involves describing the student's strengths and weaknesses. Step 2 requires a description of general education teachers' expectations and instructional demands. Step 3 consists of comparing the student's skills with course expectations. Step 4 involves planning for and monitoring instruction. In steps 5 and 6, special education teachers provide support to general education teachers as they implement the accommodations and monitor student progress. Teachers engage in a cooperative monitoring process where they identify a specific problem and recommend specific accommodations. The teachers specify the person who will implement the accommodation and develop a series of monitoring questions (e.g., Is the student listening in class? Is she participating more? Does he understand the reading material?). These questions guide the assessment process to determine the effectiveness of the accommodations. In Figure 2.2, an example of a student inventory is presented. Together, both general and special education teachers complete the inventory to assess the student's abilities in relation to the demands of the setting. Then, they develop a plan to target specific problem areas.

Co-Teaching

Co-teaching is the delivery of instruction by two or more teachers, in which each person brings specialized knowledge to the lesson (Bauwens & Hourcade, 1994). The purpose of co-teaching is to unite expertise to present instructional content. Co-teaching is based on the assumption that the team can bring to the classroom combined knowledge and expertise that will greatly enhance instruction. Team members can meet individual students' needs more adequately than one teacher. Teachers who choose to co-teach are committed to joint decision making and ownership of instructional planning, implementation, and evaluation.

For example, a speech/language pathologist and a special education teacher can combine their expertise to produce a lesson rich in language and content development. Or, special education and general education teachers could work collaboratively to plan, teach, and evaluate a lesson presented in the general education classroom. There are many variations of co-teaching partnerships, including teaming for one instructional period, teaming for the entire day, or having a special education and general education team assigned to one class all year (Cook & Friend, 1993). Co-

Figure 2.2
Sample inventory

Student inventory (elementary level)

Date reviewed _____

Student: _____ Primary disability: _____ Age: _____ Grade: 1 2 3 4 5

School: _____ Special ed. teacher: _____

Basic achievement: Reading level: _____ Source: _____ Math level: _____ Source: _____

Special education support:
Extensive (more than ½ time) _____   Moderate (1–3 hours per day) _____   Occasional (less than 1 hr./day) _____

+ Strengths (commensurate with nondisabled peers)	0 Weaknesses in general class settings
Information input (how student learns)	Information output (how student responds)
_____ Textbook	Essay _____
_____ Worksheets	Written reports _____
_____ Workbooks	Short answer _____
_____ Oral presentation	Creative writing _____
_____ Discussion	Worksheets/Workbooks _____
_____ A-V Materials	
_____ Hands-on Experiences	Multiple choice/Matching _____
_____ Observation	True/False _____
_____ Boardwork (oral)	Math word problems _____
_____ Boardwork (copying)	Computation _____
_____ Reference material	
_____ Computers	
	Demo./Lab. projects _____
_____ Teacher-directed activity	Art or media projects _____
_____ Independent work	Maps, charts, or graphs _____
_____ Peer tutors	Oral responses _____
_____ With a teacher	Oral reports _____
_____ With an aide	Group discussion _____
_____ In a small group	Boardwork _____
_____ With the whole class	Discovery/Critical think. _____
Other:	Other:

General suggestions: _____
_____
_____

IEP Goals: _____
_____
_____
_____

Figure 2.2
Continued

Problem checklist
(Check only chronic difficulties which occur in the regular class.)

Learning problems

_____ Asking questions in class
_____ Categorizing
_____ Class discussion
_____ Completing assignments
_____ Following directions
_____ Getting started
_____ Independent work skills
_____ Learning from demonstrations
_____ Learning from oral presentations
_____ Learning from tape recordings
_____ Listening
_____ Mathematics
_____ Oral expression
_____ Organization
_____ Paying attention
_____ Reading content material
_____ Recalling specific information
_____ Remembering (general skills)
_____ Seeing relationships
_____ Staying on task
_____ Study skills & learning strategies
_____ Taking notes
_____ Taking tests
_____ Thinking skills
_____ Transferring information or skills
_____ Understanding content vocabulary
_____ Working in groups
_____ Writing

Behavior problems

List behaviors which have been found to be troublesome for this student in his or her general education classes. Rank these in order of importance (1=top priority).

Behavior	Rank
_____	_____
_____	_____
_____	_____
_____	_____
_____	_____

Management technique(s) found helpful
by other teachers:

_____

_____

_____

_____

_____

_____

_____

Manual dexterity (describe): _____
_____

Classroom organization needed: _____
_____

Effective rewards and reinforcers: _____
_____

Medical, physical, or sensory problems: _____
_____
_____

Hall behavior (describe): _____
_____

Playground/Recess behavior: _____
_____

Social skills and peer acceptance: _____
_____

Responses to authority (describe): _____
_____
_____

Comments (include preferences parents have voiced regarding methods, home routines, or support to be given):

Source: From *A Guide to Cooperative Consultation*, by R. H. Riegel, 1988, Jason Court, MI: RHR Consultation Services. Copyright 1988 by RHR Consultation Services. Reprinted with permission.

teachers may be general education teachers, special education teachers, counselors, and speech/language pathologists. The players will depend on the instructional objectives and students' needs.

Implementing a co-teaching arrangement requires certain procedures. First, teachers must mutually define roles in the teaming relationship as they pertain to instruction, behavior management, and evaluation. Specifying role responsibilities can prevent ambiguities and miscommunication. Second, team members need to spend time discussing instructional philosophies to determine if a mutual, collaborative relationship can be established. This is important in developing team rapport. Third, teachers must explain what they and their students can hope to gain from a team effort. Such disclosure can promote effective communication right from the start of a teaming relationship. Fourth, team members should convey to students the teachers' roles and how instruction and discipline will be handled in the classroom. Ideally, both teachers should maintain a similar level of authority when working with the students. Finally, team members need to meet regularly to work through problems, evaluate student progress, communicate with families, and plan further instruction.

Collaborative consultation, cooperative consultation, and co-teaching can be used effectively to promote the success of students with learning and behavior problems in the general education setting. Careful planning, communication, and regular meetings are important for all three options. It is also important to consider how these options will promote the academic success of students with special needs in general education settings. Table 2.1 provides information about possible barriers and solutions in collaborative consultation, cooperative consultation, and co-teaching.

Collaborating with Paraprofessionals

As you read, think about . . .
1. Describing ways to get to know your paraprofessional.
2. Designing a meeting with your paraprofessional to define roles and responsibilities.
3. Developing a training program for paraprofessionals.
4. Developing an evaluation instrument for supervisory purposes.

Paraprofessionals are individuals who work with teachers in a supportive role; they are members of the instructional team in classrooms and other educational settings. According to Mandell and Schram (1983), paraprofessionals usually possess less than a baccalaureate degree; however, with increased emphasis on training, many paraprofessionals possess education beyond high school and, in some cases, an associate degree. In a study on the demographics of paraprofessionals, Blalock (1990) found that of 136 individuals working in a large school district in a southwestern state, 92 percent were female, 54 percent were Hispanic, 34 percent were ages 30 to 39, 38 percent were 40 to 49, and 78 percent had a high school diploma or had obtained a GED. Typically, paraprofessionals must possess a high school diploma or equivalent; salary is usually commensurate with this level of education, thereby making this group of individuals underpaid for some of the responsibilities and tasks to which they are assigned.

Table 2.1 Barriers and Solutions to Developing Collaborative Partnerships

Barriers to professional collaborative partnerships	Solutions to professional collaborative partnerships
1. Time	1. Identify times during the day that are mutually acceptable; avoid "giving away" time that is needed for mental health (e.g., lunch, time after the duty day ends). Work with administrators to identify joint planning times for collaborating.
2. Territories	2. Discuss roles in the collaborative process and how individual expertise can be mutually demonstrated.
3. Lack of follow-through on responsibilities	3. Use problem-solving and conflict-resolution techniques discussed in the chapter.
4. Role ambiguity	4. List the roles and responsibilities of each collaborative member.
5. Differences in values, perceptions, and philosophies	5. Discuss these areas; use self-disclosure, I-messages, if necessary, and active listening techniques.
Barriers to paraprofessional collaborative partnerships	**Solutions to paraprofessional collaborative partnerships**
1. Time	1. Try to set aside 30 minutes several days a week before or after school to discuss students' progress.
2. Roles and responsibilities	2. Discuss roles and responsibilities clearly so each person knows his or her duties.
3. Age	3. Tap the expertise of paraprofessionals who have been working at the school longer than the teacher; help build the self-confidence of new paraprofessionals.
Barriers to parental collaborative partnerships	**Solutions to parental collaborative partnerships**
1. Time	1. Find times to meet with parents that are mutually agreeable. This may necessitate early morning or late afternoon meetings to accommodate busy schedules.
2. Language	2. Have an interpreter present during meetings. Be sure written communication is in the parents' primary language.
3. Professional jargon	3. Avoid technical terms and acronyms that may be unfamiliar to parents.

Paraprofessionals can contribute significantly to implementing appropriate educational programs for students with learning and behavior problems; their skills are an important part of developing collaborative partnerships in schools. In this section, we discuss a rationale for recognizing paraprofessionals as important members of special education collaborative teams. We present ideas that can be considered when developing collaborative partnerships with paraprofessionals. Suggestions for overcoming common barriers associated with working collaboratively with paraprofessionals are presented in Table 2.1.

The Need for Collaborative Partnerships

At one time, paraprofessionals spent most of their time performing clerical duties; monitoring halls, playground, and cafeteria; and supervising students who were being disciplined for behavioral infractions. However, the role of the paraprofessional has evolved with increased awareness of the valuable contributions they can make in educational settings. Increased training opportunities have led many paraprofessionals to develop important skills that can benefit educational teams.

According to Blalock (1991), paraprofessionals have been in great demand since the 1960s to help deliver services to students with disabilities; today, that demand continues as more students are in general education settings and require more services than general educators can reasonably provide. In addition to working in special education and general education classes, paraprofessionals can help students outside of school; this may involve riding public transportation with students to their job sites, assisting students with disabilities on job site tasks, and participating with students and teachers in community activities designed to promote recreational and social skills. Thus, as options expand for providing services and effective instruction to youngsters with learning and behavior problems, the need for paraprofessionals continues to evolve.

Developing Collaborative Partnerships

Several areas must be considered when developing collaborative partnerships with paraprofessionals, including the establishment of roles, supervision and training, and teaming. This section describes considerations for each of these areas.

Roles and Responsibilities

Clear definitions of job descriptions, roles, and responsibilities promote communication between teachers and paraprofessionals and foster appropriate expectations. Paraprofessionals and teachers should review each other's job description so that each is apprised of the requirements of the positions. Typically, job descriptions include a definition of the job, general responsibilities, and specific hiring requirements (e.g., amount of education, contractual duty day, length of school year). Because of the guidelines provided, reviewing job descriptions is a good way to begin a discussion about roles and responsibilities. The job description usually relays information that school district administrative personnel feel is important for particular roles; thus, teachers and paraprofessionals must abide by the established job guidelines.

Once job descriptions have been reviewed, teachers and paraprofessionals can work together to identify specific roles and responsibilities and delineate responsibilities pertaining to each role. For example, roles might include instruction, administration, behavior management, assessment, and communication with families and other professionals. Together, teachers and paraprofessionals can develop a responsibilities list for each role and identify areas for training, philosophical discussion, and further explanation (Blalock, 1991). Table 2.2 lists roles and responsibilities for paraprofessionals. Teachers have the responsibility to develop, implement, and evaluate their students' Individualized Education Programs (IEPs), and to look out for students' well-being, but paraprofessionals can greatly assist in supporting these endeavors.

Specifying roles is not only important for clarifying classroom responsibilities; it is also important for establishing the teacher's authority as the paraprofessional's supervisor and evaluator. The dynamics between the teacher and paraprofessional can be influenced by the paraprofessional's age, length of employment, and community connection (e.g., knowledge of the family's problems, relationship with commu-

Table 2.2
Roles and
Responsibilities for
Paraprofessionals

Role

The special education paraprofessional's role is to assist the teacher in performing instructional, behavioral, clerical, and evaluative classroom tasks.

Possible responsibilities

1. Score informal student assessments.
2. Conduct clerical tasks to maintain classroom organization and management.
3. Implement behavior management programs designed jointly with the teacher.
4. Work with general education teacher to facilitate instructional adaptations for mainstreamed students.
5. Reinforce and review skill instruction.
6. Monitor student progress by recording data.
7. Meet regularly with the classroom teacher to discuss specific student needs, instructional programs, successes, and concerns.
8. Work with students in community job-related settings.
9. Escort students during hallway, recess, and lunch activities.
10. Construct instructional materials.
11. Attend professional meetings.
12. Escort students to and from bus transportation.
13. Provide small-group and individual instruction.
14. Help teachers prepare for the next day.

nity members). Often, the paraprofessional is older than the teacher, has been at the school longer, and has strong community connections with families, businesses, and children. These dynamics must be respected, but not allowed to undermine the teacher's role as the paraprofessional's supervisor and as the contractually responsible person for the students' education.

Through effective communication techniques, teachers can tap the valuable knowledge paraprofessionals might possess due to their connections with the school and community. Alternatively, teachers may have to be particularly sensitive to the needs of younger paraprofessionals if they lack experience and educational expertise. Thus, it is important for teachers to invest time in establishing rapport and in team-building behaviors so that a truly collaborative partnership can be nurtured.

Supervision and Training

Teachers are typically responsible for supervising and evaluating the paraprofessionals with whom they work. Building principals may also share in the supervisory and evaluative process, but teachers usually assume the majority of this responsibility.

Ongoing communication is key to any supervisory situation. Paraprofessionals should be given opportunities to determine how they will be supervised and evaluated. Teachers and paraprofessionals must review job descriptions, roles, and responsibilities as a starting point in the supervisory process. Specific tasks and expectations should be communicated effectively to reduce role ambiguity and misinterpretations. At a minimum, weekly meetings are recommended to review the paraprofessional's tasks and job performance. Paraprofessionals should be informed about the positive and negative aspects of their performance on a regular basis.

Teachers could examine their supervisory style to determine practices that foster collegial relationships. An authoritarian style probably won't promote a spirit of collaboration, while a sharing, direct approach where the teacher and paraprofessional have an equal opportunity to reflect on strengths and weaknesses could facilitate a collaborative partnership. Paraprofessionals also should have an opportunity to openly discuss practices by their supervisors that affect communication and the fulfillment of role responsibilities.

To serve in the role of supervisor and evaluator, the teacher should probably have training in effective supervisory practices and evaluation criteria. If training is not available, teachers could seek assistance from their building principal and special education coordinator in identifying ways to make supervision promote collaborative relationships. These resources can also inform teachers of proper school district procedures for conducting employee evaluations. School districts often have career ladders for paraprofessionals in which promotion depends on positive evaluations; therefore, it is in everyone's best interest for teachers to learn about (1) evaluation criteria, (2) ways to conduct an evaluation (e.g., providing feedback, stating strengths and weaknesses, problem solving, conflict resolution), and (3) techniques to help paraprofessionals improve on any weaknesses.

Vasa, Steckelberg, and Hoffman (1986) recommend that the paraprofessional evaluation process include a self-evaluation, a parent evaluation, an observation checklist by the teacher, and the school district classified personnel evaluation. The data from these evaluations across different sources and experiences should yield a descriptive profile of the paraprofessional from which specific strengths and weaknesses could be identified and a subsequent follow-up plan could be developed to foster growth.

Training paraprofessionals is a critical element of effective supervisory practices. It is not enough to tell someone about weaknesses without offering options for improvement. School district human resources offices could team with teachers to determine specific areas in which paraprofessionals might benefit from in-service training. Many paraprofessionals may be working for the first time with children who have disabilities and might not possess knowledge about students' educational, medical, and language needs, for example. Paraprofessionals may have effective interpersonal skills and a caring attitude, but may lack skills specific to the populations with whom they are working. Therefore, school district administrators should consider teaching these individuals how to work with students of all types of disabilities in special education and general education settings.

There are several training options. First, community colleges can provide classes to develop skills paraprofessionals will need in public schools. School district and community college personnel could easily develop a curriculum to serve this training need. Second, teachers can provide informal training in their classrooms as they work with children. By modeling, prompting, and "thinking aloud" situations, teachers can instruct paraprofessionals in the skills they will need to work effectively with students. Teachers and paraprofessionals can meet periodically; in these meetings, teachers can correct problems and reinforce successes. Third, school district and university personnel could collaborate to provide several in-service training opportunities for paraprofessionals (Blalock, 1991). Scenario 2.1 presents an example of a collaborative training program for paraprofessionals that a public school and a university developed together.

Scenario 2.1

A Public School–University Collaborative Paraprofessional Training Program
In Albuquerque, New Mexico, school district administrators in special education, classified personnel, and special education faculty at the University of New Mexico conducted a joint training effort. Basic and advanced training strands were developed based on needs assessment data from paraprofessionals and teachers. Paraprofessionals could select topics of interest relevant to their particular situation. Training topics included: (1) the role of the paraprofessional, (2) teaming skills (both teacher and paraprofessional were asked to attend), (3) assertive discipline, (4) behavior management, (5) information about different exceptionalities, (6) effective communication skills, (7) sign language, (8) community-based instruction, (9) working with students with physical disabilities, (10) problem-solving skills, (11) instructional techniques, and (12) ways to observe and record instances of inappropriate behavior. Training occurred during and after the school day and ranged from awareness to skill building. The success of this training program hinged on the presence of a career ladder in the school district for paraprofessionals, where advancement depended on the accrual of specific numbers of in-service or college hours or both. Therefore, the in-service training benefited paraprofessionals, teachers, and students as more training hours were accrued to foster professional development and economic status. ■

Collaborating with Families

As you read, think about . . .

1. Designing a parent handbook that describes your program.
2. Describing ways to learn more about your families and school community.
3. Designing an agenda for a home visit.
4. Developing a parent-involvement program.
5. Designing an agenda for your first parent conference.
6. Developing ways to foster ethnic, cultural, and linguistic diversity in your classroom.
7. Explaining ways to work effectively with an interpreter.
8. Developing ways to promote positive communication with families throughout the year.

Families are an integral part of the school community; they know their children better than anyone and can provide critical information that can aid in understanding students' individual needs. For years, families have been influential in developing special education services; this influence continues to affect schools as educational reform efforts at the elementary and secondary levels contribute to the modification and creation of service delivery options for youngsters with learning and behavior problems. In this section, we talk about the importance of developing collaborative partnerships with families, and situations in which this collaboration can be facilitated. Possible barriers and solutions to working with families are discussed in Table 2.1.

The Need for Collaborative Partnerships with Families

There is a great need to collaborate with families. Families have contributed significantly to establishing special education as a field. They have formed organizations, raised revenue, initiated litigation, pushed for legislation, formed advocacy groups, and demanded free, appropriate public education in the least restrictive environment for all students with disabilities. They have clout.

Collaboration with families should be a major goal of all schools. As Pugach and Johnson so aptly noted, our "students are all members of families first and students second" (1995, p. 225). Therefore, we need to recognize the powerful effect that families have on the students with whom we work, and we ought to nurture collaborative relationships with families and family members. We cannot view children with learning and behavior problems in isolation; they are members of the total school community, the community at large, and their families (Smith & Luckasson, 1995). Therefore, we must come to know our students' families, understand their dynamics, and only then can we begin to develop effective, collaborative partnerships.

Developing Collaborative Partnerships with Families

Collaborative efforts with students' families can be developed through a family systems approach where families' needs and support are defined according to resources, interactions, functions, and the life cycle (Turnbull & Turnbull, 1990). For example, home-school collaboration efforts can be greatly enhanced if teachers are aware of (1) the family unit (e.g., one- or two-parent family, extended family); (2) resources families need to function; (3) family interactions that may affect the children's mental health and school success; (4) families' economic, vocational, and educational needs; and (5) the adult and child development cycles that influence how individuals cope with and respond to their environments.

As part of the family systems approach, educators must understand that families of children with disabilities will probably need different types of support systems that change as children mature. Families may have specific issues, such as reactions to a family member with a disability, economic needs, and future planning needs. Educators should listen to these needs and help families acquire appropriate support services. A child with a learning disability may not manifest this disability until he or she enters school; families may question instructional programs and placements and may wonder what the future holds for their child's postsecondary education. For families of children with behavior problems, school may be just another arena in which difficulties surface and negative encounters with authorities occur. By viewing the development of collaborative partnerships through a family systems approach, educators can individualize their interactions with families based on each family's unique configuration and needs.

Professionals and paraprofessionals also need to address values and perceptions as they work with children and family members. A teacher's value system and ways of perceiving information can, on occasion, impede or promote effective home-school communication and collaboration. Individuals learn values and perceptions from significant adults, home environments, peers, cultural and ethnic groups, and religious and social affiliations, to name a few. Unfortunately, it is too easy to judge or label another person's value system and perceptions based on misconceptions, stereotypes, miscommunication, and one's own value and perceptual systems.

Today's students represent a rich cultural and linguistic heritage; many children also come from a spectrum of socioeconomic environments ranging from homelessness to considerable affluence. The challenge for educators is to become more sensitive to all types of diversity, to become more educated about differences in values and perceptions, and to focus on ways of promoting collaborative home-school relationships. "Reality checks" with families are important to ensure that families' perceptions of schools are based on what is actually happening in the classroom. For instance, when a family member asks a child, "What did you do in school today?" and the child responds, "Nothing," it portrays a rather inactive, boring school day. Family members may draw conclusions based on their value systems and perceptions of what "should" be going on in classrooms. Scenario 2.2 illustrates an example of home-school communication that speaks to the importance of teachers' communicating regularly with family members.

Scenario 2.2

Example of Home-School Communication

Gus's mother tried to sit down with him each night to talk about the day's events and to review homework. On Monday, she learned that Gus was struggling with algebra and that the homework was much too difficult for him. When asked about how the teacher presented the problems in class, Gus reported that the teacher didn't really teach the problems that were given for homework, but went over other problem types. Gus's mother found this to be troublesome; it didn't seem right that the teacher would focus on one type of problem and then assign another type for homework. What was going on in that classroom? She made a mental note that she would call the teacher tomorrow and find out how Gus was doing in class and what types of problems were being taught. The next day, Gus's mother spoke to the algebra teacher and learned that her son asked many good questions during instruction, but also tended to talk to his neighbors. The teacher explained that it was his practice to teach the even-numbered problems and to assign the odd-numbered problems for homework; he did admit, however, that some of the odd-numbered problems required knowledge that had not been taught. The teacher and Gus's mother agreed to monitor Gus's classroom behavior more closely and decided that the teacher would not assign homework problems that had not been taught.

Questions?
1. *What perceptions and values do you think are evident in this scenario?*
2. *How was a collaborative relationship established?*
3. *How would you have handled this if you were the teacher?*
4. *How would you have handled this if you were Gus's mother?*
5. *What do you think about the resolution?* ■

Teachers need to try to convey information about school activities to families and to show families that they want to establish a collaboration. In this section, we describe how parent conferences and home-school communication can promote effective communication with family members.

Parent-Teacher Conferences

The parent-teacher conference is probably one of the most common, frequently planned forums for families and teachers to develop collaborative, communicative partnerships (Pugach & Johnson, 1995). Parent-teacher conferences can be used to establish rapport with family members, convey information about class activities, identify a student's strengths and weaknesses, and discover values and perceptions that can be nurtured to promote collaboration and communication. According to Turnbull and Turnbull (1990) there are four purposes for parent-teacher conferences:

1. To share information about the child's educational progress
2. To work together in finding solutions to problems

3. To establish rapport and joint responsibility for the child's educational program
4 To exchange home and school information that might contribute to a better understanding of the child's progress and individual needs

There are three stages of an effective parent-teacher conference: preconference, conference, and postconference (Kroth, 1985). Specific actions can occur during each stage to foster collaboration and communication (Pugach & Johnson, 1995). A description of the steps involved in each stage appears in Table 2.3. Tips for Teachers provides information to help teachers prepare for, implement, and follow up on parent-teacher conferences. These conferences are a critical component of collaborative relationships; time must be given to this endeavor to ensure success.

Tips for Teachers

Promoting Successful Parent-Teacher Conferences
1. Invite students to participate in conferences as appropriate.
2. Prepare written information to give parents about their child's progress.
3. Be honest with parents.
4. Involve parents in planning for their child's educational program.
5. Involve parents in establishing a home-school behavior management program.
6. Know the school community and learn about values and perceptions before the conferences.
7. Read confidential information about the child; know the child.
8. Avoid making judgments and preaching.
9. Know that parents may be at different coping stages in accepting their child's disability and other family issues.
10. Avoid monopolizing the conversation.
11. Tell parents you don't know if you're really not sure about something; follow up with accurate information.
12. Work with school administrators to offer child care during conferences.
13. Make home visits to conduct conferences when appropriate (see chapter 4).
14. Maintain a sense of humor.
15. Recognize when emotions are escalating and use defusing techniques.
16. Provide a classroom environment rich in cultural and ethnic heritage; ensure that communication will be promoted if parents do not speak English as their primary language. ■

Home-School Communication
Families are important members of the school community; therefore, establishing rapport and effective communication procedures at the beginning of the school year are key factors in promoting collaborative partnerships.

Oftentimes, an initial contact with families focuses on a concern or problem (e.g., disciplinary issues, a lack of homework, truancy) that requires parental notification and action. Smith and Rivera (1993) suggest that at the beginning of the school year and throughout the year, teachers let families know about the positive—good news about class activities, student progress, and behavior go a long way in building communication bridges that foster collaboration. Then, if a contact must be made regarding concerns, teachers have a positive foundation on which they can discuss current issues. Several techniques can be used to build communication (see Ref-

Table 2.3
Stages of
Parent-Teacher
Conferences

Preconference stage

1. Notify families of the conference's time, date, and purpose. Notification should be written in the primary language spoken at home. Provide options for conference times and dates that are convenient for them as well as for teachers (and other professionals, such as counselors, who might be attending the conference). In many families, both parents now work, and in single-parent homes, the parent is usually employed full time; thus, flexibility in conference times and dates is important to increase the likelihood of parental participation (Smith & Rivera, 1993).

2. Review evaluation data that describe how the child is progressing academically, socially, and behaviorally. Prepare a summary of important data and information that will help families understand their child's progress. Samples of work can be gathered as evidence of progress or need for remediation. Share with families the plans for promoting academic success and remediating instructional problems.

3. Develop an agenda for the meeting, including a starting and stopping time, questions that will be asked, a statement of purpose for the meeting, and a time to develop a plan, if necessary. Ask family members what topics they would like to discuss as part of the agenda.

4. Make the environment foster a collaborative spirit. Provide chairs that are designed for adults (a problem at the primary level), remove barriers (such as teacher desks), and eliminate distractions (such as intercom interruptions or hallway noise).

5. Identify other key professionals and paraprofessionals, such as the general education teacher, who might contribute important information to the conference. This is especially important if the child works with a speech and language pathologist. The challenge is to ensure that there are not too many professionals present, as this might be intimidating to families. An initial parent-teacher conference might be a good approach, followed by a second meeting with other professionals, as needed. Rapport and trust can be built in the first meeting.

6. Make arrangements for an interpreter if English is not the parents' primary language or if sign language is needed. In some school communities, a home-school liaison delivers the conference information so that families can communicate with school personnel right from the start of the school year.

Conference stage

1. Provide a warm welcome; meet family members at the door and guide them to the conference meeting table. A comfortable environment paves the way for a positive start.

2. Present the agenda and be sure that parents' questions and concerns are readily noted for discussion. Specify the time limit, which will help keep the conversation on track.

3. Begin with an explanation and display of the child's strengths. Showing work samples and describing positive situations can begin to establish rapport and trust.

4. Apprise family members of their child's progress and the instructional plan. Talk to families about ways to support instruction at home and tips for developing effective study and homework habits.

5. Provide an opportunity for family members to discuss their concerns throughout the conference. Do not give them only the last few minutes to "ask questions."

6. Watch for nonverbal and verbal signs of discomfort, anger, joy, and so forth. In situations where feelings begin to escalate, acknowledge information conveyed by family members.

7. Jot down important points during the conference; however, check with families about this practice, as it may hinder communication. Writing on carbon paper provides copies of the notes for each participant and thus eliminates the "secrecy" of note taking. Writing is especially critical if a plan of action must be developed where families and teachers agree on responsibilities for solving a problem.

8. End on a positive note, summarizing issues, successes, and plans for improvement. This can foster trust and increase the chance that other conferences will occur.

continued

Table 2.3
Continued

Postconference stage

1. Review any notes that were taken during the conference to see if specific activities must be planned for the following school day. If an agreement is made that certain activities (e.g., moving the child's desk, talking to the child alone more often) will occur, then teachers probably need to be sure that action is taken the following school day.

2. As needed, discuss with other professionals concerns about the child and follow-up plans to address the concerns. This may require an additional conference to be scheduled or stronger home-school communication efforts to be established.

erences and Suggested Readings, "Collaborating with Families," for resources that contain communication ideas). Smith and Rivera (1993) and Turnbull and Turnbull (1990) offer several suggestions for promoting communication. For example, teachers could send home weekly or monthly newsletters describing events, special student recognition, important dates, and so forth. Keep in mind that particular students and some secondary level students in general may not want to be singled out; recognizing groups of students might be one way to address this issue. As a language arts activity, students could participate in the design, layout, and production of the newsletter, especially with the many desktop publishing software programs now available for students of all ages.

Teachers could periodically send home notes recognizing a child's accomplishments. This can be done quietly with the student to minimize public display (which is especially important at the secondary level). Experience has shown that many secondary students do indeed like the special recognition; the key point is how the teacher handles it. Elementary students usually can deal with public recognition.

Teachers could make telephone calls periodically informing families of their child's progress. Calling families and telling them "I just wanted to tell you the good news..." can help tremendously in building communication and trust.

Another form of home-school communication is sending home certificates that emphasize a particular area of improvement—finishing homework, accomplishing a goal, getting along with peers—to recognize an accomplishment toward which the child has been working. This is particularly important if families and teachers have established a plan of action to remedy a problem.

Students could collect weekly samples of work and take them home to their families. This informs family members how their children are progressing with the skills that were designated as areas to focus on for the semester or school year. Samples could include good work and work that needs improvement (with an "improved" paper included as well). This shows that students are progressing with their academic goals.

Copies of discipline plans should be shared with families, as they might want to know how their children will be disciplined; be sure the principal approves the plan before it is sent home. Some teachers ask parents to sign a form that shows that they have seen the discipline plan.

Establishing parent groups is a wonderful way to form a home-school communication network; the school's counselor could co-lead such groups. Teachers who have been teaching for several years are probably ready to begin a monthly or bisemester parent group that focuses on a topic of concern (e.g., finishing homework, establishing study skills, building self-esteem, ways to promote reading) for many families. Leading this group with a counselor will ensure that a qualified professional can address any issues beyond the realm of the teacher. If the parent group has child care provided, more family members might be able to participate in the group.

Some teachers try to involve families in the classroom. There are many ways in which teachers can solicit parent involvement. For instance, families can come to class on a regular basis to read with students during reading time. They can share a special skill or information from a trip. Families can work as individual tutors; be sure to provide some initial training and be specific about tasks they should do. Families can offer ethnic and cultural experiences (e.g., cooking specialty dishes), which may be beyond the realm of the teacher, but which are critical to promoting diversity acceptance in schools. Holidays are a wonderful time, in particular, to involve families who can share cultural and ethnic traditions and customs. For example, if teachers are permitted to discuss holiday traditions, Christian, African, and Jewish winter holidays can be shared with children. Families can help teachers make bulletin board displays and learning materials—have a designated night to explain these needs to families and just see the wonderful items you get in response! Grandparents are an untapped source of classroom volunteers. Many grandparents would love the opportunity to work in their grandchildren's classrooms and schools. For instance, in one school in Albuquerque, New Mexico, grandparents participated in a schoolwide reading program.

Weekly report cards that require a signature are another way to keep families informed, to signal areas of growth and concern and to share a note about a special achievement. These regular report cards also permit children the opportunity to discuss their progress with their families.

Developing communication bridges takes time and effort. Teachers must also be aware of cultural and linguistic factors when working with families. Frequent positive and informative communication written in the parent's primary language is important. In the long run, the benefits are usually great and promote the type of home-school communication that contributes to children's progress.

● ●

Foundation Skills for Collaborating

As you read, think about . . .

1. Describing a situation in which you were involved that consisted of a major communication breakdown. Analyze what went wrong and how the problem can be avoided.
2. Observing a two-way conversation and identifying positive and negative nonverbal communication.
3. Developing a plan to promote more effective listening with a communication partner.
4. Identifying a specific problem and implementing the problem-solving steps discussed in this section. Evaluate how the plan worked.
5. Describing a situation in which you were communicating and conflict arose. Specify the circumstances that precipitated the conflict and how it was resolved.
6. Researching ways people of different cultural and ethnic groups communicate, show respect and discipline children. Remember not to overgeneralize or stereotype people, but to identify those customs and traditions that seem to dominate a group.

Establishing collaborative partnerships with professionals, paraprofessionals, and families is necessary for effective schools. Underlying these collaborative efforts there should be effective interpersonal and communicative skills, problem-solving skills, and awareness of cultural and linguistic diversity. Partnerships involve working with people; to do this well, teachers must have foundation skills that foster collaboration. In this section, we discuss interpersonal and communicative skills, problem-solving and conflict-resolution skills, and multicultural and linguistic diversity considerations that can develop a foundation for effective working relationships.

Interpersonal and Communicative Skills

Heron and Harris (1993) conceptualized the communication process as consisting of a conceived message that is encoded and transmitted, and a received message that is decoded and comprehended. For this process to occur successfully, the speaker and listener must possess an array of skills. For instance, successful communication requires effective listening, encoding, and decoding skills. Participants in the communication process have to interpret and transmit nonverbal signals, and they must possess interpersonal skills that foster interactions. According to West, Idol, and Cannon (1989), effective communicative participants have caring, respect, rapport, and enthusiasm, flexibility. They can take risks, listen, and give credit to others.

Listening is an important skill to develop for improving communicative interactions. Listening involves maintaining appropriate eye contact, acknowledging the speaker's message with verbal feedback, and maintaining appropriate nonverbal signals. Deterrents to effective listening include (1) being preoccupied and not listening, (2) talking more than listening, (3) second-guessing what the speaker will say and responding inappropriately, (4) making judgments, (5) being distrustful, (6) using language not appropriate to the situation (e.g., too technical, unmindful of cultural and ethnic values and perceptions) (West, Idol, & Cannon, 1989), (7) fatigue, (8) strong emotions, and (9) specific words chosen to convey messages (Kroth, 1985). Through careful self-analysis and feedback from speakers, listeners can improve their skills so that more effective communication occurs.

One of the most effective types of listening is called **active listening** (Gordon, 1980). The purpose of active listening is to engage the listener in the message being sent, to demonstrate to the speaker that the listener is interested in the message, to enable the speaker to convey specific concerns, and to provide feedback to the speaker to ensure that the message was correctly received and perceived. Active listening can be used effectively in many types of interactions, particularly during emotionally charged conversations. There are six types of active listening:

1. Acknowledging—tells the speaker you are listening; may include appropriate nonverbal signals and verbal comments.
2. Paraphrasing—the listener provides feedback to the speaker about the received, perceived message by repeating back to the speaker in his or her own words the message that was conveyed.
3. Reflecting—involves telling the speaker the feelings he or she is verbalizing.
4. Clarifying—asks for more specific information to help the listener better understand the message.
5. Elaboration—involves asking the speaker to provide more information about an idea or the message to broaden the content conveyed to the listener.

6. Summarizing—requires the listener to reiterate the main ideas of the conversation and the actions that will be taken, if any. Summarizing gives closure to a conversation and provides feedback for all members about the key points discussed.

Messages conveyed verbally can be analyzed in terms of how the message is being received, the nonverbal language emitted by the listener, and the feedback from the listener that signals accurate interpretation. West, Idol, and Cannon (1989) recommend specific procedures for facilitating effective verbal communication. First, before speaking, organize your thoughts to be sure that they are relevant to the conversation and can be stated succinctly. Second, demonstrate good listening behaviors to show that you are indeed interested in the speaker's message. Third, use feedback to show that you are listening and understanding the speaker's message. Fourth, avoid being judgmental and evaluative. Fifth, be aware of extraneous factors (e.g., a receiver who doesn't feel well or who has a personal crisis, a parent who may be very angry at another professional yet unconsciously projects the anger onto you, a paraprofessional who feels that the tasks she or he is assigned are demeaning) that may interfere with the communication process. Sixth, try not to use technical, educational jargon. Be specific without using acronyms that the listener may not know.

Because people are so busy today, they often communicate in writing. Professionals may communicate with each other via newsletters, Internet, and notes. Written communication could include a signature, date, and request for a response (West, Idol, & Cannon, 1993). Although written communication reduces the need for face-to-face interactions, participants must be sure that written messages are conveyed appropriately to ensure accurate interpretation. For example, written messages containing spelling or syntactical errors send a message that the writer has not proofread his or her work, or lacks some basic skills. Jargon must be used cautiously in written communication. Long, detailed messages can lose their effectiveness because of their complexity or because the recipient lacks time to read them.

Nonverbal communication is another interactive and communicative skill that requires careful analysis to ensure that the speaker is emitting appropriate signals and that the listener is comprehending the intended message. According to Heron and Harris (1993) and West, Idol, and Cannon (1989), nonverbal communication includes facial expressions, body posturing and movement, use of space, and touch. Nonverbal messages are a powerful form of communication because they tend to be more genuine and they may be more easily conveyed than emotionally laden verbal messages (Miller, 1986).

Facial expressions can be very informative about trust, disdain, and interest. Elevated eyebrows, little or regular eye contact, smiles, and frowns convey specific messages to speakers. Facing the speaker, crossing one's arms, and sitting in a relaxed position are all examples of body posturing and movement that need to be recognized as speakers and listeners interact. Keeping about two to four feet between speakers and listeners is an acceptable use of space when participants know each other and can interact comfortably. Finally, touch is a form of communication that needs to be monitored carefully. Some people are not comfortable with touching arms or hugging, for instance. This is an area that can develop rapport, but must be handled carefully.

Probably one of the most important factors in nonverbal communication is the cultural and ethnic values of people with whom interactions are occurring. For example, in the Navajo culture, children who are being disciplined and who are showing respect do not establish eye contact; they tend to look down. When fostering effective interpersonal and communicative interactions, it is extremely important that all participants be cognizant of the customs and values of people with whom they are working. Tips for Teachers provides ideas about promoting more effective interpersonal and communicative skills.

Promoting Interpersonal and Communicative Skills

1. Engage in active listening techniques.
2. Use body posture (e.g., leaning forward, arms uncrossed), body movement (e.g., nodding head), and facial expression (e.g., eye contact, smiles) to convey that you are open, interested, and listening.
3. Have an interpreter available if family members do not speak English as their primary language.
4. Be aware of values, perceptions, and culture of both teacher and family.
5. Avoid behaviors (e.g., giving advice, minimizing feelings, demonstrating resistance) that may produce negative interactions. ■

Problem-Solving and Conflict-Resolution Skills

In most collaborative partnership endeavors, a plan is developed for the benefit of a student. Very often, professionals, paraprofessionals, and families face complex problems that require careful consideration and action to help children; these interactions may be plagued with some element of conflict that must be resolved so that partnerships can move forward with their plans.

As participants develop a plan for a student, conflicts can arise. For example, two professionals may be working on a plan for a student and one member may fall short of implementing his or her agreed-upon tasks. In this situation, conflict could easily arise due to lack of carry-through of the plan for the student. This issue would need to be addressed in a constructive manner that would facilitate progress toward implementing the plan. Participants who enter into collaborative partnerships of any type must consider effective problem-solving and conflict-resolution skills.

Problem solving is the identification, implementation, and evaluation of a plan to solve a mutually agreed-upon problem. Problem solving can probably be accomplished best when participants in the communicative, collaborative process (1) assess the current situation using specific variables (e.g., behavior, time, situational factors, achievement information, nonverbal signals, verbal comments), (2) identify together the specific behavior that is of concern (e.g., homework completion, reading comprehension, tardy arrival at collaboration meetings, follow-through on collaboration plans), (3) specify objectives for solving the problem, (4) develop a plan of action, including tasks, persons responsible, and time lines, and (5) evaluate the plan periodically (Heron & Harris, 1993).

Conflict is a disagreement of interests or ideas (Guralnik, 1984). In a collaborative relationship, conflict may stem from differences in opinions about strategies, facts, or values. Conflict may arise if people feel that they are being forced into situations (e.g., working together, having students with disabilities in their classrooms full time, implementing a strategy for which no training occurred), if roles (e.g., special education teacher as consultant) are not clearly defined, if philosophies (e.g., humanistic, disciplinarian) clash, if levels of expertise and professional development don't match the demands of the situation (e.g., a first-year teacher is asked to chair a committee), if interpersonal styles (e.g., introvert, extrovert, direct, indirect) clash, and if people are resistant to change (e.g., issues of "territory," power, and interest in trying new research-based ideas) (Heron & Harris, 1993; West, Idol, & Cannon, 1989). Conflict is inevitable even in the best of circumstances; therefore, developing conflict-resolution skills is beneficial.

Several guidelines for conflict resolution are:

- Don't expect the conflict to go away; it may diminish, but if problems and feelings are not discussed, they will reemerge at another time.
- Confront conflict when it occurs by stating your feelings with an I-message. For example, "I'm feeling uncomfortable with this situation," "I'm sensing that maybe we're not on the same wavelength," "I think your body language is telling me you're not pleased with this arrangement." In essence, this is a reality check. You can test whether your perceptions are accurate. If not, discussing the situation as you perceive it at that time could prevent further misperceptions and problems.
- Avoid being judgmental or accusatory, "You're not listening," "You're late again," "That idea didn't work the last time and it won't work this time."
- Use self-disclosure if appropriate: "I'm feeling really unsure about how to handle this problem and could use some assistance."
- Maintain open, ongoing communication, even if it is just notes to other members. A major source of conflict is the lack of communication between partners and the perceived (or actual) notion that one person is moving ahead without talking through the plan.
- Use active listening: send I-messages, paraphrase, summarize, clarify. These techniques can go a long way in developing a better understanding of how members feel and how they perceive situations.
- Discuss conflict at a time when members aren't pressed to return to their classroom or are in the midst of a situation that might interfere with conflict resolution. Timing is an important consideration.
- Use the problem-solving steps described above to reach consensus and identify a plan of action. By using problem-solving steps, members can focus on a procedure that promotes communication, discussion, and resolution.
- Recognize that sometimes conflicts are not resolved and that for the time being, partnerships may be terminated. Many reasons (e.g., a lack of interest, power issues, insecurity, bad timing, mistrust, inability to establish congruent objectives) account for members' inability to resolve conflict. Focus on letting go and finding an alternative productive way to handle the situation if further action is required.

Multicultural and Linguistic Diversity Considerations

We have already discussed several considerations for working more effectively with individuals from diverse cultural, ethnic, and linguistic heritages. For example, we mentioned the importance of recognizing diverse values and perceptions and of both oral and written communication with people in their primary language. We also noted the issue of being aware of different communication (verbal and nonverbal) styles when establishing collaborative partnerships. We now present demographics that reflect a changing society, and we discuss competencies that educators can develop to foster more effective communication and collaboration.

The cultural, ethnic, racial, and linguistic composition of American society is changing dramatically. According to Baca and Cervantes (1989), there are nearly 8 million school-age students who represent ethnic, racial, and linguistic backgrounds other than the historically dominant European American influence. These students may qualify for a range of services, including bilingual programs and limited English proficiency programs. Additionally, approximately one million of these students require special education services. Given these statistics, it behooves educators to learn to work with diverse populations so that individual student needs, including special education needs, can be met adequately. Many in today's society have moved from valuing an assimilative "melting pot" to espousing a "cultural pluralism" theory in which cultural and ethnic diversity can be recognized as a strength and in which people are allowed to exercise their diversity, rather than conforming to one set of standards and values.

Harris (1991) developed a set of consultation competencies for educators who work with culturally and linguistically diverse students with special needs. Such educators should know about: (1) their perspectives (i.e., beliefs, values) about students with special needs from diverse backgrounds and the professionals who work with them, (2) roles (e.g., purpose of collaboration, players) of collaborative partners, (3) interpersonal, communicative, and problem-solving skills (e.g., values, perceptions, and beliefs of partners) needed to promote successful collaboration, and (4) appropriate assessment and instructional strategies (e.g., language and cultural considerations for assessment, specific strategies, adapting curricula).

In any discussion of multicultural diversity, it is important to keep in mind that the notion of "culture" permeates all of society and all our interactions. We all belong to some cultural group distinguishable by customs, traditions, beliefs, foods, dress, and so forth. Additionally, cultural groups may be distinguished by a specific ethnicity, religious affiliation, or racial background. Culture emerges in group interactions, clubs, and social gatherings. Heron and Harris (1993) pointed out that in schools, there is a culture specific to co-teaching, cooperative teaching, collaborative consultation, and family units. Thus, educators must be aware of their own cultural style, how they have been socialized professionally, and the cultural style of other collaborative members.

Summary

It is important for educators to develop collaborative partnerships with professionals, paraprofessionals, and families. When working with other professionals, teachers should use a variety of procedures to ensure an effective collaboration. Collaborative consultation, cooperative consultation, and co-teaching can help facilitate communication and can assist teachers in meeting the needs of students in special and general education classrooms.

Professionals who work with paraprofessionals can promote collaborative partnerships by defining roles and responsibilities, using effective supervisory practices, and fostering training opportunities in school districts. Paraprofessionals are invaluable team members who can offer critical support for professionals.

The success of collaboration endeavors relies heavily on the development and utilization of basic foundation skills. Collaborative members need to be skilled in appropriate interpersonal and communicative skills that foster trust, respect, caring, and openness. It is important to have effective problem-solving and conflict-resolution skills for coping with issues constructively. An awareness of diversity issues, particularly as they relate to communication styles, is critical for fostering open communication.

Study and Discussion Questions

1. Describe effective practices for collaborating with professionals.
2. Explain ways in which teachers and paraprofessionals can work together effectively.
3. Discuss practices that promote collaborative partnerships with families.
4. Describe skills needed for effective collaborative partnerships.
5. Develop a lesson that is co-taught with a general education teacher.
6. Design a behavior management plan that involves co-teaching with a general education teacher.
7. Develop a lesson that involves your paraprofessional. Specify roles and responsibilities.
8. Design a parent group on a topic of your choice.
9. Describe a possible source of conflict between families and teachers and design a plan for resolving the conflict.
10. Describe other barriers and solutions for communicating effectively with professionals, paraprofessionals, and families.

● ●

References and Suggested Readings

Idol, L., Nevin, A., & Paolucci-Whitcomb, P. (1994). *Collaborative consultation* (2nd ed.). Austin, TX: PRO-ED.

Nevin, A., Thousand, J., Paolucci-Whitcomb, P., & Villa, R. (1990). Collaborative consultation: Empowering public school personnel to provide heterogeneous schooling for all—or, Who rang that bell? *Journal of Educational and Psychological Consultation, 1,* 41–67.

Collaborating with Professionals

Bauwens, J., & Hourcade, J. J. (1991). Making co-teaching a mainstreaming strategy. *Preventing School Failure, 35*(4), 19–23.

Bauwens, J., & Hourcade, J. J. (1994). *Cooperative teaching: Rebuilding the schoolhouse for all students.* Austin, TX: PRO-ED.

Bauwens, J., Hourcade, J. J., & Friend, M. (1989). Cooperative teaching: A model for general and special education integration. *Remedial and Special Education, 10*(2), 17–22.

Chalfant, J. C., & Van Dusen Pysh, M. (1989). Teacher assistance teams: Five descriptive studies on 96 teams. *Remedial and Special Education, 10*(6), 49–58.

Cook, L., & Friend, M. (1993). Educational leadership for teacher collaboration. In B. Billingsley (Ed.), *Program leadership for serving students with disabilities* (pp. 421–444). Richmond, VA: Virginia Department of Education.

Dunn, L. M. (1968). Special education for the mildly retarded—Is much of it justifiable? *Exceptional Children, 35*(1), 5–22.

Friend, M., & Bursuck, W. (1996). *Including students with special needs.* Boston: Allyn & Bacon.

Friend, M., & Cook, L. (1992). The new mainstreaming: How it really works. *Instructor, 101*(7), 30–32, 34, 36.

Fuchs, D., Fuchs, L., & Bahr, M. (1990). Mainstream assistance teams: A scientific basis for the art of consultation. *Exceptional Children, 57*(2), 128–139.

Garcia, S. B., & Ortiz, A. A. (1988). Preventing inappropriate referrals of language minority students to special education. *National Clearinghouse for Bilingual Education—New Focus, 5,* 1–12.

Graden, J., Casey, A., & Christenson, S. (1985). Implementing a prereferral intervention system: Part I. The model. *Exceptional Children, 51,* 377–384.

Harris, K. C. (1991). An expanded view on consultation competencies for educators serving culturally and linguistically diverse exceptional students. *Teacher Education and Special Education, 14*(1), 25–29.

Heron, T. E., & Swanson, P. (1991). Establishing a consultation assistance team: A four-step practical procedure. *Journal of Educational and Psychological Consultation, 2*(1), 95–98.

Hudson, P., & Fradd, S. (1990). Cooperative planning for learners with limited English proficiency. *Teaching Exceptional Children, 23*(1), 16–21.

Idol, L. (1988). A rationale and guidelines for establishing special education consultation programs. *Remedial and Special Education, 9*(6), 48–58.

Idol, L. (1990). The scientific art of consultation. *Journal of Educational and Psychological Consultation, 1*(1), 3–22.

Idol, L., Nevin, A., & Paolucci-Whitcomb, P. (1994). *Collaborative consultation* (2nd ed.). Austin, TX: PRO-ED.

Riegel, R. H. (1988). *A guide to cooperative consultation.* Jason Court, MI: RHR Consultation Services.

Robinson, S. M. (1991). Collaborative consultation. In B. Y. L. Wong (Ed.), *Learning about learning disabilities* (pp. 441–463). San Diego, CA: Academic Press.

Villa, R. A., Thousand, J. S., Paolucci-Whitcomb, P., & Nevin, A. (1990). In search of new paradigms for collaborative consultation. *Journal of Educational and Psychological Consultation, 1*(4), 279–292.

West, J. F., & Idol, L. (1990). The nature of consultation vs. collaboration: An interview with Walter B. Pryzwansky. *The Consulting Edge, 2*(1), 1–2.

Collaborating with Paraprofessionals

Blalock, G. (1990). *Paraprofessional training program activity, 1989–1990.* Unpublished report, University of New Mexico, Albuquerque.

Blalock, G. (1991). Paraprofessionals: Critical team members in our special education programs. *Intervention in School and Clinic, 26*(4), 200–214.

Blalock, G., Polloway, E. A., & Patton, J. (1989). Strategies for working with significant others. In E. A. Polloway, J. Patton, J. Payne, & R. Payne (Eds.), *Strategies for teaching students with learning and behavior problems* (4th ed., pp. 125–146). Columbus, OH: Merrill.

Mandell, B. R., & Schram, B. (1983). *Human services: An introduction.* New York: Wiley.

Pickett, A. L. (Ed.). (1987). *Career ladders and a training model for the (re)training of direct service workers in community based programs for people with developmental disabilities.* New York: City University of New York, New Careers Training Laboratory.

Vasa, S. F., Steckelberg, A. L., & Hoffman, P. (1986). *Resource guide for the development of policies and practices in the use of paraprofessionals in special education.* Lincoln, NE: University of Nebraska, Department of Special Education and Communication Disorders.

Collaborating with Families

Harry, B. (1992). *Cultural diversity, families, and the special education system: Communication and empowerment.* New York: Teachers College Press.

Kroth, R. L. (1985). *Communicating with parents of exceptional children: Improving parent-teacher relationships* (2nd ed.). Denver, CO: Love.

Lobato, D. J. (1990). *Brothers, sisters, and special needs.* Baltimore: Brookes.

Pugach, M. C., & Johnson, L. J. (1995). *Collaborative practitioners, collaborative schools.* Denver, CO: Love.

Ramey, S. L., Krauss, M. W., & Simeonsson, R. J. (1989). Research on families: Current assessment and future opportunities. *American Journal on Mental Retardation, 94,* ii–vi.

Simpson, R. L. (1990). *Conferencing parents of exceptional children* (2nd ed.). Austin, TX: PRO-ED.

Smith, D. D., & Luckasson, R. (1995). *Introduction to special education—Teaching in an age of challenge* (2nd ed.). Boston: Allyn & Bacon.

Smith, D. D., & Rivera, D. (1993). *Effective discipline* (2nd ed.). Austin, TX: PRO-ED.

Turnbull, A. P., & Turnbull, H. R., III. (1990). *Families, professionals, and exceptionality: A special partnership* (2nd ed.). Columbus, OH: Merrill.

Foundation Skills for Collaborating

Baca, L. M., & Cervantes, H. T. (1989). *The bilingual special education interface* (2nd ed.). Columbus, OH: Merrill.

Gordon, T. (1980). *Leadership effectiveness training.* New York: Wyden.

Guralnik, D. B. (Ed.). (1984). *Webster's new world dictionary* (rev. ed.). New York: Warner Books.

Harris, K. C. (1991). An expanded view on consultation competencies for educators serving culturally and linguistically diverse exceptional students. *Teacher Education and Special Education, 14*(1), 25–29.

Heron, T. E., & Harris, K. C. (1993). *The educational consultant* (3rd ed.). Austin, TX: PRO-ED.

Kroth, R. L. (1985). *Communicating with parents of exceptional children: Improving parent-teacher relationships* (2nd ed.). Denver, CO: Love.

Miller, P. W. (1986). *Nonverbal communications* (2nd ed.). Washington, DC: National Education Association.

West, J. F., Idol, L., & Cannon, G. (1989). *Collaboration in the schools: An inservice and preservice curriculum for teachers, support staff and administrators.* Austin, TX: PRO-ED.

Chapter 3
The Individualized Education Program Process

In 1990, Congress enacted the Individuals with Disabilities Education Act (IDEA; P.L. 101–476), which is the reauthorization of the Education for All Handicapped Children Act (P.L. 94–142) and the Education of the Handicapped Act amendments (P.L. 99–457). P.L. 94–142 required that all children and youth with disabilities from ages 3 to 21 receive appropriate educational services and an Individualized Education Program (IEP). P.L. 99–457 amendments added an educational provision to families who have children, up to age three, and included Individualized Family Service Plans (IFSP). These three laws entitle all students with disabilities to an education and include many safeguards to protect students' and parents' rights to a free, appropriate public education. These laws are far-reaching and have direct impact on the entire educational system. They have drastically changed the roles and responsibilities of parents and school personnel (administrators, diagnosticians, counselors, and teachers).

The purpose of this chapter is to identify and discuss the steps of the Individualized Education Program (IEP) process. This process plays a major role in special education, because it is through this process that appropriate, individualized services are established for children and youth with special needs and legal safeguards are established for their parents or guardians. In this chapter, the authors provide an overview of the IEP process as set forth by IDEA, and discuss the seven steps of the IEP process.

Making Connections

Before you read, consider characteristics of students with learning and behavior problems discussed in chapter 1; think about how those characteristics contribute to learning difficulties and how you can use effective teaching techniques to address these learning problems. Review ideas presented in chapter 2 for building collaborative partnerships with professionals and working effectively with family members; consider how these partnerships will be important when you identify students with learning difficulties as needing special education services. Finally, identify the communication skills you need when you work with professionals and families to develop appropriate educational programs for students with special needs.

Objectives

After studying this chapter, the reader will be able to

1. Identify the seven major provisions of IDEA and the seven steps of the Individualized Education Program (IEP) process.

2. Describe the prereferral and referral processes.

3. Explain the purposes of assessment, describe formal and informal assessment techniques, and discuss the assessment debate.

4. Describe the purpose of the identification step of the Individualized Education Program (IEP) process.

5. Explain the action taken during the analysis of services step in the IEP process.

6. Describe service delivery models that can be discussed during the placement step of the IEP process, and the debate surrounding these models.

7. Describe the purpose of the instructional-decision-making step and the components of the IEP.

8. Explain three types of evaluation that occur under the program evaluation step of the IEP process.

●●

Overview of the Individualized Education Program Process

As you read, think about ...

1. Applying the provisions of IDEA to the development of appropriate educational services for students with special needs.
2. Explaining what you think occurs in each of the seven steps of the IEP process.
3. Describing ways to work with families from culturally and linguistically diverse backgrounds during the IEP process.
4. Identifying the role of the general education teacher during the IEP process.
5. Explaining the IEP process to parents or guardians and general educators.

IDEA requires that all children and youth with disabilities from ages 3 to 21 be provided with appropriate educational services. This law includes seven major provisions: (1) a free, appropriate public education (FAPE), (2) notification and procedural rights for parents or guardians, (3) identification, (4) necessary related services, (5) individualized assessments, (6) individualized education programs (IEPs), and (7) placement in the least restrictive environment (LRE) (Smith & Luckasson, 1995). Each state is required to submit documented evidence that efforts were made to locate every preschool-aged and school-aged person with disabilities. The law states that every student with a disability is entitled to participate in activities enjoyed by youngsters without disabilities (e.g., transportation, counseling, recreation, physical education, employment, special interest groups, athletics, and clubs). The law also requires that before being placed in special education and related services, students receive complete, nondiscriminatory, individual evaluations (i.e., tests administered in the student's primary language by properly trained personnel).

For every school-aged student identified as having a disability, an *Individual Education Program (IEP)* must be developed, implemented, and evaluated. For each preschooler under the age of six, the *Individualized Family Service Plan (IFSP)* must include instruction for the child and the family. A role for parents is included in these IFSPs, so they can be active and knowledgeable in assisting in their child's progress. By the time the student is 16, he or she must have an **Individualized Transition Plan (ITP),** developed for him or her. Often a component of the IEP, this plan prepares special education students for the transition from secondary school to adult life. The ITP must specify and evaluate the transition services (e.g., rehabilitation, vocational, postsecondary, recreational, personal) that students need for adjustment to adulthood. (See chapter 14 for additional information about the ITP.)

The components of the IEP, IFSP, and ITP are specified in the law, as are the steps to follow that qualify youngsters for these special services. The IEP requires a set of **annual goals** to be written for each student and requires teachers, parents or guardians, and other administrators to meet. As a check and balance, parents, guardians, or administrators can initiate **due process hearings.** When properly implemented, the Individualized Education Program process improves educational programs for all students with disabilities.

To be able to fulfill the requirements of IDEA and implement the seven steps of the IEP process, teachers must be familiar with the process and possess specific knowledge (assessment instruments and procedures, curricula) and skills (writing annual goals and short-term objectives, conducting task analyses, modifying instructional materials). Therefore, this chapter provides information about the seven steps of the IEP process, writing an IEP, and the skills needed to complete these activities.

The IEP process includes seven steps for school personnel to follow, from the initial referral for special educational services to the evaluation of services provided to those eligible. The IEP process steps (Smith & Luckasson, 1995) include:

1. Referral
2. Assessment
3. Identification
4. Analysis of services
5. Placement
6. Instructional decision making
7. Program evaluation

The flow chart in Figure 3.1 illustrates the steps and intended sequence of the IEP process required by law.

Referral/Prereferral

As you read, think about...

1. Explaining prereferral techniques that teachers can use to meet the needs of students with special needs better in the general education classroom.
2. Assuming the role of the special education teacher and developing a collaborative plan with the general education teacher to assist a student with reading difficulties.
3. As a prereferral technique, developing a home-school plan with a child's parent or guardian and the general education teacher.
4. Developing an assessment plan to monitor student progress in the general education setting to determine whether the prereferral technique is successful.
5. Developing questions you might ask the special services committee members about a child who is being referred.

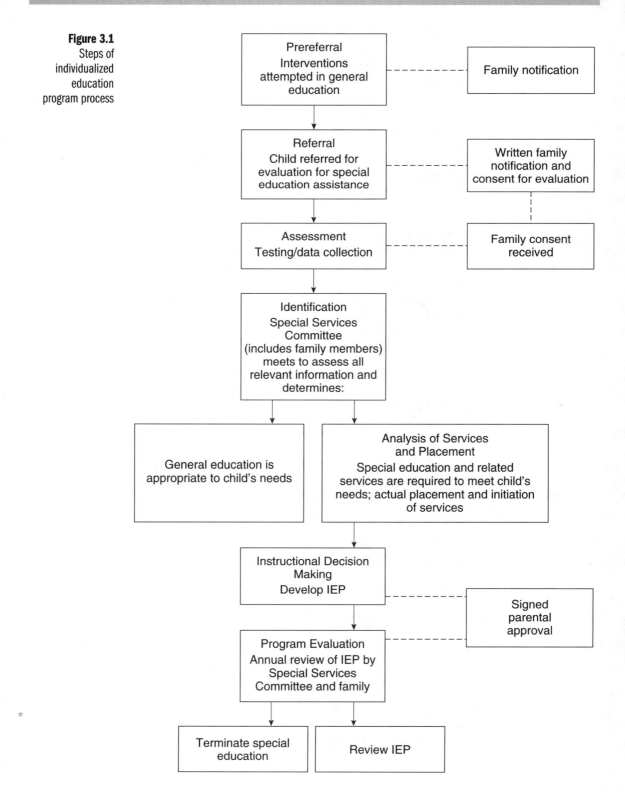

Figure 3.1
Steps of individualized education program process

Very often, the **special services committee** members will identify interventions that the classroom teacher could try with the student. This is considered the **prereferral step.** General classroom teachers are expected to confer informally with colleagues to identify alternative intervention strategies. Interventions might include special seating, curricular adaptations, and instructional modifications (see chapters 5, 10, 11, 12, and 13 for additional adaptation and modification suggestions). Typically, when prereferral interventions are implemented, teachers monitor student progress by using techniques such as **curriculum–based assessment,** data measurement systems (e.g., duration, latency, rate, time sampling), and anecdotal notes (see chapter 6 for an explanation of these measurement techniques). During the prereferral stage, parents or guardians should be notified about their child's academic or social problems, usually by the general education teacher. A home-school plan may be necessary to help alleviate specific classroom problems. A collaborative plan may be all that is necessary to foster student success.

Many school districts have initiated some structure at the prereferral stage through the special services committee. For instance, some programs (e.g., Teacher Assistance Teams, Chalfant & Van Dusen Pysh, 1989; Collaboration in the Schools, West, Idol, & Cannon, 1989) give general education teachers a problem-solving approach to determine and assess alternative classroom interventions. In some cases, these programs have reduced the number of referrals to special education. If, however, prereferral interventions yield little student progress, the special services committee may call for a formal evaluation of the student. It should be noted that a waiver of prereferral interventions would be appropriate if the disability is obviously severe enough to warrant immediate **referral** for special education assessment.

Children are referred for special education services in a variety of ways for a variety of reasons. Not every student referred qualifies for assistance from specially trained personnel. Although some might argue that all children should receive the benefits of special education (reduced class size, individualized instruction), these services are expensive and are intended for those who have disabilities. Some parents know that their child will need special education before that child starts school (for example, parents of students with severe disabilities). Preschoolers whose language development is delayed are usually identified as potential students for the **speech and language pathologist**. However, most students who receive special services are initially referred by the general classroom teacher. Sometimes, the referral occurs very early in a student's academic career; other times, referral does not occur until middle elementary grades. Although not as common, some students are not identified until middle or high school, when the curricular and setting demands become most difficult.

The referring teacher notifies the principal and the special services committee about a student who is having difficulties in school. This special services committee, sometimes referred to as the appraisal and review committee or the child study team, should be composed of relevant school personnel. Permanent committee members should be the school's special education teacher(s), principal, counselor, and school psychologist. Rotating members are the child's classroom teacher, the child's parents or guardians, and the social service agency representatives who deal with the child and the family.

The primary referring agent, usually the general classroom teacher, should indicate to the special services committee the reasons for the referral and provide some data or justification. Information from general screening instruments, prereferral interventions, classroom academic performance in relation to classmates, and observations about social behavior problems should accompany a written request for referral. After reviewing the referral request and considering information from additional school personnel (supplemental service teachers such as the physical education teacher, the music teacher, or the art teacher), the special service committee may decide that a formal evaluation or assessment is necessary.

Before the formal evaluation can begin, the child's parents or guardians must receive a written notification of the referral and a written request for permission to conduct an evaluation. The parents or guardians must then give their written permission. If they have been kept apprised of their child's progress, such notification may simply be a formality to initiate assessment, rather than a shock that classroom problems are occurring.

• •

Assessment

As you read, think about . . .
1. Identifying the purposes of assessment.
2. Describing assessment issues pertaining to youngsters from culturally and linguistically diverse backgrounds.
3. Designing a set of assessment questions that can be answered during the formal and informal assessment process.
4. Describing the types of information that can be obtained from developmental and school history.
5. Comparing and contrasting formal and informal assessment techniques.
6. Summarizing the issues pertinent to the assessment debate.
7. Describing appropriate ways to discuss with families the assessment process results.

Because special education is expensive and is intended for those students whose disability requires a specially designed program of instruction, students must qualify for these services. There is a range of special services available. Some students need only limited special support services (speech or language therapy, adapted physical education) and can remain with their class for a regular academic education. Others require intensive educational and social programs that utilize the expertise of many highly trained specialists.

Currently, most diagnostic information relies heavily on standardized tests. Although there continues to be considerable debate about the appropriateness and usefulness of standardized assessment instruments, the major issues are not resolved, and traditional testing procedures are used nationally. It is important for all special educators to know about traditional assessment instruments and procedures, whether they believe in their merits or not. If teachers are to be active, participating members in the IEP process, they must be cognizant of commonly used evaluation methods, their purposes, and appropriate uses. (See the section on assessment in the references and suggested readings section for more detailed information.)

The **assessment step** of the Individualized Education Program process involves gathering data from a variety of sources and individuals to develop a profile of the referred student. This is an important step in the process because, by law and according to good professional practice, an identification decision for special education services must be based on information from a variety of reliable and valid sources, including developmental history, school history, and formal and informal assessment techniques.

Assessing students with suspected disabilities is defined as "the systematic process of gathering educationally relevant information to make legal and instructional decisions about the provision of special education services" (McLoughlin & Lewis, 1995). Educational assessment is conducted to determine (1) whether the student's academic and social difficulties are due to a disability, (2) whether the student requires special education services, and (3) the most appropriate types of special education services that are needed, based on all available information about the child. The purpose of the assessment step is to answer specific questions to assist professionals and parents or guardians in making valid decisions about students' individual needs. According to McLoughlin and Lewis (1995, p. 18), the following questions should be answered during the assessment step:

1. Is there a school performance problem?
2. If there is a school performance problem, is it related to a disability?
3. What is the level of academic achievement and what are the student's strengths and weaknesses in learning?
4. What is the level of intellectual performance and adaptive behavior?
5. What is the level of development of specific learning abilities and learning strategies?
6. What is the status of classroom behavior and social-emotional development?
7. What are the student's educational needs?
8. What is the level of reading, mathematics, written language, and oral language achievement; what are the student's strengths and weaknesses in these areas?
9. What is the relationship of learning problems to general considerations for classroom success: general learning ability, specific abilities and strategies, behavior, and social-emotional development?
10. What is the relationship of learning problems to medical, social, and cultural factors?
11. What are the educational needs and annual goals?
12. What kind of special education and related services are necessary?
13. What is the least restrictive and most appropriate educational placement?
14. How effective is the educational program?

There are many categories of diagnostic tests and procedures. Each of these is used in one of several ways to identify and serve students with disabilities. Within the IEP process, these assessments might be used for referral, identification, classification, placement, instructional decision making, or program evaluation.

In most states, for students to be placed in special education classrooms, they must meet their state's standards for a particular categorical classification (e.g., learning disabilities, emotional disturbance, mental retardation). For example, to qualify for services from a learning disabilities teacher, the student must (1) be of average or above average intelligence, (2) be behind academically (often specified as two or more years behind and as having what is considered a significant discrepancy between potential and achievement), and (3) be without physical impairments, mental retardation, or severe emotional disturbance.

For these students, various types of tests are included in their assessment batteries: intelligence, overall academic achievement (and usually several specific achievement tests), acuity, and often learning style. For students with mental retardation, adaptive behavior scales also are included. A classroom observation is often a required component of the identification process, for students with learning disabilities. For students with behavioral disorders, a behavior rating scale is completed by various individuals with whom the child interacts.

Developmental History

Parents or guardians can supply a great deal of important information about the development of their child. When developing a diagnostic profile of a student, the school diagnostician asks parents or guardians a series of questions about their child's birth, developmental milestones, illnesses, social skills, and interests. This case history can provide basic information that helps the school diagnostician to understand the child's overall development better. However, because recall of developmental history may be sketchy or not completely accurate, diagnosticians should not rely too heavily on developmental history information: this information should be interpreted within the total context of assessment data.

School History

School records can be a valuable source of information about the student's academic and social progress. Records of attendance, achievement scores, curricular materials, anecdotal notes, and student work can be assembled to provide a composite overview of the student's progression through the grades. The information can be used to document particular problems that might have been evident in earlier grades, such as attendance patterns, previously implemented techniques, classroom and behavioral interactions, and teacher concerns. Again, although this is important information, some pieces, such as anecdotal notes, may need to be interpreted cautiously because of reliability issues.

Formal Assessment

Formal assessment typically refers to the administration of standardized, norm-referenced tests that yield information about student performance. These tests are administered by school psychologists or diagnosticians to determine identification, eligibility, and academic, social, and behavioral strengths and weaknesses. A variety of formal assessment instruments, such as intelligence tests, achievement tests, behavioral rating scales, adaptive behavior measures, and process tests, are used to answer assessment questions about the reasons for academic or social difficulty. These tests must be administered and scored according to procedures in the test manual, and should determine how a student performs compared with other students of a similar age and grade. Table 3.1 lists some formal assessment instruments often used during the assessment step. Although the list is not exhaustive, it is representative of formal assessment instruments administered to develop a diagnostic profile of a youngster.

The formal assessment process is multidisciplinary. Professionals from different fields may be involved in assessing the student for a particular reason. For example,

Table 3.1
Examples of
Formal Assessment
Instruments

Intelligence and aptitude

Detroit Tests of Learning Aptitude-P2
(Hammill & Bryant, 1991)

Detroit Tests of Learning Aptitude-3
(Hammill, 1991)

Kaufman Assessment Battery for Children
(Kaufman & Kaufman, 1983)

Stanford-Binet Intelligence Scale (4th ed.)
(Thorndike, Hagen, & Sottler, 1986)

System of Multicultural Pluralistic Assessment
(Mercer & Lewis, 1977)

Wechsler Intelligence Scales for Children-III
(Wechsler, 1991)

*Woodcock-Johnson Psycho-Educational Battery-
Revised* (Woodcock & Johnson, 1989)

Academic achievement

Diagnostic Achievement Battery-2
(Newcomer, 1990)

Diagnostic Achievement Test for Adolescents
(Newcomer & Bryant, 1986)

Kaufman Test of Educational Achievement
(Kaufman & Kaufman, 1985)

Peabody Individual Achievement Test-Revised
(Dunn & Markwardt, 1989)

Wide Range Achievement Test-Revised
(Jastak & Wilkinson, 1984)

*Woodcock-Johnson Psycho-Educational Battery-
Revised* (Woodcock & Johnson, 1989)

Adaptive behavior

AAMR (Adaptive Behavior Scale-School Edition)
(Nihira, Leland, & Lambert, 1993)

Adaptive Behavior Inventory (Brown & Leigh, 1986)

Specific learning abilities

Bender Gestalt Test for Young Children
(Koppitz, 1975)

*Developmental Test of Visual-Motor Integration-
Third Ed.* (Beery, 1989)

*Developmental Test of Visual Perception-
Second Ed.* (Hammill, Pearson, & Voress, 1993)

*Goldman-Fristoe-Woodcock Test of Auditory
Discrimination* (Goldman, Fristoe,
& Woodcock, 1990)

Reading measures

Formal Reading Inventory (Wiederholt, 1985)

Gray Oral Reading Test-3
(Wiederholt & Bryant, 1991)

Test of Reading Comprehension (rev. ed.)
(Brown, Hammill, & Wiederholt, 1986)

Woodcock Reading Mastery Tests-Revised
(Woodcock, 1987)

Mathematics measures

Key Math Revised (Connolly, 1988)

Test of Mathematical Abilities-2
(Brown, Cronin, & McEntire, 1994)

Written language measures

Test of Written Language-2
(Hammill & Larsen, 1988)

Test of Written Spelling-3
(Larsen & Hammill, 1994)

Woodcock Language Proficiency Battery
(Woodcock, 1980)

Oral language measures

Test of Language Development-P:2
(Newcomer & Hammill, 1988)

the speech and language pathologist very often evaluates the child's abilities in expressive and receptive language. For students with suspected learning disabilities, this is important because of the pervasive language problems demonstrated by a large number of these students (Mercer, 1991). All students referred for formal assessment have vision and hearing **acuity evaluations.** Typically, acuity screening occurs at the school level conducted by the nurse; more formal evaluation may be conducted by an audiologist or optometrist. Some students with suspected learning disabilities may also be evaluated by a pediatrician or neurologist to obtain information about various behavioral characteristics (e.g., hyperactivity, motor problems).

After instruments have been administered and evaluations have been conducted using a multidisciplinary approach, a case report is written that specifies (1) student demographic information, (2) reason for the referral, (3) prereferral assessment information, (4) a summary of developmental and school histories, (5) tests administered, (6) test results reported as derived scores, (7) analyses of the results, (8) presence or absence of a disability that requires special education and related services and the basis for the determination, and (9) instructional recommendations.

Informal Assessment

Informal assessment measures directly link school performance with the curriculum. Student progress within the designated curriculum is monitored on a regular basis by techniques that measure the skills learned. Results can be used to (1) modify instruction, (2) plan instructional objectives, and (3) document current levels of performance in terms of the instructed curricula. Informal assessment techniques typically refer to curriculum-based measures, error analyses, **authentic assessments, portfolio assessments,** and **criterion-referenced tests** (see Table 3.2 for a sample listing of informal assessment techniques). Teachers have made great strides using such measures appropriately to effect instructional decision making. Continued

Table 3.2
Examples of Informal Assessment Techniques

Authentic assessment	**Clinical interviews**
Oral reports	"Think-aloud"
Experiments	**Portfolio assessment**
Essays	Taped samples of academic work
Reports	Performance-based assessment measures
Curriculum-based assessment/measurement	Written samples of academic work
Spelling	Error analyses
Reading	Teacher anecdotal notes
Mathematics	Student self-reflection notes
Written expression	Logs
Content area subjects	Behavioral observation notes
Measurable observations of academic and social behaviors	**Work sample analysis**
Time sampling	Miscue analysis
Frequency	Job site analysis
Latency	Spelling products
Duration	Mathematics products
Antecedent behavior consequence log	Written samples
Social skills	**Anecdotal notes**
Behavioral observations	Social skills
Criterion-referenced tests	Behavioral observations
Diagnostic Comprehensive Inventory of Basic Skills (Brigance, 1983)	**Checklists**
	Curricular scope and sequence
Diagnostic Inventory of Basic Mathematics Skills (Enright, 1983)	Social and behavioral skills

research and training are necessary, however, to develop reliable and valid informal assessment measures and to instruct teachers in doing data analysis and program planning (Rivera, 1993; Taylor, Tindal, Fuchs, & Bryant, 1993). See chapter 6 for more detailed information about informal assessment measures.

The Assessment Debate

A great deal of controversy has surrounded the formal assessment process, which is the administration of diagnostic standardized tests to determine strengths and weaknesses and the presence of a disability. Critics (Deno, 1989; Marston, 1989; Shapiro & Derr, 1990; Ysseldyke, 1986; Ysseldyke, Algozzine, & Epps, 1983) of standardized diagnostic tests cite many reasons for their dissatisfaction with traditional assessment methods, including: (1) discriminatory practices, (2) overidentification of students from culturally and linguistically diverse backgrounds as having disabilities, (3) inability to discriminate between low achievement and learning disabilities (Epps, Ysseldyke, & McGue, 1984), (4) questionable statistical procedures for determining a severe discrepancy between potential and achievement (Dangel & Ensminger, 1988; Reynolds, 1985), and (5) cultural and linguistic bias of assessment information (Frame, Clarizio, & Porter, 1984).

Ysseldyke (Ysseldyke, Algozzine, Shinn, & McGue, 1982) suggests that diagnostic tests do not guarantee accurate identification of those students who have disabilities and those who do not. His findings indicate that students who have behavioral problems are the ones who are referred to diagnosticians, who then find ways to classify students as having disabilities so they can receive special education services. Furthermore, the entire diagnostic process has also been criticized as not being cost-effective. Some school districts even spend more money in the referral, identification, and placement process than they do educating students in classrooms.

Additional criticisms have been leveled against standardized testing of all students. Some educators question the degree to which standardized tests accurately measure student progress and provide instructionally relevant information. Opponents of traditional testing support the adoption of alternative approaches to assessment, including techniques such as portfolio assessments, performance-based assessments, and authentic assessments (Feurer & Fulton, 1993; Wesson & King, 1992; Worthern, 1993). Linked to school reform, these alternative assessment approaches are popular as a result of interest in (1) examining student achievement and ongoing progress more directly, (2) focusing more on analyzing processes rather than just products, (3) identifying assessment options to traditional standardized testing procedures, and (4) measuring higher-order thinking and problem-solving skills rather than only basic skills.

The debate about formally assessing school-aged children for special education services has raged for years. The issues in question include the following: What is the purpose of the diagnosis? Who should do the diagnosis? Who should interpret the results of the diagnosis? Does testing violate a child's right to privacy? What are the appropriate uses of the assessment information? What practices can prevent students from culturally and linguistically diverse backgrounds from being overidentified as having disabilities and underidentified as gifted? The meanings and implications of these questions are interpreted differently from school district to school district. One perspective, however, can be offered for the testing issue: Standardized tests can only be justified if they are used correctly and are useful to the school system, teacher, parents, *and* the child.

Identification

As you read, think about...

1. Reviewing your state's eligibility criteria for students to receive special education categorical (or noncategorical) services.
2. Examining assessment information and developing a profile of a youngster to determine if she or he qualifies for special education services.
3 Interviewing various professionals (e.g., speech and language pathologist, learning disabilities teacher) to determine the types of assessment information they offer to the special services committee during the identification process.
4. Observing a special services committee meeting to learn about the information discussed and the decision-making process used to identify students as being eligible for special education services.
5. Interviewing a diagnostician or school psychologist to learn about techniques used to minimize the misidentification of students from culturally and linguistically backgrounds as having disabilities.

In the **identification step** of the IEP process, the multidisciplinary team closely examines all information gathered about the child's current level of performance. Professionals try to answer assessment questions (see questions 1 through 14 in the list under Assessment) to determine whether the school performance problems result from a disability and warrant special educational services. The assessment information is compared with state-established eligibility guidelines for learning and behavioral disabilities and a decision is reached about the most appropriate educational interventions for the child, which may include special education services or some other type of school intervention.

Analysis of Services

As you read, think about...

1. Discussing the roles of professionals in related services.
2. Explaining assessment information that might suggest the need for related services.
3. Hypothesizing potential problems and solutions when scheduling related services.

If a student is declared eligible for special education services, the special service committee's fourth step in the IEP process, the **analysis of services step** is to recommend appropriate **related services** to meet the child's individual needs (see question 12 under Assessment). A variety of services, such as occupational therapy, speech or language therapy, counseling, and adapted physical education, are available to meet students' specific learning and behavioral needs. These services are noted on the IEP and are initiated once parents or guardians grant permission for placement in special education.

Placement

As you read, think about . . .

1. Explaining service delivery options to parents based on the individual needs of their children.
2. Describing the array of services.
3. Establishing a collaborative plan with a general education teacher in whose classroom a student with special needs will be placed all day.
4. Establishing a collaborative plan with a general education teacher in whose classroom a student with special needs will be placed for part of the day, in addition to spending part of the day in your resource program.
5. Explaining the types of needs exhibited by elementary- and secondary-level students for whom a general classroom, resource program, or self-contained program would be the most appropriate educational placement.

Once students have been identified as being eligible for special education services and those services have been specified, the fifth step is to determine the most appropriate **placement** in the least restrictive environment based on individual student needs (see question 13 in the list under Assessment). Traditionally, a full **continuum of services** has been available from which a staffing committee selects the most appropriate special education placement. The continuum is a linear model from most to least restrictive environments and is based on the premise that students progress sequentially through each special educational placement environment (e.g., self-contained program to resource-room program). Smith and Luckasson (1995) offer another model for program placement consideration known as the **array of services.** This model requires professionals to make placement decisions about the least restrictive environment by examining (1) intensity of services, (2) instructional considerations, (3) location of services, (4) types of personnel, (5) duration of services, (6) individual and family values, and (7) the level of the disability's severity (i.e., mild, moderate, severe). For example, the special services committee might consider all available information and the "array" factors and deem it appropriate that a student stay in the general education setting. The general education teacher would receive consultative services from the special education teacher on program adaptations. In addition, the student would receive specialized academic instruction from the special education teacher in a part-time resource-program setting for some period of time.

Some professionals (e.g., Stainback & Stainback, 1989) argue that students with learning and behavioral difficulties are best served in fully inclusive settings for the entire school day, which implies that special education services merge with general education instruction to meet the needs of students within the general education classroom. These professionals say that special education pull-out services have not achieved desired outcomes and that a student should not receive fragmented services from different teachers in a school that may not be in the child's neighborhood. The fully inclusive setting is a widely debated topic among professionals (e.g., Hallahan & Kauffman, 1995), parents, and other guardians. Professional organizations, such as the Council for Learning Disabilities (1993), the Council for Exceptional Children—Division for Learning Disabilities (1993), the Council for Exceptional Children—Council for Children with Behavioral Disorders (1988), and the National Joint Committee on Learning Disabilities (1993), have taken a stand against the "indiscriminate full-time placement" of students with learning and behavior problems in the general education classroom with the elimination of service delivery options. Professionals are well advised to seek placement and service options that meet individual needs as guaranteed by IDEA.

● ●

Instructional Decision Making

As you read, think about . . .

1. Selecting a student, analyzing assessment data, and determining present levels of academic and social performance.
2. Projecting desired educational outcomes for the student in 1 as the basis for developing annual goals.
3. Writing annual goals for the student in 1.
4. Describing ways to involve families in determining annual goals for the child.
5. Writing a task analysis for an annual goal evaluation criteria.
6. Developing instructional behavioral objectives for one annual goal.
7. Considering ways to infuse cultural diversity awareness into teaching.

Once a student is identified as having a disability and is declared eligible for special education, decisions must be made regarding the educational program that he or she will receive (see question 11 under Assessment). The IEP requires that annual goals be specified for every special service provided for a student. Each student's yearly instructional program needs to be specified and sequenced. A student's performance levels should be stated in detail. Information about a student's **current levels of performance** should be provided, rather than just his or her scores on achievement tests. The IEP also requires evaluation of the student's program and of the instructional interventions used to promote academic and social growth (see chapter 6 for additional evaluation techniques). The authors now present some of the components of **instructional decision making,** along with an explanation of the IEP writing process.

Annual Goals

For more than two decades, teachers have specified the desired outcomes of their instruction in terms of annual goals for progress in children's behavior. Annual goals are usually global. It is more efficient to instruct and easier to coordinate services when annual goals are specified in behavioral terms. If wording is precise in behavioral statements and if outcomes are described in a certain way, measurement and evaluation will be much more reliable. The behavior must be specified in observable terms and must state criteria for mastery. An example of a poor annual goal is: "Johnny and his classmates will like each other better." Although this goal is worthy, it is imprecise, is unsuitable for reliable measurement, and does not include a provision for mastery. Without more specificity, independent observers will not be able to measure or collect data on the behavior of interest. Table 3.3 provides examples of annual goals and **instructional objectives** that are stated behaviorally.

Table 3.3
Annual Goals
and Instructional
Objectives

Annual goal: to tell time using a standard clockface with arabic numerals with 100% accuracy.

Abbreviated objective	Instructional objectives		Criterion
Hand discrimination	2.01 The student points to and names both the hour and minute hands	2.01	with 100% accuracy within 15 seconds

Hour hand	2.02 The student names all hour hand placements
	  2.02.01 The student states the hour for exact hour hand placements
	  2.02.02 The student states the hour for any hour hand placement
		2.02
		(.01–
		.02)
			with 100% accuracy within 10 seconds

Minute hand	2.03 The student states all minute hand placements
	  2.03.01 The student states the minute for minute hand placements on any interval of five
	  2.03.02 The student states the minute for exact minute hand placements
	  2.03.03 The student says fractions of hours using the minute hand (e.g., quarter after)
		2.03
		(.01–
		.03)
			with 100% accuracy within 10 seconds

Combination of hour and minute hands	2.04 The student tells the correct time using both the hour and minute hands
	  2.04.01 The student tells the time for the "o'clock" times
	  2.04.02 The student tells time for all intervals of five minutes
	  2.04.03 The student tells time for fractions of the hour
		2.04
		(.01–
		.04)
			with 100% accuracy within 10 seconds

Task Analysis

For instruction to be efficient, annual goals and instructional objectives must be sequenced; that is, their order of presentation must be determined. Lists of goals and objectives can be helpful to teachers as they decide what will constitute students' instructional programs. Without a sequence, however, teachers cannot know *when* an objective should become the target of instruction. The purpose of a **task analysis** is to determine the priority of goals and objectives and provide a plan for the sequence of instruction.

Teachers do not have to conduct task analyses for every skill they teach. In fact, teachers should not spend valuable time conducting unnecessary task analyses. For students who profit from the standard mathematics sequences used as outlines for elementary basal texts, the sequence of instruction is already determined through the combined efforts of researchers and professionals from that discipline.

In some cases, however, a textbook does not include an area that particular students need to master. For example, the use and understanding of time is a very important area that is often neglected or inadequately covered in mathematics texts. In such instances, teachers should search for already available instructional materials. (Only if appropriate instructional programs are not available should teachers create their own sequences and materials. The time involved in developing good instructional materials often far exceeds an already busy teacher's resources.) If teachers located instructional materials from a variety of sources, teachers must conduct a task analysis to determine the best order in which to teach the materials.

There are various ways to structure the task analysis process. Some processes specify the interventions to be used, as well as the sequence of instruction to follow when teaching a skill. Occasionally, systems are quite complex. Simple systems that provide an outline or blueprint of the instructional sequence are sufficient to guide teachers in their instructional planning. A teacher sequencing instructional units, for example, needs to make only a skeletal outline of the proposed ordering of objectives. When developing an IEP, the teacher should flesh out annual goals and instructional objectives from the abbreviated outline in the task analysis.

Writing the IEP

According to IDEA, once the special services committee decides that a child is eligible for special education and its related services, and before the child begins receiving these services, the IEP must be written. The IEP is a communication, management, and administrative tool. Although it provides guidelines for the content of a student's educational program, it need not be an instructional plan.

The law specifies a number of requirements for the IEP and its content. Table 3.4 indicates the items that must be included in each IEP. A portion of one student's IEP, shown in Figure 3.2, delineates only three annual goal areas. For most students, a substantial number of annual goals and their ensuing instructional objectives are necessary.

As specified by law, the IEP is developed by a team of people, including the student's teacher(s), an agency or school representative qualified to supervise the provision of special education, the student's parent(s) or guardian(s), and (if appropriate) the student. Although some school districts do not insist that the student's teacher(s) for the coming academic year be present, it is advantageous if they can give their input from the beginning, when a student's yearly program is being developed. The teacher for the coming year must implement the IEP, select educational programs and materials, write daily lesson plans, and evaluate student progress toward the goals and objectives stated in the IEP, so his or her involvement is critical in the early developmental stages. Competent specialists can help develop IEPs and should insist on participating. Also, the student's general education teacher should be included to maintain consistency within the child's total program.

Implementation of the IEP begins the first day the student comes to class. Related services specified in the IEP should be initiated according to the schedule indicated. It is advisable, even necessary, to monitor goals and objectives continually if efficient progress is to be made. Each day throughout the school year, all those concerned with the student's educational performance and progress should be concerned with attaining the IEP goals and objectives. The responsibility is onerous, but the result can be rewarding.

Although the law does not mandate continual evaluation of student performance (evaluation and review are only necessary annually), the student may well fall short of the stated goals without frequent monitoring of the planned program. The law does mandate that each student's goals and objectives be monitored and that criteria for mastery be indicated.

Table 3.4
IEP Information

Area	Specifications
1. Present levels of performance	1. A statement of the child's present levels of educational performance should be provided for at least each of the following areas: a. Academic achievement b. Social adaptation c. Prevocational and vocational skills d. Psychomotor skills e. Self-help skills
2. Annual goals	1. Annual goal statements should be included for each of the areas listed above. 2. These should describe the educational performance levels expected at the end of the year. 3. They should be individually tailored for each student in line with information provided for present functioning levels.
3. Instructional objectives	1. Instructional objectives should be developed for each of the annual goals. 2. These should be measurable intermediate steps leading to the attainment of the stated goals. 3. Appropriate criteria and evaluation procedures must be delineated to indicate whether the objectives have been achieved.
4. Special and related services	1. A description of the kind of education services required should be included. 2. A justification for the type of special education class placement is required (resource room, partially self contained, etc.). 3. A listing of specialized related services must be included (language therapy, physical education, etc.). 4. Projected dates for the initiation and anticipated duration of service should be provided.
5. General education	1. A description of the extent to which the student will participate in regular education programs must be included. 2. Care must be taken to ensure that the student receives an appropriate education in the least restrictive setting possible.
6. Responsibility	1. Individuals responsible for implementing and monitoring the student's IEP must be designated.
7. Evaluation	1. Methods and procedures to be used to review each IEP must be specified. 2. A schedule for review must be indicated. 3. Reviews must take place at least annually.
8. Family involvement	1. The family members of the student should be encouraged to help develop the IEP goals and objectives. 2. They must be aware of the content of the IEP. 3. They must demonstrate approval of the IEP by signing it.

Parent Involvement

It is important to remember that the IEP requires parent participation. Parents should be present at the IEP meeting and, as much as possible, should participate in the entire process. This means that the IEP should *not* be written and finalized before teachers meet with the student's parents. Teachers must remember that parents are important resources, and a positive relationship with parents is critical to the overall growth of their children.

Figure 3.2
Sample Individualized Education Program plan form with individualized program goals in one subject area

Carleen Jones	September 15
(Student's name)	(Date)
6/15/79	9
(Birthdate)	(Age)
Ms. Lock	Valley Vista
(Teacher)	(School)
September 2	
(Date of last assessment)	

Prioritized Annual Goals:

1. Articulation deficits will be remediated.
2. Computational arithmetic skills (addition, subtraction, and multiplication facts, and processes like carrying and borrowing) will be mastered.
3. Decoding skills in reading will be mastered.

Description of Student's Program:

Special Education Resource Room, General Education 4th grade, and Speech Therapy.

Present levels of performance

Strengths:

Carleen relates well with her peers and does not display any social behavior problems.

She follows instructions and seems to benefit greatly from individualized instruction.

Weaknesses:

She has an articulation problem that interferes with her oral language, which results in her hesitancy to speak before the group.

She is several grade levels behind in reading and does not demonstrate sufficient word attack skills.

She is behind her classmates in computational arithmetic and has not mastered many basic facts.

Committee Members Present:

Mr. Petre	Ms. Pepe (Gen. Ed.)
(Diagnostician)	(Teacher)
Mr. & Mrs. Jones	Mr. Martinez
(Parent or guardian advocate)	(School representative)
Mr. Porec—Speech	Ms. Lock (Sp. Ed.)

Computational Arithmetic

(Area)

Carleen Jones

(Student's name)

September 15

(Date)

Annual Goal: To demonstrate mastery of computational facts from three computational areas (addition, subtraction, and multiplication) and to demonstrate mastery of process problems for two computational areas (addition and subtraction).

Review Dates: 11/15   2/15   4/15

Instructional objectives	Methods, materials, and procedures	Person responsible	Start date	Target date	Date objective met	Comments and revisions
1. Carleen will solve all addition facts by meeting the criterion of correct rate (CR) score of 25 and an error rate (ER) score of 0.	Teacher-made worksheets, flash cards, error drill, free time reinforcement.	Ms. Lock	9/15	10/15		
2. Carleen will solve all subtraction facts by meeting the criterion of CR at 25 and ER at 0.	Teacher-made worksheets, language mastery, error drill, free time reinforcement.	Ms. Lock	10/15	12/15		
3. Carleen will solve all multiplication facts by meeting the criterion of CR at 20 and ER at 0.	Teacher-made worksheets, crib sheet, certificate from general education teacher.	Ms. Lock and Ms. Pepe	1/15	3/15		
4. Carleen will compute addition problems that require regrouping by achieving three consecutive scores of 95% or better.	Teacher-made worksheets, teacher demonstrations, certificate of success.	Ms. Lock	10/1	11/5		
5. Carleen will calculate subtraction problems that do not require regrouping by achieving three consecutive scores of 95% or better.	Teacher-made worksheets, demonstrations, response cost for errors (minutes from recess).	Ms. Lock	11/5	11/25		

The student's parents must be informed of the evaluation results and the ensuing decisions and recommendations about their child's educational program. Parents are to be included in the IEP meeting (at which their child's Individual Education Program for the academic year is developed). They must be notified of the date, place, and time of the meeting. If they cannot attend, parent conferences, telephone calls, and home meetings may be used instead. In most cases, parents and schools are in agreement and share their concerns and program recommendations. Parents do have the right to challenge the committee's evaluation or program recommendations. In instances where agreement cannot be reached between the two parties, a due process hearing may be called; decisions are then made by an impartial hearing officer.

Parents should be encouraged to participate actively in developing the goals and objectives included in their child's IEP. They must at least be aware of its content and indicate their approval by signing the IEP. The intent is that parents' involvement in their child's educational program will continue after they approve the IEP. Unfortunately, some parents' interest and concern stop once they have met their legal commitment by signing the IEP. If, however, a more complete educational program is to be implemented, parents and teachers should work together throughout the academic year.

Once the IEP is written, communication and dialogue with the parents should continue. Although formal parent conferences are held several times a year at most schools, more frequent communication can lead to joint partnerships between school and home. Parents can become instructional resources, assisting teachers in helping students to acquire, maintain, and generalize social and academic skills learned at school.

The Individualized Family Service Plan (IFSP)

Some children may be diagnosed at birth or during the preschool years as having a disability or as being at risk for a disability. These children are entitled to early intervention programs and the development of an Individualized Family Service Plan (IFSP). Although the emphasis of this book is on school-age students, the IFSP is presented so that the reader is introduced to all three plans (i.e., IEP, IFSP, ITP). It is beyond the scope of the book to expand the discussion of the IFSP any further.

The purpose of the IFSP is to identify specific developmental goals for the child and to identify and implement interventions and resources to support the family in attaining these goals. The IFSP is developed as a collaborative effort between the family and the professionals (e.g., speech and language pathologist, occupational therapist, social worker) with whom the family will interact as their child receives services. The IFSP must include annual goals, a description of the child's developmental abilities, outcomes, services, time lines, designation of a service manager, and transition methods. The IFSP is meant to be a formal plan for an early intervention program to meet the developmental needs of young children who have a disability or may be at risk for a disability. The IFSP also ensures proper continuation of services and interventions to assist families and children in making the transition from early intervention programs into kindergarten.

The Individualized Transition Plan (ITP)

IDEA states that students who require transitional services should have an ITP that provides interagency linkages and designates skills and services that the students will need to make a successful transition to adulthood. The ITP requires interagency collaborative planning to meet students' individual needs. Thus, professionals from postsecondary institutions, vocational rehabilitation, social work, counseling, and health services may team their efforts to develop a comprehensive plan for each youngster. Parents or guardians and the student should also be part of the process, one that will have major ramifications for continued services after high school. Each ITP should include annual goals to achieve outcomes in the areas of (1) employment, (2) community integration, (3) independent residential living, and (4) recreation and leisure activities (Smith & Luckasson, 1995). These ITP goals may complement the IEP or may be written as a supplement to the student's educational plan. In both cases, ITP goals should be identified and initiated by the time the student is 16 to ensure careful transition planning throughout the high school years.

ITPs assist professionals, parents or guardians, and students in long-range planning to promote smooth transitions to adulthood. They designate specific outcomes that students should achieve, which in turn have implications for secondary instruction and curriculum. In addition, ITPs provide a mechanism for interagency collaboration and promote communication among schools, agencies, parents or guardians, and students in preparing for the many facets and demands of adulthood (see chapter 14 for additional information about ITPs and transition).

● ●

Progralm Evaluation

As you read, think about . . .

1. Identifying ways to monitor academic and social progress.
2. Designing a school day that consists of evaluating student progress.
3. Identifying ways to involve students in evaluating their own progress.

The last assessment question (see question 14 in the list under Assessment) posed by McLoughlin and Lewis (1995) relates to the effectiveness of the educational program. **Program evaluation,** which is the final step in the IEP process, involves three types of evaluation: formative evaluation of student progress, annual review and update of the IEP goals and objectives, and a comprehensive reevaluation of the student.

Student progress on the IEP annual goals and instructional objectives must be monitored and documented frequently throughout the school year. Formative evaluation means that teachers collect assessment information regularly; they can use this information to make instructional decisions about the appropriateness of instructional methodology and the effectiveness of the educational program in helping the student meet IEP goals and objectives. Various tests and assessment procedures (e.g., criterion-referenced tests, achievement tests) can facilitate program evaluation, but the best way to evaluate the program is to use the direct and daily curriculum-based assessments. By using frequent assessment procedures that determine the effectiveness of curricular and instructional interventions, teachers can immediately document student progress.

The IEP must be reviewed annually to summarize and note student progress and to consider adding new annual goals and instructional objectives. The annual review involves the special services committee, parents or guardians, and the student, when appropriate. Teachers should be prepared to summarize the academic and social accomplishments based on formative evaluation information and to identify new curricula for instruction. At this time, a change in placement may be recommended, special education services may be added or eliminated, and general classroom instructional and curricular accommodations may be reevaluated.

By law, students receiving special education services must undergo a comprehensive reevaluation every three years. This process is an important safeguard for students, as it provides updated assessment information about current levels of performance from which the special services committee can make appropriate decisions about identification, analysis of services, placement, and IEP goals and objectives. In some cases, students may no longer require special education services or may need only limited support to succeed in the general education curriculum. For others, a change in placement may be appropriate.

Summary

IDEA requires that students with special needs from ages 3 to 21 receive appropriate educational services, including proper assessment practices, procedural safeguards for parents or guardians, the implementation of an IEP, and the delivery of services in the LRE. The Individualized Family Service Plan (IFSP), Individualized Education Program (IEP), and Individualized Transition Plan (ITP) provide explanations of educational services and instructional emphases to ensure proper intervention at all age levels.

The Individualized Education Program process consists of seven steps: referral (including prereferral), assessment, identification, analysis of services, placement, instructional decision making, and program evaluation. Each of these steps includes specific provisions to guarantee the rights of students and their parents or guardians. Each step is designed to focus on the student's specific needs and to seek information that will benefit the child's educational progress. The IEP process is a multidisciplinary approach that involves many professionals, the child, and the child's family. Although debate continues about assessment practices and service delivery models, collaboration between professionals and family members is crucial to ensure that the IEP is implemented correctly and that the student is making the type of academic and social progress he or she is capable of achieving.

Study and Discussion Questions

1. Identify the seven major provisions of IDEA and the seven steps of the Individualized Education Program (IEP) process.
2. Describe the prereferral and referral processes.
3. Explain the purposes of assessment, describe formal and informal assessment techniques, and discuss the assessment debate.
4. Describe the purpose of the identification step in the Individualized Education Program (IEP) process.
5. Explain the action taken during the analysis of services step in the IEP process.
6. Describe service delivery models that can be discussed during the placement step of the IEP process and the debate surrounding these models.

7. Describe the purpose of the instructional-decision-making step and the components of the IEP.
8. Explain three types of evaluation that occur under the program evaluation step of the IEP process.
9. Discuss the role of parents or guardians and professionals in the IEP process.
10. Develop a task analysis for an academic skill.
11. Write a set of instructional objectives for Travis, a fourth grader who frequently disrupts class during silent reading time and is a poor independent reader.

● ●

References and Suggested Readings

Overview of the Individualized Education Program Process

Smith, D. D., & Luckasson, R. (1995). *Introduction to special education—Teaching in an age of challenge* (2nd ed.). Boston: Allyn & Bacon.

Referral/Prereferral

Chalfant, J. C., & Van Dusen Pysh, M. (1989). Teacher assistance teams: Five descriptive studies on 96 teams. *Remedial and Special Education, 10*(6), 49–58.

West, J. F., Idol, L., & Cannon, G. (1989). *Collaboration in the schools: An inservice and preservice curriculum for teachers, support staff and administrators.* Austin, TX: PRO-ED.

White, R., & Calhoun, M. L. (1987). From referral to placement: Teachers' perceptions of their responsibilities. *Exceptional Children, 53,* 460–468.

Assessment

McLoughlin, J. A., & Lewis, R. B. (1995). *Assessing special students* (4th ed.). Columbus, OH: Merrill.

Formal Assessment

Mercer, C. D. (1991). *Students with learning disabilities* (4th ed.). Columbus, OH: Merrill.

Salvia, J., & Ysseldyke, J. (1991). *Assessment* (5th ed.). Boston: Houghton Mifflin.

Taylor, R. L. (1993). *Assessment of exceptional students: Educational and psychological procedures* (3rd ed.). Boston: Allyn & Bacon.

Informal Assessment

Coutinho, M., & Malouf, D. (1993). Performance assessment and children with disabilities: Issues and possibilities. *Teaching Exceptional Children, 25*(4), 62–67.

Deno, S. L., Mirkin, P. K., & Wesson, C. (1984). How to write effective data-based IEPs. *Teaching Exceptional Children, 16*(2), 99–109.

Fuchs, L. S., Fuchs, D., Hamlett, C. L., & Stecker, P. M. (1992). Effects of curriculum-based measurement and consultation on teacher planning and student achievement in mathematics operations. *American Educational Research Journal, 28,* 617–641.

Nolet, V. (1992). Classroom-based measurement and portfolio assessment. *Diagnostique, 18*(1), 5–26.

Rivera, D. M. (1993). Performance, authentic, and portfolio assessments: Emerging alternative assessment in search of an empirical basis. *Diagnostique, 18*(4), 325–334.

Taylor, R. L., Tindal, G., Fuchs, L., & Bryant, B. R. (1993). Assessment in the nineties: A possible glance into the future. *Diagnostique, 18*(2), 113–122.

Wesson, C. L., & King, R. P. (1992). The role of curriculum-based measurement in portfolio assessment. *Diagnostique, 18*(1), 27–37.

Wolf, K. (1991). The school teacher's portfolio: Issues in design, implementation, and evaluation. *Phi Delta Kappan, 73*(2), 130–136.

Debate

Dangel, H. L., & Ensminger, E. E. (1988). The use of a discrepancy formula with LD students. *Learning Disabilities Focus, 4*(1), 24–31.

Deno, S. L. (1989). Curriculum-based measurement and special education services: A fundamental and direct relationship. In M. R. Shinn (Ed.), *Curriculum-based measurement: Assessing special children* (pp. 1–17). New York: Guilford Press.

Epps, S., Ysseldyke, J. E., & McGue, M. (1984). "I know one when I see one"—Differentiating LD from non-LD students. *Learning Disabilities Quarterly, 7,* 89–101.

Evans, L. (1990). A conceptual overview of the regression discrepancy model for evaluating severe discrepancies between IQ and achievement scores. *Journal of Learning Disabilities, 23,* 406–412.

Feuer, M. J., & Fulton, K. (1993). The many faces of performance assessment. *Phi Delta Kappan, 74*(6), 478.

Frame, R. E., Clarizio, H. F., & Porter, A. (1984). Diagnostic and prescriptive bias in school psychologists' reports of a learning disabled child. *Journal of Learning Disabilities, 17,* 12–15.

Marston, D. B. (1989). A curriculum-based measurement approach to assessing academic performance: What it is and why do it. In M. R. Shinn (Ed.), *Curriculum-based measurement: Assessing special children* (pp. 18–78). New York: Guilford Press.

Reynolds, C. (1985). Measuring the aptitude-achievement discrepancy in learning disability diagnosis. *Remedial and Special Education, 6,* 37–55.

Rivers, D., & Smith, T. (1988). Traditional eligibility criteria for identifying students as specific learning disabled. *Journal of Learning Disabilities, 21,* 642–644.

Shapiro, E. S., & Derr, T. F. (1990). Curriculum-based assessment. In T. B. Gutkin & C. R. Reynolds (Eds.), *The handbook of school psychology* (pp. 365–386). New York: Wiley.

Shinn, M. R., Tindal, G. A., Spira, D., & Marston, D. (1987). Practice of learning disabilities as social policy. *Learning Disability Quarterly, 10,* 17–28.

Siegel, L. (1989). IQ is irrelevant to the definition of learning disabilities. *Journal of Learning Disabilities, 22,* 506–546.

Sinclair, E., & Alexson, J. (1986). Learning disabilities discrepancy formulas: Similarities and differences among them. *Learning Disabilities Research, 1,* 112–118.

Wesson, C. L., & King, R. P. (1992). The role of curriculum-based measurement in portfolio assessment. *Diagnostique, 18*(1), 27–37.

Worthern, B. R. (1993). Critical issues that will determine the future of alternative assessment. *Phi Delta Kappan, 74*(6), 444–454.

Ysseldyke, J. (1986). Use of assessment information to make decisions about students. In R. J. Morris & B. Blatt (Eds.), *Special education research trends.* New York: Pergamon Press.

Ysseldyke, J. E., Algozzine, B., & Epps, S. (1983). A logical and empirical analysis of current practice in classifying students handicapped. *Exceptional Children, 50,* 160–166.

Ysseldyke, J. E., Algozzine, B., Shinn, M., & McGue, M. (1982). Similarities and differences between low achievers and students labeled learning disabled. *Journal of Special Education, 16,* 73–85.

Placement

Council for Exceptional Children—Council for Children with Behavioral Disorders. (1988). *Position statement on the regular education initiative.* Reston, VA: Author.

Council for Exceptional Children—Division for Learning Disabilities. (1993). *Inclusion: What does it mean for students with learning disabilities?* Reston, VA: Author.

Council for Learning Disabilities. (1993, April). Position statement. *Learning Disability Quarterly, 16,* 126.

Hallahan, D. P., & Kauffman, J. M. (Eds.). (1995). *The illusion of full inclusion.* Austin, TX: PRO-ED.

National Joint Committee on Learning Disabilities. (1993, January). *A reaction to "full inclusion": A reaffirmation of the rights of students with learning disabilities to a continuum of services.* Author.

Smith, D. D., & Luckasson, R. (1995). *Introduction to special education—Teaching in an age of challenge* (2nd ed.). Boston: Allyn & Bacon.

Stainback, S., & Stainback, W. (1989). No more teachers of students with severe handicaps. *TASH Newsletter, 15,* 9–10.

Instructional Decision Making

La Mar, K., & Rosenberg, B. (1988). *Synthesis of individual transition plans: Format and process.* Sacramento: California State Department of Education.

Neubert, D. A., Tilson, G. P., & Ianacone, R. N. (1989). Postsecondary transition needs and employment patterns of individuals with mild disabilities. *Exceptional Children, 55,* 494–500.

Smith, D. D., & Luckasson, R. (1995). *Introduction to special education: Teaching in an age of challenge* (2nd ed.). Boston: Allyn & Bacon.

Trapani, C. (1990). *Transition goals for adolescents with learning disabilities.* Boston: College-Hill.

Program Evaluation

McLoughlin, J. A., & Lewis, R. B. (1995). *Assessing special students* (4th ed.). Columbus, OH: Merrill.

Chapter 4
Designing Instruction

Teaching and learning are complex behaviors that require attention to and coordination of a number of factors. Several of these were discussed in chapter 1, including the characteristics of learners, teachers, and the environment. For example, teachers must be familiar with the learning characteristics and attitudes their students bring to the classroom. This information assists teachers in designing appropriate instructional programs and meeting individual student needs. Teachers also must be familiar with techniques designed to promote positive classroom environments and incorporate principles of effective teaching. As noted in chapter 3, Individualized Education Program (IEP) annual goals and instructional objectives form the basis of all instructional programs. Therefore, teachers must be familiar with their students' IEPs before planning instruction.

In addition, teachers need to understand specific phases of teaching so that effective instruction and learning can occur. In chapters 4, 5, and 6, the authors discuss the Phases of Teaching Model. In this chapter, we present the Phases of Teaching Model and discuss the designing instruction phase of teaching. The implementing instruction and evaluating instruction phases of teaching are discussed in chapters 5 and 6, respectively. In these three chapters, there are tips and scenarios to help readers conceptualize the features of instructional design, implementation, and evaluation. While reading these three chapters, the reader should try to construct the whole picture of teaching.

Making Connections

Before you read, recall the chapter 1 discussion about characteristics of students with learning and behavior problems and how those characteristics might affect the learning process. Review the characteristics of effective teaching; think about designing a lesson that promotes those characteristics. Consider designing a lesson with another teacher to help students with special needs acquire skills in the general education setting. Finally, review the components of the Individualized Education Program discussed in chapter 3 in preparation for the content in this chapter.

Objectives

After studying this chapter, the reader will be able to

1. Identify the phases and the components of the Phases of Teaching Model.
2. Describe factors relating to the learner.
3. Explain considerations for designing curriculum and instruction.
4. Explain classroom and behavior management considerations.
5. Describe considerations for beginning and ending the school year.

● ●

The Phases of Teaching Model

Teaching can be conceptualized as consisting of three phases: designing instruction, implementing instruction, and evaluating and modifying instruction. During each phase, teachers address certain components so that effective teaching and successful learning can occur. Table 4.1 shows the Phases of Teaching Model, which includes the three phases and the specific components for each phase.

The designing instruction phase focuses on the learner, curriculum and instruction, and classroom and behavior management. During this phase, teachers make decisions about what they will teach, how they will teach, which resources they will use for instructional purposes, and under what conditions they will teach. In this phase, teachers also examine IEPs and other pertinent student information, identify stages of learning and establish current levels of instructional performance, identify the **curriculum,** select **instructional materials,** select **instructional arrangements,** and develop **instructional plans.** Teachers also perform **noninstructional tasks,** such as addressing environmental considerations, establishing schedules, and setting classroom rules and expectations.

Table 4.1
Phases of
Teaching Model

Designing instruction	Implementing instruction	Evaluating instruction
The learner	**Approaches to instruction**	**Curriculum-based assessment**
Personal and social factors	Behavioral	Purpose
Academic factors: stages of learning	Strategic	Design
	Holistic/constructivist	Data collection and analysis procedures
Curriculum and instruction		Pairing instruction and evaluation
Curricular selection and organization	**Other types of instruction**	
Instructional materials	Remedial	**Teacher observation and analysis**
Instructional arrangements	Tutorial	Anecdotal logs
Instructional plans	Adaptive	Antecedent-behavior-consequence analysis
Classroom and behavior management	**Delivery of instruction**	Observational recording
Environmental considerations	Instructional steps	Work sample analysis
Schedules	Instructional management	"Think-aloud" interviews
Rules and expectations	Instructional language	
		Portfolio assessment
Considerations for starting and ending the school year	**Homework**	Content selection
Starting the school year	Research findings	Analysis
Ending the school year	Homework practices	Cautions and considerations
	Technology	
	Instructional technology	
	Assistive technology	

The implementing instruction phase is when actual teaching occurs. Students' instructional needs dictate teachers' approach to material and the instructional objectives. Teaching means melding instruction, curriculum, management, teacher behavior, environmental awareness, and evaluation into an integrated system of instruction in which many components occur simultaneously and warrant attention. The key to this phase is the teacher's ability to pull it all together. For many teachers, it takes several years with strong instructional support, constructive teacher evaluations, and master-teacher mentoring to pull the components of teaching together into coherent, effective lessons.

The evaluating instruction phase is another important phase of teaching, because teachers need to determine whether or not students are benefiting from instructional interventions and making satisfactory progress toward IEP goals. Because students with learning and behavior problems tend to be academically delayed, it is critical to obtain evaluation information to determine the effectiveness of instruction. This must be accomplished in a timely fashion to ensure both effective and efficient instruction and to minimize further academic delay. Evaluation results also help the teacher know whether the student is ready to tackle new instructional objectives.

The Phases of Teaching Model of instruction is presented in this book as an example of how to organize and manage instructional phases and components that promote effective teaching.

Phase One: Designing Instruction

By designing instruction, teachers establish an effective foundation for implementing and evaluating instruction. Specifically, teachers need to consider their students' educational needs, curricular and instructional components, classroom and behavior management components that will foster effective instruction, and considerations for starting and ending the school year. The model is intended to help teachers conceptualize the "pieces" of teaching that drive instructional planning, implementation, and evaluation.

The Learner

As you read, think about...
1. Designing interview questions that you would use to discover information about your students.
2. Explaining the information you would like to know when visiting your students' homes and neighborhoods.
3. Comparing and contrasting the learning behaviors of students (or yourself) when first learning a skill, when mastering a skill, and when applying a skill to a new situation.
4. Describing ways to foster a classroom setting that recognizes cultural, linguistic, and ethnic diversity.

Students bring to school a rich heritage of cultural, linguistic, and ethnic diversity coupled with a wide range of familial experiences. The home environments in which students are raised contribute significantly to their attitudes toward learning. Students with learning and behavior difficulties also have self-concepts and motivational levels that have been influenced by successful and unsuccessful academic and social interactions.

Before teachers design an instructional program, they must identify the personal, social, and academic needs of their students (refer to chapter 1 for a review of learner characteristics). Teachers must develop a good understanding of the diverse backgrounds and experiences students bring to the educational setting, and they must also know the academic levels at which students are performing in order to plan effective instruction.

Personal and Social Factors

Students' personal and social factors include their attitudes, beliefs, experiences, and backgrounds. These factors influence students' perceptions of school and learning, and how they approach the teacher and classroom situation. It is important for teachers to get to know their students quickly and to accentuate positive personal and social factors. At the beginning of the school year, or when new students join the class, teachers can get to know their students through a variety of methods. For example, teachers have found interest inventories, home visits, and group activities such as "corners" useful ways of identifying students' personal and social factors. Here is an explanation of each of those methods:

1. *Interest inventories.* Many teachers have students complete inventories to determine their interests, likes, and dislikes. For example, the interest inventory might ask: "What is your favorite movie?"; "What was the last book you read?"; "What is your favorite sport?"; "What do you like to do after school?"; "What do you like to do with your family on the weekends?"; "Who would you most want to be like?"; "What is your favorite color?"; "What is your favorite television show?"

For older students, interest inventory information could be obtained in an interview format in which students could use a set list of questions to interview a classmate. The interviewer would then have to share some of the information with other students.

A teacher can use information from the interest inventory to initiate discussions, decide which books to select for the reading center, or identify a topic for group work. Interest inventory answers also can provide teachers with important information about students' backgrounds and experiences.

2. *Home visits.* Making home visits is one of the best ways for teachers to learn about their students. Meeting parents and their children at home presents a different environmental arrangement than the classroom. In many cases, families may be more at ease meeting the teacher in their home than at school. Parents often provide valuable information about their children and home situation that can be used wisely in the classroom setting. Home visits must be conducted judiciously, however. In some cases, they might not be advisable. Some parents or guardians prefer that teachers not visit them at home. In addition, teachers may not be comfortable in certain community environments. Cautions considered, home visits are valuable tools to inform teachers about their students and the life experiences they bring to school.

3. *Corners.* Corners (Andrini, 1991) can be fun and interesting for both teachers and students. Teachers designate each corner of the classroom as representing a

response for a statement. Students listen to the statement, then go to the corner with the response that best describes their perceptions about the topic. For instance, the statement might be "There is too much violence on television"; the corner response choices might be: strongly agree, agree, disagree, strongly disagree. Students would move to the corner with the response of their choice, then discuss with other students in the same corner their reasons for selecting that choice. The types of statements and responses would vary according to students' ages. This is a good activity to generate discussion and to help teachers know their students better.

An important consideration for teachers in getting to know their students is to develop an appreciation for cultural, ethnic, and linguistic backgrounds. First, teachers should become aware of the diversity in their classrooms by visiting with families and students. Second, teachers should include experiences and activities in their curriculum that speak to the cultural and ethnic diversity found in their classroom, in the community, and in general. It is ideal to promote awareness of a variety of heritages on an ongoing basis, rather than just when a particular holiday occurs. Third, teachers can infuse into instruction some of the general principles of acknowledging cultural and ethnic diversity found in Spotlight on Diversity.

General Principles of Acknowledging Cultural, Ethnic, and Linguistic Diversity

- Encourage students to use their primary language during the school day.
- Establish a tutoring program with people who can tutor students in their primary language.
- Have books written in other languages available in the classroom.
- Display pictures of various cultures represented in the school.
- Display pictures of culturally diverse people in professions and high-status occupations.
- Encourage all parents to get involved with class activities.
- Take into account students' sociocultural backgrounds and their effects on oral language, reading and writing, and second-language learning. ●

Source: Compiled and adapted from *New Voices: Second Language Learning and Teaching: A Handbook for Primary Teachers* by New Zealand Department of Education, 1988, Wellington: Department of Education; cited in "A Theoretical Framework for Bilingual Special Education" by J. Cummings, 1989, *Exceptional Children, 56,* pp. 113–114; cited in "An Optimal Learning Environment for Rosemary" by N. T. Ruiz, 1989, *Exceptional Children, 56,* p. 134; and cited in *Introduction to Special Education—Teaching in an Age of Challenge* (2nd ed., p. 62), by D. D. Smith and R. Luckasson, 1995, Boston: Allyn & Bacon.

Academic Factors

As discussed in chapter 3, many decisions are made about a student's instructional program when the Individualized Education Program (IEP) is developed. These decisions include the identification of annual goals and instructional objectives. Therefore, before planning instruction, teachers should examine students' IEPs to determine the academic and social annual goals and instructional objectives for which they are responsible.

Given an annual goal, teachers could conduct a task analysis (see chapter 3) and informal assessment to pinpoint specific objectives for which instruction must be designed. Informal assessment results could tell teachers areas in which students require instruction and the stages of learning in which they are functioning.

Stages of Learning

All learners pass through various **stages of learning** every time they master and integrate a new skill. Those who design students' educational programs must anticipate and plan for these stages (Idol, 1989). Researchers have shown that knowing students' stages of learning is important for selecting appropriate instructional interventions. For example, in classic **applied behavioral analysis** research, Ayllon and Azrin (1964) and Hopkins (1968) discovered that rewards are not always effective for promoting academic mastery; instructions had to be used first to get the **target behavior** to a level at which rewards were effective. In other words, there had to be some level of correct responding before **reinforcement** could be instituted. Another research study designed by Smith and Lovitt (1976) showed that students had to learn to solve computational arithmetic problems before reinforcement was effective. However, when some level of proficiency and accuracy had been obtained, reinforcement was influential. Since then, a number of studies have shown that certain instructional procedures are best applied in particular situations (see "References and Suggested Readings" in the stages of learning section at the end of this chapter).

Five stages of learning have been identified. These stages are: acquisition (initial and advanced), proficiency, maintenance, generalization, and adaption (problem solving). A diagram of these stages and students' learning levels appears in Figure 4.1. Stages are applicable while students are learning skills and increasing their performance levels.

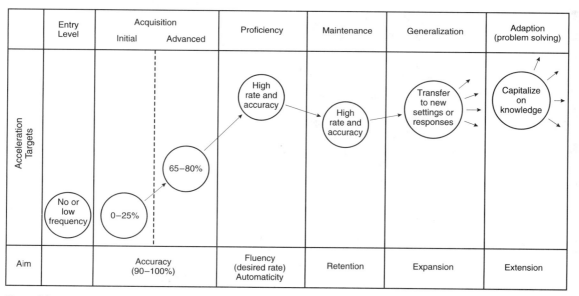

Figure 4.1
Stages of learning that lead to ultimate mastery through continual increases in a skill's frequency

During acquisition, the learner could enter the learning process with no knowledge of how to perform a task accurately. After a period of instruction, some learners demonstrate that they can perform the task or skill with 90 to 100 percent accuracy; they have passed through the acquisition stage of learning. Others require further direct instruction at the acquisition stage of learning to attain sufficiently high levels of accuracy to indicate mastery. During the acquisition stage, the aim is for the individual to learn how to perform the skills accurately. This is not where the educational process should stop, however. The individual must also be able to perform the skill quickly enough to execute it automatically.

During the proficiency stage of learning, the aim is for the learner to perform the task with both quality (accuracy) and sufficient quantity (fluency). The interventions differ from those used in the acquisition stage; they direct the learner to increase fluency of performance. It is very important for learners to reach proficient levels of performance. For example, if a student can correctly form the letters of the alphabet, but does so too slowly, he or she will not be able to complete assignments that require writing as a basic tool (written composition, spelling tests) in a timely manner. The student who writes slowly might not be able to keep up with the teacher's dictation of spelling words on weekly tests. Students need to be able to perform tasks fluently so they can complete work accurately and within the designated time period. Hasselbring, Goin, and Bransford (1988) note that students should be able to perform lower-level cognitive skills automatically and fluently so that they can place more emphasis on those higher-order skills that extend knowledge and learning. Mastering skills so that they require little cognitive processing is known as **automaticity.**

Once the learner achieves proficient levels of performance, he or she enters the maintenance stage of learning. The intent is for the learned behavior to remain at the high levels of the two previous stages. Retention of learning is important to all teachers and their students. For some students, this is the most frustrating stage of learning; learned skills are often not retained once direct instruction is withdrawn. Many teachers set aims in the proficiency situation slightly higher than necessary to anticipate this loss in fluency. For individuals who tend to retain too little fluency of performance, teachers must plan for maintenance by periodically evaluating retention and implementing direct intervention on an as-needed basis.

After the maintenance stage comes the generalization stage of learning, in which the learner should be able to perform the learned behavior in all appropriate situations, regardless of the setting. For many students, skills learned in the classroom do not appear automatically in other settings, with other people, or with various materials. For example, a student might have mastered a learning strategy to develop themes in English class. In history class, however, the student does not apply the strategy when asked to write a report. Another student might have demonstrated the ability to regroup when subtracting a one-digit number from a two-digit number, but not be able to rename when subtracting two digits from two digits. These students must learn to generalize (Stokes & Baer, 1977). Some researchers (Ellis, Lenz, & Sabornie, 1987) recommend that the concept of generalization be introduced to students during the acquisition stage of learning, and specifically programmed following demonstration of skill mastery (Deshler & Schumaker, 1986).

The last stage of learning is often referred to as adaption, or problem solving. This stage requires the student to capitalize on previous learning and to extend knowledge and skills already acquired. In new situations, the learner must be able to solve problems. It is important to teach students to extend their knowledge and skills. Students need to be flexible and able to make decisions based on previous learning. Problem solving is a neglected area in many students' educational programs and needs to be integrated throughout the school years.

Teachers need to be aware of these stages of learning, because the entry level (e.g., acquisition, proficiency) of each student influences the teacher's selection of instructional interventions and accountability systems. Interventions that are most efficient and effective in one stage of learning might not be suitable in another. The measurement systems chosen to evaluate instruction differ depending on the stage at which the student is functioning (more details about this are given in chapter 6). Because the stages of learning are so important, we stress their influence on instruction throughout this text. Scenario 4.1 presents an example of how one student progressed through the stages of learning over time.

Scenario 4.1

Example of Stages of Learning

Ryan was a third-grade student who was identified as having a learning disability in mathematics. The Individualized Education Program specified annual goals and instructional objectives in mathematics, including word problems. Ryan's special education teacher conducted a task analysis for solving word problems and administered informal assessment techniques to determine the instructional objective for instruction. Assessment data showed that Ryan could solve one-step word problems, but did not generalize this knowledge to two-step problems. He was at the acquisition (0 percent accuracy) stage of learning in solving two-step word problems using basic computational algorithms.

The teacher used direct instruction to teach Ryan a strategy for solving two-step word problems (acquisition stage). The teacher discussed with Ryan the importance of solving two-step problems, explaining that many daily activities require problem solving (generalization). Ryan also worked on developing fluency with basic facts, because facts were part of the word problem information that had to be manipulated (proficiency stage for facts). It took Ryan three days to reach mastery (90 percent accuracy) in stating the steps of the problem-solving strategy. Ryan then worked in a cooperative learning group with his peers to solve one-step (maintenance stage) and two-step word problems. The group worked together for a week until it was determined through curriculum-based assessment that students could solve two-step problems proficiently.

Once Ryan demonstrated mastery (90 percent accuracy) in solving two-step word problems using the strategy, his general education teacher asked him to solve two-step story problems. The special education served as a consultant in case there were generalization problems (generalization stage). The general education teacher learned Ryan's new strategy for solving two-step word problems; Ryan was asked to use the strategy when solving problems from his textbook. Ryan worked with a partner in a peer tutoring situation to develop word problems using meaningful situations (adaption). They shared these problems with other students who were asked to solve peer problems. ■

In the following section, we talk about curricular and instructional considerations for the designing instruction phase. Teachers use IEP annual goals, instructional objectives, and informal assessment information to select curricular areas in need of instruction and to develop their lesson plans accordingly.

Curriculum and Instruction

As you read, think about...

1. Designing the curriculum for a content area that you would like to teach. Design the curriculum for only one grade level.
2. Comparing and contrasting the secondary level curriculum for students wishing to pursue a college education and vocational training education.
3. Enhancing the reading and mathematics curriculum for elementary level students with severe academic difficulties.
4. Analyzing a secondary level content area textbook using the guidelines presented in this section, and preparing a list of strengths, weaknesses, and recommendations for improvement.
5. Brainstorming materials to use in addition to textbooks.
6. Analyzing instructional workbooks and making recommendations for ways to use these materials.
7. Comparing and contrasting teacher-mediated and student-mediated instructional arrangements.
8. Using the peer learning arrangement to write a lesson plan for an instructional objective (use Figure 4.5, which appears later in this chapter, as a model).
9. Working in a cooperative learning group to develop a unit plan.

In the curriculum and instruction component of the designing instruction phase, teachers use IEP annual goals and objectives to make decisions about the content to be taught and to develop instructional plans. When making these decisions, teachers must consider (1) curricular selection and organization, (2) instructional materials, (3) instructional arrangements, and (4) instructional plans. We will now discuss these four instructional areas.

Curricular Selection and Organization

Armstrong (1989) described curriculum as a plan for the selection and organization of student experiences to change and develop behaviors. As depicted in Table 4.2, curricular selection criteria greatly influence what is taught to students with learning and behavior problems. Curriculum can be organized into various areas and across disciplines using a theme-based, integrated approach to instruction.

Selection Criteria

Curricular selection must match the annual goals and objectives designated on students' IEPs. For example, if an annual goal and instructional objective specify that

Table 4.2
Curricular
Selection
Considerations

Individualized education program: annual goals and instructional objectives
Life goals
Elementary/Secondary level
Resources and textbooks
Service delivery programs
Graduation/Diploma requirements

the student will develop reading comprehension skills, then the teacher might select a learning strategies curriculum coupled with subject area reading material as the content for teaching.

Teachers should not be the only ones making decisions about the curriculum that students learn to prepare them for life experiences. Students and their parents should be consulted regarding the life goals they want the student to achieve. Teachers, students (as appropriate), and parents can establish realistic life goals, based on students' strengths and weaknesses, and select curricula and experiences to address these goals. This process can occur at the elementary and secondary level; parents and students should begin thinking about life goals at an early age and modify them accordingly as the student moves through the grades.

The level of schooling, elementary or secondary, will affect the curriculum being taught. For example, it is common for academic and social skills to be the curricular content at the elementary level (Polloway, Patton, Epstein, & Smith, 1989). For students with learning and behavior problems, emphasis must be placed on remediating deficit academic skills and developing appropriate social skills for successful interpersonal relationships.

At the secondary level, curricular options for students with learning and behavior problems will vary according to **transition** and life goals, including postsecondary career choices. Selecting curricular options should be a significant part of planning for students' transition to adulthood. According to the National Joint Committee on Learning Disabilities (1994), successful transition planning includes students' developing appropriate social skills, learning effective studying and test-taking skills, exploring postsecondary entrance requirements, and selecting courses that meet those requirements. Thus, the core curriculum requirements, course electives, and job-related experiences will vary according to the postsecondary choices that students with disabilities and their parents make. Secondary-level curricular selection will depend on whether students are seeking a college education, vocational training, or immediate employment following graduation (Polloway et al., 1989). Middle and high school special education curricula must also address issues pertaining to transition. Thus, curricula should include training in social skills, functional life skills, career education, and learning strategies.

The resources available to teachers greatly influence curricular selection. Most school districts have curriculum guides for general and special education detailing the content areas, goals, and objectives to be covered. Special education curriculum is developed for those students with learning and behavior problems severe enough to warrant curricular alternatives to those offered in general education. For example, more emphasis is placed on **functional life skills** and career development skills for students with severe learning and behavior problems, and mastery of academic skills is emphasized less. Curriculum might include **functional academics,** social skills, career exploration, and on-the-job training.

The textbook is probably the most influential factor in determining the curriculum and focus of instruction at the elementary and secondary level. Thus, youngsters must be capable of reading textbooks, comprehending the content, synthesizing a large amount of information that may have limited review and practice opportunities, working independently, and functioning at an appropriate level for that textbook's curriculum. For youngsters with special needs, curriculum and instruction that are driven primarily by textbooks may be problematic. Some of the issues pertaining to textbook curricular selection are discussed later in this chapter.

Service delivery programs chosen to provide special education services to young-sters also affect the curriculum chosen for instruction. Students with learning and behavior problems who receive most, if not all, of their education in a general educa-tion classroom are typically expected to complete that classroom's curriculum. This implies that students must be capable of learning from textbooks and limited teacher interactions. Students with disabilities who receive special education services in a resource or self-contained program (or other delivery program) may receive instruc-tion in curriculum that is task-analyzed in greater detail or presented at a slower pace than what is presented in the general education classroom.

High school graduation and diploma requirements are yet another factor to con-sider when selecting curriculum. National educational reform efforts (National Asso-ciation of School Boards of Education, 1992) to improve the quality of school curriculum and instruction called for student competencies in academic areas, such as mathematics, science, and language arts. Many school districts offer graduation and diploma options for students with learning and behavior problems, based on indi-viduals' needs. For example, college-bound students have to satisfy specific core course graduation requirements, while students with more severe disabilities may receive a diploma after achieving IEP goals and objectives. Therefore, the type of diploma students seek and the graduation requirements they must satisfy often dic-tate the curriculum selected for individual students. We now turn our attention to five major curricular areas. These areas cover a wide variety of curricular content to meet the diverse needs of students with learning and behavior problems.

Curricular Areas

The five major curricular areas discussed in this chapter are: **academic skills,** func-tional life skills, **social skills, career skills,** and **learning strategies.** Each area represents a body of information that has a specific emphasis to help meet the needs of students with learning and behavior problems. The curricular areas selected for instructional design depend on the criteria discussed previously, such as IEP annual goals and objectives, students' life goals, outcomes identified for youngsters, and level of schooling (i.e., elementary, middle, high school).

1. *Academic skills* (discussed further in chapters 10, 11, 12, and 13). Stu-dents with learning and behavior difficulties require instruction in basic aca-demic skills, including reading, language arts, and mathematics. Instruction focuses on teaching youngsters skills comparable with those of their peers. The approach taken to deliver academic skills instruction will vary depending on educators' teaching preferences (e.g., constructivism, direct instruction—see chapter 5 for a discussion of various instructional approaches). Regard-less, the intent is the same—to teach students academic skills deemed impor-tant by school officials. To master these skills, students with disabilities usually require intensive academic instruction, including more task-analyzed curricular objectives, more practice opportunities, and maintenance and gen-eralization activities to promote the application of skill learning. Few would argue the merits of selecting an academic skills area as a curricular emphasis for students at the elementary and secondary grades; however, teachers must also choose other areas to ensure that individual learning needs are fully addressed.

2. *Functional life skills* (see chapter 14 for further information). Functional life skills enable students to manage everyday living independently and successfully. Researchers (Brolin, 1992; Clark, 1994; Edgar, 1987; Sitlington & Frank, 1993) have shown that many students with learning and behavior problems leave school without the necessary skills to be independent adults; thus, educators must provide a comprehensive curriculum, including basic functional life skills, to prepare youngsters for adulthood.

Functional life skills differ for various academic areas. For example, in mathematics, functional life skills might include estimating, balancing a checkbook, making change, measuring, understanding credit cards, and reviewing pay stubs. Reading skills might include understanding signs, labels, information commonly displayed in everyday life, a newspaper, a job application form, and recipes. Word processing and keyboard skills, writing one's signature, completing a job application form legibly, and writing instructions might all be considered functional life skills in the area of written expression. Once specific functional life skills are identified for instructional purposes, teachers must pick one or two ways to teach the skills. First, teachers can infuse instruction of these skills into current curriculum. For example, functional life skills could be taught as part of an instructional unit of study, included in a learning center, and integrated into a content area of instruction (e.g., geometry, language arts, history). Second, teachers can incorporate those skills necessary for successful independent living in a course of instruction. For instance, in a high school course featuring "consumer skills" or "life skills," students would learn those skills necessary to make successful transitions to adulthood (e.g., see Cronin & Patton, 1993, and chapter 14).

3. *Social skills* (see chapter 8 for additional information). It is well documented that some students with learning and behavior problems lack socialization skills (Bender, 1989; Bos & Vaughn, 1994; Stone & LaGreca, 1990) and must be taught directly. Social skills curricula (Elias & Clabby, 1989; Hazel, Schumaker, Sherman, & Sheldon-Wildgen, 1981) have been developed to teach youngsters with social skills deficits or who are at risk for social difficulties. Social skills can be categorized into a variety of domains, such as communication skills, problem-solving skills, self-related skills, and task-related skills (Schumaker, Hazel, & Pederson, 1988; Walker et al., 1988). Students should begin learning these skills at the elementary level, and activities should be planned that require students to practice and generalize their social skills knowledge.

4. *Career skills* (refer to chapter 14 for further discussion). Career education is considered a major curriculum that promotes a successful transition to adulthood (Wiles & Bondi, 1993). It consists of four areas: (1) values, attitudes, and habits, (2) human relationships, (3) occupational information, and (4) acquisition of job and daily living skills (Clark & Kolstoe, 1995). According to the Division on Career Development of the Council for Exceptional Children, career development is a lifelong process that must be emphasized at all levels of schooling through direct instruction and programming (Clark, Carlson, Fisher, Cook, & D'Alonzo, 1991). Cronin and Patton (1993) identify several ways to address career education in the curriculum, including infusing career skills into present course content and developing specific courses that focus on life skills and include career development (see chapter 14).

5. *Learning strategies* (see chapter 5 for additional information and chapters 10, 11, 12, and 13 for specific examples). A **learning strategy** is a routine or procedure that enables the learner to acquire and utilize knowledge. Learning strategy training is based on the notion that youngsters with learning problems lack efficient and effective cognitive strategies (Ellis & Friend, 1991; Wong, 1991) and the metacognitive skills (Fleischner & Garnett, 1987; Wong & Wong, 1986) to address tasks successfully. Consequently, students may become overly dependent on the teacher for assistance, utilize inefficient or effective strategies, or develop motivational problems (Torgesen, 1977).

A large body of research documents specific strategies that students with learning and behavior problems can learn to help them cope with academic and behavioral tasks. Learning strategy instruction teaches students how to learn and how to use self-regulation skills (e.g., planning, monitoring, testing, revising, and evaluating) (Baker & Brown, 1984). Strategy instruction has proven effective in teaching mainly secondary level students to engage more effectively in reading comprehension, mathematics problem solving, written language, and study skills tasks. Strategy instruction is recommended as an important part of a total curriculum for students with learning difficulties (Deshler, Schumaker, Lenz, & Ellis, 1984). For instance, researchers at the University of Kansas have developed the Learning Strategies Curriculum, which includes teaching paraphrasing, test-taking skills, and sentence writing (see chapters 10 and 13 for more about these and other strategies). As with other curricular areas already described, teachers must decide how to infuse strategy curriculum into existing course content and ensure that students are indeed generalizing strategic training to their courses and study situations.

We now present information about integrating curricular content into thematic lessons. Curricular integration enables students to apply the skills they have learned or that require additional practice across disciplines.

Curricular Integration

We define curricular integration as teaching across the disciplines or content areas based on a theme. For example, the theme "dinosaurs" could be taught by emphasizing skills from mathematics, the fine arts, literature, science, social studies, and language arts. Here are several benefits to organizing curriculum with an integrated theme-based approach:

1. Integrated curriculum helps students make connections across curricular areas as they apply skills within a meaningful context (theme). Integrated curriculum, based on a theme, has support from professional organizations (e.g., the National Council of Teachers of Mathematics, 1989) who call for teachers to help students make "connections" across the disciplines and content areas.
2. Integrating curriculum offers students, for whom the learning stages of maintenance, generalization, and adaption are an issue, an opportunity to apply and adapt previously mastered skills.
3. Theme-based integrated curriculum can be individualized by including instructional objectives appropriate for the diverse learning needs of students in the classroom.

4. Integrated curriculum provides an opportunity to infuse student experiences and cultural backgrounds into the curriculum chosen for instruction.

The integrated curricular approach to instruction is intuitively appealing, offers some exciting instructional opportunities for teachers and students, and has some field testing to support the concept (e.g., Kataoka & Patton, 1989; Rhodes & Dudley-Marling, 1988). However, Willis (1994) offers some cautionary notes and suggestions for integrating curriculum. Educators must be cautious about interdisciplinary content selected for themes. A theme must have sufficient depth in each content area. According to Willis (1994), "In selecting concepts for such units, teachers often choose what fits best with the theme, rather than emphasizing the ideas that are most important and useful within the discipline" (p. 4). Teachers can avoid this by carefully analyzing **curriculum guides** or having discussions with content area teachers at the secondary level. An explanation of developing integrated curricular units appears later in this chapter in the "Instructional Plans" section. Figure 4.2 depicts an example of instructional objectives and activities for a **theme-based integrated curriculum** on sunflowers.

Instructional Materials

When developing lessons, teachers must decide which materials to choose that will supplement instruction and provide meaningful activities for learning skills and concepts. **Instructional materials** refer to any type of material (e.g., textbooks, kits, **manipulatives,** games, playing cards) used to convey instructional content to students. Instructional materials may be used when concepts are first presented to youngsters, during independent practice activities, and during peer-group instruction. For example, students may use math rods during place value instruction, complete reading comprehension activity books during independent seatwork, and use a scale to weigh objects during a cooperative learning science-math activity.

Teachers often acquire instructional materials from colleagues, book fairs, textbook storage rooms, libraries, catalogues, state adoption lists, resource centers, or the local "teacher" store. Teachers may also come by these materials as part of a textbook adoption cycle or through conference exhibitors. Other times, teachers may inherit a classroom that is well stocked with a variety of instructional materials, or may teach in general education classrooms where instructional materials are available.

Basal textbooks may be obtained through a school-district-wide adoption process, in which a curriculum adoption committee selects the same books for all teachers, through a site-based managed approach, in which teachers and principals at individual schools select their basals, or through the efforts of individual special education teachers who "scrounge" the book room for discards to use with their students.

There is a plethora of available instructional materials, so it is important for teachers to select materials judiciously. Teachers usually must operate within tight budgetary restrictions. The following section discusses guidelines for selecting and using instructional materials, followed by a section devoted specifically to guidelines for textbooks.

Guidelines for Selecting and Using Instructional Materials

Research on effective curricular and instructional design procedures affirms the importance of providing examples and **nonexamples;** providing teacher-guided prac-

Topic: Sunflowers

Content Areas: Mathematics, Science and Health, Fine Arts, Language Arts

Instructional Objectives:

Mathematics
Instructional objectives:
State reasonable estimations.
Measure objects to ½″ with 100% accuracy.
Graph data using a bar graph with 90% accuracy.
Solve two-step word problems with 90% accuracy.

Science and health
Instructional objectives:
State the conditions needed for plants to grow.
Follow steps in planting a garden with 100% accuracy.
Use the scientific method to conduct a science experiment.

Fine arts
Instructional objectives:
Draw pictures using different media.

Language arts
Instructional objectives:
Use descriptive language in conversation and writing.
Write an expository story using correct capitalization, punctuation, and spelling.
Read stories for pleasure.
Create a multimedia presentation of a story.

Activities: Planting a Garden

Mathematics
Measure ingredients used in planting a garden.
Discuss the selection of appropriate measurement tools.
Estimate how far apart individual seeds should be planted.
Estimate, then measure, the height of sunflowers at different developmental stages.
Graph height data daily.
Estimate the number of seeds in a sunflower, then count the seeds.
Compare student and sunflower height.
Write and solve story problems about sunflowers.

Science and health
Discuss the pros and cons of organic gardening.
Listen to a speaker discuss ways to ensure successful gardening.
Conduct a science experiment by growing sunflowers under certain conditions (e.g., light, no light, water, no water, different soils).
Harvest the sunflower seeds and cook them.
Discuss growth patterns of sunflowers, why they are called sunflowers, what parts of the country/world they grow in, what conditions are most favorable for growth, why they droop, how drooping can be prevented.

Fine arts
Draw illustrations to accompany sunflower stories.
Paint sunflower pictures with accompanying descriptive words.
Create a sunflower song.
Take photos of sunflowers to be used in a multimedia/interactive story on the computer.
Design a sunflower T-shirt.
Design sunflower art work that could be given as presents.
Make a collage using sunflower seeds.
Use the leaves for rubbings and tracings.

Language arts
Read about organic gardening.
Read directions for planting seeds.
Keep a journal documenting the growth of the sunflower.
Write adjectives to describe sunflowers.
Spell "gardening" words.
Using the prewriting, writing, and editing stages of story development, write a story about the sunflowers.
Download photos into the computer and develop stories using word processing.
Read sunflower stories.
Develop a story or poem, "The Day in the Life of a Sunflower."

Figure 4.2
Theme-based integrated curriculum

tice opportunities and independent student practice opportunities; reviewing and integrating skills and concepts; teaching strategies; and checking for student understanding (Engelmann & Carnine, 1991). Ideally, instructional materials should therefore reflect these important curricular and instructional needs. For example, if a particular material is limited in practice opportunities, then teachers must provide supplemental practice opportunities to ensure that students master skills and concepts. Teachers should consider these curricular and instructional requirements when selecting and using instructional materials. As research has shown, students exhibit greater academic gains when teachers select materials and instructional programs that meet learners' needs and include assessment procedures to monitor progress (Fuchs & Deno, 1991).

When selecting and using instructional materials, teachers should consider the students, the content and methodology, and evaluation. Teachers should also think about whether there is an appropriate match between learner needs and the instructional material. Table 4.3 presents questions relative to the student, instructional content and methodology, and evaluation procedures to serve as guidelines for selecting and using instructional materials.

The first part of the table poses questions relating to the learner. Teachers can determine a student's current levels of functioning by examining assessment data gathered during the referral, identification, and placement process and by administering informal assessments. Then, the teacher can select instructional materials that match the instructional level of functioning, and IEP annual goals and objectives.

Table 4.3
Guidelines for Selecting and Using Instructional Materials

Questions relating to the learner	Yes	No	Comments
1. Do I have adequate information about my students' present levels of functioning?	yes	no	
2. Will the instructional material meet Individualized Education Program (IEP) annual goals and instructional objectives?	yes	no	
3. Will my students respond favorably to the instructional material?	yes	no	
Questions relating to the content and methodology			
1. Is the content age-appropriate?	yes	no	
2. Does the instructional material specify a sequence of skills and contain adequate scope of the content area?	yes	no	
3. Is information on teaching strategies included?	yes	no	
4. Are there sufficient opportunities to practice new skills?	yes	no	
5. Are generalization and maintenance activities included?	yes	no	
6. Can the instructional material be adapted?	yes	no	
7. Can I afford the instructional material?	yes	no	
Questions relating to student progress			
1. Are guidelines given for determining appropriate placement of students within a given skill sequence?	yes	no	
2. Are assessment forms included for documenting student progress?	yes	no	
3. Do I need to devise guidelines for monitoring student progress?	yes	no	

Source: Adapted from "Evaluation Criteria for the Selection of Materials and Instructional Programs," by A. Babkie, P. Goldstein, and D. Rivera, 1992, *LD Forum, 17*(2), pp. 10–14.

Graham (1985) noted that if students have positive attitudes, they will learn much more from instructional materials; thus, teachers need to take into account potential student responses and motivation as part of the selection process. Motivational issues such as students' desire to learn the information and interest in the topic should be considered, as well as the presentation format of the instructional materials.

The middle of Table 4.3 includes questions relating to instructional content and methodology. When examining instructional materials, teachers should determine their purpose, goals and objectives, target audience, and academic area (Babkie, Goldstein, & Rivera, 1992). Age-appropriateness of instructional materials should be a primary concern as part of the selection process. For example, **high-interest/low vocabulary materials** can be used with older students who have limited vocabularies. These materials focus on topics that appeal to older students, such as current events, sports, and entertainment personalities, yet are written at certain grade levels (e.g., second grade, third grade) to account for limited **word recognition** reading abilities.

Teachers can identify and prioritize the skills that students need to learn in each content area, and then select instructional materials that match content skills with students' needs. Additionally, there should be a match between the teacher's task analysis of the skills or objectives to be learned and the skill sequence of the instructional materials. For example, if telling time is an annual goal specified on a student's IEP, then the teacher needs to select materials that provide the adequate scope and sequence to meet their students' varied time-telling abilities (e.g., telling time to the hour, to the half hour, to five minutes, to a minute).

Some instructional materials can be used independently by students, while others require teacher-directed instruction. Thus, the instructional methodology in the materials also will vary. For example, some instructional materials might include directions, models, practice opportunities, reinforcement systems, and enrichment activities, which could all be used for maintenance and generalization purposes. Other materials might consist of language development picture cards that can be used only during direct instruction. Thus, teachers must examine the methodology presented in the teacher's guide (if such a guide exists) to determine how the instructional material can best be used in a lesson.

Teachers often need to modify instructional materials to meet an individual learner's needs. Some instructional materials offer suggestions for adaptations, such as extension exercises or alternative methodologies. Other adaptations might include adding more practice options, using portions of the material, rewording complex directions, breaking components down into smaller instructional activities, requiring a different student response format (see the section on adapting instruction in chapter 5 for additional information). Finally, teachers must consider the expense of the instructional material in relation to what it offers. Teachers should consider the durability of the instructional material, hidden costs (e.g., replenishing consumable materials), student-material match, and need for supplemental materials and adaptations.

The last part of Table 4.3 asks questions relating to the evaluation of students' progress. Teachers must determine where to begin a student in a particular instructional material's skill sequence. Also, teachers should check to see if forms are included to monitor student progress. If not, then teachers must identify ways to record students' data, such as charting their progress and constructing a checklist to record mastered skills. Teachers must have guidelines for analyzing data to make decisions about how well the student is progressing in the instructional material. For example, if a student scores between 50 and 60 percent accuracy on a skill for two weeks, is this student making progress or should the teacher have changed the instructional strategy or material? In other words, how long will the student be allowed to show little or no progress before the teacher intervenes? To answer this question, teachers can use data-monitoring guidelines (see "Data Collection and Analysis Procedures" in chapter 6). It is necessary to have guidelines for evaluating data to ensure that students are making good academic gains.

Guidelines for Textbooks

Researchers (Fiore & Cook, 1994) have shown that basal textbooks are the most widely used instructional material in all elementary and secondary classrooms for mathematics (Cawley & Parmar, in press; Rivera, Bryant, & Fowler, 1996), social studies (Bean, Zigmond, & Hartman, 1994; Chall & Conard, 1991), and science (Yager, 1989). Thus, the curriculum and instruction in many classrooms may be driven by the content in textbooks.

At first glance, basal texts may be a logical choice to drive instruction. However, upon careful examination of the curricular and instructional design, it becomes apparent that teachers should use basal texts judiciously. For example, mathematics textbooks are based on the **spiral curriculum** instructional approach (International Association for the Evaluation of Educational Achievement, 1987), which means that teachers must cover a large number of skills during the school year, often at the expense of individual student's content mastery (Cawley & Parmar, 1990; Engelmann, Carnine, & Steely, 1991). Social studies textbooks in general education settings have been found to lack explanations, content goals, and effective presentation formats (Beck, McKeown, & Gromoll, 1989). Very often, basal texts offer limited opportunities to practice skills and concepts, which may be problematic for students who need time to engage in activities that promote understanding, mastery, and generalization (Vale, 1980). Textbooks are written according to grade levels and usually do not address the range of developmental abilities (e.g., reading, mathematics, language) found in most classrooms (Cawley & Parmar, 1990). Textbooks may be written at reading levels more difficult than the actual grade level in which they are used (Chall & Conard, 1991). They may ask questions that tap primarily lower-order cognitive skills (Armbruster & Ostertag, 1987). For example, textbooks may only require the student to recall facts, instead of interpreting information. Additionally, textbooks may lack pictorial and graphic cues to prompt students, organizational features that help students make connections between concepts, and explicit strategies that promote conceptual understanding (Engelmann et al., 1991). (See chapter 10 for a technique to determine the reading level of a textbook.)

As a result of problems found in most textbooks, teachers must carefully examine textbooks to use with students who have disabilities. This implies, of course, that teachers have the freedom to select the books they will use for instructional purposes; if not, then they must make adaptations (see chapter 5). Here are guidelines to consider when selecting textbooks:

1. Examine the **scope and sequence** of skills and concepts and compare to IEP annual goals and instructional objectives. Review the teacher's guide to identify curricular and instructional goals.

2. Study the organization of the textbook, looking for reference tools, such as a table of contents, index, glossary; formatting assistance, such as content headings, boldface, margin notes, graphics; and directions.

3. Identify study tools, such as boldfaced or italicized key words or vocabulary, "signal words" (e.g., first, second, next) to prompt important information, graphics to illustrate key information, comprehension prompts (e.g., pictures, graphics), content section and end-of-chapter lower- and higher-order comprehension questions, and chapter objectives as advance organizers.

4. Review textbooks for cultural, ethnic, racial, disabilities, and gender representations free of stereotypes and token inclusions. Look for accurate representations of cultural, ethnic, and racial heritage, particularly in social studies books.

5. Examine teachers' guides for enrichment and extension activities that provide adequate practice opportunities and maintenance and generalization activities.

6. Determine whether the teachers' guides include strategies that teach students how to learn and apply concepts and skills. Look for strategies that help students make connections between concrete experiences and abstract representations.

7. Analyze the language structure, vocabulary, and readability of textbooks.

By conducting a careful examination of available instructional materials and selecting materials based on individual learners' needs, teachers can feel confident that their materials will reinforce instructional objectives and be appropriate for their students' ability levels. Next, we discuss teachers' choices about how to deliver instruction to meet individual students' needs.

Instructional Arrangements

Instructional arrangements refer to the ways in which the instructional process is structured to promote student learning. There are two major types of instructional arrangements: teacher-mediated and student-mediated. In the teacher-mediated arrangement, three general options are available: whole-group, small-group, and one-to-one instruction. In the student-mediated arrangement, three more options are generally applied: peer tutoring, cooperative learning, and learning centers (Bos & Vaughn, 1994; Mercer & Mercer, 1993). Each type of instructional arrangement suggests roles for teachers and students and methods of instructional delivery. A discussion of each instructional arrangement follows.

Teacher-Mediated Instruction

In whole-group instruction, the teacher presents a lesson to the entire class. This arrangement works well at the elementary and secondary levels when common instructional objectives are identified, the teacher delivers a lesson (usually using a direct instructional approach—see chapter 5), and students are expected to respond orally or in writing. Typically, teachers select whole-group instruction for teaching content area subjects, such as science, social studies, and health; this is particularly true at the secondary level.

Researchers have shown that **whole-group instruction** has proven effective for students of varying abilities (Gersten, Carnine, & Woodward, 1987). Whole-group instruction allows students to hear responses from peers and the teacher to work individually with students after delivering instruction. The disadvantages of this arrangement include limited **corrective feedback** (which may be problematic for students with disabilities), pacing that may be too fast for some students, and lack of instructional relevance (i.e., instructional objectives may not be appropriate for certain students). Teachers must be sure that when they select whole-group instruction as the instructional arrangement, the objectives are appropriate for most of the students, and time can be allocated for students who require further individualized instruction.

In **small group instruction** a teacher works with a group of two to six students. The purpose of small-group instruction varies according to instructional levels and students' individual needs. Students are usually grouped homogeneously to facilitate instruction. For example, in reading or mathematics, students reading at about the same reading level or requiring instruction on the same math objective would be grouped together. Another reason to group students is to provide additional instruction on a previously introduced objective. Students can work toward mastering a common objective, and receive additional instruction to promote improved understanding of the concepts.

Some research supports the efficacy of this instructional arrangement (Carnine, Silbert, & Kameenui, 1990). The major advantage to small-group instruction is the ability to give students more modeling, prompting, and corrective feedback. **Pacing** can be monitored to meet students' individual needs more easily than in whole-group instruction. The challenge of small-group instruction is to ensure that the rest of the class is actively engaged with meaningful tasks. Having back-up tasks ready for those students who require teacher assistance when it is not available and for those who finish their tasks before small-group instruction concludes can assure that all students are actively involved in learning.

In **one-to-one instruction,** teachers provide instruction to individual students based on their specific learning and behavioral needs. For example, a student may need extra assistance (e.g., prompts, feedback, directions) to begin working on or mastering an instructional objective. A student's behavior may warrant individualized instruction away from other students in the classroom. Tutorial assistance might be necessary when a student prepares for an exam in a content class or to correct errors on a homework assignment.

Time and time again, one-to-one instruction has been shown to help students avoid frustration and cope with instructional demands (Bloom, 1984). Clearly, the advantage of this teacher-mediated arrangement is that individual students receive assistance that promotes their learning. On the other hand, teachers must plan tasks so other students are engaged as well. Furthermore, one-to-one instruction may not be readily available in general education classrooms because of the number of students and time constraints. Figure 4.3 depicts the three teacher-mediated instructional arrangements, and Tips for Teachers (p. 94) provides guidelines for using these arrangements.

Student-Mediated Instruction

Peer tutoring is a student-mediated instructional arrangement involving a tutor-tutee relationship. Miller, Barbetta, and Heron (cited in Miller et al., in press) identify several peer tutoring formats, including classwide peer tutoring, and small-group,

Figure 4.3
Various
instructional
approaches

Teacher working
with all the students
at once.

Teacher working
with small group of
students while other
students in
classroom are
engaged in
activities.

Teacher working
with one student
while other students
are engaged in
activities.

Teacher-Mediated Instructional Arrangements: Preparation Guidelines

Whole-group instruction

1. Determine if students possess prerequisite skills for lesson.
2. Determine instructional objective relevant for group.
3. Select intervention.
4. Identify material to be reviewed.
5. Identify vocabulary, rules, and subject matter to be presented.
6. Arrange instructional materials and media.
7. Determine evaluation method.
8. Select technique to check for understanding.
9. Develop lower- and higher-order questions.
10. Determine language of the teacher, student, and curriculum.
11. Identify ways to engage students actively.
12. Schedule length of lesson.

Small-group instruction

1. Identify students at similar instructional levels.
2. Select intervention.
3. Identify vocabulary, rules, and subject matter to be presented.
4. Arrange instructional materials.
5. Arrange environment—semicircle, small table positioned close to teacher.
6. Identify material to be reviewed.
7. Select evaluation method.
8. Develop questioning techniques and ways to check for understanding.
9. Determine language of the teacher, student, and curriculum.
10. Identify tasks that promote frequent responding and student involvement.
11. Identify tasks for students not in small group to complete, independently or with other students.
12. Develop "back-up" tasks.

One-to-one instruction

1. Identify student who requires teacher assistance (e.g., behavior, tutorial, direct instruction).
2. Identify instructional objective.
3. Determine if student possesses necessary prerequisite skills.
4. Select intervention.
5. Determine type of instruction needed (modeling, corrective feedback, prompts).
6. Identify evaluation method.
7. Identify tasks for other students to complete, independently or with other students. ■

cross-age, and home tutoring programs. Additionally, Simmons, Fuchs, Fuchs, Pate Hodge, and Mathes (1994) identify a classwide peer tutoring format in which the tutor and tutee change roles. In each format, there exists a tutor-tutee relationship, which consists of instruction and feedback as a means of providing efficient instruction to students with disabilities (Cooke, Heron, & Heward, 1983; Jenkins & Jenkins, 1988). This type of instructional arrangement could occur (1) during a set time of the day when all students work within tutor-tutee dyads, (2) as an activity for students not involved in teacher-mediated small-group instruction, (3) in other classrooms with younger students as part of a cross-age tutoring program, and (4) at home with a family member.

Research has shown that peer tutoring can be used effectively at the elementary and secondary level in mathematics (Beirne-Smith, 1991; Miller, Barbetta, Drevno, Martz, & Heron, in press), spelling (Delquadri, Greenwood, Stretton, & Hall, 1983), and reading (Heron, Heward, Cooke, & Hill, 1983; Simmons et al., 1994). Peer tutoring has been shown to be most successful when the principles of effective teaching are used, such as active student involvement, opportunities to respond, repetition, review, practice, and data collection (Beirne-Smith, 1991; Delquadri, Greenwood, Whorton, Carta, & Hall, 1986; Lerner, 1993). Additionally, peer tutors must be trained in instructional procedures and ways to deliver reinforcement. Smith and Rivera (1993) offer guidelines for establishing a peer tutoring program; the guidelines are presented in Tips for Teachers below.

Tips for Teachers

Guidelines for Establishing Peer Tutoring Programs

1. Be sure peer tutors are proficient in the skill they are tutoring.
2. Teach peer tutors how to provide specific praise.
3. Teach peer tutors a variety of ways to practice skills.
4. Teach peer tutors ways to deliver reinforcement.
5. Provide a script or key phrases to assist peer tutors in delivering instruction.
6. Provide specific rules for peer tutoring situations, such as "talk softly."
7. Be certain the peer tutor-tutee match is appropriate.
8. Provide places in the classroom for tutors and tutees to work.
9. Arrange for a cue so students can signal to tutors when assistance is needed.
10. Teach peer tutors to collect data on student progress, documenting correct and error responses. Monitor the data to determine if a change in intervention is necessary. (See chapter 6 for data collection ideas.)
11. Monitor peer tutoring to ensure that overreliance on the peer tutor is not occurring. ■

Source: Adapted from *Effective Discipline* (2nd ed., p. 104) by D. D. Smith and D. M. Rivera, 1993, Austin, TX: PRO-ED.

The advantages of this student-mediated instructional arrangement include: developing academic skills, fostering cooperative relationships, requiring less teacher support, and fostering academic support for students with learning and behavioral problems in general education settings (Mercer & Mercer, 1993). The challenges include allocating time to teach tutors their role responsibilities, monitoring tutor-tutee relationships, matching students appropriately, and monitoring student progress.

Cooperative learning is a generic term that describes student-mediated instructional techniques for achieving academic and social skills in small heterogeneous student groups (Rich, 1993). Cooperative learning is an instructional arrangement that actively involves students in discussing, problem solving, collaborating, and completing tasks. The purposes of cooperative learning are to have students work collaboratively to achieve common academic and social goals, and to be accountable to the team for their individual efforts (Johnson, Johnson, & Holubec, 1994).

Extensive research has been conducted in various academic areas (e.g., mathematics, reading, social studies) on cooperative learning with students who have disabilities, who are average achievers, and who come from diverse backgrounds. In most cases, the research has shown that students with various academic abilities tend to derive academic and social skills benefits from this instructional arrangement (Johnson & Johnson, 1986; Sharan, 1980; Slavin, Madden, & Leavey, 1984).

Six techniques for cooperative learning show up most often in the literature. Most of the techniques have group academic and social goals, arrangement of heterogeneous student groups, **task structure,** cooperation, individual and group accountability, and reward structure (Rivera, in press). Table 4.4 shows a description of the six

	Learning Together (Johnson & Johnson, 1986)	Group Investigation (Sharan, 1980)
Steps	1. Teacher explains academic task, cooperative goal struc-ture, and criteria for success to group teams. 2. Students are responsible for learning material and making sure group members learn material as well. 3. Students provide encouragement and assistance to team members. 4. Teacher monitors group work and intervenes to provide task assistance or teach collaborative skills. 5. Student work and group functioning are evaluated.	1. Teacher presents an overview of the topic to be learned. 2. Students select subarea of topic for investigation and study. 3. Within groups, students problem-solve, define roles, plan a course of action, and implement their plan. 4. Teacher monitors work of students, encouraging them to use a variety of activities and resources. 5. Students present their results to the entire class in an interactive manner. 6. Evaluation may include individual or group assessment.
Goals	1. Academic task goal. 2. Cooperative/collaborative/social goal.	1. Academic task goal. 2. Cooperative goal to accomplish task.
Student groups	1. Heterogeneous consisting of different racial and ethnic groups, students with disabilities, boys and girls. 2. Two to six students per team.	1. Heterogeneous consisting of different racial and ethnic groups, students with disabilities, boys and girls. 2. Two to six students per team.
Task structure	1. Group-paced instruction. 2. Teams work together to study topic/concept/material/problem—"we all sink or swim together." 3. Everyone must learn concepts and participate. 4. Student roles may be assigned. 5. Limited materials may be provided, necessitating interdependence. 6. Students are arranged to promote face-to-face interaction. 7. Teams construct one group product.	1. Group-paced instruction. 2. Teams work together to identify subtopic for study, to determine method of investigation, and to accomplish task. 3. Everyone is responsible for task completion and helping other members. 4. Emphasis is on higher-order thinking processes, group study, and a variety of activities.
Cooperation	1. Help each other learn material. 2. Demonstrate collaborative/social group skills (e.g., pro-viding feedback, elaborating, sharing, staying on task, doing one's share of the work).	1. Members are encouraged to help each other. 2. Members must decide together which topic to study and which learning procedures to employ.
Accountability/ Evaluation	1. Everyone is responsible for his or her own learning. 2. Everyone is responsible for ensuring other team members learn concepts. 3. Members may be asked to explain group answers, take a test, or edit another person's work. 4. Student work is evaluated.	1. Individual or group assessment occurs. 2. Team members evaluate how they worked together.
Group processing	1. Group members evaluate their ability to work as a team according to set criteria at the conclusion of their work. 2. Group members determine group skills that should be worked on to promote better collaboration.	1. Team members evaluate how effectively the team worked together.
Reward structure	1. Rewards may be assigned according to group contingency criteria in task completion or demonstration of collabora-tive skills. 2. Praise may be given as well.	1. No explicit reference to rewards was located in the literature.
Theoretical structure	1. Cooperation. 2. Motivational theory. 3. Reinforcement theory.	1. Cooperation. 2. Social-developmental theory. 3. Motivational theory.

Table 4.4
Select Models of Cooperative Learning

	Team-Assisted Individualization **(Slavin, Madden, & Leavey, 1984)**	**Jigsaw** **(Aronson, Stephar, Sikes, Blaney, & Snapp, 1978)**
Steps	1. Students are assessed and placed in individualized mathematics curricula based on ability and level. 2. Students work in teams to complete their own work and to assist other members. 3. Students assume full responsibility for management aspects of instruction such as checking and routing work. 4. Teachers provide direct instruction to small homogeneous groups of students to introduce skills, as needed. 5. Students take quizzes and their scores are used to compute a team score. Team scores determine if a certificate is earned.	1. Teaching material is divided into parts and assigned to group members. 2. Students learn how to communicate with and tutor other students. 3. Subgroups with the same material learn to meet and then share their material with the original team group members. 4. All members of the team must learn all parts of the material. 5. Teachers monitor groups providing assistance, encouragement, and direction.
Goals	1. Complete units of instruction. 2. Help team members to understand correct answers for problems.	1. Learn a part of the material, then teach this to other team members.
Student groups	1. Heterogeneous consisting of different racial and ethnic groups, students with disabilities, boys and girls. 2. Four to five students per team.	1. Heterogeneous consisting of different racial and ethnic groups, students with disabilities, boys and girls. 2. Four to seven students per team.
Task structure	1. Individually paced. 2. Students complete their own math problems and share with teammates for corrective feedback. 3. Team members provide assistance.	1. Cooperative/interdependent. 2. Students learn a section of material pertaining to a topic, then teach that material to group members.
Cooperation	1. Team members correct other members' work and provide assistance.	1. All students must work together to learn all of the material regarding a topic.
Accountability/ Evaluation	1. Team members correct papers and receive feedback after each set of four problems is completed. 2. Students take final tests to show mastery and progress. 3. Students' mastery levels and scores are used to compute team's average score.	1. All students are accountable for learning all of the material.
Reward structure	1. Weekly team average scores are computed; teams that meet criteria receive certificates.	
Theoretical structure	1. Individualization/cooperation/direct instruction. 2. Motivational theory. 3. Reinforcement theory.	1. Cooperation/peer tutoring. 2. Motivational theory.

	Student Teams and Achievement Divisions **(Slavin, Madden, & Leavey, 1984)**	**Teams–Games–Tournaments** **(Slavin, Madden, & Leavey, 1984)**
Steps	1. Teacher presents material to be studied. 2. Students work in teams to learn material. 3. Students take quizzes individually. 4. Scores from quizzes contribute to group score. 5. High-achieving teams and students receive recognition.	1. Teacher presents material to be studied. 2. Students work in teams to learn material. 3. Students compete in tournament games with peers of a similar ability answering questions about the material practiced in teams. 4. Points are awarded based on performance in tournaments. 5. Team (e.g., original cooperative learning team) scores obtained from points members accrue in tournament games. 6. Public praise is provided to winners and team standings are announced weekly.

Table 4.4
Continued

continued

	Student Teams and Achievement Divisions (Slavin, Madden, & Leavey, 1984) (continued)	Teams–Games–Tournaments (Slavin, Madden, & Leavey, 1984) (continued)
Goals	1. Students learn academic material. 2. Students help team members learn material.	1. Students learn academic material. 2. Students help team members learn material.
Student groups	1. Heterogeneous consisting of different racial and ethnic groups, students with disabilities, boys and girls. 2. Four to five students per team.	1. Heterogeneous consisting of different racial and ethnic groups, students with disabilities, boys and girls. 2. Four to five students per team.
Task structure	1. Group-paced instruction. 2. Teams work together to study worksheets using any technique. 3. Everyone must learn concepts.	1. Group-paced instruction. 2. Teams work together to study material. 3. Everyone must learn concepts.
Cooperation	1. Help each other learn material.	1. Help each other learn material so members will do well in tournaments.
Accountability/ Evaluation	1. Everyone is responsible for his or her own learning. 2. Everyone is responsible for ensuring that other team members learn concepts. 3. Each member's quiz score will be used to compute a group score.	1. Everyone is responsible for his or her own learning. 2. Everyone is responsible for ensuring that other team members learn concepts. 3. Each member's tournament points will be used to compute a group score.
Reward structure	1. Teams with high scores receive public praise. 2. Group contingency reward structure. 3. Students with outstanding individual scores receive public praise.	1. Group contingency reward structure.
Theoretical structure	1. Cooperation–Competition. 2. Motivational theory. 3. Reinforcement theory. 4. Peer tutoring model.	1. Intrateam cooperation–Interteam competition. 2. Expectancy theory of motivation. 3. Reinforcement theory. 4. Peer tutoring model.

Table 4.4
Continued

techniques. Johnson and his colleagues (1994) identify five elements of cooperative learning: positive interdependence, face-to-face interaction, individual accountability, group behaviors, and group processing (see Johnson et al., 1994 for a discussion of these elements). They view these five elements as key ingredients in promoting collaborative activities by student groups. Additionally, Kagan (1989–1990) describes activity structures for cooperative groups. Examples of these activity structures appear in Table 4.5, along with sample math activities to illustrate each structure.

In preparing for cooperative learning, teachers may want to consider the following questions:

1. What are the academic and social skills objectives?
2. What task or activity structure can be used to teach the objectives?
3. How can the elements of cooperative learning be promoted?
4. How will student groups be formed?
5. What environmental factors must be considered?
6. What management techniques will be used?
7. What is the teacher's role during group activities?
8. How will individual and group progress with instructional objectives be monitored?

	Structure	Definition	Math example
Table 4.5 Successful Cooperative Learning Activity Structures	Categorizing	Analyze and classify objects based on specific criteria.	Categorize shapes based on attributes. Categorize numbers in various ways: odd, even, multiples.
	Co-op	Study a minitopic and then present to teammates.	Study classmate preferences on certain topics and construct graphs. Construct word problems requiring a specific solution strategy and share with classmates.
	Numbered heads	After each team member numbers off, discuss the answer to a question, then the teacher calls a specific number to answer the question.	Discuss the answer to a mental computation problem. Discuss the definition of a rule or principle previously introduced.
	Round the table	Students work on problems jointly by passing the problems around the table for each member's response.	Pass a probe with multiplication facts for each member to answer a problem. Pass problems for each member to compute the next step of an algorithm.

Source: Adapted from *Cooperative Learning & Mathematics*, by B. Andrini, 1991, San Juan Capistrano, CA: Resources for Teachers.

Table 4.6 provides guidelines for cooperative learning activities.

There are several advantages to cooperative learning. First, cooperative learning activities provide opportunities for students to work together toward common goals, thus necessitating some degree of collaborative behavior. Second, group work requires verbal interactions, which gives students opportunities to develop language skills. Third, cooperative learning makes students work collaboratively to solve problems and complete tasks; this puts the responsibility of solving problems on students rather than teachers. Fourth, research has proven that cooperative learning promotes social interactions and peer acceptance.

Cooperative learning activities require extensive planning and preparation, particularly to address the guidelines discussed in Table 4.6. Teachers must ensure that all students participate fully, regardless of their group assignment. The bulk of the work should not fall on the shoulders of only a few students. O'Connor and Jenkins (1994) found that in cooperative learning groups in which the ethic of "working together" had not been established, students with lower skills were excluded from group participation. Finally, teachers must be sure that students are capable of performing instructional objectives successfully with group members and individually. Rivera (in press) suggested that cooperative learning groups be used as a "guided practice" activity following direct instruction to students on the instructional objective (see chapter 5 for a discussion about guided practice and direct instruction).

Learning centers are activity-based instructional arrangements that provide a variety of interactive, student-mediated learning opportunities; centers can be completed individually as well. Learning centers are instructional devices developed to teach and reinforce specific goals and instructional objectives. Centers are a multilevel collection of activities and materials designed to meet student interests and age levels; thus, they are appropriate for elementary- and secondary-level students and

Table 4.6
Guidelines for
Cooperative
Learning Activities

1. Academic and social skills instructional objectives
   Relate to IEP annual goals and instructional objectives.
   Teach before placing students in cooperative learning groups.
   Select social skills that students must possess to work successfully in groups.

2. Task or activity structures
   Select a task or activity structure that can be used to teach the academic objective and to promote the
      social skills objective.

3. Cooperative learning elements
   Promote the elements using different techniques:
   a. Provide specific praise for groups following the classroom rules
   b. Assign a group grade that reflects the academic efforts of all group members
   c. Assign bonus points to each group for appropriate social behaviors
   d. Administer individual reinforcers for each group member when all members are demonstrating appropriate
      academic and social skills behaviors
   e. Limit the number of materials per group so students will have to share available resources
   f. Structure activities so students depend on other group members to complete the task
   g. Call on students randomly during whole group discussion to explain their group's product
   h. Arrange the environment to promote social interactions
   i. Assign specific roles (e.g., record keeper, time keeper, encourager, materials person) that students learn before
      working in groups (Johnson, Johnson, Warring, & Maruyama, 1986)

4. Student groups
   Form groups of two to six students.
   Form heterogeneous groups.
   Provide roles for each group member.
   Start with smaller groups until students learn how to work collaboratively.

5. Environmental factors
   Select furniture (e.g., student desks, tables) that can be shifted to promote verbal interactions.
   Have materials readily accessible.

6. Management techniques
   Establish rules with consequences for group behavior.
   Establish transition guidelines for moving into groups.
   Determine how materials will be distributed.
   Determine acceptable group "voice level."
   Identify "clean-up" routine.
   Identify ways to deal with student questions (e.g., refer questions back to group members rather than
      teacher's answering questions).

7. Teacher's role
   Determine behaviors to be monitored during group work. Select data collection technique.
   Determine behaviors to praise and reinforcement system to administer.
   Determine ways to deal with groups that require additional instruction.

8. Student evaluation
   Select technique to monitor individual student progress with instructional objectives.
   Select technique to monitor group progress with instructional objectives.

students with varying abilities (e.g., reading levels, handwriting abilities). Learning centers offer students active learning opportunities that promote self-direction (e.g., working independently, self-correcting work). Centers can be based on a specific subject area, such as mathematics, writing, art, or on a theme.

The following guidelines can help teachers develop and use learning centers in elementary- and secondary-level classrooms:

1. Identify instructional objectives for centers, based on IEP annual goals, curriculum guides, assessment information about student levels of performance, and student interests.
2. Select one theme or subject area for which a learning center can be developed.
3. Develop multilevel activities to accommodate varying student needs (e.g., materials with different reading levels, tape-recorded directions).
4. Select a location for the center. Consider the demands of adjoining spaces (e.g., a reading center should be in a quiet area of the classroom). Consider the need for electrical outlets (e.g., listening center, music center). Consider the best area to accommodate several students.
5. Collect materials for centers (e.g., printers can give paper strips or cards for the writing center, nails can be obtained from construction sites for the woodworking center, reading materials can be obtained from different sources for the reading center, movie theaters can contribute posters).
6. Laminate materials to increase durability.
7. Develop materials that can be stored easily.
8. Use media to enhance learning activities (e.g., computers, card reader machines, tape recorders, filmstrip machines, opaque projectors to develop posters and activities for the centers).
9. Teach students how to use the center and media equipment.
10. Make materials self-correcting (e.g., answers provided in folders or on the back side of materials).
11. Designate an area for completed work.
12. Develop a schedule that tells students when they can attend centers and which centers to complete during the week.
13. Designate the number of students to work in a center at one time.
14. Be sure the directions are clear.
15. Design a system to record student completion of centers and progress with activities.
16. Develop center rules and consequences.

Learning centers offer students opportunities to engage in hands-on activities, to practice skills introduced during instruction, and to interact with their peers. Using self-checking materials, students can obtain immediate feedback on completed tasks. Students must also exhibit self-direction to complete the assignments, work independently, and restore the center once they are finished.

Centers do require teachers to spend time preparing, rotating, and storing the materials. Additionally, teachers must devote time to teaching students how to use centers. However, time spent in teaching students how to use the center is time well spent in the long run. We believe the benefits of using learning centers outweigh the challenges of time constraints.

In this section, we discussed curricular selection and organization, instructional materials, and instructional arrangements. Also, earlier in this chapter, we discussed the importance of obtaining informal assessment information about students' stages of learning. Now, we present information about writing instructional plans, which includes making decisions about curriculum, instructional arrangements, and stages of learning. Although you will need the content from chapters 5 and 6 to develop instructional plans, you now have a good knowledge base.

Instructional Plans

Instructional planning is one of the most important components of the designing instruction phase of teaching, because in this component, basic decisions about the "what" and "how" of teaching are made (Polloway & Patton, 1993). The time teachers spend deciding what will be taught, how instruction will be delivered, and how student progress will be evaluated enhances the time in which students are engaged and the probability that lessons will go smoothly.

Instructional plans refer to specific lesson plans that form the basis of daily instructional activities, and unit plans that focus on a specific topic taught over a period of time. Both types of planning provide a road map for teaching. Instructional plans give structure and organization to delivering instruction and evaluating student progress. We now present each type of plan, including a description, some decision-making questions, and an example.

Lesson Plans

Lesson plans are descriptions of specific instructional activities that occur during the school day. Developing lesson plans involves (1) selecting and sequencing specific curriculum, (2) identifying instructional approaches and interventions, (3) including the principles of effective teaching, and (4) designing an evaluation plan. The end product is a written plan that guides teachers through instructional activities during the school day.

When developing lesson plans, it helps to respond to specific decision-making questions that address the "what" and "how" of teaching. Here are decision-making questions, along with actions that teachers can take to help answer these questions:

1. What are the student's IEP annual goals and instructional objectives for the content area to be taught? (Select curriculum.)
2. What is the sequence of instructional objectives selected for instruction? (Conduct task analysis; state instructional objectives behaviorally, including condition, target behavior, and criterion. Conduct informal assessments— see chapter 6; examine prerequisite knowledge.)
3. Which other students share similar instructional needs? (Compare informal assessment results to determine stages of learning and to identify instructional groups.)
4. What instructional arrangements will be chosen? (Select whole-group, individualized, small-group, cooperative learning, peer tutoring.)
5. How will instruction be delivered? (Select instructional approach; consider corrective feedback; consider practice opportunities—see chapter 5.)
6. What materials and technology will be selected? (Infuse them into instructional process—see chapter 5 for technology information.)
7. What adaptations are necessary? (Consider curriculum, instruction, environment, management, materials.)
8. How will student progress be monitored? (Consider match between instructional objective and evaluation system—see chapter 6.)

9. How will the lesson be evaluated? (Consider student progress data, ability to complete the designated activity, level of student understanding during lesson, student's ability to work independently following instruction.)
10. How much time will be devoted to this lesson? (Consider length of lesson and student attention span, interest, motivation.)
11. Are the lessons cohesive? (Examine the instructional objectives and lessons to determine if the lessons provide appropriate scope, sequence, and depth.)

While developing lessons, teachers should examine how instruction will unfold for the week. In other words, what content will be taught during the week? Will students be able to make connections between lessons? Are lessons sequential so that students learn prerequisite skills? Are lessons driven by textbook content or by student instructional needs? Regardless of how instruction is delivered (see chapter 5), teachers must know the content's scope, sequence, and depth (e.g., need for practice opportunities, practice within various instructional arrangements) to maintain lesson cohesiveness.

The format of the written lesson plan varies according to individual teachers' preferences about recording lesson information. For example, the format may be as simple as a lesson plan book containing small boxes for instructional objectives, materials, and assignments (see Figure 4.4), or as complex as a form that specifies instructional objectives, instructional approach, materials, evaluation, and student groups. Beginning teachers are urged to spend time initially to develop lesson plans that will provide enough structure to promote appropriate pacing and student engaged time, yet not to spend hours laboriously developing detailed plans. Figure 4.5 illustrates a lesson plan that contains answers to the decision-making questions.

Unit Plans

Unit teaching focuses on a subject-centered or theme-based integrated curriculum (Olson & Platt, 1996). For example, a subject-centered unit on "democracy" could be developed in a social studies class. A theme-based unit could be developed on transportation, including objectives pertaining to mathematics, social studies, science, language arts, and the fine arts. Unit teaching provides opportunities for individualized instruction (Meyen, 1981), integration of cultural and ethnic activities (Banks, 1987), and cross-disciplinary instruction.

The process of developing an instructional unit consists of (1) selecting a topic and providing a rationale for the topic, (2) identifying subtopics, (3) stating goals, (4) identifying core areas, (5) developing core activities (i.e., activities for each core area that relate to the subtopics), (6) selecting resource materials, (7) specifying key vocabulary, and (8) developing an evaluation plan (Meyen, 1981). The end product is a comprehensive plan that includes a series of lesson plans spanning a period of instructional time (e.g., a week, a month, a semester). As when developing a lesson plan, teachers should answer several decision-making questions when making a unit plan. Here is a list of decision-making questions:

1. What topic will be taught? (Select topic for integrated or subject-centered curricular content.)
2. What is the rationale for teaching this topic? (Connect to IEP annual goals and instructional objectives, curriculum guides, and student interests.)
3. What are the unit's subtopics? (Brainstorm subtopics using curriculum guides.)

Figure 4.4
Example of simplified version of lesson plan

Lesson Plan, Secondary Level Resource Room Program

Times	Monday	Tuesday	Wednesday	Thursday	Friday
8:00–9:00	Language Arts, Parts of Speech: Name nouns, verbs, adjectives with 90% accuracy. Pp. 61–62.	Language Arts, Sentence Writing Strategy: State steps in strategy with 100% accuracy. Handout 3.	Collaboration Meet with 1st period "Flight Team" teachers. Update on reading comp. work.	Language Arts, Reading comp.: Read from grade-level textbook using comprehension strategy with 100% accuracy. Textbook/cue cards.	Language Arts: Review parts of speech, writing strategy, and reading strategy. Prepare for quiz on Monday.
9:10–10:10	Mathematics, Word Problems: Solve two-step word problems with 90% accuracy. Student-created problems.	Mathematics, Word Problems: Review two-step word problems. Problems from Monday.	Mathematics, Consumer Math: Solve problems with ratios and percentages with 90% accuracy. Newspaper.	Mathematics, Consumer Math: Review ratios and percentages. Work with peer/tutors to solve problems with 90% accuracy. Worksheet.	Quiz: Word problems using ratios and percentages.
10:20–11:20	Study Skills: Develop outline for social studies content with 90% accuracy. Pp. 106–108.	Study Skills: Develop outline for science content with no assistance with 90% accuracy. Pp. 82–84.	Study Skills: Review test-taking strategy for exam next Tuesday.	Study Skills: Review note-taking skill by having students take notes from lecture. Compare to "master" set of notes.	Collaboration with "Roadrunner Team" to get update on mathematics abilities of students in program.
11:30–12:00	1st lunch	1st lunch	1st lunch	1st lunch	1st lunch

4. How can cultural and ethnic diversity be infused into the unit? (Consider cultural and ethnic customs, values, holidays, famous people, history, geographic identity.)

5. What are the goals for the unit's topic and subtopics? (Develop scope and sequence of goals that will serve as basis for objectives; relate to IEP annual goals and objectives.)

6. What core areas will be emphasized in the unit? (Select content areas for the theme-based integrated unit.)

7. What core activities will be taught? (For each content area identified in number 6, specify instructional activities that relate to the subtopics and core areas; develop lesson plans by answering lesson plan decision-making questions.)

Developing effective lesson and unit plans takes time because teachers must consider so many factors. Lessons may need to be altered as instruction progresses and as teachers discover that students require additional practice time or that they are learning skills sooner than expected. In the following section, we discuss components of classroom and behavior management that are important to consider when designing instruction. Carefully designed management is the foundation of effective instruction and must receive proper attention during the design phase of instruction.

Figure 4.5
Lesson plan
example

Lesson Plan

Annual Goal: The student will compute basic facts accurately and fluently

Students: Claudia, Tzu-Lan, Bradford, Jeremy   **Dates:** 12/1–12/5   **Time:** 9:30–10:00

Instructional arrangement: Small-group instruction followed by peer tutoring

Instructional objective	Instruction	Intervention	Evaluation	Follow-up comments
1. Compute addition facts to 18 with 30 correct per minute and no more than 3 errors per minute. 2. Compute subtraction facts to 18 with 30 correct per minute and no more than 3 errors per minute. 3. Compute multiplication facts to 81 with 30 correct per minute and no more than 3 errors per minute. 4. Compute division facts to 81 with 30 correct per minute and no more than 3 errors per minute. 5. Solve story problems using basic facts with 90% accuracy.	1. Direct instruction a. Advance organizer. Review importance of knowing facts. b. Model strategy using think-aloud. c. Students state strategy steps and record in notebook. d. Check understanding of strategy steps. e. Corrective feedback for errors. f. Apply strategy to solve facts. 2. Peer tutoring a. Work in pairs with peers using peer tutoring model to practice facts. b. Solve story problems with peers.	1. Teach fact families. 2. Use error correction in peer tutoring. 3. Use benchmark for fluency building. 4. Use SOLVE strategy for solving word problems. **Materials/Technology** 1. Fact families table. 2. Strategy handout for fact families. 3. Workbook p. 63 for homework. 4. Peer tutoring folders. 5. Strategy handout for word problems. 6. Probes/graphs.	1. Students complete daily one-minute timing on facts, graphing correct and error rate scores. 2. Decision rules: a. 3 days mastery—new objective. No improvement b. 3 days—new intervention.	Day 1: Students were able to complete fact family table. Students could state how to solve fact families. Review strategy tomorrow. May need behavior management program for Claudia to keep her on task.

● ●

Classroom and Behavior Management

As you read, think about . . .

1. Designing a floor plan for your classroom.
2. Analyzing a classroom based on the environmental considerations discussed in this section.
3. Analyzing examples of schedules from elementary and secondary classes to determine events in a typical day.
4. Designing classroom rules for an elementary- and a secondary-level special education program.

Classroom and behavior management should promote organization, consistency, and parameters for students with learning and behavioral problems. Classroom management refers to managing the environment and developing schedules; behavior management includes establishing rules and expectations for appropriate student behavior. Although these components are noninstructional, classroom and behavior management warrant careful consideration, as they contribute significantly to the design and implementation of effective instruction.

Environmental Considerations

The classroom environment is an important component to consider when designing instructional programs. In this section, we discuss the physical characteristics of a classroom and the way in which the environment is organized instructionally; both influence student behavior and instructional effectiveness.

Physical Space

The physical classroom environment consists of features that a teacher must examine before making decisions about how to organize the environment for instruction. Teachers should examine the classroom for (1) electrical outlets, (2) location of chalkboards and bulletin boards, (3) physical dimensions, (4) storage units, (5) immovable features (e.g., partitions, coatracks, heating units, furniture, rugs), (6) restrooms, and (7) availability of water. Additionally, the physical location of the classroom (e.g., portable unit outside of main building, basement of main building) influences the instructional organization. For example, if a classroom is located in a portable unit adjacent to the main building and lacks sink facilities, then teachers have to plan accordingly for art activities, science, cleanup, and cooking. The availability of electrical outlets greatly influences instructional organization. If teachers plan on having learning centers that require electricity, they must consider the number and location of electrical outlets. Thus, one of the first environmental tasks in designing instruction is to examine the physical space and to determine how various features might influence instructional organization.

Instructional Organization

Instructional organization refers to the arrangement of the environment based on an overall instructional plan. After teachers develop an overall instructional plan based on what curriculum will be taught, what materials and media will be used, and what instructional arrangements will be utilized, the classroom environment can be organized to implement the instructional plan. Sketching a floor plan for organizing the classroom is a good first step.

Several environmental considerations must be addressed before implementing an instructional plan. One consideration is the type of furniture available in the classroom. For example, at the elementary level, some resource program teachers may prefer to have students work at tables, whereas self-contained program teachers might elect to have individual student desks or carrels as work spaces. At the elementary and secondary levels, special education teachers might prefer tables for small-group instruction with individual student desks for independent work. Special education itinerant teachers may have designated tables in a section of the general education classroom to conduct small-group or one-to-one instruction. Learning centers might require a table and bulletin board area. Teachers must decide which types of furniture they prefer and which are most conducive to the instructional arrangements that will be used during the day.

Selection of media is another consideration that influences instructional organization. For example, teachers who elect to construct listening centers or computer learning centers need to ensure the availability of audio media, headphones, a computer, and appropriate software. Some schools have computer labs with designated computer time for individual classes; in these cases, instruction may have to be organized according to the availability of the computer.

A third environmental consideration that influences instructional organization is traffic patterns. Traffic patterns are the paths students frequently take as they move about the classroom. The arrangement of furniture and location of instructional tools (e.g., pencil sharpener, sink, materials) may influence students' travel patterns as they move from large-group to small-group instruction, from independent seatwork to the pencil sharpener, and so forth. Teachers should observe students as they move about the classroom to determine common traffic patterns and potential trouble spots. For example, if students must work their way through a cluster of desks to get to the pencil sharpener, teachers could be inviting behavior problems and disruptions. Teachers can minimize behavior problems by (1) separating instructional areas, (2) providing adequate movement space, and (3) providing access to areas most frequented (Evertson, Emmer, Clements, & Worsham, 1994).

Students' seating arrangements are another environmental consideration that influences instructional organization and behavior management (Smith & Rivera, 1993). Teachers must decide, based on their instructional plans, how to arrange student desks and tables. For instance, at the secondary level, teachers may choose to have individual students' desks in rows facing a designated "front" of the classroom. At the elementary level, teachers might prefer more small-group work, requiring seats to be closer together. In all cases, teachers must be aware of student characteristics (e.g., the "talkers," students who are easily distracted, students who have difficulty remaining on task, social relationships) that might affect seating arrangements (Smith & Rivera, 1993).

Schedules

Developing a classroom schedule is a crucial component of effective classroom management. Schedule development can vary according to school levels, students' instructional needs, the amount of time designated for special education services, service delivery models, general education teachers' schedules, and schedules of other program teachers (e.g., physical education, adapted physical education, speech and language pathologist, music teachers, band instructor). Thus, teachers are advised before constructing a schedule to identify all the factors that may impinge on and contribute to schedule development, recognizing that schedules may change as the year progresses.

In special education programs where students spend most of their school day, teachers are usually responsible for most academic and social skills instruction. Therefore, in developing schedules, teachers should consider that different subjects need to be taught. Teachers may also need to consult with other professionals to determine scheduling needs for students who require related services, and with general education teachers to establish a schedule for students who are integrated into general education settings on a part-time basis.

In special education programs in which students spend only a portion of their day (e.g., resource programs), special education teachers at the secondary level may have students assigned to them according to the master schedule and subject area being taught. At the elementary level, special education teachers must coordinate schedules with general education teachers and related services providers. The key is to establish daily times when students with similar academic area needs (e.g., reading, written expression, mathematics) attend the special education program to receive instruction. In some elementary schools, to minimize excessive removal of students to attend various "pull-out" programs such as special education, half of the day is designated to primary-grade students being pulled out, and the other half of the day is reserved for intermediate-grade students. This provides a block of time during the day when general education teachers know that they have all of their students and when special education teachers know that they can work with a group of students of a particular age and grade level.

On a frequent, perhaps daily, basis, special education teachers consult with the general education teachers and work in the general education setting with youngsters who have disabilities. At the elementary level, consulting may occur during a planning period, before or after school, or during lunch. Special education teachers who work with youngsters in the general education setting must also work collaboratively with teachers to identify appropriate times to attend their classrooms to provide instructional assistance. At the secondary level, the master schedule of classes dictates when teachers can consult or work with students in a general education classroom. Special education teachers must identify those planning periods when teachers with whom they consult are available. They must also adjust their schedules to the class schedules of students who require in-class assistance. In some secondary schools, a "team" instructional approach is used, so a group of teachers who share students also share common planning periods and even share the delivery of instruction. In this case, special education teachers can consult and work with a group of teachers about one or more students.

Rules and Expectations

Students must know the teacher's rules and expectations for acceptable behavior. All special education teachers who work with various groups of students must know the expectations and rules, too. Behavior problems are a natural consequence when teachers do not establish clear and concise codes of conduct for the classroom. Smith and Rivera (1993) offer the following recommendations for establishing classroom expectations as part of a preventive approach to discipline problems and as a natural component of effective instructional design:

1. Establish rules with students.
2. State rules in a positive manner.
3. Convey the classroom rules and expectations to parents, other educators, and the principal.
4. Enforce rules consistently with positive or negative consequences (see chapter 7 for more information about effective behavior management interventions).

Considerations for Starting and Ending the School Year

As you read, think about . . .
1. Developing a list of activities that you will accomplish prior to the first day of school.
2. Designing activities for the first day of school.
3. Designing an outline of activities for the first week of school.
4. Developing a list of tasks that you will accomplish at the end of the school year.

The beginning and ending of the school year are filled with many clerical, administrative, and instructional responsibilities. Special education teachers may have responsibilities assigned to them from different administrators, including the building principal and the special education administrative office staff. It is usually a good idea to identify everyone's responsibilities in advance to ensure adequate preparation time. This section focuses on guidelines and considerations for beginning and ending the school year.

Starting the School Year

The beginning of the year is a hectic time filled with eager anticipation of the coming months and with meeting returning and new students. For special education teachers, many building-level meetings with the school staff and district-level meetings with special education administrators and colleagues can fill almost all of the time allocated for planning. At this time, assignments to specific programs, classrooms, and buildings may still be tentative, pending decisions about establishing a new program, establishing a caseload of students, or the availability of a classroom. Although the beginning of every year will be hectic, you can reduce that stress by taking the following actions before the first day back to school: (1) obtain a list of students for whom you are responsible, (2) read all students' IEPs and assessment information, (3) make home visits, (4) collect instructional materials and media, (5) be sure your classroom is equipped with appropriate furniture, (6) meet general education teachers with whom you will be working, (7) develop a tentative schedule, (8) identify informal assessment techniques, (9) develop a learning center, (10) get organized (set up files; arrange your room; post the rules, or develop rules with students on the first day; establish student and teacher space), (11) plan activities for the first day, (12) plan activities for the first week, (13) know the school's schedule, (14) meet the custodian and secretary, (15) obtain the budget for your supplies and materials—order as soon as possible, (16) obtain fire drill procedures to post in your classroom, (17) know which school buses your students arrive on, and (18) be sure you are familiar with the school district's general and special education policies and procedures.

Ending the School Year

Many tasks must be accomplished before summer vacation begins. Special education teachers typically must complete end-of-the-year reports about services delivered to each student with disabilities during the year. Very often, IEPs require one last update, based on recent informal assessment information. There may be staffing meetings to determine students' placement options for the following year. It is important for special education teachers to document instructional objectives that were accomplished and interventions that were effective as information for the following year's receiving teacher. If students are transitioning to a new school or graduating from high school, measures must be taken to ensure that these transitions are successful and that students' needs will be met in the next setting (see chapter 14 for more information about transition services).

Summary

As noted earlier in this chapter and as you have discovered by studying this chapter's content, teaching and learning are complex behaviors that require the coordination of many factors. We have conceptualized the instructional process as consisting of three phases: designing instruction, implementing instruction, and evaluating instruction. We have called this the Phases of Teaching Model. In this chapter, we presented an overview of this model and discussed in detail the designing instruction phase. We discussed learners, curriculum and instruction, classroom and behavior management, and considerations for beginning and ending the school year, all to illustrate the many factors that must be considered when designing instruction for students with learning and behavior problems.

Designing curriculum and instruction involves selecting and organizing various curricula specific to individual students' learning and IEP goals. Various curricular areas can be examined and selected to meet the needs of students. Teachers can choose from numerous instructional materials to supplement instructional objectives and activities. Teacher-mediated and student-mediated instructional arrangements offer options for delivering instruction to whole or small groups of students and on a one-to-one basis. Developing instructional plans is a critical aspect of designing instruction, because these plans incorporate valuable information about teaching objectives, teaching techniques, materials, and evaluation techniques.

Classroom and behavior management represent important components of instruction, as teachers must address specific environmental considerations, develop schedules, and identify rules and expectations for students. A sound, carefully conceived management program ensures that lessons will progress smoothly and that students will be engaged in the instructional process.

Finally, it is necessary for teachers to address the many noninstructional details that occur at the beginning and end of the school year. For instance, knowing about fire drill procedures and school district policies helps teachers manage their administrative responsibilities. Once teachers have addressed the many components of designing instruction, they are ready to turn their attention to teaching. In chapter 5, we continue to discuss the Phases of Teaching Model by presenting the components of the implementing instruction phase.

Study and Discussion Questions

1. Identify the phases and components of the Phases of Teaching Model.
2. Describe the learner's personal, social, and academic factors.
3. Explain considerations for designing curriculum and instruction.
4. Explain classroom and behavior management considerations.

5. Describe considerations for beginning and ending the school year.
6. Design your own criteria for selecting curriculum.
7. Compare and contrast the five curricular areas.
8. Design a theme using the integrated curricular technique.
9. Compare and contrast several secondary-level textbooks using the guidelines for evaluating textbooks in this chapter.
10. Develop a lesson for an instructional objective of your choice.
11. Develop an instructional unit that covers two weeks of instructional time.
12. Describe instructional arrangements. Identify the advantages and disadvantages to each.
13. Discuss environmental considerations for establishing classroom and behavior management.
14. Establish rules with a group of students; discuss their reasons for choosing rules.
15. Construct a weekly schedule for an elementary resource program.

● ●

References and Suggested Readings

The Learner
Personal and Social Factors

Andrini, B. (1991). *Cooperative learning and mathematics.* San Juan Capistrano, CA: Resources for Teachers.

Brown, L. (1987). Assessing socioemotional development. In D. D. Hammill (Ed.), *Assessing the abilities and instructional needs of students* (pp. 504–609). Austin, TX: PRO-ED.

Smith, D. D., & Luckasson, R. (1995). *Introduction to special education—Teaching in an age of challenge* (2nd ed.). Boston: Allyn & Bacon.

Stages of Learning

Ayllon, T., & Azrin, N. H. (1964). Reinforcement and instruction with mental patients. *Journal of the Experimental Analysis of Behavior, 7,* 327–331.

Deshler, D. D., & Schumaker, J. B. (1986). Learning strategies: An instructional alternative for low-achieving students. *Exceptional Children, 52,* 583–590.

Ellis, E. S., Lenz, B. K., & Sabornie, E. J. (1987). Generalization and adaptation of learning strategies to natural environments: Part I. Critical agents. *Remedial and Special Education, 8*(1), 6–20.

Garnett, K., & Fleischner, J. E. (1983). Automatization and basic fact performance of normal and learning disabled children. *Learning Disability Quarterly, 6,* 223–231.

Hasselbring, T. S., Goin, L. I., & Bransford, J. D. (1988). Developing math automaticity in learning handicapped children: The role of computerized drill and practice. *Focus on Exceptional Children, 20*(6), 1–7.

Hopkins, B. L. (1968). Effects of candy and social reinforcement, instructions, and reinforcement schedule learning on the modification and maintenance of smiling. *Journal of Applied Behavior Analysis, 1,* 121–129.

Idol, L. (1989). The resource/consulting teacher: An integrated model of service delivery. *Remedial and Special Education, 10*(6), 38–48.

Smith, D. D., & Lovitt, T. C. (1976). The differential effects of reinforcement contingencies on arithmetic performance. *Journal of Learning Disabilities, 9,* 21–29.

Stokes, T. F., & Baer, D. M. (1977). An implicit technology of generalization. *Journal of Applied Behavior Analysis, 10,* 349–367.

Curriculum and Instruction
Curricular Selection and Organization

Armstrong, D. G. (1989). *Developing and documenting the curriculum.* Boston: Allyn & Bacon.

Baker, L., & Brown, A. L. (1984). Cognitive monitoring in reading. In J. Flood (Ed.), *Understanding reading comprehension* (pp. 21–44). Newark, NJ: International Reading Association.

Bender, W. N. (1989). Generalization and setting specificity of behavioral deficits among learning disabled students. *Learning Disabilities Research, 4*(2), 96–100.

Bos, C. S., & Vaughn, S. (1994). *Strategies for teaching students with learning and behavior problems* (3rd ed.). Boston: Allyn & Bacon.

Brolin, D. E. (1992). *Life centered career education (LCCE) curriculum program.* Reston, VA: Council for Exceptional Children.

Clark, G. M. (1994). Is a functional curriculum approach compatible with an inclusive education model? *Teaching Exceptional Children, 26*(2), 36–39.

Clark, G. M., Carlson, B. C., Fisher, S., Cook, I. D., & D'Alonzo, B. J. (1991). *Career development for students with disabilities in elementary schools: A position statement of* the Division on Career Development. Reston, VA: Division on Career Development for Exceptional Children.

Clark, G. M., & Kolstoe, O. P. (1995). *Career development and transition education for adolescents with disabilities* (2nd ed.). Boston: Allyn & Bacon.

Cronin, M. E., & Patton, J. R. (1993). *Life skills instruction for all students with special needs: A practical guide for integrating real-life content into the curriculum.* Austin, TX: PRO-ED.

Deshler, D. D., Schumaker, J. B., Lenz, B. K., & Ellis, E. S. (1984). Academic and cognitive interventions for LD adolescents: Part II. *Journal of Learning Disabilities, 17,* 170–179.

Edgar, E. (1987). Secondary programs in special education: Are many of them justifiable? *Exceptional Children, 53,* 555–561.

Elias, M. J., & Clabby, J. F. (1989). *Social decision-making skills: A curriculum guide for the elementary grades.* Rockville, MD: Aspen.

Ellis, E. S., & Friend, P. (1991). Adolescents with learning disabilities. In B. Y. L. Wong (Ed.), *Learning about learning disabilities* (pp. 505–561). San Diego, CA: Academic Press.

Fleischner, J. E., & Garnett, K. (1987). Arithmetic difficulties. In K. Kavale, S. Forness, & M. Bender (Eds.), *Handbook of learning disabilities: Vol. 1. Dimensions and diagnosis* (pp. 189–209). Boston: Little, Brown.

Hazel, J. S., Schumaker, J. B., Sherman, J. A., & Sheldon-Wildgen, J. (1981). *ASSET: A social skills program for adolescents.* Champaign, IL: Research Press.

Kataoka, J. C., & Patton, J. R. (1989). Teaching exceptional learners: An integrated approach. *Science and Children, 16,* 52–58.

National Association of School Boards of Education. (NASBE). (1992). *Winners all.* Alexandria, VA: National Association of School Boards of Education.

National Council of Teachers of Mathematics. (1989). *Curriculum and evaluation standards for school mathematics.* Reston, VA: Author.

National Joint Committee On Learning Disabilities. (1994). *Secondary to postsecondary education transition planning for students with learning disabilities.* Position paper: Author.

Polloway, E. A., Patton, J. R., Epstein, M. H., & Smith, T. E. C. (1989). Comprehensive curriculum for students with mild handicaps. *Focus on Exceptional Children, 21*(8), 1–12.

Rhodes, L. K., & Dudley-Marling, C. (1988). *Readers and writers make a difference: A holistic approach to teaching learning disabled and remedial students.* Portsmouth, NH: Heinemann Educational Books.

Schumaker, J. B., Hazel, J. S., & Pederson, C. S. (1988). *Social skills for daily living.* Circle Pines, MN: American Guidance Service.

Sitlington, P. L., & Frank, A. R. (1993, October). *Iowa statewide follow-up study: Adult adjustment.* Des Moines: Iowa State Department of Education.

Stone, W. L., & LaGreca, A. M. (1990). The social status of children with learning disabilities: A reexamination. *Journal of Learning Disabilities, 23*(1), 32–37.

Torgesen, J. K. (1977). The role of nonspecific factors in the task performance of learning-disabled children: A theoretical assessment. *Journal of Learning Disabilities, 10,* 27–34.

Walker, H. M., McConnel, S., Holmes, D., Todis, B., Walker, J., & Golden, N. (1988). *The Walker social skills curriculum: The ACCEPTS program.* Austin, TX: PRO-ED.

Wiles, J., & Bondi, J. (1993). *Curriculum development* (4th ed.). Columbus, OH: Merrill.

Willis, S. (1994). Teaching across disciplines: Interest remains high despite concerns over coverage. *Update, 36*(10), 1, 3–4. Alexandria, VA: Supervision and Curriculum Development.

Wong, B. Y. L. (1991). The relevance of metacognition to learning disabilities. In B. Y. L. Wong (Ed.), *Learning about learning disabilities* (pp. 232–261). San Diego, CA: Academic Press.

Wong, B. Y. L., & Wong, R. (1986). Study behavior as a function of metacognitive knowledge about critical task variables: An investigation of above average, average, and learning-disabled readers. *Learning Disabilities Research, 1,* 101–111.

Instructional Materials

Armbruster, B. B., & Ostertag, J. (1987). *Questions in elementary science and social studies textbooks.* Paper presented at the American Educational Research Association, Washington, DC.

Babkie, A., Goldstein, P., & Rivera, D. (1992). Evaluation criteria for the selection of materials and instructional programs. *LD Forum, 17*(2), 10–14.

Bean, R. M., Zigmond, N., & Hartman, D. K. (1994). Adapted use of social studies textbooks in elementary classrooms. *Remedial and Special Education, 15*(4), 216–226.

Beck, I. L., McKeown, M., & Gromoll, E. W. (1989). Learning from social studies texts. *Cognition and Instruction, 6*(2), 99–153.

Cawley, J. F., & Parmar, R. S. (1990). Issues in mathematics curriculum for handicapped students. *Academic Therapy, 25*(4), 507–521.

Cawley, J. F., & Parmar, R. S. (in press). Preparing teachers to teach mathematics to students with learning disabilities. *Journal of Learning Disabilities.*

Chall, J. S., & Conrad, S. S. (1991). *Should textbooks challenge students?* New York: Teachers College Press.

Engelmann, S., & Carnine, D. (1991). *Theory of instruction: Principles and applications.* Eugene, OR: Association for Direct Instruction.

Engelmann, S., Carnine, D., & Steely, D. G. (1991). Making connections in mathematics. *Journal of Learning Disabilities, 24*(5), 92–251.

Fiore, T. A., & Cook, R. A. (1994). Adopting textbooks and other instructional materials. *Remedial and Special Education, 15*(6), 333–347.

Fuchs, L. S., & Deno, S. L. (1991). Paradigmatic distinction between instructionally relevant measurement models. *Exceptional Children, 57,* 488–500.

Graham, S. (1985). Evaluating spelling programs and materials. *Teaching Exceptional Children, 17,* 299–303.

International Association for the Evaluation of Educational Achievement. (1987). *The underachieving curriculum: Assessing U.S. school mathematics from an international perspective.* Urbana: University of Illinois Press.

Rivera, D. P., Bryant, B. R., & Fowler, L. (1996). Self-perceptions of mathematics competence of elementary and secondary learning disabilities teachers. Manuscript submitted for publication.

Vale, C. A. (1980). *National needs assessment of educational media and materials for the handicapped.* Princeton, NJ: Educational Testing Services.

Yager, R. E. (1989). A rationale for using personal relevance as a science curriculum focus in schools. *School Science and Mathematics, 89,* 144–156.

Instructional Arrangements

Andrini, B. (1991). *Cooperative learning and mathematics.* San Juan Capistrano, CA: Resources for Teachers.

Aronson, E., Stephan, C., Sikes, J., Blaney, N., & Snapp, M. (1978). *The jigsaw classroom.* Newbury Park, CA: Sage.

Becker, W. C., & Carnine, D. (1981). Direct instruction: A behavior theory model for comprehensive educational intervention with the disadvantaged. In S. W. Bijou & R. Ruiz (Eds.), *Behavior modification: Contributions to education* (pp. 145–210). Hillsdale, NJ: Erlbaum.

Beirne-Smith, M. (1991). Peer tutoring in arithmetic for children with learning disabilities. *Exceptional Children, 57*(4), 330–337.

Bloom, B. (1984). The search for methods of group instruction as effective as one-to-one tutoring. *Educational Leadership, 41*(8), 4–18.

Bos, C. S., & Vaughn, S. (1994). *Strategies for teaching students with learning and behavior problems* (3rd ed.). Boston: Allyn & Bacon.

Carnine, D., Silbert, J., & Kameenui, E. J. (1990). *Direct instruction reading* (2nd ed.). Columbus, OH: Merrill.

Cooke, N. L., Heron, T. E., & Heward, W. L. (1983). *Peer tutoring: Implementing classwide programs in the primary grades.* Columbus, OH: Special Press.

DelQuadri, J., Greenwood, C. R., Stretton, K., & Hall, R. V. (1983). The peer tutoring spelling game: A classroom procedure for increasing opportunity to respond and spelling performance. *Education and Treatment of Children, 6,* 225–239.

DelQuadri, J., Greenwood, C. R., Whorton, D., Carta, J. J., & Hall, R. V. (1986). Classwide peer tutoring. *Exceptional Children, 52,* 535–542.

Gersten, R., Carnine, D., & Woodward, J. (1987). Direct instruction research: The third decade. *Remedial and Special Education, 8*(6), 48–56.

Heron, T. E., Heward, W. L., Cooke, N. L., & Hill, D. S. (1983). Evaluation of a classwide tutoring system: First graders teach each other sight words. *Education and Treatment of Children, 6,* 137–152.

Jenkins, J., & Jenkins, L. (1988). Peer tutoring in elementary and secondary programs. In E. L. Meyen, G. A. Vergason, & R. J. Whelan (Eds.), *Effective instructional strategies for exceptional children* (pp. 335–354). Denver, CO: Love.

Johnson, D. W., & Johnson, R. T. (1986). Mainstreaming and cooperative learning strategies. *Exceptional Children, 52*(6), 553–561.

Johnson, D. W., Johnson, R. T., & Holubec, E. (1994). *The new circles of learning: Cooperation in the classroom and school.* Alexandria, VA: Association for Supervision and Curriculum Development.

Johnson, D. W., Johnson, R. T., Warring, D., & Maruyama, G. (1986). Different cooperative learning procedures and cross-handicap relationships. *Exceptional Children, 53*(3), 247–252.

Kagan, S. (1989–1990). The structural approach to cooperative learning. *Educational Leadership, 47*(4), 12–15.

Lerner, J. (1993). *Learning disabilities: Theories, diagnosis, and teaching strategies.* Boston: Houghton Mifflin.

Mercer, C. D., & Mercer, A. R. (1993). *Teaching students with learning problems* (4th ed.). Columbus, OH: Merrill.

Miller, A. D., Barbetta, P. M., Drevno, G. E., Martz, S. A., & Heron, T. E. (in press). Math peer tutoring for students with specific learning disabilities. *LD Forum.*

O'Connor, R. E., & Jenkins, J. R. (1994). *Cooperative learning as an inclusion strategy: A closer look.* Unpublished manuscript, University of Washington.

Rich, Y. (1993). *Education and instruction in the heterogeneous class.* Springfield, IL: Thomas.

Rivera, D. P. (in press) Cooperative learning for students with learning disabilities. *LD Forum.*

Sharan, S. (1980). Cooperative learning in small groups: Recent methods and effects on achievement, attitudes, and ethnic relations. *Review of Educational Research, 50*(2), 241–271.

Simmons, D. C., Fuchs, D., Fuchs, L. S., Pate Hodge, J., & Mathes, P. (1994). Importance of instructional complexity and role reciprocity to classwide peer tutoring. *Learning Disabilities Research & Practice, 9*(4), 203–212.

Slavin, R. E., Madden, N. A., & Leavey, M. (1984). Effects of team assisted individualization on the mathematics achievement of academically handicapped and nonhandicapped students. *Journal of Educational Psychology, 76*(5), 813–819.

Smith, D. D., & Rivera, D. M. (1993). *Effective discipline* (2nd ed.). Austin, TX: PRO-ED.

Instructional Plans

Banks, J. A. (1987). *Teaching strategies for ethnic students* (4th ed.). Boston: Allyn & Bacon.

Meyen, E. L. (1981). *Developing instructional units* (3rd ed.). Dubuque, IA: Brown.

Olson, J., & Platt, J. (1996). *Teaching children and adolescents with special needs* (2nd ed.). Columbus, OH: Merrill.

Polloway, E. A., & Patton, J. R. (1993). *Strategies for teaching learners with special needs* (5th ed.). Columbus, OH: Merrill.

Classroom and Behavior Management
Environmental Considerations

Evertson, C. M., Emmer, E. T., Clements, B. S., & Worsham, M. E. (1994). *Classroom management for elementary teachers* (3rd ed.). Boston: Allyn & Bacon.

Smith, D. D., & Rivera, D. M. (1993). *Effective discipline* (2nd ed.). Austin, TX: PRO-ED.

Rules and Expectations

Smith, D. D., & Rivera, D. M. (1993). *Effective discipline* (2nd ed.). Austin, TX: PRO-ED.

Chapter 5
Implementing Instruction

Making Connections

Before you read this chapter, review information about teacher characteristics and effective teaching in chapter 1. Review how to develop a task analysis and write annual goals as presented in chapter 3. Consider the lesson preparation discussed in chapter 4, including curricular selection, instructional materials, and instructional arrangements. If you have developed a lesson plan, explain how you will teach the designated instructional objectives. Finally, examine rules you have developed and describe how you will reinforce those rules with praise and consequences while teaching your lesson.

In chapter 4, the Phases of Teaching Model was presented as a way of conceptualizing and integrating the many components that comprise teaching and learning. Phase one of the teaching model, designing instruction, was also examined in chapter 4. Once teachers have invested time learning about their students, planning appropriate curriculum, and establishing classroom and behavioral parameters, the next step is to teach and then evaluate the students' learning. In this chapter, the authors discuss phase two: implementing instruction. We discuss student evaluation in chapter 6.

After studying this chapter, the reader will be able to

1. Discuss the three approaches to instruction.

2. Describe steps for the delivery of instruction.

3. Discuss effective homework practices.

4. Design ways to infuse instructional and assistive technology into the classroom.

● ●

Phase Two: Implementing Instruction

Appropriately designed instruction (e.g., knowing the stages of learning, selecting appropriate curriculum, selecting materials, developing lesson plans, establishing rules and expectations) paves the way for teachers to implement successful lessons. When implementing instruction, teachers should consider several components. First, teachers select an approach or approaches to instruction; the selection often depends on the lesson's objectives, the teacher's philosophy about teaching, and the teacher's perception of students' needs. Second, teachers may synthesize effective teaching practices by implementing and managing **instructional steps, instructional management procedures,** and **instructional language** through their delivery of instruction. Third, teachers must decide effective ways to use homework as part of instruction; research supports the use of homework in promoting students' practice and mastery of the skill being taught.

In this chapter, we build on the discussion of designing instruction presented in chapter 4 by discussing three instructional approaches that special and general education teachers commonly use. Teachers will find this information helpful when developing lesson plans. Next, we talk about the delivery of instruction in terms of specific instructional steps. Regardless of the instructional approach chosen, teachers use certain steps during instruction, including gaining student attention; describing the lesson's purpose; providing some type of instructional support, guidance, or direction; and concluding the lesson with a closure activity. As you read the next section, think about instructional steps you might use to teach a lesson. Finally, we discuss some of the current research results regarding effective homework practices and offer recommendations for implementing a homework plan in your classroom.

● ●

Approaches to Instruction

As you read, think about . . .

1. Explaining the three approaches to instruction.

2. Comparing and contrasting the three instructional approaches.

3. Describing lesson examples for the approaches.

4. Developing a lesson using one or more of the approaches.

When we set about to write this section, the task of identifying and describing approaches to instruction seemed relatively easy. However, upon closer examination, we found our special education instructional vernacular to be somewhat confusing. For example, when reading articles about instructional interventions, we encountered words such as "procedures," "strategies," "tactics," "methods," "techniques," and "approaches," which may or may not be used interchangeably to describe how students are taught. In an attempt to address this semantic entanglement, we have chosen to use specific terms to describe instruction. These terms and definitions for how to teach are presented in Table 5.1 as a frame of reference for this chapter and the remaining chapters in the book.

There are several approaches to instruction. Teachers select an approach depending on the instructional objectives, individual students' needs, stages of learning, and curricular content. We describe three that many teachers in general and special education classes use: (1) the behavioral approach, (2) the strategic approach, and (3) the holistic/constructivist approach. Each approach is characterized by a theoretical base and underlying principles. With each approach, students have different ways of engaging in learning and teachers and students assume different roles in the learning process. When designing lesson plans and implementing these approaches, teachers should consider teacher- and student-mediated arrangements (discussed in chapter 4).

Although we discuss each approach separately, it should be noted that these approaches are not mutually exclusive. Good teaching may involve combining approaches during a lesson or over the course of the school day. We believe that teachers should be aware of these approaches, know the characteristics, and be capable of combining them to promote effective instruction. Most importantly, teachers should implement those instructional approaches that have proved effective for youngsters with learning and behavior problems.

We briefly discuss the three approaches by describing each one, explaining its theoretical bases and principles, identifying some of the issues surrounding the approaches, describing classroom instruction, and presenting examples. Although we discuss the approaches here, we address implementation of the approaches, along with interventions, tactics, techniques, and methods, in chapters 8, 10, 11, 12, and 13. It should be noted that we focus more heavily on the behavioral and strategic approaches than on the holistic approach.

The Behavioral Approach

The **behavioral instructional approach** focuses on the manipulation of antecedent and consequent events to modify observable academic and social interactions (or behaviors) between individuals and their environment (Tawney & Gast, 1984). The

Table 5.1 Instructional Terms for How to Teach	Terms	Definitions
	Interventions/Tactics/Techniques/Strategies	Instructional routines used to teach and reinforce skills/concepts.
	Instructional procedures	Steps used to implement interventions/tactics/techniques.
	Methods	Instruction consisting of interventions/tactics/techniques and instructional procedures to teach and reinforce skills/concepts.
	Instructional approaches	Philosophical and theoretical orientation and explanation for instruction. Approaches embody ways in which students interact with their environment and teachers interact with students. May consist of methods, instructional procedures, and interventions/tactics/techniques.

behavioral approach is based on the principles of applied behavior analysis and operant conditioning theory, which attribute learning to the arrangement and manipulation of events following behaviors (Baer, Wolf, & Risley, 1968; Skinner, 1966). The
principles of applied behavior analysis and operant conditioning theory, described in
Table 5.2 (Tawney & Gast, 1984), can be translated to classroom instruction to promote academic and behavioral skills instruction.

Critics of the behavioral approach cite the focus on **isolated skills** (e.g., basic
facts, phonics) as limitations of instruction (Poplin, 1988). In particular, the lack of
instructional generalization of isolated skills to other related skills and academic
areas is often listed as a major drawback of the behavioral approach. Some researchers (e.g., Rivera & Bryant, 1992; Rivera & Smith, 1987) demonstrate that students
with learning and behavioral problems are indeed capable of generalizing isolated
skill instruction; when instructed on difficult skills, they generalize to easier skills
(i.e., computational problems). Thus, the lack of generalization issue with the behavioral approach may be due more to how an instructional sequence is presented than
solely to isolated skill instruction (see chapter 12 for details on the relationship
between instructional sequence and generalization).

Table 5.2
Principles of
Instructional
Approaches

Behavioral approach	Strategic approach	Holistic/Constructivist approach
Emphasis is on the interaction between the student and the environment.	Strategies serve a variety of purposes. No "best" strategy has been found to work across all domains.	Students select behaviors for learning within the context of their own goals rather than the teacher's goals.
Hypotheses of behavioral causation are avoided.	Strategy instruction should be based on the law of parsimony; that is, strategy "packages" should be kept to a minimal number of components of key ingredients.	Knowledge is a meaningful construction related to each person's experiences and interests.
Academic and social behaviors are stated precisely in observable terms.		Students work with meaningful activities and are encouraged to solve problems in a variety of ways. Teachers ask probing questions to redirect students when necessary.
Reinforcement is used to shape and modify behavior.	Strategies that work well for typical students do not necessarily work as well for students with learning and behavior disabilities.	
Data-based techniques are used to plan for and monitor instruction systematically.	Selection of strategies must be based on a student's knowledge base.	Instruction is integrated across academic areas to help students make connections rather than present isolated skill sequences.
New behaviors can be taught by reinforcing existing responses.	Students must be taught to generalize mastered strategies.	Instruction recognizes the importance of social interactions.
Instruction focuses on discrete skills.	Strategies assist students in receiving, organizing, transforming, and retrieving information efficiently and effectively.	Higher-order thinking is emphasized.
Students progress through stages of learning; there should be a match between interventions and stages of learning.	Student knowledge and procedural understandings affect learning.	Learning occurs from the whole to the parts.
	Efficient students tailor their learning activities to expected outcomes.	Learning depends on taking risks and making mistakes.

Classroom instruction based on the behavioral approach is teacher-directed; that is, the teacher arranges the instructional program by designing task-specific lessons that require certain student responses. Typically, reinforcement techniques are used to increase desirable behaviors, such as completing assignments, raising one's hand to speak, and answering problems correctly. The student's role usually involves listening to instruction and responding orally or in writing. Students receive feedback for correct and incorrect responses during a highly structured, teacher-led lesson whole- or small-group or one-to-one instruction. We now present one example of how behavioral principles can be applied to classroom instruction.

Direct Instruction

Direct instruction is a systematic approach to instructional and curricular design and classroom management. According to Gersten, Carnine, and Woodward (1987), "Research on direct instruction officially began in 1966 with the publication of Bereiter and Engelmann's *Teaching Disadvantaged Children in the Preschool*" (p. 48). Bereiter and Engelmann conceptualized direct instruction as consisting of six components: (1) **explicit strategies,** (2) **mastery learning,** (3) **error correction,** (4) teacher-directed and independent activities, (5) relevant practice utilizing a range of curricular examples, and (6) **cumulative review** (Gersten, Woodward, & Darch, 1986). (These concepts are discussed elsewhere in this chapter and throughout the book.)

Direct instruction focuses on teaching isolated skills (e.g., spelling words, telling time, learning vocabulary words) to achieve mastery. As such, it is important for teachers to give students opportunities to make generalizations about and to connect isolated skills within and across academic areas. For example, when developing proficiency of math facts, students should understand how learning math facts connects to solving computational problems, solving story problems, and using daily living skills. The direct instruction approach is most beneficial when students are acquiring (acquisition stage of learning) and becoming fluent with (proficiency stage of learning) skills.

Teachers can design and implement direct instruction lessons by following these steps:

1. Establish instructional objectives that are based on assessments of present levels of performance as noted on the Individualized Education Program (IEP) and as identified through informal assessment techniques (e.g., curriculum-based assessments—see chapter 6). The objectives should be related to IEP goals.
2. Determine the necessary prerequisite skills for the instructional objectives and whether or not students possess these prerequisite skills.
3. Sequence the instructional objectives (see task analysis information in chapter 3) and develop an instructional time line.
4. Develop explicit strategies that promote efficient and effective learning.
5. Develop an instructional format that includes **teacher-scripted instructions,** correct student responses, and presentation and practice information.
6. Provide practice opportunities until students reach mastery (mastery learning).
7. Use error correction techniques.
8. Provide praise and reinforcement for correct responses.
9. Monitor student progress.

The Strategic Approach

The **strategic instructional approach** is based on the notion of teaching students effective and efficient **cognitive** and metacognitive strategies to promote learning. Cognitive strategies (e.g., **verbal rehearsal,** categorizing information) incorporate learners' behaviors that affect how information is processed (Mayer, 1988). Metacognitive strategies are self-regulatory behaviors (e.g., self-monitoring, self-evaluating) that assist individuals in selecting, monitoring, and revising the use of cognitive strategies (Borkowski, 1992; Wong, 1991). For example, a cognitive strategy for processing reading material from a textbook might be to identify key points and underline key information; the metacognitive strategy might be to ask oneself, "Have I found all of the main ideas and supporting details?" or "Have I underlined all of the key vocabulary terms?"

Strategy instruction is based on the information processing theory, which has its roots in cognitive strategy and memory research. **Information processing theory** focuses on understanding the cognitive and metacognitive strategies that individuals use to receive, transform, store, and retrieve information (Wong, 1993; Swanson & Cooney, 1985). Thus, cognitive strategy researchers are interested in observable behaviors, as well as the mediating role of cognition and metacognition on behavior (Wong, 1993). The strategic approach to instruction is based on research findings suggesting that students with learning and behavior difficulties may be "inactive learners" who lack effective and efficient cognitive and metacognitive strategies (Torgesen, 1977). This approach has been well researched and is widely accepted as an efficacious way to promote learning for many students with learning problems at the elementary and secondary levels. The principles of strategy instruction are presented in Table 5.2 (Swanson & Cooney, 1991; Wong, 1991). (See chapters 8, 10, 11, 12, and 13 for specific strategy instruction examples).

Several issues surround the strategic approach to instruction. First, strategy instruction has been criticized for not promoting the generalization of strategies across academic areas and settings (Wong, 1993), and for students' inability to adapt strategies to meet varying setting demands. For example, a student may learn a reading comprehension strategy, but if he or she fails to use the strategy in different content-area classrooms, one must question the utility of the strategy. Although the issues of generalization and adaptation have been targeted in some strategy instruction methods (see Strategies Intervention Model, discussed below), researchers continue to address the problem. A second, related issue is the "anchoring" of strategy instruction. Strategy instruction once focused on general types of problem-solving approaches; however, now more emphasis is placed on teaching strategies within specific academic domains (e.g., reading, writing, mathematics) (Wong, 1993).

Classroom instruction based on the strategy approach is typically teacher-directed, initially involving specific procedures to teach the strategy. Strategy instruction may include teacher modeling, **thinking aloud** the use of cognitive and metacognitive strategies, and the use of **scaffolded instruction** (e.g., providing guidance through questioning). Students may be taught specific cognitive strategies, such as **mnemonics,** key words (see chapter 13), verbal rehearsal, imagery, and categorization. Students can also learn metacognitive strategies, including **self-checking, self-questioning,** and self-monitoring. Assessment is usually conducted to determine student progress in learning the strategy, followed by practice opportunities to apply the strategy in content-specific activities. Finally, instruction may become less teacher-directed and more student-directed as students take increasing responsibility for implementing strategic learning across curriculum areas (i.e., domains) and settings and for adapting strategies to present situations. Here is one example of a strategic approach to instruction.

The Strategies Intervention Model (SIM)

Probably one of the most widely known and researched strategy-based approaches to instruction is the Strategies Intervention Model (SIM) developed by Don Deshler, Gordon Alley, and Jean Schumaker at the University of Kansas Institute for Research in Learning Disabilities (UK-IRLD). Beginning in 1978, Deshler and his colleagues researched learning characteristics of students with learning disabilities and low achievement and the demands of their instructional settings. When Deshler and his colleagues found discrepancies between setting and teacher expectations and the approaches to learning that these students used to meet teacher expectations, they developed the Learning Strategies Curriculum (LSC) and instructional procedures. The researchers then packaged, field-tested, and presented these innovations for extensive training. Table 5.3 shows the components of the LSC and the instructional procedures. All of the strategies in the curriculum are taught by the same instructional procedures, including teacher-scripted lessons and extensive data collection procedures. (Persons who wish to use SIM must obtain training through certified UK-IRLD trainers. Contact the Coordinator of Training, University of Kansas, Institute for Research on Learning Disabilities, 3061 Dole Center, Lawrence, KS 66045.)

Table 5.3
Learning Strategies Curriculum and Instructional Procedures

Learning strategies curriculum

Acquisition	Storage	Expression and demonstration
Word identification	First-letter mnemonic	Sentence writing
Paraphrasing	Paired associates	Paragraphs
Self-questioning	Listening and note taking	Error monitoring
Visual imagery		Themes
Interpreting visual aids	**Participation**	Assignment completion
Multipass	Slant	Test taking
	IPlan	

Instructional procedures

Stage 1:	Pretest
Stage 2:	Describe the strategy
Stage 3:	Model using the strategy
Stage 4:	Verbal practice of the strategy steps
Stage 5:	Controlled practice in instructional reading material
Stage 6:	Advanced practice and feedback in grade-level reading material
Stage 7:	Posttest
Stage 8:	Generalization to other settings, people, materials
	Orientation, Activation, Adaptation, Maintenance

Note: Mastery testing should occur after Stages 4, 5, 6, and 7 to determine whether to continue in the instructional sequence or review to achieve mastery. Mastery testing should occur after Stages 1 and 8 to determine whether to go to another strategy or continue with the present strategy.

The Holistic/Constructivist Approach

The **holistic/constructivist instructional approach** regards learning as a process involving students' interactions with experiences that are based on their current knowledge and interests. In this approach, the teacher facilitates the learning process through the questioning process, the construction of open-ended types of activities, and the creation of an environment that promotes risk taking. In essence, this instructional approach is based on the assumption that learning is based on experiences and an integration of academic skills, rather than a series of isolated skills linked together. Principles of the holistic/constructivist approach appear in Table 5.2 (Poplin, 1988a; Pressley & Rankin, 1994; Reid, Kurkjian, & Carruthers, 1994).

The holistic/constructivist approach is based on the **social constructivist learning theory** developed by Piaget (1977) and extended by Vygotsky (1987), who viewed meaningful and interactive learning as important to children's ability to master their environments (Stone & Reid, 1994). The theory is that learning occurs when individuals make information useful by assimilating those features that pertain to their experiences and by incorporating the connections teachers help them make and understand (Stone & Reid, 1994).

Concerns about the holistic/constructivist approach to instruction abound. Although it is intuitively appealing and instructionally sound (e.g., providing a literacy base for reading instruction, helping youngsters make connections across academic domains), research is emerging that calls into question the efficacy of a holistic/constructivist approach for some students (e.g., students who are gifted, nontypical learners, and in some cases students with behavior problems). The approach does not emphasize explicit strategy training and direct instruction, which students with learning and behavior problems need (Mather, 1992; Moats & Lyon, 1993; Pressley & Rankin, 1994). For instance, literacy instruction that minimizes direct teaching of phonology, oral reading fluency, and reading comprehension strategies is problematic for youngsters with learning and behavior problems, who are at risk for academic problems and who are from culturally and linguistically diverse backgrounds (Delpit, 1988; Westby, 1993). In the area of mathematics instruction, debate continues regarding the most effective instructional approaches to be used when teaching youngsters with mathematics learning difficulties.

Classroom instruction in a holistic/constructivist approach typically involves teachers as facilitators or coaches of idea- and problem-centered learning, which is driven by student interest in the topic and exploration (Cobb, 1988). Student learning is constructed around interactions with topics based on students' experiences and knowledge. Social interactions and discussions with peers stimulate new ideas as students are encouraged to seek solutions to problems in their own ways (Reid et al., 1994). Teachers may use scaffolded instruction to guide students as they think about problems.

Although we provide several examples of holistic/constructivist approaches to instruction in this book (e.g., reciprocal teaching in chapter 10; narrative webbing in chapter 11), we strongly believe that teachers who choose to use this approach would serve their students well by combining this with other instructional approaches and by evaluating student progress (see chapter 6) systematically and regularly to determine academic growth. As Kauffman (1994) so aptly notes, "Unfortunately, too often our style has been to reject the proven but homely method for something supported only by fervent testimony or antiscientific sentiment. This may be our worst implementational sin of all" (p. 616).

Other Types of Instruction

Very often, the special education teacher's role is to select an instructional approach or type of instruction that best meets the learners' needs and the purpose of instruction. In the previous section, we discussed three instructional approaches; in this section, we present types of instruction that serve a particular purpose or need. There are three types of instruction that merit discussion: remedial, tutorial, and adaptive. These types of instruction serve a particular purpose and may or may not be used in conjunction with the three instructional approaches. We discuss each one briefly and present examples throughout chapters 10, 11, and 12.

Remedial Instruction

Remedial instruction is implemented when other interventions have proven ineffective. Typically, an entirely different method is used. Special education teachers have used remedial methods (e.g., "blending and segmenting tasks" discussed in chapter 10; techniques for "all facts" discussed in chapter 12) for years to teach academic skills when more conventional methods (e.g., basals, workbooks) have failed to teach students with learning and behavior problems. The emphasis of this type of instruction is to remediate the learning problem and to promote mastery of skills using techniques that may involve additional instructional materials, a multisensory emphasis, interventions specific to the stages of learning, and the presentation of skills in smaller instructional units.

Tutorial Instruction

Tutorial instruction focuses on short-term assistance for students who are preparing for a test, a report, an oral presentation, and so forth. Typically, the student works with the teacher or peer on the designated assignment. For example, a student might need assistance reviewing the week's spelling words in preparation for Friday's test; in this instance, the teacher and student might work together practicing the words repeatedly until mastery is achieved. At the elementary level, students might require extra assistance in preparation for a test on basic math facts. At the secondary level, students might need review sessions in preparation for an oral presentation or a content area exam. The teacher and student might also review the steps of a strategy that can be used in taking tests or writing papers. The tutorial instruction concludes once the spelling test is over or once a new area requiring tutorial instruction is initiated.

Adaptive Instruction

Adaptive instruction means making adaptations or modifications to curriculum, instruction, management, materials, and the physical environment to help students with learning and behavior problems learn more successfully. Adaptive instruction may be particularly necessary for students with learning and behavior problems, who spend more of their school day in general education settings. Both general and special education teachers must identify ways in which the instructional environment can be adapted to meet those individual students' needs.

For younger students, adaptations may be necessary because of difficulties with self-management, hyperactivity, writing problems, language difficulties, and limited reading abilities. For example, if a student has difficulty copying work from the chalkboard, then the information on the chalkboard could be given to the student on paper. Assignments could be shortened, math signs could be color-coded, more time could be permitted to complete work, and peer tutors could be assigned to help with questions. Older students may require adaptations to help them read, comprehend, and write because there is often a discrepancy between a student's reading and writing abilities and secondary-level teachers' expectations. For example, study guides could be provided to assist students with content area assignments, more activity-based lessons could be provided in class to minimize excessive textbook reading, and organizational formats could be presented to help students during the prewriting and writing stages.

Adaptations and modifications can be made in the following five areas: (1) instructional materials (e.g., fewer problems on a page), (2) instructional steps/presentation (e.g., more checking for understanding during teaching), (3) curriculum (e.g., instructional objectives task-analyzed more specifically), (4) physical environment (e.g., isolated work space), and (5) instructional management (e.g., sitting closer to the teacher) (Cheney, 1989; Hoover, 1990; Salend, 1994). Teachers should consider the following steps when planning adaptations and modifications that will meet individual students' needs:

1. Compare the student's academic abilities to the instructional and curricular levels.
2. Consider the best way for students to learn information as it relates to how content is presented and the types of student responses expected.
3. Develop adaptations and modifications as appropriate in the four areas discussed above (see chapters 10, 11, 12, and 13 for specific ways to adapt instruction).
4. Monitor student progress (see chapter 6) to determine the efficacy of the adaptations and modifications. Table 5.4 presents ideas that can be used across the content areas.

In this section, we discussed three instructional approaches that teachers typically use to teach instructional objectives, and we presented three other types of instruction that are used for a specific purpose. We now present information about the delivery of instruction, information that is applicable across instructional approaches.

Delivery of Instruction

As you read, think about . . .

1. Describing the instructional steps.
2. Designing an elementary or a secondary lesson using one of the instructional approaches described above and some or all of the steps listed below.
3. Identifying effective teaching characteristics and discussing how these would be infused into the lesson you designed.
4. Defining the boldfaced terms and providing examples of what these terms mean to you.
5. Explaining specific teaching and student behaviors for each instructional step.
6. Comparing and contrasting teaching and student behaviors across the three instructional approaches.
7. Relating the instructional steps to the stages of learning.
8. Explaining lessons you have observed or taught and thinking about how instructional management components were handled.
9. Selecting a topic to teach and identifying the language of the curriculum and teacher.

Table 5.4 Curricular and Instructional Adaptations

Textbooks/materials/worksheets

- Reduce the number of skills instructed/practiced during one lesson (found on one page or in one assignment)
- Ensure that students have enough practice opportunities to master skills presented
- Provide additional models if there are too few in the book or they are too complex
- Use the textbook as a guide for instruction
- Use visuals, graphics, and color
- Allow alternative ways (e.g., circle the correct answer, estimate the answer, tape record your answer, underline the answer, fill in the blanks, use manipulatives) to demonstrate knowledge in addition to copying problems
- Use the computer to enlarge graphics, allow for alternative responding, provide more practice, tailor practice to individuals' needs, and record student progress

Assignments

- Reduce number of problems
- Provide different types of assignments requiring different responding techniques
- Use teams
- Initiate a reinforcement system

Behavior management

- Provide advance organizer
- Use appropriate pacing
- Distribute materials when they will be used. Collect after lesson
- Provide clear, short directions
- Check for understanding frequently
- Call on students randomly
- Provide points for targeted behaviors
- Use "no homework" passes as awards
- Be sure there is an appropriate match between student ability level and instructional level
- Ask students to explain directions

Content

- Use task analysis to identify smaller instructional steps
- Examine prerequisite skills—be sure student possesses these skills
- Determine the "language" of the curriculum
- Relate skills in an integrated fashion so students develop connections

Presentation techniques

- Obtain student attention before beginning instruction
- Provide an advance organizer
- Model processes and steps
- Use the "think-aloud" process
- Maintain pacing
- Check for understanding frequently
- Teach cognitive strategies
- Use manipulatives
- Determine stage of learning and select appropriate intervention
- Use active participation techniques to maintain attention and to promote involvement
- Teach the language of the curriculum
- Have students explain procedural steps
- Have students answer questions that tap all levels of Bloom's taxonomy
- Have students identify and generate examples and nonexamples
- Use models, diagrams, and symbols

Practice techniques

- Use cooperative learning groups
- Use peer tutoring
- Use multimedia: card reader machine, overhead projector, tape recorder, record player, computers
- Provide a variety of practice opportunities where students express knowledge and comprehension in different ways (e.g., manipulatives, diagrams, problem solving, explanations)
- Ensure mastery before moving to the next skill
- Provide practice supplemental to the textbook and workbook or worksheet
- Refrain from having students complete 20–30 problems to demonstrate understanding
- Tap learning channels to vary practice: see/write, hear/write, see/say, think/do, etc.
- Have students do error drills
- Integrate curricular practice opportunities so students work on a variety of skills in one lesson

Good teaching requires teachers to synthesize and implement principles of effective teaching (presented in chapter 1), instructional steps, instructional management, and instructional language. Synthesizing all of these variables to teach a lesson can indeed be challenging. This section describes the instructional steps, instructional management procedures, and instructional language that are necessary for teaching an effective lesson. We presented questions for teachers to consider as they monitor their instruction, lessons, and students' progress.

Instructional Steps

This section describes instructional steps that teachers can use to deliver instruction. These steps consist of: (1) the **advance organizer, (2) presentation of subject matter,** (3) **guided practice,** (4) **closure,** (5) **independent practice,** and (6) **evaluation.** Researchers have shown that demonstration, guided practice, feedback, and independent practice produce higher achievement results for low-achieving students and for students with learning and behavior problems (Algozzine, Ysseldyke, & Campbell, 1994; Gersten et al., 1986; Rosenshine & Stevens, 1984). By combining effective teaching techniques with these instructional steps, teachers can pace lessons so that students remain actively engaged, rather than having time for misbehaving; elicit high rates of accurate responding; and provide models, examples, feedback, and prompts (Englert, 1984). Additionally, it is imperative that teachers check student understanding of the material frequently during instruction.

Advance Organizer

An advance organizer consists of a set of behaviors to prepare students for the lesson's content and for learning (Ausubel & Robinson, 1969; Lenz, Alley, & Schumaker, 1987). Before presenting an advance organizer, teachers must be sure that they have gained student attention. Teachers can use **signals** (discussed below in "Instructional Management Procedures") to capture student attention before beginning the lesson. By having students focused on the teacher at the onset of the lesson, teachers will spend less time reexplaining information that was previously discussed.

Typically, advance organizers consist of telling students the purpose of the lesson (objectives), motivating students and sparking their interest, and reviewing related background information. Students should be aware of the lesson's instructional objective (e.g., writing multiplication facts fluently, defining vocabulary terms). They should know what skill the teacher intends to teach and what outcome is expected of them. Teachers can prepare students for a lesson by providing a reason for learning the lesson's content and by making the lesson relevant for students. Students who see a reason for learning the content show more motivation for learning the lesson and find a way to relate to the topic. Finally, teachers should provide a review of homework before beginning the new lesson (Mastropieri & Scruggs, 1994). Review helps students warm-up for the lesson, promotes active responding, and provides teachers with information about students' current levels of understanding before they move to new material. Table 5.5 presents ideas for providing effective advance organizers.

Ask Yourself

1. Do I have the students' attention?
2. Is the instructional objective stated specifically?

Table 5.5
Advance Organizer
Ideas

Tell the student the purpose of the lesson.

State the topic of the learning activity.

Identify subtopics of the activity.

Describe background information.

State the concepts to be learned.

Motivate students by providing rationales.

Provide an organizational framework.

Tell students desired outcomes from learning activity.

Source: Adapted from "Activating the Inactive Learner: Advance Organizers in the Secondary Content Classroom," by B. K. Lenz, G. R. Alley. and J. B. Schumaker, 1987, *Learning Disability Quarterly, 10*(1), pp. 53–62.

3. Do students appear to be interested in the lesson?

4. Has there been sufficient review of background or related content?

5. Is there vocabulary that needs to be reviewed?

6. Do student homework responses reflect high levels of accuracy? ◄

Presentation of Subject Matter

Presenting subject matter to students requires specific procedures to ensure that mastery is achieved, particularly for students with learning and behavior problems. During this instructional step, teachers present specific curriculum related to the instructional objective. For example, teachers might present rules (e.g., spelling, phonics, mathematics), cognitive strategies (e.g., reading strategy, paragraph-writing strategy), and concepts (e.g., place value, science vocabulary, health). When presenting the instructional content, teachers should model correct responses and have students **imitate** the modeled responses while providing them with corrective feedback and specific praise. Students can imitate modeled responses orally, in written form, or motorically (e.g., by manipulating objects). Teachers can ask questions to promote discussion and to involve students in the lesson. In addition, teachers provide **massed practice** (i.e., extra practice) opportunities to ensure mastery of the rule and words for which the rule applies. Nonexamples can be provided, along with examples of words that use the rule. to be sure that students discriminate application of the rule correctly. Teachers should then check student understanding (see Table 5.6 for ways to **check for understanding**) of instruction by asking questions (higher- and lower-order; see "Instructional Language" below), providing sufficient **wait time** (3 to 4 seconds), and calling on students by name after questions have been asked. Theoretically, asking a question and then calling on a student by name keeps the **level of concern** moderate and promotes on-task behavior. Calling on a student and then asking a question allows other students to tune out, thereby diminishing the level of concern and on-task time.

For example, a phonics lesson could focus on the instructional objective, "Students will read words with long vowels and silent e's with 100 percent accuracy." The teacher would teach the long vowel/silent e rule and model words for which the rule applies. Students would have a turn saying the rule together and individually, then reading words with the rule followed by repeating the rule. Individual students who

Table 5.6
Ways to Check for
Understanding

Active participation cards Teacher asks question pertaining to lesson. Students respond using active participation card (yes/no; true/false) by holding card at chest level with appropriate response showing. Teachers can survey group quickly to determine correct and incorrect responses.	Yes/True
Thumbs up/down Teacher asks question pertaining to lesson. Students respond by putting thumb up (yes, true, agree) or down (no, false, disagree). Teachers can survey group quickly to determine correct and incorrect responses or student opinions.	No/False

Asking questions/giving answers
Teachers and students ask questions and provide answers to questions relating to lesson content.

Written quiz
Provide a short answer or multiple choice quiz to check understanding of material presented; this will be graded.

Oral quiz
Randomly ask students questions that require a brief explanation, true/false response, and so forth; this will be graded.

had difficulty stating the rule or reading words with the rule would receive corrective feedback (e.g., "The rule is . . . , What is the rule?"), and the teacher would provide practice opportunities for students to state the rule correctly. The teacher would also give specific praise (e.g., "Yes, that is the correct rule," "Yes, you read that word correctly using the rule.") for correct responses. Students would have sufficient opportunities to respond so that they could practice applying the rule. They would also be asked to discern between words that used the rule and those that did not.

Guided Practice

Guided practice offers students opportunities to practice skills and concepts with the teacher's direction. Some of the instructional techniques, such as modeling, prompting (see Table 5.7 for examples of hierarchy of prompts using the questioning strategy), corrective feedback, and specific praise could occur during this instructional step. Teachers could work with individuals who require further assistance to reach mastery, or with the whole group by circulating and monitoring performance. Teachers could plan guided practice activities in which students work individually at their desks, in small groups (e.g., cooperative learning), or in pairs (e.g., peer tutoring). Questioning and checking for understanding continue to be important instructional techniques to ensure student comprehension of the instructional objectives.

Ask Yourself ▶

1. Are students comprehending the lesson?
2. Is modeling effective?
3. Are all students engaged in active learning?
4. Do I need to provide more examples?
5. Are more practice opportunities necessary?
6. Do I need to give more prompts?
7. Do students understand after corrective feedback?

8. Are students making connections across skills?

9. Are students using problem-solving skills?

10. Is the instructional arrangement effective?

11. Is the skill appropriate for students?

12. Do I need to task-analyze the skill further to meet students' individual needs?

13. Are there vocabulary words that require further instruction?

14. Are the instructional materials and textbooks appropriate? ◀

Closure

Closure happens at the end of a lesson, and it provides a time for teachers and students to synthesize the lesson's activity as it relates to the instructional objective. During this instructional step, which may take only a few minutes, teachers and students (1) review the instructional objective, (2) review the lesson's activity, (3) relate learning to other contexts, and (4) discuss follow-up plans.

For example, returning to the phonics lesson example we discussed previously, teachers could review the instructional objective (e.g., "Today, we learned the long

Table 5.7
Hierarchy of
Prompts Using
Response-
Dependent
Questioning
Strategy

Step 1: Opening question
Teacher asks question about subject being presented.

Example: Asks student to make the sound of the digraph EE.

Response: Student makes correct sound; if incorrect, then proceed to Step 2.

Step 2: Constructed response
Teacher seeks correct response by prompting student to focus on specific knowledge or information from which a correct response can be constructed.

Example: Teacher says, "Think about the rule we have learned for two vowels together."

Response: Student makes correct sound; if incorrect, then proceed to Step 3.

Step 3: Multiple choice
Teacher provides choice of two responses; one of the responses is correct.

Example: "Is the sound 'ee' (makes a long e sound) or 'e' (makes short e sound)?"

Response: Student selects correct sound; if incorrect, then proceed to Step 4.

Step 4: Restricted alternative
Teacher eliminates the incorrect response from Step 3, but does not provide the answer.

Example: "EE (points to letters on chalkboard) does not make the 'e' (short e sound) sound; what is the correct sound of EE?"

Response: Student provides correct response; if incorrect, then proceed to Step 5.

Step 5: Complete model
Teacher provides correct response.

Example: Teacher points to EE on chalkboard and makes "ee" sound.

Response: Student imitates correct response.

Source: Adapted from *Direct Teaching Tactics for Exceptional Children*, by J. J. Stowitschek, C. E. Stowitschek, J. M. Hendrickson, and R. M. Day, 1984, Rockville, MD: Aspen.

vowel/silent e rule and read words containing this rule."), ask students together and individually to restate the rule and to read words for which the rule applies, and give students a mix of words (to which the rule applies and does not apply) to check discrimination ability. Teachers could ask students to state reasons for learning this rule (e.g., spelling, reading, decoding), assign homework, talk about the following day's lesson, and ask students to complete independent practice activities.

Closure activities serve to wrap up the lesson. Closure is an important part of the lesson and needs to be considered when time is allotted to instructional planning.

Ask Yourself ?

1. Do I allow enough time for closure?

2. Do all or most of the students have opportunities to engage in closure activities?

3. When I do closure activities, do I still have students who do not understand the instructional objective?

4. Are students able to relate the lesson's objective to other learning? ◄

Independent Practice

Students who have demonstrated a solid understanding of the skill (as determined during checking for understanding) are probably ready to engage in activities that do not require direct teacher supervision or guidance. Independent practice can occur in different instructional arrangements. For example, student-mediated arrangements, such as cooperative learning groups, peer tutoring pairs, **computer-assisted instruction,** or learning centers, could be developed for students to practice recently introduced skills. Students could also work independently at their desks, practicing the introduced skill and previously mastered skills (e.g., **maintenance checks, distributed practice**). Students can also do homework (see the section called "Homework" later in this chapter for guidelines) as another venue for practice. The important considerations during independent practice are that activities relate directly to the instructional objective introduced during the presentation of the subject matter, that students can work independently with a high level of success, and that students receive feedback (e.g., from the teacher or from self-correction) on work completed during this instructional step (Epstein, Polloway, Foley, & Patton, 1993).

Ask Yourself ?

1. Is the instructional arrangement effective in promoting practice on the instructional objective?

2. Are students capable of completing activities independently?

3. Are students achieving high levels of accuracy on independent practice activities?

4. Am I providing feedback opportunities for activities? ◄

Evaluation

Evaluating student progress is one of the most important instructional steps. Teachers must check for student understanding during the lesson (Gersten et al., 1986) and evaluate student ability to perform the skill after direct instruction to determine progress and intervention effectiveness (Fuchs, Fuchs, & Hamlett, 1989). Chapter 6 has further information about monitoring student progress.

Ask Yourself ▶

1. Have students demonstrated mastery of the skill presented in the lesson?
2. Do I need to reteach or model the skill?
3. Are students capable of performing the skill independently?
4. Is my instructional intervention effective?
5. Should I implement a new instructional intervention? ◀

Table 5.8 shows those instructional steps and effective practices that should be considered during instruction.

Instructional Management Procedures

Perhaps one of the most difficult components to incorporate into a lesson effortlessly is management, which consists of managing student behavior, providing effective directions, using attention signals, managing teacher behavior, and making transitions. Unfortunately, a well-designed lesson can quickly go awry if management issues surface and are not dealt with appropriately during the course of instruction.

Table 5.8
Instructional Steps and Effective Practices

Advance organizer
Gain student attention.
Provide review of relevant content.
Tell students objectives for lesson.
Motivate students for lesson.

Presentation of subject matter
Model correct responses.
Teach vocabulary.
Teach rule or relationship.
Teach strategies.
Provide prompts for correct responses.
Provide corrective feedback.
Focus on practice.
Pace instruction appropriately.
Ask questions; provide time for students to respond.
Check for understanding.

Guided practice
Provide active learning opportunities.
Provide relevant practice opportunities.

Monitor student performance.
Prompt correct responses.
Provide corrective feedback.
Ask questions; provide wait time.
Check for understanding.

Closure
Summarize lesson content.
Provide information about follow-up lessons and practice.

Independent practice
Ensure that students are ready for independent practice.
Provide relevant practice opportunities.
Evaluate progress.

Evaluation
Monitor student progress.
Record achievement results.
Determine if instruction is effective in promoting mastery.

Source: Adapted from *Effective Instruction for Special Education* (2nd ed.), by M. A. Mastropieri and T. E. Scruggs, 1994, Austin, TX: PRO-ED.

Therefore, it is worth the time to attend to management issues and procedures prior to and during instruction.

Student Behavior

Managing student behavior effectively while teaching a lesson can be quite challenging. Teachers must be aware of the specific behavioral needs of their students, plan appropriate behavioral intervention programs to meet these needs, and implement the behavioral programs while teaching. For example, several students might tend to call out during instruction, rather than raising their hands. To reduce or eliminate this inappropriate behavior, the teacher could develop a program that reinforces the students for raising their hands rather than "calling out" and that provides a negative consequence when "calling out" occurs. This program should be implemented concurrent with instruction and could consist of a simple tally mark system on the chalkboard.

In addition to implementing specific behavioral programs, teachers can manage student behavior in general with a variety of techniques. For example, pacing the lesson appropriately should help keep students on task and engaged. A lesson that is paced too quickly can cause confusion for some students; a lesson paced too slowly could create boredom, disruptive off-task behavior, and a loss of time when students could be learning. Providing reinforcement for students who follow classroom rules (e.g., raising hands, listening to others) can promote appropriate behaviors and reduce occurrences of counterproductive behaviors. Management of student behavior is discussed more fully in chapter 7.

Ask Yourself ▶

1. Have I identified the behaviors that most interfere with teaching and for which I must plan an intervention program?

2. Have I developed an intervention program that I can implement during instruction?

3. Am I being consistent with dispensing positive and negative consequences?

4. Is my behavioral intervention program making a difference?

5. How are the other students responding to the intervention program? ◀

Directions

Providing clear, concise directions can minimize students' waiting for further teacher explanations, initiating work that they do not fully understand, or forgetting what they are supposed to do. Directions should be (1) stated right before the activity, (2) limited to two or three single-step actions, and (3) checked to determine that students comprehend them before engaging in an activity. For example, before students work in pairs to complete an activity, the teacher might say: "In pairs, I want you to first (showing one finger as a visual signal) read the paragraph together; second (showing two fingers) underline words you don't know; and third (showing three fingers) write two sentences about the paragraph. What will you do first, Sarah? What will you do second, Sam? What will you do third, Steve?" Directions can be oral or written (displayed on an overhead projector), depending on students' needs. Teachers must be sure that students understand the directions before proceeding with the activity. Teachers can ensure that students understand the directions by selecting a criterion (e.g.. three) for the number of correct responses in a row and calling on (in this case) three different students to give the correct answer about the directions. This is called criterion of repetitions. The idea is not only to check for students' understanding of the directions, but also to provide enough verbal repetitions of the directions to increase the likelihood that most, if not all, students will comprehend them.

Ask Yourself ⯈

1. Do I state the directions clearly?

2. Do I give too many directions?

3. Is a visual signal necessary?

4. Are sequence words (e.g., first, second) necessary? ◀

Attention Signals

The signals teachers give to gain student attention can be visual (e.g., turning the lights off and on, standing quietly in front of the classroom and looking at students, looking at the clock), auditory (e.g., ringing a bell, playing a chord on the piano, clapping hands, snapping fingers), or verbal (e.g., "It's time to get quiet," "I'm ready to begin," "Good morning," counting backwards from five). Signals are an effective way to manage behavior and to tell students that something is going to happen. Signals must be taught so students know what the teacher is trying to convey. They must also be reinforced (e.g., "Thank you for following the signal.") and changed periodically for the sake of novelty and to maintain students' interest (Smith & Rivera, 1993).

Ask Yourself ⯈

1. Is my signal working?

2. How long does it take for students to attend to this signal?

3. Is it time to change the signal?

4. Do I reinforce students for responding to the signal? ◀

Teacher Behavior

An often overlooked component of instruction is the teacher's behavior, which can significantly affect the success of the lesson and management of student behavior. Teacher behavior consists of preparation and presence (see chapter 7 for a discussion of other teachers' behaviors, such as "with-it-ness," that contribute to effective behavior management).

Preparation   Being prepared to teach is one of the key ingredients in successful lessons. The time spent preparing and overpreparing can make all the difference in how smoothly a lesson goes. Being prepared means that teachers (1) know the objective of the lesson; (2) are familiar with students' stages of learning; (3) have selected an appropriate intervention; (4) know the instructional steps and what should occur during each step; (5) have materials, supplies, and audiovisual equipment ready; and (6) know how they will manage student behavior. Teachers who spend instructional time looking for their teacher's guide or setting up the overhead projector invite student misbehavior and lose precious instructional time and momentum. Furthermore, being overprepared means that teachers know that lessons may take less time than anticipated and are ready with a relevant, back-up activity to fill the instructional time.

Ask Yourself ?

1. Do I know the objective of the lesson?

2. Am I familiar with my students' stages of learning?

3. Do I have an appropriate intervention?

4. Do I know what I will do for each instructional step?

5. Do I have materials, supplies, and audiovisual equipment ready and close at hand?

6. Am I comfortable with ways to manage student behavior?

7. Have I anticipated student behaviors?

8. Do I have a back-up activity in case I finish early? ◀

Presence   Teacher presence can be thought of as the use of **assertive behaviors, teacher proximity,** and nonverbal communication to manage student behavior and to promote a positive classroom environment. Teacher presence can be used effectively to convey messages that prevent, reduce, or terminate undesirable behaviors and to foster behaviors that support a learning environment.

Canter (1986) describes the assertive teacher as one who establishes a classroom routine, develops structure, states behaviors expected from students, sets behavioral limits, and involves parents and administrators in the classroom discipline program. Assertive teachers articulate their expectations to students by stating, "I need you to . . ." or "I want you to . . ." and avoid asking or pleading with students to cooperate (e.g., "Would you please . . ."). Assertive teachers exert influence in the classroom, yet do so in a way that creates a supportive classroom climate and demonstrates respect for students (Smith & Rivera, 1993).

Teacher proximity means that teachers monitor and promote on-task behavior by moving about the classroom and by standing near students who may exhibit problem behaviors. For example, if a class discussion is taking place and a student appears to be off task, the teacher can stand near this student to draw him or her back into the discussion. Teachers can reduce or eliminate behavior problems simply by roaming around the classroom and remaining accessible. Teacher proximity also reinforces appropriate on-task behaviors.

Teachers' **nonverbal behavior** can also be used effectively to provide feedback to students about desirable and undesirable behaviors. For example, a teacher might use a smile, a nod, a head shake, a finger over closed lips, or a stern look. Very often, nonverbal teacher behavior can take care of problems, thus minimizing the need for more intrusive, time-consuming behavioral interventions. Teachers should take full advantage of their presence to monitor behavior and deal with appropriate and inappropriate behaviors during instruction.

Ask Yourself ?

1. During instruction, am I stating my expectations clearly to students?

2. Am I exerting my influence while I am teaching?

3. Do I need to move around the classroom more frequently?

4. Are there students whose behavior I could monitor better with more proximity?

5. What effect does my proximity have on monitoring and reinforcing behavior?

6. Is nonverbal communication effective?

7. What types of nonverbal communication are most effective? ◄

Transition

Transition is defined as "the interval between any two activities" (Evertson, Emmer, Clements, & Worsham, 1994). Thus, transitions occur before lessons begin, during the course of instruction if activities change, and after the lesson ends. According to Emmer, Evertson, Clements, and Worsham (1994) these transition times can breed management problems, such as disruptive behavior, resulting from (1) lack of teacher or student readiness, (2) unclear communication about expectations for transitions, and (3) faulty transition procedures.

Because valuable instructional time can be lost to management problems stemming from poor transitions, teachers are advised to establish a transition plan of action. Smith and Rivera (1995) offer the following transitional guidelines:

1. Teachers should offer a signal indicating to students that it is time to finish their work or that they should move to another activity within the current lesson. The finish-up signal helps students focus on concluding the activity and preparing for the next activity or lesson. For example, teachers could tell students to finish their work within ten minutes because then they will start a new group lesson. Within the lesson, teachers could also tell students that they will discuss two more questions then move on to a small-group activity.

2. Teachers should gain student attention before asking students to make a transition. Gaining attention helps quiet students and focus them on directions for transition.

3. Teachers should tell students the specific transition plan and behavioral expectations. For instance, teachers could tell younger students that they need to meet in their math groups at their designated locations and that they should go to their groups quietly.

4. Students who follow the transition plan and behavioral expectations should receive positive reinforcement; specific praise often works well in this case. For older students, a nonverbal signal reinforcing the correct behavior would probably be appropriate.

Ask Yourself ▶

1. How do students handle transitions before, during, and after lessons?

2. Am I giving students enough time to complete their activity before transitioning to the next activity or lesson?

3. Do I have an effective transition plan that takes into consideration students' specific behavioral needs?

4. Am I communicating my expectations clearly? ◄

Scenario 5.1 illustrates how a teacher might implement the instructional steps and management. It takes time, practice, and mentoring for a teacher to synthesize instructional steps and management effectively; even then, most teachers will acknowledge that some lessons will be problematic for unforeseen reasons. Treat these as learning experiences!

Scenario 5.1

Hypothetical Lesson: Instructional Steps and Management

One week, Ms. Reid spent several days conducting assessment in division facts to determine the stage of learning for three of her students; all three students were in the acquisition stage of learning and required instruction in division facts. Ms. Reid decided to use direct instruction to teach the facts coupled with manipulatives and practice problems. She designed a lesson plan that included an instructional objective for her lesson, direct instruction steps, materials, and evaluation methods.

Ms. Reid selected small-group instruction as the instructional arrangement because so few students in the group required instruction in the same skill. She knew that two of the students liked to talk to each other, so she made a mental note to be sure that those students did not sit next to each other.

On Monday, Ms. Reid called the four students to the small-group instruction table where they could sit comfortably around the table and she could interact closely with them. She gained their attention with a verbal cue signal, then gave them specific instructions about her expectations for their behavior while in small-group instruction.

Ms. Reid told the students the purpose of instruction, then began the lesson. She introduced division vocabulary and had the students practice the vocabulary words through repetition and individual responding. She then introduced the concept of division by using manipulatives (stored on a bookcase behind her table). She modeled the use of the manipulatives to illustrate division, then gave each student manipulatives to follow her lead.

Ms. Reid provided specific praise to individual students for quiet, on-task behavior. At one point, she leaned across the table and tapped one student on the shoulder as a reminder to return to the task at hand. Ms. Reid asked each student many questions to check understanding. She provided numerous examples of division facts and asked the students to show division using the manipulatives. She showed the manipulatives in specific patterns and asked for division facts to represent the patterns.

Corrective feedback and prompts were provided for incorrect responses. At one point, she placed her hand on top of one student's manipulatives to quiet off-task play with the devices. She kept a checklist of correct and incorrect responses to determine student progress.

At the end of the lesson, Ms. Reid removed the manipulatives and asked students to define the vocabulary words again and to summarize their learning. She told them that tomorrow they would work in pairs with more manipulatives and pictures.

Instructional Language

Instructional programs for students with learning and behavior problems should be designed to teach new concepts and facts, new strategies for thinking and problem solving, and appropriate social-communicative behaviors that allow students to succeed during instruction. Listening, speaking, reading, and writing are all language skills that can be used for learning in the classroom. Therefore, teachers must have knowledge of the role language plays in teaching and learning. The next section describes the linguistic interaction that occurs during instruction and discusses instructional questioning.

Curriculum-Student-Teacher Interactions

The responsibility for making the classroom a successful learning and instructional environment lies with the teacher. Figure 5.1 shows the triadic interactive relation-

Figure 5.1
Language interaction in curriculum and instruction

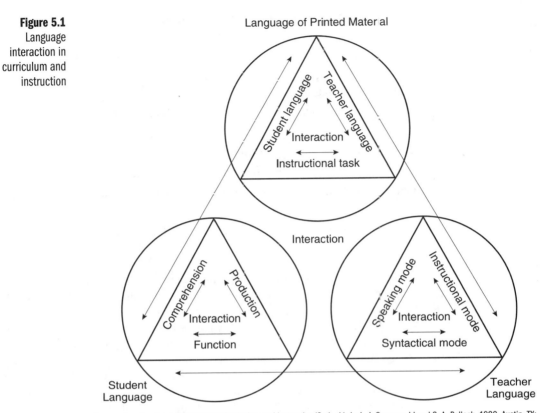

Source: From *Language Interaction in Curriculum and Instruction* (2nd ed.), by L. J. Gruenewald and S. A. Pollack, 1990, Austin, TX: PRO-ED. Copyright 1990 by PRO-ED. Reprinted with permission.

ship that exists between the curriculum, student, and teacher in any academic setting (Gruenewald & Pollack, 1990). Figure 5.1 shows that multiple language interactions can occur during the instructional process.

Teachers must examine any curricular material and instructional task closely to determine which language skills (e.g., vocabulary, reading level, syntactical complexity) students need to be successful. It may be necessary to teach prerequisite skills or modify curricular material before introducing new material. Teachers must also be aware of the language skills that the new material presents and should tailor instruction accordingly.

Students interact with both the teacher and the printed material many times each day as they participate in classroom activities and complete academic tasks. They bring to the learning process diverse abilities in comprehending and producing language. Their abilities to use language appropriately within social contexts and instructional arrangements (e.g., cooperative learning, peer tutoring) may vary. Teachers should take these abilities into consideration when planning and delivering instruction. Additionally, teachers must remember the language needs of students from culturally and linguistically diverse backgrounds who possess academic learning problems. See the Spotlight on Diversity for suggestions on addressing the language needs of these students during instruction.

Spotlight on Diversity

Instructional Language Considerations

- Encourage students to use their new language skills.
- Use modeling, activity-based learning, and technology for introducing and practicing skills.
- Rephrase important points, directions, and questions.
- Use student experiences by relating new material to students' backgrounds.
- Provide manipulatives.
- Integrate language development into subject instruction.
- Use a variety of media to develop language competencies.
- Provide students with opportunities to work in student-mediated arrangements. ●

Source: Adapted from *Effective Mainstreaming (2nd ed.), by S. J. Salend, 1994, New York: Macmillan.*

Teachers prepare instructional materials to present to students and discuss the material with students before, while, and after they complete assignments. Thus, teachers must be aware of the language they use while instructing (e.g., speaking rate, syntactical and semantic complexity, nonverbal language). Teachers need to be aware of each student's language comprehension and production deficits and strengths so that they can make appropriate adaptations in oral instructions and in any printed materials they present to the students. Teachers also should be aware of students' difficulties in managing oral and written forms of communication and engaging in group conversations. Teachers can manage many of the interactions within the language triad. If teachers recognize their influential positions, they can meet some important teaching goals with students who have learning and behavior difficulties.

Teachers can implement specific guidelines and adaptations to enhance language interactions within the triad. The printed materials in classroom curricula introduce students to new facts and challenge students to practice new learning strategies. Teachers should present students with printed academic material that is written in a language form and style that students can understand. The passages, directions, and questions in many textbooks and workbooks require students to comprehend compound and complex sentences. These materials also require students to think about objects and events that they cannot presently see, touch, or hear. The complex and abstract nature of many academic materials demands that their language be simplified or augmented if students are to learn the concepts or facts at hand (Wiig & Semel, 1984). The complex sentences and implicit words used in many workbooks and texts can be simplified without sacrificing the author's intent. Table 5.9 provides some guidelines for noting semantic and grammatical complexity in spoken and written passages and adapting them for students with learning and behavior problems. Teachers can present such adaptations to students orally (e.g., "Cross out *collections* and write in *groups*"), in the form of revised worksheets, or in student-mediated arrangements so that students can assist one another with the information.

Students may need extra time to comprehend and respond to complex and abstract questions, directions, and teachers' instructions. Student language could be developed through the use of small-group work and hands-on activities. Teachers can

Table 5.9
Examples of
Classroom
Language Adapted
for Complexity of
Message

Instruction/Questions	Adaptation	Focus
(Math)		
Ring the accurate answer in each problem.	Draw a circle around the correct answer.	Vocabulary
(Science)		
Why are location and motion important to people?	What is motion? Why is it important to people? What is location? Why is it important to people?	High-level question; multiple concepts
(Math)		
Write numbers on the second ruler, color it yellow, and cut it out to use in class.	Write the numbers 1–6 on the empty ruler below. Color the ruler yellow. Cut out the ruler. Use the ruler to measure your pencil.	Long sentence; multiple steps; vague pronoun referent
(Reading)		
The characters in the story were too upset to do anything constructive when they discovered the burglar. What would you do?	Who were the characters in the story? How did they feel when they found the burglar in the house? What would you do if you found a burglar in your house?	Complex sentence; vocabulary; high-level question

enhance learning by monitoring their rate of speech, the complexity of their sentences, and their choice of questions during instruction (Gruenewald & Pollack, 1990). Salend (1994) offers the following suggestions to promote effective communication during instruction: Use words that are familiar to students, paraphrase new vocabulary and key phrases, limit the use of idioms, control sentence length and complexity, highlight new words through variations in intonation, ask questions, and check for understanding.

Additionally, teachers should evaluate the content and form of their conversations with students in the classroom. For instance, do most classroom interactions consist of comments or questions? Extensive questioning certainly challenges students to think; however, students with learning and behavior difficulties may also benefit from having teachers describe, demonstrate, and relate new concepts and materials to previously existing information. After students have had an opportunity to synthesize the new material, teachers can ask questions to facilitate recall and reorganization of new and old thoughts.

Instructional Questioning

When special and general education teachers decide to question students, they should select their questions thoughtfully (Blank & Marquis, 1987). Some questions demand more thinking than others. If questions are too complex, students may find it difficult to express knowledge they possess about a particular topic. They may recognize some of the words in the question, but be unsure of what to say. Teachers may erroneously interpret students' inadequate responses to mean that the students have no knowledge about the topic. By using an easier question, teachers may discover students' true knowledge.

A hierarchy of questions and directives appears in Table 5.10. Questions that require only recall of simple facts (levels 1 and 2) are generally easier than those that

Table 5.10
A Hierarchy of
Questions and
Directives

Level	Questions/Statements
Level 1: Matching perception At this level, the simplest level, the child must be able to apply identifying, naming, or imitating language to what he or she sees in the everyday world.	What is this? What did you see? Show me the circle.
Level 2: Selective analysis of perception At this level, the child must focus more selectively on specific aspects of material and integrate separate components into a unified whole, describing, completing a sentence, giving an example, or selecting an object by two characteristics.	What is happening? Find something that is . . . Finish the sentence
Level 3: Reordering perception The child must restructure or reorder perceptions according to constraints imposed through language (excluding assuming role of another or following directions in correct sequence).	Find the things that are not . . . What will happen next? What would she say?
Level 4: Reasoning about perception The formulations at this level, the most complex level, require the child to go beyond immediate perceptions and to talk about logical relationships between objects and events (predicting, explaining, or finding a logical solution).	What will happen if . . . Why should we use that? What could you do?

Source: From "The Language of Instruction: The Hidden Complexities," by L. Berlin, M. Blank, and S. Rose, 1980, *Topics in Language Disorders and Learning Disabilities, 1*, p. 52. Copyright 1980 by Aspen Publications. Reprinted with permission.

require reasoning, evaluation, or comparisons (levels 3 and 4). The higher-level questions demand more thinking and frequently require more time for students to produce an acceptable answer. If teachers appreciate the demands of the questions they ask, they can present students with questions and directives that appropriately tap students' knowledge. In time, teachers can challenge students to expand their thinking and answer more complex questions.

Ask Yourself ?

1. What are the language demands of the curricular materials?

2. How do language demands change across various instructional arrangements?

3. What are the language strengths and needs of my students?

4. What language complexities do I use that require modification to meet students' needs? ◄

Homework

As you read, think about . . .

1. Summarizing the research findings about effective homework practices for students with learning and behavior problems.
2. Designing your homework policy and communicating this policy to your principal and students' parents.
3. Designing homework for some of the lessons you have written.
4. Describing how you will implement the research findings about homework into your own practices with homework in the classroom.
5. Designing a handout for parents that communicates effective and ineffective homework practices by families.

Cooper (1989) defines homework as "tasks assigned to students by schoolteachers that are meant to be carried out during nonschool hours" (p. 7). Other researchers define homework more specifically as being a teacher-directed, IEP-related, and evaluated activity that helps students maintain skills (Heller, Spooner, Anderson, & Mims, 1988).

The role and efficacy of homework have become increasingly important issues in light of results from national studies (e.g., U.S. Department of Education, 1990) suggesting that the percentage of students in elementary- and secondary-level schools expected to do homework has increased in the last decade. This increase of homework assignments can be linked to two major trends. The first trend has been national commissions' scrutiny of American public education (e.g., Goals 2000, 1994), which resulted in critical reports and specific recommendations for increased educational standards and academic improvement. Research showed that students should spend up to two hours (elementary students up to one hour) a day on homework assignments (Cooper & Nye, 1994). The implications of these academic recommendations for students with learning and behavior problems must be examined closely.

The second trend has been a substantial body of research demonstrating the positive effect of high levels of academic engaged time on student achievement and learning (e.g., Sindelar, Smith, Harriman, Hale, & Wilson, 1986; Thurlow, Ysseldyke, Wotruba, & Algozzine, 1993). Students should be involved in activities that relate to instructional objectives and should be expected to reach mastery levels through direct instructional techniques, including relevant practice opportunities (e.g., homework).

Cooper (1989) identifies positive effects of homework, including improved achievement and learning, improved attitude and study skills, more self-discipline, and greater parent involvement; the potential negative effects include fatigue, loss of leisure time, parents' abilities to provide assistance, and cheating. He also notes five major factors that potentially influence the effects of homework: student characteristics, assignment characteristics, classroom factors, home factors, and classroom follow-up. These effects and factors have been discussed in the literature, and recommendations have been made for appropriate practices. We will now examine research findings about homework practices and make research-based recommendations for "best practice" in homework.

Research Findings

Two bodies of literature on homework practices have emerged in the last decade: research practices in general education settings, which have implications for students with disabilities who receive most of their education in general education classrooms, and more recently, research specifically targeting students with mild disabilities.

General education research has focused on variables related to homework effectiveness and teacher practices. Research findings comparing homework with no homework and homework with in-class study generally support the effectiveness of homework on the academic achievement of certain types of students. That student population includes those without disabilities and those with no definitive preference for subject matter (Cooper & Nye, 1994). In a national survey of homework policies, Roderique, Polloway, Cumblad, Epstein, and Bursuck (1994) found that on average, elementary students received homework three nights weekly, requiring about 40 minutes; middle school students worked four nights for about an hour; and high school students had homework requiring about one hour and 40 minutes four nights a week.

Research has shown that teachers typically assign homework for practice and extension opportunities and to allow students time to complete unfinished in-class work (Cooper & Nye, 1994; Polloway, Epstein, Bursuck, Jayanthi, & Cumblad, 1994). Research findings (Epstein et al., 1993; Polloway et al., 1994) have suggested that parent involvement in homework practices, teacher discussions of homework assignments, and student consequences for incomplete homework all influence the effectiveness of homework.

The special education research suggests that students with disabilities have more difficulties with homework than do their peers without disabilities (Epstein et al., 1993; Salend & Schliff, 1989). These difficulties could be attributed to learning and behavioral characteristics (e.g., lack of selective attention, inability to ask for assistance, difficulty with task behavior, lack of learning strategies, and poor study skills) and to ineffective teacher practices (e.g., limited homework explanations, assignment of tasks that are too difficult, limited feedback). For example, Salend and Schliff (1989) found that almost 50 percent of special education teachers working with youngsters who had learning disabilities did not discuss, review, or grade homework assignments.

Teacher and student monitoring of assignments has been reported as promoting effective practices for students with disabilities. Strukoff, McLaughlin, and Bialozor (1987) monitored the effects of giving parents report cards reflecting assignment completion; results showed a significant increase in completion and accuracy of homework. Trammel, Schloss, and Alper (1994) had eight students ages 13 to 16 with learning disabilities use self-monitoring, self-evaluation, and self-graphing. This successfully promoted homework completion and accuracy. These studies demonstrate the importance of teacher or student monitoring in fostering successful homework practices.

Rosenberg (1989) conducted two investigations on the effects of homework on the basic skills of students with learning disabilities. In his second study, he found that the rate of homework completion (i.e., greater than 90 percent returned assignments), accuracy (i.e., greater than 80 percent), and structured parental involvement made homework more effective in helping students to acquire basic skills. Rosenberg notes that homework should be used for additional independent practice following direct instruction; homework on skills for which students demonstrate little knowledge is not effective. Teachers must also ensure that there are consequences for homework completion and incompletion.

Finally, in a survey of homework experiences of elementary and junior high students in regular, resource, and self-contained special education classrooms, Bryan and Nelson (1994) found that students in resource room programs had more negative feelings about homework than students in regular classrooms and self-contained special education programs. The students had negative feelings about their understanding of assignments, the purpose of the assignments, and teacher feedback. These students tended to view homework as boring; they also perceived themselves as doing poorly on homework as compared with their peers in the other settings. The research findings suggested that teachers must consider students' opinions and perspectives when designing homework assignments.

Homework Practices

Based on the results of this research on general and special education teachers' homework practices, we can see several ways to make homework more effective.

First, special and general education teachers must work collaboratively to be sure that a homework assignment is appropriate for individual students. Second, teachers must be sure that students understand the assignments and that consequences for compliance and noncompliance exist. Third, parents can participate in the process in a structured manner so that they are clear about the assignment. Fourth, homework should involve skills that students can practice independently; students should have demonstrated acquisition of the skills and should now need further practice to reach mastery. Fifth, students with learning and behavioral problems should be taught specific study skills to help them approach homework tasks more efficiently and effectively. Tips for Teachers presents additional ideas to foster effective homework practices.

Tips for Teachers

Homework

1. Develop a homework policy stating expectations; share the policy with students, parents, and administrators.
2. Work collaboratively with general education teachers to ensure that homework assignments are modified to meet individual learners' needs.
3. Explain homework assignments; check for understanding.
4. Make homework an opportunity for independent practice, rather than an introduction to a new, untaught skill.
5. Assign reasonable amounts of homework frequently.
6. Check homework daily; provide incentive and rewards for completion and accuracy.
7. Involve parents in a structured format: Provide specific guidelines for assistance, request assistance with rewards and incentives, provide feedback about homework completion and accuracy, and request feedback about problems that occur with homework assignments.
8. Teach skills necessary for successful homework completion, such as study skills, learning strategies, and problem-solving skills.
9. Establish a routine homework system designating how homework is handled each day (i.e., where to turn it in, checking and providing feedback to students, rewarding for completion and accuracy).
10. Involve students in self-monitoring, including correction and evaluation. ■

Technology

As you read, think about . . .

1. Reviewing the Technology Act discussed in chapter 1.
2. Describing different types of instructional technology with which you are familiar.
3. Designing a plan for infusing instructional technology into peer tutoring, cooperative learning, and whole-group instruction.
4. Comparing and contrasting instructional and assistive technology.
5. Designing a plan for infusing an assistive technology device into cooperative learning for an elementary and secondary student with a severe reading or writing problem.
6. Providing a rationale for family members about the role of assistive technology.

Technology plays a major role in today's society. Technology tremendously influences our life, whether we read about technology in the newspaper; use a home computer to manage business or complete homework; access the local library's computer to conduct a reference search; program our home to automatically turn on the lights, the heater, or a coffee pot; or watch television using a personal satellite dish.

In schools, the impact of technology also is being felt as elementary- and secondary-level teachers become more comfortable with the various technologies and ways to use them in the classroom. It is common to find district- or school-based technology experts whose role is to assist teachers in using technology for instruction and to update their knowledge about technology. For students with learning and behavior problems, technology can not only augment instruction, but also help them compensate for specific disabilities. We now discuss instructional and assistive technology by (1) defining the terms, (2) providing examples, (3) discussing selection considerations, and (4) describing infusion techniques.

Instructional Technology

It is hard to find a school today that does not have some form of technology that can be used to facilitate instruction. According to the International Association for the Evaluation of Education Achievement (IEA), 99 percent of schools have installed computers and 85 percent of the students use them (Anderson, 1993). Instructional technology is a major component of American education; however, the need for teacher education in instructional technology is still great. For instance, a 1992 study that IEA did of 2,500 schools in Austria, Germany, Japan, the Netherlands, and the United States found that the U.S. places greater emphasis on using computers to learn content area skills, provides students with less formal instruction in computer use, offers less in-service training to teachers in computer technology, and is more likely to have **multimedia technologies** (e.g., CD-ROMs, videodiscs) than the other countries in the study. This section is designed to provide the reader with basic information about instructional technology; however, it is beyond the scope of this book to offer an exhaustive discussion. For additional information, we suggest that you refer to this chapter's "References and Suggested Readings" and that you contact some of the technology publishing companies (see Table 5.11) for catalogues. Chapters 10 through 13 also present technology ideas and software suggestions.

Definition and Advantages

Instructional technology is defined as scientific devices that facilitate instruction by offering teachers a means of extending, augmenting, individualizing, and enriching learning. Instructional technology can be very motivating for students who typically find textbook learning and lecturing dull or difficult. Although instructional technology is not a cure-all, when used appropriately as an instructional tool, it can provide another avenue for classroom learning. Lewis (1993) cites the following advantages of instructional technology for students with learning and behavior problems: (1) drill and practice software to promote mastery of skills, (2) development of writing abilities, (3) simulations and problem-solving opportunities, (4) access to the curriculum, (5) individualized learning, and (6) a motivator.

Table 5.11
Technology
Publishing
Companies

Ablenet, Inc., 1081 Tenth Avenue S.E., Minneapolis, MN 55414

Adaptive Devices Group, 1278 North Farris, Fresno, CA 93728

Brøderbund Software, P.O. Box 6121, Novato, CA 94948

Cambridge Development Laboratory, Inc., 214 Third Avenue, Waltham, MA 02154

Claris Corporation, 5201 Patrick Henry Drive, Santa Clara, CA 95052

Closing the Gap, P.O. Box 68, Henderson, MN 56044

CompuServe, 5000 Arlington Centre Blvd., P.O. Box 20212, Columbus, OH 43220

Compu-Teach, 78 Olive Street, New Haven, CT 06511

Davidson & Associates, Inc., 19840 Pioneer Ave., Torrance, CA 90503

Discis Knowledge Research, Inc., NYCCPO Box 45099, 5150 Yonge St., Toronto, Ontario, M2N 6N2 Canada

Don Johnston Developmental Equipment, Inc., P.O. 639, 1000 N. Rand Rd., Building 115, Wauconda, IL 60084

Dragon Systems, Inc., 320 Nevada St., Newton, MA 02160

Franklin Learning Resources, The Education Division of Franklin Computer, 122 Burrs Rd., Mt. Holly, NJ 08060

Hartley Courseware, Inc., 133 Bridge St., P.O. Box 419, Dimondale, MI 48821

International Society for Technology in Education, 1787 Agate St., Eugene, OR 97403

MECC, 6160 Summit Dr. North, Minneapolis, MN 55430

Spinnaker Software, 201 Broadway, Cambridge, MA 02139

Tom Synder Productions, 80 Coolidge Rd., Watertown, MA 02172

WINGS for Learning/Sunburst Communications, 1600 Green Hills Rd., P.O. Box 66002, Scotts Valley, CA 95067

Types

Although there are many types of instructional technology, we discuss only four because of space limitations. Software is the first type of instructional technology. A proliferation of educational software is available for a variety of hardware. Software is available for most content areas, allowing teachers to supplement instruction and offering users many options. Educational software typically consists of text (words), graphics (e.g., pictures, animation), directions, feedback or error correction procedures, and remedial activities (i.e., extra practice on an area in which mastery was not achieved). Documentation (a teacher's guide and general directions) usually accompanies educational software and may include an explanation of the software or even actual lessons and extended activities. It is important to evaluate software when selecting it for classroom instruction; evaluation guidelines are offered below in the section called "Software Selection."

A second type of instructional technology is information technology, which is accessed through telecommunications. In this case, the computer is connected to a **modem** that allows users access to information worldwide. Students could correspond with other students in various regions of the country to share information or to develop writing skills. Students could communicate with experts around the world on a subject of interest or study. Teachers could also correspond with other professionals to broaden their expertise in a subject area or to gain wider access to resources to supplement instruction. Informational technology might include access to bulletin boards, data bases, and consumer information; the possibilities are endless and continue to expand.

Multimedia, a third type of instructional technology, is the combination of graphics, sound, text, or video in a format intended to enhance the content. For example, a CD-ROM story can feature explanations of contextual clues, definitions of vocabulary, and an auditory presentation of the text. Instruction on a particular subject could include a video clip or a branching program for extra practice. Videodiscs are also becoming popular as a way of presenting interactive curriculum with sound and video; teachers can provide practice opportunities, and evaluate student learning following the videodisc lesson.

A fourth type of instructional technology is the presentation of lessons using a computer and projection panel. In this case, teachers use technology as an instructional tool in their lessons. Many teachers develop lessons by using word processing programs or presentation software (i.e., software that is designed for formal presentations and includes clip art, graphics, and text options). These lessons can be saved for future use and modified to meet individual students' needs. Through the use of projection panels connected to computers, these lessons can be presented to large or small groups of students. Some publishing companies now produce instructional materials that can be used with an overhead projector; this enables teachers to present a lesson to the class. Students can observe, participate in the lesson, or interact with materials at their desks based on the teacher's model. Thus, the computer and overhead projector can create some exciting learning activities and opportunities.

Software Selection

Appropriate software selection for students with learning difficulties is imperative. Teachers must examine the software instructional design before purchasing it. Educational software should include instructional features that promote effective learning for students who require extra practice and feedback. Software should contain simple, easy-to-follow directions, models, examples, positive corrective feedback, extra practice opportunities (branching), an appropriate reading level, pacing options, and documentation of students' progress. Table 5.12 contains examples of different types of software, and Table 5.13 contains information for software evaluation and selection.

Infusing Instructional Technology into Teaching

Instructional technology has great potential as a teaching tool. Technology-assisted instruction, which includes multimedia, videodiscs, computers, projection panels and computers, and informational technology, is underutilized in today's classrooms. For instance, computers are too often used as a reinforcer for good behavior, as a filler after work is completed, or only in the computer lab on the designated computer day. In some cases, teachers lack everyday access to technology because schools can't afford to purchase overhead projectors, videodiscs, and computers for all classrooms; in other cases, teachers lack sufficient training in infusing technology into a lesson. Therefore, teachers are challenged to increase their access to and knowledge about instructional technology.

Treat instructional technology as you would treat any other supplemental material or resource. The following suggestions should help you infuse instructional technology into your lessons:

Table 5.12
Types of Software

Type	Purpose	Strengths
Tutorial	1. Designed to present new information. 2. Introduces new skills and concepts. 3. Prerequisite skills may be necessary.	1. Provides practice on new skills and concepts. 2. May present sequence of skills. 3. Can be used to supplement direct instruction. 4. Can be used in student-mediated arrangements.
Drill and practice	1. Reinforces skills previously taught. 2. Provides practice opportunities on skills and concepts. 3. Provides feedback regarding progress.	1. Provide the extra practice in skills and concepts that students with learning and behavior problems may require. 2. Can continue providing necessary practice for students to reach mastery.
Simulation	1. Presents decision-making and cause-effect situations. 2. De-emphasizes "right or wrong" answers.	1. Gives students opportunities to make decisions and to witness the results of those decisions. 2. Provides opportunities to analyze situations and apply problem-solving skills.
Games	1. Presents learning in a fun, gamelike situation. 2. May have various effects such as animation and sound to simulate a game format. 3. May have points for correct scores.	1. May be appealing to some students while reinforcing skills.

Source: Adapted from *Special Education Technology: Classroom Application,* by R. Lewis, 1993, Pacific Grove, CA: Brooks/Cole.

1. Select the instructional objective to be taught based on assessment data (see chapters 3 and 6).
2. Select the instructional approach and design the steps for instruction.
3. Select materials, books, and technology (e.g., software, multimedia) that can be used to promote mastery of the instructional objective.
4. Select an instructional arrangement (e.g., teacher-mediated, which may require a computer, projection panel and screen; student-mediated, which may require careful selection of peer tutors or cooperative learning groups) that will be used for instruction, guided practice, and independent practice.
5. Arrange the environment to facilitate the use of the instructional technology (e.g., access to power strips, tables to accommodate a small group of students and a work space, access to a screen, proximity of the computer and the printer).
6. Prepare an evaluation plan to monitor student progress and to evaluate the effectiveness of the instructional technology (e.g., Did students understand how to use the technology? What type of assistance did students require? How did students use the information supplied through technology? Was the technology more beneficial than a conventional technique?).

Instructional technology can be used as a tool to facilitate students' learning. For some students with special needs, however, assistive technology devices are necessary to promote access to curriculum and instruction. We now discuss assistive tech-

Table 5.13
Guidelines for
Software
Evaluation and
Selection

A. Basic information

Name of software _____

Publisher _____   Cost _____

Hardware _____

Network copy _____   Cost _____

B. Software description

Software grade level(s) _____

Software instructional area(s) _____

Reading level of software text (if applicable) _____

Purpose _____

_____ Tutorial   _____ Remediation   _____ Drill and practice

_____ Simulation   _____ Game   _____ Problem solving

Instructional objectives   _____ Yes   _____ No   List objectives if stated _____

_____

Information presentation (check any that apply)

_____ Speech   _____ Music   _____ Graphics

_____ Text   _____ Animation

Visuals (check any that apply)

_____ Color   _____ Black and white   _____ Screen too busy

_____ Graphics enhance rather than distract from purpose

_____ Print legible   _____ Print size age-appropriate

Sound (check any that apply)   _____ Yes   _____ No

_____ Sound is clear/audible   _____ Speech is audible

_____ Sound is distracting   _____ Rate of speech is appropriate

Overall impressions/concerns _____

_____

C. Instructional design

Directions are clear, easy to read, and short	_____ Yes	_____ No
Examples or models are provided	_____ Yes	_____ No
Pacing is appropriate	_____ Yes	_____ No
Practice opportunities are provided	_____ Yes	_____ No
Corrective feedback is provided	_____ Yes	_____ No
Corrective feedback is stated positively	_____ Yes	_____ No
Difficulty level is individualized	_____ Yes	_____ No
Branching is available for extra practice	_____ Yes	_____ No
Reinforcement (visual and/or auditory) is present	_____ Yes	_____ No
A record-keeping/evaluation option is available	_____ Yes	_____ No

Overall impressions/concerns _____

_____

Table 5.13
Continued

D. Software content

Appropriate to stated objectives	____ Yes	____ No
Factual and accurate	____ Yes	____ No
Free of gender-cultural-racial bias	____ Yes	____ No
Related to school's curriculum	____ Yes	____ No
Related to student's IEP	____ Yes	____ No
Sufficient scope and sequence	____ Yes	____ No

Overall impressions/concerns _____

_____

E. Technical considerations

User demands (respond to any that apply)
Academic _____

_____

Physical/Motor _____
Computer knowledge _____
Technical vocabulary _____
Problem solving _____

Functions (check any that apply)
____ Save work in progress   ____ Print in progress   ____ Alter sound
____ Return to main menu at any point in program   ____ Change pace

Teacher demands (respond to any that apply)
Amount of instruction to students for using software _____

_____

Installation procedures _____
Level of student monitoring _____
Preparation needed before using software _____

Teacher assistance (respond to any that apply)
Documentation _____

_____

Enrichment activities/Lesson plans _____

_____

Field test/Research data _____
Overall impressions or concerns _____

_____

nology, which is becoming increasingly popular as a means of teaching students with learning and behavior difficulties.

Assistive Technology

Students with disabilities should have equal access to curriculum and instruction. Therefore, not only must special education teachers select appropriate curriculum and design effective instruction to meet individual needs, but they must also ensure that students with disabilities can readily access this curriculum and instruction. Different disabilities hinder students' ability to succeed academically. For example, students could have difficulty with writing because of a fine motor problem (i.e., holding the pencil, forming letters), with reading because of a severe reading disability, or with number recognition because of a memory problem. These students would have limited access to writing, reading, or mathematics because of their disabilities. Assistive technology devices can help students with special needs such as these. The next section provides an overview of assistive technology; suggestions for using various assistive technology devices appear in chapters 10 through 13.

Definition and Advantages

According to the Technology-Related Assistance for Individuals with Disabilities Act of 1988, an assistive technology device is "any item, piece of equipment, or product system, whether acquired commercially off-the-shelf, modified, or customized, that is used to increase, maintain, or improve the functional capabilities of individuals with disabilities" (p. 102, Stat., 1046). Assistive technology gives individuals with disabilities unprecedented opportunities and access. Once used solely by persons with sensory or motor impairments, assistive technology devices are increasingly used by individuals with a variety of learning and behavior problems (Bryant & Rivera, 1995). Assistive technology is not a panacea, but is one of many options that can be used to enhance and complement other instructional techniques.

Types

Assistive technology devices can be classified as nontechnological or technological (Lewis, 1993). Examples of nontechnological devices include a pencil grip, eyeglasses, a timer, and a tape recorder. Technological devices include alternative keyboards, scanners, and speech synthesis.

Assistive technology devices allow students more access to the instructional environment; that is, assistive technology devices can help students to compensate for their specific disabilities. For example, if a student has a severe writing problem (e.g., dysgraphia) and needs to write a report for a social studies class, the student could tape record his or her report. The student would still be expected to include all components in the report and have a "page length" similar to other students' reports, but the method for demonstrating knowledge would be different. Another example might be a student who uses a word processing program to develop stories. If this student has difficulty using a traditional keyboard, he or she could use an adapted keyboard. In both examples, the students meet the same expectations as their peer group, but they access instruction and demonstrate knowledge differently. Table 5.14 presents examples of assistive technology devices and their possible **compensatory instructional** uses for students with learning difficulties.

Selecting Assistive Technology Devices

When determining appropriate assistive technology devices, teachers and students should (1) examine the setting demands and expectations, (2) identify the abilities needed to address the setting demands successfully, (3) determine the student's functional abilities and weaknesses, and (4) select an appropriate device. Thus, the selection of assistive technology devices is accomplished through a problem-solving approach. For example, the teacher might require students to write stories (setting demand). Students would need story-writing skills and the ability to use a pencil (req-

Table 5.14
Examples of
Assistive Technology
Devices

Technological

1. Optical character recognition (OCR) system: Printed text is scanned into the computer and read to the user via speech synthesis
2. Speech recognition: A system consisting of hardware, software, and headphones; the user dictates text and the system prints the text on the screen
3. Large screen monitors: Monitors that are 17" or larger and that accommodate large print
4. Alternative keyboards: Keyboards that are adjusted with key guards (plastic keyboard overlay to ensure only one key is struck at one time) or other means (e.g., switch, touch screen) for entering information into the computer

Compensatory possibility

1. Students with severe reading disabilities have access to printed material, textbooks, handouts, worksheets
2. Students with serious written communication problems or fine motor problems can generate printed text through this system
3. Students with reading problems can be presented with fewer words to read at one time, making the amount of content manageable
4. Students with fine motor problems can have access to the process of entering information into the computer

Nontechnological

1. Pencil grip: Piece of rubber or plastic placed on a pencil where it is held for writing
2. Tape recorder

Compensatory possibility

1. Students with fine motor problems have larger instrument to grasp for more writing control
2. Students with writing problems can tape their responses; students with reading problems can hear the text presented orally

uisite abilities). In this example, our student can hold a pencil (functional ability), but has difficulty with conventional pencils (weakness), so a pencil grip might be a recommended compensatory technique to help the student grasp the pencil firmly and write the story. In another example, the student may be required to use a calculator to check her arithmetic on a worksheet (setting demand). However, this student may have difficulty accessing the small keys (weakness and requisite ability); therefore a large-keyed calculator is selected for her. Table 5.15 shows a problem-solving approach to selecting appropriate assistive technology devices to help students compensate for their weaknesses.

Table 5.15
Assistive Technology
Problem Solving

Task	Requisite abilities	Functional strengths	Functional limitations	Technology solutions
Read chapter from social studies textbook	Comprehend material	Ability to understand technical vocabulary	Ability to decode	Reader
	Use cognitive and metacognitive strategies		Ability to apply cognitive and metacognitive strategies	Books on tape
	Interpret context clues	Vision and hearing		Optical character recognition/speech synthesis
	Use composition genres			
	Define vocabulary			

Source: Adapted from *Cooperative Learning: Teaching in an Age of Technology*, by B. R. Bryant and D. P. Rivera, November, 1995, paper presented at the meeting of the Learning Disabilities Association of Texas, Austin.

The selection of assistive technology devices is an ongoing process as students mature and situations change. Certainly, families must be involved in the selection process, as family members play a crucial role in the acceptance and use of the device in all settings. They can determine the child's specific needs at home and can explain to the teacher how the needs affect learning and schoolwork. This information can help in selecting a device that is helpful across settings. Family members may require training to learn how to use the device and to offer support to the child. Finally, they may need help in understanding that assistive technology devices are compensatory tools intended to promote equitable access.

Infusing Assistive Technology Devices into Teaching

Selecting an appropriate assistive technology device is a good beginning; next, teachers must develop a plan for infusing the device into their classroom. Here are some considerations for developing and implementing this plan:

1. Become familiar with the device. If the device is new to you, try it out, experiment with it, read the documentation, and seek assistance. Have an extra set of batteries available, an additional power strip, extra computer paper, and extra printer cartridges or ribbons, if necessary. Know your local or school technology expert—have his or her number handy.
2. Write instructional objectives and an instructional plan for infusion of the device.
3. Become familiar with how the device promotes access to learning and the classroom. This is important, in case you need to justify the use of the device to family members, the student, and other professionals.
4. Check your classroom environment to ensure that the device can be used easily. Check for physical obstacles (e.g., table size for a computer and scanner, table space for an alternative keyboard, access to electrical outlets) and location considerations (e.g., computer in the corner of the room for small-group work, talking calculator that may distract other students if used around students' desks).
5. Develop a lesson and check to be sure that the student can access the curriculum and instruction by using his or her device. (Can the student see the teacher? Does the device distract from instruction? Does the student need more response time? Is instructional pacing appropriate?)
6. Evaluate instruction and the use of the device. (Was the student able to keep up with the other students using the device? Was the device distracting to the student? How did the device promote accessibility? Is the student learning?)

Instructional and assistive technology are important components of instruction. They can be used effectively to help students with learning and behavior problems be more successful in elementary- and secondary-level settings. The challenge is to become more familiar with the technologies and to move forward in infusing them into classroom instruction at all levels.

Summary

The focus of this chapter was on the implementing instruction phase of teaching. We discussed the behavioral, strategic, and holistic/constructivist approach to instruction. Although these approaches vary somewhat in instructional principles and procedures, they can be used throughout the school day to teach specific instructional objectives. Additionally, remedial, tutorial, and adaptive instruction plays a role in teaching youngsters with learning and behavior problems, depending on the instructional purpose and students' specific needs. These instructional approaches and types of instruction can work equally well with elementary- and secondary-level students and with various instructional objectives that are identified on students' IEPs.

Perhaps one of the most challenging parts of teaching is pulling together the components into a coherent, successful lesson. This takes time and practice. As teachers use the instructional steps, they must consider ways to manage student behavior effectively and ways to use their own presence as an effective management technique. Additionally, teachers need to monitor their instructional language and be aware of the language abilities and diversity students bring to the learning environment.

Teachers must decide on the role of homework to assist students in mastering instructional objectives, and must choose effective management techniques for monitoring homework completion and accuracy. Teachers must also consider the role of the family in the homework process and explore ways to promote appropriate homework practices at home.

We presented information about instructional and assistive technology and how it can facilitate instructional opportunities and successes for students with special needs. We discussed the definitions, types, selection guidelines, and infusion process to acquaint the reader with technology-assisted instruction.

We have talked about designing and implementing instruction. We will now focus on the next important piece of the teaching model—instructional evaluation.

Study and Discussion Questions

1. Discuss the three approaches to instruction.
2. Describe steps for the delivery of instruction.
3. Discuss effective homework practices.
4. Design ways to infuse instructional and assistive technology into instruction.
5. Describe a tutorial lesson that you might plan.
6. Explain behavior management techniques that you would consider when implementing a lesson.
7. Write an instructional objective and state the instructional language.
8. Provide a plan for transitioning students from large-group instruction to working independently at their desks.
9. Brainstorm signals that can be used to attain student attention.
10. Develop an evaluation plan for selecting educational software.
11. Use the problem-solving chart in Table 5.15 to evaluate a student's potential need for assistive technology.

References and Suggested Readings

Approaches to Instruction
Behavioral Approach

Baer, D. M., Wolf, M. M., & Risley, T. R. (1968). Some current dimensions of applied behavior analysis. *Journal of Applied Behavior Analysis, 1*(1), 91–97.

Becker, W. C., & Carnine, D. (1981). Direct instruction: A behavior theory model for comprehensive educational intervention with the disadvantaged. In S. W. Bijou & R. Ruiz (Eds.), *Behavior modification: Contributions to education* (pp. 145–210). Hillsdale, NJ: Erlbaum.

Bereiter, C., & Engelmann, S. (1966). *Teaching disadvantaged children in the preschool.* Englewood Cliffs, NJ: Prentice-Hall.

Carnine, D., Silbert, J., & Kameenui, E. (1990). *Direct instruction reading.* Columbus, OH: Merrill.

Engelmann, S., & Carnine, D. (1991). *Theory of instruction: Principles and applications.* Eugene, OR: Association for Direct Instruction.

Engelmann, S., Carnine, D., & Steely, D. G. (1991). Making connections in mathematics. *Journal of Learning Disabilities, 24*(5), 292–303.

Garnett, K., & Fleischner, J. E. (1983). Automatization and basic fact performance of normal and learning disabled children. *Learning Disability Quarterly, 6,* 223–230.

Gersten, R., Carnine, D., & Woodward, J. (1987). Direct instruction research: The third decade. *Remedial and Special Education, 8*(6), 48–56.

Gersten, R., Woodward, J., & Darch, C. (1986). Direct instruction: A research-based approach to curriculum design and teaching. *Exceptional Children, 53*(1), 17–31.

Hasselbring, T. S., Goin, L. I., & Bransford, J. D. (1988). Developing math automaticity in learning handicapped children: The role of computerized drill and practice. *Focus on Exceptional Children, 20*(6), 1–7.

Poplin, M. (1988). The reductionistic fallacy in learning disabilities: Replicating the past by reducing the present. *Journal of Learning Disabilities, 21*(7), 389–400.

Rivera, D. M., & Bryant, B. R. (1992). Mathematics instruction for students with special needs. *Intervention in School and Clinic, 28*(2), 71–86.

Rivera, D. M., & Smith, D. D. (1987). Influence of modeling on acquisition and generalization of computational skills: A summary of research findings from three sites. *Learning Disability Quarterly, 10,* 69–80.

Skinner, B. F. (1966). *The behavior of organisms: An experimental analysis.* New York: Appleton-Century-Crofts.

Tawney, J. W., & Gast, D. L. (1984). *Single subject research in special education.* Columbus, OH: Merrill.

Strategic Approach

Borkowski, J. (1992). Metacognitive theory: A framework for teaching literacy, writing, and math skills. *Journal of Learning Disabilities, 25,* 253–257.

Deshler, D. D., & Schumaker, J. B. (1986). Learning strategies: An instructional alternative for low-achieving adolescents. *Exceptional Children, 52,* 583–590.

Ellis, E. S. (1993). Integrative strategy instruction: A potential model for teaching content area subjects to adolescents with learning disabilities. *Journal of Learning Disabilities, 26*(6), 358–383.

Ellis, E. S., Lenz, B. K., & Sabornie, E. J. (1987). Generalization and adaptation of learning strategies to natural environments: Part I. Critical agents. *Remedial and Special Education, 8*(1), 6–21.

Hollingsworth, M., & Woodward, J. (1993). Integrated learning: Explicit strategies and their role in problem-solving instruction for students with learning disabilities. *Exceptional Children, 59*(5), 444–455.

Mayer, R. E. (1988). Models for understanding. *Review of Educational Research, 59*(1), 43–64.

Swanson, H. L., & Cooney, J. B. (1985). Strategy transformations in learning disabled children. *Learning Disability Quarterly, 8,* 221–231.

Swanson, H. L., & Cooney, J. B. (1991). Learning disabilities and memory. In B. Y. L. Wong (Ed.), *Learning about learning disabilities* (pp. 104–129). San Diego, CA: Academic Press.

Torgesen, J. K. (1977). The role of nonspecific factors in the task performance of learning-disabled children: A theoretical assessment. *Journal of Learning Disabilities, 10,* 27–34.

Wong, B. Y. L. (1991). The relevance of metacognition to learning disabilities. In B. Y. L. Wong (Ed.), *Learning about learning disabilities* (pp. 232–261). San Diego, CA: Academic Press.

Wong, B. Y. L. (1993). Pursuing an elusive goal: Molding strategic teachers and learners. *Journal of Learning Disabilities, 26*(6), 354–357.

Holistic/Constructivist Approach

Cobb, P. (1988). Tension between theories of learning and instruction in mathematics education. *Educational Psychologist, 23,* 87–104.

Delpit, L. D. (1988). The silenced dialogue: Power and pedagogy in educating other people's children. *Harvard Educational Review, 58,* 280–298.

Kauffman, J. M. (1994). Places of change: Special education's power and identity in an era of educational reform. *Journal of Learning Disabilities, 27*(10), 610–618.

Mather, N. (1992). Whole language reading instruction for students with learning disabilities: Caught in the cross fire. *Learning Disabilities Research & Practice, 7,* 87–95.

Moats, L. C., & Lyon, G. R. (1993). Learning disabilities in the United States: Advocacy, science, and the future of the field. *Journal of Learning Disabilities, 26,* 282–294.

Piaget, J. (1977). *The development of thought: Equilibrium of cognitive structures.* New York: Viking Press.

Poplin, M. (1988a). Holistic/constructivist principles of the teaching/learning process: Implications for the field of learning disabilities. *Journal of Learning Disabilities, 21*(7), 401–416.

Poplin, M. (1988b). The reductionistic fallacy in learning disabilities: Replicating the past by reducing the present. *Journal of Learning Disabilities, 21*(7), 389–400.

Poplin, M. S., & Stone, S. (1992). Paradigm shifts in instructional strategies. From reductionism to holistic/constructivism. In W. Stainback & S. Stainback (Eds.), *Controversial issues confronting special education: Divergent perspectives* (pp. 153–179). Boston: Allyn & Bacon.

Pressley, M., & Rankin, J. (1994). More about whole language methods of reading instruction for students at risk for early reading failure. *Learning Disabilities Research and Practice, 9*(3), 157–168.

Reid, D. K., Kurkjian, C., & Carruthers, S. S. (1994). Special education teachers interpret constructivist teaching. *Remedial and Special Education, 15*(5), 267–280.

Stone, C. A., & Reid, D. K. (1994). Social and individual forces in learning: Implications for instruction of children with learning difficulties. *Learning Disability Quarterly, 17*(1), 72–86.

Westby, C. E. (1993). Counterpoint: There may be holes in whole language. *American Speech-Language-Hearing Association Special Interest Division 10 Newsletter* (pp. 11–16). Rockville, MD: American Speech-Language-Hearing Association.

Vygotsky, L. S. (1987). Thinking and speech. In R. Rieber & A. S. Canon (Eds.), *Collected works of L. S. Vygotsky; Vol 1. Problems of general psychology.* New York: Plenum.

Other Types of Instruction

Cheney, C. O. (1989). The systematic adaptation of instructional materials and techniques for problem learners. *Academic Therapy, 25*(1), 25–31.

Hoover, J. J. (1990). Curriculum adaptation: A five-step process for classroom implementation. *Academic Therapy, 25*(4), 407–415.

Salend, S. J. (1994). *Effective mainstreaming: Creating inclusive classrooms* (2nd ed.). New York: Macmillan.

Delivery of Instruction
Instructional Steps

Algozzine, B., Ysseldyke, J. E., & Campbell, P. (1994). Strategies and tactics for effective instruction. *Teaching Exceptional Children, 26*(3), 34–36.

Ausubel, D. P., & Robinson, F. G. (1969). *School learning: An introduction to educational psychology.* New York: Holt, Rinehart & Winston.

Englert, C. S. (1984). Effective direct instruction practices in special education settings. *Remedial and Special Education 5*(2), 38–47.

Epstein, M. H., Polloway, E. A., Foley, R. M., & Patton, J. R. (1993). Homework: A comparison of teachers' and parents' perceptions of the problems experienced by students identified as having behavioral disorders, learning disabilities, or no disabilities. *Remedial and Special Education, 14*(5), 40–50.

Fuchs, L. S., Fuchs, D., & Hamlett, C. L. (1989). Effects of instructional use of curriculum-based measurement to enhance instruction programs. *Remedial and Special Education, 10*(2), 43–52.

Gersten, R., Woodward, J., & Darch, C. (1986). Direct instruction: A research-based approach to curriculum design and teaching. *Exceptional Children, 53*(1), 17–31.

Lenz, B. K., Alley, G. R., & Schumaker, J. B. (1987). Activating the inactive learner: Advance organizers in the secondary content classroom. *Learning Disability Quarterly, 10*(1), 53–62.

Mastropieri, M. A., & Scruggs, T. E. (1994). *Effective instruction for special education* (2nd ed.). Austin, TX: PRO-ED.

Rosenshine, B., & Stevens, R. (1984). Classroom instruction in reading. In D. Pearson (Ed.), *Handbook of research on teaching* (pp. 681–744). New York: Longman.

Stowitschek, J. J., Stowitschek, C. E., Hendrickson, J. M., & Day, R. M. (1984). *Direct teaching tactics for exceptional children.* Rockville, MD: Aspen.

Instructional Management Procedures

Canter, L. (1986). *Assertive discipline: A take-charge approach for today's educator.* Los Angeles: Canter.

Emmer, E. T., Evertson, C. M., Clements, B. S., & Worsham, M. E. (1994). *Classroom management for secondary teachers* (3rd ed.). Boston: Allyn & Bacon.

Evertson, C. M., Emmer, E. T., Clements, B. S., & Worsham, M. E. (1994). *Classroom management for elementary teachers* (3rd ed.). Boston: Allyn & Bacon.

Smith, D. D., & Rivera, D. M. (1993). *Effective discipline* (2nd ed.). Austin, TX: PRO-ED.

Smith, D. D., & Rivera, D. P. (1995). Discipline in special education and general education settings. *Focus on Exceptional Children, 27*(5), 1–14.

Instructional Language

Berlin, L., Blank, M., & Rose, S. (1980). The language of instruction: The hidden complexities. *Topics in Language Disorders and Learning Disabilities, 1,* 52.

Blank, M., & Marquis, A. (1987). *Directing discourse.* Tucson, AZ: Communication Skill Builders.

Gruenewald, L. J., & Pollack, S. A. (1990). *Language interaction in curriculum and instruction* (2nd ed.). Austin, TX: PRO-ED.

Salend, S. J. (1994). *Effective mainstreaming: Creating inclusive classrooms* (2nd ed.). New York: Macmillan.

Silliman, E. R., & Wilkinson, L. C. (1994). Discourse scaffolds for classroom intervention. In G. P. Wallach & K. G. Butler, *Language learning disabilities in school-age children and adolescents* (pp. 27–52). Columbus, OH: Merrill.

Wiig, E. H., & Semel, E. M. (1984). *Language assessment and intervention for the learning disabled* (2nd ed.). New York: Macmillan.

Homework

Bryan, T., & Nelson, C. (1994). Doing homework: Perspectives of elementary and junior high school students. *Journal of Learning Disabilities, 27*(8), 488–499.

Cooper, H. (1989). *Homework.* White Plains, NY: Longman.

Cooper, H., & Nye, B. (1994). Homework for students with learning disabilities: The implications of research on policy and practice. *Journal of Learning Disabilities, 27*(8), 470–480.

Epstein, M. H., Polloway, E. A., Foley, R. M., & Patton, J. R. (1993). Homework: A comparison of teachers' and parents' perceptions of the problems experienced by students identified as having behavioral disorders, learning disabilities, or no disabilities. *Remedial and Special Education, 14*(5), 40–50.

Goals 2000: Educate America Act, P.L. 103-227 (1994).

Heller, H. W., Spooner, F., Anderson, D., & Mims, A. (1988). Homework: A review of special education practices in the Southwest. *Teacher Education and Special Education, 11,* 43–51.

Polloway, E. A., Epstein, M. H., Bursuck, W. D., Jayanthi, M., & Cumblad, C. (1994). Homework practices of general education teachers. *Journal of Learning Disabilities, 27*(8), 500–509.

Roderique, T. W., Polloway, E. A., Cumblad, C., Epstein, M. H., & Bursuck, W. D. (1994). Homework: A survey of policies in the United States. *Journal of Learning Disabilities, 27*(8), 481–487.

Rosenberg, M. S. (1989). The effects of daily homework assignments on the acquisition of basic skills by students with learning disabilities. *Journal of Learning Disabilities, 22*(5), 314–323.

Salend, S. J., & Schliff, J. (1989). An examination of the homework practices of teachers of students with learning disabilities. *Journal of Learning Disabilities, 22,* 621–623.

Sindelar, P. T., Smith, M. A., Harriman, N. E., Hale, R. L., & Wilson, R. J. (1986). Teacher effectiveness in special education programs. *The Journal of Special Education, 20,* 195–207.

Strukoff, P. M., McLaughlin, T. F., & Bialozor, R. C. (1987). The effects of a daily report card system in increasing homework completion and accuracy in a special education setting. *Techniques: A Journal for Remedial Education and Counseling, 3,* 19–26.

Thurlow, M., Ysseldyke, J., Wotruba, J., & Algozzine, B. (1993). Instruction in special education classrooms under varying student-teacher ratios. *The Elementary School Journal, 93,* 305–320.

Trammel, D. L., Schloss, P. J., & Alper, S. (1994). Using self-recording, evaluation, and graphing to increase completion of homework assignments. *Journal of Learning Disabilities, 27*(2), 75–81.

U.S. Department of Education. (1990). Reading and writing proficiency remains low. *Daily Education News,* 1–7.

U.S. Department of Education. (1992). *Fourteenth annual report to Congress on the implementation of the Individuals with Disabilities Education Act.* Washington, DC: Author.

Technology
Instructional Technology

Anderson, R. E. (Ed.). (1993). *Computers in American schools 1992: An overview.* Minneapolis: University of Minnesota, International Association for the Evaluation of Education Achievement.

Behrmann, M. M. (1988). *Integrating computers into the curriculum: A handbook for special educators.* Boston: College-Hill.

Bruder, I. (1991). Guide to multimedia: How it changes the way we teach and learn. *Electronic Learning, 11*(1), 22–26.

Church, G., & Bender, M. (1989). *Teaching with computers: A curriculum for special educators.* Boston: College-Hill.

Fritz, M. (1991). Videodisc update: The power of visual learning. *Technology & Learning, 12*(3), 39–50.

Lewis, R. B. (1993). *Special education technology: Classroom application.* Pacific Grove, CA: Brooks/Cole.

MacArthur, C. A., & Malouf, D. B. (1991). Teachers' beliefs, plans, and decisions about computer-based instruction. *Journal of Special Education, 25*(5), 44–72.

Malouf, D. B., Morariu, J., Coulson, D. B., & Maiden, V. S. (1989). Special education teachers' preferences for sources of software evaluation information. *Journal of Special Education Technology, 9*(3), 144–155.

Assistive Technology

Behrmann, M. M. (1994). Assistive technology for students with mild disabilities. *Intervention in School and Clinic, 30*(2), 70–83.

Bryant, B. R., Rivera, D., & Warde, B. (1993). Technology as a means to an end: Facilitating success at the college level. *LD Forum, 19*(1), 13–18.

Bryant, B. R., & Rivera, D. P. (1995, November). *Cooperative learning: Teaching in an age of technology.* Paper presented at the meeting of the Learning Disabilities Association of Texas, Austin.

Hanley, T. V., Appel, L. S., & Harris, C. D. (1988). Technological innovation in the context of special education systems: A qualitative and structured research approach. *Journal of Special Education Technology, 9*(2), 98–108.

Lewis, R. B. (1993). *Special education technology: Classroom application.* Pacific Grove, CA: Brooks/Cole.

MacArthur, C. A. (1993). Beyond word processing: Computer support for writing processes. *LD Forum, 19*(1), 22–27.

Raskind, M., & Shaw, T. (1995, March). *Assistive technology for students with learning disabilities: An overview.* Paper presented at the meeting of the Texas Assistive Technology Partnership, Austin, TX.

Rivera, D. P., Erin, J., Lock, R., Allan, J., & Resta, P. (in press). Infusing assistive technology into a teacher preparation program in learning disabilities. *Journal of Learning Disabilities.*

Technology-Related Assistance for Individuals with Disabilities Act of 1988 and amendments (Catalogue No. 850, Senate Rep. 100–438). Washington, DC: U.S. Government Printing Office.

Chapter 6
Evaluating Instruction

Making Connections

Before you read, think about the role of assessment in designing the Individualized Education Program, as discussed in chapter 3. Review the types of assessments presented in chapter 3 and the controversy surrounding assessment practices. Examine the stages of learning information that was discussed in chapter 4; think about ways in which assessments can be used to identify stages of learning for instructional purposes. Now, consider ways to monitor students' progress on instructional objectives and to evaluate whether or not students are making adequate progress.

In chapter 3, we discussed formal and informal assessment measures, and we provided specific examples of measures for both types of assessments. We noted that formal assessment refers to the administration of standardized, norm-referenced tests for the purposes of determining disability identification, eligibility for special education services, and academic and social strengths and weaknesses as compared to the peer group. Informal assessment typically measures students' academic and social performance in relation to specific curriculum. The results of informal assessment can be used to plan instructional objectives, modify instruction, document progress, and evaluate program effectiveness.

Objectives
After studying this chapter, the reader will be able to

1. Describe the development and implementation of curriculum-based assessment.

2. Explain types of teacher observation and analysis techniques.

3. Describe how to design and use portfolio assessment.

Both formal and informal assessment measures play a major role in the special education assessment process, and when used as intended, they yield important information about students from which an assessment profile can be developed. (It is beyond the scope of this book to provide a thorough description and analysis of both formal and informal assessment measures and practices; for additional readings, see References and Suggested Readings at the end of this chapter.) Table 6.1 summarizes the assessment questions discussed in chapter 3 and suggests formal and informal assessment measures that can be used to answer the questions.

In chapters 4 and 5, you read about two phases of teaching—designing and implementing instruction. Equally as important is the evaluating instruction phase, because the information obtained here determines whether or not students are pro-

Table 6.1
Assessment Purposes, Questions, and Measures/ Techniques

Purposes and questions	Measures/Techniques
Identification and eligibility	
Is there a school performance problem?	Norm-referenced assessment instruments
Is the problem related to a disability?	Curriculum-based assessment measures
How does the student's performance compare with those in his or her peer group?	
What are the student's overall strengths and weaknesses in academic and social areas?	
What is the current level of performance for academic and social skills?	
Instructional diagnosis	
Does this student possess the prerequisite skills to learn new skills and concepts?	Norm-referenced assessment instruments
What does this student comprehend about the concepts or skills?	Curriculum-based assessment measures (frequency, duration, percent, rate)
What strategies does this student use to learn the skills or concepts?	Work sample analysis/Error analysis
	"Think-aloud" cognitive problem solving
Why doesn't this student generalize previously taught material to newly presented material?	
Does the student require more practice?	
Program evaluation	
Has the student achieved mastery as compared with his or her peer group and his or her previous levels of performance?	Norm-referenced assessment instruments
	Curriculum-based assessment measures
Is the instructional intervention effective?	
What modifications and reteaching are necessary?	

Source: Adapted from *Curriculum and Evaluation Standards* (1989), by the National Council of Teachers of Mathematics, Reston: VA.

gressing academically and socially according to the Individualized Education Program's annual goals and instructional objectives. The focus of this chapter is on informal assessment measures and techniques that can be used to evaluate and monitor instruction, and to determine program effectiveness.

Phase Three: Evaluating Instruction

The evaluating instruction phase of the Phases of Teaching Model includes components that relate to helping teachers select appropriate instructional objectives, monitor student progress regularly, and determine whether or not the instructional program is moving students forward to mastery. Children are sent to school to gain knowledge and enhance their abilities. They are expected to learn how to perform academic tasks, interact with others in socially appropriate ways, and develop skills to make them productive members of society. It is teachers' awesome responsibility to achieve these overall goals. Society has charged the schools and the educational system with the obligations of meeting these somewhat ambiguous yet quite ambitious goals for each individual.

It is not impossible to monitor students' learning. In fact, evaluation of student performance has been typical school routine for many years. Traditionally, students' progress is measured at the beginning and at the end of each school year, and before each grade report. This noncontinuous system, however, does not provide teachers with ongoing feedback about the effectiveness of teaching procedures. Those who teach students with learning and behavior difficulties need more precise, frequent evaluation techniques. Collecting information about students' progress, particularly in relation to the Individualized Education Program, should be an integral part of the instructional process.

In chapter 3, the authors introduced examples of informal assessment techniques and data collection systems. We will now discuss the components of evaluating instruction more fully. The three components discussed here include: curriculum-based assessment, teacher observation and analysis assessment, and portfolio assessment. These components can assist teachers in developing a profile of students and in making good instructional decisions.

Curriculum-Based Assessment

As you read, think about . . .

1. Explaining the purposes of curriculum-based assessment.
2. Designing a curriculum-based assessment using the steps described below.
3. Describing the reasons for collecting data.
4. Comparing and contrasting the data collection systems explained in this chapter.
5. Explaining the rationale for data calculations and how they are used to analyze data.
6. Constructing a graph using data display and data calculations features.
7. Designing a lesson using each step in pairing instruction and evaluation.

Curriculum-based assessment (CBA) has gained popularity as a technique for measuring student performance as it relates to curricular goals and instructional techniques. Educators use assessment measures that not only determine how students are performing in relation to the peer group (e.g., standardized tests), but also determine how students are performing in relation to the daily curriculum and instruction. Assessment procedures must be versatile yet valid to assist educators in designing, implementing, and evaluating instruction to meet the needs of an increasingly diverse student population. With CBA, the assessment content matches the curriculum content. The teacher uses material from the students' curricula to determine where students should be placed, what their instructional objectives should be, and how they are progressing. In this section, we describe (1) the purposes of CBA, (2) how to design curriculum-based assessment, (3) data collection and analysis procedures, and (4) the procedures for pairing instruction and evaluation. (See "References and Suggested Readings" for literature on curriculum-based measurement and precision teaching; both are excellent examples of CBA that use graphing, decision-making rules, and intervention recommendations to guide the instructional process.)

Purposes

Curriculum-based assessment has several purposes. The purposes include:

1. Directly measuring the curriculum being taught
2. Establishing a link between students' IEPs and classroom instruction
3. Providing a means for monitoring student progress and evaluating the effectiveness of the intervention being used to teach the instructional objective
4. Obtaining data during the prereferral stage about students' progress in the general education setting with no special education services
5. Providing a more culturally fair means of assessing the progress of youngsters from culturally and linguistically diverse backgrounds
6. Determining initial placement in a sequence of skills

CBA offers teachers an alternative to standardized testing for monitoring and evaluating instructional programs and student progress.

Designing Curriculum-Based Assessment

There are two types of curriculum-based assessment: one identifies the initial instructional objective to target for instruction, and the other measures students' progress with the identified instructional objective. We discuss procedures for designing CBA based on IEP goals and objectives. These CBAs are applicable to oral reading, mathematics, and language arts. To assess progress in social studies and science, teachers may want to use textbook chapter tests, teacher-made tests, and oral discussions and questioning. For written expression assessment, teachers could use the procedures described below, or analyze written work for the presence of story elements, mechanics (e.g., spelling, handwriting, grammar, punctuation, capitalization), or writing components (e.g., ideas, sequence, development, main ideas and supporting details—see the "Work Sample Analysis" section below). For story problem solving and reading comprehension, teachers could use the procedures described below, or the "think-aloud" procedures described later in this chapter.

Placement

To identify instructional placement within the designated curriculum (see chapter 4 for a discussion of curricular selection), initial assessment must occur to determine specific instructional objectives to be taught. To begin with, teachers should refer to the IEP and identify the annual goals.

This way, teachers can begin to develop an idea of the content and skill areas that require instruction. The next step is to design the placement CBA. Taylor (1993) lists five steps to follow when constructing curriculum-based assessment for instructional placement purposes (some school districts have CBAs already designed and some instructional materials may contain CBAs):

Step 1. **Identify the annual goal skill to be assessed**

Examine the student's annual goals on the Individualized Education Program (IEP). An example of an annual goal might be: The student will add whole numbers.

Step 2. **Identify the instructional objectives (task analysis)**

Task-analyze step 1 into smaller steps that can become instructional objectives. Instructional objectives for the annual goal identified in step 1 might include: two-digit + one-digit numbers with no regrouping to the tens and hundreds place, two-digit + two-digit numbers with no regrouping, three-digit + two-digit numbers with no regrouping, three-digit + three-digit numbers with no regrouping, two-digit + one-digit numbers with regrouping, two-digit + two-digit numbers with regrouping, three-digit + two-digit numbers with regrouping, and three-digit + three-digit numbers with regrouping. Each of these steps could be treated as an instructional objective, depending on the student's ability level.

Step 3. **Develop test items for each instructional objective**

Develop sufficient items (3 to 4) for each objective to ensure that the student has enough opportunities to respond in the time frame allowed in the testing situation. Develop several versions of the CBA for testing across several days.

Step 4. **Determine standards of performance (mastery levels)**

Identify a **performance standard** for each objective. You can state the criterion as the percentage correct (90 percent accuracy) or as a rate (100 correct words per minute) (see the "Data Collection Systems" section below for a discussion of data collection systems). To determine an appropriate performance standard or criterion, (1) have students in the general education classroom perform the skill (take the average of those scores as the criterion), (2) use a percentage correct criterion or fluency criterion (acceptable percentage correct criteria usually range from 85 to 100, depending on the skill; fluency criteria depend on the skill), or (3) use the school district performance standards.

Step 5. **Administer and interpret the CBA instrument**

Have students take the CBA several times; one administration is not sufficient to obtain an accurate picture of students' instructional abilities. Students should know the time limits in which they will work and the standards that apply (e.g., work quickly, skip problems you don't know, reduce fractions, show your work, finish all of the pages). Analyze test item results for each instructional objective; the scores can be averaged to determine the student's instructional levels of performance. Plan to teach instructional objectives with results that fall below the criterion level.

Progress Monitoring

Once specific content area instructional objectives have been selected (in the example above, three digits + two digits with regrouping might be selected if the scores fell below the established criterion level), teachers can develop "probes" containing items for the identified instructional objective. **Probes** contain items based on the instructional objective; they may include worksheets with math facts, words to decode, or sentences with grammar that needs to be corrected; reading passages; or spelling words. Probes should contain only items that reflect the instructional objective. For example, if three digits + two digits with regrouping is chosen for instruction, then probes should contain only those types of problems (e.g., $586 + 84 =$, $694 + 98 =$). Probes determine pre-instructional ability with the designated instructional objective and regularly assess students' progress with the objective and intervention. Procedures for using both types of CBAs—placement and progress monitoring—are discussed in the "Procedures for Pairing Instruction and Evaluation" section, below.

We now give an overview of data collection procedures that have been used in classrooms for over two decades. We discuss data collection systems, data analysis procedures, and data display ideas. The section includes guidelines for choosing data collection systems and techniques for analyzing, evaluating, and visually depicting the data.

Data Collection and Analysis Procedures

A major component of curriculum-based assessment is collecting and evaluating data for determining a student's placement and progress in an instructional sequence. Teachers must select an appropriate data collection system that can accurately measure the targeted skill, and must implement specific data analysis procedures to determine if their intervention is indeed making a difference with the students. In this section, we discuss three important data collection and analysis procedures: **data collection systems, data calculations and analyses,** and **data displays.**

Data Collection Systems

The purpose of collecting information on student performance is to evaluate the teacher's and student's progress toward achieving goals and objectives. To justify the time spent measuring, the data collected must be meaningful. Therefore, the information gathered should relate directly to the target behavior. If oral reading is the current behavior of concern, the student should read aloud from an assigned reader to measure his or her progress.

Direct measurement of the specified behavior alone, however, does not guarantee meaningful data. Student performance must be evaluated across time. This means that direct data should be gathered daily or at least frequently. Teachers who do not see the student daily should measure the target behavior each time the student receives instruction.

The data gathered must be of equivalent or comparable scale, so that one day's performance can be judged against other days' performances to assess whether progress has been made. To have equivalent data, several factors must be constant. First, the behavior measured must remain the same across time. If rate of oral reading is the target behavior, the child should read orally from comparable passages each day—rather than having oral reading on Monday, silent reading on Tuesday, oral reading comprehension on Wednesday, and so on. These other reading targets might also need to be assessed frequently, but they are separate targets, not interchangeable ones. The measurement system chosen must also remain constant. If timing the reading rate is the appropriate measurement system, it must be used consistently. Interspersing one system with another renders all the data meaningless.

To determine whether the scheduled instruction has been responsible for changes in student performance, it is important to keep other situational variables as constant as possible. For example, if a child is asked to read orally in the morning one day, after lunch the next day, and before recess the following day, the changes in that student's oral reading might not be due to the materials presented or the instruction given. Likewise, if the location of the student's reading desk is changed daily, variations in performance might be more attributable to those moves than to actual change in reading ability. Naturally, everything cannot be held constant. The student's health or the events that happened the previous evening or during the morning on the way to school can affect the way a student performs at school. Frequent measures of performance, however, place those variables in perspective, and give an accurate picture of the student's abilities in target areas.

It is important to choose a measurement system that adequately reflects the target behavior, is sensitive to changes in performance, and can be implemented with relative ease. A number of different measurement systems are available. They render different kinds of information and are applicable to specific situations. The remainder of this section, "Data Collection Systems," discusses the advantages and disadvantages of each measurement system.

Frequency   The simplest system of data collection is frequency. Frequency data indicate the number of times a behavior occurred. Each time teachers observe the behavior, they can make hatch marks on an index card taped to a convenient place. Data can be collected by aides, volunteers, peers, or the target student.

Many situations lend themselves well to the frequency system. For example, the number of disruptive acts, talk-outs, out-of-seats, correct math problems, correct spelling words, and instances of tardiness can all be measured by the collection of frequency data. Frequency data should not be used in all situations. Systematic measurement devices are needed to translate behavioral occurrences so that one day's performance can be compared with another's, and so that the teacher can determine how often the behavior occurs across time.

Merely counting the frequency of the behavior, however, does not guarantee commonality of the data. Let's suppose that Liz talks back to the music teacher a lot. The teacher decides to count how many times this happens. According to the teacher's data, Liz talked back five times on Monday, Tuesday, and Wednesday, four times on Thursday, and three times on Friday. Can the teacher accurately say that Liz's performance has improved? That is impossible to determine from the data provided, for there is no indication whether session time was held constant. If music period lasted for fifty minutes on Monday, forty minutes on Tuesday and Wednesday, twenty minutes on Thursday, and only ten minutes on Friday, Liz's behavior did not improve across the week. In fact, she was even worse on Friday than Monday! This example demonstrates that if frequency data are to be kept, session time must be held constant.

A corollary is also true. If the number of correct responses is the target of interest, the number of opportunities to respond must be held constant (rather than session time). If frequency data are used in this situation, the only way to determine whether spelling accuracy increases is to keep the number of dictated spelling words the same each time.

Duration   Sometimes the important question is not "How many times does a certain behavior occur?" but rather "How long does the behavior last?" To illustrate this point, two students' tantrums were compared. Both students had two tantrums during the school day. One student's tantrums lasted a total of two minutes. In this case, the teacher decided that, for the present, no direct action was warranted, but that she would monitor the student's tantrums periodically to be certain that neither the frequency nor the duration warranted remediation. The second student presented another problem. He also had an average of only two tantrums each day, but the average time spent having tantrums over a week was forty-five minutes daily. Although this student did not have a high frequency of tantrums, the high duration indicated a need for remediation. In some cases, both the frequency *and* duration of a social behavior are of concern. When this occurs, both aspects of the target behavior can be measured concurrently.

Duration data are not difficult to obtain if the teacher has a stopwatch. Each time a tantrum begins, the teacher or another student starts the watch. When the tantrum ceases, the watch is stopped, but the accumulated time is not erased. When another tantrum begins, the stopwatch is started. The process is repeated until the observation period ends. The stopwatch reveals the amount of time the student spent having tantrums.

As with frequency data, a major precaution must be considered when keeping duration data. For the same reasons that the number of opportunities or the session time must be held constant in the frequency situation, session time must remain the same for all data collection sessions. If data are kept for the whole day or even for the morning, the time is of sufficient length so that the teacher need not be concerned that each daily recording session is equivalent to the minute. When duration data cannot be collected over an entire school day, morning, or afternoon, a precise observation time (for example, thirty minutes) should be established.

Percent   When neither frequency nor duration data can be collected appropriately because situational variables cannot be controlled, it is necessary to translate the data into a ratio so that comparisons can be made from one day's data to another. If the number of spelling words included on each test is the same, frequency data (counting the number of correctly spelled words) are appropriate. If, however, the number of words presented varies per test, the raw data must be converted to an equivalent form. A comparable situation exists for duration data. When observation time cannot be held constant, the raw data must be translated into another form to ensure that the data have meaning and can serve to evaluate and reflect changes in student performance accurately across time. Percent scores (percent correct, percent of occurrence) can serve this purpose.

This measurement system gives an indication of the quality or the accuracy of performance. Percent correct does not give information about the quantity or amount of work completed, but is a very appropriate measurement system when the accuracy of student performance is of concern.

Percent correct scores are calculated with the following formula:

$$\frac{\text{number of correct responses}}{\text{number of correct and incorrect responses}} \times 100 = \text{percent correct}$$

For example, the percent correct score for one day's spelling test is determined by dividing the number of correctly spelled words by the total number of words on the test, multiplied by 100 (to remove the decimal point). Kyle spelled four words correctly on a fifteen-word test. The percent correct score was calculated by dividing 4 by 15 and then multiplying the quotient by 100. In this case, the correct score was 27 percent.

The number of opportunities to respond affects the score a student can obtain, as does the student's performance. If there are only five questions on one social studies quiz and thirty questions on the next quiz, a student who misses only one question on each test receives vastly different percentage scores (80 percent and 97 percent, respectively). To remedy this situation, some teachers make certain that all quizzes are of sufficient length so that scores are not biased, as in the above example.

When session time is not held constant while duration data are collected, the raw data must be transformed into a ratio so the data can be compared with each other. Therefore, in these instances, two different kinds of information must be gathered for each session: the length of observation time, and the total amount of time the student is engaged in the target activity. The percentage of occurrence score is obtained with the following formula:

$$\frac{\text{number of minutes engaged in target behavior}}{\text{session time}} \times 100 = \text{percent of occurrence}$$

It should be remembered that although session time may vary from day to day when this type of percentage score is used, it is advisable to keep the observation times comparable and not allow great fluctuations.

Rate   Speed of performance is important for almost everything adults do, particularly in job situations. Unfortunately, it is an area that special education teachers often neglect, because they are so concerned with instilling student accuracy. In many academic situations, however, indication of accuracy is not sufficient to evaluate a student's true academic progress. It is possible to get every item on a test correct, but to fail academically because assignments are not completed on time. Students who are learning to become better silent readers, for example, must be able to read passages accurately, but also quickly enough to keep up with classmates. In these instances, both *accuracy* and *speed* (quality and quantity) of student performance are of vital importance.

Percent correct scores indicate the quality of a student's performance. Rate provides a measure of quantity. Together, correct rate and error rate scores show the quality *and* quantity of student achievement. As Figure 6.1 shows, percentage scores reflect only one aspect of student performance. Once a student achieves 100 percent, a ceiling is reached. It appears that the student cannot improve anymore. The rate graph of Erin's performance on the same multiplication fact worksheets reveals that

Figure 6.1

Comparison of percent correct and error rate scores for the same task

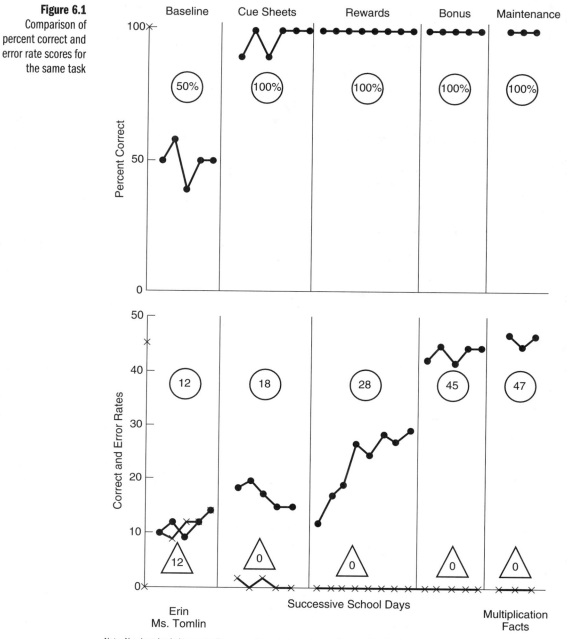

Note: Numbers in circles are median scores for each phase. Interventions are listed at the top of each phase.

her speed of performance is unsatisfactory, even though her percent correct scores are 100.

Rate is a measurement system that gives an indication of speed of performance. In oral reading, the teacher can hear each word read. In silent reading, the teacher is not able to determine how accurately the student read each word in the passage; a test of comprehension has to serve this purpose. By calculating reading rate, however, it is possible to assess students' proficiency or speed of reading. This is accomplished by dividing the number of words read during a silent reading session by the time it took to complete the passage.

There are two ways to determine the amount of time it took a student to complete a passage. One is to have the students write on a page the times they began and concluded the passage, then the teacher subtracts the start time from the stop time. Another is to provide them with stopwatches and have them start the watch when they begin reading and stop the watch when they complete the passage. The number of words read is obtained either by counting the words in the section, or by using a text with precounted passages.

In this example of students' completing a passage, it is impossible to gain information about the quality and quantity of performance by using one measurement system. Percent of comprehension questions answered correctly and rate of silent reading have to be used. For many academic areas, however, it is possible to gain an indication of speed of performance and accuracy through the use of one measurement system, such as correct and error rates. Oral reading, calculation of math facts, and other job skills lend themselves well to the correct and error rate measurement system.

Unlike percent correct, in which only one score per evaluation session is sufficient, two scores per session are required for correct and error rate. With percent, the correct percentage score is inversely related to the incorrect percentage score. A perfect score is always 100 percent and never more than that; it is impossible to obtain a correct percentage score of 150 percent. Therefore, if the correct percentage score is 90 percent, the error percentage score is 10 percent. If the correct percentage score is 60 percent, the error percentage score is 40 percent. Correct and error rate scores are not so related. Error rate scores for an entire school week can be zero and the correct rates can be different each day (Monday's correct rate was 30, the error rate was 0; Tuesday's correct rate was 45, error rate 0; Wednesday's correct rate 46, error rate 0; Thursday's correct rate 42, error rate 0; Friday's correct rate 55, error rate 0). Although it might be impossible for a correct rate to go above a certain level, that is a function of the target area and not the measurement system itself. For example, it is possible to read silently at a rate of 300 words per minute, to read orally at a correct rate of 175, and to calculate 75 math facts per minute. One might even surpass these scores, while one cannot surpass 100 percent.

Correct and error rates can be calculated with these two formulas:

$$\frac{\text{number of correct responses}}{\text{session time (minutes)}} = \text{correct rate}$$

$$\frac{\text{number of incorrect responses}}{\text{session time (minutes)}} = \text{error rate}$$

Since the correct and error rate measurement system is commonly employed in oral reading, that situation is used for illustration. Jennie was a poor reader and her teacher decided that until substantial changes in her reading skills were noted, Jennie's reading progress would be monitored daily. Each day, Jennie read orally to her teacher from her assigned basal text for five minutes. As Jennie read, the teacher marked those words read incorrectly in her copy of the text. At the conclusion of the session, the teacher counted the number of errors made and the number of correctly read words. On one day, Jennie read a total of 205 words correctly and made 15 errors. These raw data were calculated into correct and error rate scores by dividing by five minutes (session time). Therefore, the correct rate for this day was 41 (205 ÷ 5 = 41 correct words per minute) and the error rate was 3 (15 ÷ 5 = 3 incorrect words per minute). Both scores were necessary to evaluate Jennie's progress, because they are not dependent on each other (the knowledge of one score does not yield the information necessary to determine the other). It is possible for her correct rate scores to increase, decrease, or stay the same, while her error rate scores stay the same, decrease, or increase.

Table 6.2 summarizes those data collection systems teachers are most likely to employ. They range in sophistication from frequency to rate and can be applied appropriately in social and academic situations.

Data Calculations and Analyses

Once data are gathered, it is necessary to perform several calculations to render the data more meaningful. When the effectiveness of an intervention strategy is being evaluated, comparative scores can be useful. It is important to be able to compare a student's performance in one condition to the next, so that a judgment about whether or not a procedure should be discontinued can be made. The following discussions center on those calculations that give the data referents.

Central Tendency   There are three different ways to calculate **central tendency** for the data within a condition: mean, median, and mode. The mode is the score

Measurement system	Definition	Formula	Limitations
Frequency	The number of occurrences; how often the behavior occurs	Count or tally	Session time or number of opportunities must be held constant
Duration	The total amount of time the individual engages in an activity; how long the behavior lasts	Cumulative time; time of each episode added together	Session time must be held constant
Percent correct	The ratio between correct and incorrect responses	$\frac{\text{no. of correct responses}}{\text{no. of correct + incorrect responses}} \times 100$	Data are biased by the number of opportunities—only an indication of accuracy with no indication of quantity or speed of performance
Percent of occurrence	The ratio between the amount of time the student engages in the target activity and session time	$\frac{\text{no. of minutes engaged in the target activity}}{\text{session time}} \times 100$	Data are biased if some sessions are very short in length
Rate	The speed at which an activity is performed, stated as a per-minute score	$\frac{\text{no. of responses}}{\text{time}}$	Sheer rate provides no indication of quality of performance, only quantity
Correct rate and error rate	The number of correct and error responses made per minute	$\frac{\text{no. of correct responses}}{\text{session time}}$ $\frac{\text{no. of incorrect responses}}{\text{session time}}$	Correct rate and error rate cannot be used alone; both scores must be kept per session

Table 6.2
Summary of Data Collection Systems

occurring most often and one that serves no purpose for the evaluation of student performance. The mean and median are, however, useful measures. The mean is the average score (total of all scores within a condition, divided by the number of scores). The median is the middle score by rank order; with practice, it is very simple to determine. First, count the number of scores in the condition. Divide that by two to determine which place is in the middle. Using rank order (not temporal sequence), count until you reach that place. The score in the middle place is the median. See Figure 6.2 for examples.

Another way to determine the median score follows the same general theme, but instead of using a raw data sheet (and the actual scores), the teacher uses graphed data. In this second method, the teacher again counts the number of scores in a phase, but then uses the horizontal lines on the graph to help determine the rank order of the scores. See Figure 6.3 for an example.

A score representing central tendency, *either* a mean *or* median, should be calculated for each set of scores for every condition. If correct and error rate scores are used, then two scores of central tendency are calculated for each condition.

Trend   Although we give no details here about precise ways of calculating **trend lines,** it is important to consider the trend or direction of the data when evaluating a student. Data can follow three basic trends: they can increase, decrease, or be flat. One reason that it is not sufficient to use only the mean or median is illustrated in Figure 6.3. In A, the median scores for each condition are the same—18; the profile shown is that which most people envision when the medians or means are the same for two conditions. The two conditions shown in B also have the same median scores, but the trends and interpretation of the data are different. C reveals an entirely different situation. If one considers only the central tendency scores for each condition, one could conclude that the student improved greatly from one condition to the next. When one considers the *trend,* however, one sees that there is no improvement at all, only a maintenance of the trend initiated in the first condition. Both the scores of cen-

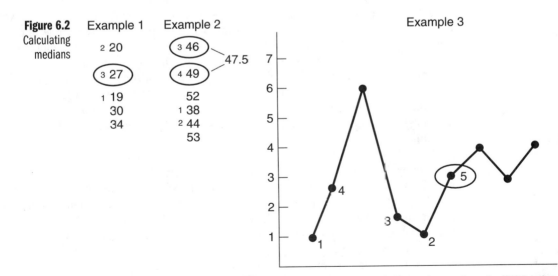

Figure 6.2
Calculating medians

Note: In Example 1, there are five scores; the third (27) score is the median. In Example 2, there are six scores; the median (47.5) is halfway between scores 3 and 4. In Example 3, there are nine scores; the fifth score (3) is the median.

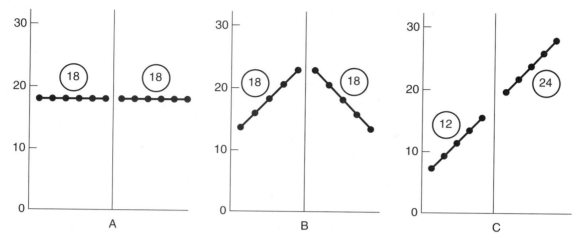

Figure 6.3
Possible combinations of data trends and middle scores and their relation to interpretation of results

Note: It is important to note the central tendency (mean or median) for each condition, but the trend of the data should also be considered. In A, no improvement across conditions was noted. In B, the central tendency scores for both conditions are the same, but the trends of the data are different: in this case, the student's performance worsened. In C, the student's performance improved across conditions; the trend indicates that the improvement continued during the second condition. The intervention scheduled during the second condition cannot be credited for the improvement indicated by the changes in central tendency scores.

tral tendency and the trend or direction of the data must be considered before declaring a tactic successful, because of the changes noted from one condition to the next.

Figure 6.4 shows examples of possible variations in correct and error rate trend patterns. These patterns are important to note for analysis purposes. Figure 6.4 also illustrates that correct rate and error rate scores are independent of one another. Correct rate scores are indicated by dots; error rate scores are indicated by Xs. The top row of graphs (A, B, and C) displays data that indicate student improvement. In case A, the student's error rate scores are remaining the same. In case B, the reverse is true; the student is making fewer errors, while not showing any change in correct performance. Case C is what every teacher wishes for: overall improvement in both measures of performance. In the middle row of graphs (D, E, and F), the students are not improving at all. In case D, both sets of scores are remaining static. In case E, both correct and error rate scores are accelerating at approximately the same pace; the student is merely doing his or her work faster. In the last graph, case F, the student is slowing down across time, but proportionally. The quality of performance has not improved as overall production has vastly decreased. The bottom row of examples (cases G, H, and I) are all those instances teachers hope not to see. In case G, correct rate scores are remaining static while the error rate scores are accelerating, and in case H, the student's error rates are remaining the same, but correct rates are rapidly decelerating. The last example is every teacher's nightmare. The student started out performing the task relatively well on the first day of measurement, but performance deteriorated across time so that by the final day, the student's error rate score exceeded the correct rate score.

The importance of examining both scores should become apparent as one looks only at the correct rates for case E. The correct rate scores were increasing and one might feel that the student's performance was improving. When one evaluates the

Figure 6.4
Patterns of possible
correct rate and
error rate

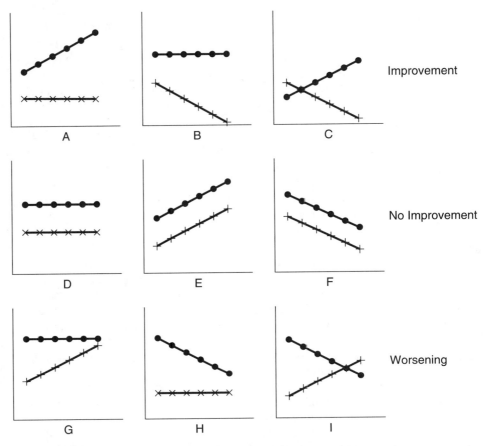

Note: Correct rate scores (dots) and error rate scores (Xs) are not reciprocal; one set of scores may decrease, while the other set may also decrease, stay at the same level, or increase. In the top row, all three graphs indicate improvement, although the data patterns differ. In the second row, all three graphs indicate no improvement. In the bottom row, performance is worsening.

error rate scores, however, one finds the contrary to be true. If one were to study the error rate pattern that appears in case F, one might feel that the student's performance was improving, for the error rate scores are decreasing. When the correct rate scores also are considered, however, one can see that the student is not getting any better at all. From these examples, one can see that although correct and error rate information are gathered simultaneously, they are not dependent measures: Both are needed to evaluate student performance accurately when quality and quantity (proficiency) of student performance is of concern.

Aim Scores   There are two general types of **aim scores** possible for individual students: long-term and short-term. The long-term goal for a student might be to read fast enough to keep up with classmates in the in-class reading assignments in social studies, since the student's present functioning level is far below that level. Therefore, several goals (and aim scores) are established for this student: one that is attainable in the near future and one that is the ultimate aim. In fact, as student performance improves, a number of short-term aims might be established in the course of reaching the final goal.

Sometimes aim scores are referred to as levels of mastery. In percent situations, teachers often demand three days above 90 percent before moving the student to a new task. Some even require three consecutive days at 100 percent. Why these particular criteria are used, no one knows. Keeping some pupils from learning new skills because they cannot obtain three consecutive 100 percent scores does not seem pragmatic. The teacher should judge what the aim score should be for an individual and what information should he learned. It is important, however, for the teacher to make such a determination before or while initiating instruction.

Aim scores also are used in rate situations. Many refer to these aim scores as **desired rates.** In general, students should be able to function with their classmates. One way to determine aim scores is to test the skills of sample students from the regular classroom to which the student is returning or is a member. If members of the regular class calculate math facts at a rate of 40 correct facts per minute, the target student should be able to do about the same. Otherwise, the student cannot succeed in this situation.

Criteria for Change of Phase   There should be two different criteria for concluding a **phase:** failure of a tactic or attainment of the aim score. It is vital to instructional planning to know when a tactic is insufficiently effective or totally ineffective. Sometimes an intervention does not work for a particular student; after three days of very little or no change in the data, another intervention should be scheduled. In some cases, an intervention is effective for a while, but then ceases to be. In such instances, it is important to know when substantial change is not occurring so that another intervention can be added to or substituted for the first. Some criteria guidelines are available. Change the intervention if the data are flat or worsening after three days of instruction (some teachers wait a week). Change the intervention objective if the aim is reached two out of three consecutive days. Of course, other guidelines can be developed. The important point is to establish guidelines so that ineffective procedures are not followed too long.

When criterion for mastery or the aim score is reached and maintained for several days, new procedures should be implemented. If the aim score is reached during an intervention condition, it is advisable to discontinue the intervention procedures to determine whether the student can remain at the desired levels of performance without the help of the intervention procedure. If the preestablished aim score level is maintained, it is time to move on to the next step in the instructional sequence.

Data Display

Data gathered on student performance are easier to evaluate if transformed into a visual display as they are collected. When data are presented graphically, analysis becomes obvious and evaluation almost automatic. In fact, students have been known to improve their performance after seeing such graphs.

Data should be graphed when collected and not after long intervals. Many times, the need to change intervention strategies becomes apparent only when the data are displayed visually. Time lost because data were not analyzed cannot be justified.

Raw Data Form   As data are being collected, scores describing student performance (math worksheets, spelling tests, pages of creative writing) can soon be overwhelming; it is advisable to transpose the data to one sheet of paper for easy reference. The same is true for other products of student performance that do not leave a permanent record (oral reading, social behavior, and oral language). In these cases, it is even more important that data be stored in a convenient place in an orderly fashion. A sample data sheet appears in Figure 6.5. Other versions can be developed to suit individuals and specific learning situations better.

Setting Up a Graph   Student performance data are displayed most conveniently on a graph. Several different kinds of graph paper are available. The most commonly used is the standard arithmetic graph paper available in most bookstores. Some teachers prefer using semilogarithmic graph paper when charting rate data, but as can be seen in Figure 6.6, an arithmetic grid is acceptable for graphing rates. We now discuss standard procedures to follow when setting up a graph, such a labeling the axis and noting preestablished criteria.

The scores are shown on the *ordinate,* or vertical axis (a line that goes up and down). The axis must be labeled with the name of the measurement system used (frequency, duration, percent correct, rate per minute), and hatch marks should be noted

Figure 6.5
Sample raw data sheet

Student's name _____   Subject area _____

Teacher's name _____   Specific target _____

Data D/M/Y	Day	Number		Percent Correct	Time	Rate	
		Correct	Error			Correct	Error
/ /	M						
	T						
	W						
	T						
	F						
/ /	M						
	T						
	W						
	T						
	F						
/ /	M						
	T						
	W						
	T						
	F						
/ /	M						
	T						
	W						
	T						
	F						

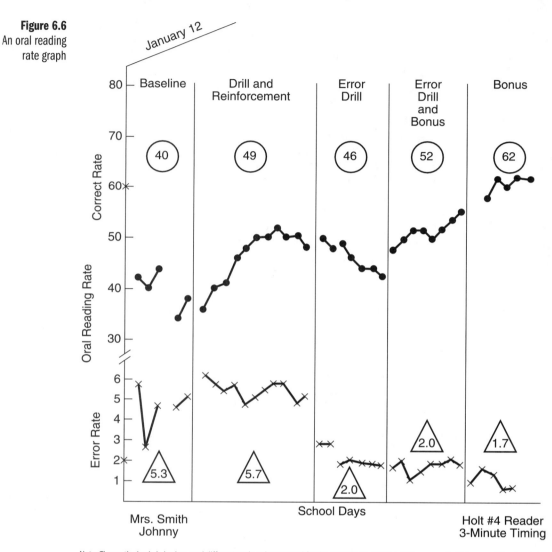

Figure 6.6
An oral reading rate graph

Note: The vertical axis is broken, and different scale units are used for the correct rate (dots) and the error rate (Xs) scores. The aim scores for each are indicated by stars on the vertical axis. Each condition is labeled to indicate the procedures in effect. Also, central tendency scores for each condition are noted. Because daily correct rate and error rates were calculated, two central tendency scores appear for each condition. The correct rate central tendencies are circled; error rates are shown inside large triangles.

for quick reference when plotting specific scores (for example, 25, 50, 75, and 100 for percent; 5, 10, 15, and 20 for frequency).

If rate is the measure chosen, a special arrangement of the vertical axis may be required. If a student's correct and error rate scores are close together, there is no need for any change in the vertical axis. Most often, the correct rate scores cluster in one area of the graph and the error rate scores in another. In the typical arrangement of a graph, changes in correct rate scores are clearly visible.

Error rate scores can present a different problem, however. A number of plots are possible between a score of one and zero (.2, .1, .5). Without some adjustment of the vertical axis, changes in error rate performance go unnoticed. For this reason, many teachers break the vertical axis into two parts: one for the correct rate scores, and one for the error rate scores. The correct rate axis must be deep enough to allow for change in performance, both positive and negative. Therefore, it is advisable to get an estimate of a student's correct rate performance before making the graph.

Teachers can determine the arrangement of the vertical axis for error rate scores by looking at student performance and the possible scores. If a student initially makes about ten errors per minute, room must be left for scores of ten and those slightly above that level. Also, the teacher should provide a place to enter a zero score and room for those scores that can fall between zero and one (.5, .2). A sample rate graph is shown in Figure 6.6.

Session days are represented on the *abscissa,* or horizontal axis (a line that goes across the page). This axis is labeled in accordance with the frequency of data collection. If the teacher is in a resource room and sees the student only three times a week, the abscissa is labeled "Session days." If data are collected daily, the horizontal axis is labeled "School days." Some teachers like to see the days of each week cluster together. To accomplish this, the horizontal axis is labeled "Successive calendar days," and day lines are held for Saturday and Sunday, although they are never used.

Once the abscissa is labeled, the days are represented by vertical lines that cross the horizontal axis. If "School days" is the label chosen, the lines representing Monday, Tuesday, Wednesday, and so on, always represent those days. If a student was absent on Monday, that day line is left open and Tuesday's data are plotted on the line designated for Tuesday.

It is necessary to have the following information clearly visible on every graph so that one student's chart is not confused with another's or a math chart is not thought to be a chart for reading. The teacher's name should be on the graph. If more than one person teaches the student, their names should also appear somewhere on the chart. The homeroom teacher's name always should be noted to facilitate compilation of a student's graphs for any given year. Besides the names of the teacher(s) and the student, information about the target behavior sufficient to distinguish one graph from another is necessary. In some cases, a brief notation such as "oral reading from the Holt #4 reader" is enough; in other situations, more information is needed about the target behavior and materials used.

The date for the first data plot should be indicated on the graph. Often, it is desirable to indicate the day line that stands for the first data day of each month.

Along the vertical axis, additional data notations can appear. It is helpful to both student and teacher to place stars on the vertical axis at the levels of the short-term aim scores. The notations and aim scores for both correct and error rates appear on the sample graph shown in Figure 6.6.

Entering Data on Graph   Data plots are placed on a graph in such a way that the scores fall directly *on* day lines (vertical lines) and at the appropriate gradients as indicated on the vertical axis. The score of 12 percent is placed on the day line for the day on which it was collected at the correct level for 12 percent—between the 10 percent and 15 percent designated places.

Plots are connected within a phase or condition. When a student is absent, that day line is left blank and the plots preceding and subsequent to the absence are *not* connected. No-chance days (hearing test, fire drill, field trip, teacher lost the data) are noted on the graph with a blank day line, but the data before and after a no-chance day *are* connected.

If Saturday and Sunday day lines are included in a graph, they are left blank, because no data are collected on these days. In this situation, Friday and Monday plots are *not* connected, so a week's set of data cluster together visually. If the graph is labeled "School days," there are no day lines to represent Saturday and Sunday, and the Friday and Monday data plots *are* connected.

If correct rate and error rate are used as the measures of performance, two plots appear on each day line, one for each rate. To distinguish these two sets of data, a dot is used to indicate correct rate and an X is used for the error rate score. Correct rate plots are connected only to other correct rates, and the error rates are connected only to error rates. An example is provided in Figure 6.6.

A change in condition is indicated by a solid vertical line drawn between the two day lines that represent the last plot for one condition and the first plot for a new condition. This line is referred to as a **phase change line** and separates the data from two different conditions. To separate the data from two phases visually, plots are *not* connected across phase change lines. Also, each phase is labeled so the teacher quickly can recall the procedures used in each different phase.

To indicate central tendency, either the mean or median must be calculated for each condition and each set of scores. After the calculations are completed at the conclusion of each phase, the score is entered on the graph in the middle of the phase, but not in such a way that it covers the data. Usually, a large circle is drawn around it. If correct rate and error rate scores are used, there are two central tendency scores per phase. The correct rate central tendency score is placed in a large, open circle, while the error rate central tendency score is placed in a large, open triangle.

Checklist   To ensure that all the steps necessary to construct a meaningful evaluation graph are completed, a checklist is provided in Table 6.3. This checklist also serves as a summary of this section of the chapter.

Procedures for Pairing Instruction and Evaluation

The section on curriculum-based assessment has served as an overview of the procedures teachers follow to evaluate the intervention strategies they select for individual students. These evaluation procedures test such influences by judging the amount of progress made or not made in a given situation. When pairing instruction and evaluation, teachers follow a general (although clearly not linear) sequence of steps, as they establish the structure necessary to evaluate instruction. A general delineation of those steps follows.

Prebaseline

During the prebaseline stage of the evaluation process, teachers seek answers to some fundamental questions. What instructional objectives need remediation? Which and what level of materials should be utilized? Which measurement system should be selected?

Teachers can answer these critical questions through systematic observation and testing. They can use an initial curriculum-based assessment to determine which

Table 6.3
Checklist for
Constructing
Evaluation Graphs

Done

1. Set up graph.
____   a. Draw abscissa line (horizontal axis).
____   b. Draw ordinate line (vertical axis).
____   c. Label abscissa.
____   d. Label ordinate.
____   e. Note target (spelling, etc.; indicate material used).
____   f. Note teacher's name.
____   g. Note student's name.
____   h. Date graph.
____   i. Note aim score(s).
2. Calculate data.
____   a. Set up raw data sheet.
____   b. Calculate scores.
3. Plot data.
____   a. Place plot(s) on appropriate day line.
____   b. Connect plots for successive data days.
____   c. Do not connect plots if student was absent.
____   d. Connect plots for no-chance days.
____   e. Note phase changes with a solid vertical line.
____   f. Label phase.
4. Analyze data.
____   a. Calculate either mean or median scores by condition.
____   b. Enter scores of central tendency on graph for each phase.

instructional objectives need remediation. Once the teachers has identified the instructional objectives and determined the level of the student's performance, it is easier to select the measurement and evaluation design.

Before formal data collection procedures are implemented, a number of other details must be handled. First, a consistent time and place for data collection must be established. Formats for data collection and analysis must be designed. A raw data sheet must be developed. A graph should be set up to reflect the needs of the data system.

Baseline

During the baseline step and all of the steps that follow, data are collected and plotted regularly using probes. Systematic and frequent assessment of the student's performance is conducted to obtain knowledge about the characteristics of the target behavior. The student's initial performance levels are judged against a long-range aim score, and a short-term aim is established. After systematically observing the student's performance the teacher can choose an initial intervention strategy. Criteria for change of phase are set. Once the teacher feels confident that she or he understands the student and his or her performance characteristics, a central tendency score is calculated and the baseline phase terminated.

Intervention Conditions

During instructional conditions, the student is learning to perform a target objective at more desirable levels of performance or is learning not to exhibit undesirable behavior. During **intervention conditions,** a specific intervention procedure is applied systematically and consistently each day of instruction. Again, evaluation data are collected, plotted, and analyzed to ensure that desired changes in student performance continually occur. If a tactic loses its effectiveness, and meets the criteria for change of phase, another tactic is added to the first, or a new strategy is scheduled. The changes in procedures are submitted to the same evaluation system. Once the desired change is achieved, the aim score or mastery criterion reached, and a score of central tendency calculated, the intervention procedures are discontinued.

Maintenance

The last phase of daily or frequent data collection is designed to ensure the **maintenance** of the desired level of performance without the intervention strategy. Can the student perform the task on his or her own? This is the ultimate test of the teaching procedures implemented. Once the student demonstrates mastery or achievement of the aim score, frequent testing of the target behavior can be stopped.

Posttest

After the target skill is learned and maintained, it is important to be certain that it remains at the desired levels. Therefore, weekly **posttests** are recommended for a while, followed by monthly posttests for the remainder of the school year. It is important to monitor student performance, for the monitoring process in and of itself can facilitate retention.

• •

Teacher Observation and Analysis Assessment

As you read, think about . . .

1. Observing a student and collecting anecdotal notes for a period of time.
2. Designing a work sample analysis data collection form for analyzing a specific skill.
3. Recording the processes explained by a student during a "think-aloud" assessment session and analyzing the effect of the strategies.
4. Observing a student for an hour, maintaining an antecedent behavior consequence log, and analyzing the data.

In addition to the data collection systems discussed earlier in this chapter, specific observational and analytical assessment techniques can be used to gather further information about students' academic and social progress. Anecdotal logs, antecedent behavior consequence analysis, observational recording, work sample analysis, and "think-aloud" procedures can yield useful information and, when coupled with more precise data, can produce a learning profile of the student, target specific concerns, and document progress. These data techniques may be more sensitive than the other data collection systems to factors that could be interfering with or contributing to the learning process. Additionally, these data techniques can shed light on inefficient strategies that students might be using in the learning process. We offer a discussion of each technique.

Anecdotal Logs

Historically, teachers kept information about their students in **anecdotal logs.** Most often such records were kept in diary format through an abbreviated narrative; naughty or otherwise unacceptable social behavior was noted at the end of the school day (see Figure 6.7 for an example).

Although teachers made attempts to keep daily records of student behavior, the value of the information was questionable. Because the notes were taken at the end of the day, the recollections of a tired teacher over a six-hour period had to be trusted. The accuracy and detail of these records were suspect at best, for they depended on the teacher's memory and subjective feelings. Although the reliability of the measurement is in doubt, a busy teacher can use this system initially. The teacher should note occurrences of certain behaviors to determine whether their frequency is sufficient to warrant the scheduling of a complex data collection system.

Antecedent Behavior Consequence (ABC) Analysis

A more sophisticated form of anecdotal record keeping is available for monitoring social behavior as it naturally occurs. The **Antecedent Behavior Consequence (ABC) analysis** method lends some structure and organization to the collection of observational information. Instead of relying on recollection at the end of a school day or an academic period, the teacher is required to keep a record of classroom or playground events *as they occur.* The notations are organized on a time basis. Events that precede the target behavior, or **antecedent events,** are noted in the first column of a prepared form (see Figure 6.8). The behavior of concern for a target student is marked in the middle column, and **consequent events,** or events occurring subsequent to the behavior, are indicated in the last column.

This system is helpful when teachers are attempting to specify exactly what problem behavior should be considered for remediation. For example, a teacher often indi-

Figure 6.7
Anecdotal records
for recording
behavioral
information

Figure 6.8
ABC analysis
reporting form

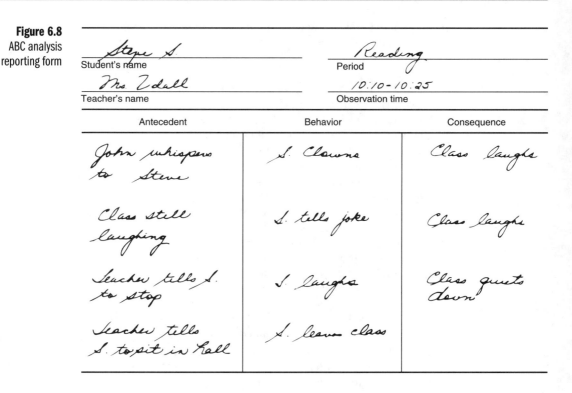

Student's name _Steve S._   Period _Reading_

Teacher's name _Mrs. Udall_   Observation time _10:10–10:25_

Antecedent	Behavior	Consequence
John whispers to Steve	S. clowns	Class laughs
Class still laughing	S. tells joke	Class laughs
Teacher tells S. to stop	S. laughs	Class quiets down
Teacher tells S. to sit in hall	S. leaves class	

cates that a student is "aggressive," but is not certain about the forms the student's aggression takes, the frequency of such acts, the victims of the aggression, or what events tend to stimulate these episodes.

After watching an aggressive student on the playground for several days and keeping a record of his behavior using this format, one teacher was able to define the behavior more precisely. Bill's aggression, for example, consisted of distinct components: not following the rules of the game, hitting and kicking others, and swearing. By counting the number of times each of these categories of behavior occurred, the teacher had a rough estimate of the frequency of occurrences and which was the most prevalent.

The ABC analysis method of note taking also yields additional useful information. Other children who are directly or indirectly involved in the target student's acts of aggression can be identified. For example, Bill only exhibited aggressive behavior when Tom and Susie were present, and Pete most frequently was the victim. Information about other students who might be contributing to the situation can help the teacher take steps to reduce aggressive occurrences in the future. Also, certain environmental situations tend to be present when the aggressive acts occur. In Bill's case, the probability of trouble increased when he was playing baseball. The variables contributing to problematic behavioral episodes are almost infinite in number, but being cognizant of their presence and their interactive capabilities certainly facilitates the selection of an appropriate intervention strategy.

Both forms of anecdotal notes, the traditional log and the ABC analysis, are useful initially to pinpoint and define social behaviors. However, both methods are too cumbersome to implement for a long period of time, because they require the teacher to make records of behavior in longhand and do not allow for quick review of behavioral changes noted over days, weeks, or months. Once the target behavior is identified, the teacher should select a measurement system to evaluate changes in student performance.

Observational Recording

This data collection system was designed to evaluate social behavior through the observation of students' actions and interactions. Only a brief discussion follows because these procedures require the use of outside personnel and are too complex for busy teachers to implement alone. Readers who require more details about **observational measurement systems** should refer to References and Suggested Readings at the end of this chapter. Although classroom teachers are not likely to select one of these complex systems, they should be aware of their existence and characteristics, for situations might arise warranting their use.

There are essentially two versions of observational recording systems: continuous and sampling. In the continuous system, data are kept for a period of time and everything occurring in that period is recorded through the use of observational codes. This system provides a complete "transcript" of the behavioral incident that transpires during the prescribed time. The difficulties involved with collecting, and analyzing the voluminous amount of data generated using this system, are enormous. Computerized data collection systems are available in which a data collector can enter information about the target environment into a tape recorder, which allows for computerized analysis later.

Time sampling procedures have been used and refined over a long period of time. The sampling method does not require all incidents to be recorded, but requires events to be recorded during slices of time. In these cases, fixed time samples might be used. For example, an hour can be divided into twelve five-minute intervals. At the end of every five minutes, the teacher could count the number of children out of their seats. The teacher averages the number of children who were out of their seats each of the twelve times. This average comprises the day's data.

Since the teacher is not able to collect the data and teach concurrently, outside personnel are necessary to ensure that the data are collected accurately and reliably. One suggestion is to seek help from a neighboring college's psychology or special education department, after gaining permission from the school's administration.

Work Sample Analysis

"Work sample analysis is used to study the correct and incorrect responses made in a student's work" (McLoughlin & Lewis, 1995, p. 9). Teachers can examine student work to identify types and frequencies of errors. This information can help teachers establish instructional objectives or select a new intervention.

The most common type of work sample analysis is **error analysis.** Researchers (e.g., Ashlock, 1986; Enright, 1983) have documented the importance of knowing the types of errors students make and planning subsequent instruction to remediate the problems.

Error analysis is easy to conduct. The teacher (1) examines work sample products, (2) documents error types, (3) asks students to explain how they arrived at an erroneous solution, and (4) makes instructional recommendations. For instance, in mathematics, the teacher could (1) examine story problems completed by students, (2) record the percentage correct, (3) examine each problem to determine types of errors (e.g., erroneous computation, incorrect diagram to depict information, incorrect use of "key word" technique), (4) ask students to explain how the problems were solved, and (5) identify additional instructional objectives, based on the error types and student explanations. In oral reading, the teacher could record error types (e.g., substitutions, omissions, additions), record the number of errors, and if the number of incorrect responses is significant, plan a remedial program.

The error analysis procedure can produce good information for designing the instructional program. The important piece is to be sure to ask students to explain their answers. Through careful analysis of work samples coupled with student explanations, teachers can pinpoint faulty conceptual or procedural knowledge that can then be remediated.

"Think-Aloud" Interviews

A "think-aloud" interview is a type of process assessment aimed at identifying, as much as possible, the cognitive strategies students use to solve mathematics problems (McLoughlin & Lewis, 1995), comprehend reading material, solve a social problem, conduct a science experiment, and so forth. In the think-aloud interview, students are asked to share their thought process as they perform a task. Interview questions might include: (1) "What are you thinking?" (2) "How will you solve this task or problem?" (3) "What is another way to solve the problem?" (4) "What do you think the answer might be and why do you think that?" and (5) "How would you explain this problem to another student?"

Several factors must be present for the think-aloud interview to be used appropriately. First, teachers must be good observers of student performance. Second, they must be knowledgeable about the scope and sequence of curriculum. Third, teachers must be familiar with cognitive strategies (McLoughlin & Lewis, 1995). For example, if a student is asked to explain (think out loud) how to add a group of four blocks to a group of five blocks, and the student puts the two groups together and then starts counting from one to arrive at the answer, the teacher knows that this student must be assessed (interviewed) further to determine knowledge of numbers and groups, and to assess ability with the "count on" addition strategy (counting by a designated number such as 2, 3, 5). Some of the interview questions might include, "What is an easier way to count all the blocks besides starting with one?" and (given five blocks) "What different arrangements can you make with the blocks to show five?"

Through the "think-aloud" interview procedure, the teacher can begin to understand how the student is approaching the problem or task, and what strategies the student is using. This information may lead the teacher to develop new instructional objectives or to change the intervention. Along with other data, the interview information can help teachers better understand the processes students use to solve problems or tasks and the effectiveness of these processes.

The final section of this chapter focuses on portfolio assessment, in which the teacher collects a variety of student work and makes decisions about students' progress over a period of time.

● ●

Portfolio Assessment

As you read, think about . . .

1. Describing the reasons for the popularity of portfolio assessment.
2. Explaining ways in which portfolio assessment can be used with other traditional methods of assessment and with the evaluation procedures described above.
3. Describing hypothetical content for portfolio assessment in three academic content areas.
4. Explaining the cautions associated with portfolio assessment.

A great deal of interest has been generated in portfolio assessment as a means of monitoring student learning and evaluating the effectiveness of instructional programs and decision making (e.g., Paulson, Paulson, & Meyer, 1991; Swicegood, 1994; Valencia, 1990; Wolf, 1991). Portfolio assessment is defined as "a purposeful collection of student work that exhibits the student's efforts, progress, and achievements in one or more areas. The collection should include student participation in selecting content, the criteria for selection, the criteria for judging merit, and evidence of student self-reflection" (Paulson et al., p. 60).

Portfolio assessment is being used to examine student progress as it relates to curricular objectives and instructional methods, to focus more on process rather than just on product, to measure more directly student academic achievement and classroom learning, and to assist teachers in evaluating the effectiveness of their instruction (Wesson & King, 1992). Recently, portfolio assessment (e.g., Paulson et al., 1991; Swicegood, 1994) has received widespread interest as a viable means of establishing an index of student learning and evaluating the effectiveness of instructional programs and decision making.

Although complete agreement is lacking on what constitutes portfolio assessment (e.g., some researchers equate educational portfolios to artists' portfolios, while other researchers argue the differences between instructional and assessment portfolios; descriptions of portfolio content and format vary) (Nolet, 1992), certain characteristics emerge frequently in portfolio descriptions. Those characteristics are discussed in terms of content selection and analysis.

Content Selection

The main purpose of portfolio assessment is to document student progress and guide instructional decision making on a regular basis in a particular content area. Therefore, the items selected for portfolio assessment should: be a valid reflection of the curricular goals, be done on a designated time line, include student products and processes that are derived from different instructional techniques, and represent a variety of situations (e.g., contrived and spontaneous) in which student work is generated (Rivera, 1994).

For students with learning and behavior problems, the items selected for inclusion in the portfolio should relate to curricular goals and objectives contained in the Individualized Education Program (IEP), which typically include academic and social skills. Measures of behavior and adaptive functioning, academic and literacy growth, strategic learning and self-regulation, and language and cultural aspects could be included in the portfolio and linked to the IEP (Swicegood, 1994). Portfolio assessment should include data that portray student progress in the designated curriculum when specific instructional procedures have been implemented. Examples of data that may be contained in the portfolio include "raw data" (e.g., essays, a handwriting paper, a set of story problems, a tape of oral reading, a poem, math problems); "summarizing data" (e.g., inventories, norm-referenced tests, rating scales) for evaluation purposes (Valencia, 1990); and curriculum-based data (e.g., anecdotal notes, ABC logs, academic graphs) (Wesson & King, 1992).

Analysis

Students with learning and behavior problems typically lack specific academic skills and effective cognitive strategies to promote efficient learning. Therefore, portfolio assessment should include examples of completed products (e.g., math problems) with analyses that document the types of strategies employed. For instance, samples of completed story problems could be part of a portfolio assessment. The problems could be analyzed in terms of (1) correct or incorrect answers, (2) computational skills, (3) reading errors, (4) syntactical errors, (5) the strategy used to solve the problem, and (6) visual aids (e.g., tallies, pictures, graphs). Teachers could use think-aloud, observation, and error analysis to assess the product and process to determine problem-solving strengths and weaknesses. This information could be recorded in the portfolio and used often to document student progress.

Frequent measures of student progress can assist teachers in monitoring learning and implementing decision-making criteria. For example, fluency in oral reading could be measured (timed) twice weekly to determine the effect of the instructional intervention. The teacher could collect rate data and conduct an analysis of student growth. Decisions regarding rate of student progress could be implemented and a graph of progress could be stored in the portfolio until reading fluency is timed again. Portfolio items should be collected and assessed frequently to determine if instructional techniques are indeed promoting student academic growth.

Teachers usually include in portfolios samples of work generated under different conditions. These data could be useful in discerning under which conditions each student with a learning difficulty functions best. For example, cooperative learning and peer tutoring are two popular instructional arrangements, but teachers must keep anecdotal notes, samples of work, and student self-reflections (self-reports about their progress) to ensure that all students are making progress academically and socially. As the range of academic skills and the diversity of learning styles increase, teachers must use valid assessment practices to ensure that all students profit from instruction. Different types of accommodations, adaptations, and compensatory techniques should be specified and used to make frequent decisions about effective learning conditions. For younger students, portfolio assessment can be used to monitor and document academic and social learning, whereas with older students, transition and vocational assessments can be analyzed as well. Tips for Teachers presents guidelines for developing and implementing of classroom portfolios.

Tips for Teachers

Guidelines for Developing and Using Portfolio Assessment

1. Decide who will be involved in developing the portfolio.
2. Decide the purposes of the portfolio: to show growth over time, to show the student's error patterns and corrections, to trace the developmental steps of a

project, or to document strategies and instructional arrangements used when a product was developed.

3. Decide the curricular focus of the portfolio. Specify the goals and objectives.
4. Involve the student in collecting and analyzing the work.
5. Design on a storage and management system for the students' portfolios.
6. Develop a communication system with parents so that portfolios can be viewed and discussed.
7. Establish evaluation criteria for analyzing student work. ▪

Cautions and Considerations

Although we acknowledge the potential merits of portfolio assessment as a means of evaluating student mastery of IEP annual goals, instructional objectives, and instructional effectiveness, we also recommend that teachers use portfolio assessment judiciously. As Valencia (1990) notes, "If the goals of instruction are not specified, portfolios have the potential to become unfocused holding files for odds and ends, or worse, a place to collect more isolated skills tests" (p. 339). We would add the need for systematic data analysis and linkage to the IEP. Additionally, teachers of students with learning and behavior problems are advised to consider some of the issues typically raised with portfolio assessment. Coutinho and Malouf (1993) point out that "relatively little is known about the use of this approach with students with disabilities, the implications of large-scale performance assessment programs for these students, and the role of special educators in implementing the approach" (p. 63).

Perhaps the most often discussed concern and consideration in the portfolio assessment literature is the limited empirical support that validates portfolio assessment as a technically sound procedure for making instructional decisions about student progress (Herman, 1992). Questions have been raised about the reliability of scoring procedures and the validity of some items found in portfolios purporting to document progress in a particular academic area. It is often unclear how much a portfolio must contain to reflect student strengths and weaknesses or to measure progress adequately.

Studies need to be conducted with students who have learning and behavior problems to determine (1) the effectiveness of portfolio assessment; (2) the role of student self-reflection in the process; (3) content items that are beneficial in developing an instructional profile; (4) the frequency with which teachers must monitor progress using this procedure to make effective instructional decisions; (5) the role of portfolio assessment, if any, in program placement decisions, and (6) ways in which this approach should be united with traditional, standardized assessment procedures.

Summary

The focus of this chapter was on the evaluating instruction phase. This phase, which follows the designing instruction and implementing instruction phases, represents the third ingredient for teaching and learning. We discussed assessment for proper instructional placement in the curriculum and ongoing assessment of student progress. We presented a variety of data collection systems that, when used appropriately with data analysis procedures, should yield valuable information about student progress and program effectiveness. Suggestions were offered for visually depicting the data so that students and teachers can view the learning trends. Teacher observa-

Table 6.4
Graphing Practice

Aim: 100%; CR 40, ER 1			
Date	# Correct	# Wrong	Phase
10/2	30	5	
	35	10	
	25	5	Baseline
	30	10	
	35	10	
10/9	25	10	
	25	5	
	40	5	
	40	5	Cue sheet
	55	2	
	55	0	
	50	0	
10/17	100	2	
	125	0	
	150	0	Cue sheet and rewards
	185	1	
	200	0	
	200	0	
10/24	210	0	
	220	0	Maintenance
	215	0	

tion and analysis assessment techniques were presented as ways to collect additional information about students, including factors such as the influence of other students, seating arrangements, behavioral consequences, and strategies that students use to tackle tasks and problems. Finally, we presented a discussion about the development and use of portfolio assessment. Although this is a common assessment technique, teachers are advised to use portfolio assessment wisely in collecting student information and in making decisions about progress. Now that we have concluded a discussion of the phases and components of teaching, we turn our attention to effective teaching methodology for social and academic skills.

Study and Discussion Questions

1. Describe the development and implementation of curriculum-based assessment.
2. Explain examples of teacher observation and analysis techniques.
3. Describe how to design and use portfolio assessment.
4. Explain how to collect data and teach concurrently.
5. Identify data collection techniques to match instructional objectives.
6. Explain how to translate data into report card grades.
7. Use a lesson plan you have developed and explain how CBA will be used to evaluate instruction. Include the data collection and analysis procedures.
8. Describe how you will manage data collection and analysis procedures (e.g., by using file folders to store graphs, individual student file folders).
9. Conduct a work sample analysis or think-aloud procedure with an elementary- and secondary-level student with learning problems.

10. Discuss portfolio assessment. Explain how to implement this for math and reading skills. Describe the contents of the portfolio and ways in which analysis will be conducted.
11. Give three reasons for graphing data collected on student performance.
12. Create a percentage and a rate (daily session time was held constant at five minutes) graph for Heather's multiplication fact performance. See Table 6.4 for the data on her performance.

● ●

References and Suggested Readings

National Council of Teachers of Mathematics. (1989). *Curriculum and evaluation standards*. Reston, VA: Author.

Curriculum-Based Assessment

Baer, D. M., Wolf, M. M., & Risley, T. R. (1968). Some current dimensions of applied behavior analysis. *Journal of Applied Behavior Analysis, 1*(1), 91–97.

Bentz, J. L., & Fuchs, L. S. (1993). Teacher judgment of student mastery of math skills. *Diagnostique, 18*(3), 219–232.

Deno, S. L. (1989). Curriculum-based measurement and special education services: A fundamental and direct relationship. In M. R. Shinn (Ed.), *Curriculum-based measurement: Assessing special children* (pp. 1–17). New York: Guilford Press.

Fuchs, D., Fernstrom, P., Reeder, P., Bowers, J., & Gilman, S. (1992). Vaulting barriers to mainstreaming with curriculum-based measurement and transenvironmental programming. *Preventing School Failure, 36*(2), 34–38.

Fuchs, L. S. (1992). Classwide decisionmaking with computerized curriculum-based measurement. *Preventing School Failure, 36*(2), 30–33.

Fuchs, L. S., & Deno, S. L. (1991). Paradigmatic distinction between instructionally relevant measurement models. *Exceptional Children, 57,* 488–500.

Fuchs, L. S., Fuchs, D., & Hamlett, C. L. (1989). Effects of instructional use of curriculum-based measurement to enhance instruction programs. *Remedial and Special Education, 10*(2), 43–52.

Fuchs, L. S., Fuchs, D., Hamlett, C. L., & Allinder, R. (1989). The reliability and validity of skills analysis within curriculum-based measurement. *Diagnostique, 14,* 203–221.

Fuchs, L. S., Fuchs, D., Hamlett, C. L., & Allinder, R. (1991). The contribution of skills analysis to curriculum-based measurement in spelling. *Exceptional Children, 57,* 443–452.

Fuchs, L. S., Fuchs, D., Hamlett, C. L., & Whinnery, K. W. (1991). Effects of goal line feedback on level, slope, and stability of performance within curriculum-based measurement. *Learning Disabilities Research and Practice 6*(2), 66–74.

Shinn, M., Rosenfeld, S., & Knutson, N. (1989). Curriculum-based assessment: A comparison of models. *School Psychology Review, 18,* 299–316.

Taylor, R. L. (1993). *Assessment of exceptional students: Educational and psychological procedures* (3rd ed.). Boston: Allyn & Bacon.

Teacher Observation and Analysis Assessment

Ashlock, R. B. (1986). *Error patterns in computation: A semi-programmed approach* (4th ed.). Columbus, OH: Merrill.

Enright, B. E. (1983). *Enright diagnostic inventory of basic arithmetic skills.* North Billerica, MA: Curriculum Associates.

McLoughlin, J. A., & Lewis, R. B. (1995). *Assessing special students* (4th ed.). Columbus, OH: Merrill.

Portfolio Assessment

Coutinho, M., & Malouf, D. (1993). Performance assessment and children with disabilities: Issues and possibilities. *Teaching Exceptional Children, 25*(4), 63–67.

Herman, J. L. (1992). What research tells us about good research. *Educational Leadership, 49*(8), 74–78.

Nolet, V. (1992). Classroom-based measurement and portfolio assessment. *Diagnostique, 18*(1), 5–26.

Paulson, F. L., Paulson, P. R., & Meyer, C. A. (1991). What makes a portfolio a portfolio? *Educational Leadership, 48*(5), 60–63.

Rivera, D. (1994). Portfolio assessment. *LD Forum, 19*(4), 14–17.

Swicegood, P. (1994). Portfolio-based assessment practices. *Intervention in School and Clinic, 30*(1), 6–15.

Valencia, S. (1990). A portfolio approach to classroom reading assessment: The whys, whats, and hows. *The Reading Teacher, 43*(4), 338–340.

Wesson, C. L., & King, R. P. (1992). The role of curriculum-based measurement in portfolio assessment. *Diagnostique, 18*(1), 27–37.

Wolf, K. (1991). The school teacher's portfolio: Issues in design, implementation, and evaluation. *Phi Delta Kappan, 73*(2), 130–136.

Chapter 7
Generic Interventions that Improve Behavior

Making Connections

Before you read, consider the discussions in chapters 4 and 5 regarding preparing for and addressing behavioral concerns. Before instruction occurs, teachers must determine their classroom rules and expectations and be aware of individual students' behavioral needs. Review your classroom rules; your own behavior, which can promote effective behavioral responses; and instructional management techniques. Consider your options for those times when even the best planning efforts cannot prevent the unforeseen disruptive behavior. Think about how the collaborative relationships between professionals and parents can foster effective schoolwide and classroom-based behavior. Remember that stages of learning apply to learning new behavioral patterns and that the role of reinforcement must be considered as indivualized behavioral programs are developed.

Many educators associate the notion of improving students' behaviors with the reduction of classroom disruption. Concern about students who disrupt the learning environment is justified because educators recognize that for learning to occur, a system of order must be established that specifies parameters for acceptable behavior and provides consequences for appropriate and inappropriate behaviors. If even the smallest disruption continues, it can inhibit or impair the learning of an entire class. Generally, minor disruptions can be reduced or eliminated by applying simple interventions or changes in the educational routine; however, more serious behavioral disruptions necessitate more complicated interventions, which require more teacher time to apply. Because the learning environment for an entire school can be affected negatively (e.g., excessive rules, punitive environment, reduced student freedom) by serious behavioral disruptions, educational programs that foster positive learning environments must be put into place for the benefit of all students.

Objectives

After studying this chapter, the reader will be able to

1. Explain preventive measures to decrease the occurrence of inappropriate behaviors.

2. Provide examples of interventions that eliminate mild levels of inappropriate behaviors.

3. Give examples of interventions that reduce moderate levels of disruptive behaviors.

4. Provide descriptions of and rationales for using interventions to minimize or eliminate more serious behavioral infractions.

To begin promoting positive learning environments, educators must become more informed about the social and behavioral norms of various cultural, ethnic, and racial groups and how these norms may be manifested in classroom settings and interact with the norms of educational environments and professionals. Educators must develop an understanding of how students from diverse backgrounds perceive the rules and expectations imposed by teachers and how students respond to social settings, group work, and teachers' disciplinary procedures. Furthermore, educators should develop an understanding of how families perceive school environments and the discipline of their children. As educators become better informed about the diverse norms within their classroom, they can strive to integrate these values and perceptions into a more cohesive behavioral and discipline plan. Considerations for developing a better understanding of diverse norms are presented in Spotlight on Diversity.

Spotlight on Diversity

Considerations for Developing an Understanding of Diverse Behavioral Norms and Expectations

- Consider how diverse groups perceive authority figures.

- Learn how individuals from different cultural, ethnic, and racial groups respond to authority figures.

- Develop an understanding for and appreciation of how individuals from diverse groups assert their individuality and their ethnic, cultural, or racial identity.

- Become familiar with the nonverbal communication norms of diverse groups.

- Become familiar with different groups' norms for educational achievement and lack of academic success.

- Recognize that each person has his or her own identity in addition to an identity with a specific cultural, ethnic, and racial group; avoid stereotyping people.

- Develop an understanding of different dialects, recognizing that individuals use dialectic differences to relate to specific groups.

- Consider the connection between the development of antisocial behavior (e.g., gangs, drugs or alcohol, weapons) and the lack of academic and social success; consider that antisocial behavior may be the only form of status for some students.

- Develop an understanding of how individuals respond to teachers' expectations of working quietly, sitting for long periods of time, working individually, working in groups, achieving academic success, getting the correct answer, and engaging in competitive behavior. ●

Source: Adapted from "Culturally Diverse Students," by D. F. Reed, 1993, in J. W. Wood (Ed.), *Mainstreaming: A Practical Approach for Teachers* (2nd ed., pp.123–154), Columbus, OH: Merrill. Copyright 1993 by Merrill.

As educators attempt to reduce disruptions by putting various disciplinary actions into place, they must also ensure that selected interventions do not alter a positive educational climate where students can explore, discover, and learn. Sometimes, teachers respond to behavioral disruptions with interventions that are too severe or that require too much time to implement. Smith and Rivera (1993) developed the Intervention Ladder (see Figure 7.1) as a guide for reducing disruptions in school settings. According to Smith and Rivera, the intervention should match the infraction. Tactics on the lower end of the Intervention Ladder are sufficient to reduce most disruptions at school. Less intrusive and less severe tactics should be tried first.

Figure 7.1
The intervention ladder

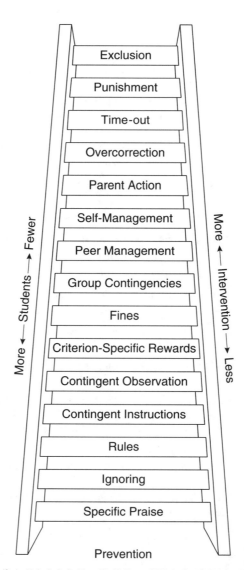

Source: From *Effective Discipline* (2nd ed.), by D. D. Smith and D. M. Rivera, 1993, Austin, TX: PRO-ED. Copyright 1993 by PRO-ED. Reprinted with permission.

In this chapter, the authors explain the Intervention Ladder and provide descriptions of a variety of interventions that can be used to prevent, minimize, and eliminate inappropriate behaviors. We organize our discussion of interventions according to how involved the teacher must be to implement the intervention successfully and how severe the behavioral infraction is.

● ●

Prevention

As you read, think about . . .

1. Identifying reasons that behavior problems occur.
2. Describing situations that may produce behavior problems in the elementary- and secondary-level classroom.
3. Discussing teachers' behaviors that might contribute to inappropriate students' behaviors.
4. Brainstorming ways in which behavior problems could be prevented.
5. Explaining how members of the school community could work collaboratively to prevent behavior problems.

In chapter 5, we talked about the importance of instructional management techniques (e.g., teacher presence, signals, transitions, directions) that must be implemented to promote successful teaching and learning. Certainly, these are good effective, preventive measures to address potential behavioral concerns. Preventing behavior problems could be viewed as an intervention; therefore, prevention is placed at the bottom of the Intervention Ladder to signify that educators should implement preventive techniques from the first day of school. Only when the preventive interventions (discussed below) prove ineffective should teachers select more intrusive tactics, which we describe later in this chapter.

To establish an effective plan, teachers must understand why behavior problems occur. Many behavior problems can be avoided if educators recognize and respond to situations before they become problematic. We begin by discussing reasons for behavior problems and offering ways in which some of these problems can be prevented.

Why Behavior Problems Occur

School conduct problems occur for many reasons. First, students might be either bored or frustrated with the academic materials presented to them. One important study (Center, Deitz, & Kaufman, 1982) found a strong correlation between task difficulty and inappropriate behavior. The relationship is dramatic and clear. For students who misbehave because the instructional material is either too difficult or too easy, simply adjusting the curricular demands will eliminate most of the disruption that these students create.

A second reason for misbehavior may be lack of motivation for learning. Some students see little reason for tackling the academic tasks of the day. They may fail to understand the relevance of the tasks or the way in which activities are presented. For this group of students, teachers must ensure instructional relevancy and identify creative ways of presenting tasks.

A third possible reason for inappropriate behavior is that students may not understand when certain behaviors are permissible and when they are not. Often a fine line exists between what is acceptable deportment and what is not; many students have difficulty understanding the limits of acceptable behavior.

Fourth, behavior problems can result from the teacher's inconsistent messages and behavior. Teachers must be consistent about their expectations and the consequences of not meeting those expectations. For example, if a teacher considers a certain noise level acceptable during group interchanges, then that level should be tolerated during all such times. It is unreasonable to expect students to adjust their noise level when cues and instructions are lacking.

A fifth possible reason for behavior problems may stem from family problems at home. Some children are faced with problematic and dysfunctional family situations. The emotional problems resulting from dysfunctional family dynamics could easily translate into classroom disruptive behaviors.

A sixth reason for behavior problems is the teacher's lack of awareness of classroom activities and pupil behavior at all times. Teachers must always be able to see all students in the classroom and be aware of behavioral interactions. Nooks and crannies may offer students "private space," but they also impede teachers' abilities to be informed of classroom behavioral activities. Similarly, teachers who position themselves in the classroom so that visibility is limited are inviting behavioral problems that they cannot see or stop.

Preventive Measures

Numerous measures can be used to prevent discipline problems. We now describe some of those measures and refer the reader to the "Prevention" section in References and Suggested Readings for further information.

1. Review assessment information to identify academic and social strengths and weaknesses, current levels of performance, and IEP goals. Select appropriate instructional objectives that will challenge students but not create unnecessary academic frustration.
2. Develop class activities that encourage youngsters to become actively involved in learning. Create exciting learning experiences (e.g., class plays, group assignments, mock TV news productions of historical events, field trips) to encourage student involvement in a subject. Relate learning to students' interests and to relevant reasons for studying information.
3. Help students learn to discriminate between the behavioral options in each school situation and match that situation with the proper behavioral response. For example, at the secondary level, students must be able to adapt to different classroom rules as they change classes throughout the day and interact with different teacher expectations. Students must make discriminations between hall or playground behavior and behavior during small-group or whole-class instruction.
4. Communicate specifically and carefully, so youngsters understand what is expected of them in a variety of different school situations. All members of the school community—parents, maintenance staff, administrative staff, students, and teachers—must have a common understanding of what constitutes expected and acceptable behavior in the classroom, lunchroom, playground, and hallway.

5. Maintain **"with-it-ness"** by knowing what is happening in the classroom at all times. Structure the classroom physical environment to maximize visibility of all students and position the teacher work space to promote access to students. Teachers must have "eyes in the back of their heads" and let students know that this is the case.
6. Motivate students by providing activity-based tasks, small-group work, and reinforcement for appropriate behavior.

Although teachers may institute preventive measures in their classrooms, some students need direct interventions to decrease their disruptive behaviors. For them, the tactics found on the Intervention Ladder need to be implemented. It is important to remember, however, that tactics found lower on the ladder should be tried first, for they are less serious, are less intrusive upon the learning environment, take less of the teacher's time to implement, disrupt positive learning environments least, and are often effective. We now turn our discussion to interventions found on the Intervention Ladder.

● ●

Mild Interventions

As you read, think about . . .

1. Identifying behaviors for which children can be praised to promote positive behavior in the classroom.
2. Establishing an ignoring intervention plan to eliminate an inappropriate behavior.
3. Listing specific rules that foster a positive classroom environment and the ability of the teacher to instruct.

We begin our discussion of interventions by describing specific praise, ignoring, and rules. Mild interventions are relatively easy to administer, and work effectively for most students. In many situations, they are the first choice for addressing classroom behavior problems. Table 7.1 provides examples and cautions for all of the interventions presented in this chapter; Table 7.2 explains ways to implement mild interventions. As with any instructional program, the intervention must be evaluated; evaluation techniques can be found in chapter 6.

Specific Praise

Specific praise—complimenting or verbally rewarding others for their accomplishments—is a simple, natural human act that can bring about substantial changes in performance. This form of teacher attention and feedback has been studied for many years; unfortunately, research findings have shown that although it is a powerful and extremely easy intervention to use, it is underutilized in many classroom settings. For example, research results from one study showed a strong correlation between the number of positive statements and the grade level: Teachers of elementary students had the highest approval and disapproval rates; by middle school, students were reprimanded more often than they were praised (White, 1975). Thus, one of the simplest interventions available for better discipline remains untapped in many classrooms.

Specific praise and a teacher's attention can produce remarkable changes in students' social and academic performance. One need only watch a group of kindergart-

Tactic	Example	Caution
Specific praise	"Steve, thank you for raising your hand to speak."	The praise must be precise and tailored to the student's age level.
Ignoring	When Juan came to the teacher's desk and interrupted the teacher, she paid no attention to him.	The student being ignored must really want the teacher's attention.
Rules	After several weeks of school, the students reviewed the guidelines about the behavior expected for each member. They had established a classroom code of conduct and decided on consequences for infractions of the rules.	Rules should be positively stated and general; the list should not be too long (5–7 rules).
Contingent instructions	While Alex was writing on his desk, the teacher went to him and said quietly, "Don't write on your desk, Alex."	Instructions need to be concise, direct, and delivered quietly during or immediately after the inappropriate behavior.
Contingent observation	During a group math activity, Steve was disruptive. His teacher had him return to his desk for 5 minutes while the others continued the math activity.	The observation period need not be long, and the student should be allowed to rejoin the group after sitting quietly for a short period of time.
Criterion-specific rewards	Because Gus was not tardy for a week, he was allowed 10 minutes of extra free time on Friday afternoon.	All students should have the opportunity to earn rewards. Otherwise, they might purposely misbehave to be put on a reinforcement schedule.
Fines	Sara became ineligible for this week's monitor duty because she was disruptive in class.	Students should not lose the opportunity to receive a reward or privilege too early in the week; the ratio of units of reward needs to be greater than the fines.
Group contingencies		
Dependent	Maria earned the whole class 5 extra minutes of lunch because she completed her assignment accurately and on time.	The student should be capable of performing the targeted behavior.
Independent	Each student who returned to class on time after the assembly was excused from one homework assignment.	The reward needs to be important to all the group's members.
Interdependent	When the entire class was not disruptive during the science activity for a week, the weekly spelling test was canceled.	Any student who is unable to meet the group's goal should have an individually set goal.
Peer management		
Behavioral managers	After being trained in behavioral techniques, Tzu-Lan became Beth's behavioral manager. Tzu-Lan modeled correct behavior and reinforced Beth's appropriate behavior.	Students need to implement a program that is carefully designed and supervised.
Environmental restructuring	Jeremy kept disturbing the class during seatwork assignments. In the past, the class laughed at Jeremy, which encouraged his disruption. After discussion and training sessions, the class learned to praise his quiet working behavior and ignore his disruptions.	The peer group needs to discuss and role-play the situation so that their reactions to a target peer are appropriate.
Self-management		
Self-regulation	When Phillip realized that he and Chad were about to fight, he left the hallway and returned to his classroom.	Students must be taught to analyze their behavior and predict their reactions in situations through discussions and role-playing.

Table 7.1
Tactic Examples and Cautions

Self-evaluation	Robin marked each time she talked out during class on a record sheet kept on her desk. At the end of each class period, she totaled the tallies and graphed the score.	Students need to be taught to collect data on their own performance and graph the results. Teachers need to check periodically for accuracy.
Self-reinforcement	Because Lonnie did not get into trouble one day on the playground, he scheduled 10 minutes of earned time at the end of the day.	Students need to be guided to select realistic goals and rewards.
Parent action	Jason's behavior necessitated an intervention plan that involved working closely with his parents. Weekly conferences were scheduled to ensure continuity between home and school.	Parents should be a part of the school community from the first day of school. Thus, parents will be informed of their child's behavior throughout the school year.
Overcorrection		
Positive practice	Megan pushed her way into class after lunch. For the next 3 school days, she had to hold the classroom door open for her peers. This made her the last one returning to class after lunch.	Short practice sessions (3 to 5 minutes) are sufficient to cause behavior change.
Restitution	Gail tipped over her desk intentionally. As a consequence, she had to straighten a section of the classroom.	The restitution must be directly related to the infraction.
Time-out		
Exclusion	Susan was very noisy during PE, so her teacher had her return to her homeroom.	A supervised place where the student can be sent must be prearranged.
Seclusion	Whenever John had a temper tantrum, he was sent to a time-out room for at least 3 minutes.	School officials' and parents' permission must be obtained. A proper time-out room that meets standard guidelines (in size, lighting, ventilation, and supervision) needs to be arranged. Data on its use must be collected.
Punishment	Judy had to stay after school to complete her homework for refusing to do her seatwork assignment.	The punishment and the person who delivers it can become negatively associated.
Exclusion		
In-school supervision	After considerable disruptive conduct in English, Jane was assigned to spend 3 days in the counselor's office.	The room needs to be designated and an adult continually assigned for supervision.
Suspension	A hearing was held because Norman destroyed school property and threatened other students even after a variety of interventions had been tried. It was decided that Norman would be suspended for 3 days.	Plans for supervising a suspended youngster should be established with the parent.
Expulsion	School personnel had tried all available means to control Jon's conduct. Despite their attempts, Jon fought with other students, threatened his teachers, and destroyed the learning environment. After a formal hearing, Jon was expelled from school for a month.	The possibility that an expelled student will find nonschool activities more interesting and rewarding must be considered.

Table 7.1
Continued

ners react when their teacher praises one of them for being ready to begin group time. Praise is effective when it is specific and tailored to the age and personality of the person. For instance, teachers cannot praise 10th-grade students in the same way they do 1st graders. Older students might not respond favorably to a teacher who praises them publicly, but a private word can mean a great deal.

Table 7.2
Mild Intervention
Implementation
Ideas

Intervention	Implementation ideas
Specific praise	1. Identify the student and behavior to be praised.
	2. Gain the student's attention.
	3. Provide a positive comment about the desired behavior.
	4. Do this publicly or privately, depending on the situation and student.
	5. Provide specific praise orally or in writing.
Ignoring	1. Identify whose attention the target student is seeking; that person should do the ignoring.
	2. Ignore the student when the behavior occurs.
	3. Praise the student when the behavior doesn't occur.
Rules	1. Involve students in generating a list of rules (no more than 7).
	2. Phrase rules positively.
	3. Identify and apply positive and negative consequences consistently.
	4. Teach the rules; praise students for following the rules.
	5. Share rules with parents and administrators.

Praise can serve as a reward for proper conduct, and also as a reminder and as feedback about a teacher's expectations for students. Before scheduling elaborate programs aimed at changing minor conduct problems, teachers should examine the amount of praise they give to determine whether they could use praise to produce more positive changes in their students' performance.

Ignoring

Ignoring is the planned, systematic withdrawal of attention by the individual whose attention is sought. The landmark research that clearly demonstrated the power of adult attention on nursery school children's behavior was conducted more than thirty years ago (Allen, Hart, Buell, Harris, & Wolf, 1964). That work showed that behavior correlates with the application and withdrawal of teacher attention.

Ignoring is effective only when it is consistently applied. The person applying the tactic must be important to the individual whose behavior needs improvement, and this person must persist in carrying out the tactic in all circumstances. According to Bacon (1990), "When the behavior fails to gain the desired attention, the behavior will eventually stop. Before the behavior stops, it may escalate to an unpleasant level in an attempt to demand teacher attention" (p. 608). Thus, teachers must implement the ignoring intervention consistently, even during the brief escalation period.

Adult attention is extremely important to younger children. That is why those teachers see immediate, and often dramatic, changes when they praise or ignore their students. However, as children get older, the attention of the peer group increases in importance, and the teacher's influence lessens. That is why ignoring older youngsters when they are tardy, talk out of turn, or clown around is ineffective.

Evertson, Emmer, Clements, and Worsham (1994) suggest that ignoring is an appropriate tactic in response to a minor infraction. If the behavior is unlikely to persist and speaking to the student would interfere with teaching, then ignoring is a logical choice. Of course, there are instances when ignoring is not the appropriate tactic. For example, it is inappropriate when the other students have ceased to pay attention to instruction or when the student's behavior is dangerous or harmful to the learning environment or to individuals. Ignoring is a subtle tactic, and might not produce change fast enough for some situations. Breaking school windows, threatening others, or fighting will probably not be influenced quickly enough by ignoring. In such cases, more stringent procedures found higher on the Intervention Ladder will be necessary.

Rules

Rules are a necessary part of society. They provide parameters and predictability to monitor behavior. Without rules, individuals are left to establish their own guidelines for creating consistency and some sense of security in their world (Windell, 1991). Unfortunately, some students do not conform to teachers' expectations for classroom settings because they do not understand what is required of them. They do not understand the demands of the settings. Often, educators assume that youngsters know how they are supposed to act in particular situations. They feel that all students should know they are to be quiet and work on their assignments independently during seatwork time, come to class on time, and listen and take notes during lectures. The codes of school conduct are often implied and not delineated carefully. In some school situations, students learn about the existence of a rule only when they break it and are punished for the infraction. A discovery method for learning school rules and codes of conduct is inefficient. Rules must be established, taught, reinforced, and reviewed regularly.

Rules of conduct are usually inconsistent. In some cases, the rules change; in other cases, the range of tolerance or the limits of acceptable behavior vary. Some teachers allow considerable freedom of movement or noise during class time; others do not. Conforming to different settings and different teachers' styles requires considerable discrimination skills. Students with learning and behavior problems often lack such skills. Establishing classroom rules and having discussions about them can facilitate a better understanding of school expectations and lead to increased compliance for many youngsters.

For some children with learning and behavior problems, preliminary interventions may not eliminate or reduce behavioral concerns; thus, moderate interventions become necessary. We now present a discussion about several interventions that fall higher on the Intervention Ladder, which means that more teacher time will be required to implement these interventions.

● ●

Moderate Interventions

As you read, think about...

1. Identifying ways to deliver contingent instructions during teaching.
2. Establishing a criterion-specific reward system to promote oral reading fluency.
3. Identifying the cautions in using a fine system.
4. Describing how interdependent group contingencies can be used to promote appropriate behavior.
5. Establishing a behavioral manager system to promote academic and behavioral success in the classroom.
6. Developing ways to foster self-management in the classroom.
7. Establishing ways to work effectively with parents when home-school intervention plans are necessary.

Once teachers have tried mild interventions and found little success in changing inappropriate behaviors, they must identify interventions that are more likely to produce desirable behavioral change and a positive instructional climate. Interventions on the ladder that fall into this category include contingent instructions, contingent observation, criterion-specific rewards, fines, group contingencies, peer management, self-management, and parent action. Moderate interventions require more planning, more implementation time, and careful monitoring of student progress and reaction to the intervention. The reader is referred to Table 7.1 for examples and cautions, and Table 7.3 for implementation ideas.

Contingent Instructions

Establishing rules usually reduces many instances of classroom disruption but does not eliminate them. Some students might not understand the implication of the rules, others might have forgotten a rule, and still others may break rules simply to be disobedient. When a rule is broken or unacceptable behavior occurs, there must be a consequence.

Contingent instructions is an intervention implemented after the target behavior occurs; the teacher quietly and on a one-to-one basis tells the individual not to engage in that specific activity. For example, if the rule is "raise your hand to speak" and a student continues to call out during class discussion, the teacher can walk over to the student, quietly remind him or her about the rule, and tell the student not to call out again.

A few research studies have shown the positive effects of contingent instructions (O'Leary, Kaufman, Kass, & Drabman, 1970; Roberts & Smith, 1977). Findings from these studies demonstrate that contingent instructions can be used successfully when: (1) they are specific, (2) they immediately follow the target behavior, and (3) they do not draw class attention to either the behavior or the student. Baron (1988) found that students resist changing their inappropriate behavior if criticism is not delivered in a considerate manner. Although contingent instructions will not help all youngsters reach a desired level of appropriate behavior, teachers can implement the strategy early, before trying other interventions found higher on the Intervention Ladder.

Contingent Observation

Contingent observation is a form of time-out (discussed later in this chapter) requiring the student to be removed from a reinforcing situation (Gast & Nelson, 1977). A youngster is removed from a group activity for not participating properly, but may still watch the activity from a removed vantage point for a short period of time.

The advantage of this tactic is that the student does not lose instructional time and can watch others participating appropriately. Hopefully, the activity from which the student is temporarily excluded will be desirable enough to warrant appropriate behavior and the invitation to rejoin the group. The key is to ensure that the contingent observation period is not so long that the student loses interest in rejoining the group and becomes disruptive even when isolated from the group. Scenario 7.1 illustrates the correct application of contingent observation.

Table 7.3
Moderate
Intervention
Implementation
Ideas

Intervention	Implementation ideas
Contingent instructions	1. Implement right after rule is broken. 2. Stand close to student and talk quietly to him or her. 3. Provide information about broken rule and expected behavior. 4. Praise student when appropriate behavior occurs.
Contingent observation	1. Provide warning. 2. If behavior occurs again, remove student to area of room where he or she can observe class activity. 3. Set short time for isolation and tell student that rejoining the group is contingent on sitting quietly. 4. Ignore the student. 5. Provide quiet reminder about appropriate behavior when student rejoins group.
Criterion-specific rewards	1. Identify target behavior. 2. Establish criterion for behavior. 3. Select the schedule of reinforcement. 4. Reward students for achieving the mastery level.
Fines	1. Decide on the privilege that will be fined, based on the occurrence of the target behavior. 2. Be sure students desire privilege. 3. Match the fine to the infraction.
Group contingencies (in general for dependent, independent, and interdependent contingencies)	1. Identify target behavior. 2. Identify criterion level for reward. 3. Collect data on student progress.
Peer management (for behavioral managers and environmental restructuring)	1. Explain the steps in the intervention process. 2. Provide instruction in the systematic use of giving praise, modeling, giving directions, and ignoring. 3. Provide rewards.
Self-management (in general for self-regulation, self-evaluation, and self-reinforcement)	1. Identify behaviors for which self-management is an appropriate intervention. 2. Teach problem-solving skills. 3. Model; have students imitate process. 4. Provide feedback.
Parent action	1. Implement a parent-contact system at the beginning of the school year. 2. Establish a parent-involvement program in the classroom. 3. Develop a specific intervention plan with parents if necessary. 4. Maintain frequent contact; provide feedback about the program's success to parents and students.

Scenario **7.1**

Example of Contingent Observation

Ms. Caldwell asked Gus to take his chair and sit away from the group because he could not share appropriately during the cooperative learning math activity. Ms. Caldwell told Gus that he had to leave the group because he could not share with the other students and that he must sit quietly for three minutes before he could rejoin the group. She set the timer for three minutes. Students continued to work on solv-

ing problems and constructing graphs in their groups. After three minutes of sitting quietly, Gus was permitted to rejoin the group with a private reminder to share the manipulatives if he wanted to continue with the group work. ■

Criterion-Specific Rewards

Criterion-specific rewards means that students earn privileges only when they reach desirable levels of the target behavior. Rewards to students for improving their academic or behavioral skills can come in a variety of forms, ranging from tangible representations of improvement to earning privileges, free time, or honors. Rewards can be very effective in encouraging students of all ages to conform to classroom and school rules and to improve behaviorally and academically as individuals and as members of groups.

Reinforcement is a technique that encourages a student to repeat a desirable behavior. Reinforcement is applied after a behavior occurs. An event is a **reinforcer** only if it causes an increase in the target behavior. What might be a reinforcer for one student might not be for another. Except in the case of **primary reinforcers** (food, sleep, water), it cannot be assumed that any tactic is a reinforcer. Data must be kept to determine this.

Many teachers like to reduce undesirable behavior by rewarding a behavior that is incompatible with it. For example, students cannot be out-of-seat when they are in their seats; they cannot be talking out of turn when they are raising their hands to speak. Many alternative behaviors can be rewarded. Teachers should try to reinforce positive behavior before they implement tactics that center on inappropriate or undesirable conduct.

In many cases, for students with learning and behavior problems, direct intervention on an inappropriate or undesirable behavior is necessary. We now discuss techniques for identifying rewards and establishing schedules of reinforcement.

Identifying Rewards

Most rewards used in school situations are termed **secondary reinforcers,** because their value must be learned. Events such as free time, for example, are not naturally reinforcing; the teacher must arrange for students to learn their reinforcing value. Students will not work for library time if they do not know what library time is, or that it can be fun and interesting. Many of the events that are highly motivating in school can be used as positive reinforcers, but students must first be aware of their reinforcing value. This can be accomplished through discussions or periods in which students can try out potential reinforcers.

For instance, Mr. O'Ryan permitted students to interact with a variety of activities they selected for 30 minutes one Friday afternoon. He had games, weaving activities, poster art, and audiotapes of current popular music (previously screened and approved). After the 30 minutes of self-selection, he told the students that beginning on Monday, they could choose one activity as their reward for reaching the desired accuracy level on three assignments. Mr. O'Ryan knew that he would have to change activities periodically to maintain interest level and provide other self-selection times to teach the reinforcing value of the rewards, but in the long run, he hoped to improve academic performance and on-task behavior.

From this example, it is clear that rewards do not need to be expensive, tangible, or complicated. Because the selection of rewards (reinforcers) is key to using reinforcement procedures effectively, students should be active participants in the selection of those items or activities that they strive to earn. Probably the best way to select reinforcers is to ask students what they would like to earn as rewards for their accomplishments. Table 7.4 provides a list of suggested rewards (Smith & Rivera, 1993).

The rewards that students work for must be highly desirable to them. Individuals' tastes and preferences change. What is important to third graders might not be to ninth graders. What is important to students one week might not be the next. Therefore, students should be allowed to work for a variety of rewards and participate in their selection.

Establishing Schedules of Reinforcement

When teachers use reinforcement, they typically apply a schedule that organizes and systematizes the earning of rewards. A number of different types of schedules are available that assist in this process. **Fixed ratio (FR) schedules of reinforcement** are used when the individual receives a unit of reinforcement after a specified number of occurrences of a target behavior. This is probably the most common schedule of reinforcement used in academic situations, for it allows the teacher to count the num-

Table 7.4
Rewards Suggested
by Students

Working with a friend in the hall	Obtaining legal hall passes
Collecting the lunch money	Running errands for the teacher
Taking attendance	Taking notes to other teachers
Taking the attendance cards to the office	Taking good work to the principal or counselor
Running off dittos and collating papers	Free time for special projects
Early dismissal	Extra recess
Writing something on a ditto master and running it off	Sticker on a behavioral report card
Sitting at the teacher's desk to do the assigned seatwork	Lunchtime basketball games, with the teacher serving as referee
Viewing noneducational videotapes on Friday afternoon	Popcorn during educational films
Extra shop or PE time	Special parties
Special picnic lunches or food treats	Field trips
Attendance at assemblies	Special art projects
Working on games or puzzles	Listening to the radio
Typing on a typewriter	Decorating the bulletin board
Extra library time	Being a group leader
Helping the class line up at the door	Leading the class to the library
Reading a magazine	Lunch with the teacher
Listening to a tape with headphones	Taking a note home to parents
Working on the computer	Watering the plants
Feeding the class animals	Receiving a homework pass for one night
Sitting next to a friend	Going to another classroom as a cross-age tutor

Source: From *Effective Discipline* (2nd ed.), by D. D. Smith and D. M. Rivera, 1993, Austin, TX: PRO-ED. Copyright 1993 by PRO-ED. Reprinted with permission.

ber of correct responses that a student makes, apply the ratio, and deliver the specified amount of reinforcement. For example, the teacher taught Jeremy to solve subtraction problems. He then had 10 problems to complete independently. The teacher applied a fixed ratio schedule of reinforcement of 9:1—one unit of reinforcement would be given for nine correct problems.

The **fixed interval (FI) reinforcement schedule** allows for reinforcement for a selected period of appropriate behavior. FI schedules are usually applied to improve social behavior, on-task behavior, study time, or "attending." A kitchen timer can be used to indicate when the fixed time period has passed. For example, Sue needed to increase the amount of time she spent in her seat calculating problems in her arithmetic workbook. The teacher selected a FI schedule of 5:1. For each five-minute time period over the twenty-minute arithmetic study time planned for each day, Sue could earn one point. Each point was exchangeable for an extra minute of recess time. A total of four extra minutes of recess could be earned each day. A kitchen timer was set for five minutes. If Sue was in her seat working on her assignment during the five-minute segment, she received one point. If she was out of her seat during that segment, she did not receive a point. The timer was then reset and another five-minute segment was initiated.

With both the ratio and interval schedules of reinforcement, schedules may either be fixed or variable. In the fixed situations, the time period set or the number of responses required is constant. In some cases, better performance is noted when students are not as certain about reinforcement delivery. Then, variable schedules are more useful.

The **variable interval (VI) schedule,** is usually used for social behavior. As with the fixed interval, reinforcement is delivered according to segments or amounts of time, but the time segments differ.

One common application of a variable interval schedule is the "timer game" (see "Group Contingencies" later in the chapter). A kitchen timer is set to ring on average every five minutes (a schedule of 5:1). Sometimes it will ring after one minute, sometimes after nine minutes, sometimes after three minutes, and so on. Anyone in his or her seat working on the assignment when the bell rings receives a point. Anyone not behaving appropriately when the bell rings does not receive a point. At the end of the period, the team or student with the most points wins. Because of the unpredictability of when reinforcement can be earned, students tend to behave consistently better throughout the entire period.

Variable ratio (VR) schedules of reinforcement are similar to fixed ratio schedules, but here once a ratio is determined, an average of that number is applied per session. VR schedules can also be applied when the maintenance of social behaviors is of concern. Peggy's maintenance of excellent behavior in social studies class could be encouraged with a VR schedule. She would not know which days of "perfect" behavior in social studies earned her reinforcement and which days did not.

Fines

Just as students can be reinforced or rewarded for improvement, they can lose privileges when their performance is unsatisfactory. **Fines,** often referred to in the research literature as **response cost,** are usually tied to rewards. A student can earn a privilege through good behavior and can lose that privilege because of poor behavior. As with rewards, the schedule for fines should be predetermined, and not set during or immediately after the infraction when tempers and feelings might result in fines that are too stringent.

In many school situations, students are given privileges even when they do not earn them. For example, attendance at school plays, assemblies, field trips, and sporting events are allowed, regardless of student deportment. Participation and attendance in such activities or specially arranged events could be earned or lost, depending on students' behavior. One caution must be raised, however. Some events and activities are not enjoyable to all youngsters. Students who do not want to participate might misbehave purposely to avoid having to attend a school event. Scenario 7.2 illustrates this point.

Scenario 7.2

Example of Fines

At Jefferson Middle School, the periods between classes had become quite disorderly. Books were carelessly thrown about in the halls, students engaged in pushing matches, and some students' language was inappropriate. The school staff worked collaboratively to institute a fine system (after trying other tactics). Monitors stood in the halls between classes and distributed penalty cards to those who were disorderly (these cards had been defined to the student body). Anyone receiving a penalty card could not attend that week's assembly. Unfortunately, the monitors noticed an increase in inappropriate behavior and the consequent distribution of penalty cards. Upon asking certain students, the staff members learned that the students generally viewed assemblies as boring and did not want to attend them; the penalty card was a way to be excused. ■

Teachers must also be careful not to levy fines that negate the possibility of earning a privilege early in the reward period. For example, on Monday each child in the sixth grade was given one card that served as a pass to view on Friday a video recording of the book they were reading. Any child who displayed improper conduct in the hallway during period change was fined that card. Throughout the week, behavior during period change grew worse because those youngsters who were fined on Monday lost all chance of attending the video. They had no reason left to behave properly. Each day, the number of such children increased, and disruption increased to a level greater than it was originally. When fines are used, students must not lose the incentive to keep working.

Group Contingencies

Group contingencies are interventions that teachers and students like, because they can be arranged as classroom games. Group contingencies use the peer group as a resource to encourage positive changes in behavior. They also can add an element of fun to the school program. Litow and Pumroy (1975) classify group contingencies into three types: dependent, independent, and interdependent. Although they vary as to who earns and who receives the reward, they all involve students as a group of peers.

Dependent Group Contingencies

In the **dependent group contingency** situation, the whole class receives reinforcement if a classmate earns it. Dependent group contingencies have proven to be effective strategies if one student's behavior needs modification. For instance, a student and the students sitting around her might get to leave for lunch several minutes early because she stayed in her seat the entire period.

Dependent group contingencies can make peers involved in improving their classmate's behavior; however, before this contingency system is employed, teachers should determine that target individuals are capable of earning reinforcement for the group. If they are not, their peers might inflict penalties on them because they failed and the group was denied its due reward.

Independent Group Contingencies

Independent group contingencies eliminate the competitive element present in many group contingency situations. When the independent version is used, a group goal is stated, but students earn reinforcement for themselves as they meet the goals set for the group. For instance, students can, with the teacher's assistance, keep track of their own inappropriate behavior during an academic period. Students whose daily score for inappropriate behavior is below the group goal can leave for recess five minutes early; those who exceed the goal must stay in the classroom and continue working until the designated recess period begins. An advantage of independent group contingencies is that the entire class is not denied the reward because of the behavior of a few.

Interdependent Group Contingencies

When **interdependent group contingencies** are applied, the behavior of the whole class determines whether reinforcement is received. All who participate in inappropriate activity also participate in its consequences. Because a student's behavior is often encouraged by the group, this system appeals to many teachers. This type of group contingency is effective for all age groups and is the most commonly used group contingency.

When interdependent group contingencies are used, it is important for the teacher to be certain that the children involved are capable of the requisite behavior. If not, undue pressure could be placed on the individual who causes the group to lose its opportunity for reinforcement. When one child consistently ruins the chances for the group, an individual contingency program could be arranged for that pupil, while the others participate in the group contingency. The teacher must also plan for the possibility that several students might actually enjoy subverting the program for the group. If this occurs, the teacher must make special arrangements for the subversive students. Interdependent group contingency programs can be quite effective, particularly when the peer group's attention and reactions are what causes undesirable behavior to occur.

Educators have found that interdependent group contingencies can influence a variety of behaviors, ranging from general disruptions and classroom noise to tardiness. They have reduced the number of off-topic comments in group discussion time by tallying appropriate and inappropriate comments with different colored pencils. That difference could cause students to earn or lose different levels of rewards. As rewards, teachers have used listening to popular music while working, free activity periods, extra minutes of physical education, or additional art or science time. Scenario 7.3 presents four examples of interdependent group contingencies.

Scenario 7.3

Examples of Interdependent Group Contingencies

Example one: The flip chart (Sulzbacher & Houser, 1968)

Some of the children in Ms. Dela Garza's classroom engaged in acts that greatly bothered her (using and talking about what the researchers referred to as the "naughty finger"). These students quickly realized that Ms. Dela Garza became upset and embarrassed when any of them did these things. As an intervention, the teacher placed a flip chart at the front of the room. On it were cards with the numbers 0 to 10. The first card showing was 10. This indicated that the students had 10 minutes of a special recess at the end of the day. For each transgression, the teacher flipped a card, revealing a lower number and indicating that the class lost one minute from their special recess time. Even on the first day of intervention, this reduced the frequency of the target behavior substantially. The nice feature of this intervention is that the teacher is not required to spend much time managing a complex record-keeping system and the teacher regained instructional time that had been lost to the confusion and disruption of the inappropriate behavior.

Example two: The good behavior game (Barrish, Saunders, & Wolf, 1969)

In the good behavior game, the class is divided into two or more teams. Each time a team member violates a rule (talking out of turn, being out-of-seat), that team receives a point. At the end of the period, the team with the fewest points wins the game and might or might not receive a reward or privilege. If all teams have very few points, they all win; if all teams have too many points, they all lose. The good behavior game can be used to reduce disruption in such settings as assemblies, lunch periods, sports, and field trips.

Example three: The time game (Broden, Hall, Dunlap, & Clark, 1970)

The time game has a format similar to the good behavior game, but a kitchen timer is used. Using a variable interval schedule, possibly 5:1, the teacher sets the clock to ring at different times, averaging every five minutes. The students cannot predict when the bell is going to ring. When it does ring, each team gets a point if all members are engaged in the proper activity (studying, completing assignments). At the end of the game, teams with more points than a minimum that the teacher has set win the game.

Example four: Cooperative learning behavior teams (Maurer, 1988)

In cooperative learning behavior teams, students are divided into teams of three to four students. The group should include no more than one student who displays disruptive behavior. A target behavior should be selected for all the groups to work on as they complete group activities. A group receives a point whenever any member of the group exhibits the target behavior. Each group's goal is to have accumulated the least number of points. Therefore, group members must work together to act appropriately and not receive points. ■

Peer Management

Using children to help each other is not a new concept. In fact, as early as the first century, the Romans used tutoring as an integral part of the instructional process. Educators are most familiar with **peer management** as it is applied in tutoring situations. However, **behavioral management,** which uses a one-to-one tutoring format, and **environmental restructuring,** which relies on an entire group, can be applied to the improvement of students' social behavior. These two techniques are discussed in the next sections.

Behavioral Managers

Peers can help classmates improve their social behavior by establishing a situation much like tutoring. As in other tutoring arrangements, however, educators must consider a number of factors. The children need to be carefully selected. The tutor, referred to as the **behavioral manager** in social situations, needs to be matched with the other youngster(s). The behavioral manager selected cannot be too powerful or too authoritarian. Some mutual respect between the youngsters should exist or be fostered. Behavioral managers need to be trained, be proficient in the skill they are assigned, and be able to follow through with the program designed by the teacher. Behavioral managers need to know how to provide instructions, as well as feedback, praise, and reinforcement procedures. They also need defined space in which to work. Finally, behavioral managers need to be rewarded for their efforts, possibly through a dependent group contingency arrangement.

Lovitt, Lovitt, Eaton, & Kirkwood (1973) report a clever use of a classmate serving as a behavioral manager. The students, two nine-year-old boys with learning problems, usually sat near each other in class. One of the students tended to engage in inappropriate and distracting verbal behavior, which the authors generically referred to as "bathroom language." During the intervention condition, when that student used inappropriate language, the peer manager said, "I don't like it when you say _____." Then he picked up his schoolwork and moved to another desk, away from the other child. Within a short period of time, the frequency of this type of language dropped to zero and remained at that level. Most likely, the use of a classmate as the behavioral manager (rather than the teacher) created a positive atmosphere for both boys and released the teacher from interfering in the situation.

When carefully monitored, peers can effectively be used as behavioral managers to help develop a more positive classroom environment. Since in many situations peers encourage inappropriate behavior, it seems worthwhile to encourage them to develop more positive behavior in each other.

Environmental Restructuring

In many situations, a student misbehaves because his or her classmates continually reinforce that behavior. The "class clown" only engages in silly behavior because he is reinforced by the peer group: They laugh at his antics, pay attention to him, and like his jokes. Through discussion sessions, modeling, role playing, and considerable practice, the class can learn not to react or reinforce inappropriate behavior from a peer. The peer group can also learn to praise proper conduct from a misbehaving or inappropriate peer. This is not easy to accomplish and takes considerable time. In some situations, however, it might be well worth the effort, for all parties involved can learn that they are responsible for the behavior that occurs in their classroom or at their school.

Self-Management

Self-management procedures have received considerable attention from researchers and teachers lately. These procedures encourage students to become actively involved in their educational programs. For those who could be called inactive learners, these procedures might serve to change their overall orientation toward learning and school. Besides being excellent interventions that help to improve students' behavior, they also teach valuable skills needed in life. They help students learn to manage their time, control their behavior, and develop independence.

Studies have shown that self-management techniques are effective for elementary (Hughes & Boyle, 1991) and secondary (Schloss, 1987) students. In addition to promoting youngsters' academic and social skills, self-management techniques are appealing because they actively involve the individual in the learning process. Ellis and Friend (1991) found that adolescent students with learning problems tended to rely on their teachers to achieve classroom success, rather than taking a more active role in the instructional process. Naturally, such an overreliance is counterproductive to achieving independence; self-management techniques can be used to promote more independence and decision-making skills. Many comprehensive reviews have been written on self-management techniques (Lovitt, 1995). In the following sections, we discuss three general types of self-management techniques: self-regulation, self-evaluation, and self-reinforcement. These techniques may be used independently or as an entire treatment package. It should be noted that self-management is higher on the Intervention Ladder because of the amount of teacher time needed to institute various self-management techniques. Teachers could also teach self-management techniques as a way to prevent misbehavior.

Self-Regulation

The aim of self-control tactics is for individuals to monitor their own behavior. For example, in some instances students determine when and how much study time they need to increase academic performance. In other instances, they do not engage in inappropriate behavior because they know which situations precipitate those events and seek to avoid them.

These procedures are usually employed in an attempt to reduce undesirable behavior patterns. A series of activities is employed, with controlled relaxation as one of the usual components. One example of a self-control strategy for aggression is called the *turtle technique* (Robin, Schneider, & Dolnick, 1977). The student delays reacting to a situation and assumes the turtle position (eyes closed, fists clenched, and head on desk), which relaxes him or her and restrains the aggression. The child then thinks of alternative ways to deal with the situation.

Many self-control instructional programs include the following targets: anticipating consequences, appreciating feelings, and managing frustration, inhibition, and delay. These are important skills for all individuals to master, but for those who seem unable to regulate their own behavior, they are critical.

Teachers can use **self-regulation** tactics to help students achieve self-control for the target behaviors. Some of these techniques include: (1) using self-talk as a reminder to exhibit behavioral control, (2) counting softly to aid as a "cooling down" technique, and (3) removing oneself from a situation to a quiet area until one regains self-control. As teachers work with students to select appropriate self-regulatory techniques, they should keep the following items in mind: evaluation data of previously implemented self-regulatory techniques, the setting in which the target behavior is occurring, the student's age and ability level, and the target behavior that the teacher and student seek to eliminate (Smith & Rivera, 1993).

Self-Evaluation

There are many components of **self-evaluation.** Sometimes they are used together as an intervention package, and sometimes only one component is utilized. One form of self-evaluation allows students to correct their own work. **Self-correction** can be useful to busy teachers (because it saves teacher time) and students receive helpful and immediate feedback about the accuracy of their work. Many teachers periodically check students' self-corrected papers and find that students correct their own assignments with high accuracy. This also encourages students to be more actively involved in their learning, which leads to less inappropriate behavior in class.

When **self-recording** or **self-monitoring** is implemented, students keep records on their own behavior. Simple frequency measurements are easy for youngsters to use, and in many cases the mere act of keeping data on their own behavior causes positive changes in performance. When **self-reporting** is used, students are required to report to the teacher and sometimes to the class about their performance. Many students enjoy and are further motivated by a tactic called **self-graphing.** Here, students are responsible for their own evaluation graphs (see chapter 6), and many educators report substantial improvement in a variety of behaviors when students produce a visual display of their performance.

Excellent research data have been accumulated for over twenty years on the ways in which self-recording and self-evaluation promote academic and behavioral improvement. In one of the first studies of self-recording, Broden, Hall, and Mitts (1971) determined that students became less disruptive and more studious merely by keeping records of the time they spent studying and talking. The use of self-records has caused increased amounts of attention-to-task (Hallahan, Marshall, & Lloyd, 1981) and thereby less disruption. Kneedler and Hallahan (1981) also found that students do not have to be accurate in their self-recording for the procedure to be effective.

Self-Reinforcement

When this procedure is used, the students, rather than the teacher, determine the reinforcement schedule and the rewards given for improvement. One of the first studies of this kind (Lovitt & Curtiss, 1969) showed that students can determine their own reinforcement schedules. In that study, student performance was much better when students determined the reinforcement schedule than when the teacher set the schedule. Although there has been considerable debate about whether self-imposed contingencies are better than teacher-imposed arrangements, it appears that **self-reinforcement** is superior. In one study (Dickerson & Creedon, 1981), students performed better in the self-reinforcement condition than they did when the teachers were in control. They also noted an excellent by-product of this tactic—the students reminded each other to be quiet and do their assignments and actually praised themselves and each other for improvement.

Many educators who use self-management procedures strongly recommend that all three types—self-regulation, self-evaluation, and self-reinforcement—be used together. Each procedure has considerable power, and together they tend to cause even greater improvement. Self-management encourages active involvement, which frequently causes students to maintain their improvement for longer periods of time. Once implemented, self-management saves a teacher considerable time, because the students are responsible for much of their educational programs. This frees the teacher to work individually with students and oversee the class's progress without being bogged down by time-consuming tasks.

Parent Action

Parents (or other family members) should be actively involved in and informed about their child's educational program throughout the school year. In chapters 2 and 3, the authors talked about communicating and working effectively with parents. Clearly, communication between home and school should be continuous. Parents should be kept informed of positive as well as negative behaviors and the success of interventions to eliminate inappropriate behavior. Too often, parents are not aware of behavioral concerns until more serious interventions are necessary.

Asking parents to be directly involved in solving school-related problems should be reserved until other methods, such as those previously described, have been tried. Direct parent involvement in remediation efforts requires extensive communication to ensure that whatever home-school intervention plan is established is carried out and implemented accurately. Thus, **parent action** is higher on the Intervention Ladder because of the degree of teacher and parent time required to implement a behavioral program.

Parents and educators can serve as partners in students' educational programs. Parents could determine part of their children's weekly allowances based on weekly behavioral reports from their teachers. As a reward for improved behavior at school, parents could provide their children with extra allowances, more time reading a bedtime book, extra minutes of television, or a special dinner. They also could take the children to a movie, a sporting event, or some other special activity.

There are several important considerations for parents who are arranging a reinforcement system at home. Parents must be able to deliver the reward; a reward earned but not received can result in worsened performance. Many parents need to be guided in choosing reasonable rewards. Some parents who use fines are too harsh. Parents need guidance in determining the severity of fines. Throughout school-home intervention plans, educators need to supervise the program and be certain that ongoing communication exists.

● ●

More Serious Interventions

As you read, think about . . .
1. Identifying behaviors for which overcorrection might be appropriate.
2. Developing a letter for parents describing time-out procedures that will be used in your classroom.
3. Identifying the negative aspects of punishment and exclusion.

Infrequently, teachers must address certain behaviors (e.g., fighting, displaying injurious behavior, cutting classes) by using more intrusive, time-consuming interventions. Mild and moderate interventions may already have been tried. The nature of the specific behavior may require interventions higher on the Intervention Ladder. More serious interventions require careful planning and evaluation, time, as well as administrative and family support. Very often, other school community members (e.g., the principal, a counselor, a parent) may be involved with the teacher as she or he works with a youngster to eliminate an inappropriate behavior. We discuss several interventions that fall in the "serious" section of the ladder due to the time required to implement them appropriately and due to the type of behavior displayed. These interventions include overcorrection, time-out, punishment, and exclusion. See Table 7.1 for examples and cautions, and Table 7.5 for implementation ideas.

Overcorrection

Overcorrection procedures have gained considerable popularity in schools recently for three reasons: they have an educational component, students must take responsibility for their actions, and overcorrection procedures are effective. There are two kinds of overcorrection, *positive practice* and *restitution*.

Positive Practice Overcorrection

Positive practice overcorrection requires the student to "overpractice" a form of the desired behavior. Table 7.6 provides examples of positive practice and how they might be implemented. Scenario 7.4 illustrates the application of positive practice overcorrection.

Scenario **7.4**

Example of Positive Practice Overcorrection

As a group of Mr. Garcia's students entered the classroom, they bumped, pushed, and yelled at one another. It took Mr. Garcia several minutes of instructional time just to obtain quiet in the classroom so he could teach. He had tried several inter-

Table 7.5
Serious Intervention Implementation Ideas

Intervention	Implementation ideas
Overcorrection (in general for positive practice and restitution)	1. Match the types of overcorrection with the degree of the disruptive behavior. 2. Implement overcorrection procedure immediately after the behavior. 3. Design a correction procedure that focuses on positive behavior.
Time-out (in general for exclusion and seclusion time-outs)	1. Limit time-out time to 3 minutes. 2. Provide positive reinforcement for alternative behaviors. 3. Provide a warning before implementing time-out procedures. 4. Avoid lectures before or during time-out procedures. 5. Remain calm and matter-of-fact.
Punishment	1. Use only when the behavior is very serious or dangerous. 2. Try other techniques first. 3. Inform parents of procedures. 4. Provide no threats or warnings. 5. Stop the behavior as soon as it is observed.
Exclusion (for in-school supervision, suspension, and expulsion)	1. Provide official notice of policies and procedures to parents. 2. Work collaboratively with the school community to develop and implement procedures. 3. Inform parents and students of their due process rights. 4. Maintain formal records. 5. Work with other school authorities as necessary.

Table 7.6
Examples of
Positive Practice
Overcorrection

Undesirable act	Positive practice procedure
1. Nail biting	Hold hands at side for one minute
2. Noisy classroom transition	Spend the recess period practicing coming to class quietly and beginning assignment independently
3. Autisticlike gestures	Hold hand stiff for fifteen seconds
4. Poor spelling on a composition assignment	Look up all words spelled incorrectly in dictionary and write a paragraph about each word
5. Use of slang words	Practice using correct words in phrases
6. Agitation and disruption	Required relaxation
7. Talking out of turn	Raise hand and wait for teacher to call on student during five-minute practice sessions

ventions on the Intervention Ladder, but achieved no success in eliminating the disruptive behavior. He then used a positive practice overcorrection technique. Each time the group of students did not enter the classroom quietly and in an orderly fashion, he had the students return to the hall and practice the proper way of entering the room. They had to repeat this tactic twice and had to work harder to catch up with the other students, who had begun their work. ■

A study involving a group of students who talked out of turn excessively (Azrin & Powers, 1975) showed how positive practice could effect changes. During the recess period, rather than going outside, students had to practice raising their hands and obtaining permission to speak without disturbing other students in the class. Positive practice can be used to practice misspelled words on a spelling test, errors on a math facts test, and vocabulary words from a content lesson. Extra practice on a skill or behavior is a benefit of positive practice; however, teachers should ensure that the number of practice opportunities are reasonable (e.g., spell misspelled words five, not ten, times).

Restitutional Overcorrection

The form of overcorrection that has drawn the most attention from educators and parents is **restitutional overcorrection.** The notion of restitution is supported in many phases of society today, particularly in the court system. Victims are being repaid for losses incurred from crimes. In school situations, restitutional overcorrection requires the individual to restore the environment to an improved state. Table 7.7 lists examples of implementing this tactic.

Restitutional overcorrection has several advantages. First, it makes individuals responsible for their actions. For example, if Jeremy disrupts the class by throwing over desks and scattering books around the floor, he must restore the learning environment. With other procedures, Jeremy might be punished for his actions, but others are left with the task of righting the classroom furniture. Second, because the offending student is not removed from the classroom, that individual does not lose instructional time.

Burke (1992) suggests guidelines for using restitution overcorrection. First, teachers should actually observe the student committing the inappropriate behavior; that is, the student who is receiving the restitution intervention should be the student

Table 7.7
Examples of
Restitution
Overcorrection

Undesirable act	Restitution procedure
1. Throw and overturn furniture	Restore whole room to a pleasant appearance, straighten furniture, dust and clean whole room
2. Break or destroy others' property	Earn money needed to purchase replacements
3. Write on desk	Clean all desks in class
4. Write obscenities on wall	Paint whole wall
5. Steal	Return item stolen and an additional item
6. Chew objects	Cleanse mouth with antiseptic
7. Throw rocks on playground	Pick up litter and rocks to clear ground

who actually committed the act. Second, the restitution overcorrection consequence should match the infraction. Third, even if teacher prompts are necessary, the student should be expected to perform the restitution. Fourth, the restitution intervention should not be enjoyable to the student.

Although overcorrection is an appealing tactic, it is aversive and rather negative. Educators need to remember that there are many other tactics lower on the Intervention Ladder that should be tried before overcorrection procedures if the behavior warrants such intervention. Matching the misbehavior with an appropriate intervention is an important guideline to remember.

Time-out

Time-out might well be one of the most controversial tactics found on the Intervention Ladder, largely because of this tactic's frequent misuse and misapplication. As with reinforcement, the use of time-out can be documented as early as the 1800s when Itard tried to teach Victor, the wild child (Lane, 1976). Olson (1935) also describes an isolation technique: In general, the careful teacher attempts to avoid situations in which a child is given the feeling of being cut off from a group. An occasional child, however, may "go to pieces" so completely as to disrupt either the comfort or activities of his associates in a room. Nursery school teachers, in particular, have found it highly advantageous to remove such a child from the group to a place where he may relax and acquire control without being a distracting influence or attracting the attention he may be seeking. In some instances special rooms have been set aside for this purpose. The isolation technique must be used skillfully in order to be an educational experience for the child, gradually modifying him in the direction of greater control. This goal may be defeated if the child regards the treatment simply as punishment and develops a feeling of antagonism toward the teacher (pp. 378–379).

Time-out did not gain widespread use until the 1970s, and it has been used most extensively in special education classes. Time-out is simply removing an individual from an environment that is reinforcing and maintaining inappropriate behavior. Contingent observation, which was discussed earlier in this chapter, is a form of time-out.

The next form of time-out is **exclusion time-out**, which requires that the student be removed from the learning activity. The educational components of contingent observation are missing, for the student cannot observe the appropriate performance of his or her peers. A disruptive student might be excused from music and requested to return to homeroom.

The most severe variation of time-out (and the one most publicized), **seclusion time-out,** necessitates the use of an isolation room. The misbehaving student is removed from the classroom and spends a specified amount of time alone. After an act of aggression, for example, a student is instructed to go to the time-out room for three minutes. When seclusion time-out is used, several important precautions must be taken, because of the furor over seclusion time-out and because of several court actions placed against residential facilities for individuals with disabilities that use time-outs. An appropriate place or room must be found. It should be well lighted, properly ventilated, sizable (at least six feet by six feet), safe, and unlocked. Preferably, the room should have a window so the student can be observed periodically (Gast & Nelson, 1977a, 1977b). If a room cannot be found where an adult can monitor the student's actions, another intervention should be scheduled. For the teacher's protection against lawsuits, the school principal should be consulted next. If the school administration agrees that seclusion time-out is necessary, the parents should be contacted and their permission obtained. Once time-out is initiated, precise records on its use should be kept. A sample data sheet is provided in Figure 7.2. On that sheet, the number of times a student goes to the time-out room and the amount of time spent there are noted.

The duration of time-out should also be predetermined (anywhere from one to five minutes is usually sufficient). It is advisable for release to be contingent upon good behavior. Many educators use an extension release clause or a changeover delay procedure. This extends time-out for fifteen seconds if the student is misbehaving while time-out is scheduled to end; to be released, the student must act appropriately for at least the last fifteen seconds of the time-out.

There are many concerns about time-out and its use in school. For some students, time-out could be reinforcing, for they are removed from what they might view

Figure 7.2
Sample record sheet to be posted near the door of seclusion time-out room

Day	Date	Time Time-out Initiated	Total Time in Time-out	Description of Behavior in Time-out

Student's name _____   Target behavior _____

as an unpleasant situation. Inappropriateness may even increase during a time-out for this reason. When the learning process is not enjoyable and teachers do not compensate for the often boring and repetitive activities they plan for their students, even time-out, a tactic designed to be unpleasant, can become a more attractive alternative to students. For students who find the academic situation frustrating and even punishing at times, time-out may cause increases rather than decreases in the target behaviors.

There are some very undesirable features of seclusion time-out, and careful consideration must be given to the seriousness of the behavioral infraction before time-out is scheduled. The implementation of time-out is costly to both student and teacher. The student loses valuable instructional time, and the teacher is forced to schedule an intervention that can be difficult to manage.

Time-out and its variations can be very effective tools for teachers who are trying to eliminate or greatly reduce behaviors that interfere with the learning process. Implementation should occur with care and caution. The student's performance should warrant time-out either because it was unaltered by other tactics or because the transgressions are serious.

Punishment

Although most of the tactics discussed in this chapter can be called punishers, for the sake of clarity, **punishment** here includes those tactics involving the application of aversive consequences. Punishment, then, is the second severe tactic found on the Intervention Ladder. Although no research studies have investigated punishment's effectiveness with students with mild to moderate disabilities (Polsgrove & Rieth, 1983), its use by school administrators and their staffs is widespread (Rose, 1983). One reason for this could be its effectiveness. It has, however, many negative aspects. Children often associate the aversive technique with the person who administers it. Punishment increases the likelihood of the student's trying to escape the situation associated with the person doing the punishment. Its influence does not usually generalize across settings, so often it needs to be applied in all situations in which the behavior occurs. Punishment is not a behavior-building technique, for new skills are not taught through this method.

There are other negative features of punishment that educators need to know. Some children may simply substitute another undesirable behavior for the one that was punished. Punishment can also put fear into the classroom environment; children perform because they are afraid not to. This does not foster a good learning environment in which children feel free to explore and discover.

For these reasons, educators should carefully consider whether punishment should be used in school settings. Many other, less aversive procedures are available that do not have such negative potential. The controversy over punishment has raged for years. Olson (1935) stated that punishment has no real place in "modern" schools. He believed that using punishment was a sign of incompetence and inefficiency and that direct and rewarding consequences were more effective. Despite concerns about the use of punishment, more and more states are approving, through various court decisions, the use of punishment in the schools. The prevalence of its use is unknown. Clearly when it is used, its full impact must be monitored, and those students who are punished should receive rewards for appropriate performances.

Exclusion

Only a brief discussion is given here about **exclusion** because states and school districts differ greatly in their policies about excluding students with and without disabilities from school. Generally, there are three kinds of exclusion: **in-school supervision, suspension,** and **expulsion.** The first is a mild form of exclusion and requires the student to spend time in a study hall under the supervision of an adult. One might even consider this procedure a form of time-out. In-school suspension has been used in many middle and high school settings with considerable success in reducing tardiness to classes, hallway disruptions, and various school rule violations. It can be most useful to have a designated room, supervised by a teacher or paraprofessional, for such instances when students lose the privilege of attending an assembly, field trip, or other school event. When an in-school suspension room is always available, teachers do not have to make special arrangements for students who need to be dismissed from a class because they are disrupting their peers' learning or have lost a privilege.

The other two forms of exclusion require the youngster to stay away from school for some defined period of time. Both these procedures have serious ramifications and need to be carefully considered before they are applied. Under these conditions, students lose valuable instructional time, and may fall far behind in their academic subjects, which could contribute to further frustration with school and more behavioral problems. Another difficulty with these procedures is that students may not be supervised while they are excluded from school. When this occurs, they might prefer being away from school to being in school. Students might misbehave again when they return to school, so they can be dismissed again. School officials must consider these negative possibilities before they exclude youngsters from school.

Summary

Several interventions have been presented in this chapter that aim at reducing or eliminating misconduct in school settings. Table 7.1 summarizes these interventions and includes some cautions that educators must consider for each one. Educators must develop an understanding of their students' cultural, ethnic, and linguistic backgrounds, particularly as this information relates to ways that students interact with peers and adults.

The Intervention Ladder should serve as a reminder that many mild interventions are available for dealing with inappropriate behaviors. These mild interventions should be tried before more elaborate, expensive, or intrusive moderate and serious interventions. For most infractions in school settings, those interventions found lower on the ladder will be effective with the majority of youngsters. For those few youngsters who do not respond favorably to mild interventions, the interventions found higher on the ladder may prove necessary.

Study and Discussion Questions

1. Describe the rationale for the Intervention Ladder.
2. Explain preventive measures to decrease the occurrence of inappropriate behaviors.

3. Describe preventive measures that can be used to address the following behaviors:
   • the student likes to talk to other students
   • the student talks loudly
   • the student is easily interrupted when working
4. Provide examples of interventions that eliminate mild levels of inappropriate behaviors, and behaviors for which they could be used.
5. Provide examples of behaviors that warrant the use of interventions from the upper half of the Intervention Ladder.
6. Give examples of interventions that reduce moderate levels of disruptive behaviors.
7. Describe reasons that behavior problems occur.
8. Provide descriptions of and rationales for using interventions to minimize or eliminate more serious behavioral infractions.
9. Describe behaviors from your own experience as a teacher and interventions that you might try to eliminate the behaviors.

References and Suggested Readings

Reed, D. F. (1993). Culturally diverse students. In J. W. Wood (Ed.), *Mainstreaming: A practical approach for teachers* (2nd ed., pp. 123–154). Columbus, OH: Merrill.

Smith, D. D., & Rivera, D. M. (1993). Effective discipline (2nd ed.). Austin, TX: PRO-ED.

Prevention

Center, D. B., Deitz, S. M., & Kaufman, N. E. (1982). Student ability, task difficulty, and inappropriate classroom behavior: A study of children with behavioral disorders. *Behavior Modification, 6,* 355–374.

Cone, J. P., DeLawyer, D. D., & Wolfe, V. V. (1985). Assessing parent participation: The parent/family involvement index. *Exceptional Children, 51,* 417–424.

DeLuke, S. V., & Knoblock, P. (1987). Teacher behavior as preventive discipline. *Teaching Exceptional Children, 20,* 18–24.

Fafard, M. (1987). Preventing discipline problems in inner-city special education programs. *Teaching Exceptional Children, 20,* 44.

Rieth, H. J., & Bickel, D. D. (1986). Effective schools, classrooms, and instructions: Implications for special education. *Exceptional Children, 52,* 489–500.

Rieth, H., & Evertson, C. (1988). Variables related to the effective instruction of difficult-to-teach children. *Focus on Exceptional Children, 20*(5), 1–8.

Slade, D., & Callaghan, T. (1988). Preventing management problems. *Academic Therapy, 23*(3), 229–235.

Smith, D. D., & Rivera, D. M. (1993). *Effective discipline* (2nd ed.). Austin, TX: PRO-ED.

Smith, D. D., & Rivera, D. P. (1995). Discipline in special education and general education settings. *Focus on Exceptional Children, 27*(5), 1–14.

Mild Interventions
Specific Praise

Gable, R., Hendrickson, J., Young, C., Shores, R., & Stowitschek, J. (1983). A comparison of teacher approval statements across categories of exceptionality. *Journal of Special Education Technology, 6,* 15–22.

Morsink, C. V., Soar, R. S., Soar, R. M., & Thomas, R. (1986). Research on teaching: Opening the door to special education classrooms. *Exceptional Children, 53,* 32–40.

Thurlow, M., Graden, J., Greener, J., & Ysseldyke, J. (1983). LD and non-LD students' opportunities to learn. *Learning Disability Quarterly, 6,* 172–183.

White, M. A. (1975). Natural rates of teacher approval and disapproval in the classroom. *Journal of Applied Behavior Analysis, 8,* 367–372.

Ignoring

Allen, K. E., Hart, B. M., Buell, J. S., Harris, F. R., & Wolf, M. M. (1964). Effects of social reinforcement in isolate behavior of a nursery school child. *Child Development, 35,* 511–518.

Bacon, E. H. (1990). Using negative consequences effectively. *Academic Therapy, 25,* 599–611.

Evertson, C. M., Emmer, E. T., Clements, B. S., & Worsham, M. E. (1994). *Classroom management for elementary teachers* (3rd ed.). Boston: Allyn & Bacon.

Hall, R. V., Fox, R., Willard, D., Goldsmith, L., Emerson, M., Owen, M., Davis, F., & Porcia, E. (1971). The teacher as observer and experimenter in the modification of disputing and talking-out behavior. *Journal of Applied Behavior Analysis, 4,* 141–149.

Rules

Colvin, G., Sugai, G., & Patching, B. (1993). Precorrection: An instructional approach for managing predictable problem behaviors. *Intervention in School and Clinic, 28*(3), 143–150.

Duke, D. L. (1980). *Managing student behavior problems.* New York: Teachers College Press.

Evertson, C. M., Emmer, E. T., Clements, B. S., & Worsham, M. E. (1994). *Classroom management for elementary teachers* (2nd ed.). Englewood Cliffs, NJ: Prentice-Hall.

O'Melia, M. C., & Rosenberg, M. S. (1989). Classroom management: Preventing behavior problems in classrooms for students with learning disabilities. *LD Forum, 15*(1), 23–26.

Rosenberg, M. S. (1986). Maximizing the effectiveness of structured management programs: Implementing rule-review procedures with disruptive and distractible students. *Behavioral Disorders, 11,* 239–248.

Windell, J. (1991). *Discipline: A source of 50 failsafe techniques for parents.* New York: Macmillan.

Moderate Interventions
Contingent Instructions

Baron, R. A. (1988). Negative effects of destructive criticism: Impact on conflict, self-efficacy, and task performance. *Journal of Applied Psychology, 73,* 199–207.

O'Leary, K. D., Kaufman, K. F., Kass, R. E., & Drabman, R. S. (1970). The effects of loud and soft reprimands on the behavior of disruptive students. *Exceptional Children, 37,* 145–155.

Roberts, M. B., & Smith, D. D. (1977). The influence of contingent instructions on the social behavior of a young boy. *School Applications of Learning Theory, 9,* 24–42.

Van Houten, R., Nau, P. A., McKenzie-Keating, D. E., Sameoto, D., & Colavecchia, B. (1982). An analysis of some variables influencing the effectiveness of reprimands. *Journal of Applied Behavior Analysis, 15,* 65–83.

Contingent Observation

Gast, D. L., & Nelson, C. M. (1977). Timeout in the classroom: Implications for special education. *Exceptional Children, 43,* 461–464.

Mace, C. F., Page, T. J., Ivancic, M. T., & O'Brien, S. (1986). Effectiveness of brief timeout with and without contingent delay: A comparative analysis. *Journal of Applied Behavior Analysis, 19,* 79–86.

Criterion-Specific Rewards

Axelrod, S. (1983). *Behavior modification for the classroom.* New York: McGraw-Hill.

Deitz, D. E. D., & Repp, A. C. (1983). Reducing behavior through reinforcement. *Exceptional Education Quarterly, 3,* 34–36.

Gallagher, P. A. (1988). *Teaching students with behavior disorders: Techniques and activities for classroom instruction.* Denver, CO: Love.

Myles, B. S., Moran, M. R., Ormsbee, C. K., & Downing, J. A. (1992). Guidelines for establishing and maintaining token economies. *Intervention in School and Clinic, 27*(3), 164–169.

Smith, D. D., & Rivera, D. M. (1993). *Effective discipline* (2nd ed.). Austin, TX: PRO-ED.

Fines

Polsgrove, L., & Rieth, H. (1983). Procedures for reducing children's inappropriate behavior in special education settings. *Exceptional Education Quarterly, 3,* 20–33.

Rapport, M. D., Murphy, H. A., & Bailey, J. S. (1982). Ritalin vs. response cost in the control of hyperactive children: A within subject comparison. *Journal of Applied Behavioral Analysis, 15,* 205–216.

Salend, S. J., & Allen, E. M. (1985). A comparison of self-managed response-cost systems on learning disabled children. *Journal of School Psychology, 23,* 59–67.

Sindelar, P. T., Honsaker, M. S., & Jenkins, J. R. (1982). Response cost and reinforcement contingencies of managing the behavior of distractible children in tutorial settings. *Learning Disability Quarterly, 5,* 3–13.

Walker, H. M. (1983). Applications of response cost in school settings: Outcomes, issues, and recommendations. *Exceptional Education Quarterly, 3,* 47–55.

Group Contingencies

Barrish, H. H., Saunders, M., & Wolf, M. M. (1969). Good behavior game: Effects of individual contingencies for group consequences on disruptive behavior in a classroom. *Journal of Applied Behavior Analysis, 2,* 119–124.

Broden, M., Hall, R. V., Dunlap, A., & Clark, R. (1970). Effects of teacher attention and a token reinforcement system in a junior high school special education class. *Exceptional Children, 36,* 341–349.

Litow, L., & Pumroy, D. K. (1975). A brief review of classroom group-oriented contingencies. *Journal of Applied Behavior Analysis, 8,* 341–347.

Maurer, R. (1988). *Special education discipline handbook.* West Nyack, NY: Center for Applied Research in Education.

Salend, S. J. (1987). Group-oriented behavior management strategies. *Teaching Exceptional Children, 20,* 53–55.

Salend, S. J., & Gordon, B. (1987). A group-oriented timeout ribbon procedure. *Behavioral Disorders, 12,* 131–137.

Salend, S. J., & Lamb, E. M. (1986). The effectiveness of a group-managed interdependent contingency system. *Learning Disability Quarterly, 9,* 268–274.

Salend, S. J., Reynolds, C. J., & Coyle, E. M. (1989). Individualizing the good behavior game across type and frequency of behavior with emotionally disturbed adolescents. *Behavior Modification, 13,* 108–126.

Sulzbacher, S. I., & Houser, J. E. (1968). A tactic to eliminate disruptive behaviors in the classroom: Group contingent consequences. *American Journal of Mental Deficiency, 73,* 88–90.

Peer Management

Dougherty, B. S., Fowler, S. A., & Paine, S. C. (1985). The uses of peer monitors to reduce negative interaction during recess. *Journal of Applied Behavior Analysis, 18,* 141–153.

Endsley, W. R. (1980). *Peer tutorial instruction.* Englewood Cliffs, NJ: Educational Technology.

Fowler, S. A. (1986). Peer-monitoring and self-monitoring: Alternatives to traditional teacher management. *Exceptional Children, 52,* 573–581.

Kerr, M. M., Strain, P. S., & Ragland, E. U. (1982). Teacher-mediated peer feedback treatment of behaviorally handicapped children. *Behavior Modification, 6*(4), 277–290.

Krouse, J., Gerber, M. M., & Kauffman, J. M. (1981). Peer tutoring: Procedures, promises, and unresolved issues. *Exceptional Education Quarterly, 1,* 107–115.

Lovitt, T. C., Lovitt, A. O., Eaton, M. D., & Kirkwood, M. (1973). The deceleration of inappropriate comments by a natural consequence. *Journal of School Psychology, 11,* 148–154.

Self-Management

Bornstein, P. H. (1985). Self-instructional training: A commentary and state-of-the-art. *Journal of Applied Behavior Analysis, 18,* 69–72.

Broden, M., Hall, R. V., & Mitts, B. (1971). The effect of self-recording on the classroom behavior of two eighth-grade students. *Journal of Applied Behavior Analysis, 4,* 191–199.

Dickerson, E. A., & Creedon, C. F. (1981). Self-selection of standards by children: The relative effectiveness of pupil-selected and teacher-selected standards of performance. *Journal of Applied Behavior Analysis, 14,* 425–433.

Ellis, E. S., & Friend, P. (1991). Adolescents with learning disabilities. In B. Y. L. Wong (Ed.), *Learning about learning disabilities* (pp. 505–561). San Diego, CA: Academic Press.

Fantuzzo, J. W., & Clement, P. W. (1981). Generalization of the effects of teacher- and self-administered tokens to non-treated students. *Journal of Applied Behavior Analysis, 14,* 435–447.

Hallahan, D. P., Kneedler, R. D., & Lloyd, J. W. (1983). Cognitive behavior modification techniques for learning disabled children: Self-instruction self-monitoring. In J. D. McKinney & F. Feagans (Eds.), *Current topics in learning disabilities* (Vol. 1). Norwood, NJ: Ablex.

Hallahan, D. P., Lloyd, J. W., Kneedler, R. D., & Marshall, K. J. (1982). A comparison of the effects of self- versus teacher-assessment of on-task behavior. *Behavior Therapy, 13,* 715–723.

Hallahan, D. P., Marshall, K. J., & Lloyd, J. W. (1981). Self-recording during group instruction: Effects on attention to task. *Learning Disability Quarterly, 4,* 407–413.

Hughes, C. A., & Boyle, J. R. (1991). Effects of self-monitoring for on-task behavior and task productivity on elementary students with moderate mental retardation. *Education and Treatment of Children, 14,* 96–111.

Karoly, P., & Kanger, F. H. (1982). *Self-management and behavior change: From theory to practice.* New York: Pergamon Press.

Kneedler, R. D., & Hallahan, D. P. (1981). Self-monitoring of on-task behavior with learning disabled children: Current studies and directions. *Exceptional Education Quarterly, 2,* 73–82.

Lovitt, T. C. (1995). *Tactics for teaching* (2nd ed.). Columbus, OH: Merrill.

Lovitt, T. C., & Curtiss, K. A. (1969). Academic response rate as a function of teacher- and self-imposed contingencies. *Journal of Applied Behavior Analysis, 2,* 49–53.

Paris, S. B., & Oka, E. R. (1986). Self-regulated learning among exceptional children. *Exceptional Children, 53,* 103–108.

Rhode, G., Morgan, D. P., & Young, K. R. (1983). Generalization and maintenance of treatment gains of behaviorally handicapped students from resource rooms to regular classrooms using self-evaluation procedures. *Journal of Applied Behavior Analysis, 16,* 171–188.

Robin, A., Schneider, M., & Dolnick, M. (1977). The turtle technique: An extended case study of self-control in the classroom. In K. D. O'Leary & S. G. O'Leary (Eds.), *Classroom management: The successful use of behavior modification* (2nd ed.). New York: Pergamon Press.

Schloss, P. J. (1987). Self-management strategies for adolescents entering the work force. *Teaching Exceptional Children, 19*(4), 39–43.

Smith, D. D., & Rivera, D. M. (1993). *Effective discipline* (2nd ed.). Austin, TX: PRO-ED.

Stevenson, H. C., & Fantuzzo, J. W. (1984). Application of the "generalization man" to a self-control intervention with school-aged children. *Applied Behavior Analysis, 17,* 203–212.

Workman, E. A., & Katz, A. M. (1995). *Teaching behavioral self-control to students.* Austin, TX: PRO-ED.

Parent Action

Birenbaum, A., & Cohen, H. J. (1993). On the importance of helping families: Policy implications from a national study. *Mental Retardation, 31,* 67–74.

Kroth, R. L. (1985). *Communicating with parents of exceptional children: Improving parent-teacher relationships* (2nd ed.). Denver, CO: Love.

Lobato, D. J. (1990). *Brothers, sisters, and special needs.* Baltimore: Brookes.

Nelson, C. M., Rutherford, R. B., Center, D. B., & Walker, H. M. (1991). Do public schools have an obligation to serve troubled children and youth? *Exceptional Children, 57,* 406–415.

Simpson, R. L. (1990). *Conferencing parents of exceptional children* (2nd ed.). Austin, TX: PRO-ED.

Turnbull, H. R., & Turnbull, A. P. (Eds.). (1985). *Parents speak out: Then and now.* Columbus, OH: Merrill.

More Serious Interventions
Overcorrection

Azrin, N. H., & Powers, M. A. (1975). Eliminating classroom disturbances of emotionally disturbed children by positive practice procedures. *Behavior Therapy, 6,* 525–534.

Burke, J. C. (1992). *Decreasing classroom behavior problems.* San Diego, CA: Singular Publishing Group.

Carey, R. G., & Bucher, B. (1983). Positive practice overcorrection: The effects of duration of positive practice on acquisition and response reduction. *Journal of Applied Behavior Analysis, 16,* 101–109.

Foxx, R. M., & Bechtel, D. R. (1983). Overcorrection: A review and analysis. In S. Axelrod & J. Apsche (Eds.), *The effects of punishment on human behavior.* New York: Academic Press.

Time-out

Bacon, E. H. (1990). Using negative consequences effectively. *Academic Therapy, 25,* 599–611.

Barton, L. E., Brulle, A. R., & Repp, A. (1987). Effects of differential scheduling of timeout to reduce maladaptive responding. *Exceptional Children, 53*(4), 351–356.

Brantner, J. P., & Doherty, M. A. (1983). A review of timeout: A conceptual and methodological analysis. In S. Axelrod & J. Apsche (Eds.), *The effects of punishment on human behavior.* New York: Academic Press.

Gast, D. L., & Nelson, C. M. (1977a). Legal and ethical considerations for the use of timeout in special education settings. *The Journal of Special Education, 11,* 457–467.

Gast, D. L., & Nelson, C. M. (1977b). Timeout in the classroom: Implications for special education. *Exceptional Children, 43,* 461–464.

Lane, H. (1976). *The wild boy of Aveyron.* Cambridge, MA: Harvard University Press.

Mace, C. F., Page, T. J., Ivancic, M. T., & O'Brien, S. (1986). Effectiveness of brief timeout with and without contingent delay: A comparative analysis. *Journal of Applied Behavior Analysis, 19,* 79–86.

Olson, W. C. (1935). The diagnosis and treatment of behavior disorders of children. In the thirty-fourth yearbook of the National Society for the Study of Education (Eds.), *Educational diagnosis.* Bloomington, IL: Public Schools.

Punishment

Newsome, C., Favell, J. E., & Rincover, A. (1983). Side effects of punishment. In S. Axelrod & J. Apsche (Eds.), *The effects of punishment on human behavior.* New York: Academic Press.

Olson, W. C. (1935). The diagnosis and treatment of behavior disorders of children. In the thirty-fourth yearbook of the National Society for the Study of Education (Eds.), *Educational diagnosis.* Bloomington, IL: Public Schools.

Polsgrove, L., & Rieth, H. (1983). Procedures for reducing children's inappropriate behavior in special education settings. *Exceptional Education Quarterly, 3,* 20–33.

Rose, T. L. (1983). A survey of corporal punishment of mildly handicapped students. *Exceptional Education Quarterly, 3,* 9–19.

Wood, F. H., & Braaten, S. (1983). Developing guidelines for the use of punishing interventions in schools. *Exceptional Education Quarterly, 3,* 68–75.

Exclusion

Bartlett, L. (1989). Disciplining handicapped students: Legal issues in light of *Honig v. Doe. Exceptional Children, 55,* 357–366.

Craft, N., & Haussman, S. (1983). Suspension and expulsion of handicapped individuals. *Exceptional Children, 49,* 524–527.

Yell, M. L. (1989). *Honig v. Doe:* The suspension of handicapped students. *Exceptional Children, 56,* 60–69.

Chapter 8
Social Skills

Regardless of the setting (school, home, workplace, leisure activity), being socially competent and possessing effective social skills enhances individuals' quality of life. Unlike their counterparts, individuals with learning and behavior problems tend to have difficulty with an array of social behaviors including, for example, choosing appropriate social behaviors for different situations, predicting behavioral consequences, reading social cues, and adapting their behavior in social situations (Hazel & Schumaker, 1988; Pearl, Donahue, & Bryan, 1986).

Making Connections

Before you read, think about social skills that students with learning and behavior problems need in order to be successful in general education classroom settings and in other settings outside of the classroom. Compare this list of skills with what you know about social skills deficits among some students with disabilities. Describe how these deficits are problematic for students and teachers. Briefly review the behavioral interventions discussed in chapter 7. Review how some of these interventions can be used to promote effective social skills.

Objectives

After studying this chapter, the reader will be able to

1. Explain the construct of social competence.

2. Identify and explain curricular topics for social skills intervention.

3. Describe interventions for social skills targeted for instruction.

Although educators have developed and researched many procedures that reduce disruptive classroom behaviors (see chapter 7 for suggested interventions), the development of social skills alone cannot be equated with the development of **social competence.** Many youngsters, particularly children who are withdrawn, do not present conduct problems to their teachers and therefore do not receive instructional programs aimed at improving classroom behavior. However, most of these youngsters, and many others, do not develop the social skills and competence necessary for successful social interactions.

Social skills are used in the multidimensional process called social competence. This complex set of abilities facilitates interactions. When effective, social interactions elicit others' positive reactions and reduce the probability that they will respond negatively. The application of social skills must be flexible; different skills must be used, depending upon the situation and social context. The result contributes to acceptance by others.

Deficits in social skills occur throughout all groups of students with learning and behavior problems. Therefore, the development of social competence is of utmost concern to many educators. This is especially true because of the least restrictive environment requirements of P.L. 101–476 and P.L. 99–457 and the trend of "inclusive" classrooms. As youngsters with disabilities return to general education classrooms for some or all of their educational programs, their deficits in social skills are more obvious and classroom teachers seek to remediate these problems. To succeed in these least restrictive environments, students must be able to compete academically *and* socially. Although academic remediation and improvement are extremely important, social skills development must also be a high priority for those students in need of such remediation. Special education teachers who provide consultant services to general education teachers must be sure that social skills are targeted for instruction and student progress is monitored accordingly.

Social skills training is important because individuals who lack appropriate social skills and competence will probably have difficulties as children (Haager & Vaughn, 1995) and adjustment problems as adults in vocational, personal, and recreational areas (Neubert, Tilson, & Ianacone, 1989; Weller, 1989). Although social skills training has only recently been acknowledged as an important part of the school curriculum, training programs have shown promising results regarding educators' ability to remediate social deficits, such as peer interaction skills and social acceptance of students with learning and behavior problems (Cartledge & Milburn, 1986; Vaughn, McIntosh, & Spencer-Rowe, 1991). Thus, educators should include social skills targets on the IEPs of students who do not interact with others successfully. For example, social skills annual goals could include a focus on developing interactive and decision-making abilities. Instructional objectives might include developing communication skills to promote more effective social interaction and problem-solving skills to foster decision making.

In this chapter, the authors focus on social skills curriculum and instruction for elementary- and secondary-level youngsters with learning and behavior problems. We explain the general construct of social competence under which social skills training and other skills are included, discuss topics that can be included in a social skills curriculum, and discuss a variety of instructional tactics that educators can use to remediate social skills deficits. Additionally, we suggest social and behavioral considerations for teaching students from culturally and linguistically diverse backgrounds.

Nature of Social Competence

As you read, think about . . .

1. Describing the construct of social competence.
2. Identifying areas that constitute social competence.
3. Describing behaviors of individuals for whom social competence is problematic.
4. Identifying social skills training that might be beneficial in remediating social competence deficits.
5. Explaining the three categories of social competence deficits.

Social competence is the general construct that is used to explain social behavior, social acceptance, and the use of social skills (Haager & Vaughn, 1995). It is this construct under which social skills training occurs. Social competence can be assigned to individuals who are proficient in and generalize their use of social skills. It consists of social cognition, social interaction, social effectiveness, and decision making. All of these areas require social skills training and each is discussed separately under the section called "Topics for Instruction."

Gresham and Reschly (1988) suggest that individuals who do not display social competence fall into several categories. The first they term a skill deficit. The necessary behavior(s) are not in the individuals' repertoires. The members of the second group have a performance deficit; individuals possess the necessary skills, but do not apply them at the appropriate times or places. The third kind is a self-control deficit. In these cases, the individuals do not control their behaviors, and high rates of aversive behaviors often result. Those who have skill deficits could be considered in the acquisition and proficiency stages of learning. In these cases, the goal of instruction is for students to learn the target behavior or groups of behavior so they are mastered at a set level of accuracy and fluency. In the second case, when the individual is capable of performing the desired responses but does not apply them (generalization stage), one could say that the individual is not generalizing previous learning to different settings where the behavior should occur. Students who display excesses of behavior must reduce or eliminate their occurrences (see chapter 7 for suggested remediation strategies for reducing excesses of behavior). Therefore, just as with academic behaviors, it appears that the stages of learning theory (presented in chapter 4) are relevant to the instruction of social skills.

Social competence, then, is the ultimate goal of social skills training efforts. Many students with special needs require direct instruction in some or all of the skills that constitute social competence so that they can succeed in their interactions on the job, at home, and during leisure activities.

Topics for Instruction

As you read, think about...

1. Defining and explaining the five areas that comprise social competence.
2. Describing behaviors that suggest strengths and weaknesses in each of the five areas.
3. Describing social situations in which social competency areas are important.
4. Summarizing the research for the competency areas.

Although a verified taxonomy for social skills training does not exist, there has been considerable research about a variety of skills that fall within the realm of social skills training. Also, a number of social skills curricula and instructional programs have been developed recently. These products can assist educators in planning instruction in this important area. Tables 8.1, 8.2, and 8.3 show the topics of instruction included in three well-researched social skills curricula. Analysis of these curricula reveals a vast number of targets for educators to address.

Research about social skills and social competence has focused on clusters of behaviors organized and named differently from those listed in most curricula. Therefore, the list found in Figure 8.1 was developed to show another schema for social competence. This list is not intended to represent another curriculum model, but rather to present the results of the research literature concisely. Throughout these

Table 8.1
Stephens's Social
Skills Curriculum

Self-related behaviors	Environmental behaviors
Accepting consequences	Care for the environment
Ethical behavior	Dealing with emergencies
Expressing feelings	Lunchroom behavior
Positive attitude toward self	Movement around environment
Responsible behavior	
Self-care	
Task-related behaviors	**Interpersonal behaviors**
Asking and answering questions	Accepting authority
Attending behavior	Coping with conflict
Classroom discussion	Gaining attention
Completing tasks	Greeting others
Following directions	Helping others
Group activities	Making conversation
Independent work	Participating in organized play
On-task behavior	Exhibiting positive attitude toward others
Performing before others	Playing informally
Quality of work	Respecting own and others' property

Source: From *Social Skills in the Classroom*, by T. M. Stephens, 1978, Columbus, OH: Cedar Press. Copyright 1978 by Cedar Press. Reprinted with permission.

Table 8.2
The Walker Social
Skills Curriculum

Area I: Classroom skills

Listening to the teacher (sitting quietly and looking at . . .)

When the teacher asks you to do something (doing it)

Doing your best work (following directions and writing neatly)

Following classroom rules

Area II: Basic interaction skills

Eye contact

Using the right voice

Starting (finding someone to talk to)

Listening (looking at the person and paying attention)

Answering (saying something after someone talks to you)

Making sense (talking about the same things)

Taking turns talking

Asking questions

Continuing to talk (keeping the talking going)

Area III: Getting along skills

Using the polite words (saying nice things at the right time)

Sharing

Following rules (playing the game the same way as everyone else)

Assisting others (doing nice things for others when they need help)

Touching the right way

Area IV: Making friends

Good grooming (washing hands and face, brushing teeth, wearing clean clothes)

Smiling

Complimenting

Friendship making (starting conversation, taking turns talking, inviting)

Area V: Coping skills

When someone says no (finding another way to play)

When you express anger

When someone teases you

When someone tries to hurt you

When someone tells you to do something you can't do

When things don't go right

Source: From *The Walker Social Skills Curriculum: The ACCEPTS Program*, by H. M. Walker et al., 1988, Austin, TX: PRO-ED. Copyright 1988 by PRO-ED. Reprinted with permission.

discussions, it is important to remember that recent research (see References and Suggested Readings at the end of the chapter) has shown that social skills can be taught and peer acceptance improved.

According to Vaughn and Haager (1994), peer acceptance is considered to be an indicator of successful social adjustment in school and the workplace. Studies on peer acceptance and rejection of students with learning and behavior problems have

Table 8.3
Social Skills for
Daily Living

Orientation: Body basics

Kit 1: Conversation and friendship skills

Active listening

Greeting

Saying goodbye

Answering questions

Asking questions

Introducing yourself

Interrupting correctly

Conversation

Making friends

Kit 2: Skills for getting along with others

Accepting thanks

Saying thanks

Accepting compliments

Giving compliments

Apologizing

Accepting no

Resisting peer pressure

Responding to teasing

Accepting criticism

Giving criticism

Kit 3: Problem-solving skills

Following instructions

Getting help

Asking for feedback

Giving rationales

Solving problems

Persuasion

Negotiation

Joining group activities

Starting activities with others

Giving help

Source: From *Social Skills for Daily Living*. by J. B. Schumaker, J. S. Hazel, and C. S. Pederson, 1988, Circle Pines, MN: American Guidance Service. Copyright 1988 by American Guidance Service. Inc. All rights reserved. Reprinted with permission.

produced equivocal results. For instance, some researchers found that students with learning problems at the elementary level were rated lower in peer acceptance than their average-achieving peer group (Bursuck, 1989; La Greca & Stone, 1990). Other research findings showed that students with learning problems *and* low-achieving peers were less accepted than their average- and high-achieving peers (Haager & Vaughn, 1995). Peer acceptance has also been noted outside of the classroom setting. For instance, parents of youngsters with learning problems observe that their chil-

Figure 8.1
Social competence

Social Cognition	Social Interaction	Social Effectiveness	Decision Making
Role-taking	Cooperation	Acceptance	Predict consequences
Perception	Play	Peer	Social reasoning
Comprehension	Sharing	Adults	Problem solving
Interpretation	Communication	Appearance	
	Interchange	Assertiveness	
	Social conventions	Compliance	
	Deference	Nondisruption	
	Manners		

Figure 8.1
Social competence

dren may have fewer friends and memberships in organizations than children without learning problems (McConaughy & Ritter, 1985). Many students with special needs are not as socially active as their typical counterparts (Deshler & Schumaker, 1983). They go out less frequently, attend fewer sporting events, and participate less in extracurricular activities. Researchers have shown that social interaction skills, such as communication and interpersonal attitudes, correlate highly with employment success (Strawser, 1988; Weller, 1989). Poor social interaction skills have been identified as a major cause of adult maladjustment for persons with learning problems (Cartledge, 1989; Mellard & Hazel, 1992). Although, some students with learning problems may not experience social rejection (Sabornie, 1990) or may be well accepted by peers away from school (Roberts, Pratt, & Leach, 1991), there are clearly students with learning and behavior problems who require social skills training.

Social Cognition

To interact with others effectively, individuals must comprehend each other's implicit and explicit messages. They must also understand the social context and situation. **Social cognition** is the ability to gather information from the social field, process that information, determine its importance, and formulate a direction for positive action. This requires a considerable degree of experience and sophistication, which many persons with special needs do not possess.

To comprehend social situations, individuals also need to understand other people's emotional state. To do this requires an ability to understand other people's viewpoints. In the research literature, this ability is called **role taking.** Role taking relates to social perception because it requires a person to determine what someone else is thinking and feeling. It also forces that individual to see things from a different perspective. Role-taking skills can be improved through a number of activities. For example, students can make up several versions of the same story. The "Three Little Pigs" could be told from two perspectives: the pigs' and the wolf's. Role-taking skills are also refined through acting. Students could put on a class play, where extra time in discussion would be spent talking about the characters, their feelings, and emotions.

Social comprehension, which may be improved by enhanced role-taking abilities, requires the individual to perceive the words that others use, their tone of voice, and their nonverbal expressions. The research evidence is clear: Many students with special needs—whether watching a videotape or television show or participating in real-life situations—do not perceive or comprehend social situations well. This might be due to an inability to discriminate social cues, make inferences, or understand the importance of information conveyed implicitly or received subtly in social situations.

Evidence from research and clinical practice indicates that social cognition is developmental. For many it improves with age; for those who do not gain these skills independently, social cognition can be improved through direct instruction. Therefore, teachers need to consider social cognition targets (sensitivity, perception, comprehension, interpretation) and use opportunities for instruction that arise during the school day. Also, lessons aimed at teaching these social cognition skills need to be scheduled for students who have skill deficits in this area.

Social Interaction

People interact with each other in a variety of ways. Very young children interact with each other primarily through play. In play situations, children learn to cooperate, establish and follow rules, and share. Although play remains a part of people's lives through adulthood, **social interaction** assumes a greater communicative function as individuals become older. As with play, communicative interaction requires facility with a number of complex behaviors. Someone must initiate. For those participating, an interchange of giving and taking turns and remaining on topic is required for the interaction to continue. Then, the interaction needs to be terminated. The communicative situation requires individuals to ask open-ended questions and select and engage in conversational topics.

Social interaction requires complex skills and abilities that interplay with each other. Several skills contribute to successful social interactions: eye contact, duration and latency of replies, compliance, requesting new behaviors or topics, loudness of speech, gestures, and general affect. Effective social interactions also require individuals to discriminate the proper place and time for their interactions. Engaging in conversation about the games to play at recess is not appropriate during seatwork assignments. Manners and other social conventions also determine the appropriateness of when and how to interact with others. Introductions and greetings vary by the setting and the person. The way one greets an employer is different from the way one greets a friend. In that regard, individuals must learn that interactions with authority figures are different; there is an expectation of deferential respect and attentiveness.

The social context in which interactions occur, and the way they vary, makes it difficult to master the skills that constitute social interaction. These difficulties are compounded for individuals who come from a culture different from the dominant one. For example, making eye contact when participating in a conversation is expected in the dominant culture. It is considered rude in the Navajo and other Native American cultures. This fact raises several questions that have yet to be answered by educators. For example, exactly what social skills should educators teach students from different cultures? Can these students be taught to discriminate cultural settings and the appropriateness of various interaction styles depending on the cultural situation? Who should teach these skills? (See Spotlight on Diversity.)

Social and Behavioral Considerations

- Children learn social and cultural norms and rules through the socialization process.
- Violations of cultural norms result in sanctions.
- Tolerance for rule violations and endorsement of actions conforming to rules vary across cultures.

- Rules of nonverbal communication are influenced by cultural variability, cultural subgroups (e.g., gender, age, socioeconomic status, race), and environmental (e.g., work, school, recreation) norms.
- Cultural norms influence home environments, the need for privacy, the use of interpersonal space (Ramirez, 1989), and touching behavior (Anderson & Fenichel, 1989).
- The importance of and adherence to the concept of time vary across cultures.
- Expressions of respect for adults, such as establishing eye contact, asking questions, and using formal titles, vary across cultures (Ramirez, 1989).
- Competition and cooperation may be viewed differently across cultures (Roberts, Bell, & Salend, 1991). ●

Social Effectiveness

Social effectiveness, sometimes referred to as social integration, implies acceptance from peers and others. The product of social effectiveness is social status. This status, particularly from the peer group, is important to most individuals. Peer acceptance requires a number of skills and attributes, such as friendliness, social visibility, outgoingness, social participation, nurturance and reinforcement of peers, kindness, and sensitivity. The result is making and maintaining friendships, an aspect of peer acceptance.

Social skills instructional programs (Schumaker, Hazel, & Pederson, 1988; Walker et al., 1988) typically include components on how to make friends. Interestingly, a relationship exists between having friends and being well groomed (being neat and clean, especially in dress). The importance of good grooming skills was identified in a study conducted by Schumaker, Wildgen, and Sherman (1982). They found that students with special needs tend to be less able in a number of factors relating to appearance (pleasant facial expression, posture, grooming, clothing neatness, general attractiveness) than their regular education counterparts. Verbal and nonverbal interactions (such as smiling, complimenting others, initiating conversations, and taking turns) also seem to relate to social effectiveness.

Another factor that contributes to social effectiveness for school-aged youngsters is their classroom behavior. Drabman and Patterson (1981) maintain that disruptive students are less popular than those who follow rules and behave according to teacher's expectations for the class. This may be one reason that many students with special needs are not valued by their peers. These authors suggest that once such inappropriate behavior is reduced or eliminated (see chapter 7 for suggestions on remediation), these students' social status also improves.

Assertiveness

Another aspect of social effectiveness—assertiveness—has become an important component of social skills training. Assertiveness, viewed as an important element of **self-determination** (discussed more fully in chapter 14), is a skill that students and adults must learn in order to express their needs and desires, to interact effectively with peers, and to advocate for themselves in a variety of situations (Hoffman & Field, 1995; Martin & Marshall, 1995). There are many facets of assertiveness, and each has some social benefits. For example, students must know when and how to say "no" to peers or others who demand their participation in or submission to an inappropriate behavior. Assertiveness helps students avoid being victims. Assertiveness, like other social skills, can be developed through direct instruction (as described in the "Instructional Methods and Techniques" section of this chapter).

Social effectiveness requires proficiency in the skills discussed in this section, as well as those identified in "Social Cognition and Social Interaction." Merely interacting with others does not guarantee effectiveness, nor does possessing the skills discussed in these two sections. Students must decide when to use and apply them at the appropriate times and places.

Decision Making

Although most students seem to understand what is deemed acceptable behavior at school and in society, many seem unable to choose socially acceptable behaviors in specific situations. For example, when a conflictual situation is described, they cannot identify the problem. They cannot provide options for handling the situation or predict the consequences for the solutions they suggest. They cannot arrive at the best way to behave or react in situations similar to the one presented to them. Bryan and Bryan (1986) maintain that many youngsters with special needs tend to select antisocial behaviors, particularly when pressured by their peers. The link between juvenile delinquency and mild disabilities might relate to poor decision-making skills and inabilities to solve social problems.

A curriculum that teaches **decision-making abilities** should include a variety of skills. Martin and Marshall (1995) and Wehmeyer (1995) offer the following skills for inclusion in a decision-making program:

1. Determine the demands of the situation.
2. Set goals and standards for the situation.
3. Determine information that will assist in decision making.
4. Use past experiences to form solutions for new problems.
5. Brainstorm solutions considering cause and effect.
6. Consider the best solution based on specific selection criteria.
7. Develop a plan; seek assistance as needed.
8. Evaluate the plan; modify as necessary.

Problem Solving

Problem solving is an area in which many students need considerable instruction. Whether solving a mathematical problem or a problem in a social situation, these students are unable to arrive at appropriate solutions. Meichenbaum (1979) states that problem-solving deficits "include selecting the first solution the child thinks of without developing alternatives or examining consequences, thus failing to conceptualize alternative options of action" (p. 24). He believes that children need to develop social reasoning skills, with which they come up with alternative solutions to simple conflict situations and predict the consequences of their solutions. He suggests that training sessions can take the form of group games in which children are encouraged to think and reason, rather than elicit set responses. Table 8.4 shows the components of social problem-solving training as advocated by Meichenbaum. These steps should be helpful to teachers as they design instructional programs for students deficient in these important skill areas.

Table 8.4
Meichenbaum's
Components of
Problem-Solving
Training

Prerequisite skill	(Pre)	Look for signs of upset, or "not so good," feelings.
Problem definition	(1)	Know exactly what the problem is.
Goal statement	(2)	Decide on your goal.
Impulse delay	(3)	Stop and think before you act.
Generation of alternatives	(4)	Think of as many solutions as you can to solve your problem.
Consideration of consequences	(5)	Think of the different things that will happen after you implement each solution.
Implementation	(6)	When you think you have a really good solution, try it.
Recycle	(Post)	If your first solution doesn't work, be sure to try other solutions.

Source: From "Teaching Children Self-Control," by D. Meichenbaum, 1979, in B. B. Lahey and A. E. Kazdin, (Eds.), *Advances in Clinical Child Psychology* (Vol. 2), New York: Plenum Press. Copyright 1979 by Plenum Press. Reprinted with permission.

Instructional Methods and Techniques

As you read, think about . . .

1. Describing specific interventions that are used to teach social competence.
2. Devising an intervention program for teaching cooperation skills.
3. Explaining how modeling can be used to teach social conventions.
4. Discussing the role of assertiveness training in self-determination curriculum and ways to teach youngsters to be assertive.
5. Developing a problem-solving curriculum that can be infused into current curriculum and taught throughout the school day.
6. Identifying ways to help students generalize social skills training across settings.
7. Explaining how to teach students self-control.

The training of social competence areas has benefited greatly from the cognitive (strategic) and behavioral approaches to instruction. Over the last fifteen years, intervention research efforts have focused on cognitive-behavioral tactics to teach social skills and to promote generalization (Montague, 1988; Vaughn, Lancelotta, & Minnis, 1988). Specifically, training tactics that have proven effective include modeling, coaching, behavior rehearsal, role playing, problem solving, mnemonics, feedback, and prompting (Warger, 1990).

In this section, we discuss several topics of instruction that illustrate how specific social skills can be taught. Because many of the same procedures are used to teach students different social skills, descriptions are provided only in specific areas to serve as examples of how they can be implemented. Table 8.5 provides a more thorough listing of social skills and suggested remediation procedures that research and practice have proven successful.

Acquisition of Cooperation Skills

Coaching is a tactic that teachers can use to teach many different social skills. We discuss it only to show how this procedure can be applied. Coaching involves having a trainer give guidance and feedback on appropriate social behaviors in natural environments. Tactics such as modeling, prompting, and rehearsal can be used to promote

Table 8.5
Social Skills
Training Tactics

Instructional target	Stage of learning	Possible tactics
Social cognition		
Interpretation	Acquisition	Role playing
		Coaching
		Discussions
Perception	Acquisition	Role taking
		Acting in dramas
		Role playing
		Retelling stories
		Role taking
		Coaching
Social interaction		
Peer interaction	Acquisition	Modeling
		Group contingencies
		Peer pairing
		Behavioral management
		Dispensing reinforcement
		Adult-mediated prompting
		Social praise
Conventions	Acquisition	Self-management
		Self-instruction
		Coaching
		Role playing
		Rehearsals
		Verbal rehearsal
		Behavioral rehearsal
		Modeling live film
		Coaching
		Peer tutoring
	Maintenance and generalization	Rationales
		"Surprise" visits
		Variable reinforcement
Social effectiveness		
Appearance	Acquisition	Modeling
		Instructions
		Coaching
		Group discussions
Assertiveness	Acquisition	Role playing
		Reinforcement
		Coaching
		Modeling
		Peers
		Videotapes
		Adults
		Instructions
		Discussions
		Behavioral rehearsal and feedback

continued

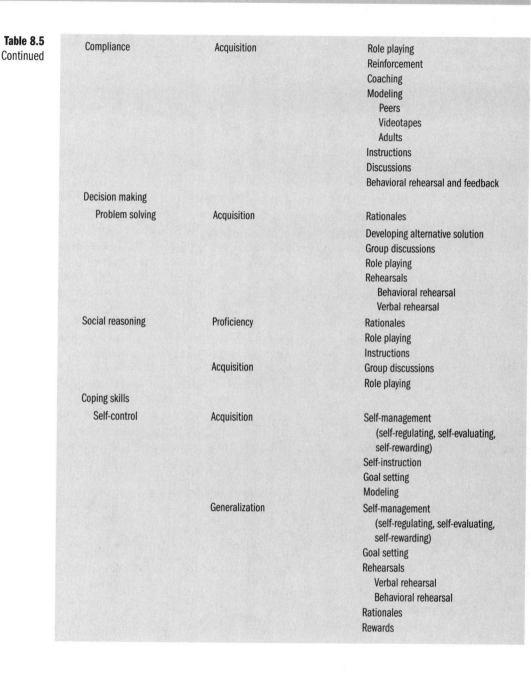

Table 8.5
Continued

Compliance	Acquisition	Role playing
		Reinforcement
		Coaching
		Modeling
		Peers
		Videotapes
		Adults
		Instructions
		Discussions
		Behavioral rehearsal and feedback
Decision making		
Problem solving	Acquisition	Rationales
		Developing alternative solution
		Group discussions
		Role playing
		Rehearsals
		Behavioral rehearsal
		Verbal rehearsal
Social reasoning	Proficiency	Rationales
		Role playing
		Instructions
	Acquisition	Group discussions
		Role playing
Coping skills		
Self-control	Acquisition	Self-management
		(self-regulating, self-evaluating, self-rewarding)
		Self-instruction
		Goal setting
		Modeling
	Generalization	Self-management
		(self-regulating, self-evaluating, self-rewarding)
		Goal setting
		Rehearsals
		Verbal rehearsal
		Behavioral rehearsal
		Rationales
		Rewards

the occurrence of the behavior (Warger, 1990). In coaching, the student receives direct verbal instructions, and then rehearses the target skill in a nonthreatening situation. The following steps could be used in a coaching situation (Gresham, 1981):

1. Presentations of rules or standards for the target behavior.
2. Rehearsing the skill with the coach or peer partner.
3. Feedback from the coach on the rehearsed performance.
4. Discussions and suggestions for future performances.

For older students who are working in cooperative group instructional arrangements, teachers might target social skills that are important for cooperative group learning. Prior to group work, teachers could construct contrived situations in which students role-play particular behaviors while being coached by the teacher. First, the teacher might model the appropriate cooperative behaviors. Second, the teacher could provide examples and nonexamples of the target cooperative skills. Third, students could practice the desired social behaviors with the teacher providing verbal prompts and placing posters containing written prompts around the room. Finally, students could discuss their group's work and make recommendations for future group activities that involve cooperative behaviors.

Montague (1988) investigated how coaching behaviors (e.g., modeling, rehearsal, prompting, practice, feedback, reinforcement) affected the abilities of students with learning disabilities, behavior disorders, or mental retardation to learn job-related social skills. Results showed that the tactics were effective in teaching the targeted behaviors in contrived situations. Thus, coaching tactics can be used successfully across school-age populations to promote appropriate social skills.

Acquisition of Social Conventions

As with coaching, modeling has been used to teach a variety of social skills. It is described here to illustrate how it can be effectively used to teach youngsters how to interact in a job interview. Regardless of the skill taught and regardless of its application, the relevant features of this procedure remain much the same.

Modeling social skills comes in two general forms: live modeling and symbolic modeling. In live modeling, one person (perhaps a counselor) role-plays the employer interviewing applicants for a position. Another person (possibly the teacher) plays the part of the applicant. In the symbolic modeling situation, videotapes or films of actual interviews are used. Students need to see both models of the interview situation.

For the situation just described, it is advisable to pair modeling procedures with other procedures. For example, before the demonstration, the teacher should engage the students in a discussion about the importance of job interviews and guide the students to watch for specific behaviors on the part of the applicant (greetings used, deference, tone of voice, gestures, smiling). Afterward, to follow up the observation period, the teacher holds a discussion session that analyzes the demonstration. The students then practice a mock interview. Students are paired and take turns being the employer and applicant. Here, they rehearse the good skills they observed and avoid the negative ones. Throughout these practice sessions, the teacher coaches, provides feedback, and praises students for the appropriate application of social conventions.

Gresham (1981) points out that for modeling to be effective, the target student(s) must attend to the model, retain the information presented, have the ability to execute the skill that was demonstrated, and possess the motivation necessary to apply and practice the skill. When modeling and peers are paired, the cautions discussed in chapter 7 about the selection and use of peers in tutoring must be considered.

Modeling has been used extensively and has proven effective across a variety of studies to teach social conventions. For instance, LaGreca and Mesibov (1981) used modeling and other tactics to promote conversation skills and greeting and interaction skills in students with learning disabilities. They found that students with learning disabilities improved their performance on targeted skills, although not to the level of the average-functioning control group of students. In another study, 40 students with learning disabilities (treatment and control groups) received training that included modeling to promote attending to the speaker, greeting, making requests, and complying with requests. Significant results were noted between groups in social skills acquisitions, although no differences were found between groups in peer ratings or teacher expectations social skills abilities.

As an instructional tactic, modeling has been shown repeatedly to be effective across disability groups and research areas (academics and social skills). It is relatively simple to implement, takes little teacher time, and can be used in a variety of settings and across age groups.

Acquisition of Assertiveness Skills

Few studies have been conducted to study how assertiveness can be developed in children. Assertiveness relates to social effectiveness and is required in even the simplest situations (asking for objects controlled by others, requesting assistance, seeking a chance to participate).

Assertiveness instruction is gaining in popularity as educators become increasingly aware of the need for youngsters with learning and behavior problems to be able to advocate for themselves, particularly as they get older and transition into adult roles (e.g., educational, vocational, recreational, social). Specifically, assertiveness training is a part of self-determination curricula (see chapter 14 for additional information), which is becoming more prevalent in today's classrooms. Assertiveness training includes the skill of expressing one's wants and needs appropriately, stating one's rights, identifying support systems, and conducting one's affairs (Martin & Marshall, 1995). Instructional tactics include problem solving, brainstorming, discussions, and role playing (Wehmeyer, 1995). Assertiveness training (and self-determination skills) can be infused into current course curricula, such as career education (Wehmeyer, 1995). Although self-determination skills, including assertiveness training, can be taught in the elementary grades, Ward (1988) points out that adolescence with its pending transition to adulthood is a particularly critical time to teach self-determination and assertiveness skills.

Social Skills Problem Solving

In one study, Hazel, Schumaker, Sherman, and Sheldon (1982) taught youngsters to improve their social problem-solving skills through a systematic training program. The students were presented with a situation in which they were required to describe a social problem, generate three solutions to the problem, evaluate the consequences of each solution, choose the best one, and decide how to implement the solution they selected. The researchers cited the following examples of problem situations: asking a parent for a later curfew, and not having enough time to complete an assignment. Instruction was presented in role-playing situations. The group leader modeled the skill and the students verbally and behaviorally rehearsed the skill through role playing and group discussions. The final test of skill acquisition was for the students to role-play the problem-solving skill with a novel situation. The results of this study indicate that students with cognitive processing difficulties did not learn to solve problems as well as those who did not display such deficits. Students with poor cognitive skills might need more time to acquire and master the abilities to generate different solutions and select ones that best fit a given problem.

Teachers who need to train students to solve social problems better might use a group of interventions together, as Hazel et al. (1982) did. Meichenbaum's problem-solving components (found in Table 8.4) could serve as the framework for lesson plans. Actual problems that occur at school could be used for developing discussion. The teacher would describe the social problem and lead students in group discussions in which they analyzed the problem and generated possible solutions.

Adelman and Taylor (1982) present another approach to teaching interpersonal problem-solving skills. The tactics they used to teach students to solve social problems are found in Table 8.6. These researchers maintain that students do not solve their interpersonal problems because they are not motivated to do so. Their premise is that students need to be motivated to learn; this motivation needs to be instilled before skill remediation begins. Once students are eager to learn a skill, it is less difficult for the teacher to instruct them. Maintenance and generalization are also enhanced. To increase motivation, they emphasize that the time and effort the student puts into learning a skill is worthwhile, that there is value in the outcome, and that the student's expectations of the results should be realistic. This motivational technique, which many teachers call providing **rationales,** is clearly a sound instructional procedure.

Table 8.6
Initial Steps for Enhancing and Maintaining Motivation to Solve Interpersonal Problems

Such activities as direct discussion, responses to direct questions, sentence completion, Q-sort items, role playing, audiovisual presentation, etc.[a] are used as vehicles for presenting or eliciting and clarifying the following:

1. Specific times when the individual experiences interpersonal problems (without assigning blame).
2. The form of the problems (again, no judgments are made).
3. The individual's perceptions of the causes of the problems.[b]
4. A broader analysis of possible causes (e.g., the individual's thoughts about other possible reasons and about how other people might interpret the situation; the intervener's examples of other perceptions and beliefs).
5. Any reasons the individual might have for wanting the interpersonal problems not to occur and for why they might continue.
6. A list of other possible reasons for people's non wanting to be involved in such problems.
7. The reasons that appear to be personally important to the individual and why they are significant, underscoring those which are the individual's most important reasons for not wanting to be involved in such problems.
8. General ways in which the individual can deal appropriately and effectively with such problems (e.g., avoiding them, using available skills, and developing new skills).
9. The individual's (1) general desire not to continue to experience interpersonal problems, (2) specific reasons for wanting this, and (3) desire to take some action.
10. The available alternatives for avoiding problems, using acquired skills, and developing new skills.
11. The available options related to activities and objectives associated with learning new skills (e.g., the specific activities and materials, mutual expectations).
12. Specific choices in the form of a mutually agreeable plan of action for pursuing alternatives related to steps 10 and 11.

Any step can be repeated as necessary, especially because of new information. Also, once the skill development activities are initiated, some of the above steps must be repeated in order to maintain an individual's motivation over time.

[a] Videotapes are particularly useful to make points vividly (e.g., to portray others in comparable situations, to present others as models).
[b] Each step does not require a separate session (e.g., steps 1–3 can be accomplished in one session).

Source: From "Enhancing the Motivation and Skills Needed to Overcome Interpersonal Problems," by H. S. Adelman and L. Taylor, 1982, *Learning Disability Quarterly, 5.* Copyright 1982 by the Council for Learning Disabilities. Reprinted with permission.

Social Skills Generalization

Deshler and Schumaker (1983) report that students do generalize their learning of social skills if they are programmed for this generalization. As with all learning, teachers cannot expect that generalization will occur without direct instructional efforts. In a preliminary report of the field-test results of Deshler and Schumaker's social skills training program, students did generalize skills that were taught through role playing and verbal and behavioral rehearsal to normal school situations. The researchers tested this generalization by observing "surprise situations" and found that the trained students generalized their learning well. It appears that generalization was enhanced because once a skill was mastered in the training sessions, the teachers set up surprise situations. In these situations, the teachers tested the students' ability to apply the newly learned skill and gave immediate feedback about the adequacy of the students' responses. If, for example, a student is learning to accept criticism, teachers could schedule intermittent testings of this skill to determine if it is maintained and applied in those situations where it should be. Once the student masters the skill in these situations, he or she is encouraged to set goals for using this skill outside the testing situation.

Self-Control

The authors discussed self-control and self-management strategies in some detail in chapter 7. Because developing self-control is such an important part of attaining social competence, we present strategies that can help teachers train students to develop and generalize these skills. Meichenbaum (1979) devised a helpful hierarchy (see Table 8.7) that organizes the general topics of instruction that should be included when teaching self-control. Whether the particular skill is delaying gratification, controlling one's temper, persisting in completing a task or meeting a goal, or participating effectively in an extracurricular school activity, the steps that Meichenbaum outlines should help teachers in developing complete lesson plans.

The development of social competence is a comprehensive goal that teachers and their students need to address. Social skills can be taught one by one. However, teachers must retain a vision of the overall construct of social competence if their students are to be competent in those social skills needed for independent adulthood.

Summary

Although many students with special needs are not socially competent, direct instruction aimed at the development of social skills is not typically included in the overall school curriculum. This area is now gaining more attention from researchers, teachers, and those who develop instructional materials.

Being socially competent requires the use of many sophisticated and often subtle skills. Socially competent individuals interact with others well. They understand social situations and other people's feelings and viewpoints. Such individuals understand the conventions of society and can discriminate different social contexts and adapt their behavior accordingly. By understanding different social contexts, they are able to make decisions, gain acceptance from others, and cope well with their environments.

Table 8.7
Meichenbaum's
Strategies for
Self-Control

Strategy 1: Developing and maintaining commitment

a. Substitute more adaptive self-attributions about nature of problem.

b. What "if-then" relationships do you see between certain actions and particular outcomes?

c. Identify and systematically anticipate several positive outcomes of your new behavior.

Strategy 2: Observing one's activities

a. What do you say to yourself about:
   (i) the behavior you want to change?
   (ii) your ability to change it?
   (iii) your progress?

b. Under what circumstances do you currently engage in the behavior you want to change?

c. How frequently or how much do you currently engage in the behavior you want to change?

Strategy 3: Planning the environment

a. Establish a supportive environment: teach family, friends, and associates how you would like them to help.

b. Modify the stimuli or cues that evoke the behavior you want to change.
   (i) External: Rearrange your physical environment.
   (ii) Internal: Alter undesirable internal cues, such as thoughts and images.

c. Develop a contract that specifies goals, behavior needed to attain those goals, and consequences for success and failure.

Strategy 4: Arranging consequences (behavioral programming)

a. Self-reward
   (i) Covert: Plan positive thoughts to follow successful actions.
   (ii) Overt: Plan to give yourself or have someone give you a reward for success (e.g., playing golf on Saturday, a gift).

b. Self-punishment
   (i) Covert: Plan negative thoughts or images to follow undesired actions immediately.
   (ii) Overt: Withhold a selected pleasant activity (e.g., watching your favorite TV show) or take away something you have (e.g., fine yourself $1 for each occurrence of undesirable behavior).

Source: From "Teaching Children Self-Control," by D. Meichenbaum, 1979, in B. B. Lahey and A. E. Kazdin, (Eds.), *Advances in Clinical Child Psychology* (Vol. 2), New York: Plenum Press. Copyright 1979 by Plenum Press. Reprinted with permission.

Because many students with special needs are unable to sustain friendships, decide what behaviors are expected and correct in particular situations, or understand social contexts, they frequently do not adjust well at school or home. This can also lead to difficulties in adult life, such as problems on the job. Less is known about how to teach social skills to students effectively than is known about more traditional content (e.g., mathematics, reading, written language). Regardless, teachers need to remember that the direct instructional techniques can cause substantial improvement in skills that constitute social competence.

Study and Discussion Questions

1. Explain the construct of social competence.
2. Identify and explain curricular topics for social skills intervention.
3. Describe interventions for social skills targeted for instruction.
4. Discuss the implications of teaching social skills to students who do not come from the dominant culture in the United States, and how you would handle such situations.

5. Develop a lesson plan for teaching improved grooming and appearance to secondary students.
6. Describe how the consultant special education teacher could work with the general classroom teacher to promote social skills in students with learning and behavior problems.
7. Develop a social skills curriculum and describe how you would infuse instruction of this curriculum into the content of other subjects.

● ●

References and Suggested Readings

Cartledge, G., & Milburn, J. F. (Eds.). (1986). *Teaching social skills to children: Innovative approaches* (2nd ed.). New York: Pergamon Press.

Hazel, J. S., & Schumaker, J. B. (1988). Social skills and learning disabilities: Current issues and recommendations for future research. In J. F. Kavanagh & T. J. Truss, Jr. (Eds.), *Learning disabilities: Proceedings of the national conference* (pp. 293–344). Parkton, MD: York Press.

Neubert, D. A., Tilson, G. P., & Ianacone, R. N. (1989). Postsecondary transition needs and employment patterns of individuals with mild disabilities. *Exceptional Children, 55,* 494–500.

Pearl, R., Donahue, M., & Bryan, T. (1986). Social relationships of learning-disabled children. In J. K. Torgesen & B. Y. L. Wong (Eds.), *Psychological and educational perspectives on learning disabilities* (pp. 193–224). Orlando, FL: Academic Press.

Vaughn, S., McIntosh, R. M., & Spencer-Rowe, J. (1991). Peer rejection is a stubborn thing: Increasing peer acceptance of rejected students with learning disabilities. *Learning Disabilities Research and Practice, 6,* 83–88.

Weller, C. (1989). *Investigation of subtypes and severities of learning disabled adults* (Report No. 133FH80023). Washington, DC: National Institute for Disability and Rehabilitation Research.

Nature of Social Competence

Bender, W. N., & Smith, J. K. (1990). Classroom behavior of children and adolescents with learning disabilities: A meta-analysis. *Journal of Learning Disabilities, 23,* 298–305.

Bender, W. N., & Wall, M. E. (1994). Social-emotional development of students with learning disabilities. *Learning Disability Quarterly, 17,* 323–341.

Bursuck, W. D., & Asher, S. R. (1986). The relationship between social competence and achievement in elementary school children. *Journal of Clinical Child Psychology, 15,* 41–49.

Gresham, F. M. (1981). Social skills training with handicapped children: A review. *Review of Educational Research, 51,* 139–176.

Gresham, F. M., & Reschly, D. J. (1988). Issues in the conceptualization, classification, and assessment of social skills in the mildly handicapped. In T. Kratochwill (Ed.), *Advances in school psychology* (pp. 203–247). Hillsdale, NJ: Erlbaum.

Haager, D., & Vaughn, S. (1995). Parent, teacher, peer, and self-reports of the social competence of students with learning disabilities. *Journal of Learning Disabilities, 28*(4), 205–215, 231.

Hollinger, J. D. (1987). Social skills for behaviorally disordered children in preparation for mainstreaming: Theory, practice, and new directions. *Remedial and Special Education, 8*(4), 17–27.

McConaughy, S. H., & Ritter, D. R. (1985). Social competence and behavioral problems of learning disabled boys aged 6–11. *Journal of Learning Disabilities, 18,* 547–553.

Roberts, C., & Zubrick, S. (1993). Factors influencing the social status of children with mild academic disabilities in regular classrooms. *Exceptional Children, 59*(3), 192–202.

Schloss, P., Schloss, C., Wood, C. E., & Kiehl, W. S. (1986). A critical review of social skills research with behaviorally disordered students. *Behavioral Disorders, 12*(1), 1–14.

Vaughn, S., & Haager, D. (1994). Social competence as a multifaceted construct: How do students with learning disabilities fare? *Learning Disability Quarterly, 17,* 253–266.

Walker, H. M., Sherin, M. R., O'Neill, R. E., & Ramsey, E. (1987). Longitudinal assessment of the development of antisocial behavior in boys: Rationale, methodology, and first year results. *Remedial and Special Education, 8*(4), 7–16, 27.

Topics for Instruction

Bursuck, W. (1989). A comparison of students with learning disabilities to low achieving and higher achieving students on three dimensions of social competence. *Journal of Learning Disabilities, 22,* 188–194.

Cartledge, G. (1989). Social skills and vocational success for workers with learning disabilities. *Rehabilitation Counseling Bulletin, 33,* 74–79.

Deshler, D. D., & Schumaker, J. B. (1983). Social skills of learning disabled adolescents: Characteristics and intervention. *Topics in Learning and Learning Disabilities, 3*(2), 15–23.

Gresham, F. M. (1981). Social skills training with handicapped children: A review. *Review of Educational Research, 51,* 139–176.

Haager, D., & Vaughn, S. (1995). Parent, teacher, peer, and self-reports of the social competence of students with learning disabilities. *Journal of Learning Disabilities, 28*(4), 205–215, 231.

Hoffman, A., & Field, S. (1995). Promoting self-determination through effective curriculum development. *Intervention in School and Clinic, 30*(3), 134–141.

LaGreca, A. M., & Mesibov, G. B. (1981). Facilitating interpersonal functioning with peers in learning disabled children. *Journal of Learning Disabilities, 14,* 197–199, 238.

LaGreca, A. M., & Stone, W. L. (1990). LD status and achievement: Confounding variables in the study of children's social status, self-esteem, and behavioral functioning. *Journal of Learning Disabilities, 23,* 483–490.

Martin, J. E., & Marshall, L. H. (1995). ChoiceMaker: A comprehensive self-determination transition program. *Intervention in School and Clinic, 30*(3), 147–156.

McConaughy, S. H., & Ritter, D. R. (1985). Social competence and behavioral problems of learning disabled boys aged 6–11. *Journal of Learning Disabilities, 18,* 547–553.

Mellard, D. F., & Hazel, J. S. (1992). Social competencies as a pathway to successful life transitions. *Learning Disability Quarterly, 15,* 251–271.

Montague, M. (1988). Job-related social skills training for adolescents with handicaps. *Career Development for Exceptional Individuals, 11,* 26–41.

Roberts, C., Pratt, C., & Leach, D. (1991). Classroom and playground interaction of students with and without disabilities. *Exceptional Children, 57,* 212–224.

Sabornie, E. J. (1990). Extended sociometric status of adolescents with mild handicaps: A cross-categorical perspective. *Exceptionality, 1,* 197–209.

Schumaker, J. B., Hazel, J. S., & Pederson, C. S. (1988). *Social skills for daily living.* Circle Pines, MN: American Guidance Service.

Stephens, T. M. (1978). *Social skills in the classroom.* Columbus, OH: Cedars Press.

Strawser, S. (1988). *The effect of academic, functional, adaptive, and severity factors on career success of learning disabled adults: Implications for secondary transition curriculum* (Report No. 158HH60006). Washington, DC: U.S. Department of Education, Office of Special Education and Rehabilitative Services.

Vaughn, S., & Haager, D. (1994). Social competence as a multifaceted construct: How do students with learning disabilities fare? *Learning Disability Quarterly, 17,* 253–266.

Vaughn, S., Lancelotta, G. X., & Minnis, S. (1988). Social strategy training and peer involvement: Increasing peer acceptance of a female LD student. *Learning Disabilities Focus, 4,* 32–37.

Walker, H. M., McConnell, S., Holmes, D., Todis, B., Walker, J., & Golden, N. (1988). *The Walker social skills curricula: The ACCEPTS program.* Austin, TX: PRO-ED.

Warger, C. L. (1990). *Can social skills for employment be taught? Using cognitive-behavioral procedures with adolescents with mild disabilities.* ERIC/OSEP Clearinghouse on Handicapped and Gifted Children. Reston, VA: Council for Exceptional Children.

Weller, C. (1989). *Investigation of subtypes and severities of learning disabled adults* (Report No. 133FH80023). Washington, DC: National Institute for Disability and Rehabilitation Research.

Social Cognition

Cartledge, G., Studpay, D., & Kaczala, C. (1986). Social skills and social perception of LD and nonhandicapped elementary students. *Learning Disability Quarterly, 9,* 226–234.

Jackson, S. C., Enright, R. D., & Murdock, J. Y. (1987). Social perception problems in learning disabled youth: Developmental lag versus perceptual deficit. *Journal of Learning Disabilities, 20,* 361–364.

Renick, M. J., & Harter, S. (1989). Impact of social comparisons on the developing self-perceptions of learning disabled students. *Journal of Education Psychology, 81,* 631–638.

Social Interaction

Anderson, P. P., & Fenichel, E. S. (1989). *Serving culturally diverse families of infants and toddlers with disabilities.* Washington, DC: National Center for Clinical Infant Programs.

Kistner, J. A., & Gatlin, D. (1989). Correlates of peer rejection among children with learning disabilities. *Learning Disability Quarterly, 12* 133–140.

Ramirez, O. (1989). Mexican American children and adolescents. In J. T. Gibbs & L. N. Huang (Eds.), *Children of color: Psychological interventions with minority youth* (pp. 224–250). San Francisco: Jossey-Bass.

Roberts, G. W., Bell, L. A., & Salend, S. J. (1991). Negotiating change for multicultural education: A consultation model. *Journal of Educational and Psychological Consultation, 2*(4), 12–16.

Sainato, D. M., Maheady, L., & Shook, G. L. (1986). The effects of a classroom manager role on the social interaction patterns and social status of withdrawn kindergarten children. *Journal of Applied Behavior Analysis, 19,* 187–195.

Strain, P. S., & Odom, S. L. (1986). Peer social initiations: Effective intervention for social skills development of exceptional children. *Exceptional Children, 52,* 543–551.

Van Bourgondien, M. E. (1987). Children's responses to retarded peers as a function of social behaviors, labeling, and age. *Exceptional Children, 53,* 432–439.

Vaughn, S., Hogan, A., Kouzekanani, K., & Shapiro, S. (1990). Peer acceptance, self-perceptions, and social skills of learning disabled students prior to identification. *Journal of Educational Psychology, 82,* 101–106.

Vaughn, S., McIntosh, R., Schumm, J. S., Haager, D., & Callwood, D. (1993). Social status, peer acceptance, and reciprocal friendships revisited. *Learning Disabilities Research and Practice, 8*(2), 82–88.

Social Effectiveness

Deshler, D. D., & Schumaker, J. B. (1983). Social skills of learning disabled adolescents: Characteristics and intervention. *Topics in Learning and Learning Disabilities, 3*(2), 15–23.

Drabman, R. S., & Patterson, J. N. (1981). Disruptive behavior and the social standing of exceptional children. *Exceptional Education Quarterly, 1,* 45–55.

Schumaker, J. B., Hazel, J. S., & Peterson, C. S. (1988). *Social skills for daily living.* Circle Pines, MN: American Guidance Service.

Schumaker, J. B., Wildgen, J. S., & Sherman, J. A. (1982). Social interaction of learning disabled junior high students in their regular classrooms: An observational analysis. *Journal of Learning Disabilities, 15,* 355–358.

Walker, H. M., McConnell, S., Holmes, D., Todis, B., Walker, J., & Golden, N. (1988). *The Walker social skills curricula: The ACCEPTS program. Austin, TX: PRO-ED.*

Assertiveness

Combs, M. L., & Slaby, D. A. (1977). Social skills training with children. In B. B. Lahey & A. E. Kazkin (Eds.), *Advances in Clinical Child Psychology* (Vol. 1). New York: Plenum Press.

Hoffman, A., & Field, S. (1995). Promoting self-determination through effective curriculum development. *Intervention in School and Clinic, 30*(3), 134–141.

Martin, J. E., & Marshall, L. H. (1995). ChoiceMaker: A comprehensive self-determination transition program. *Intervention in School and Clinic, 30*(3), 147–156.

Wehmeyer, M. L. (1995). Policy supporting self-determination in the environments of children with disabilities. *Education and Training in Mental Retardation and Developmental Disabilities* (March), 3–14.

Decision Making

Bryan, T. H., & Bryan, J. F. (1986). *Understanding learning disabilities.* Palo Alto, CA: Mayfield.

Martin, J. E., & Marshall, L. H. (1995). ChoiceMaker: A comprehensive self-determination transition program. *Intervention in School and Clinic, 30*(3), 147–156.

Wehmeyer, M. L. (1995). Policy supporting self-determination in the environments of children with disabilities. *Education and Training in Mental Retardation and Developmental Disabilities* (March), 3–14.

Problem Solving

Adelman, H. S., & Taylor, L. (1982). Enhancing the motivation and skills needed to overcome interpersonal problems. *Learning Disability Quarterly, 5,* 438–445.

Bash, M. A. S., & Camp, B. W. (1986). Teacher training in the think aloud classroom program. In G. Cartledge & J. F. Milburn (Eds.), *Teaching social skills to children: Innovative approaches* (2nd ed.). New York: Pergamon Press.

Foss, G., Auty, W. P., & Irvin, L. K. (1989). A comparative evaluation of modeling, problem-solving, and behavioral rehearsal for teaching employment-related interpersonal skills to secondary students with mental retardation. *Education and Training of the Mentally Retarded, 24*(19), 17–27.

Hazel, S. J., Schumaker, J. B., Sherman, J. A., & Sheldon, J. (1982). Application of a group training program in social skills and problem solving to learning disabled and non–learning disabled youth. *Learning Disability Quarterly, 5,* 398–408.

Meichenbaum, D. (1979). Teaching children self-control. In B. B. Lahey & A. E. Kazdin (Eds.), *Advances in clinical child psychology, Vol. 2.* New York: Plenum Press.

Schumaker, J. B., Hazel, J. S., Sherman, J. A., & Sheldon, J. (1982). Social skill performances of learning disabled, non–learning disabled, and delinquent adolescents. *Learning Disability Quarterly, 5,* 388–397.

Montague, M. (1988). Job-related social skills training for adolescents with handicaps. *Career Development for Exceptional Individuals, 11,* 26–41.

Vaughn, S., Lancelotta, G. X., & Minnis, S. (1988). Social strategy training and peer involvement: Increasing peer acceptance of a female LD student. *Learning Disabilities Focus, 4,* 32–37.

Warger, C. L. (1990). *Can social skills for employment be taught? Using cognitive-behavioral procedures with adolescents with mild disabilities.* ERIC/OSEP Clearinghouse on Handicapped and Gifted Children. Reston, VA: Council for Exceptional Children.

Acquisition of Cooperative Skills

Gresham, F. M. (1981). Social skills training with handicapped children: A review. *Review of Educational Research, 51,* 139–176.

La Greca, A. M., & Mesibov, G. B. (1981). Facilitating interpersonal functioning with peers in learning disabled children. *Journal of Learning Disabilities, 14,* 197–199, 238.

Montague, M. (1988). Job-related social skills training for adolescents with handicaps. *Career Development for Exceptional Individuals, 11,* 26–41.

Warger, C. L. (1990). *Can social skills for employment be taught? Using cognitive-behavioral procedures with adolescents with mild disabilities.* ERIC/OSEP Clearinghouse on Handicapped and Gifted Children. Reston, VA: Council for Exceptional Children.

Social Convention Acquisition

Gresham, F. M. (1981). Social skills training with handicapped children: A review. *Review of Educational Research, 51,* 139–176.

La Greca, A. M., & Mesibov, G. B. (1981). Facilitating interpersonal functioning with peers in learning disabled children. *Journal of Learning Disabilities, 14,* 197–199, 238.

Acquisition of Assertiveness Skills

Martin, J. E., & Marshall, L. H. (1995). ChoiceMaker: A comprehensive self-determination transition program. *Intervention in School and Clinic, 30*(3), 147–156.

Ward, M. J. (1988). The many facets of self-determination. National Information Center for Children and Youth with Handicaps. *Transition Summary, 5,* 2–3.

Wehmeyer, M. L. (1995). Policy supporting self-determination in the environments of children with disabilities. *Education and Training in Mental Retardation and Developmental Disabilities* (March), 3–14.

Social Skills Problem Solving

Adelman, H. S., & Taylor, L. (1982). Enhancing the motivation and skills needed to overcome interpersonal problems. *Learning Disability Quarterly, 5,* 438–445.

Hazel, S. J., Schumaker, J. B., Sherman, J. A., & Sheldon, J. (1982). Application of a group training program in social skills and problem solving to learning disabled and non–learning disabled youth. *Learning Disability Quarterly, 5,* 398–408.

Social Skills Generalization

Blackbourn, J. M. (1989). Acquisition and generalization of social skills in elementary-aged children with learning disabilities. *Journal of Learning Disabilities, 22,* 28–34.

Deshler, D. D., & Schumaker, J. B. (1983). Social skills of learning disabled adolescents: Characteristics and intervention. *Topics in Learning and Learning Disabilities, 3*(2), 15–23.

Foxx, R. M., McMorrow, M. J., Bittle, R. G., & Ness, J. (1986). A critical review of social skills generalization in two natural settings. *Journal of Applied Behavior Analysis, 19,* 299–305.

Schloss, P., Schloss, C., Wood, C. E., & Kiehl, W. S. (1986). A critical review of social skills research with behaviorally disordered students. *Behavioral Disorders, 12*(1), 1–14.

Self-Control

Gresham, F. M. (1981). Social skills training with handicapped children: A review. *Review of Educational Research, 51,* 139–176.

Meichenbaum, D. (1979). Teaching children self-control. In B. B. Lahey and A. E. Kazdin (Eds.), *Advances in clinical child psychology* (Vol. 2). New York: Plenum Press.

Chapter 9
Generic Interventions that Improve Academic Performance

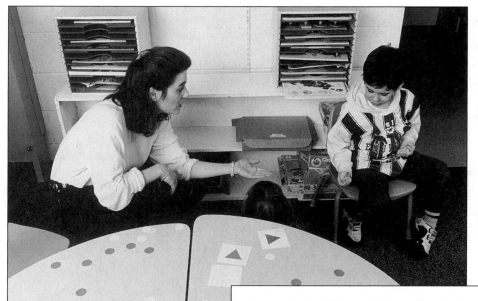

Making Connections

Before you read, review the section called "Critical Teaching Skills" in chapter 1. Consider how these skills are implemented as part of effective teaching. Notice the importance of matching instruction to the learner's level. Think about how you would work with a paraprofessional, as discussed in chapter 2, to implement academic instruction when teaching students with special needs. Review the explanations of stages of learning presented in chapter 4; explain how you would use curriculum-based assessment (discussed in chapter 6) to determine students' stages of learning for various academic skills. Now, consider interventions you might use for students who must learn a new skill, become more proficient with a skill, maintain a skill that was mastered, generalize a skill to a new situation, or adapt learning to meet the setting demands. Finally, consider how data collection and analysis, discussed in chapter 6, can be used to monitor students' progress as they move through the stages of learning during instruction.

In general, when children achieve overall academic success, both teachers and students work in partnership. The teacher's role is to present a curriculum that helps students acquire knowledge of many subjects and learn a wide variety of complex skills. For this to occur efficiently, the teacher must create a positive learning environment and select the effective interventions. The student, ultimately, must not only possess the skills needed to perform the task, but also must perform these functions:

- Understand the requirements of a task.

- Use an appropriate strategy for solving the problem or doing the task.

- Know which skills to use in performing the task.

- Use the appropriate strategy in an organized, rather than random, fashion.

- Assess how well he or she applied skills to requisite steps in the task or problem's completion.

These goals of instruction can be achieved when a positive learning environment exists, when students' curricula are well planned, and when teaching tactics are selected to produce maximal learning. This chapter summarizes a number of interventions that research and practice have shown to facilitate learning. The purpose is to provide teachers with a number of intervention strategies so teachers can match them with diverse students who have individual learning styles and needs.

Objectives

After studying this chapter, the reader will be able to

1. Explain the initial acquisition stage of learning interventions.
2. Describe interventions for the advanced acquisition stage of learning.
3. Provide examples of interventions for the proficiency stage of learning.
4. Explain interventions for the maintenance stage of learning.
5. Discuss generalization and interventions to promote this stage of learning.
6. Describe the adaption stage of learning and interventions for this stage.

There are many ways to organize information about general remedial interventions. One way is to classify interventions by the time they are usually applied (e.g., before, during, or after the student performs the task). Another way is by the purpose of the procedure. Using this system, one would categorize a tactic according to whether it increases or decreases the frequency of the target behavior. Although both are functional methods of organizing interventions, to rely on either of these schemes is to fail to recognize the complexity of educational situations.

Both research and practice have shown that the effectiveness of many interventions depends on the student's entry level or stage of learning. Certain tactics are most effective when a youngster is first learning how to perform a task; others seem influential only when that student needs to become more skilled in its execution. For example, the tactics teachers use to teach sight words or arithmetic facts are different from those used to teach fluency in reading or computation. The student will probably improve the most when his or her stage of learning is matched with an intervention.

In this chapter, the authors present discussions of tactics by stage of learning. We discuss tactics specific to certain academic tasks in later chapters of this text.

Initial Acquisition Stage

As you read, think about ...

1. Analyzing data to determine if the student is in the initial acquisition stage of learning.
2. Identifying skills for which the initial acquisition stage of learning interventions would be most appropriate.
3. Determining data collection techniques to monitor the interventions chosen.
4. Identifying ways to determine when students have moved to the advanced acquisition stage of learning.
5. Designing a lesson plan to teach an instructional objective using an intervention discussed in this section; include data collection and analysis procedures.

As discussed in chapter 4, the initial acquisition stage of learning occurs when an individual is beginning to learn a skill. Here, the student's entry level might be as low as 0 percent, indicating that the entire skill must be learned and mastered. Some students might be able to perform part of the skill, but because they cannot complete the entire task, their correct scores are initially low. The tactics discussed in this section are most appropriately applied when the student needs to learn how to execute a task or answer the material presented. In these cases, most teachers evaluate the influence of their instructional programs by measuring student performance in terms of percent correct scores (see chapter 6 for a review of evaluation procedures).

Physical Guidance

This tactic is used when motor skills are involved. **Physical guidance,** sometimes referred to as molding or manual guidance, requires the teacher to participate in executing the skill. When teachers take preschool children's hands to help them cut paper, the tactic of physical guidance is being used. Handwriting, assembly tasks, and many vocational skills can be initially acquired through the use of physical guidance. A speech clinician helping a student to pronounce a deficient articulation sound often physically guides the correct formation of the student's lips. This direct contact with students should be used only in the early phases of acquiring a skill and should be *faded* (gradually eliminated) as soon as possible.

Shaping

This procedure involves carefully reinforcing successive approximations of the target response. The student is rewarded first for attempting to perform the new skill. Gradually, rewards are offered only as the student performs closer and closer approximations of the skill. Finally, only accurate responses are rewarded.

Elaine is learning how to play tennis. She is learning how to swing the racket. At first, her coach praises her for any swing in the right direction. Soon, she is praised only when the racket is positioned correctly and the swing is straight. After a while, praise is only given when the swing is correct and Elaine follows through with the racket. Gradually, her coach shapes a correct swing, and eventually she is praised only for completely accurate (although not yet proficient) swings of the racket.

Shaping can be useful in building new skills. Certainly handwriting is a prime target for using shaping procedures. At first, an approximation of the correct formation of a letter is rewarded; later, only better and better attempts at letter formation are rewarded. Rather than having students learn through trial and error, shaping allows less chance of learning incorrect responses.

Modeling

Showing someone how to perform a skill is a most efficient way of teaching new response patterns to individuals. **Modeling** is best used when teaching academic subjects. Modeling means demonstrating the desired behavior to one or more observers. The observers are then required to imitate the skill. The observer's ability to imitate is crucial to the process. Because the imitative skill is innate and comes early in normal human development, teachers normally do not have to teach it. Most children come to school already possessing a developed set of imitative skills. It is primarily through the modeling-imitation paradigm that infants, toddlers, and preschool children learn a wide variety of language, social, and academic skills before starting school.

Since showing someone else how to do a task is probably the most natural teaching skill that humans possess, it is one that teachers need not learn. It is important, however, to remember to demonstrate tasks carefully, completely, and slowly. In many cases, it is helpful to verbalize the steps that must be followed to execute the skill accurately. Having the learner repeat the modeled steps before completing the skill independently ensures accuracy.

Modeling can be used with either groups or individuals. If a group uses modeling, however, the teacher should be certain that all the students are at the same stage of learning. If the students are at different levels, instruction may not be appropriate for some students. A pupil who is more advanced than the others will be wasting instructional time. In these situations, it is best to individualize.

In academic situations, modeling is most thoroughly researched in computational arithmetic, so we discuss this tactic in more detail in chapter 12. Modeling is appropriately applied in other areas as well. Whether the new skill is how to use a software program, how to compute arithmetic problems, how to write cursive, or how to use a learning strategy, modeling can be a most effective instructional tool.

Match-to-Sample

This initial acquisition tactic is included in many commercially available workbooks. The student is provided with the correct answer and is required to select from a number of choices the item matching the one provided initially. For example, in a letter identification worksheet, the student is shown a series of letters in the first column and must circle its match in the corresponding row.

Another form of **match-to-sample** is the cue sheet. Sample letters (cues) written in cursive above the blackboard allow students to match their letters to the properly formed ones on the cue sheet. Multiplication tables that students can use when solving problems are a variation of this tactic. In this case, the emphasis is on solving computational problems and not on multiplication facts. A multiplication table containing facts and answers serves as a clue for students to refer to as they solve more difficult computational problems. Match-to-sample interventions are appropriate only in the initial phases of acquisition and should be gradually eliminated so the student is required to perform the skill independently.

Telling

Verbal directions to help students acquire new skills have always been used in education. Unfortunately, many youngsters seem not to profit from instructions. Most likely, this is due to adults' careless application of instructions. **Telling** students how to perform the target skill can be efficient when students are acquiring skills, but communication must be conveyed with more care and concern than usual. Instructions must be consistent and specific to the goals the instructor has for the student. For example, for students learning to write better themes, teachers might instruct them to vary their sentence beginnings, expand the length of their sentences, and use more elaboration.

Teachers have a propensity for using instructions. Many teachers make more than 200 instructional statements a day. Most of these, however, are not specific to either students or situations. When instructions are provided systematically, they can serve efficiently to direct students to perform a desired skill without time-consuming, elaborate, or expensive educational procedures.

Cueing and Prompting

These procedures are used during the early acquisition phase, but do not necessarily stimulate first occurrences of the target behavior. Both **cueing** and **prompting** help students to make a correct response and can be added to the tactics just discussed.

There are three kinds of cues: movement, position, and redundancy. When movement cues are provided, the teacher points to, touches, or taps the item that represents the correct choice. When position cues are used, the correct choice is placed closest to the student. Redundancy cues pair the correct response with a particular property. For example, the correct choice might be physically larger than the other items.

Prompts often are used in reading. Here, teachers first form their lips as though to say the correct initial sound, then actually say the first sound of the unknown word, then sound out the word in its phonetic units. Any time students have figured out the correct response, they are encouraged to provide it. Prompts provide students with hints in the hope that the correct response will be uttered before the answer must be provided.

Time Delay

In many remedial classroom situations, teachers need to find interventions that teach skills with and without their assistance. Such interventions are useful for work performed in one-to-one instruction, small groups, work stations, or independently.

Time delay is an intervention that includes a stimulus (e.g., question, arithmetic fact, spelling word), a timed pause, a student response (correct, incorrect, or no response), and the correct response. Time delay can be used to teach spelling words, arithmetic facts, numeral or letter recognition, sight word recognition, vocabulary words, and a foreign language.

For example, in spelling, the teacher dictates a word. During the silence of 20 to 25 seconds, the student is to spell (orally or on paper) the word. The correct spelling is then provided by the teacher, a peer tutor, an answer sheet, or an audiotape. As the student makes subsequent attempts to spell the word list, the timed pause is shorter.

In mathematics, basic facts can be presented to students on flashcards with a five-second time delay. Students can then record or say their answer, depending on how the teacher has structured instruction. Anyone who has studied a foreign language by listening to audiotapes has experienced the time delay procedure. The voice on the tape says the word or phrase in a foreign language; in the segment of silence, the student is to provide the answer or repeat what was previously heard, and the audio then restates the original word or phrase. Time delay has considerable potential because it is easy for the teacher to administer, it places the student in control of the instructional situation, and it can be easily discontinued when the skill is mastered.

Flow Lists

Some students have difficulty memorizing large amounts of information, but can remember items presented in small groups. Many teachers have found **flow lists** most useful with such children in subjects such as spelling and arithmetic. When this tactic is used, the student's daily spelling list might comprise only five words. Once the student spells any word correctly three days in a row, it is dropped from the daily spelling list and another one is added. Using this system ensures that the student knows the information taught before instruction is discontinued. However, many teachers also schedule periodic review tests to be certain that learning is maintained. If a student forgets a word, the word is recycled through the flow list. An example of a flow list data sheet for addition facts is found in Figure 9.1.

Advance Organizers

The research conducted at the Kansas University Institute for Research and Learning Disabilities (UK-IRLD) revealed that few teachers provide students with advance

Figure 9.1
Addition fact flow
list data sheet

Name _____ John _____   Addition Fact Form

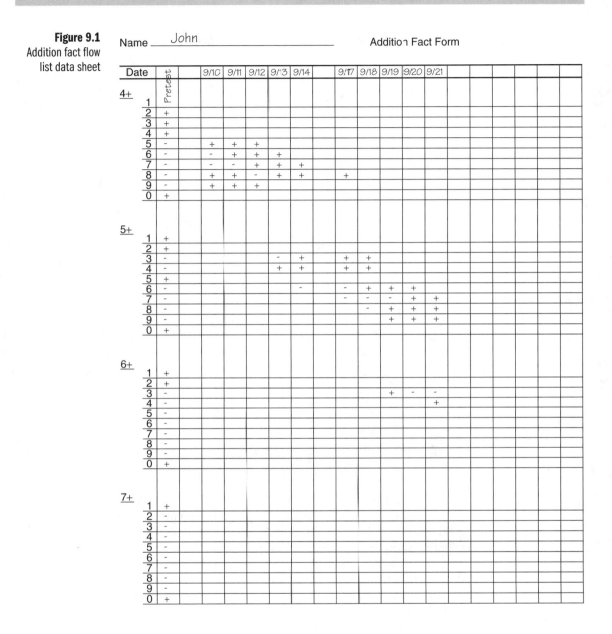

organizers (Deshler, Warner, Schumaker, & Alley, 1983); that is, teachers do not tell students what the lecture or lesson is about and why the information presented is important. However, when informed instruction (Paris & Jacobs, 1984) is used, it has been found that students who are made aware of a reading task before they read a passage, for example, score higher on comprehension tests on those passages. Simply stated, teachers who introduce their lectures or assignments clearly find that their students learn the information better, whether the subject to be learned is history, science, or English (Lenz, Alley, & Schumaker, 1987). (Advance organizers were discussed in more detail in chapter 5.)

Reinforcement (Rewards)

We covered reinforcement procedures in some depth earlier (see chapter 7 for a review of reinforcement theory, selecting reinforcers, and cautions teachers should take). Regardless of the specific form that reinforcement takes (praise, tokens, privileges), it should be delivered according to a schedule. These schedules vary in appropriateness, depending on the characteristics of the learner and the stage of learning in which the reinforcement is being applied. For example, the continuous reinforcement (CRF) schedule is only appropriately applied in the initial acquisition stage of learning. In this situation, the student earns a unit of reinforcement for each occurrence of the target behavior. With other fixed ratio (FR) schedules, the student earns rewards after so many occurrences of the target behavior. For example, John might earn 1 unit of reinforcement for every 10 correct arithmetic problems, because his schedule of reinforcement was set at an FR of 10:1. FR schedules are most commonly used to motivate students for academic learning, and they are most useful for that purpose.

● ●

Advanced Acquisition Stage

As you read, think about...

1. Analyzing data to determine if the student is in the advanced acquisition stage of learning.
2. Identifying academic performances that suggest the student is in the advanced acquisition stage of learning.
3. Developing a lesson that uses one of the interventions found in the advanced acquisition section.
4. Designing a peer tutoring program to promote mastery of skills for students in the advanced acquisition stage of learning.
5. Identifying how to manage instruction when a group of students is in the initial and advanced acquisition stage of learning for the same skill.

Many times, students in the initial acquisition stage of learning receive carefully planned instruction, and then indicate by their percent correct scores (90 to 100 percent) that they have mastered the target skill. Sometimes, the percent correct scores indicate that the students have learned most of the skill, but have not mastered it. In these cases, students seem not to be able to meet mastery criterion (three days above 90 percent) due to either inefficient learning or careless errors. The tactics described earlier were insufficient to elicit sufficient learning for the students to advance. They did not make students proficient at a given task; they failed also in preparing them for the next skill in the curriculum. The tactics described next are usually ineffective in the initial acquisition period, but help students achieve mastery. They are frequently referred to as *refinement tactics*.

Feedback

The purpose of **feedback** is to inform students about the accuracy of their responses. Feedback tactics form a category that falls along a continuum (ranging from a simple yes or no, right or wrong, to more thorough and complex forms reminiscent of instructional tactics). Some of these versions of feedback are more effective than others. Telling a student which answers are correct and which are incorrect is far superior to identifying only correct answers. Although many teachers of youngsters with disabilities feel that these students have already experienced too much failure and therefore want to ignore their errors, excusing errors constitutes an unnecessary form of over-protection. Student performance improves more when correct and incorrect responses are identified.

For many students, it is most helpful to be reinstructed on incorrect answers. The teacher might demonstrate again how to solve a long division problem or punctuate a compound sentence.

Telling

Specific instructions carefully applied can be useful in increasing student's academic performance. Simply telling youngsters to be more careful as they do their assignments can contribute to increases in their percent correct scores. Smith and Lovitt (1976) found that some of their students made careless errors in their arithmetic assignments and therefore did not reach percentage scores that indicated mastery. These students' scores averaged about 75 percent. Telling the students to be more careful as they computed the problem was sufficient, and the students obtained scores indicating mastery (in these cases, three consecutive days at 100 percent).

For students who have acquired the basic processes but whose accuracy is still of concern, further explanation or redirection might be helpful. Sometimes only minor instructional statements relating to the way the student is completing the assignment facilitate final acquisition of the task. Once this is accomplished, proficiency can become the target.

Drill

Drill can also bring about necessary increases in accuracy. There are several varieties of drill that, when specifically applied, can facilitate mastery of many academic areas, such as sight words, arithmetic facts, spelling, handwriting, and punctuation. For students who are unsure of the correct answer and get the correct solution one day and not the next, drill specifically on those items can be sufficient to increase accuracy. New response drill can also be helpful. Here, the teacher might select words from the upcoming reading passage that students have a high probability of missing, and drill students on those words before they read independently. Both these forms of drill, new response and error, can be accomplished through the use of flash-cards, card reader machines, or computer programs.

Positive Practice Overcorrection

In chapter 7, two forms of overcorrection (restitution and positive practice) were discussed. One of these procedures, positive practice, can be applied to academic instruction. When students have not completely acquired a skill and exhibit inconsistent results, this form of overpractice can be helpful. For example, for students who misspell words written in themes or reports, teachers can require those students to write each word correctly five times, look up and rewrite those words' definitions in the dictionary, and break them into syllables. This is the application of positive practice overcorrection for spelling. Similar applications can be made for most academic situations, and they have proven effective in eliminating many errors students make.

Reward for Accuracy

Sometimes students need an incentive to put out the extra effort required to achieve mastery level percentage scores. Various incentive systems can be applied to increase accuracy. Students could receive extra bonuses or privileges for perfect papers. Special certificates of commendation, perfect papers placed on a bulletin board, notes home to parents, extra recess or leisure time, and other special activities could be scheduled for final mastery of academic tasks.

Fines

For some students, directions, drill, or rewards do not increase accuracy. For those who seem to have a motivational problem and who make inconsistent and careless mistakes, losing privileges for committing errors can stimulate increased percentage scores. This tactic of fining students for unsatisfactory performance, also referred to as response cost, can be most effective for some students. Withdrawing minutes from recess or taking away privileges can encourage students to reduce errors in arithmetic, spelling, or written composition. One caution about this technique should be noted, however. The teacher must be certain that the student can perform the desired task before levying fines. It is unfair to punish students for things they are incapable of doing. When the teacher is certain that the reason for unsatisfactory scores is not a lack of ability or knowledge, but rather an unwillingness to provide the correct answer, fines might well be a beneficial tactic to select.

Peer Tutoring

As discussed in chapters 4 and 7, using children to teach their classmates is not a new concept. When its purpose is to improve academic performance, it is called tutoring. Many such systems have been explored in schools. Probably the most common is cross-age tutoring. Here, an older student teaches a younger one. Same-age or classmate tutoring is also effective when arrangements cannot be made for an older student to tutor. Tutoring can be applied in a wide variety of academic situations: written expression, arithmetic computation and problem solving, reading orally and answering comprehension questions, studying for tests in content subjects such as history or social studies, and completing homework assignments.

If peer tutoring is to be employed successfully, several things must be considered. First, the tutors must be carefully selected. There must be a good fit between the two students (it is best if tutors work in pairs and not with small groups). The tutors must be trained. They need to be proficient in the skills they are to teach, as well as in teaching skills. Tutors should participate in training sessions in which they learn how to use instructions, feedback, praise, and reinforcement properly. Tutors also need to receive rewards themselves for their work.

In classrooms where students' abilities vary widely, teachers should consider tutoring for the faster and slower students. Tutoring may also be helpful for classes with a large number of students. One-to-one or individualized instruction is beneficial for most students, but is expensive in teacher time. Therefore, in many classrooms, individualization is viewed as unfeasible. Using peer tutors allows teachers to individualize instruction for those students who need extra assistance to master academic skills.

The Puzzle or Jigsaw Technique

Using this intervention, a group of students work together to solve a problem or complete a task, with each member assigned a specific activity. For example, three high school students are assigned the group task of proofing and correcting a poorly written term paper by an anonymous person (perhaps the teacher). One student is assigned the job of correcting all capitalization errors, another is to correct the punctuation, and the other corrects the spelling mistakes. When they have each completed their corrections, they discuss the reasons for their corrections and go through the paper together as a group.

This intervention has several advantages. It encourages group involvement and increased attention to the learning task. In many cases, it can also lead to a better understanding of assignments because the students share, discuss, and model the steps followed to arrive at the correct solution to the problem or task.

Proficiency Stage

As you read, think about . . .

1. Analyzing data to determine if the student is in the proficiency stage of learning.
2. Identifying skills for which fluency is important.
3. Determining data collection techniques to monitor the interventions chosen.
4. Comparing and contrasting the interventions described in this stage of learning with those interventions presented in the acquisition stage of learning.
5. Designing a lesson plan to teach an instructional objective using an intervention discussed in this section; include data collection and analysis procedures.

A number of instructional tactics facilitate proficiency or fluency. Modeling, telling, drilling, and reinforcement can improve both the quality and quantity of students' academic performances. This, of course, is the aim of instruction, once students have acquired or learned how to perform the targeted skill. In the proficiency stage of learning, the interventions scheduled should help students retain their high levels of accuracy while increasing their speed. To judge the effectiveness of these interventions, teachers evaluate student performance in terms of correct and error rate scores (see chapter 6 for a review).

Modeling

Modeling is most commonly and appropriately applied in the acquisition stage. However, modeling has proven instrumental in building proficiency in some students' academic performances. Smith (1979), for example, used a modeling tactic to increase students' oral reading rates. The teacher read the first passage from the students' basal text at the desired rate (approximately 100 words per minute). The students then continued reading from the text for the allotted time. Modeling substantially and positively influenced the students' oral reading performances. Although there are few examples of the use of modeling in building proficiency, modeling is natural to the instructional situation; it is easy to schedule and might be a worthwhile tactic to try.

Telling

Another simple tactic natural to instructional situations is frequently underused. Sometimes students do not know what is expected of them. Are they supposed to fill the math period with the seatwork given to them at the beginning of the period? Are they supposed to concentrate on accuracy? If students understand the teacher's aims, they might improve their performance without any elaborate techniques. Some teachers report that simply clarifying goals for students helps students to achieve desired results. This technique works particularly well when students are told to read faster or compute as many problems as they can. This might be a good first tactic to apply when fluency or proficiency must be enhanced.

Drill

A tactic to improve fluency used in schools for many, many years is drill and practice. Music teachers help students become more proficient at playing musical instruments by insisting on drill and practice. The purpose of these tactics is to get the target skill at an automatic level of functioning. Handwriting is taught almost exclusively through the use of these tactics. Drill on errors seems to enhance oral reading, handwriting, and computational arithmetic. Error drill can improve fluency or rates of performance, because errors often interrupt individuals' flow of responding. Without these interruptions, students move through academic tasks more proficiently.

To help students become more proficient at basic academic tasks, many teachers schedule time for speed-building activities. For example, in reading, many teachers use a procedure called repeated readings. Here, the student rereads the same passage orally until a desired rate is achieved. Gradually, the student's improvement with this one passage transfers to reading new material. Flashcards can increase students' rates of producing correct answers.

Many students, however, find drill uninteresting and refuse to practice tasks over and over when drill alone is scheduled. Some teachers add incentives to the drill procedures so that these students will practice sufficiently. Others vary the drill and practice activities so they are more interesting and gamelike. For example, it is not uncommon to have a mathematics teacher say long series of arithmetic facts rather quickly. The student who can arrive at the solution, despite the rather fast delivery of the problems, is the winner.

The introduction of computers to schools has many advantages. One of these is the opportunity for drill and practice (see the "Instruction and Technology" section in chapter 5). Certain software allows youngsters to practice arithmetic facts in gamelike situations. Such programs encourage accuracy and fluency on what are frequently laborious tasks. Metronomes (or pacers) set at a designated beat can be used for building fluency in basic facts, sight words, recognition, and so forth. Each beat requires a response. There are many ways in which teachers can promote fluency or proficiency. Teacher drills, software, and metronomes are just three examples of fluency-building activities.

Reinforcement

We discussed reinforcement procedures in some detail in chapter 7 and earlier in this chapter. Here, we address reinforcement procedures that are typically used to increase proficiency.

Premack Principle

This principle, sometimes called Gramma's rule, arranges the time in which activities are scheduled. Those activities the student likes to engage in (high-strength) follow those activities the student does not like or does not voluntarily engage in very much (low-strength).

In some cases, rescheduling the academic routine can effect positive changes in student performance. Some students fritter away time when given an assignment they do not like. If that assignment were scheduled first, and an activity enjoyable to the students followed, they would have an incentive to complete the tedious activity so they could move on to one they liked. For example, if Ruth hates arithmetic and loves reading, arithmetic seatwork would be given to her first. The longer she spends on the arithmetic assignment (both completing it and correcting errors made), the less time she has left for reading. Before resorting to more complicated or elaborate intervention procedures, teachers might consider applying the Premack Principle by rescheduling academic assignments according to student preferences.

Free Time

Contingent free time is the most common application of the Premack Principle in classroom situations. With contingent free time, students earn minutes to spend in activities of their choice by improving their academic performance. Free time is earned by using an FR schedule of reinforcement (discussed in chapter 7). The teacher or student might have determined that for every two study questions found at the end of the social studies text that are answered correctly, the student can earn one minute of free time (FR2). Once enough free time minutes are accumulated, the student can choose an activity from a number of selections (working on a science project, leisure reading, programming the computer).

Go–No Go Contingencies

These contingency arrangements are merely adaptions of FR schedules. They are referred to in the research literature as differentially reinforcing higher rates of responding (DRH) and differentially reinforcing lower rates of responding (DRL) schedules. These schedules do not determine what (free time, points, privileges) the student earns for improved performance, but rather what level of accuracy the student should demonstrate.

In FR schedules, reinforcement is earned for every set number of correct responses. If Billy is given an FR5 schedule for correctly spelled words on a weekly test, then for every five words correctly spelled, he can earn one minute of free time. If there are twenty words on the weekly test, he could earn four minutes of free time each week. If he only spells five words correctly, he would earn one minute of free time. This, however, is unfortunate, for he would receive reinforcement for an unsatisfactory performance, and Billy's teacher wants him to score a minimum of 75 percent on those tests. By adding a go–no go contingency, Billy receives reinforcement only when his score surpasses a certain level. Billy would earn his minutes of free time only when he correctly spells at least fifteen words. Thus, reinforcement is earned only when a minimally acceptable level of performance is achieved.

Go–no go contingencies are used frequently in oral reading, where the teacher might be concerned about correct rate and error rate scores simultaneously. She wants a student's correct reading rates to increase and the error rates to decrease.

Minimally acceptable scores can be set for both these rates. For example, it could be arranged that Tiffany would not receive any free time unless her correct rate exceeded sixty-five, and her error rate was lower than five on any one day. Once her scores indicated improvement beyond these minimal levels, the FR schedules would be applied.

Maintenance Stage

As you read, think about...

1. Analyzing data to determine if the student is in the maintenance stage of learning.
2. Designing instructional plans that include maintenance interventions for mastered skills.
3. Determining data collection techniques to monitor the interventions chosen.
4. Explaining ways to manage instruction of students in the acquisition, proficiency, and maintenance stages of learning.
5. Designing a learning center or using technology to promote maintenance of mastered skills.

In the maintenance stage of learning, the aim is for the student to retain the mastery levels of performance attained when direct instruction was in effect. Both accuracy and proficiency should remain at acceptable levels. In some cases, maintenance is conducted without any intervention to determine whether the student can actually perform the skill without any help from the teacher. In other cases, the student receives infrequent reinforcement for satisfactory performance during the maintenance stage. Unfortunately, not many academic and behavioral researchers have devoted their energies to the study of retention.

Once mastery levels are achieved, it is important that students maintain them. For example, once a youngster reaches a mastery level of performance in oral reading, fluency must be retained in order for that student to keep up with the peer group. Merely practicing oral reading skills should help to retain satisfactory reading levels. If reading is dropped from the curriculum and no longer receives attention from the teacher or student once it is "mastered," performance levels will decrease. Academic learning is not like riding a bike, particularly for those who have had difficulty mastering a given academic skill in the first place. One important key to retention is continued practice, although on a periodic basis. For many students, however, practice alone is not enough. For them, direct though infrequent intervention is required for some time to ensure that learning is retained. We now present some tactics that facilitate maintenance and retention.

Overlearning

This procedure has received little attention from researchers lately, but it has merit and should be reinvestigated as a maintenance procedure. **Overlearning** requires the student to practice a task well beyond the level of mastery. This concept probably gave rise to the notion that three or even five consecutive scores be above a predetermined level before the student moves on to learn more difficult tasks. If a teacher were to incorporate overlearning into the teaching process, students would have to demonstrate mastery for a longer time than is typically used. Snell made the point that if overlearning is used, "repeated practice or review distributed over time rather than massed into a brief time period" should facilitate long-term retention (1978, p. 363). Overlearning should be an integral part of the teaching routine for learners with disabilities, because it tends to improve retention and generalization.

Variable Ratio Schedules

In fixed ratio schedules of reinforcement, rewards are delivered after a set number of correct responses or a set amount of time has been recorded. Variable schedules provide students with reinforcement in such a way that the student cannot predict when the opportunity for reinforcement will occur. In a sense, this keeps the student on guard, performing as best as possible. Usually, variable schedules lead to consistent performance with higher and more constant rates.

Variable ratio (VR) schedules are not usually recommended for direct application to academic subjects, for if the ratio changed daily, one day's performance would be worth more units of reinforcement than another day's performance. However, an interesting application of VR schedules can be applied to academic subjects when long-term maintenance is of concern. For example, Steve was a poor reader but finally reached his long-term goal score. His teacher was afraid that he would not maintain his now proficient rate of oral reading. During intervention, Steve received reinforcement using a fixed ratio of 15:1 for correct rate. During long-term follow-up, the teacher read with Steve three days a week. She told him that they were going to play a game. Some days, he would receive reinforcement for his reading assignment, and some days he would not. He would never know in advance which days "counted." Initially, she applied a VR of 2:1 to his reading sessions, so on the average, every other reading session earned him reinforcement (using the fixed ratio schedule of the intervention condition to determine the exact amount of reinforcement earned). Gradually, the VR scheduled was reduced. By the end of the school year, reinforcement was earned only periodically. Through the use of this technique, however, Steve not only maintained his proficient oral reading rate, but also continued to improve.

VR schedules for academic situations must be applied carefully. Using these schedules for cases such as Steve's, however, might help students maintain desirable performances.

Social Reinforcement

Social reinforcement (praise and adult and peer approval) is underutilized as a planned intervention. Often, after months and months of direct instruction, the student achieves proficiency of skills. These accomplishments are put behind both student and teacher. All intervention is discontinued; no reminders are provided to use these newly mastered skills. No wonder teachers frequently note that once instruction is completed, academic performance decreases. In particular, for youngsters who seem to have retention problems, continued and periodic feedback and praise for using their newly learned skills are warranted.

Statements like "Gee, you remembered to borrow here," could alleviate this situation. The power of praise is well documented. If used on a variable schedule, praise can serve to remind the student of what the desired behavior actually is, provide feedback about the fine points of the newly mastered skill, and show the teacher's approval of the student's efforts to use academic skills appropriately. In some situations, the peers can be encouraged to praise classmates for continued academic improvement. Social reinforcement might well be sufficient to keep a former target behavior within a youngster's repertoire.

Intrinsic Reinforcement

The hope is that students will eventually work to maintain proficient levels of basic skills because they enjoy the product of those skills. All teachers hope that their students will eventually enjoy reading and that they will read without outside encouragement. Certainly, this is the ultimate goal of the educational process. Unfortunately, many students do not achieve this goal in all school-related areas. Teachers must strive continually to help their students attain such proficient levels of performance that **intrinsic reinforcement** will in fact guarantee maintenance.

Generalization Stage

As you read, think about . . .

1. Designing a data collection system to monitor generalization.
2. Developing a plan with the general education teacher to promote skill generalization.
3. Designing a lesson plan to promote generalization of a mastered skill to a new environment, people, and materials.
4. Designing an instructional arrangement that fosters generalization of mastered skills.

As discussed in chapter 4 in the section on stages of learning, many students with special needs do not automatically generalize or transfer their learning to new settings or situations. In some cases, researchers have found that careful, direct instruction on the target skill will cause some students to generalize that skill to other, closely related skills. For example, a number of studies (Lloyd, Saltzman, & Kauffman, 1981; Rivera & Smith, 1987) have shown that tactics such as modeling and demonstration promote generalization in computational arithmetic. However, it does not happen for all children in this way. For many youngsters, generalization in and of itself needs to be a target for instruction (Stokes & Baer, 1977). Stokes and Baer (1977) postulate that generalization might well be a skill that must be taught to those who are deficient in its application.

Several guidelines about generalization may be helpful:

1. Do not expect it to occur.
2. Extend the contingencies used in the teaching situation to the generalization settings also.
3. Plan to implement the original, effective intervention procedure in the generalization situations.

Once students do generalize, teachers must remind, reinforce, and praise them, because generalization is an important aspect of academic achievement. Guidelines (Ellis, Lenz, & Sabornie, 1987a, 1987b; Rivera, Cook, & O'Malley, 1992; Vaughn, Bos, & Lund, 1986) to promote the occurrence of generalization are presented in Tips for Teachers.

Generalization Techniques

1. Use cooperative planning.
2. Prompt students to identify when certain instructional strategies and skills are appropriate.
3. Have students prompt each other to use instructional strategies and skills.
4. Provide intermittent reinforcement for students who generalize skills.
5. Encourage students to monitor their own use of strategies and skills (e.g., using a checklist to record when a strategy is used, keeping a record of grades).
6. Prompt students to develop and use cue cards in the general education setting.
7. Discuss with students when and how instructional strategies and skills can be used.
8. Review the students' grades in general education classes.
9. Model aloud adaptive thinking; that is, use an instructional strategy to perform the skill.
10. Ask general education teachers to expect students to generalize skills; have them tell students that they are aware of the skills that were taught in the special education classroom and that they expect the skills to be implemented.
11. Provide extra credit for students who generalize.
12. Team-teach strategies in the general classroom.

Rationales

Many teachers have found that when students understand the importance of applying newly mastered skills to different settings or situations, generalization is more likely to occur. Deshler and Schumaker, through their work at the KUIRLD, found that many students who had mastered various learning strategies did not use their new learning skills in general classroom settings. The students did not generalize. However, when students were told why they should apply learning strategies to these settings, and accepted these rationales, they did generalize.

Transfer Activities

After students have mastered a skill or learning strategy and have demonstrated that mastery in the special setting, they need to use their newly learned skills in other settings. If, for example, students have learned a strategy that will help them write themes, they need to apply that strategy in history and English classes. If students do not generalize their strategy use, the following techniques might be helpful. Cue cards, which summarize a learning strategy, can serve as reminders to apply the strategy in the regular education setting. Also, having group discussions and making lists about classes and situations in which this technique would be useful encourages generalization. The special education teacher can arrange for practice sessions in which students complete assignments similar to those given in the history class. The students would receive guided practice and benefit from doing the exercise in a more controlled setting.

Varying Stimulus Conditions

Generalization may be facilitated by **varying stimulus conditions**—introducing extraneous, irrelevant, or distracting stimuli; changing instructors and instructional settings; and changing class size. Teaching the student what and what not to respond to and reinforcing only correct responses in a variety of settings in the presence of different people also seem to promote generalization. If those in the youngster's environment (parents, siblings, and other teachers) do not carry out and extend remedial efforts consistently, little maintenance or generalization will occur.

Self-Management

Self-control procedures (discussed in detail in chapter 7) also foster generalization. Students who have great difficulty generalizing from one setting to another could work with their teacher to set a goal for generalizing a specific skill in a particular setting. They might develop a behavioral contract to implement this goal. Then, the students would monitor their own behavior, take data on their performance, and reward themselves for meeting their goals.

Cooperative Planning

Too often, special education and general education teachers do not share information about the progress made by individual students whom they both serve. In part, this is because of the busy schedules that teachers keep. Sometimes it is due to the unfortunate distance between these two fields and their administrative organizations. It is important for special educators to communicate with the other teachers who work with their pupils. Communication will lead to better academic programming for the student, for the teachers can discuss individuals' strengths, weaknesses, and recent progress. With an open dialogue, cooperative planning about students' programs can occur.

When special and general education teachers hold periodic conferences about those students about whom they are mutually concerned, they can share information about what particular students have learned in each classroom. The special education teacher, for example, can indicate what skills and strategies students have mastered in the special education setting. If students are not applying those skills in the general education setting, the teachers can discuss ways they can both encourage generalization. The general education teacher might cue a student to use a strategy when appropriate; the special education teacher might provide specific instructions, arrange for practice sessions, or train a peer tutor to assist the special education student (see chapter 2 for more about collaboration between teachers).

• •

Problem-Solving (Adaption) Stage

As you read, think about . . .

1. Developing a portfolio of student work that demonstrates effective problem-solving (adaption) skills.
2. Infusing a technology learning center into a classroom environment to promote problem-solving skills.
3. Developing a collaborative lesson plan with the general education teacher to foster problem-solving skills in different environments.
4. Developing a cognitive strategy to teach problem-solving skills.
5. Designing a lesson plan to teach an instructional objective that focuses on problem solving, using an intervention discussed in this section. Include data collection and analysis procedures. Use the instructional steps to teach the lesson.

Problem solving is the ability to extend knowledge and skills to novel situations. The inability to solve problems might be one of the greatest weaknesses of students with special needs (Havertape & Kass, 1978) and is an area that must gain more attention from researchers, curriculum materials developers, and teachers. Problem solving involves a number of skills that fall on a continuum. The dimensions of problem solving range from being able to figure out how to perform an academic task to solving the most pressing problems facing humankind. Although the depth of abilities to solve problems probably relates to the innate characteristics of individuals, various degrees of problem solving can be taught.

People use many components or individual skills when they solve problems. Being aware of requisite elements, such as those listed in Table 9.1, might help teachers to plan more complete educational programs for their students. For example, if Crista has difficulty solving problems because she cannot categorize information, direct instruction on that skill is warranted. She might be assigned to work on a computer game to improve her categorization skills. Eric, who cannot identify similarities among groups of items, could be asked to find the common elements of the things he has in his desk.

Guided Instruction

When teachers hold guided group discussions, students are taught to understand a problem, relate it to a simpler one, find different ways to solve it, and check their solutions. Although youngsters probably need some adult guidance, teachers must be cautious not to dominate the discussions. Rather, through open-ended questions, they should guide the students when they need direction.

Students seem to develop better problem-solving skills when they work in small groups. Problem-solving instruction might provide good opportunities to integrate group activities into the instructional routine. In most special education classrooms, instruction is individualized and group activities are limited. Although individualization produces excellent academic improvement, it does not foster cooperation and communicative interaction. Group activities centered on solving problems could alleviate this situation.

A number of conditions exist that can improve children's abilities to solve problems. Some of those are found in Table 9.2. Guidelines are also available for teachers to follow as they plan and conduct problem-solving activities; those are found in Table 9.3.

Table 9.1
Component Skills of
Problem Solving

Flexibility

Categorizing

Persistence

Decision making

Recognizing patterns

Determining relationships

Identifying irrelevant items

Finding similarities

Analyzing

Estimating

Table 9.2
Conditions and
Activities that
Improve Problem
Solving

Have a plan of attack.

Have an overall approach.

Practice generating and testing solutions.

Retell problem in your own words.

Use imagery.

It is important to remember that, above all, students need to have continued practice in generating and testing solutions to solve problems. This means that time needs to be devoted to this important stage of learning.

Problem-Solving Strategy

The problem-solving strategy involves a series of sequential steps. It can be taught to youngsters using a cognitive-behavioral modification teaching sequence that consists of: (1) the teacher's modeling aloud the desired behavior or cognitive strategy, (2) the student's completing the modeled steps by verbalizing his or her actions while working the problem, (3) the teacher's providing corrective feedback, and (4) instruction's being provided in generalizing the strategy or skill. Following is a description of the problem-solving strategy.

1. First, children must be able to obtain the information required to solve the problem. This step could involve brainstorming with peers, conducting research, or engaging in group discussions to obtain the information.
2. Second, students must understand what is to be solved; that is, they must be able to articulate the problem (teacher modeling).
3. Third, students must determine what information and solution techniques the problem demands (teacher modeling; student brainstorming and verbalizations).
4. Fourth, students must establish criteria for solution selection (teacher modeling and asking questions; student discussions).
5. Fifth, students must generate and evaluate hypotheses using the criteria previously established.
6. Sixth, students should implement the solution.

Table 9.3
Teacher Guidelines
for Problem-Solving
Activities

Present real-life problems.

Present problems with several or no solutions.

Present problems within students' experiences.

Provide many opportunities to solve problems.

Allow students to experiment and discover.

Ask open-ended questions.

Assist students in collecting data.

Reward different methods of approaching the problem.

Reward different solutions.

7. Seventh, students should regroup to evaluate the solution periodically. For many students with learning and behavior problems, this process will require substantial guidance from the teacher. Figure 9.2 is helpful in teaching and having youngsters remember the strategy.

Figure 9.2
An illustration from a comprehensive problem-solving program

What is my problem?

How can I solve it?

Am I using my plan?   How did I do?

Source: From *Think Aloud: Increasing Social and Cognitive Skills—A Problem-Solving Program for Children,* by B. W. Camp and M. A. S. Bash, 1985, Champaign, IL: Research Press. Copyright 1981 by the authors. Reprinted with permission.

Summary

As students learn new skills, they pass through several stages of learning. Many instructional procedures are effective in only one of these stages and are ineffective in the others. Table 9.4 lists tactics that tend to be most effective in each stage of learning. Table 9.5 describes implementation ideas. Unfortunately, teachers cannot simply match their students' behavioral descriptions to the categories provided in this table and be guaranteed successful remediation programs. All students are individuals, and what is effective for one student might not be for another. The purpose of this chapter has been to help teachers better select those procedures with the highest *probability* of affecting improvement by reviewing those basic, generic procedures that can be applied across a variety of academic skills. Tactics limited to one particular academic subject (reading, mathematics) are described in later chapters.

Study and Discussion Questions

1. Explain interventions for the initial acquisition stage of learning.
2. Describe interventions for the advanced acquisition stage of learning.
3. Provide examples of interventions for the proficiency stage of learning.
4. Explain interventions for the maintenance stage of learning.
5. Discuss generalization and interventions to promote this stage of learning.
6. Describe the adaption stage of learning and interventions for this stage.
7. Discuss the stages of learning theory as it applies to academic instruction.

Acquisition		Proficiency	Maintenance	Generalization	Problem solving (adaption)
Initial	**Advanced**				
Physical guidance	Feedback	Modeling	Overlearning	Rationales	Guided instruction
Shaping	Telling	Telling	Intermittent reinforcement	Reinforcement	Problem-solving strategy training
Modeling	Drill	Drill	VR schedules	Instructions	Transfer activities
Match-to-sample	Error drill	Error drill	Speed drill	Social reinforcement	
Telling	New response drill	New response drill	Social reinforcement	Self-management	
Cues	Positive practice overcorrection	Repeated practice	Praise	Cooperative planning	
Movement		Flashcards	Feedback	Transfer activities	
Position	Puzzle technique	Computer games	Intrinsic reinforcement	Varying stimulus conditions	
Redundancy	Reward for accuracy	Reinforcement			
Prompts	Fines	Premack Principle			
Time delay	Peer tutoring	Free time			
Flow list	Cross-age tutoring	FR schedules			
Advance organizers	Classmate tutoring	Go–no go contingencies			
Reinforcement	Self-management				
	Self-instruction				
	Self-correction				

Table 9.4
Generic Academic Tactics by Stage of Learning

Table 9.5
Implementation
ideas

Intervention	Implementation ideas
Physical guidance	1. Conduct motor response physically with child. 2. Be sure teacher's and student's motor movements match. 3. Move to partial physical guidance as quickly as possible.
Shaping	1. Develop task analysis with terminal objective. 2. Teach each subskill of task analysis to mastery.
Modeling	1. Use think-aloud procedure. 2. Provide opportunities for students to imitate modeled behavior under teacher supervision.
Match-to-sample	1. Provide lots of opportunities for students to match items to sample. 2. Have students note sample and item similarities.
Telling	1. Be specific about the desired response. 2. Tell orally or in writing.
Cues	1. Have students explain why response is correct. 2. Have students imitate correct response.
Prompts	1. Have students imitate correct response. 2. Provide prompt only after unassisted attempt fails to produce correct answer.
Time delay	1. Shorten latency period as quickly as possible. 2. Determine average latency period between stimulus and response for typical learner. 3. Use different media for practice opportunities.
Flow list	1. Determine student's optimal number of words, facts, etc., that can be learned to mastery in one day. 2. Determine number of consecutive days allowed for incorrect responses to be made. 3. Plan on periodic reviews.
Advance organizers	1. Provide students with a reason for learning the instructional objective. 2. Involve students as much as possible. 3. Discuss where the skill can be used besides just in the classroom.
Reinforcement (acquisition, proficiency, maintenance)	1. Determine reinforcers for which students will work. 2. Change reinforcers to avoid satiation. 3. Learn the reinforcement schedule as soon as possible; match schedule to stage of learning and needs of students. 4. Have students keep track of points earned.
Feedback (acquisition, maintenance)	1. Provide specific, corrective feedback. 2. Pair feedback with specific praise.
Drill (acquisition, proficiency)	1. Move from consistent to novel drill activities to maintain interest. 2. Use computers appropriately for drill activities. 3. Provide consistent amount of time to practice activity before evaluation phase.
Positive practice overcorrection	1. Provide reasonable number of practice opportunities. 2. Be sure practice is correct.
Puzzle technique	1. Select tasks that have parts for groups of students to learn. 2. Model for students how to teach their peers their parts. 3. Provide practice opportunities to learn students' parts.

continued

Table 9.5
Continued

Reward for accuracy	1. Determine reward for which students will work.
	2. Determine appropriate instructional objective for which reward is necessary (may be task-analyzed).
	3. Move from reinforcer to intrinsic reinforcement as soon as possible.
Fines	1. Use tactic after other interventions have been tried.
	2. Be sure students are interested in the task and prefer the task to the fine.
	3. Avoid fines that leave students few alternatives to improve their academic performance.
Peer tutoring	1. Match tutors and tutees carefully.
	2. Teach tutors to teach and reinforce.
	3. Provide reinforcers for tutors.
Self-management	1. Model correct self-management technique.
	2. Conference with students frequently to monitor use of self-management technique.
	3. Promote problem-solving behaviors.
Repeated practice	1. Provide novel drill-and-practice opportunities.
	2. Have students check their own work.
	3. Use various student-mediated instructional arrangements.
	4. Have students practice only errors (slice of skill).
Flashcards	1. Pair with peer tutoring.
	2. Provide self-correcting materials.
	3. Include evaluation procedure.
Computer games	1. Evaluate software before sharing with students.
	2. Teach students how to use software appropriately.
	3. Pair with peer tutoring or cooperative learning.
	4. Include a variety of types of software (drill, problem-solving)
Premack principle	1. Determine a strong reinforcer.
	2. Be sure the work required to earn the reinforcer is reasonable.
Free time	1. Use as a reinforcer.
	2. Limit amount of time.
	3. Teach use of free time activities.
Overlearning	1. Determine level of mastery.
	2. Determine reasonable amount of overlearning to occur (number of extra days, number of extra problems).
Praise/Social reinforcement	1. Be specific.
	2. Provide in writing or orally.
	3. Provide age-appropriate praise.
Intrinsic reinforcement	1. Learn external reinforcement systems; move to variable ratio and interval as soon as possible.
	2. Ask students to describe how they feel about their successful academic performance.
Rationales	1. Provide during advance organizer.
	2. Explain to students reasons for learning skill.
	3. Have students explain reasons for learning skill.
	4. Have students describe various environments in which skill is necessary.
Instructions	1. Teach students to generalize across environments, people, and materials.
	2. Provide written instructions (cue cards) that can be used as needed.

Table 9.5
Continued

Cooperative planning	1. Work with general education teachers and parents to promote generalization of skills.
	2. Develop a generalization plan; evaluate periodically.
Guided instruction	1. Move from direct instruction to guided instruction in which students do more problem solving and generating of solutions.
	2. Teach students a problem-solving strategy.
	3. Provide scaffolded instruction as necessary.
	4. Provide feedback.
	5. Teach students ways of adapting to new situations.
Problem-solving strategy training	1. Use direct instruction to teach the strategy.
	2. Be sure students know strategy steps.
	3. Provide role-playing situations.
	4. Monitor use and generalization of strategy.
Transfer activities	1. Provide specific activities across environments that require students to generalize and adapt their learning.
	2. Use role playing and think-aloud to teach generalization and adaption.
	3. Use community-based instruction and field trips as opportunities to generalize and solve problems.

References and Suggested Readings

Initial Acquisition Stage
Modeling
Bandura, A. (1969). *Principles of behavior modification.* New York: Holt, Rinehart & Winston.

Hendrickson, J. M., & Gable, R. A. (1981). The use of modeling tactics to promote academic skill development of exceptional learners. *Journal of Special Education Technology, 4*(3), 20–29.

Rivera, D. M., & Smith, D. D. (1987). Influence of modeling on acquisition and generalization of computational skills: A summary of research findings from three sites. *Learning Disability Quarterly, 10*, 69–80.

Telling
Kraetsch, G. (1981). The effect of oral instructions and training on the expansion of written language. *Learning Disability Quarterly, 4*, 82–90.

Smith, D. D., & Lovitt, T. C. (1975). The use of modeling techniques to influence the acquisition of computational arithmetic skills in learning-disabled children. In E. Ramp & G. Semb (Eds.), *Behavior analysis: Areas of research and application.* Englewood Cliffs, NJ: Prentice-Hall.

Time Delay
Cybriwsky, C. A., & Schuster, J. W. (1990). Using constant time delay procedures to teach multiplication facts. *Remedial and Special Education, 11*(1), 54–59.

Kinney, P. G., Stevens, K. B., & Schuster, J. W. (1988). The effects of CAI and time delay: A systematic program for teaching spelling. *Journal of Special Education Technology, 9,* 61–72.

Koscinski, S. T., & Gast, D. L. (1993). Computer-assisted instruction with constant time delay to teach multiplication facts to students with learning disabilities. *Learning Disabilities Research & Practice, 8*(3), 157–168.

Schuster, J. W., Stevens, K. B., & Doak, P. K. (1990). Using time delay to teach word definitions. *Journal of Special Education, 24,* 306–318.

Stevens, K. B., & Schuster, J. W. (1987). Effects of a constant time delay procedure on the written spelling performance of a learning disabled student. *Learning Disability Quarterly, 10,* 9–16.

Stevens, K. B., & Schuster, J. W. (1988). Time delay: Systematic instruction for academic tasks. *Remedial and Special Education, 9*(5), 16–21.

Advance Organizers
Deshler, D. D., Warner, M. M., Schumaker, J. B., & Alley, G. R. (1983). Learning strategies intervention model: Key components and current status. In J. D. McKinney & F. Feagans (Eds.), *Current topics in learning disabilities* (Vol. 1). Norwood, NJ: Ablex.

Lenz, B. K., Alley, G. R., & Schumaker, J. B. (1987). Activating the inactive learner: Advance organizers in the secondary content classroom. *Learning Disability Quarterly, 10,* 53–62.

Paris, S. G., & Jacobs, J. E. (1984). The benefits of informed instruction for children's reading awareness and comprehension skills. *Child Development, 55,* 2083–2093.

Advanced Acquisition Stage
Feedback
Bruni, J. V. (1982). Problem solving for the primary grades. *Arithmetic Teacher, 29*(6), 10–15.

Gable, R. A., & Hendrickson, J. M. (1979). Teacher feedback: Its use and impact on learner performance. *Journal of Special Education Technology, 3,* 29–35.

Telling
Smith, D. D., & Lovitt, T. C. (1975). The use of modeling techniques to influence the acquisition of computational arithmetic skills in learning-disabled children. In E. Ramp & G. Semb (Eds.), *Behavior analysis: Areas of research and application.* Englewood Cliffs, NJ: Prentice-Hall.

Drill
Haring, N. G., Lovitt, T. C., Eaton, M. D., & Hansen, C. L. (1978). *The fourth R: Research in the classroom.* Columbus, OH: Merrill.

Fines
Lovitt, T. C., & Smith, D. D. (1974). Using withdrawal of positive reinforcement to alter subtraction performance. *Exceptional Children. 40,* 357–358.

Walker, H. M. (1983). Applications of response cost in school settings: Outcomes, issues, and recommendations. *Exceptional Education Quarterly, 3,* 47–55.

Peer Tutoring
Chiang, B., Thorpe, H. W., & Darch, D. B. (1980). Effects of cross-age tutoring on word recognition performance of learning disabled students. *Learning Disability Quarterly, 3,* 11–19.

Delquadri, J., Greenwood, C. R., Whorton, D., Carta, J. J., & Hall, R. V. (1986). Classwide peer tutoring. *Exceptional Children, 52,* 535–542.

Fowler, S. A. (1986). Peer monitoring and self-monitoring: Alternatives to traditional teacher management. *Exceptional Children, 52,* 573–581.

Greenwood, C. R., Dinwiddie, G., Terry, B., Wade, L., Stanley, S. O., Thibadeau, S., & Delquadri, J. C. (1984). Teacher-versus-peer mediated instruction: An eco-behavioral analysis of achievement outcomes. *Journal of Applied Behavior Analysis, 17,* 521–538.

Johnson, D. W., & Johnson, R. T. (1986). Mainstreaming and cooperative learning strategies. *Exceptional Children, 52*(6), 553–561.

Picott, H. E., Fantuzzo, J. W., & Clement, P. W. (1986). The effects of reciprocal peer tutoring and group contingencies on the academic performance of elementary school children. *Journal of Applied Behavior Analysis, 19,* 93–98.

Proficiency Stage
Modeling
Smith, D. D. (1979). The improvement of children's oral reading through the use of teacher modeling. *Journal of Learning Disabilities, 12,* 172–175.

Reinforcement
Cowen, R. J., Jones, F. H., & Bellack, A. S. (1979). Grandma's rule with group contingencies—A cost-effective means of classroom management. *Behavior Modification, 3,* 397–418.

Roberts, M., & Smith, D. D. (1980). The relationship among correct and error oral reading rates and comprehension. *Learning Disability Quarterly, 3,* 54–64.

Smith, D. D., & Lovitt, T. C. (1976). The differential effects of reinforcement contingencies on arithmetic performance. *Journal of Learning Disabilities, 9,* 11–29.

Maintenance Stage
Overlearning
Snell, M. D. (Ed.) (1978). *Systematic instruction of the moderately and severely handicapped.* Columbus, OH: Merrill.

Variable Ratio Schedules
Hendersen, H., Jenson, W. R., & Erken, N. (1986). Focus article: Variable interval reinforcement for increasing on-task behavior in classrooms. *Education and Treatment of Children, 9,* 250–263.

Social Reinforcement
Kelly, M. L., & Stokes, T. F. (1984). Student-teacher contracting with goal setting for maintenance. *Behavior Modification, 8*(2), 223–244.

Generalization Stage
Deshler, D. D., Alley, G. R., Warner, M. M., & Schumaker, J. B. (1981). Instructional practices for promoting skill acquisition and generalization in severely learning disabled adolescents. *Learning Disability Quarterly, 4,* 415–421.

Ellis, E. S. (1986). The role of motivation and pedagogy on the generalization of cognitive strategy training. *Journal of Learning Disabilities, 19,* 66–70.

Ellis, E. S., Lenz, B. K., & Sabornie, E. J. (1987a). Generalization and adaptation of learning strategies to natural environments: Part 1. Critical agents. *Remedial and Special Education, 8*(1), 6–21.

Ellis, E. S., Lenz, B. K., & Sabornie, E. J. (1987b). Generalization and adaptation of learning strategies to natural environments: Part 2. Research into practice. *Remedial and Special Education, 8*(2), 6–23.

Lloyd, J., Saltzman, N. J., & Kauffman, J. M. (1981). Predictable generalization in academic learning as a result of preskills and strategy training. *Learning Disability Quarterly, 4,* 203–216.

Rivera, D. M., Cook, D., & O'Malley, J. (1992). Techniques to promote the occurrence of generalization of strategies from the special education classroom to the regular education setting. *LD Forum, 17*(3), 5–8.

Rivera, D., & Smith, D. D. (1987). *Facilitating generalization for computation arithmetic.* Albuquerque: University of New Mexico, Special Education Department.

Schmidt, J. L. (1983). Conditions that promote generalization. *The Pointer, 27*(2), 8–10.

Stokes, T. F., & Baer, D. M. (1977). An implicit technology of generalization. *Journal of Applied Behavior Analysis, 10,* 349–367.

Vaughn, S., Bos, C. S., & Lund, K. A. (1986). But they can do it in my room: Strategies for promoting generalization. *Teaching Exceptional Children, 18,* 176–180.

Rationales

Deshler, D. D., & Schumaker, J. B (1983). Social skills of learning disabled adolescents: Characteristics and intervention. *Topics in Learning and Learning Disabilities, 3*(2), 15–23.

Self-Management

Blandford, B. J., & Lloyd, J. W. (1987). Effects of a self-instructional procedure on handwriting. *Journal of Learning Disabilities, 20,* 342–346.

Lovitt, T. C. (1995). *Tactics for teaching* (2nd ed.). Columbus, OH: Merrill.

Problem-Solving (Adaption) Stage

Camp, B. W., & Bash, M. A. S. (1981). *Think aloud: Increasing social and cognitive skills—A problem-solving program for children.* Champaign, IL: Research Press.

Havertape, J. F., & Kass, C. E. (1978). Examination of problem solving in learning disabled adolescents through verbalized self-instructions. *Learning Disability Quarterly, 1,* 94–103.

Kahney, H. (1986). *Problem solving: A cognitive approach.* Philadelphia: Open University Press.

Sliff, B. D., Weiss, J., & Bell, T. (1985). Separability of metacognition: Problem solving in learning disabled and regular students. *Journal of Educational Psychology, 77*(4), 437–445.

Smith, D. D., & Robinson, S. (1986). Educating the learning disabled. In R. J. Morris & B. Blatt (Eds.), *Special education: Research trends.* New York: Pergamon Press.

Chapter 10
Reading

Making Connections

Before you read this chapter, examine Individualized Education Programs at the elementary and secondary levels to find listed reading annual goals and identify how they are intended to be taught. Note the materials and evaluation methods that are to be used. Review reading tests (see chapter 3) typically used to assess reading abilities and examine actual test results if possible. Review the curricular models presented in chapter 4; think about the role of reading in each model. Reexamine the instructional approaches described in chapter 5; consider how those approaches are applied to reading instruction. Think about the reading curriculum, the skills that are being taught, and specific reading strategies that are used to promote reading comprehension.

The ability to read and comprehend the written word has long been considered an indicator of intellectual competence. More recently, reading has also come to be seen as a functional tool that allows each individual to develop and maintain employment skills and to participate more fully in the social and recreational activities of daily life. Because underachievement in reading is a common problem of students with special needs, it is critical for teachers to select appropriate reading strategies.

This chapter was written by Drs. Brian R. Bryant and Diane Pedrotty Rivera, The University of Texas at Austin.

Objectives

After studying this chapter, the reader will be able to

1. Describe how reading is acquired through instruction.
2. Identify and explain how the components of reading instruction relate to different reading acquisition models.
3. Provide explanations of reading instructional components.

Bryant and Wiederholt (1990) demonstrated that children with reading problems have difficulties in a variety of tasks, including (1) blending letters to form nonsense words (e.g., sut, crog), (2) identifying lists of whole words, (3) recognizing smaller words embedded in larger words, (4) using various structural analysis clues (i.e., inflectional endings, affixes, contractions, compounds) to decode words, (5) sequencing words to form sentences, (6) reading continuous print fluently, and (7) comprehending the meaning of the passages they have read orally. In addition, Deshler, Ellis, and Lenz (1996) reviewed the literature and identified characteristics of good and poor adolescent readers. Table 10.1 summarizes their findings.

Many researchers have identified **phonological awareness** (i.e., the ability to recognize speech sounds and blend them into meaningful units) as being a critical factor in acquiring reading skills (Perfetti, Beck, Bell, & Hughes, 1987; Torgesen & Bryant, 1994; Wagner & Torgesen, 1987), and particularly in acquiring the skills associated with word recognition (Lyon, 1995). The lack of efficient **decoding skills** (i.e., converting letter combinations to words) gets in the way of oral reading fluency (i.e., the ability to read quickly and effortlessly) and **reading comprehension** abilities. Research is also showing that deficiencies in decoding and single word recognition are the most significant types of reading problems (Olson, Forsberg, Wise, & Rack, 1994; Stanovich, 1986) and are predictive of reading comprehension difficulties (Lyon, 1995).

Many effective teaching practices have been identified for youngsters who have learning problems, are at risk for academic difficulties, or are from culturally and linguistically diverse backgrounds. These practices for teaching reading include (1) **code emphasis** content, which includes direct instruction in phonological processing, (2) oral reading fluency development, and (3) reading comprehension strategies (Lyon, 1995, Mather, 1992; Moats & Lyon 1993; Pressley & Rankin, 1994; Westby, 1993).

Table 10.1
Summary of
Research Findings
Differentiating
Good and Poor
Adolescent Readers

Good readers . . .	Poor readers . . .
are aware of variables that interact in reading.	are less aware of variables that interact in reading.
are able to identify main ideas from a passage and determine their relative importance.	have difficulty identifying a passage's main ideas and determining their relative importance.
use headings, subheadings, and other text features to aid in comprehension.	struggle with making connections between headings, subheadings, and the text features and text meaning.
attempt to correct comprehension breakdowns by rereading material.	tend to move through the text, even if they do not understand what they have read.
employ a variety of reading strategies and adapt their reading to the material.	have few alternative reading strategies in their repertoire.
bring considerable experiences and background knowledge to the reading process.	have limited experience and prior knowledge to help them understand new material.

In this chapter, we describe the nature of reading and its components. We discuss approaches to reading instruction and provide strategies and interventions that have proven effective in improving students' reading skills. The instructional interventions have been validated by case study, sound research methodology, and student progress data.

Nature of Reading

As you read, think about . . .

1. Developing your own definition of reading.
2. Describing how the models of reading relate to instructional approaches discussed in chapter 5.
3. Developing your own philosophy of reading and noting how teachers' reading philosophies can affect how they collaborate with one another to improve their students' reading skills.
4. Describing how reading problems can delay a student's overall academic growth.
5. Using techniques in chapter 6 to assess student placement and progress with reading.

Reading is a complex act that is difficult to understand fully. Huey's statement in 1908 reflects reading's complexity:

> To completely understand what we do when we read would almost be the acme of . . . achievement, for it would be to describe very many of the most intricate workings of the human mind, as well as to unravel the tangled story of the most remarkable specific performance that civilization has learned in all its history. (p. 6)

Although over 90 years have passed since Huey's statement, researchers still have not explained completely the act we call reading. However, we can point to a body of literature and research that has accumulated on the topic to provide a glimpse of how individuals acquire the ability to read. In the next section, we define reading, discuss three approaches and issues to reading instruction, and describe curricular and instructional design features.

Definition of Reading Literacy

Wiederholt and Bryant (1987) state that defining reading "is more than an exercise in polemics. It is necessary in scientific endeavors to use words in a precise manner. Imprecise word use causes confusion and misinterpretation of what the writers and speakers are intending to convey" (p. 165). Yet, when defining reading, authors "do not provide any insight into reading or the way it is being discussed, [which] can lead to contentious debates" (Smith, 1988, p. 165). We provide this section because it gives the reader of this text a conceptual framework upon which to build throughout this chapter.

Almost all definitions of reading share one common property: that is, they all stress that it involves gaining meaning from printed or written symbols (Wiederholt & Bryant, 1987). For example, *Webster's II New Riverside University Dictionary* (1984) gives the following definitions:

1. To examine or grasp the meaning of (written or printed characters, words, or sentences). 2. To utter or express aloud (written or printed materials). 3. To interpret the meaning or nature of through close examination or observation. 4. To determine the intent, moods, thoughts of. 5. To attribute (a particular meaning) to something read.

If reading is a combination of decoding and comprehension, then one would have to argue that simply decoding without comprehending what is being read would not truly be reading. For instance, many children can rapidly read single words written in a column (researchers refer to this as *calling* words), but when asked what the individual words mean, they are unable to provide an answer.

Complexity of vocabulary is only one potential barrier to comprehension, however. Wiederholt and Bryant (1987) provide the following passage from *Great Books of the Western World* (Hutchison, 1952) to show how complex syntax can also diminish comprehension:

> The latter of the two queens, whose name was Victocris, a wiser princess than her predecessor, not only left behind her, as memorials of her occupancy of the throne, the works which I shall presently describe, but also observing the great power and restless enterprise of the Medes, who had taken so large a number of cities, and among them Vinoveh, and expecting to be attached in her turn, made all possible exertions to increase the defenses of her empire. (p. 41)

Most people would have great difficulty comprehending this passage, even though they might call all the words correctly. Thus, we would argue that a person who can pronounce the words in the passage but is not able to understand the writer's intent is not reading. This is not to say that the individual is a nonreader—it simply means that the person cannot read or comprehend this particular passage. To summarize, we believe that reading is the act of decoding print or written symbols and understanding the intent conveyed by the writer.

Approaches and Issues in Reading Instruction

For as long as there have been reading instructional programs, there has been debate about how best to teach reading; this is true in both the special and general education literature. Research has been conducted on the various techniques, but there has never been one approach that has been guaranteed to work with all children. Why? Although there is no simple explanation about why some children learn to read with one approach while others do not, it is a simple fact that all children are different from each other. They come to school with different experiences, different health histories, different attitudes, different learning styles, and so forth. In other words, because children are unique in their attributes, they respond to reading curricula differently.

Over the past 30 years, several approaches to reading acquisition have been popularized. There has been the "look-say method," wherein children are taught a series of words to be memorized; the "phonics method," where letter-sound associations are taught; the "alternate alphabet method," in which early readers learn a contrived alphabet system that provides a perfect one-to-one correspondence between letters and sounds (in our conventional alphabet, there is not a perfect correspondence); and a collection of other reading programs, most of which contain elements of the "look-say" and "phonics" approaches.

After examining several attempts to describe how reading is taught, Harris and Sipay (1980) divided reading approaches into three categories: bottom-up, top-down, and interactive. We prefer to use different terms to describe the philosophies associated with each approach: "decoding-to-comprehend," "comprehending-to-decode," and "decoding-comprehending interaction."

Decoding-to-Comprehend Approach

The decoding-to-comprehend approach is based on the premise that written language is a graphic code of spoken language that must be "decoded," or translated into its more natural form. With this approach, the sound-symbol correspondences (sometimes referred to as grapheme-phoneme correspondences) are learned and applied to written text. Once this has been accomplished, the reader associates meaning with the spoken word.

As an example, consider the word *cat*. The decoding-to-comprehend advocate would teach the sound commonly associated with each letter (i.e., see *c*, think /k/, see *a*, think /a/, see *t*, think /t/). The sounds are then blended together to form /kat/, which the reader then associates with a furry creature.

With this reading approach, comprehension occurs as a result of translating the graphic code into a more familiar spoken code. Only after the code is broken can a person understand what the writer intends to convey. If the writer consistently conveys information using words that are not in the reader's spoken language, comprehension is unlikely to occur.

Synthetic phonics programs, which teach the sounds associated with the letters that represent them, are examples of the decoding-to-comprehend approach. Such programs use a controlled vocabulary and have a strong drill-and-practice emphasis. Phonics rules are stressed (e.g., "When two vowels go walking, the first one does the talking"—example *toad; "c* is pronounced *s* if the vowel after it is *i* or *e*"—example *ceiling*).

Issues regarding this reading approach focus on the merits of memorizing English rules and learning reading skills in isolation. Critics of the decoding-to-comprehend approach note that English is not a consistent language, in that phonics rules do not generalize completely (e.g., *dead* does not follow the "two vowels go walking" rule). Critics also argue that studying decoding skills in isolation is boring and fails to make the connection between these skills and the act of reading literature. Advocates of the phonics approach counter that exceptions to rules are relatively rare, are of little overall importance, and are easy to learn.

Comprehending-to-Decode Approach

The comprehending-to-decode approach is based on the idea that the reader's cognitive and linguistic competencies are the primary factors in constructing meaning from print. Frank Smith (1988), a leading proponent of this approach, characterizes the differences between the two approaches:

> Reading is less a matter of extracting sound from print than of bringing meaning to print. The sounds that are supposed to reveal the meaning of sequences of letters cannot in fact be produced unless a probable mean-

ing can be determined in advance. It is a universal fact of reading rather than a defect of English spelling that the effort to read through decoding is largely futile and unnecessary.... [R]eading and learning to read are essentially meaningful activities; they are not passive and mechanical but purposeful and rational, dependent on the prior knowledge and expectations of the reader (or learner). Reading is a matter of making sense of written words rather than decoding print to sound. (p. 2)

The comprehending-to-decode approach is demonstrated best by the "whole language" approach, in which reading and writing are taught together and skills are taught within the context of literature, rather than in isolation. Mather (1992) reviewed the whole-language movement and identified several positive instructional features. These include student access to and appreciation of quality literature, a language-rich environment, a low level of boredom in reading activities, and good comprehension skills. However, Mathers and others (e.g., Pressley & Rankin, 1994) point out that the lack of instructional focus on reading skill acquisition may be detrimental to students who have reading disabilities. In fact, there is little research that supports the comprehending-to-decode approach when used alone with students who have learning and behavior problems.

Decoding-Comprehending Interaction Approach

The decoding-comprehending interaction approach provides a middle ground to the top-down and bottom-up debate. The decoding-comprehending interaction approach views reading as a process of moving back and forth from a decoding-to-comprehend process to a comprehending-to-decode process, depending on the difficulty of the material being read and the reader's skills. Goodman, Smith, Meredith, and Goodman (1987) explain this process as follows:

The reader's focus is always on making sense of the text. Attention is on meaning, and anything else such as letters, words or grammar only gets full attention when the reader has trouble getting to the meaning. Each cycle is tentative and may not be completed if the reader can move on directly to meaning. (p. 207)

In other words, the philosophy of this approach maintains that readers use whatever strategies they need to comprehend the text. Decoding strategies are used to read unfamiliar words, and the context of the passage contributes to an overall understanding of the material. Comprehension is, therefore, adversely affected when the reader is lacking an actual skill or a piece of knowledge related to the text. Teachers who use the decoding-comprehending interaction model recognize the benefits of reading for meaning and being exposed to literature, while maintaining the need to build reading fluency through skill acquisition, particularly for students who experience reading problems.

Curricular and Instructional Design Features

By definition, children with reading disabilities do not read well. Although this may seem a simplistic description, the reality is that these children have not responded to whatever reading approach has been used with them. Proponents of the comprehending-to-decode model cannot argue that their approach works for all children because it is simply not so. Likewise, proponents of the decoding-to-comprehend approach cannot claim 100 percent success either.

Historically, remedial reading methods have taken either the "more of the same," approach, in which the students are subjected to the same curriculum that has failed (except instruction is given in higher dosages), or the "let's try something new" approach, in which the students are moved away from the standard curriculum and exposed to a different one. At times, these approaches are successful, but at other times, the students continue their pattern of frustration and failure.

Students learn differently, so teachers need to have a wide variety of teaching methods and strategies at their disposal. There are basic curricular and instructional features of reading instruction that have proven effective with many students who have reading disabilities (Lewis, 1983). We discuss these features here.

Direct Teaching

We believe that students with reading disabilities must be taught how to read. Whatever approach is used, teachers must actively engage students in the instructional process. Lewis (1983) describes direct teaching as occurring when the instructor demonstrates, models, defines, and explains. Students with reading disabilities have demonstrated that they do not learn to read vicariously. These students require the teacher's direct involvement in instruction and correction when the student errs.

Teach Skills

Students need to be taught how to decode and comprehend fluently. Regardless of the reading approach selected, teachers must identify and specifically teach reading skills. Students need to learn skills in word recognition and word identification. Vocabulary instruction is an important part of overall reading instruction because of the link between vocabulary knowledge and reading comprehension abilities (Carlisle, 1993). Therefore, vocabulary development is an important skill to promote in students with reading problems. Many students with reading disabilities can benefit greatly from strategic instruction to foster comprehension skill development. Students also need to be taught effective ways to comprehend reading material. The development of solid reading comprehension skills can span a student's elementary and secondary years.

Teach Automaticity

Good readers read with apparent effortlessness. The reason for this is quite simple: Reading becomes an automatic act. Reading skills that are taught as tools for fluent reading are so ingrained that they no longer require the student's attention. Yet automaticity does not occur unless teachers teach it. Practice builds reading fluency and automaticity. Lack of automaticity with word recognition and word identification skills may hinder students' abilities to comprehend reading material. LaBerge and Samuels (1974) note that movement from accuracy to automaticity is necessary to acquire both fluent reading and good comprehension.

Teach Generalization Strategies

Reading skills must generalize to overall performance. That is, students should use reading skills regardless of the material being covered. Students need to learn specific strategies for generalizing their basic reading skills to science texts, social studies texts, and so forth. In this way, the critical bridge from "learning to read" to "reading to learn" is constructed.

Expose Children to Literature

Beyond teaching reading to give students access to content area curriculum, reading allows people to experience what others write about. That is, the body of literature that has accumulated over time allows readers to enjoy time travel with Jules Verne and experience Margaret's growing pains thanks to Judy Blume. Fortunately, many of today's reading textbooks include a sampling of literary works. Remedial programs should include popular novels, mysteries, and other literature.

Skills for Instruction

As you read, think about . . .

1. Explaining how the components of reading relate to one another.
2. Identifying how the components of reading relate to the approaches to teaching reading noted earlier.
3. Discussing how a child's background and experiences can affect his or her acquisition of reading skills.
4. Describing the author-reader connection.

In this chapter, we will focus on four components of reading acquisition and development: decoding letters and words in print, comprehending words and ideas in print, reading with fluency, and content area reading. Figure 10.1 provides a diagram of topics for reading instruction.

As an introduction to this section, we provide in Table 10.2 a description of the five stages of reading acquisition that Chall offers in her 1983 text, *Stages of Reading Development*. These developmental stages show how many of the discrete skills discussed below are used concurrently during the reading process. Moreover, these stages provide the foundation for building the skills at the heart of the reading curriculum in today's schools.

Figure 10.1
Topics for reading instruction

Reading

Decoding	Comprehension	Fluency	Content area
Word recognition	Understanding words	Tone–Volume	Comprehension
Basic sight words	Words in context	Inflection	Reading rate
Other sight words	Words in isolation	Print conventions	Technical vocabulary
Word identification	Understanding ideas	Rate	Text structures
Letter identification	Literal		
Phonetic analysis	Factual recall		
Structural analysis	Sequence		
Contextual analysis	Inferential		
	Judgments		
	Drawing conclusions		
	Anticipating outcome		
	Cause-Effect		

Table 10.2
Stages of Reading

Stage 0. Prereading: birth to age 6. During this stage, children who grow up in literate surroundings are exposed to letters, words, and books. As a result, the children develop many of the requisite abilities (commonly called readiness skills) associated with early reading success. Such skills include top-to-bottom and left-to-right orientation skills associated with books, control over syntax and words, and auditory and visual discrimination.

Stage 1. Initial reading, or decoding, stage: grades 1–2, ages 6–7. During this stage, children learn the arbitrary sets of letters and associate these with the corresponding parts of spoken words. Children gain insight about the nature of English spelling and the alphabetic principle.

Stage 2. Confirmation, fluency, ungluing from print: grades 2–3, ages 7–8. With the decoding skills, the syntax, and the vocabulary developed at earlier stages, students can take advantage of these skills and concentrate on the meaning of a story or book. Of importance during this stage is the reader's ability to use context to gain fluency and speed. In addition, children master some of the more complex phonic elements.

Stage 3. Reading for learning the new—a first step: middle school, ages 9–13. Once students have "learned to read," they are ready to "read to learn." As children read at this stage, they should gain factual information, learn new concepts, and as a result, learn how to accomplish new tasks. Word meaning and students' prior knowledge are increasingly important, but students still use decoding skills learned earlier to derive meaning.

Stage 4. Multiple viewpoints: high school, ages 14–18. The difference between this stage and stage 3 is that in stage 4, students learn to deal with more than one point of view in reading. By having been introduced to basic concepts in stage 3, students in stage 4 are prepared to be exposed to different interpretations and theories of, for instance, Columbus's "discovery" of America. The views of Native Americans, Spanish historians, and others provide alternative renditions of the historical accounts that can be discussed and debated.

Stage 5. Construction and reconstruction—a world view: College, Ages 18 and above. At this stage, students are able to use the printed materials that are of interest to them selectively. Readers learn to construct knowledge for themselves from what they read. They can balance their comprehension of the ideas read, their analysis of them, and their own ideas of them.

Source: Adapted from *Stages of Reading Development*, by J. S. Chall, 1983, New York: McGraw-Hill.

Decoding Letters and Words in Print

The first component of reading relates to decoding (i.e., converting letter combinations to words). Common sense dictates that people who cannot identify words in print have difficulty making sense of anything written. So severe is some people's inability to decode that over 100 years ago Kussmaul (1877) introduced the term *word blindness* to describe an inability to understand words. Although Kussmaul's application of the term initially related to spoken language, it was generalized to reading in subsequent years (Hinshelwood, 1917).

Decoding requires the reader to recognize common vocabulary words and to apply word analysis and word attack skills. These decoding skills help youngsters decipher words more readily. We now examine two subcomponents of decoding, word recognition and word identification.

Word Recognition

Word recognition is synonymous with sight vocabulary. Cooper, Warncke, and Shipman (1990) provided two definitions of sight vocabulary or sight words, as they are commonly called. The first definition views sight vocabulary as "those words that are instantly recognized by the reader" (p. 58). In this context, a developing reader's sight vocabulary is constantly expanding as access to print increases. Through continuous exposure to words in print, the reader sees the same words over and over and no longer needs to analyze them.

The second definition that Cooper et al. (1990) offer is that sight vocabulary is "those words that are taught or learned as whole words" (p. 58). Cooper et al. provide three circumstances for teaching words as whole units:

1. When the word to be taught has an irregular spelling pattern, therefore defying analysis using regular phonic or structural generalizations. Examples: *have, come, said.*
2. When the reader needs to know the word, but hasn't yet learned the generalizations that would apply to its pronunciation. Examples: *old, find, night.* In the case of these words, the students would not have learned the exceptions to the short-vowel generalization; therefore, they would not be expected to know that all of these vowel sounds are governed by another set of generalizations.
3. When the word must be learned for success in reading because it occurs so frequently in printed material. These words form a special category of words often known as basic sight words, structure words, or high-frequency words.

Several sight word lists have been created to help teachers determine which words most commonly appear in print and therefore which words should be taught to be recognized at sight. The Dolch Word List (Johnson, 1971; see Table 10.3) is an example of a sight word list; it provides 220 commonly used words.

Word Identification

Word identification is used here synonymously with *word analysis* and *word attack*. It describes the reading strategies employed to decode unknown words. This ability includes all aspects of alphabet knowledge, including the ability to discriminate between letters, associate sounds with letters, and analyze the phonetic and structural aspects of words. In this section, the areas within word identification are divided into four categories: (1) letter identification, (2) phonetic analysis, (3) structural analysis, and (4) contextual analysis.

Letter Identification   Letter identification includes the ability to know the letter names and to match uppercase and lowercase letters. Research has demonstrated that knowledge of letter names, per se, does not predict reading success, but almost every reading program includes some letter naming and matching capital letters with their lowercase counterparts.

Phonetic Analysis   Phonetic analysis, or phonics, refers to decoding via the alphabetic principle of making connections between units of print and units of sound (Stanovich, 1992). Phonetic analysis uses common elements to form these print-sound relationships:

1. *Consonants* are the letters *b, c, d, f, g, h, j, k, l, m, n, p, q, r, s, t, v, x,* and *z* (*w* and *y* also can be consonants), which represent speech sounds wherein the airflow is stopped or constricted within the oral mechanism by the tongue, teeth, or lips, either in isolation or in some combination. All consonants except *c* and *g* are fairly consistent in their sound correspondences. Hard sounds, as in *can* and *goat*, versus soft sounds, as in *cent* and *gym*, tend to be based on the letter that

Table 10.3
Dolch List

preprimer	primer	first	second	third
1. the	45. when	89. many	133. know	177. don't
2. of	46. who	90. before	134. while	178. does
3. and	47. will	91. must	135. last	179. got
4. to	48. more	92. through	136. might	180. united
5. a	49. no	93. back	137. us	181. left
6. in	50. if	94. years	138. great	182. number
7. that	51. out	95. where	139. old	183. course
8. is	52. so	96. much	140. year	184. war
9. was	53. said	97. your	141. off	185. until
10. he	54. what	98. may	142. come	186. always
11. for	55. up	99. well	143. since	187. away
12. it	56. its	100. down	144. against	188. something
13. with	57. about	101. should	145. go	189. fact
14. as	58. into	102. because	146. came	190. through
15. his	59. than	103. each	147. right	191. water
16. on	60. them	104. just	148. used	192. less
17. be	61. can	105. those	149. take	193. public
18. at	62. only	106. people	150. three	194. put
19. by	63. other	107. Mr.	151. states	195. thing
20. I	64. new	108. how	152. himself	196. almost
21. this	65. some	109. too	153. few	197. hand
22. had	66. could	110. little	154. house	198. enough
23. not	67. time	111. state	155. use	199. far
24. are	68. these	112. good	156. during	200. took
25. but	69. two	113. very	157. without	201. head
26. from	70. may	114. make	158. again	202. yet
27. or	71. then	115. would	159. place	203. government
28. have	72. do	116. still	160. American	204. system
29. an	73. first	117. own	161. around	205. better
30. they	74. any	118. see	162. however	206. set
31. which	75. my	119. men	163. home	207. told
32. one	76. now	120. work	164. small	208. nothing
33. you	77. such	121. long	165. found	209. night
34. were	78. like	122. get	166. Mrs.	210. end
35. her	79. our	123. here	167. thought	211. why
36. all	80. over	124. between	168. went	212. called
37. she	81. man	125. both	169. say	213. didn't
38. there	82. me	126. life	170. part	214. eyes
39. would	83. even	127. being	171. once	215. find
40. their	84. most	128. under	172. general	216. going
41. we	85. made	129. never	173. high	217. look
42. him	86. after	130. day	174. upon	218. asked
43. been	87. also	131. same	175. school	219. later
44. has	88. did	132. another	176. every	220. knew

Source: From "The Dolch List Reexamined," by D. D. Johnson, 1971, *The Reading Teacher, 24,* pp. 455–456. Copyright 1971 by International Reading Association. Reprinted with permission. All rights reserved.

follows the consonant. For instance, the letters *i* and *e* following a *c* or *g* will usually result in a soft pronunciation of the consonant.

2. *Consonant blends* occur when two or three consonants combine to form a distinct sound that captures elements of each consonant's sound. For instance, the *bl* that appears in the word *blend* is a blend. Other blends are *br, cl, cr, dr, dw, fl, fr, gl, gr, pl, pr, sc, scr, sk, skr, sm, sn, sp, spr, st, str, sw, tr,* and *tw.*

3. Like consonant blends, *consonant digraphs* can be formed by combining two consonants. Unlike blends, however, the consonant digraph takes on its own unique sound (e.g., *ch* in *ch*air), represents the sound of one of the contributing consonants (e.g., *pn* in *pn*eumonia), or represents the sound of another grapheme (e.g., *gh* in lau*gh*). Common consonant digraphs include *ch, ck, gh, kn, ph, pn, sh, th, wh,* and *wr.*

4. *Vowels* are the letters *a, e, i, o,* and *u* (and sometimes *y* and *w*). These graphemes represent speech sounds in which the airflow is not constricted in the oral mechanism.

   Long vowels are those in which the name of the letter is heard. The *a* in *a*te, *i* in *i*ce, the first *e* in g*e*ne, and *o* in g*o* are examples of long vowel sounds.

   Short vowels are vowels whose sounds do not correspond to their name. Examples of short vowels are the *a* in b*a*t, *e* in *e*gg, *i* in *i*n, *o* in l*o*t, *u* in b*u*g, and *y* in m*y*th.

5. *Vowel digraphs* are similar to consonant digraphs in that they are composed of two consecutive vowels that combine to produce a single *long* or *short vowel* sound. This sound may or may not be the same as one of the contributing vowels. Vowel digraphs include *ai* in p*ai*n or s*ai*d, *ay* in r*ay*, *ea* in s*ea*l or d*ea*d, *ee* in m*ee*t, *ie* in p*ie*ce, and *oa* in g*oa*t or br*oa*d. Because vowel digraphs must appear in the same syllable, the *ea* in r*ea*ct would not be considered a digraph.

6. *Diphthongs* are the vowel equivalent to consonant blends. These combinations of two vowels result in the sounds of both contributing vowels being heard. Examples include *oi* in b*oi*l and *oy* in c*oy*. Similar to digraphs, diphthongs must be in the same syllable; thus, the *oy* in c*oy*ote would not be considered a diphthong.

7. *Schwa* is the name of the unique, unstressed, short *u* sound symbolized by the / / in a dictionary. Examples of schwa include comm*a* and f*o*rsaken.

Structural Analysis   *Structural analysis* involves using the structural attributes of words and their importance in decoding unknown words. Spache and Spache (1986) maintain that the purpose of training in structural analysis is "the development of the habit of recognition by larger, more meaningful units within words" (p. 492). Structural analysis components include prefixes, suffixes, inflectional endings, compound words, and contractions.

In considering structural analysis components, it is helpful to know that a *morpheme* is the smallest meaningful unit in language. The word *cat* is a morpheme because it conveys meaning. But the letter *s* is also a morpheme because when it follows *cat*, it adds meaning. Because *s* cannot stand alone as a meaningful unit, we call *s* in this case a *bound morpheme. Cat* is a *free morpheme,* because it has meaning even when it stands alone.

Prefixes and suffixes are bound morphemes known as *affixes.* A *prefix* is a bound morpheme that appears before a free morpheme (e.g., *dis*associate). A *suffix* is a bound morpheme that appears at the end of a free morpheme (e.g., collaborat*or*).

Inflectional endings are special bound morphemes that, like suffixes, come at the end of words. These endings change the meaning of a word with regard to possession (e.g., rabbit*'s*), comparison (e.g., long*er*), number (e.g., rat*s*), and tense (e.g., walk*ed*). In these cases, the inflectional endings changed the meaning of the free morphemes *rabbit* (to show ownership), *long* (to show relative distance), *rat* (to show more than one), and *walk* (to show past tense).

Compound words are two free morphemes strung together to form a new word that retains the meaningful elements of the contributing morphemes. For example, *playground* is a compound word that means "an area (ground) in which to play." Other compound words are *basketball, doghouse,* and *toothpick. Bulletin* would not be considered a compound word; even though it contains two free morphemes, *bullet* and *in,* the word has nothing to do with the meanings associated with each morpheme.

Contractions are single words created by combining two or more words and substituting an apostrophe for missing letters. For example, the contraction *isn't* is a combination of *is not,* with an apostrophe taking the place of the letter *o.*

Contextual Analysis   *Contextual analysis* is the use of textual meaning and clues to help identify an unknown word. For instance, consider a passage that reads, "Tom pulled his little red wagon behind him" and a reader who can read only the words: "Tom pulled his little red _____ behind him." Using semantic and syntactic abilities, the reader could fill in the blank with a word that makes sense. Bryant and Wiederholt (1990) note that readers tend to use context clues in combination with other word attack skills, in this case, by filling in the blank with a word that makes sense *and* that begins with *w.*

Comprehending Words and Ideas in Print

Decoding is necessary to identify what words the writer has chosen to get his or her point across, but it is an insufficient exercise if the reader doesn't know what the words mean or what message the writer is conveying. Although the understanding of words and the understanding of ideas are inextricably tied to one another in the comprehension process, we choose to separate them for discussion's sake.

Understanding Words

Earlier, we used the term *sight vocabulary* to describe words that can be decoded without analysis (i.e., words that have either been learned as whole units or that have been automatized through continuous exposure). Here, we introduce the term **meaning vocabulary,** which simply means that an individual understands the meaning of a word. This is not to say that an individual has to know the dictionary definition of a word, but that he or she can recognize or use the word appropriately in the context of continuous speech. We agree with Spache and Spache (1986), who inferred that some readers have developed such automaticity in their word attack abilities that they can pronounce a series of words, even though they have no idea what the words mean. If the reader knows the meaning of the words that are being read, then the words are in the person's meaning vocabulary and he or she is able to understand individual words in print.

McGee and Richgels (1990) provided a list of vocabulary skills that proficient readers can accomplish:

Describe pictures

Classify objects

Identify and understand concrete nouns (dog, cat, man, horse)

Identify and understand pronouns (it, she, he, they, us, we)

Identify synonyms, antonyms, and homonyms

Identify descriptive words

Identify and understand abstract words (love, honesty)

Cheek and Collins (1985) note that there are several kinds of vocabularies. A person's **general vocabulary** consists of words that are used on a regular basis during conversation. A **specialized vocabulary** is made up of words that have multiple meanings, depending on the context. For instance, the word *range* may be in a person's general vocabulary when it refers to a series of mountains, but it moves into the specialized vocabulary when used in statistics to describe the lowest and highest numbers inclusive in a data set. A **technical vocabulary** refers to those words that are used in a particular content area (e.g., decoding when used to describe a reading act).

As readers mature, their vocabularies expand with their reading material. High school and college students encounter words in their readings that, through the use of context and glossaries, expand their meaning vocabularies. In fact, this chapter has probably introduced new technical vocabularies and new specialized vocabularies to each reader.

Understanding words is more than simply having words in one's meaning vocabulary. It also involves using many of the skills described earlier that are associated with decoding. For instance, knowing the meaning of prefixes, suffixes, and inflectional endings helps a person comprehend a combination of free and bound morphemes (e.g., mis-manage-ment). The ability to use context clues to derive meaning is also important. For example, a reader may not know the word *magnanimous* in the sentence, "The philanthropist's donation to the Boy Scouts of America was a *magnanimous* gesture." It is probable, however, that the reader can use the context of the sentence to understand that *magnanimous* is a positive attribute.

Understanding Ideas

In their review of research on reading comprehension, Barr and Johnson (1991) cite the work of several authors who attempted to identify subareas of reading comprehension. In 1968, for example, Davis identified seven separate comprehension skills: recalling word meanings; using context to make word meaning inferences; answering questions about explicit or implicit parts of the content; weaving together ideas from the content; recognizing a writer's purpose, attitude, tone, and mood; identifying a writer's technique; and following the structure of a passage.

Others, however, have disputed Davis's division of comprehension and have come up with subareas of their own. When we discuss comprehension of ideas in print, we hold that only two types of comprehension are paramount: literal and inferential. *Literal comprehension* deals specifically with the material on the printed page. An example of literal comprehension would be reading a passage on Mount Vesuvius and being able to regurgitate factual information obtained in the passage (e.g., Vesuvius destroyed the city of Pompeii and there were no known survivors). *Inferential comprehension* requires the reader to go beyond the facts stated in the passage, perhaps to project one's ideas as to the writer's thoughts and feelings or those of the people who were being affected by the volcano.

Identifying why some students have difficulty comprehending print has challenged researchers for decades. To examine the potential breakdowns most effectively, it is helpful to identify the components that have some bearing on the reading process. We provide information here on factors associated with the author and the reader.

Author Component   Brown, Hammill, and Wiederholt (1986) noted that reading comprehension is closely tied to the author's understanding and skill. Within this are included (1) intended meaning, (2) expectations about the reader, and (3) the expression of the intended meaning.

Authors' intentions are probably never reconstructed exactly in the minds of their readers, for several reasons. The meaning may be fuzzy in the author's mind. The author may also lack the skills needed to bring the ideas to the mind of the reader. Brown et al. (1986) note that written language never can fully characterize the author's actual intentions, because life experiences and specific language competence are unique to each reader.

The author's expectations about the reader also affect the reader's comprehension. Authors usually have expectations about the reader that influence the elements they use in written language. Vocabulary selection, complexity of syntax, and the organization of material are all the author's choices. When authors have grossly misjudged their audience, they create a comprehension problem. When the reader does not have the background that the author assumes, the reader is unlikely to understand the writing.

Another author component that can affect meaning involves readability. In the past, when writers spoke of readability or text difficulty, they were primarily referring to such matters as the number of different words among the total number of words, the syllabic length of words, the number of words per sentence, and the complexity of the sentence structure (i.e., simple versus complex and compound sentences). In this vein, several readability formulas (e.g., the Fry formula—see Figure 10.2) have been established. Klare (1984) summarized the research on readability formulas and suggests that these formulas can be used with caution to provide a general indication of readability, but the formulas cannot be interpreted as providing *exact* indicators of a given text's readability.

The manner in which authors aid readers in organizing the text information prior to reading also affects reading comprehension. Ausubel (1968) recommends that authors write "advanced organizers" (i.e., an outline of major and minor subordinate ideas) to help readers better understand the author's intention.

Written language influences a reader's understanding, as well. Written language is thought to employ much more syntactic complexity than spoken language. Written language sometimes employs a formal sentence structure (e.g., "Bowing awkwardly, he left the room"), which may present special problems for comprehension. Authors who use complex syntax may be interfering with the reader's ability to comprehend.

Reader Component   Brown et al. (1986) note three factors associated with the reader's role in comprehension. These include (1) the reader's expectations about the text or the author, (2) the reader's experience with language in its written form, and (3) the reader's prior knowledge and experience.

Reader expectations are believed to be predictions about ideas or specific language elements that are either confirmed or not confirmed as one reads. The reader

Figure 10.2
The Fry
Readability Scale

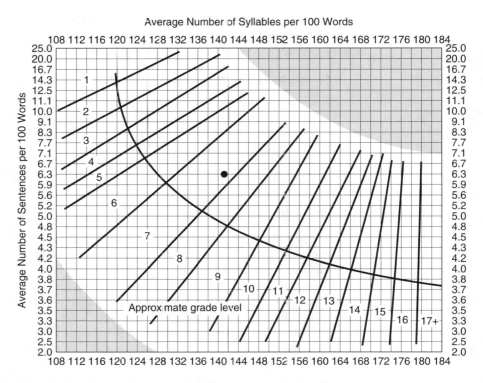

Directions: Randomly select three 100-word passages from a book or an article. Plot average number of syllables and average number of sentences per 100 words on graph to determine the grade level of the material. Choose more passages per book if great variability is observed and conclude that the book has uneven readability. Few books will fall in gray area, but when they do, grade-level scores are invalid.

Count proper nouns, numerals, and initializations as words. Count a syllable for each symbol. For example, "1945" is 1 word and 4 syllables and "IRA" is 1 word and 3 syllables.

Example:	Syllables	Sentences
1st hundred words	124	6.6
2nd hundred words	141	5.5
3rd hundred words	158	6.8
Average	141	6.3

Readability 7th grade (see dot plotted on graph)

Source: From *Reading Instruction for Classroom and Clinic* (p. 232), by E. B. Fry, 1972. New York: McGraw-Hill. Copyright 1972 by McGraw-Hill. Reprinted with permission.

is not always conscious of making such predictions. Implicit knowledge of what is permissible, either in language or in life, influences expectations. For example, careful attention to "The boy up ran the hill," would make most readers reread the sentence, because the word order does not fit our expectations about language. Also, reading that "The sun went down in a bright green blaze," should trigger some curiosity about the meaning or perhaps the truth of such a reported event.

Reader language is also an important part of the reader component. A reader's general language competence provides access to comprehension. The role of the reader's language is usually assumed to be important by writers, but often rather vaguely.

Prior knowledge and experience affect the student's understanding of the ideas expressed in the text. Comprehension builds on what is already known, so a reader who has no prior knowledge of life in a big city is likely to have problems understanding a social studies chapter dealing with that topic. Forming relationships from one unknown to another unknown is sure to affect the ability to comprehend a text. A reader who is unfamiliar with numerous concepts in a passage will have great difficulty comprehending what is being read.

Reading with Fluency

Adams (1990) observes, "The most salient characteristic of skillful readers is the speed and effortlessness with which they seem able to breeze through text" (p. 409). The ability to read with speed and effortlessness is called *fluency.* Duffy and Roehler (1986) describe fluency in greater detail: "Fluent reading reflects the reader's clear understanding of the words used, the topic, the author's purpose, and the text structure and is evidenced by correct intonation and an absence of interruptions" (p. 472). After reviewing the reading disability literature, Lyon (1995) states that a lack of fluent word recognition is the most frequently cited factor in reading disorders.

Reading fluency is an important skill for mature readers who must often read large quantities of material for school assignments. Fluency is influenced by numerous factors (e.g., purpose for reading, content), and there are different fluency expectations for oral and silent reading. Guzak (1985) reported reading rates for both silent and oral reading (see Table 10.4). As the table shows, the rates are similar at the early reading levels, with the silent reading rate becoming much higher beginning at the third grade. Table 10.5 provides fluency rates for letters, words, and words in context.

Content Area Reading

Content area textbooks (e.g., science, social studies) require students to use a variety of skills to obtain meaning from often difficult reading material about subjects which they may have little background knowledge. Students must be fairly proficient with

Table 10.4
Standard Reading
Inventory Minimum
Speeds

Grade	Oral (wpm)	Silent (wpm)
1	60	60
2	70	70
3	90	120
4	120	150
5	120	170
6	150	245
7 and above	150	300

Table 10.5
Precision Teaching
Rates

Pinpoint	Standard
See/Say isolated sounds	60–80 sounds/minute
See/Say phonetic words	60–80 words/minute
Think/Say Alphabet (forward/backward)	400+ letters/minute
See/Say letter names	80–100 letters/minute
See/Say sight words	80–120 words/minute
See/Say words/context (oral reading)	200+ words/minute
See/Think words/context (silent reading)	400+ words/minute
Think/Say ideas or facts	15–30 ideas/minute

Source: From *Training Manual* (8th ed), by Precision Teaching Project, 1984, Great Falls, MT: Precision Teaching Materials. Copyright 1984 by Precision Teaching Project. Reprinted with permission.

reading comprehension strategies, reading rate, technical vocabulary, and various text structure organizations to understand complex reading material. These skills become more important as the student progresses through school. In the elementary grades, the task is to learn to read from a textbook (Huhn, 1980). The task of secondary students is to learn subject matter from textbooks; this task requires proficiency with a variety of reading skills and assumes mastery with them. The next section of this chapter offers ideas about how to foster content area reading skills; other ideas appear in chapter 13.

Instructional Methods and Techniques

As you read, think about ...

1. Describing ways to promote a reading literacy classroom environment at the elementary and secondary levels.
2. Developing an IEP in reading for a secondary-level student with severe reading problems.
3. Designing a collaborative plan with the elementary-level general education teacher whose class includes four students with reading disabilities.
4. Designing a reading lesson to promote oral reading fluency and decoding skills.
5. Developing a lesson that teaches reading comprehension strategies, including a generalization component.
6. Applying interventions in chapter 9 to reading instruction.
7. Devising ways to promote textbook instruction at the secondary level for students with severe reading disabilities.
8. Designing an instructional unit that includes instruction to foster reading skills and promote literacy.

Reading is a complex, developmental process that requires abilities in decoding, comprehension, fluency, and understanding content area material. Earlier in this chapter, we discussed three reading approaches, each of which is based on a particular philosophy of reading instruction. We endorse the interactive approach because it emphasizes decoding, building oral reading fluency, and fostering comprehension skills, while exposing students to literature. Reading skills must be taught directly to youngsters with reading disabilities. These students must also develop comprehension skills so that they can gain meaning from text. Thus, students are probably best served by teachers who possess broad knowledge of reading methods and interventions to meet their students' individual instructional needs.

In this section, we address each reading skill, as discussed in the "Skills for Instruction" section, by presenting a variety of reading methods and techniques, which are listed in Table 10.6. The narratives provide more detail on selected research-based tactics and strategies for elementary- and secondary-level students.

Table 10.6
Reading Teaching Tactics

Instructional target	Stage of learning	Possible tactic
Word recognition	Acquisition	Time delay
		Flow list
		Reinforcement
		Drill
		Positive practice
		Reward for accuracy
		Peer tutoring
		Word repetition
		Card reader practice
	Proficiency	Computer games
		FR
		Go–no go contingencies
		Pacing
Word identification	Acquisition	Modeling
		Telling
		Cues
		Prompts
		Time delay
		Flow list
		Reinforcement
		Drill
		Positive practice
		Reward for accuracy
		Peer tutoring
		Letter-sound correspondence
		Blending and segmenting tasks
		Decoding using structural analysis
		Word expansion
	Proficiency	Modeling
		Drill
		Go–no go contingencies
Understanding words	Acquisition	Match-to-sample
		Prompting
		Time delay
		Flow list
		Feedback

Instructional target	Stage of learning	Possible tactic
Table 10.6 Continued		
Understanding Words (continued)	Acquisition (continued)	Drill
		Fuzzle technique
		Feer tutoring
		Learning vocabulary out of context
		Learning vocabulary through reading exercises
		Advance organizer
	Generalization	Feinforcement
Understanding ideas	Acquisition	Match-to sample
		Fuzzle technique
		Feer tutoring
		Story mapping
		Faraphrasing
		Feciprocal teaching
		Structured questions
	Proficiency	Free description technique
	Generalization	Fationales
		Feinforcement
		Self-management
		Cooperative planning
		Transfer activities
Oral reading fluency	Acquisition	Modeling
		Feinforcement
		Drill
		Fositive practice
		Feward for accuracy
		Feer tutoring
		Error correction procedures
	Proficiency	Freviewing
		Modeling
		Telling
		Drill
		Go–no go contingencies
		Repeated readings
		Skip and drill
		Fhrase-cued text reading
	Generalization	Fationales
		Feinforcement
		Self-management
Content area reading	Acquisition	Modeling
		Cues
		Frompts

continued

Instructional target	Stage of learning	Possible tactic
Content area reading (continued)	Acquisition (continued)	Peer tutoring
		POSSE strategy
		Multipass
		K-W -L strategy
		Study guides
	Generalization	Reinforcement
		Instructions
		Cooperative planning
	Problem solving (adaption)	Guide instruction
		Transfer activities

Table 10.6 Continued

Suggestions for adapting reading instruction in the general education classroom appear in Adapting Instruction; information about technology as it relates to reading instruction can be found in Focus on Technology.

Adapting Reading Instruction for the General Education Setting

Elementary

1. Provide many opportunities for students to practice oral reading fluency.
2. Use different student-mediated instructional arrangements to help students with difficult reading material.
3. Build sight word vocabulary.
4. Teach students to blend and segment sounds through direct instruction.
5. Teach students strategies to promote reading comprehension.
6. Use technology to increase access to the reading curriculum.

Secondary

1. Use high-interest—low vocabulary material.
2. Teach reading comprehension strategies.
3. Provide study guides to help students comprehend content area material.
4. Use different student-mediated instructional arrangements to facilitate reading comprehension.
5. Use technology to increase access to the reading curriculum.
6. Teach a functional sight vocabulary. ■

Technology that Aids Students in Reading

• **Instructional technology**

1. Software programs exist for teaching a variety of reading skills (e.g., word recognition, comprehension, fluency). Care should be taken to relate the skills being taught to the general curriculum.
2. Software programs often require the use of features that may not be available on some computers. Also, some software is not available for different types of computers. Therefore, become a knowledgeable consumer.

3. Instructional software programs are often used as reinforcement for successful accomplishment of paper-and-pencil tasks. In classrooms where this occurs, computers are often placed in the corner of the room and are not incorporated into the general learning structure. Try to incorporate technology into the curricular mainstream. There are several software programs that can be used effectively in cooperative learning groups.

● **Assistive technology**

1. Tape recorders offer a nontechnology solution to providing access to written material. Volunteers record texts or magazine articles for people who cannot read.

2. Optical character recognition, screen reader software, and speech synthesis are technology solutions to print access. They allow material to be scanned into a computer, which "reads aloud" the material as it appears on the screen. Such devices allow for a higher degree of independence than nontechnology solutions. ●

Decoding Letters and Words in Print

The first problem in learning to read is that the learner must know some words. There is a considerable difference of opinion about exactly what strategies should be used to teach those initial words. We now provide suggestions for teaching skills in word recognition and word identification.

Word Recognition: Sight Words

Word Repetition (acquisition stage)   There are two instances when sight word instruction of limited duration may be appropriate. The first instance is with elementary students who possess a very limited sight vocabulary (fewer than 60 words). Developing a sight vocabulary of 90 to 100 words provides a base for teaching many other skills. The second instance is with secondary students with no functional reading skills and students who have serious reading impairments. They need to develop recognition of "survival words"; training in a minimum (50 to 100 words) sight word vocabulary might be most appropriate.

Word repetition is an excellent technique to facilitate sight word acquisition. There are several daily steps in this technique:

1. Select and write on index cards three to five unknown basic (or survival) sight words (the Brigance Inventory of Comprehensive Skills [Curriculum Associates] contains basic and functional sight word lists).
2. Have the student practice the words (e.g., through peer tutoring or with a card reader machine) until mastery.
3. Test the student using the trials to criterion procedure (see Figure 10.3).
4. Review the previously learned words (maintenance check) after completing the trials to criterion procedure for the day's words.

Card Reader Practice (acquisition stage)   Students can practice their sight words by using the card reader machine (see chapter 12 for an explanation of card reader instruction). Words can be recorded on cards for students to practice as part

Figure 10.3
Trials to criterion
procedure

Criterion = Five consecutive correct trials of all words pronounced correctly.

1. Test the student after sufficient practice time has been allowed.

2. Collect the sight words printed on the index cards.

3. Present each word for the student to read within four seconds. On a record-keeping sheet (see below) mark each word read as right (+) or wrong (−) under Trial 1.

4. Present each word again to be read within four seconds and mark it right or wrong on the record-keeping sheet under Trial 2.

5. Repeat Step 4 for each subsequent trial until the student has read all of the sight words correctly in five consecutive trials.

6. Count the number of trials taken to achieve the criterion of five consecutive correct trials for all of the sight words. Graph the number of trials.

Date	Words	\multicolumn{12}{c}{Trials}	# Trials to Criterion
		1	2	3	4	5	6	7	8	9	10	11	12	12 trials to criterion (5 consecutive correct responses for all words)
3/12	what	+	+	−	+	+	+	+	+	+	+	+	+	
	because	−	−	−	−	+	−	−	+	+	+	+	+	
	are	−	−	−	+	−	−	+	+	+	+	+	+	

of their daily reading program. Teachers (or peers) can test students on their words and use the trials to criterion procedure (see Figure 10.3) to record student progress.

Pacing Practice (proficiency stage)   Develop a list of unknown sight words (Freeman & McLaughlin, 1984). Tape record the list for students to hear the words being pronounced; encourage students to follow along with the tape. Be sure to record the words fluently (about 80 words per minute). After pacing practice, students can read the words fluently to the teacher (or peer) for their one-minute timing. Correct and error rates should be graphed and performance monitored closely.

Word Identification

Letter-Sound Correspondence—Phonetic Analysis   Many traditional phonics programs begin with teaching letter-sound correspondence (Carnine, Silbert, & Kameenui, 1990). Teachers can use a direct instruction procedure for this, following an introductory format in the first one or two lessons in which a new letter appears. Here are the steps for the introductory format:

1. Teacher writes the letter/sound to be learned on the board and provides basic directions to students. "When I touch under the letter, you say the sound. Keep saying the sound as long as I touch it."

2. Teacher models the sound.
3. Teacher leads by responding with the group.
4. Teacher tests by having the group repeat sound several times, then prompts students with, "Your turn, say it by yourselves."
5. Teacher tests individuals in groups.

Data can be collected on individual student performance with acquiring the letter-sound correspondences. One-minute timings can be conducted to determine proficiency (see Table 10.5 for proficiency rates).

Blending and Segmenting Tasks—Phonetic Analysis   It is important to teach students to blend (e.g., /m/ /a/ /p/ = "map") and segment (e.g., tell the sounds you hear in "map") sounds during or before formal reading instruction (Adams, 1990; Simmons, Gunn, Smith, & Kameenui, 1995). Blending and segmenting abilities can be fostered by:

1. Selecting words with fewer phonemes (e.g., consonant-vowel-consonant, or CVC, pattern). Include additional phonemes (e.g., blends) once students master easier patterns.
2. Selecting words with phonemes that have continuous sounds (e.g., /m/, /r/, /f/, /s/) then add phonemes with stop sounds (e.g., /t/, /k/, /p/, /d/). Continuous sounds are easier to blend for beginning readers.
3. Building sound patterns. For example, teachers can develop lists of words showing: (1) individually segmented sounds to blend, (2) phonograms (vowel spelling patterns) to blend, and (3) words with predictable patterns to read (see below).

1	2	3
m-a-t	m at	mat
r-u-n	r un	run
tr-a-p	tr ap	trap

Structural Analysis   Learning the meanings of root words, prefixes, and suffixes can help students decode larger words (Lovitt, 1995). Several procedures are recommended to teach students how to analyze words structurally:

1. Prepare lists of words containing root words, suffixes, and prefixes. Have students circle the root words and underline the suffixes or prefixes. Have students explain the meaning of the words through a matching exercise (meaning to word) or by writing a short explanation.
2. Present a list of words and have students add prefixes or suffixes to modify their meanings. For instance, they should add the prefix "re" to make words mean "again": reexamine, redecorate, rethink.
3. Teach syllabication rules. Provide practice opportunities for students to divide words using the rules and to state the rule given specific words.
4. Provide a list of root words. Have students add suffixes to the words by rewriting the words, stating the rule if letter changes occur (e.g., y to i add es), and providing a meaning.

Word Expansion   Word expansion techniques use known words to teach new words, through the addition of prefixes, suffixes, and inflectional endings (Lovitt,

1984, 1995). This tactic incorporates aspects of both structural and contextual analysis into a three-step teaching procedure:

1. Six to ten words not instantly recognized by the student are printed on individual index cards, with a sentence containing the selected word written on the back of each card. The students are to practice the sentences.
2. The identified words are systematically expanded by adding inflectional endings, suffixes, and prefixes. Level I contains the simpler endings of s, ed, d, and ing, while level 4 contains a number of more difficult affixes, such as ex, pre, sion, and ness.
3. In this step, the children use the words in a variety of contexts. As an example, Lovitt (1984) suggests that if the emphasis is on vocabulary development, the students might be asked to classify the sight words and their expansions into categories, such as words that are plurals and words that are past tense.

Comprehending Words and Ideas in Print

Comprehension consists of two main categories: understanding words (see chapter 13 for additional vocabulary development teaching techniques) and understanding ideas. We now discuss strategies, methods, and techniques for both categories.

Understanding Words

Learning Vocabulary Out of Context   The dictionary approach is traditional instruction in which students look up unknown words in the dictionary and record their definitions. Because of the possible number of definitions for words, students should have a good conceptual and contextual understanding of the words for which they are locating definitions. Otherwise, this approach may not be that effective in promoting vocabulary development (Carlisle, 1993).

Computer-assisted instruction can be used to teach students vocabulary words and definitions in isolation (Johnson, Gersten, & Carnine, 1987). However, transfer instruction (words learned in isolation to reading passages) must occur if students are to improve their comprehension of the passages containing the vocabulary words. Transfer instruction could consist of (1) having students learn their vocabulary words in isolation, (2) locating these words in reading passages, (3) reviewing their definitions, (4) reading the passages containing the words, and (5) paraphrasing the meaning of the passages.

Learning Vocabulary through Reading Exercises   A variety of reading experiences may help students acquire vocabulary because of the connection between extensive reading and vocabulary development (Carlisle, 1993). Varied reading experiences could include listening to audiotaped stories, interacting with stories on CD-ROMs, listening to stories read by teachers or classroom volunteers, and having a peer-sharing reading time. Some software publishing companies are producing children's stories on CD-ROMs with an interactive feature. By clicking on pictures or words, students can hear definitions that relate specifically to the reading material at hand. Carlisle stresses that the incidental learning of vocabulary words through reading experiences may have to be paired with repeated exposures to word usage and meanings to develop vocabulary.

Prereading activities also help students learn vocabulary words more readily. Providing an advance organizer for a story and discussing some of the key ideas (e.g., setting, problem, characters) could give students a framework for vocabulary development. Bos and Anders (1990) used *interactive vocabulary instruction* activities to foster vocabulary learning and reading comprehension. They used semantic maps, hierarchical relation maps (see chapter 13), and a cloze procedure (in which students predict missing words in a paragraph based on contextual meaning).

Vocabulary development can be enhanced through high frequency, richness, and extension. High frequency can be accomplished with daily instructional time designated for teaching vocabulary words that students must learn for a particular unit or story. Words can be taught in semantic groups to facilitate comprehension and an understanding of word relations. Richness of instruction can include locating definitions of the words, providing contexts containing the words, asking students to create contexts for their words, and discovering how their words relate to each other. Finally, children can be challenged to use their words outside of the classroom by applying the words to other contexts and activities (McKeown & Beck, 1988).

Understanding Ideas

Free Description Technique   Lovitt (1995) notes that the free description technique eliminates teachers' preparation of comprehension questions, requires students to make passage-dependent responses, rather than guessing, and requires students to describe what they read.

Here are steps for this simple and useful procedure. The teacher role and response are identified by *T* and the student response by *S*. This procedure requires solo and cooperative efforts by both the teacher and the student.

1. *T:* Defines response desired from the student. If the student is a young child, the teacher should simply require that the student tell simple facts about the story. These facts would include a comment about a story's theme, a noun plus an action verb (two facts), an adjective or adverb that describes a noun or verb, and a preposition that describes a location.
2. *T:* Provides examples and nonexamples of facts.
3. *T:* Models saying facts for child (i.e., the boy wore a red shirt, his dog was big and black, his bike was old).
4. *T & S:* Count facts together (those given by teacher).
5. *T & S:* Discuss correct and incorrect responses.
6. *S:* Reads passage; then says facts (thirty seconds to one minute).
7. *T:* Counts number of correct and incorrect facts, as they are provided by S.
8. *T:* Provides feedback to S at end of session. Indicates how present performance compares with previous effort.
9. *T or S:* Plots numbers on chart.
10. *T:* Critiques student performance, provides feedback on errors, gives suggestions for improvement.

Story Mapping for Narrative Themes   Another technique designed to provide students with a strategy for approaching a story is one that has been identified as *story grammars* or *story mapping* (Idol, 1987). The purpose of this technique is to provide students with a guide to understanding written narrative.

There are six story elements:

Setting: Introduction of main characters, time, place.
Beginning: Event that triggers the story.
Reaction: Response of main characters, what they do—goal?
Attempt: What effort do the characters make to attain goal?
Outcome: Results of attempt to reach goal.
Ending: Consequences of the main characters' action and final response.

Several procedures have been suggested to assist students in mapping a story. One is a sorting task that requires students to arrange a jumbled short story in the correct order of the various elements as just indicated. Another task requires students to sort the sentences for each of the elements into separate piles. Idol (1987) reported an application of the story mapping procedure with a focus on written language.

An example of a story map appears in Figure 10.4. Idol used three phases to teach students how to use the story map to assist in comprehending the story. First, she modeled how to (1) read a story, (2) stop at points in the story where information for each component of the map appeared, and (3) fill in the story map. Students completed their maps with the same information during modeling. Second, students were asked to read a story independently and complete their story maps, receiving teacher assistance as necessary. Finally, students read a story, completed a map, and then answered teachers' questions about the story. This process is called model, lead, test.

Paraphrasing   The paraphrasing strategy is a technique designed to help students improve recall of main ideas and specific facts (Schumaker, Denton, & Deshler, 1984). This strategy requires students to complete three activities for every paragraph they read. They must find the main idea, identify at least two details that relate to the main idea, and restate (paraphrase) the content of the main idea and details in their own words. As with all the learning strategies developed at the UK-IRLD, students use a mnemonic device (RAP), in this case to help them remember the steps that must be followed to complete the strategy accurately. (See the steps below to know more about the RAP [*r*ead, *a*sk, *p*ut] strategy.)

Steps for paraphrasing

Step 1 **R**ead a paragraph.

Step 2 **A**sk yourself, "What were the main ideas and details in this paragraph?"

Step 3 **P**ut the main idea and details into your own words.

To help students learn this strategy, many teachers model its application. They read aloud the first paragraph of a chapter in one of the student's textbooks. Then, the teachers show students how to use the RAP strategy with that paragraph. Teachers repeat the process with the second paragraph, with the students participating in some of the RAP steps. Throughout the lesson, the students apply more and more of the strategy to ensuing paragraphs. Some teachers use the jigsaw technique (see chapter 9) while teaching RAP to their students. Each student is assigned a part of

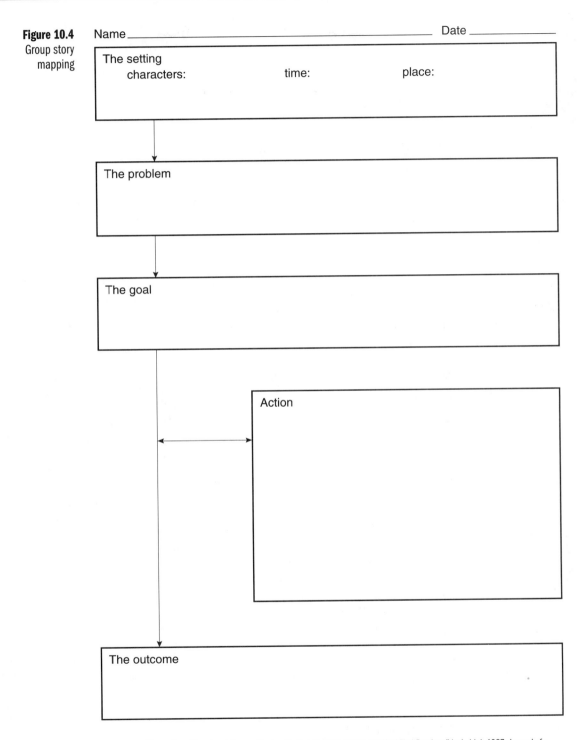

Figure 10.4
Group story mapping

Name _____ Date _____

The setting
  characters: time: place:

The problem

The goal

Action

The outcome

Source: From "Group Story Mapping: A Comprehension Strategy for Both Skilled and Unskilled Readers," by L. Idol, 1987, *Journal of Learning Disabilities, 20*, p. 199. Copyright 1987 by PRO-ED. Reprinted with permission.

the strategy to complete for each paragraph read. One student might identify the main idea, several others might identify the details about the main idea, and another student might paraphrase the paragraph.

Students who have been taught this strategy to mastery, through all the acquisition and generalization steps, have substantially improved their reading comprehension scores. During the pretest, for example, students' average comprehension percentage score from reading passages from their assigned grade-level texts was only 48 percent. However, after learning the RAP strategy, these students obtained an average score of 84 percent. Clearly, this strategy can assist students in understanding and remembering information presented in typical high school social studies and science books. Such ability contributes to students' ability to succeed in general education classes in which students are expected to gain information from books often written above their reading abilities.

Reciprocal Teaching   Reciprocal teaching is an instructional procedure that uses group discussion as a means of facilitating reading comprehension (Palincsar & Brown, 1986). Reciprocal teaching consists of dialogue between students and the teacher that is structured around four strategies. Both the students and the teacher assume the roles of leader and respondent, depending on the questions asked, students' ability to respond, and the extent to which reciprocal teaching has been used with students.

The four strategies include asking questions, summarizing information, clarifying, and making predictions. Initially, the teacher models his or her thinking processes aloud as the reading task unfolds. For example, the teacher might read the story's title aloud and ask, "What is this story about?" The teacher might brainstorm ideas about the story based on the title, summarize the ideas into one sentence, and make a prediction about the story's meaning. As the story is read aloud, the teacher could continue with this process, which requires stopping during the story and asking oneself questions about vocabulary or what might happen next. After modeling this process, teachers can begin working with their students in small groups to promote reading comprehension strategically. Teachers should encourage students to ask questions, to clarify information for their peers, and to make predictions. Moreover, teachers should move out of the leader role as soon as students are comfortable assuming such a role themselves. As such, reciprocal teaching involves group discussion, scaffolded instruction, and group problem solving (Palincsar & Brown, 1988).

Structured Questions   Prior to reading, teachers can give students a set of comprehension questions to answer as they are reading material. Literal or inferential questions could pertain to the elements of the story, vocabulary words, paraphrases of paragraph material, and summaries. Students could answer the questions individually or in small, cooperative learning groups. Additionally, peer tutors could assist with decoding words. Upon completion, teachers could work with the entire class or group to discuss students' answers to the questions.

Reading with Fluency

Error Correction Procedures   There are five common error correction procedures thought to be efficient in improving either, or perhaps both, oral reading accu-

Table 10.7 Common Error Correction Procedures for Reading Skills	Drill	Error words are noted and usually printed on individual index cards. Words are then presented individually to the student. The teacher supplies word, and the student repeats. Procedure continues until the student says all words correctly, usually to some criterion (certain number of errors, usually tied to some number of consecutive presentations).
	Phonic analysis	The learner is directed to note specific phonetic elements of the error word and is told to sound out each element.
	Sentence repetition	Each error word is supplied correctly by the teacher, followed by correct production by the student and completion of the sentence. The student then rereads the sentence containing the error word. If a second error occurs, the word correction by the teacher and student is repeated, but not the entire sentence.
	Word meaning	Each error word is supplied by the teacher, with the student repeating the word. This is followed by the teacher's asking, "What does this word mean?" If the student does not know, the teacher provides definition or synonym, and the student repeats meaning. Oral reading resumes at point of corrected word. If error occurs again, error procedure is repeated. At end of each page, a list of all words missed is presented. Student reads each word and repeats any definition provided earlier. If any word or meaning error occurs, the correction procedure is repeated.
	Word supply	Any error word is supplied by the teacher. The student is usually required to look at the error word and repeat it.

racy and fluency (Rosenberg, 1986; Singh & Singh, 1985). The procedures include drill, phonic analysis. sentence repetition, word meaning, and word supply (see Table 10.7 for a description of the procedures). These procedures have been studied with elementary- and secondary-level students with reading disabilities. Although the results were equivocal about which error correction procedure worked best, researchers generally found that the word supply procedure was not as effective as the other four procedures.

Probably the most appropriate time to use the word supply correction procedure is during one-minute fluency timings: Teacher should tell students words they don't know during the timing so as not to detract from fluency. Unknown words that were supplied can be noted and targeted for further instruction upon conclusion of the one-minute timing.

Previewing   Previewing has been used to describe a wide range of procedures. Lovitt (1995) describes a technique where students practice on either error words or new words. For example, if a student reads a passage and misses five words, those five words are practiced for five minutes following the reading session. These cards are added to words missed in other reading sessions. Before the next reading session, the student identifies all the words a few times. The student then reads the assigned text. Missed words are identified and the cycle of error word practice is again completed.

Rose (1984) describes two previewing (sometimes termed prepractice) procedures: silent and listening. Here are descriptions of the two procedures:

Silent
1. Student reads passage silently.
2. Student tells teacher when silent reading is completed.
3. Student reads passage to teacher.

Listening
1. Teacher reads assigned passage to student, who follows along as teacher reads.
2. Student reads passage to teacher.

Repeated Readings   This tactic is supported by the automaticity theory that LaBerge and Samuels (1974) proposed. The assumption is that once the reader can decode fluently, he or she can work on comprehending what is read (Lauritzen, 1982; Lovitt, 1995). Although there are many slight variations, these are steps for the repeated readings procedure.

1. Determine the student's average correct word-per-minute (wpm) rate over a two- or three-day period.
2. Set a target that is 10 to 15 percent higher than the best rate or the average rate.
3. Tell the student his or her present rate and the target rate.
4. Have the student read the passage. Collect a one-minute sample, but have the student complete the entire passage selected.
5. Tell the student the results of the reading.
   a. If the target was obtained, move to the next passage and set a new target. Repeat the process.
   b. If the target is not reached, then practice takes place. Practice can focus on specific errors, rereading of the most difficult spots, or any other type of practice thought to be appropriate for the student. Coaching by the teacher, such as "Look ahead as you read" or "Skip the words you don't know," may also be provided.

After practice, the student reads again and is timed. This process continues for five readings (others use as few as three or as many as seven). Depending on results, the student returns to more practice or moves to the next passage. Students move to the next passage after ten attempts, even if the criterion is not met.

Skip and Drill   Skip and drill is an effective method for developing oral reading fluency skills of students who read at about the first-grade level (e.g., know some sight words, can blend CVC words). This remedial method works well with those students who read haltingly and make careless errors (Lovitt, 1995). Skip and drill involves the following steps:

1. Begin at the place in the basal reader at which correct rates of 45 to 65 words per minute, incorrect rates of 4 to 8 words per minute, and 50 to 75 percent correct comprehension scores can be achieved.
2. Divide the stories in the book into six sections.
3. Develop 10 comprehension questions for each story, including recall, sequential, inferential, and judgmental questions.
4. Select a story where the student is placed and collect one-minute baseline for three days on correct and error rates and comprehension accuracy (percent correct). Chart the scores.
5. Calculate the average baseline scores after three days and compute 25 percent improvement figures for correct and error rates and comprehension.

6. Begin a new story. Have the student practice for about 10 minutes. Then, have the student read orally for one minute—mark errors, note rate (correct and error) and comprehension scores. If the student's three scores meet the improvement scores computed in step 5, then have the student skip the remaining stories in that section of the book. On the following day, the student would begin reading the first story in the next section of the book. If the student's three scores do not meet the improvement scores, then have the student read the next story in that section of the book.

7. Begin the "drill" phase if all three improvement scores are not achieved on the same day after five days of practice. If the correct rate is low, then schedule five one-minute timings. If the error rate is high, then do error drill on unknown words. If comprehension is the problem, have the student reread the passage silently to find answers to the questions. The student can tell the teacher these answers or write them down.

Phrase-Cued Text Reading   Phrase-cued text reading is a procedure that helps elementary- and secondary-level students develop syntactic awareness and reading fluency in conventional texts (Rasinski, 1994). Phrase-cued text consists of explicitly marked boundaries delineating naturally occurring and rule-bound syntactic and linguistic segments in written passages. Here is an example:

> Teachers of special needs students/ should show them ways/ to interact/ with the reading material/ so that/ comprehension is increased.//

The purpose of phrase-cued text is to show students which phrase "chunks" to read fluently. The reading material should be practiced orally and the phrases read as units. Teachers can model the procedure and then ask students to read their cued passages. Teachers should explain to students that most good readers read text in phrases and although this procedure is awkward at first, it will help them learn about phrases and become more fluent readers. The following steps are recommended to implement phrase-cued text reading.

1. Identify and copy a 250-word reading passage written at the student's instructional level.
2. Mark phrase breaks with a slash (/) mark. Mark sentence boundaries with a double slash (//).
3. Discuss the rationale and procedures for the phrase-cued technique.
4. Model.
5. Have the student read the cued text two or three times.
6. Have the student read the same text without the slash cues.
7. Conduct a one-minute timing to collect correct and error rate data. Monitor student performance.

Content Area Reading

POSSE Strategy   This strategy combines cognitive and metacognitive processing through the use of an acronym to cue specific instructional steps and a self-questioning technique to promote self-monitoring behavior (Englert & Mariage, 1990). A semantic map, which is a graphic organizer, is used to help students see and "map" the important reading information. The POSSE strategy enables students to use brainstorming, mapping, text structure organization, and evaluation.

The teacher presents the POSSE strategy steps by modeling the process aloud. There are three phases in the strategy: prereading, reading, and postreading. Students learn the acronym, POSSE, and learn how to apply the strategy to textbook reading. Here are the POSSE steps:

Prereading
1. **P**redict the ideas of the story based on information from the title, heading, pictures, and first paragraph. Record the ideas on the POSSE strategy sheet (see Figure 10.5).
2. **O**rganize the ideas into categories and develop the semantic map on the sheet.

Reading
1. **S**earch for the text structure by identifying the author's categories, main ideas, and details.
2. **S**ummarize the main idea and identify sections of the article that tell what each paragraph is about. Put main ideas in a circle and details on the adjacent lines of the sheet.

Postreading
1. **E**valuate the work by changing the main ideas into questions to determine if the supporting details match. Compare the two semantic maps to confirm information. Clarify new words and information. Predict upcoming information in the article.

Lovitt (1995) recommends that teachers evaluate students' ability to generate main ideas and retell facts from the stories. Additionally, students could work in cooperative learning or reciprocal teaching groups to complete the POSSE strategy worksheet.

Multipass   Multipass is a complex strategy taught through a 10-step process (Schumaker, Deshler, Alley, Warner, & Denton, 1982). The strategy involves modeling, verbal rehearsal, feedback, and testing at various points. The instructional steps discussed in chapter 5 under the Learning Strategies Curriculum can be used to teach the multipass strategy.

The multipass strategy consists of three substrategies (survey, size-up, and sort-out) that focus student attention on the material for a particular purpose.

Survey Pass
This pass (movement through the text) is to familiarize the student with the chapter's organization and main ideas. Students complete seven steps, including reading the title, introductory paragraph, and the major subtitles.

Size-up Pass
This pass is designed to help students gain specific information. The student is required here to include paraphrasing and looking for textual clues, such as italics and boldfaced print. These steps are followed by the student reading the content material.

Figure 10.5
POSSE strategy
sheet

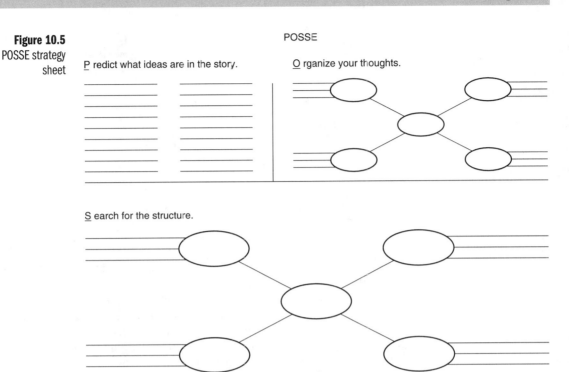

POSSE

P redict what ideas are in the story.

O rganize your thoughts.

S earch for the structure.

S ummarize   Summarize the main idea in your own words.
E valuate   Ask a question about the main idea. Compare. Clarify. Predict.

Source: From "Send for the POSSE: Structuring the Comprehension Dialogue," by C. S. Englert and T. V. Mariage, 1990, *Academic Therapy*, 25(4), p. 475. Copyright 1990 by PRO-ED. Reprinted by permission.

Sort-out Pass
This part of the strategy requires the students to test themselves on the material in the chapter. Students follow four steps that require them to think about where answers to a question would be found and to skim to locate needed information.

K-W-L Strategy   The K-W-L strategy (Ogle, 1986) can assist students in reading expository text. Students can use the worksheet in Figure 10.6 to record ideas specific to each step in the strategy. The steps of the strategy include:

1. **K**—What information do I know? Teachers and students discuss what they know about the topic. They brainstorm to generate ideas and discussion. Then, students categorize the information brainstormed to predict what they expect to read about.
2. **W**—What information do I want to discover? This step requires students to discuss and record questions they wish to pursue during their reading. Group discussion occurs, followed by students' writing their question on the K-W-L worksheet.
3. **L**—What did I learn and what would I like to learn? Students write what they have learned and check their questions to see if they obtained answers. Students also identify information that they still need to learn.

Figure 10.6
K-W-L strategy
worksheet

K—What I know.	W—What I want to find out.	L—What I learned and what I still need to learn.
Categories I expect to see.		

Source: From "A Teaching Model that Develops Active Reading of Expository Text," by D. M. Ogle, 1986, *The Reading Teacher, 39*, p. 565. Copyright 1986 by the International Reading Association. Reprinted with permission.

Study Guides   Study guides (Armbruster, Anderson, & Meyer, 1991; Hudson, Lignugaris-Kraft, & Miller, 1993; Lovitt & Horton, 1987) are designed to enhance reading comprehension by actively engaging students in the reading process through the use of short-answer questions, fill-in-the-blanks statements (frames) with page referents, and matching exercises. Researchers have demonstrated that study guides can be used most effectively when students read passages independently and teachers assist them in completing the study guide information, or when students complete the study guide independently, followed by teacher review and correction. Study guides can be used effectively during the guided practice and independent practice steps of instruction; however, teacher feedback and correction must follow both steps. Additionally, study guide formats should match test question formats to produce the best student gains. For example, Bergerud, Horton, and Lovitt (1988) found that students did not fare well on a test that asked them to label a diagram when they had used a study guide format that required short answers. This finding suggests that students should probably use different types of study guide formats to learn reading material. Figure 10.7 shows different types of study guide formats for students to use when studying content area material at the elementary and secondary levels.

Figure 10.7
Study guide
formats

1. Fill in the blanks

At the heart of the commotion in Boston was an organization known as _____ (p. 40). The members of the organization included famous people such as _____, _____, _____, _____ (p. 40).

The _____ (p. 45) called for an American boycott against British _____ (p. 45). The result of the boycott was that King George _____ _____ (p. 46).

2. Short answer questions

1. Who were the Sons of Liberty?

2. Why was the Sons of Liberty organization formed?

3. What was the effect of the Townshend Act?

Source: Adapted from "Using Content Enhancements to Improve the Performance of Adolescents with Learning Disabilities in Content Classes," by P. Hudson, B. Lignugaris-Kraft, and T. Miller, 1993, *Learning Disabilities Research & Practice, 8*(2), pp. 106–126.

Technology

Instructional and assistive technologies play an important role in remedial and compensatory strategies for students with reading deficits. An often asked question is "When do you stop trying to remediate? When should you begin compensatory strategies?" We do not believe that the two strategies are mutually exclusive. That is, we would advocate applying effective, research-based remedial strategies in conjunction with compensatory technology-based interventions.

Consider the case of a fourth-grade boy who has a reading problem that interferes with his ability to access material in his history text. Remedial strategies could include software programs that focus on strengthening his decoding and comprehension skills, while simultaneous instruction in assistive technology could allow the student to gain information from the text. In this way, the student stays on level with his peers in content knowledge. There are indications that the use of assistive technology devices as compensatory tools can actually contribute to improved reading performance (Raskind & Shaw, 1995). In this section, we briefly present information pertaining to instructional and assistive technologies as they relate to reading.

Instructional Technology

The last decade has seen the rapid increase in the number of software programs designed to teach reading skills. Lewis (1993) cites software that has been designed to teach reading readiness, beginning sight words, phonics skills, comprehension, and computer-based whole-language activities.

The Reading and Me program (Davis & Associates) is a set of disks that provides practice activities in such areas as matching, discrimination, and categorization; phonics (e.g., selecting beginning and ending consonants); and whole words (e.g., matching words to pictures). Like most computer programs, the Reading and Me curriculum takes advantage of the computer's ability to "talk" to the user.

The Twistaplot Reading Adventures (Scholastic) is a program with a series of stories that allows students to change the stories' plots. One program is the Haunted House adventure from the Tales of Mystery disk. The student helps a friend in trouble at an old haunted house by making decisions that affect the outcome of the story. Lewis (1993) notes that the reading levels of the software programs vary significantly, and cautions that some programs contain a vast amount of reading between adventuresome activities.

Much other instructional software exists for teaching reading skills, including Reading Realities (Teacher Support Software), Inference: School Days (Learning Well), Comprehension Reading Series (Hartley), Talking Reader Rabbit (Learning Company), and Ugly Duckling (Byte Work). When selecting these or other computer software programs, one must be a knowledgeable and cautious consumer. Few commercial software programs have research demonstrating their effectiveness. Also, many of the software programs require special supports (e.g., CD-ROM, speech synthesis) that do not come as standard equipment on some computers. Don't hesitate to ask questions when dealing with software publishing companies.

Assistive Technology

One way to understand the impact of assistive technology on reading is to recall Kussmaul's use of the term "word blindness." We like the term "print blindness" to make an analogy between reading disability and blindness, particularly as print blindness relates to using assistive technology devices as compensatory tools. The reason for this is quite simple: Most of the technologies that are of benefit to individuals with reading disabilities were first created for individuals with visual impairments. Here, we discuss three technologies that give students with reading problems access to curriculum: tape recorders, optical character recognition, and screen reader systems.

Tape Recorders   A nontechnology solution to accessing print is to have the material recorded so that the student can listen to the material presented in print. Thousands of books exist on tape and are available through Talking Books and Recordings for the Blind. People need not have visual impairments to use the services provided by these organizations—people with reading disabilities are also eligible to use these services.

Many schools choose to do their own recording, using volunteers (e.g., parents, members of service groups, students) to do the taping. Although this is a possible solution, tape recording is problematic if the recorder is not familiar with the technical vocabulary that may appear in some content area texts (i.e., mispronunciations can be problematic) or if readers are not readily available.

Optical Character Recognition   Many students with reading disabilities benefit from the use of optical character recognition (OCR) to convert print documents into a format that they can use. These systems are often called scanners and they resemble standard copy machines both in appearance and purpose. When a copy machine is used, the page being copied is placed on a glass plate and the machine makes a copy of the page. Instead of making a visible, hard copy of the page, OCR systems have two options for output. Some OCR systems can convert directly from print to speech output using a speech synthesizer. In this case, a speech synthesizer (see a more complete description below) electronically "reads aloud" the print. Other OCR systems convert from print to a personal computer file that may be read using a screen reader package and speech synthesizer.

The Clearinghouse on Computer Accommodations, a federal agency, offers several considerations for using OCR systems. The first consideration is the quality of the printed material to be scanned. Although some OCR systems are able to scan and recognize low-quality materials, many systems recognize only high-quality printed text. To date, no OCR systems are able to recognize handwritten material reliably.

The second consideration relates to the format of the printed material to be scanned. Some OCR devices can only scan and recognize materials on a standard 8½-by-11-inch page that is printed in top-to-bottom fashion. Other systems are able to copy materials printed sideways on the page. There are also differences in how scanning devices handle text that appears in multiple columns.

Other considerations involve whether the scanner has an automatic page feed for multipage documents or how well the scanner can handle pages of print when they are still part of a bound book. Some OCR systems have difficulty with the print that is next to the bound edge of the text. The same copying problem exists in standard copy machines.

Screen Reader Systems   Students with reading disabilities can access the information on a computer screen by listening to the screen contents being spoken. This *screen reading system* consists of a speech synthesizer working with a computer's screen reader software package. The screen reader software allows the student to select the portion of the screen (e.g., a word, a sentence, a paragraph, a page) sent to the synthesizer for speech output. The speech synthesizer is the actual hardware device that converts the selected words and paragraphs on the screen into speech output.

Screen reader software directs the output (i.e. material on the screen) to the speech synthesizer. There are several screen reader software products available that offer the option to hear an individual letter, a whole word, or sentences and paragraphs.

Not all screen readers will work with every speech synthesizer on the market. Before selecting the screen reader software, teachers should match the software with the speech synthesizer to confirm that they will work together.

There are several **speech synthesizers** available; these devices differ primarily in voice quality, size, and expense. Some synthesizers output a very monotone and mechanical sounding "voice," while others offer speech output that is more modulating and humanlike. Although inexperienced speech synthesis users understand human sounding output more easily, experienced users prefer mechanical speech because of its processing speed.

An individual's speech output requirements and preferences are influenced by numerous factors, including (1) how often and for how long the person is going to be using synthetic speech, (2) the familiarity of information to which the person is listening, (3) the presence of any hearing impairment that might make a certain synthesizer or voice much more understandable than another, and (4) the desired rate of output.

Summary

Learning to read is a complex process, laden with frustrations for students who encounter many difficulties, and filled with rewards for those who quickly and easily master the task. Students arrive at the schoolroom door with the expectation that they will learn to read. National literacy statistics clearly indicate that not all individuals attain this goal, even though they may possess a high school diploma. Although experts disagree as to the exact percentage, a substantial number of the students referred for special education services will exhibit moderate to severe disabilities in reading. Therefore, provision of a structured and comprehensive program of reading instruction is of critical importance.

A successful reading program must include consideration of decoding, comprehension, building fluency, and of individual students' content area abilities. Instruction must be tailored to individual needs. The decoding versus meaning debate, which has continued endlessly in texts and journals, has done little to instruct professionals in how to teach either skill. A comprehensive and effective reading program must include instruction in both areas. This chapter's sections about decoding and meaning provide specific procedures for teaching these skills, including some techniques for direct instruction.

Instruction in decoding must focus on both accuracy and fluency, while instruction in meaning must move from word comprehension to literal and inferential comprehension of sentences and paragraphs. Students may fall behind in content area subjects that require specific reading skills. Yet with instruction aimed at developing effective content area reading, some students can function in general education classrooms given the proper adaptations and special education instruction. Students need to learn specific strategies for obtaining meaning from content materials.

Finally, with the advent of assistive and instructional technologies, reading problems can be circumvented to allow access to print material and to foster comprehension. Technology holds great promise for individuals with reading disabilities; efficacy studies and promoting the infusion of technology into instruction are areas that require further emphasis.

Study and Discussion Questions

1. Describe the nature of reading acquisition and instruction.
2. Identify and explain how the components of reading instruction relate to different reading acquisition models.
3. Provide explanations of reading instructional components.
4. List and describe three procedures for improving oral reading fluency.
5. Develop a lesson plan to improve teaching of comprehension skills.
6. Describe ways to foster reading in the content area skills.
7. Discuss how to infuse technology into a reading program.

References and Suggested Readings

Bryant, B. R., & Wiederholt, J. L. (1990). *Gray Oral Reading Test: Diagnostic.* Austin, TX: PRO-ED.

Deshler, D. D., Ellis, E. S., & Lenz, B. K. (1996). *Teaching adolescents with learning disabilities* (2nd ed.). Denver, CO: Love.

Lyon, G. R. (1995). Learning disabilities. In E. Marsh & R. Barkley, *Childhood psychopathology.* New York: Guilford Press.

Mather, N. (1992). Whole language reading instruction for students with learning disabilities: Caught in the cross fire. *Learning Disabilities Research & Practice, 7,* 87–95.

Moats, L. C., & Lyon, G. R. (1993). Learning disabilities in the United States: Advocacy, science, and the future of the field. *Journal of Learning Disabilities, 26,* 282–294.

Olson, R., Forsberg, H., Wise, B., & Rack, J. (1994). Measurement of word recognition, orthographic, and phonological skills. In G. R. Lyon (Ed.), *Frames of reference for the assessment of learning disabilities* (pp. 243–278). Baltimore: Brookes.

Perfetti, C. A., Beck, I., Bell, L., & Hughes, C. (1987). Phonemic knowledge and learning to read are reciprocal: A longitudinal study of first grade children. *Merrill-Palmer Quarterly, 33,* 283–319.

Pressley, M., & Rankin, J. (1994). More about whole language methods of reading instruction for students at risk for early reading failure. *Learning Disabilities Research and Practice, 9*(3), 157–168.

Stanovich, K. E. (1986). Matthew effects in reading: Some consequences of individual differences in the acquisition of literacy. *Reading Research Quarterly, 21,* 360–407.

Torgesen, J. K., & Bryant, B. R. (1994). *Phonological awareness training for reading.* Austin, TX: PRO-ED.

Wagner, R. K., & Torgesen, J. K. (1987). The nature of phonological processing and its causal role in the acquisition of reading skills. *Psychological Bulletin, 101,* 192–212.

Westby, C. E. (1993). Counterpoint: There may be holes in whole language. *American Speech-Language-Hearing Association Special Interest Division 10 Newsletter* (pp. 11–16). Rockville, MD: American Speech-Language-Hearing Association.

Nature of Reading

Carlisle, J. F. (1993). Selecting approaches to vocabulary instruction for the reading disabled. *Learning Disabilities Research & Practice, 8*(2), 97–105.

Carnine, D., Silbert, J., & Kameenui, E. J. (1990). *Direct instruction reading* (2nd ed.). Columbus, OH: Merrill.

Delpit, L. D. (1988). The silenced dialogue: Power and pedagogy in educating other people's children. *Harvard Educational Review, 58,* 280–298.

Dolch, E. W. (1936). A basic sight vocabulary. *Elementary School Journal, 36,* 456–460.

Ekwall, E. E. (1985). *Locating and correcting reading difficulties* (4th ed.). Columbus, OH: Merrill.

Fry, E. B., Kress, J. E., Fountoukidis, D. L., & Polk, J. K., (1993). *The reading teacher's* book *of lists* (3rd ed.). Des Moines, IA: Authors.

Goodman, K. S., Smith, E. B., Meredith, R., & Goodman, Y. M. (1987). *Language and thinking in school* (3rd ed.). New York: Owen.

Guralnik, D. B. (Ed.) (1984). *Webster's new world dictionary* (rev. ed.). New York: Warner Communications.

Hammill, D. D., & McNutt, G. (1981). *The correlates of reading: The consensus of thirty years of correlational research.* Austin, TX: PRO-ED.

Harris, A. J., & Sipay, E. R. (1980). *How to increase reading ability* (7th ed.). New York: Longman.

Huey, E. B. (1908). *The psychology and pedagogy of reading.* New York: Macmillan.

Hutchison, R. M. (Ed.). (1952). Great books of the western world. Chicago: Encyclopedia Britannica.

LaBerge, D., & Samuels, S. I. (1974). Toward a theory of automatic information processing in reading. In H. Singer & R. D. Riddell (Eds.), *Theories, models, and processes of readiness* (2nd ed., pp. 549–579), Newark, DE: International Reading Association.

Lewis, R. B. (1983). Learning disabilities and reading: Instructional recommendations from current research. *Exceptional Children, 50*(3), 230–240.

Smith, F. (1988). *Understanding reading* (4th ed.). Hillsdale, NJ: Erlbaum.

Spache, G. (1981). *Diagnosing and correcting reading disabilities.* Boston: Allyn & Bacon.

Webster's II New Riverside University Dictionary (1984). Boston: Riverside.

Wiederholt, J. L., & Bryant, B. R. (1987). *Assessing the reading abilities and instructional needs of students.* Austin, TX: PRO-ED.

Zigmond, N., Vallecorsa, A., & Leihardt, G. (1980). Reading instruction for students with learning disabilities. *Topics in Language Disorders, 1*(1), 89–98.

Skills Instruction and Instructional Methods and Techniques

Chall, J. S. (1983). *Stages of reading development.* New York: McGraw-Hill.

Decoding Letters and Words in Print

Adams, M. J. (1990). *Beginning to read: Thinking and learning about print.* Cambridge, MA: MIT Press.

Bryant, B. R., & Wiederholt, J. L. (1990). *Gray Oral Reading Test: Diagnostic.* Austin, TX: PRO-ED.

Carnine, D., Silbert, J., & Kameenui, E. J. (1990). *Direct instruction reading* (2nd ed.). Columbus, OH: Merrill.

Cooper, J. D., Warncke, E. W., & Shipman, D. A. (1990). *The what and how of reading instruction.* Columbus, OH: Merrill.

Ekwall, E. E. (1985). *Locating and correcting reading difficulties* (4th ed.). Columbus, OH: Merrill.

Fleisher, L. S., & Jenkins, J. R. (1983). The effect of word- and comprehension-emphasis instruction on reading performance. *Learning Disability Quarterly, 6,* 146–153.

Freeman, T. J., & McLaughlin, T. F. (1984). Effects of a taped-words treatment procedure on learning disabled students' sight-word oral reading. *Learning Disability Quarterly, 7,* 49–54.

Hinshelwood, J. (1917). *Congenital word-blindness.* London: Lewis.

Johnson, D. D. (1971). The Dolch list reexamined. *The Reading Teacher, 24,* 455–456.

Jones, K. M., Torgesen, J. K., & Sexton, M. A. (1987). Using computer guided practice to increase decoding fluency in learning disabled children: A study using the Hint and Hunt I Program. *Journal of Learning Disabilities, 20,* 122–128.

Kavale, K. (1982). Meta-analysis of the relationship between visual perceptual skills and reading achievement. *Journal of Learning Disabilities, 15,* 42–51.

Kussmaul, A. (1877). Disturbance of speech. *Encyclopedia of Practical Medicine, 14,* 581–587.

Samuels, S. J. (1981). Some essentials of decoding. *Exceptional Education Quarterly, 2*(1), 11–25.

Simmons, D. C., Gunn, B., Smith, S. B., & Kameenui, E. J. (1995). Phonological awareness: Applications of instructional design. *LD Forum, 19*(2), 7–10.

Spache, G. D., & Spache, E. B. (1986). *Reading in the elementary school* (5th ed.). Boston: Allyn & Bacon.

Stanovich, K. E. (1992). Speculations on the causes and consequences of individual assumptions and their implications for reading instruction. In P. B. Gough, L. C. Ehri, & R. Treiman (Eds.), *Reading acquisition* (pp. 307–342). Hillsdale, NJ: Erlbaum.

Wilson, R. M., & Cleland, C. J. (1985). *Diagnostic and remedial reading for classroom and clinic* (5th ed.). Columbus, OH: Merrill.

Comprehending Words and Ideas in Print

Ausubel, D. O. (1968). *Educational psychology: A cognitive view.* New York: Holt, Rinehart, & Winston.

Barr, R., & Johnson, B. (1991). *Teaching reading in elementary classrooms: Developing independent readers.* New York: Longman.

Bos, C. S., & Anders, P. L. (1990). Effects of interactive vocabulary instruction on the vocabulary learning and reading comprehension of junior-high learning disabled students. *Learning Disability Quarterly, 13,* 31–42.

Brown, V., Hammill, D., & Wiederholt, J. L. (1986). *Test of Reading Comprehension.* Austin, TX: PRO-ED.

Carlisle, J. F. (1993). Selecting approaches to vocabulary instruction for the reading disabled. *Learning Disabilities Research & Practice, 8*(2), 97–105.

Chan, L. K. S., Cole, P. G., & Barfett, S. (1987). Comprehension monitoring: Detection and identification of text inconsistencies by LD and normal students. *Learning Disability Quarterly, 10,* 114–124.

Cheek, E. H., & Collins, M. D. (1985). *Strategies for reading success.* Columbus, OH: Merrill.

Darch, C., & Kameenui, E. J. (1987). Teaching LD students critical reading skills: A systematic replication. *Learning Disability Quarterly, 10,* 82–91.

Englert, C. S., & Thomas, C. C. (1987). Sensitivity to text structure in reading and writing: A comparison of learning disabled and non-learning disabled students. *Learning Disability Quarterly, 10,* 93–105.

Fleisher, L. S., & Jenkins, J. R. (1983). The effect of word- and comprehension-emphasis instruction on reading performance. *Learning Disability Quarterly, 6,* 146–153.

Fry, E. B. (1972). *Reading instruction for classroom and clinic.* New York: McGraw-Hill.

Idol, L. (1987). Group story mapping: A comprehension strategy for both skilled and unskilled readers. *Journal of Learning Disabilities, 20,* 196–205.

Jenkins, J. R., Stein, M. L., & Osborn, J. R. (1981). What next after decoding? Instruction and research in comprehension. *Exceptional Education Quarterly, 2*(1), 27–39.

Johnson, G., Gersten, R., & Carnine, D. (1987). Effects of instructional design variables on vocabulary acquisition of learning disabled students: A study of computer-assisted instruction. *Journal of Learning Disabilities, 20,* 206–213.

Klare, G. R. (1984). *Readability.* In D. Pearson (Ed.), *Handbook of reading research* (pp. 681–744). New York: Longman.

Lovitt, T. C. (1995). *Tactics for teaching* (2nd ed.). Columbus, OH: Merrill.

McGee, L. M., & Richgels, D. J. (1990). *Literacy's beginnings: Supporting young readers and writers.* Boston: Allyn & Bacon.

McKeown, M. G., & Beck, I. L. (1988). Learning vocabulary: Different ways for different goals. *Remedial and Special Education, 9*(1), 42–52.

Palincsar, A. S., & Brown, A. L. (1986). Interactive teaching to promote independent learning from text. *The Reading Teacher, 39*(8), 771–777.

Palincsar, A. S., & Brown, A. L. (1988). Teaching and practicing thinking skills to promote comprehension in the context of group problem solving. *Remedial and Special Education, 9*(1), 53–59.

Roberts, M., & Smith, D. D. (1980). The relationship among correct and error oral reading rates and comprehension. *Learning Disability Quarterly, 3,* 54–64.

Schumaker, J. B., Denton, P. H., & Deshler, D. D. (1984). *The paraphrasing strategy.* Lawrence: University of Kansas Press.

Spache, G. D., & Spache, E. B. (1986). *Reading in the elementary school* (5th ed.). Boston: Allyn & Bacon.

Wong, B. Y. L., & Jones, W. (1982). Increasing metacomprehension in learning disabled and normally achieving students through self-questioning training. *Learning Disability Quarterly, 5,* 228–240.

Reading with Fluency

Adams, M. J. (1990). *Beginning to read: Thinking and learning about print.* Cambridge, MA: MIT Press.

Duffy, G. G., & Roehler, L. R. (1986). *Improving classroom reading instruction: A decision-making approach.* Wilkes-Barre, PA: Bookkeepers.

Guthrie, F. M., & Cunningham, P. M. (1982). Teaching decoding skills in educable mentally handicapped children. *The Reading Teacher, 35,* 554–559.

Guzak, F. (1985). *Diagnostic reading instruction in the elementary grades.* New York: Harper & Row.

Lauritzen, C. (1982). A modification of repeated readings for group instruction. *The Reading Teacher, 35,* 456–458.

Lovitt, T. C. (1995). *Tactics for teaching* (2nd ed.). Columbus, OH: Merrill.

Lyon, G. R. (1995). Learning disabilities. In E. Marsh & R. Barkley, *Childhood psychopathology.* New York: Guilford Press.

Precision Teaching Project. (1984). *Training manual* (8th ed.). Great Falls, MT: Precision Teaching Materials.

Rasinski, T. V. (1994). Developing syntactic sensitivity in reading through phrase-cued texts. *Intervention in School and Clinic, 29*(3), 165–168.

Rose, T. L. (1984). The effects of two prepractice procedures on oral reading. *Journal of Learning Disabilities, 17,* 544–548.

Rose, T. L., & Beattie, J. R. (1986). Relative effects of teacher-directed and taped previewing on oral reading. *Learning Disability Quarterly, 59,* 193–199.

Rosenberg, M. S. (1986). Error-correction during oral reading: A comparison of three techniques. *Learning Disability Quarterly, 9,* 182–192.

Samuels, S. J. (1981). Some essentials of decoding. *Exceptional Education Quarterly, 2*(1), 11–25.

Singh, J., & Singh, N. N. (1985). Comparison of word-supply and word-analysis error-correction procedure on oral reading by mentally retarded children. *American Journal of Mental Deficiency, 90,* 64–70.

Content Area Reading

Armbruster, B. B., Anderson, T. H., & Meyer, J. L. (1991). Improving content area reading using instructional graphics. *Reading Research Quarterly, 26*(4), 393–416.

Bergerud, D., Lovitt, T. C., & Horton, S. (1988). The effectiveness of textbook adaptations in life science for high school students with learning disabilities. *Journal of Learning Disabilities, 21,* 70–76.

Darch, C., & Gersten, R. (1986). Direction-setting activities in reading comprehension: A comparison of two approaches. *Learning Disability Quarterly, 9,* 235–243.

Englert, C. S., & Mariage, T. V. (1990). Send for the POSSE: Structuring the comprehension dialogue. *Academic Therapy, 25*(4), 473–487.

Hudson, P., Lignugaris-Kraft, B., & Miller, T. (1993). Using content enhancements to improve the performance of adolescents with learning disabilities in content classes. *Learning Disabilities Research & Practice, 8*(2), 106–126.

Huhn, R. H. (1980). Readiness as a variable influencing comprehension in content area reading at the secondary level: A cognitive view. *Learning Disability Quarterly, 3,* 323–339.

Klauer, K. J. (1984). Intentional and incidental learning with instructional texts: A meta-analysis for 1970–1980. *American Educational Research Journal, 21,* 323–339.

Lovitt, T. C., & Horton, S. (1987). How to develop study guides. *Journal of Reading, Writing, and Learning Disabilities, 3,* 213–221.

Ogle, D. M. (1986). A teaching model that develops active reading of expository text. *The Reading Teacher, 39,* 564–570.

Schumaker, J. B., Deshler, D. D., Alley, G. R., Warner, M. M., & Denton, P. H. (1982). Multipass: A learning strategy for improving reading comprehension. *Learning Disability Quarterly, 5,* 295–304.

Technology

Boone, R., & Higgins, K. (1993). Hypermedia basal readers: Three years of school-based research. *Journal of Special Education Technology, 12*(2), 86–106.

Higgins, K., & Boone, R. (1991). Hypermedia CAI: A supplement to an elementary school basal reader program. *Journal of Special Education Technology, 11*(1), 1–15.

Juel, C., Griffith, P., & Gough, P. (1986). Acquisition of literacy: A longitudinal study of children in first and second grade. *Journal of Educational Psychology, 78,* 243–255.

Lewis, R. B. (1993). *Special education technology: Classroom application.* Pacific Grove, CA: Brooks/Cole.

Lovitt, T. C. (1995). *Tactic for teaching* (2nd ed.). Columbus, OH: Merrill.

Raskind, M., & Shaw, T. (1995, March). *Assistive technology for students with learning disabilities: An overview.* Paper presented at the meeting of the Texas Assistive Technology Partnership, Austin, TX.

Smith, F. (1985). *Reading without nonsense* (2nd ed.). New York: Teachers College Press.

Smith, F. (1988). *Understanding reading* (4th ed.). Hillsdale, NJ: Erlbaum.

Torgesen, J. K. (1986). Computers and cognition in reading: A focus on decoding fluency. *Exceptional Children, 53,* 157–162.

Ysseldyke, J. E., & Algozzine, B. (1983). Where to begin to diagnose reading problems. *Topics in Learning Disabilities, 2*(4), 60–69.

Chapter 11
Written Communication

Writing is important for all students, regardless of grade level. It is one proof of how well they are learning academic subjects. Very often, their academic achievement is related directly to their ability to express themselves in writing. For instance, students take spelling tests, write letters, and write stories, all of which require efficient writing abilities. Thus, students need to possess a range of writing abilities (e.g., generating content, using correct punctuation and capitalization, using appropriate penmanship). Writing is also an important life skill for personal communication, postsecondary education, and adult adjustment.

Research shows that elementary and secondary students with written communication learning problems are unable to express themselves successfully. For example, in comparison with their typical, same-age peers, students with learning problems write fewer, shorter, less cohesive narrative stories and include fewer story elements. They typically lack effective writing strategies, detect and edit fewer errors, and generate fewer words and sentences. Students with learning problems tend to rely on others for assistance to solve writing problems, rather than on their knowledge of the writing process. In other words, students lack confidence and ability and seek assistance more often than their peers who possess adequate writing skills.

In this chapter, we discuss three main skills areas: the nature of written communication instruction, the components and goals for instruction, and strategies for instructing elementary and secondary students. We offer suggestions for adapting written communication instruction in the general education setting and for using technology as part of the written communication curriculum.

Making Connections

Before you read, consider the role of written communication across the curriculum, and the curricular models discussed in chapter 4. Review the instructional arrangements in chapter 4 by thinking about how written communication skills and processes could be taught within those instructional contexts. Think about ways to teach writing using the instructional approaches described in chapter 5. Examine the evaluation procedures presented in chapters 3 and 6; decide on a "best practice" for evaluating students' written products. Using information from chapter 2, identify ways you would work with the general education teacher to adapt written communication instruction in the elementary and secondary general education setting. Finally, develop a list of techniques that parents could use at home that could promote written communication skills.

Objectives
After studying this chapter, the reader will be able to

1. Describe the nature of written communication instruction.

2. Identify and explain components of written communication instruction.

3. Provide instructional examples for each component of written communication.

●●

Nature of Written Communication

As you read, think about . . .
1. Providing a definition of writing literacy and naming its components.
2. Explaining issues surrounding written communication instruction.
3. Identifying writing curricular and instructional design features.
4. Designing written communication lessons according to each instructional approach presented in chapter 5.
5. Task-analyzing one skill of written communication.

Most students with special needs are deficient in written communication. Because many of them can communicate with others orally, their inabilities to transmit thoughts in a logical, cohesive fashion become more apparent when they are required to write. In this section, we offer a definition of written communication literacy, provide information about issues in this area, discuss features of effective curricular and instructional design, and examine instructional approaches as they pertain to written communication.

Definition of Written Communication Literacy

Written communication literacy consists of the ability to plan, organize, and produce written products that convey understandable, coherent, legible messages to various audiences. Inherent in this ability is knowledge of the mechanical components (discussed below) of written communication. Therefore, instruction should focus on developing skills that lead students to acquire and be proficient with written communication abilities.

Issues in Written Communication Instruction

Over the past decade, written communication instruction has attained a prominent role in all classroom settings. Spurred by national interest in improving academic skills, research findings in cognitive psychology, and an emphasis on writing in postsecondary settings and adult life, written communication instruction warrants teachers' attention across all academic subjects (Graham & Harris, 1988a, 1988b; Scardamalia & Bereiter, 1986). As a result, more instructional time has been allotted to writing, and increased written communication competency testing has been implemented nationwide (Graham & Harris, 1988a).

In special education, an emerging body of research on written communication instruction and students with learning difficulties identifies specific learning characteristics, instructional strengths and weaknesses, and efficacy of intervention programs. Newcomer et al. (1988) raise five major issues pertaining to this body of research that warrant discussion. First, the research has focused on the writing process (discussed below) with relatively less attention devoted to developing mechanical skills (i.e., spelling, grammar, punctuation, capitalization). This is problematic because of the great difficulties that students with learning difficulties have with mechanical skills. The issue is how best to address instruction in mechanics, yet retain an emphasis on developing the writing process.

The second issue relates to peer conferencing, often mentioned as an effective feedback and editing activity in the writing process. Peer conferencing infers that peers have abilities in reading and critiquing stories, skills that students with special needs may lack. Thus, it is important to be aware of students' abilities to understand and critique text structures, use mechanical skills, edit, and provide socially acceptable, constructive feedback.

The third issue that Newcomer and her colleagues (1988) raise centers on the efficacy of instructional methods. They recommend using methods such as journal writing or expressive writing, so that students can select their own topics and style of writing, and thereby possibly increase creativity and fluency, without being critiqued on mechanical skills and story structure. Student performance must be monitored carefully to ensure that students with special needs are indeed benefiting from instructional methods.

The fourth issue focuses on assessment. It is important to determine how assessment will be conducted and which criteria to use in judging improvement in written communication. The fifth issue surrounds the need for continued research on the written communication abilities of and instruction for students with learning problems. Newcomer et al. (1988) advise that research findings in writing involving typically achieving students require validation before being generalized to students with learning problems.

Curricular and Instructional Design Features

Research is being conducted on intervention programs and curricula that help students with learning problems write better. Although further research is needed, some emerging design features are most promising for students with special needs. The authors have adapted these features from the work of Graham and Harris (1988a) and discuss them below.

Teach Goal Setting

Students should be taught to set specific goals for writing improvement. These goals should correspond to the teacher's instructional objectives and can be monitored through conferences and documentation of results. Goal setting is likely to motivate students to use cognitive strategies for writing (Scardamalia & Bereiter, 1986). Moreover, in a study involving students with learning disabilities, Harris and Graham (1985) found that goal setting, which included specifying the amount and type of items to include in their stories, graphing results, monitoring their progress, and setting new goals, prompted learning.

Teach Different Types of Writing Structures

Students with special needs require instruction in various writing structures, such as narrative and expository writing. Although students may include some components of writing genres, such as story beginnings and endings, their abilities to develop various types of writing are limited. Instruction can focus on the different types of writing structures, their characteristics, and specific cognitive and metacognitive strategies for developing them. Modeling is an excellent tactic for demonstrating types of writing and characteristics; modeling can also be used to teach explicit cognitive strategies for employing the genres. The instructional steps presented in chapter 5 are another excellent vehicle for teaching students structural elements of different genres (Graham & Harris, 1988a; Scardamalia & Bereiter, 1986).

Teach Mechanical Skills

Students with learning difficulties must be taught specific **mechanical skills** (e.g., spelling, capitalization, punctuation, grammar). Direct instruction techniques can be effective in teaching these skills. Graham (1982) recommends that mechanical skills not be taught during designated composition writing time. We recommend that mechanical skills, including specific techniques such as cue cards and prompting, be taught before composition writing, to promote generalization of mechanical skills to composition writing (see chapter 9 for generalization techniques). Writing with spelling errors, legibility problems, poor sentence structure, grammatical mistakes, and misuse of capitalization and punctuation distracts the reader from the content. Worse yet, it may be a detriment to a student's acceptance into postsecondary education (a practice that is occurring in some states), landing a job, or self-expression in everyday situations. Granted, word processing programs with spelling and grammar checking systems can help to circumvent some mechanical difficulties, but they do not solve all of the problems.

Develop Writing Skills Within the Context of Other Subject Areas

Writing instruction can be integrated into other subject areas and thematic units. For example, students can be responsible for producing high-quality written work in social studies, science, and other classes. Secondary-level content area teachers can work collaboratively to develop instructional objectives, such as writing skills, that all the student's teachers emphasize and monitor. Similarly, elementary teachers can, for example, emphasize cognitive strategies taught during writing that should be used to write a paper in social studies.

Promote a Writing Environment

Like reading and mathematics, writing can easily be emphasized throughout the school day in a variety of contexts at both the elementary and secondary levels. Teachers can provide students with many opportunities for students to practice their written language skills. For instance, teachers can create a writing center that features an array of writing tools and paper. Figure 11.1 depicts a writing center that could be established to stimulate creative writing and to reinforce previously taught writing skills. Other possibilities include having a display area for students' writing, modeling writing, having students think aloud while working through the writing process, using the overhead projector to generate compositions showing the writing process, establishing a post office, and having students write, write, write!

Instructional Approaches

Written communication instruction is best characterized as a combination of the behavioral, strategic, and holistic approaches (see chapter 5 for a review of these

Figure 11.1
Writing center

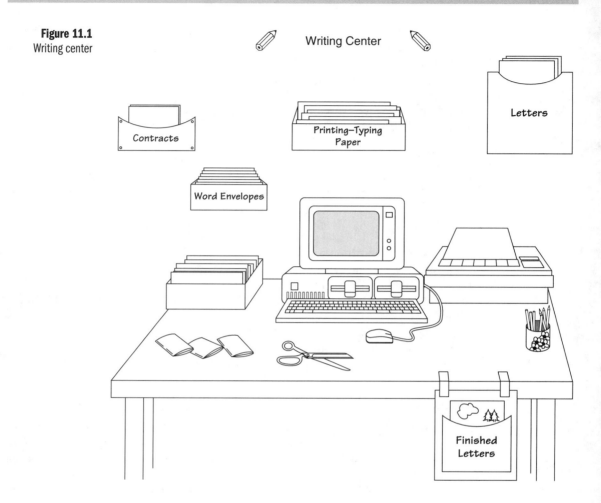

three approaches). In developing instructional programs for written communication, teachers must select the best instructional approach or combination of approaches, and make further choices based on the IEP's annual goals and instructional objectives.

Skills for Instruction

As you read, think about...

1. Describing the steps you go through when writing a paper.
2. Developing a curriculum for written communication.
3. Identifying written communication skills that students will need as adults.
4. Examining IEPs to determine annual goals, instructional objectives, and materials currently recommended for instructional purposes.
5. Examining IEPs to determine how assistive and instructional technology is being used to promote instruction.

Although educators may not totally agree on which instructional approach best teaches written communication, most authorities do agree on the components of instruction. Figure 11.2 lists the three major instructional components that must be addressed to promote mastery of written communication: the means for writing, the mechanical skills that promote better understanding of the message, and the actual process of writing. The list does not suggest a linear progression of instruction with advancement contingent on mastery of previous skills. Rather, written communication instruction is interactive; various skills in the list are taught concurrently, specific skills are isolated for direct instruction, and other skills are promoted during the writing process.

Means of Written Communication

There are various means of putting information into the written mode. At school, handwriting is the most commonly used form; certainly, it is the means students use to take notes, write in-class themes and term papers, and take tests. At home, business, and schools, typing and word processing have gained popularity and are becoming the norm. For students whose handwriting is poor—and this is particularly true for most students with special needs—knowing how to type and use a computer and word processing program can compensate for poor handwriting. Moreover, these skills allow them to concentrate their efforts on content rather than form. Students freed from the constraints of handwriting often improve the spelling, grammar, and organization of their written assignments.

Prewriting Skills

Before children can learn to write letters and symbols, they must possess some prerequisite skills. For example, students must be able to hold a pencil correctly, draw straight lines at different angles, draw curved lines at different angles, draw freehand lines, and draw a variety of shapes in which lines are joined and crossed at specific points. Students also need good spatial orientation and directional sense to succeed in handwriting. It is important, for example, for students to understand the concepts of left-to-right, up-and-down sequencing. It is possible to teach these concepts concurrently with letter formation, but instruction proceeds most efficiently if these skills have already been mastered.

Before handwriting instruction is actually initiated, the teacher must determine the handedness of each student. Some 11 percent of the population is lefthanded, and accommodations must be made for those students. For example, when writing at a chalkboard, the right-handed student stands to the left and the left-handed student

Figure 11.2
Topics for written
communication
instruction

Means	Mechanics	Composition Process	
Prerequisites	Spelling	Prewriting	Writing
Handwriting	Word Division	Planning	Semantics
Legibility	Capitalization	Purpose	Sentences
Manuscript	Grammar	Ideation	Paragraphs
Cursive	Punctuation	Topic Selection	Postwriting
Word Processing		Audience	Editing
Typing		Organization	Revision
		Types of Writing	

stands to the right of the letters or symbols being written. The left-handed student should place the top of the paper in a clockwise position (to the right), while the right-handed child should place the paper square to the body or turned slightly to the left. Because the writing motion for left-handed persons requires them to push rather than pull their pens, care must be taken to find a pen with a point that moves easily across paper. Left-handed youngsters should not be allowed to cup their hands over the letters being formed, because this is not a comfortable position and because it impairs later speed and proficiency.

Some students have difficulty holding a pencil correctly; their hands slip too far down. Some teachers suggest that a grip be placed on a pencil for students with poor motor abilities. A ball of clay or piece of sponge molded around the pencil approximately three-quarters of an inch from the pencil point might help students with this problem. Other students with minor motor problems have an easier time writing with thicker pencils. Teachers should allow students to find and use the size most comfortable for them until later, when and if their fine motor skills are better developed.

Manuscript (Printing) and Cursive

The debate about teaching students to use the manuscript form of handwriting seems perpetual. Although this is relatively easy to teach young children and does more closely match the print that appears in basal readers, this skill is taught and used for only a few years, and then dropped from the curriculum. Long ago, Strauss and Lehtinen (1951, p. 187) suggested that students with learning problems not be taught manuscript writing but instead learn only the cursive. They wrote:

> We have found it advantageous for several reasons to make an early start in teaching connected writing to the brain-injured child and to omit specific instruction in the manuscript form. The perceptional disturbances of the brain-injured child act as a definite handicap in acceptably spacing letters and words. Perception of a word form as a unified whole is aided when the letters of the word are actually joined to form a whole. Connected or cursive writing also seems to lend itself more effectively to developing a kinesthetic perception of word forms.

For students who have a propensity to reverse letters, instruction in manuscript should be discontinued and instruction in cursive initiated. Because of the way letters are formed and joined in cursive writing, the opportunity for making reversals decreases when students use cursive. The confusion between *b* and *d*, and *p* and *q*, is not as common with cursive because the letters have more definitive characteristics.

One other reason for not teaching manuscript printing to youngsters with academic problems is efficiency of learning and instruction. Why spend time teaching a skill that is soon discontinued from the school curriculum? For students who have a difficult time mastering academic tasks, it is more beneficial to spend classroom instructional time on the skill expected in the later school years. Unfortunately, for some students, there is no choice. If a student must use manuscript in the general education setting, then that student needs to acquire and become proficient in its use.

Whether students begin learning to write using the manuscript or cursive mode seems to be more of an administrative decision than one based on empirical findings. In some school districts, children first learn to print. In others, manuscript is not presented and students begin their writing experiences with the cursive form. There is not a definite instructional sequence that begins with manuscript writing and termi- nates with mastery of the cursive system. When manuscript is taught first, instruc- tion on cursive usually begins in the middle of the second grade or beginning of the third grade. Regardless, there is no evidence that mastery of manuscript writing is a prerequisite to success in learning the cursive form.

As with all other academic areas, teachers must address at least three stages of learning that teachers address when teaching students to write: acquisition, profi- ciency, and maintenance. A substantial amount of time is spent in schools teaching students how to write using the cursive system. Children spend hours practicing cor- rect letter formation. Once the skill is acquired, however, teachers can help students become proficient. Youngsters must be able to write fast enough to be able to com- plete assignments in other academic areas (history, social studies, literature). If a student is not proficient in writing skills, other subject areas will suffer. For example, if a student is too slow in forming letters, dictation is an impossible task. Spelling assignments are unfinished, possibly not because of a spelling deficiency, but because of a writing deficiency.

Typing/Keyboarding

There is little evidence available to guide teachers on many important aspects relat- ing to the relationship between written communication skills and typing. For exam- ple, at what point are students ready to learn to type? Does typing positively influence students' writing form and content? Since the introduction of computers into school settings, however, there is growing evidence that being able to type enhances written communication skills. Individuals for whom handwriting is laborious and difficult fre- quently avoid all writing tasks. This ultimately could lead them to select careers that do not require them to write, not because their interests direct them to those occupa- tions, but because they seek to avoid writing.

Word Processing

Although one does not have to be a proficient typist to use a word processing program with a computer, as with handwriting, proficiency is ultimately necessary. Without proficiency in keyboarding skills (memorizing location of keys, numbers, punctuation, and space bar), attention cannot be focused on the content of what is being written.

Because of the availability of computers in schools and at home, many young- sters are learning to use the computer as a writing tool. A number of easy-to-use word processing programs are available. Once a program is mastered, the student's transition to more powerful and complex programs is relatively easy.

Reversals

Written reversals are most predominant when students print. It is important for teachers to remember that most young children make reversals when first learning to write. This is part of the normal developmental process and should not be viewed as unacceptable. Several early studies of young children's academic performance clearly indicate that reversals correlate with age (the younger the student, the higher the probability of reversals in written work). Davidson (1934, 1935) and Hildreth (1934) demonstrated that with increasing maturity and experience, children's frequency of reversing letters and symbols decreases. In those studies, practically all kindergarten children confused *b* and *d,* and *q* and *p.* This tendency was still prevalent among first graders, but to a lesser degree. Whether these data suggest that no direct remediation efforts are necessary until second grade has not been answered through research. Logically, it seems that teachers should not adopt a laissez-faire attitude about reversals in young children and should at least provide corrective feedback when they occur. On the other hand, referral to special education merely because a kindergartner reverses letters does not seem reasonable either.

A substantial amount of literature is available indicating that reversal problems in students' written work can be remediated through direct instructional techniques. Through modeling and corrective feedback, Stromer (1977) remediated several students' number and letter reversal tendencies. Hasazi and Hasazi (1972) remediated a student's digit reversals (writing 21 for 12) through an ignoring and praising procedure. Smith and Lovitt (1973) remediated a boy's *b/d* reversal problem by showing him his error (written by the teacher on an index card and used as corrective feedback) and instructing the boy not to write a *b* for a *d*. One interesting feature of this study is the finding that, at least for this child, the frequency of reversals related to the position the letter had in the word (initial, medial, or final). During instruction, they tried to remediate the letter (*d*) and the position (initial) most frequently in error. As that letter in that position was corrected, the student's pervasive *b/d* reversal problem was eliminated. Certainly, the data available indicate that teachers should try direct remediation efforts with students who have a tendency to reverse letters or numbers.

Mechanics of Written Communication

Possessing manuscript, cursive, typing, keyboarding, or word processing skills certainly does not guarantee proficiency in written communication. They are only the means by which information is put onto paper. When students have mastered at least one skill, instruction can be initiated on the mechanics of written communication.

Unfortunately, mastery of oral communication does not ensure mastery of written communication. Although the basic rules used to communicate orally are the same as those for writing, tolerance for incorrect usage is greater in oral communication. When readers see words on paper, they expect correct spelling, grammar, capitalization, and punctuation; variation in sentence construction; and some consistency in style. Figure 11.3 shows phonetic spelling and grammar correlated to a youngster's oral language. This child grew up in the Ozark region of Missouri, and his written communication abilities reflect his regional upbringing. Regardless of where individuals are from, they are expected to use standard English in their written communication. The mechanics of written communication are fairly precise, and the demands on the learner are considerable.

Spelling

Spelling is difficult for many youngsters because standard English does not follow consistent rules. There seem to be as many exceptions to the rules as there are rules. For students with learning difficulties, spelling should be a particular area of concern because they are much poorer spellers than other students, including even low achievers (Gerber, 1984; Gerber & Hall, 1987).

Recently, many teachers have changed their spelling curriculum so that it includes words students hear and use daily. Most teachers, however, have retained the

Figure 11.3
Sample of a child's
writing that reflects
his oral language
dialect

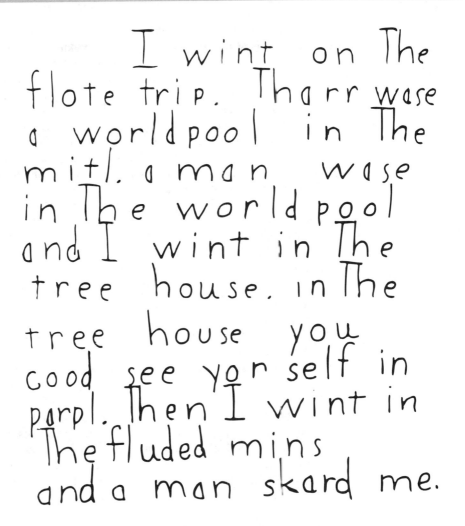

I wint on The flote trip. Tharr wase a worldpool in The mitl. a man wase in The worldpool and I wint in The tree house. in The tree house you cood see yor self in parpl. Then I wint in The fluded mins and a man skard me.

traditional approach for teaching spelling, a critical part of which is the spelling work-book. Although a number of different publishers have their own versions, they are remarkably similar. A list, usually twenty to twenty-five words, is generally presented on Monday. Every day, the teacher has the students do a different type of exercise (one day they read a paragraph with the new words, another day they practice dictionary and phonetic spellings). The culminating experience is usually a Friday test. Such has been the practice for years, and probably will remain so. There are several reasons for retaining the status quo. First, the procedure works for some youngsters and they become better spellers. Second, at least thirty minutes of the school day is planned for the teacher; the lesson plan and student materials are also provided.

Many students with learning problems are unable to learn to spell through the traditional approach. These students require added interventions such as those dis-cussed in the "Instructional Methods and Techniques" section later in this chapter, and some may need a radically different program. For example, *Corrective Spelling Through Morphographics* has been remarkably successful with a variety of students above the fourth-grade level. This packaged program consists of 140 lessons and includes student workbooks, daily lessons, and a student evaluation system. The program teaches spelling through morphographs: prefixes, suffixes, and root words. For groups of students who have difficulty in mastering spelling, this program and its approach might be an excellent alternative to the spelling tradition.

Word Division   Breaking words into syllables is a useful skill. It can help students spell better. Also, it is required when a word is broken at the end of a line of writing and is completed on the following line. Although most word processing programs automatically move whole words to the next line of type, students must still complete many assignments in manuscript or cursive writing and, consequently, must learn to divide words. Some teachers have students say the word aloud and clap with each sound unit to learn how a word is broken. However, the most reliable method of word division is to use a dictionary or word guide. It is important to teach students to use these kinds of reference books, because they are indispensable when writing compositions.

Capitalization

Capital letters are used to distinguish proper nouns and adjectives from common nouns and adjectives and to indicate the beginning of new sentences, salutations, and direct quotations. The rules for capitalizing the first letter in specific words are straightforward and are the simplest mechanical form for students to learn. Direct instruction on capitalization begins in the early elementary grades. Practice materials can be easily adapted from standard English texts and workbooks.

Grammar

This is probably the most difficult component of the mechanics of written communication. Although the rules of grammar provide general guidelines, exceptions and variations make mastery difficult. Even youngsters with typical achievement often do not master these skills until early adulthood. No student will learn the vast number of grammatical subskills without considerable practice and guided instruction.

A number of newly developed programs and strategies teach grammatical skills while teaching sentence and paragraph writing (see the "Instructional Methods and Techniques" section for more details). Students must know nouns, verbs, subjects, and predicates. Activities in which students identify these components of sentences can begin early with simple sentences, usually by fourth or fifth grade. Once students can identify nouns and verbs, instruction in other parts of speech (pronouns, adjectives, adverbs, conjunctions, prepositions, and interjections) can occur.

Although many students with special needs will not become sophisticated writers, they can develop adequate writing skills. To do so, however, they must at least be able to use correctly the basic parts of speech necessary to form simple and compound sentences.

Punctuation

As with grammar, punctuation is now taught through structured instruction about sentence and paragraph writing. Punctuation follows consistent rules of application. As students learn to write a compound sentence, for example, they are taught that a comma is placed before the conjunction, and they learn that a period ends all sentences. As with all writing, however, if students have few opportunities to write, if instruction is not direct, and if corrective feedback is infrequent, students will not master punctuation.

Composition Process

Simply put, students do not master written communication if they are not required to write. Writing is a vital process used in daily life. Writing essays is not the typical leisure pastime of most Americans, but they need writing skills for other tasks. In some professions writing is a requirement, and for success in school it is a necessity. Figure 11.4 shows the degree to which faulty mechanical elements have hampered a high school senior's written communication.

A norm-referenced test of written language is available (McGhee, Bryant, Larsen, & Rivera, 1995) that directly measures students' writing abilities. The test uses both contrived and spontaneous writing samples to assess students' performance levels in the following areas: vocabulary, grammar, capitalization, punctuation, ideation, spell-

Figure 11.4
A high school senior's plans for after graduation

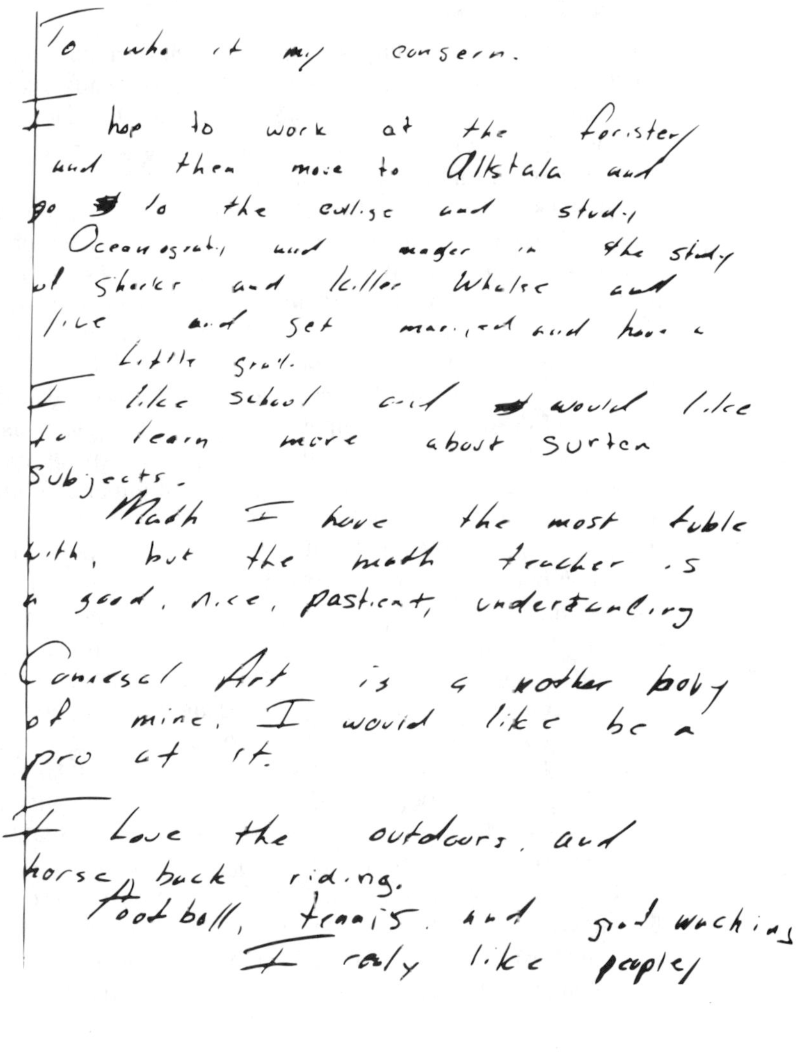
To who it my consern.

I hop to work at the foristery and then move to Alkstala and go to the cullige and study Oceanogrphy and mager in the study of Sharks and killer Whales and live and get maried and have a little grl.

I like school and would like to learn more about surten Subjects.

Math I have the most truble with, but the math teacher is a good, nice, pastient, understanding

Comersal Art is a nother hoby of mine. I would like be a pro at it.

I Love the outdoors, and horse back riding.

Football, tennis, and girl waching.

I realy like people

ing, and semantics. The test areas could easily be transformed into instructional areas for those who wish to develop their own instructional sequence in the area of written communication.

Themes, short answers, and reports are the formats of writing most commonly used in school and business. In high school, for example, students must express themselves and demonstrate their knowledge by writing book reports, themes, research papers, answers to questions at the end of chapters, and answers to questions on tests. Evaluation of the written content is biased by quality of the means used (legibility), accuracy of the mechanics used (correct spelling, punctuation, grammar), and the logical presentation of the information. Students who cannot write legibly should be allowed to type or use a word processing program, so the means of writing do not negatively influence their work's evaluation. When students can see the written product clearly, they often improve the mechanics of their writing. When students are taught to write with structure (using topic sentences, examples and explanations, and summary or concluding sentences), writing improves.

Types of Writing

Elementary and secondary students must master different types of writing as they move through their school years and into postsecondary settings. Persuasive, narrative, and expository are three examples of writing. Each type of writing has a specific purpose and contains specific content. The purpose of a piece of writing determines what type of information it will include.

In persuasive writing, the writer is trying to "sell" an opinion about a particular topic. This type of writing requires writers to take a position, describe their topic convincingly, and perhaps offer opinions about endorsing or not endorsing the stated position. Narrative writing entails the development of a story. Narrative writing requires students to have a beginning, middle, and ending; settings; characters; plots; problems and problem resolutions. Expository writing offers explanations; this writing is most common at the secondary and postsecondary level. Expository writing consists of descriptions, compare and contrast discussions, and sequences (Meyer, Brandt, & Bluth, 1980). Each of these types of expository writing requires specific content. For instance, a compare and contrast paper contains much different content from a paper that is explaining a situation.

Inherent in each type of writing is a set of questions (metacognitive strategies— self-questioning; self-regulation) that students can use to guide their writing efforts. For instance, "Have I stated all of the steps?" and "Are the steps in the correct sequence?" are questions students can use to develop an expository composition.

Little is known about the conceptual understanding of students with learning problems regarding types of writing. However, an emerging body of research suggests that they have difficulties in expository and narrative writing in terms of quality (e.g., coherence, length, development), mechanics, and revisions (MacArthur & Graham, 1987). In general, compared with their same-age, typical peers, students with special needs have minimal knowledge of writing types (Graham & Harris, 1988a) and appear to lack effective strategies to generate written compositions (Graham, Harris, & Sawyer, 1987).

For expository writing, Englert et al. (1989) found that students with learning difficulties have problems employing effective cognitive and metacognitive strategies, which hampers their writing. In particular, students may struggle with recognizing and responding to different text content found in expository writing. In narrative writing, rudimentary elements of story schema may be present, but stories may be disorganized and lack efficient development of story elements (e.g., setting, problem, characters, actions) (Graves, Semmel, & Gerber, 1994). Therefore, teachers must instruct students about different types of writing to promote students' understanding and successful writing.

The Writing Process

The writing process is an interactive activity; skilled students move through stages, which may overlap and repeat as the process unfolds and evolves (Bos, 1988). These stages have been identified differently by researchers; however, experts agree that prewriting, writing, and postwriting constitute the writing process stages (Graves, 1975).

The prewriting stage consists of two specific substages. Planning is the first substage. During planning, skilled writers decide on a purpose for writing and brainstorm ideas (ideation) related to a selected topic. They select their audience and are able to take the audience's perspective when generating their written products. This ability to take their perspective is important, because it guides decisions about what content to include to clarify the writer's intent. Writing to an audience is an important skill. The ability to adapt the content, vocabulary, and style of writing to the intended audience often separates the skilled from the unskilled writer (Flower & Hayes, 1980). Imagining how the audience will read and interpret the writing helps the writer fully understand how the composition should be constructed. In the planning substage, the student also selects a particular type of writing to guide the work. This, of course, implies that students know about types of writing in relation to their writing.

Organizing is the second substage. At this time, writers use the information generated during planning to formulate a framework for developing the written product. An outline is an excellent example of how writers can organize the information from the planning substage. Organizing is greatly influenced by the type of writing. For example, if a student is writing a story (narrative writing), then a beginning, middle, and ending would be included; thus, the outline might consist of these three major headings with subheadings of characters, plot, setting, and so forth.

During the writing stage (called drafting by some researchers), skilled writers use their organizational framework to put their ideas on paper. The writer guides the development of the paper by asking specific questions (metacognitive strategies) about the type of writing. For example, in explanatory expository writing, the writer would respond to questions such as "What is being explained?" "What happened first?" "What happened next?" and so forth (Englert, 1990). Writers refer back to the prewriting stage information, such as an organizational outline, to help them stay on track.

The postwriting stage is designated for editing and revising. During this time, writers focus on the content and on the mechanical aspects of their writing. It is common for writers to generate several drafts (writing stage) and to go through the postwriting stage several times before reaching a final product.

One key to improving writing is being able to monitor one's own errors (referred to in the research literature as *error monitoring*). Writing improves when writers use self-correction procedures (see the "Instructional Methods and Techniques" section for more details). Students must learn to proof and correct their written work. This is an important aspect in the writing process. Therefore, teachers should not only allow students to monitor for errors, but also insist upon it. Accepting first drafts of students' functional writing is only the first step in writing instruction. Working in class individually or in groups using the jigsaw technique (where one student checks for capitalization, another for spelling errors, another for punctuation) to correct drafts of student writing is a critical learning activity. Unfortunately, it is often omitted from writing instruction.

Researchers have shown that students with learning problems have difficulty identifying the stages of the writing process and using cognitive and metacognitive strategies during each stage to produce quality papers (Graham et al., 1990). They tend to lack self-regulatory skills (e.g., asking questions, adhering to text structures) and often struggle with mechanics at the expense of written quality. At the prewriting stage, students with learning difficulties generally fail to establish a purpose for writing and lack sensitivity to the needs of their audience (Englert, 1990). They tend not to engage in effective planning and organizing; rather they generate limited ideas quickly to complete the task (Graham, Harris, MacArthur, & Schwartz, 1991). In the writing stage, students with special needs tend to focus more on the mechanical aspects, instead of basing story development on a type of writing. Thus, persistent problems with writing mechanics impede content generation (Graham et al., 1991). Research has shown that during the postwriting stage, students with learning difficulties tend to edit for mechanical errors, rather than trying to improve the story's content (Wong, Wong, & Blenkisop, 1989).

Although students with learning difficulties demonstrate problems with the stages of the writing process and the mechanics of writing, promising research results have shown that these students can benefit from carefully planned instruction. For example, in two studies involving fifth- and sixth-grade students with learning disabilities, Graham and Harris (1989a, 1989b) showed that improvement in writing quality, planning, and story grammar could be obtained when students were taught to use explicit self-monitoring strategies, such as self-directed prompts and self-instruction for composing. In an earlier study involving two 12-year-old youngsters with learning disabilities, Harris and Graham (1985) found that cognitive behavioral modification techniques promoted improvement in grammar and the total number of words produced. Fortner (1986) showed that students who were exposed to daily problem-solving activities, such as brainstorming sessions, write with more expression on a greater variety of topics. She cautions teachers that students need to be encouraged to take risks and share their thoughts, even if they might be unusual or incorrect. In another study, Kraetsch (1981) also showed that written productivity and diversity can be greatly influenced by direct instructions. When her subject was told to "write as many words and ideas as you can about the picture," he did so. When told to write more, using more adverbs and adjectives, he again responded significantly to the teacher's directions.

Survival (Adult) Writing

All people should possess several writing skills if they are to cope successfully in everyday life. For many adults, the use of written communication markedly decreases once the school years are over. Society requires some basic writing abilities, however. If students are to be independent adults, they must master these skills. Unfortunately, many of these writing skills are not taught in most school settings. Only a slight modification of the educational curriculum is required for them to be included, however.

One writing skill that is very important in modern society is the signature. Not only must students learn to write their names, but they should also understand the implications of placing their signatures at the bottom of documents. Another commonly needed skill is check writing. This requires not only a signature, but also the ability to write dates and money amounts using both symbols and number names. Correct spelling of numbers is often not included in the American educational curriculum, but it is a common requirement of daily life. Spelling some numbers causes students particular difficulty. Number words should be taught as a part of any spelling curriculum. However, for those students who do not master the correct spelling of these words, there is no reason that students could not write these numbers down somewhere in the checkbook for reference. Some junior and senior high school teachers who use various token or reinforcement systems have their students write checks to purchase free time and other privileges.

Occasionally, people must fill out various forms (job applications, loan and credit applications). Most forms require that the individual print (or type) his or her name, address, phone number, social security number, and the employer's name and address. Job applications ask the individual to list former employers, provide personal references, and name the school attended. Classroom instruction on how to fill out forms and applications is advisable, and is certainly a worthwhile expenditure of instructional time. There are even commercially available workbooks for students to use to gain accuracy and some proficiency in these tasks. For many youngsters, having a prepared sheet listing all their previous employers' names and addresses and other required information is helpful for completing various forms.

Being able to write simple letters and notes is useful. Many people with special needs have relatives and friends who live in other parts of the country and find that long-distance phone calls are too expensive. Being able to write simple notes and knowing the proper way to address envelopes are valuable skills.

Note taking is another related writing skill that is both useful and necessary. Being able to write down the time and place of various appointments is vital for success in daily life, as is taking down information over the phone, including directions to places of business or friends' homes. In school, being able to take notes during classes is essential for receiving passing grades.

Instructional Methods and Techniques

As you read, think about . . .

1. Describing how to create a writing climate in the classroom at the elementary and secondary levels.
2. Developing a plan to consult with a general education social studies teacher about a student with written communication problems.
3. Designing an IEP in written communication for an elementary or secondary student who has difficulties in mechanics, means, and the writing process.
4. Developing lessons to integrate written communication skills across a day of instruction in an elementary setting.
5. Applying interventions in chapter 9 to instruction of written communication skills.
6. Developing a life skills written communication unit for secondary-level students.
7. Describing ways to teach written communication skills using different instructional approaches and instructional arrangements.

The development of written communication skills is an interactive process involving the writing process, mechanics, and means. Teachers need a variety of interventions and strategies to promote effective written communication skills.

In this section, we focus on strategies and interventions to foster many of the skills depicted in Figure 11.2 (p. 315). Table 11.1 lists a number of different instructional interventions for written language. We also offer a summary of research-based instructional interventions for elementary- and secondary-level students. We present ideas for adapting written communication instruction in the general education setting. In Tips for Teachers, we suggest ideas for implementing a writing instructional program. Finally, in Adapting Instruction we present suggestions for general education written communication instruction.

Tips for Teachers

Designing a Written Communication Program

Handwriting

1. Plan a 15–20 minute instructional period at least three times a week to provide direct instruction in handwriting.
2. Individualize handwriting letter instruction according to each student's instructional needs.
3. Monitor formation of letters to ensure correct practice.

Spelling

1. Teach spelling every day using direct instruction.
2. Draw spelling words from students' writing and from high-frequency word lists.
3. Provide periodic maintenance checks to be sure words are retained.
4. Avoid traditional instructional approaches to spelling.
5. Limit the number of words students are expected to learn daily and weekly.
6. Present spelling words initially in lists rather than sentences.
7. Have children correct their own spelling words under teacher supervision.
8. Have students pronounce their spelling words.
9. Minimize the teaching of spelling by phonic rules (especially longer words).
10. Designate in class and as homework 60–75 minutes per week for spelling instruction and practice.
11. Use the test-study-test method.
12. Avoid writing words in the air.
13. Avoid having students write their words excessively as practice.

Writing

1. Teach cognitive and metacognitive strategies for mastery.
2. Engage students in student-mediated groups to learn from each other.
3. Provide daily time for students to write.
4. Provide systematic feedback to students to promote writing improvement.
5. Avoid having students write something numerous times as punishment for an inappropriate behavior.
6. Celebrate writing by offering various writing experiences throughout the week.
7. Have students construct and publish books.
8. Display published books and have a night when students can share their stories with their parents.

Table 11.1
Tactics for Written
Communication

Instructional target	Stage of learning	Possible tactics
Means:		

Prewriting skills
  Identify letters orally
  Gross writing movements
	Acquisition	Drill
		  Group
		  Individual
		Finger painting
		Painting with a brush
		Coloring
		Practicing writing movements
		  In sand or on sandpaper
		  With finger

Hold a stylus		Painting Coloring Scribbling with a pencil Writing on a magic slate
Draw straight and curved lines at different angles		Use geometric templates Tracing Copying
Draw freehand lines		Joining two preprinted places on paper (travel from the house to the school) Dot-to-dot exercises
Left-to-right sequence		Drawing lines from go sign to stop sign Block designs

Manuscript and cursive	Acquisition	Drill practice
		  List copying
		  Paragraph copying
		10-part instructional sequence
		Five-level cursive writing program
		Copy-cover-compare
		Trace letters
		  With fingers
		  With stylus
		  That are incomplete
		Demonstration plus permanent model
		Self-guided symbol formation strategy
		Special writing paper
		Space gauges
		Arrows on where to start letters
		Slant indicators
		Large to small lines
		Error drill

continued

Table 11.1
Continued

Instructional target	Stage of learning	Possible tactics

Manuscript and cursive *(continued)*	Advanced acquisition	Self-management
		    Self-evaluation
		    Self-instruction
		    Self-correction
		    Self-selection of daily procedure

	Proficiency	Free time Rewards Warm-up Beat your own rate game Shorten session time
Reversals	Acquisition	Instructions Demonstrations
Typing/Word processing	Acquisition	Instruction on typing programs Instruction on computer programs
	Proficiency	Computer games Rewards
Mechanics:		

Spelling	Acquisition	Flow list
		Overcorrection (positive practice)
		Parent tutoring
		Distributed practice
		Copy-cover-compare
		Rewards
		    Free time
		    Privileges
		Group contingencies
		    Behavior games
		Modeling/Imitation
		Test correction
		Error drill
		Self-correction
		Self-questioning strategy
		Dictionary skills
		Computers
		Typing
		Peer tutoring
		Multisensory
		Time delay

Composition process:		
Types of writing	Acquisition	POWER strategy DEFENDS strategy Prompts

Table 11.1
Continued

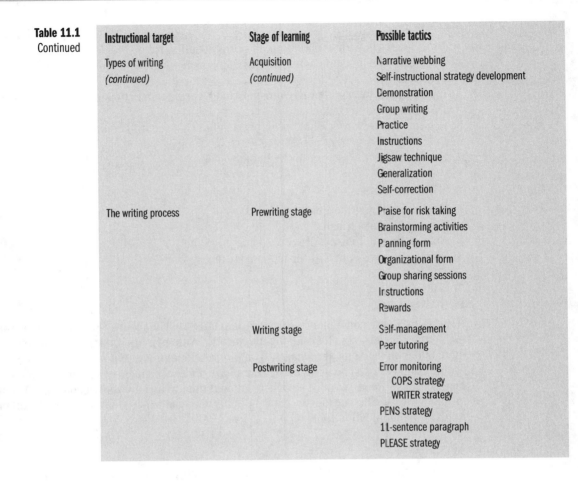

Instructional target	Stage of learning	Possible tactics
Types of writing (continued)	Acquisition (continued)	Narrative webbing
		Self-instructional strategy development
		Demonstration
		Group writing
		Practice
		Instructions
		Jigsaw technique
		Generalization
		Self-correction
The writing process	Prewriting stage	Praise for risk taking
		Brainstorming activities
		Planning form
		Organizational form
		Group sharing sessions
		Instructions
		Rewards
	Writing stage	Self-management
		Peer tutoring
	Postwriting stage	Error monitoring
		COPS strategy
		WRITER strategy
		PENS strategy
		11-sentence paragraph
		PLEASE strategy

Adapting...

Adapting Written Communication Instruction for the General Education Setting

Handwriting

1. Limit the amount students copy from the chalkboard.
2. Provide directional arrows and color-code writing paper lines to help students know correct letter formation and location of letters on lines.
3. Provide content to be copied on a sheet of paper that the student can place next to his or her writing paper for copying purposes.
4. Mark out lines on paper that students should not write on if they are to write on every other line.
5. Provide fill in the blanks for students to demonstrate knowledge, rather than asking them to write sentences.
6. Use full physical guidance intervention to teach students letter formations.
7. Have students practice handwriting every day.
8. See Focus on Technology (p. 341) for technology ideas.

Mechanics

1. Provide charts with punctuation and capitalization rules.
2. Use peer tutoring and cooperative learning as arrangements for spelling practice.
3. Individualize the number of words provided weekly to meet specific student needs.
4. Provide distributed practice.
5. Use the add-a-word spelling program and flow list record-keeping system.
6. Use direct instruction regularly to teach mechanics.
7. See Focus on Technology for technology ideas.

Writing process

1. Provide daily writing time.
2. Teach strategies to mastery.
3. Allow students to use word processing programs.
4. See Focus on Technology for technology ideas. ■

Handwriting

Handwriting is a component of written language that teachers—particularly at the elementary level—consider highly important. Although its importance seems to diminish as individuals get older, it is an instructional topic that consumes a considerable amount of school time. With a more precise sequence and more efficient instruction, students require less instructional time to acquire and become proficient in handwriting. This savings in instructional time could then be reallocated to other written communication topics.

Acquisition

Ten-Part Instructional Sequence   Towle (1978) offers a 10-part instructional sequence for handwriting instruction:

1. Copy straight lines.
2. Copy curved lines.
3. Copy letters from a model in close proximity to the student.
4. Write letters from memory (after just seeing the correct formation).
5. Copy letters from a model placed at some distance from the student (on the blackboard).
6. Write letters from memory.
7. Copy letters sequenced in words from a model in close proximity to the student.
8. Copy letters sequenced in words from a model placed at some distance from the student.
9. Copy sentences in close proximity to the student.
10. Copy sentences from a model placed at some distance from the student.

Some researchers (Towle, 1978) suggest that letters be taught in clusters; letters with common characteristics (swing up, swing over) should be taught as units. Hansen and her colleagues (Hansen, 1978), however, could not validate this system of letter presentation through their research, which found no pattern of how children acquired correct letter formation. There were no consistently troublesome letters, and no definite pattern of specific letters acquired first. All of her students learned to write, but each mastered letters in a different order.

Five-Level Cursive Writing Program   Hansen (1978) describes a five-level cursive writing program developed at the Experimental Education Unit of the University of Washington:

1. Say letter names (and print them if the child knows how).
2. Write lowercase letters.
3. Connect letters.
4. Write capital letters.
5. Write in context.

Each day while the program was in effect, the student wrote the alphabet. The student was taught and drilled daily on a maximum of five letters drawn from a pool of letters that the student could not form legibly. Once a letter was mastered (written legibly two out of three days), it was dropped from the daily list and another one was added. If a student mastered a letter without direct instruction, it was no longer included in the pool of letters from which the daily lists were drawn. Connecting letters and writing sentences were taught in similar fashion.

Teachers have used other, less comprehensive tactics to help children acquire legible handwriting. For example, students who do not use the correct slant are often given writing paper with slant indicators preprinted on the page. Students who have a tendency to write too large are given paper on which the top lines are some distance apart; as the child works down the page, the distance between the lines decreases, forcing the student to write smaller. Space gauges can be placed on a writing worksheet to help students judge the appropriate width of letters and the proper space to be left between words.

Copy-Cover-Compare Technique   When specific letters are in error, teachers often resort to the "copy-cover-compare" technique as a form of error drill. Often, an index card with problem letters correctly formed is taped to the student's desk so the student can have a referent during writing assignments. For students who have a direction problem, arrows and starting indicators can be added to the index card.

Self-Guided Symbol Formation Strategy   Graham and Madan (1981) offer a remedial technique for teaching letter formation that combines cognitive and behavioral approaches. The strategy consists of five steps:

1. Analyze a writing sample to determine consistently malformed letters.
   Table 11.2 provides suggestions of ways to analyze letter formation.
2. Select one letter for instruction that consists of modeling, tracing, and verbalization.
3. Have students trace and copy the target letter. The students should verbalize the process of making the letter, correct errors, and self-reinforce using praise or points.
4. Describe the target letter formation while the student visualizes, then writes the letter. Repeat this step until the student can write the letter five times from memory.
5. Focus on overlearning and then have students write using the target letter in context.

Table 11.2
Error Analysis for
Handwriting

Type	Definition
Letter formation	The letter is not correctly formed (an "a" is not closed, an "i" is not dotted, a "t" is not crossed).
Letter substitution	A letter or stroke is substituted for another (a capital for a lowercase letter, an "e" for an "i").
Spacing	Letters or words are either too far apart or too close together.
Spatial organization	Words or letters are not written on lines of the paper; letter size is inconsistent.
Slant	Letters are written in a variety of directions.
Illegibility	The written product is messy, with many erasures, strikeovers, and writeovers.
Speed	The product is incomplete because the student took too long to write the assignment.

Proficiency

Fluency in handwriting (or its substitutes, such as typing and word processing) is important, for without it, mastery of written language is impossible. Students need this proficiency in handwriting to succeed in spelling, dictation, note taking, and other vital areas in upper elementary, middle, or high school.

Shorten the Time   Shorten the time is a simple tactic to promote proficiency. Gradually shorten the time scheduled for completing writing assignments in class. Students could receive a reinforcer for successively shorter times for completing assignments that require writing proficiency. A go–no go contingency could be used to designate time periods and reward structures.

Warm-Up   Warm-up can be used in two ways. First, before having students do a lot of writing, ask them to take a one-minute (or 30-second) timing of the alphabet to focus on stroke formation and proficiency. Second, after recess, an assembly, or physical education, have students take a one-minute (or 30-second) timing of the alphabet. This timing tends to quiet students down, get them focused, and provide a transition from active times to quieter class time.

Beat Your Own Rate   Beat your own rate is a self-competitive tactic, in which students evaluate and graph their daily writing performance and are rewarded for increasing the number of words written in a set amount of time. Regardless of the tactic used, it is important that once letters and symbols are formed correctly, and legibility is no longer an issue, quality and quantity (proficiency) of writing become a target of instruction.

Spelling

Spelling is a well-researched topic within the written communication curriculum. A large number of tactics to improve students' spelling scores have proven effective. Some tactics modify or adapt the traditional spelling approach and are effective in increasing students' spelling scores. Many are easy to implement and make an academic subject that is often boring to students a little more interesting.

Spelling acquisition interventions are presented in Table 11.1 and several effective spelling strategies appear in Table 11.3.

Recent reviews of the spelling literature (Fulk & Stormont-Spurgin, 1995; Gordon, Vaughn, & Schumm, 1993) have revealed a number of effective interventions for

Table 11.3
Word Study
Techniques for
Learning to Spell

Fitzgerald method (Fitzgerald, 1951)

1. Look at the word carefully.
2. Say the word.
3. With eyes closed, visualize the word.
4. Cover the word, and then write it.
5. Check the spelling.
6. If the word is misspelled, repeat steps 1–5.

Horn method 1 (Horn, 1919)

1. Look at the word, and say it to yourself.
2. Close your eyes, and visualize the word.
3. Check to see if you were right. (If not, begin at step 1.)
4. Cover the word, and write it.
5. Check to see if you were right. (If not, begin at step 1.)
6. Repeat steps 4 and 5 two more times.

Horn method 2 (Horn, 1954)

1. Pronounce each word carefully.
2. Look carefully at each part of the word as you pronounce it.
3. Say the letters in sequence.
4. Attempt to recall how the word looks, then spell the word.
5. Check this attempt to recall.
6. Write the word.
7. Check this spelling attempt.
8. Repeat the above steps if necessary.

Visual-vocal method (Westerman, 1971)

1. Say word.
2. Spell word orally.
3. Say word again.
4. Spell word from memory four times correctly.

Gilstrap method (Gilstrap, 1962)

1. Look at the word, and say it softly. If it has more than one part, say it again, part by part, looking at each part as you say it.
2. Look at the letters, and say each one. If the word has more than one part, say the letters part by part.
3. Write the word without looking at the book.

Fernald method modified

1. Make a model of the word with a crayon, grease pencil, or magic marker, saying the word as you write it.
2. Check the accuracy of the model.
3. Trace over the model with your index finger, saying the word at the same time.
4. Repeat step 3 five times.
5. Copy the word three times correctly.
6. Copy the word three times from memory correctly.

Cover-and-write method

1. Look at word. Say it.
2. Write word two times.
3. Cover and write one time.
4. Check work.
5. Write word two times.
6. Cover and write one time.
7. Check work.
8. Write word three times.
9. Cover and write one time.
10. Check work.

Wong's self-questioning strategy (Wong, 1986)

1. Do I know this word?
2. How many syllables do I hear in this word? (Write down the number.)
3. I'll spell out the word.
4. Do I have the right number of syllables down?
5. If yes, is there any part of the word I'm not sure how to spell? I'll underline that part and try spelling the word again.
6. Now, does it look right to me? If it does, I'll leave it alone. If it still doesn't look right, I'll underline the part I'm not sure how to spell and try again. (If the word I spelled does not have the right number of syllables, let me hear the word in my head again, and find the missing syllable. Then I'll go back to steps 5 and 6.)
7. When I finish spelling, I tell myself I'm a good worker. I've tried hard at spelling.

Source: From "Spelling Research and Practice: A Unified Approach," by S. Graham and L. Miller, 1979, *Focus on Exceptional Children*, *12*(2), p. 11. Copyright 1979 by Love Publishing Co. Reprinted with permission. Also from "A Cognitive Approach to Teaching Spelling," by B. Y. L. Wong, 1986, *Exceptional Children*, *53*(2), p. 172. Copyright 1986 by the Council for Exceptional Children. Reprinted with permission.

spelling instruction. Because we are mostly concerned with the acquisition stage for spelling, the interventions we discuss focus on this stage of learning.

Acquisition

There are many types of effective interventions that can be used to teach students how to spell accurately. The interventions are categorized as instructional, computer-based, student-mediated, and multisensory.

Instructional Interventions
1. Modeling with imitation
2. Test correction
3. Positive practice with reinforcement
4. Constant time delay
5. Shortened list length
6. Distributed practice over a week

Computer Interventions
1. Constant time delay
2. Drill and practice
3. Individualized spelling lists
4. Error imitation and modeling of correct responses

Student-Mediated Instructional Arrangements
1. Peer tutoring
2. Self-monitoring of attention and production

Multisensory Interventions
1. Write and say
2. Tracing letter tiles
3. Write, close eyes and visualize word, write

Knowing about tactics proven influential in improving students' spelling is important, but knowing about those tactics proven ineffective is equally important. There are two instructional techniques that research has shown to be of no instructional value. In the first one, vocabulary is presented to students in sentences or paragraphs, with the supposition that if students understand a word in context, they can learn its spelling more easily. That has not been the case. In the second technique, students are made to write their spelling words in the air, with the supposition that they would be helped to visualize the words as they traced letters and thus would be able to spell the words correctly. This also has not been the case. On the other hand, the tactics listed in Table 11.1 are verified through research and clinical practice. When seeking tactics to improve spelling performance, teachers should use these techniques.

Types of Writing

Research on types of writing involving students with learning and behavioral difficulties has centered on expository and narrative styles. We now provide several interventions and strategies as examples of ways to promote effective writing development.

Expository Writing

POWER Strategy   The POWER strategy is a mnemonic that students can learn (see chapter 5 for procedures to teach cognitive strategies) to assist them in all three stages of writing (Englert et al., 1991). The acronym stands for **P**lan, **O**rganize, **W**rite, **E**dit, and **R**evise. In the planning step, students identify their audience, purpose for writing, and supportive background information. The organizing step involves structuring the information obtained in the planning step by categories in preparation for the writing step. Editing involves monitoring the content so changes can be made in the revising step. As shown in Table 11.4, specific strategies and self-talk occur at each step of this strategy. Once students can state the steps of POWER, they are ready to move into story writing.

DEFENDS Strategy   The DEFENDS strategy was designed to promote written expression skills (Ellis & Lenz, 1987). The instructional procedures discussed in chapter 5 under the strategic instructional approach were used to field-test this strategy. The acronym stands for **D**ecide on your exact position (write down your position), **E**xamine the reasons for your position (write down two reasons and three details for each reason), **F**orm a list of points that explain each reason (sequence the reasons and details), **E**xpose your position in the first sentence, **N**ote each reason and

Table 11.4
Strategies
and Self-Talk

Writing stages	Strategies	Self-talk
Prewriting		
Plan	Identify audience.	Who am I writing for?
	Identify purpose.	Why am I writing this?
	Select a topic.	What is the main idea I'm interested in?
	Generate ideas.	What ideas do I have about the topic?
Organize	Identify type of writing.	What type of writing am I doing?
	Identify how ideas are related.	What are the similarities and differences of my ideas?
	Categorize the ideas.	What categories do I have?
	Identify text structure.	How will I organize my ideas into a framework?
	Develop an organizational framework.	
Writing	Activate organizational framework.	Am I using my framework?
	Check writing against framework.	Am I using my headings and categories on my framework?
	Think about mechanics but don't dwell on them.	Am I using my spelling, capitalization, and punctuation skills? Remember to check in revising.
Postwriting	Compare my paper to my framework.	Does the content match my framework?
	Use error monitoring strategies.	Am I using error monitoring strategies?
	Check for quality.	Does the paper make sense?
		Will my audience understand what I'm trying to say?
		Is the length appropriate?

Source: Adapted from "Making Strategies Work," by D. D. Stevens and C. S. Englert 1993, *Teaching Exceptional Children, 26*(1). p. 36.

supporting points, **D**rive home the position in your last sentence (use different wording from opening sentence), and **S**earch for errors and correct. Use the COPS and WRITER strategies listed below to supplement the DEFENDS strategy.

Narrative Writing

Prompts   Prompts are very easy to implement as a strategy to stimulate student thinking about a writing topic (Graves et al., 1994). Prompts to begin stories and prompts to end stories can be written on sentence strips and strategically located on paper. The prompts signal whether the students should begin or end their story. For example, sentence strips could contain the following prompts:

> Once upon a time; this is a story about; many years ago; from that day forward, the children got along well with each other.

Students could discuss whether the prompts would begin or end a story and brainstorm a story to go with the prompts.

Narrative Webbing   Webbing can be used to help students plan and organize ideas for story writing (Zipprich, 1995). Show students a picture of interest, followed by the display of a completed web (see Figure 11.5 for an example of a blank web). Next,

Figure 11.5
Writing web

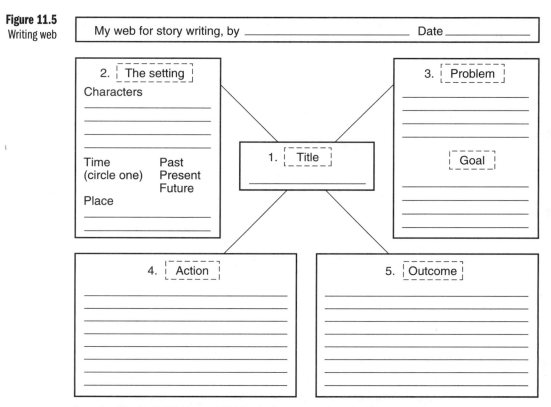

Source: From "Teaching Web Making as a Guided Planning Tool to Improve Student Narrative Writing," by M. A. Zipprich, 1995, *Remedial and Special Education, 16*(1), p. 6. Copyright 1995 by PRO-ED. Reprinted by permission.

display a new picture. Have students brainstorm ideas to complete the content for each element of the story on a blank web. Then, ask students to write a story based on the completed web's information. This intervention may facilitate planning and organization of story elements; however, students will still require instruction in mechanics (e.g., spelling, capitalization, punctuation) and story development.

Self-Instructional Strategy Development (SISD)   This strategy is based on the cognitive behavioral modification model, the learning strategies model, verbal self-regulation, and self-control (Graham & Harris, 1987). SISD instruction focuses on teaching students story elements through a mnemonic and questions:

Mnemonic: W(Who)=W(When)=W(Where); What=2; How=2

Questions: Who is the main character? When does the story take place? Where does the story take place? What does the main character do? What happens when he or she tries to do it? How does the main character feel? How does the story end?

The mnemonic and questions are taught using steps similar to those in the Learning Strategies Curriculum (discussed in chapter 5).

The Writing Process

As noted above, the process of writing involves three stages (prewriting, writing, and postwriting) that consist of specific cognitive and metacognitive activities to help guide the development of the written product. The writing process is best taught to youngsters using a combination of the instructional approaches described in chapter 5. Here are interventions and strategies that can be used to promote the stages of the writing process. When instruction in the writing stages is paired with instruction in mechanical skills and handwriting, students receive a well-rounded curriculum that should foster effective written communication abilities.

Prewriting Stage

Brainstorming   Have students brainstorm three types of words: action words, description words, and adverbs (Harris & Graham, 1985). This brainstorming will help students generate ideas before writing and demonstrate current knowledge about a topic. Then, have students categorize their information for further writing development.

Planning Form   To assist students in the planning substage of prewriting, provide a form containing boxes for information about each component (Englert, Raphael, & Anderson, 1989). For example, boxes could be designated for (1) the topic, (2) a list of ideas, (3) the types of writing, (4) the audience, and (5) the purpose of writing. This framework could be used for expository and narrative writing.

Organizational Form   Similar to the planning form, the organizational form can be used during the prewriting stage to help students organize their ideas into a framework from which they can write (Englert et. al., 1989). This form should contain space designated for each component of writing. For instance, in narrative writing, a form would contain the story elements. In compare and contrast expository writing, the form might contain boxes for the introduction, categories in which comparing and contrasting will occur, comparisons, contrasts, and an ending. Students could use the information generated during brainstorming and planning to complete the organizational form.

Writing Stage

Self-Management Techniques   Self-management techniques (e.g., self-reinforcement, self-regulation) were described in chapter 7. Those strategies are appropriate for students to implement during the writing task. Students could be given specific types of words (e.g., adjective, adverbs) to include in their stories, a length to achieve in their writing, and prompts to use their organizational form. Teachers should circulate among students during writing to offer assistance, guidance, and reinforcement as needed.

Postwriting Stage

COPS Strategy   COPS is a mnemonic that can be used during the error monitoring stage (Schumaker, Nolan, & Deshler, 1985). It can be paired with the DEFENDS strategy described above and the WRITER and PENS strategies described below. The steps for COPS are listed below; the instructional procedures from the Learning Strategies Curriculum (see chapter 5) can be used to teach the strategy.

The Most Common Mistakes in Writing (COPS)
Capitalization
   Have I capitalized the first word of the sentence?
   Have I capitalized all the proper nouns in the sentence?
Overall Appearance
   Is my handwriting easy to read, on the line, and not crowded?
   Are my words and sentences spaced correctly?
   Did I indent and write close to the margin?
Punctuation
   Did I use the right punctuation mark at the end of each sentence?
   Did I use commas and semicolons where necessary?
Spelling
   Does it look right?
   Can I sound it out?
   Have I used the dictionary?

WRITER Strategy   The WRITER strategy is a mnemonic that can be used with the DEFENDS, COPS, and PENS strategies (Schumaker et al., 1985). The steps for the WRITER strategy can be taught as a learning strategy and include the following:

Steps for Error Monitoring (WRITER)
1. Write on every other line using "PENS."
2. Read the paper for meaning.
3. Interrogate yourself using the "COPS" questions.
4. Execute a final copy.
5. Reread your paper.

Sentence Writing Acquisition and Generalization

PENS Strategy The strategy, referred to as PENS (**P**ick a formula, **E**xplore words to fit the formula, **N**ote the words, **S**ubject-verb identification), provides structure to the mechanics of writing (Schumaker & Sheldon, 1985). A prerequisite for entering the program is the ability to identify nouns, verbs, subjects, and predicates. The students are taught formulas for sentence constructions, such as those shown here:

Simple sentences:		Compound sentences:
S	V	I; cI
SS	V	
S	VV	I; I
SS	VV	

After considerable instruction with student workbooks that provide practice and drill to encourage mastery of subskills through criterion performance tests, students are taught a strategy to form their own sentences. The cognitive strategy, called PENS, is then taught to the students. They are encouraged to use this strategy in all situations where it can be applied, including in history, social studies, and English. Students are allowed to use cue cards to help them remember the strategy in as many classroom settings as possible.

1. Pick a formula.
2. Explore words to fit the formula.
3. Note the words.
4. Subject-verb identification
   a. Look for the action or state-of-being word(s) to find the verb.
   b. Ask the "who" or "what" question to find the subject.

Paragraph Writing Acquisition

Eleven-Sentence Paragraph Strategy Whether they are given a topic or are using one of their own, students begin their paragraphs with an opening topical sentence (Ray, 1986). Within the body of the paragraph, they provide three reasons that justify the opening statement. For each reason, they give an example and include an additional sentence that supports the example. The paragraph concludes with a summary statement or a rephrasing of the opening topic sentence. This paragraph-writing technique is particularly helpful to students who have difficulty organizing their thoughts or presenting their ideas logically. For example, a sample paragraph written using this technique appears in Figure 11.6. Before this child learned to write an 11-sentence paragraph, her written work was disorganized and incomplete. The steps of the 11-sentence paragraph strategy appear in Table 11.5.

PLEASE Strategy The PLEASE strategy is a metacognitive strategy designed to address problems related to prewriting planning, writing, and paragraph revision, and to facilitate problem solving (Welch, 1992). The strategy has a repertoire of actions cued by the acronym PLEASE; it is intended to promote independent writing. Following are the steps that can be taught using direct instruction procedures:

1. Pick a topic, audience, and type of writing.
2. List your ideas about the topic.
3. Evaluate your list to see if it is complete.

Figure 11.6
A student's writing
sample using the
11-sentence
paragraph
technique

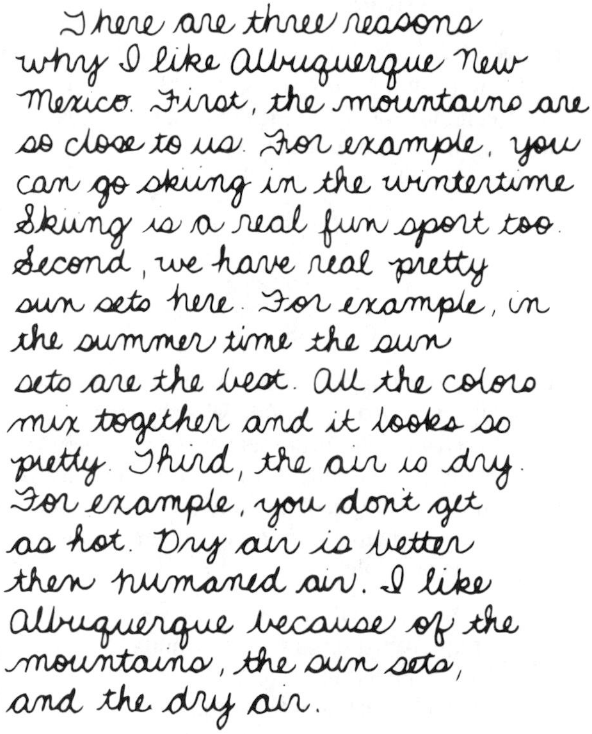

There are three reasons why I like Albuquerque New Mexico. First, the mountains are so close to us. For example, you can go skiing in the wintertime. Skiing is a real fun sport too. Second, we have real pretty sun sets here. For example, in the summer time the sun sets are the best. All the colors mix together and it looks so pretty. Third, the air is dry. For example, you don't get as hot. Dry air is better then humaned air. I like Albuquerque because of the mountains, the sun sets, and the dry air.

4. Activate the paragraph with a topic sentence.
5. **Supply** supporting sentences or details. Add expansion and clarifying sentences.
6. **End** with a concluding sentence by rephrasing the topic sentence and **Evaluate** using the COPS strategy.

Technology

Instructional and assistive technology (see chapter 5 for a more thorough discussion of instructional and assistive technology) can play an important role in written communication curriculum and instruction. Although there is limited research on how well technology can improve the written communication skills of students with special needs, emerging studies show the potential benefits of technology paired with written language instruction (MacArthur, Schwartz, & Graham, 1991).

Instructional technology, such as word processing and instructional software programs, can be used to promote written communication skills. Assistive technology devices can help students with learning and behavior problems compensate for their disability and access the written communication curriculum. With the pervasive role of computers in classrooms or school labs, students with disabilities (e.g., fine motor) that impede working with standard keyboards must have adaptive devices so that they too can access word processing or other software programs. Some students may require modifications to pencils, others may need spelling resources that have verbal and written feedback; these specific needs can be addressed with assistive technology devices.

Table 11.5
The Eleven-Sentence Paragraph

Sentence	Wording and punctuation	Example
1. Write topic sentence.	There are three reasons that . . .	There are three reasons that dance is a challenging art.
2. State the first of the three reasons. (Be sure to include comma in structure.)	First, . . .	First, dance is physically demanding.
3. Give an example.	For example, . . .	For example, it requires a great deal of physical coordination and endurance.
4. Support the example.		The dances taught require intense balancing, lifting, bending, and stretching of the body.
5. State the second reason.	Second, . . .	Second, dance is mentally stimulating.
6. Give an example.	For example, . . .	For example, it tests the dancer's ability to recall movement quickly.
7. Support the example.		It is important to have total concentration to accomplish the task well.
8. State the third reason.	Third, . . .	Third, dance is emotionally challenging.
9. Give an example.	For example, . . .	For example, the perseverance necessary is tiring.
10. Support the example.		The repetition required to achieve perfection is phenomenal.
11. Conclude with a summary, or restate topic sentence.		Dance is truly a mentally, physically, and emotionally demanding art.

Source: From *The Eleven-Sentence Paragraph*, by R. Ray, 1986, unpublished paper, University of New Mexico at Albuquerque, Department of Special Education. Reprinted by permission.

Our discussion of technology is divided into three sections: means, mechanics (focusing on spelling), and the writing process. We describe applications of technology for each of these areas and highlight examples of software currently endorsed by experts in this field. We present suggestions for infusing instructional and assistive technology into written communication programs in Focus on Technology.

 on Technology

Technology that Aids Students in Writing

● **Assistive technology**

1. **Handwriting/Keyboarding**
   Use pencil grips to provide more space and texture for student's grasp.
   Provide adapted keyboards (such as keyboard guards), touch screens, and different input devices to accommodate student needs.

2. **Spelling**
   Provide tape recorders for spelling practice.
   Use handheld electronic spell checkers.
   Have speech synthesis capabilities for verbal feedback.

3. **Writing process**
   Use word processing programs designed for children.
   Provide word prediction and grammar check software.

- **Instructional technology**
  1. **Keyboarding**
     Teaching typing skills systematically and regularly.
     Expect students to be able to use correct fingering even while not looking at the keyboard.
     Have students achieve proficiency equal to their handwriting rate.
     Avoid games that may foster incorrect form.

  2. **Spelling**
     Select spelling programs that allow teachers to input their spelling lists.
     Use software that provides sufficient practice opportunities.
     Select software that contains an evaluation system for monitoring student progress.
     Select software that allows periodic reviews of previously mastered words.
     Use software that allows word lists to be individualized.

  3. **Writing process**
     Infuse software into different instructional arrangements (e.g., peer tutoring, cooperative learning, learning center, individualized).
     Teach writing strategies concurrent with word processing programs. ●

Means

Students should receive word processing and typing instruction for many different reasons. Using this means of communication is a life skill. Computers are pervasive in American society. Word processing can facilitate writing production. Computer-generated papers may be the most legible writing some students can produce. Word processing enables students to produce neat, legible work, to correct errors, and to eliminate messy erasures, smudge marks, and torn papers commonly found in handwritten papers (Behrmann, 1994; MacArthur, 1988). Students should receive systematic instruction in using a word processing program, preferably, one designed for children. MacArthur and Schneiderman (1986) found that students with learning difficulties experienced problems with the function of the return key and ways to save and load files. Thus, students should be taught the basic features of word processing programs (e.g., menus, saving, printing) before using them to create stories.

Naturally, an inability to type is an impediment to using word processing programs successfully and can frustrate students (MacArthur, 1988). Proficiency with knowing the functions of keys (e.g., return, shift), using the space bar, and locating letters and numbers are skills students need to learn. In fact, typing proficiency was found to correlate highly with story quality (e.g., coherence, organization) when stories were written using a word processing program (MacArthur & Graham, 1987). Recommendations for word processing and typing instruction appear in Focus on Technology (MacArthur, 1988).

Several word processing and typing programs exist for student use. We do not offer an exhaustive list, nor do we endorse software programs; however, we include examples of programs so that readers can examine their merits. The word processing programs include Appleworks (Claris), Bank Street Writer (Brøderbund), Children's Writing and Publishing Center (The Learning Company), The Palmer Manuscript Method (Wings for learning/Sunburst Communications), and Typing Tutor 5 (Simon & Schuster).

Mechanics: Spelling

Both assistive and instructional technology can be used to promote spelling accuracy. Edyburn (1992) defines spelling correction technology as "a method, device, or resource that enables a writer to produce the correct spelling of a word or verify the correctness of his or her attempt at spelling a word correctly" (p. 3). Three categories of spelling correction technologies can be identified: human (e.g., proofreader, secretary), print (e.g., dictionaries [questionable value for poor spellers], thesaurus, word bank), and electronic (e.g., handheld spelling aids, word processing spell checker, word prediction programs). The "human" category is often applied in classrooms through student- and teacher-mediated instructional arrangements (e.g., peer tutoring). Peers can proofread each other's work and identify spelling errors to be corrected. Also, teachers can assist students in identifying spelling errors during a conferencing period.

Print technology is most commonly used in classrooms, yet may produce questionable results. Telling a poor speller to "look the word up in the dictionary" may be unproductive. On the other hand, personal word banks may be beneficial in helping students locate frequently used and misspelled words.

Electronic technologies are gaining popularity. Certainly, the spell check feature of most word processing programs is widely available and is helpful in correcting misspellings. However, certain limitations may be problematic for poor spellers. First, homonyms and words that are spelled correctly but misused may go undetected as spelling errors. Second, word processing spell check programs may fail to offer a correct spelling for a word in text that greatly misses the mark in spelling accuracy. Third, poor spellers may be unable to detect the correct spelling of their chosen word from a long list of possibilities (MacArthur & DeLaPaz, 1993; Raskind, 1993).

Handheld spellers are another type of electronic speller. The advantage of handheld spellers is their size and portability. Some handheld spellers (e.g., Speaking Dictionary/Thesaurus [Franklin Learning Resources]) provide word identification through speech synthesis. While this may help a student select the correct spelling of a word, the quality of speech synthesis influences the degree to which individuals can decipher electronically pronounced words.

Research on the efficacy of spell check technologies is needed. Clearly, there is value in using spell check technologies to compensate for poor spelling abilities. However, the issue remains whether or not spell check technologies improve spelling skills. Teachers should continue to provide direct instruction in spelling and use the categories of technologies described here to foster spelling accuracy.

Instructional spelling software is available to assist youngsters in practicing spelling skills. Magic Spells (Learning Company), Spellevator (MECC), and Spell It Plus! (Davidson & Associates) are examples of spelling programs that allow teachers to input students' spelling words. Activities feature games, tutorials, and drills.

The Writing Process

Word processing programs have greatly liberated students from tedious paper-and-pencil writing, which makes editing and revising difficult. Word processing and computers make students' written work accessible for teacher review; the teacher need only look at the screen (MacArthur, 1988). As students produce their work on computers, teachers can easily view the development of the written work and provide assistance (e.g., asking questions, prompting the use of a strategy or form).

Word processing programs are not the only type of software that can assist students during the writing process. Grammar software is available that can identify faulty sentence structure. This could be a valuable tool for many students who struggle to develop adequate sentences to convey their thoughts. Word prediction programs may be beneficial in story development. These programs reduce the number of keystrokes necessary to type a story. Students can enter in a designated menu a series of letters until the program predicts the correct word to insert into the student's story, based on existing grammar. Although word processing programs by themselves do not increase writing quality, they do facilitate the writing process when paired with strategic instruction in all three stages of writing (MacArthur & Graham, 1987).

Summary

Being able to write, both to express oneself and to store information, is a highly important skill. The ability to write well requires the knowledge of highly structured rules about the mechanics of our written language. For example, people need to know how to use and apply the rules of grammar, punctuation, and spelling. They need to know how to use those rules to form compositions, as well as to select and use a means so that others can understand the communication.

Writing is a necessary skill at school, home, and later in adult life. Facility with this skill can also contribute to an individual's success in the workplace. Everyone needs to develop some level of competence in communicating through the written mode, even if the skills developed are as simple as being able to write and sign checks, fill out job applications, take messages, or write reminders to oneself. The degree of mastery of this curriculum area can relate directly to the degree of independence in adult life.

The writing process was presented in this chapter with an emphasis on types of writing (expository, narrative) and the three stages of writing: prewriting, writing, and postwriting. Research shows that students with special needs typically demonstrate a range of difficulties in written communication means, mechanics, and composition. However, results also show that many students with learning and behavior problems respond favorably to direct instruction, strategic learning, and opportunities to develop writing literacy.

Numerous instructional interventions and strategies are available to teach students with learning and behavior problems effective written communication skills in the area of writing means, writing mechanics, and the composition process. In particular, interventions and strategies that are selected based on the student's stage of learning (acquisition, proficiency, maintenance, generalization) are most promising in fostering written communication skills.

Finally, technology holds great promise as a way of helping students with special needs gain greater access to the writing curriculum. Assistive and instructional technology devices can be used to help students develop their writing skills and move beyond some of their written communication barriers.

Study and Discussion Questions

1. Describe the nature of written communication instruction.
2. Identify and explain components of written communication instruction.

3. Provide instructional examples for each component of written communication.
4. Describe the written communication skills needed for successful adult adjustment.
5. Maggie, age 10, is a poor speller. She receives poor grades on her weekly spelling test in the general education classroom, and her written assignments are replete with misspelled words. Develop a lesson plan aimed at remediating Maggie's spelling deficits. Justify your intervention selection.
6. List targets for survival (adult) writing. Suggest interventions that you would use to teach these skills.
7. Discuss the benefits of teaching students to monitor for errors in their written assignments.

References and Suggested Readings

Englert, C. S., Raphael, T. E., Anderson, L. M., Gregg. S. L., & Anthony, H. M. (1989). Exposition: Reading, writing, and the metacognitive knowledge of learning disabled students. *Learning Disabilities Research, 5,* 5–24.

Espin, C., & Sindelar, P. (1988). Auditory feedback and writing: Learning disabled and non-disabled students. *Exceptional Children, 55,* 45–51.

Graham, S., Schwartz, S. S., & MacArthur, C. A. (1993). Knowledge of writing and the composing process, attitude toward writing, and self-efficacy for students with and without learning disabilities. *Journal of Learning Disabilities, 26*(4), 237–249.

Graves, A., Montague, M., & Wong, Y. (1990). The effects of procedural facilitation on the story composition of learning disabled students. *Learning Disabilities Research, 5,* 88–93.

Laughton, J., & Morris, N. (1989). Story grammar knowledge of learning disabled students. *Learning Disabilities Research, 4,* 87–95.

Montague, M., Maddux, C., & Dereshiwsky, M. (1988). Story grammar and comprehension and production of narrative prose by students with learning disabilities. *Journal of Learning Disabilities, 23,* 190–197.

Newcomer, P. L., Barenbaum, E. M., & Nodine, B. F. (1988). Comparison of the story production of LD, normal-achieving, and low-achieving children under two modes of production. *Learning Disability Quarterly, 11,* 82–96.

Nature of Written Communication
Issues in Written Communication Instruction

Barenbaum, E. M., Newcomer, P. L., & Nodine, B. F.(1987). Children's ability to write stories as a function of variation in task, age, and developmental level. *Learning Disability Quarterly, 10,* 175–188.

Graham, S., & Harris, K. R. (1988a). Instructional recommendations for teaching writing to exceptional students. *Exceptional Children, 54,* 506–512.

Graham, S., & Harris, K. R. (1988b). Research and instruction in written language: Introduction to the special issue. *Exceptional Children, 54,* 495–496.

Harris, K. R., & Graham, S. (1985). Improving learning disabled students' composition skills: Self-control strategy training. *Learning Disability Quarterly, 8,* 27–36.

Newcomer, P. L., Barenbaum, E. M., & Nodine, B. F. (1988). Comparison of the story production of LD, normal-achieving, and low-achieving children under two modes of production. *Learning Disability Quarterly, 11,* 82–96.

Scardamalia, M., & Bereiter, C. (1986). Written composition. In M. Wittrock (Ed.), *Handbook of research on teaching* (3rd ed., pp. 778–803). New York: Macmillan.

Wong, B., Wong, R., & Blenkinsop, J. (1989). Cognitive and metacognitive aspects of learning disabled adolescents' composing problems. *Learning Disability Quarterly, 12,* 300–323.

Curricular and Instructional Design Features

Graham, S. (1982). Composition research and practice: A unified approach. *Focus on Exceptional Children, 14,* 1–16.

Graham, S., & Harris, K. R. (1988a). Instructional recommendations for teaching writing to exceptional students. *Exceptional Children, 54,* 506–512.

Graham, S., & Harris, K. R. (1988b). Research and instruction in written language: Introduction to the special issue. *Exceptional Children, 54,* 495–496.

Harris, K. R., & Graham, S. (1985). Improving learning disabled students' composition skills: Self-control strategy training. *Learning Disability Quarterly, 8,* 27–36.

Scardamalia, M., & Bereiter, C. (1986). Written composition. In M. Wittrock (Ed.), *Handbook of research on teaching* (3rd ed., pp. 778–803). New York: MacMillan.

Skills for Instruction and Instructional Methods and Techniques
Means of Written Communication

Davidson, H. P. (1934). A study of reversals in young children. *Journal of Genetic Psychology, 45,* 452–465.

Davidson, H. P. (1935). A study of confusing letters b, d, p, and q. *Journal of Genetic Psychology, 47,* 458–468.

Graham, S., & Madan. A. (1981). Teaching letter formation. *Academic Therapy, 16*(4), 389–396.

Hansen, C. L. (1978). Writing skills. In N. G. Haring, T. C. Lovitt, M. D. Eaton, & C. L. Hansen, *The fourth R: Research in the classroom.* Columbus, OH: Merrill.

Hasazi, J. E., & Hasazi, S. E. (1972). Effects of teacher attention on digit-reversal behavior in an elementary school child. *Journal of Applied Behavior Analysis, 5,* 157–162.

Hildreth, G. (1934). Reversals in reading and writing. *Journal of Educational Psychology, 25,* 1–20.

Kosiewicz, M. M., Hallanan, D. P., Lloyd, J., & Graves, A. W. (1982). Effects of self-instruction and self-correction procedures on handwritten performance. *Learning Disability Quarterly, 5,* 71–78.

Smith, D. D., & Lovitt, T. C. (1973). The educational diagnosis and remediation of written b and d reversal problems: A case study. *Journal of Learning Disabilities, 6,* 356–363.

Strauss, A. A., & Lehtinen, L. E. (1951). *Psychopathology and education of the brain injured child.* New York: Grune and Stratton.

Stromer, R. (1977). Remediating academic deficiencies in learning disabled children. *Exceptional Children, 43,* 432–440.

Towle, M. (1978). Assessment and remediation of handwriting deficits for children with learning disabilities. *Journal of Learning Disabilities, 11,* 370–377.

Mechanics of Written Communication

Broden, M., Beasley, A., & Hall, R. V. (1978). In-class spelling performance: Effects of home tutoring by a parent. *Behavior Modification, 2,* 511–530.

Bryant, N. D., Drabin, I. R., & Gettinger, M. (1981). Effects of varying unit size on spelling achievement in learning disabled children. *Journal of Learning Disabilities, 14*(4), 200–202.

Dangel, H. L. (1989). The use of student directed spelling strategies. *Academic Therapy, 25*(1), 43–51.

Dixon, R. C. (1991). The application of sameness analysis to spelling. *Journal of Learning Disabilities, 24,* 285–291.

Dixon, R. C., & Engelmann, S. (1980). *Corrective spelling through morphographs.* Chicago: Science Research Associates.

Dixon, R. C., Engelmann, S., Meier, M., Steely, D., & Wells, T. (1989). *Spelling mastery.* Chicago: Science Research Associates.

Fernald, G. M. (1943). *Remedial techniques in basic school subjects.* New York: McGraw-Hill.

Fitzgerald, J. (1951). *The teaching of spelling.* Milwaukee: Bruce.

Forest, R. G., & Sitton, R. A. (1989). *Instant spelling words for writing.* North Billerica, MA: Curriculum Associates.

Foster, K., & Torgensen, J. K. (1983). The effects of directed study on the spelling performance of two subgroups of learning disabled students. *Learning Disability Quarterly, 6,* 253–257.

Fulk, B. M., & Stormont-Spurgin, M. (1995). Spelling interventions for students with disabilities: A review. *Journal of Special Education, 28*(4), 488–513.

Gerber, M. M. (1984). Investigations of orthographic problem solving ability in learning disabled and normally achieving students. *Learning Disability Quarterly, 7,* 157–164.

Gerber, M. M. (1987). Information processing approaches to studying spelling deficiencies. *Journal of Learning Disabilities, 20*(1), 34–41.

Gerber, M. M., & Hall, R. J. (1987). Information processing approaches to studying spelling deficiencies. *Journal of Learning Disabilities, 20,* 34–42.

Gettinger, M., Bryant, N. D., & Fayne, H. R. (1982). Designing spelling instruction for learning disabled children: An emphasis on unit size, distributed practice, and training for transfer. *Journal of Special Education, 16*(4), 440–446.

Gilstrap, R. (1962). Development of independent spelling skills in the intermediate grades. *Elementary English, 39,* 481–483.

Gordon, J., Vaughn, S., & Schumm, J. S. (1993). Spelling interventions: A review of literature and implications for instruction for students with learning disabilities. *Learning Disabilities Practice, 8*(3), 175–181.

Graham, S., & Miller, L. (1979). Spelling research and practice: A unified approach. *Focus on Exceptional Children, 12*(2), 1–16.

Graham, S., & Miller, L. (1980). Handwriting research and practice: A unified approach. *Focus on Exceptional Children, 13*(2), 1–16.

Hansen, C. L. (1978). Writing skills. In N. G. Haring, T. C. Lovitt, M. D. Eaton, & C. L. Hansen, *The fourth R: Research in the classroom.* Columbus, OH: Merrill.

Horn, E. (1919). Principles of methods in teaching spelling as derived from scientific investigation. In *Eighteenth Yearbook, National Society for the Study of Education.* Bloomington, IN: Public School Publishing.

Horn, E. (1954). *Teaching spelling.* Washington, DC: American Educational Research Association.

Kauffman, J. M., Hallahan, D. P., Hass, K., Brame, T., & Boren, R. (1978). Imitating children's errors to improve their spelling performance. *Journal of Learning Disabilities, 11,* 217–222.

Kearney, C. A., & Drabman, R. S. (1993). The write-say method for improving spelling accuracy in children with learning disabilities. *Journal of Learning Disabilities, 26*(1), 52–56.

Lovitt, T. C. (1995). *Tactics for teaching* (2nd ed.). Columbus, OH: Merrill.

Mandoli, M., Mandoli, P., & McLaughlin, T. F. (1982). The effects of same-age peer tutoring on the spelling performances of a mainstreamed elementary LD student. *Learning Disability Quarterly, 5,* 185–189.

McNaughton, D., Hughes, C. A., & Clark, K. (1994). Spelling instruction for students with learning disabilities: Implications for research and practice. *Learning Disability Quarterly, 17,* 169–185.

Nulman, J. H., & Gerber, M. M. (1984). Improving spelling performance by imitating a child's errors. *Journal of Learning Disabilities, 17,* 328–334.

Ollendick, T. H., Matson, J. L., Esveldt-Dawson, K., & Shapiro, E. S. (1980). Increasing spelling achievement: An analysis of treatment procedures utilizing alternating treatments design. *Journal of Applied Behavior Analysis, 13,* 645–654.

Pratt-Struthers, J., Struthers, T. B., & Williams, R. L. (1983). The effects of the Add-A-Word spelling program on spelling accuracy during creative writing. *Education and Treatment of Children, 6,* 277–283.

Rieth, H., Axelrod, S., Anderson, R., Hathaway, R., Wood, K., & Fitzgerald, C. (1974). Influence of distributed practice and daily testing on weekly spelling tests. *Journal of Educational Research, 68,* 73–77.

Stevens, K. B., & Schuster, J. W. (1987). Effects of a constant time delay procedure on the written spelling performance of a learning disabled student. *Learning Disability Quarterly, 10,* 9–16.

Vallecorsa, A. L., Zigmond, N., & Henderson, L. M. (1985). Spelling instruction in special education classrooms: A survey of practices. *Exceptional Children, 52*(1), 19–24.

Westerman, G. S. (1971). *Spelling & writing.* San Rafael, CA: Dimensions.

Wong, B. Y. L. (1986). A cognitive approach to teaching spelling. *Exceptional Children, 53*(2), 169–173.

Composition Process

Bos, C. S. (1988). Academic interventions for learning disabilities. In K. A. Kavale (Ed.), *Learning disabilities: State of the art and practice* (pp. 98–122). Boston: Little, Brown; College-Hill.

Ellis, E. S., & Lenz, B. K. (1987). A component analysis of effective learning strategies for LD students. *Learning Disabilities Focus, 2*(2), 94–107.

Englert, C. S. (1990). Unraveling the mysteries of writing through strategy instruction. In T. E. Scruggs & B. Y. L. Wong (Eds.), *Intervention research in learning disabilities* (pp. 186–223). New York: Springer-Verlag.

Englert, C. S., & Raphael, T. E. (1989). Developing successful writers through cognitive strategy instruction. In J. E. Brophy (Ed.), *Advances in research on teaching* (Vol. 1, pp. 105–151). CT: JAI Press.

Englert, C. S., Raphael, T. E., & Anderson, L. M. (1989). *Socially-mediated instruction: Improving students' knowledge and talk about writing.* Unpublished manuscript, Michigan State University at East Lansing, Institute for Research on Teaching.

Englert, C. S., Raphael, T. E., Anderson, L. M., Anthony, H. M., & Stevens, D. D. (1991). Making strategies and self-talk visible: Writing instruction in regular and special education classrooms. *American Educational Research Journal, 23,* 337–372.

Englert, C. S., Raphael, T. E., Anderson, L. M., Gregg, S. L., & Anthony, H. M. (1989). Exposition: Reading, writing, and the metacognitive knowledge of learning disabled students. *Learning Disabilities Research, 5,* 5–24.

Englert, C. S., & Thomas, C. C. (1987). Sensitivity to text structure in reading and writing: A comparison between learning disabled and non-learning disabled students. *Learning Disability Quarterly, 10,* 93–105.

Flowers, L., & Hayes, J. R. (1980). The dynamics of composing: Making plans and juggling constraints. In L. Gregg & E. Steinberg (Eds.), *Cognitive processes in writing* (pp. 31–50). Hillsdale, NJ: Erlbaum.

Flowers, L., & Hayes, J. R. (1981). A cognitive process theory of writing. *College Composition and Communication, 35,* 365–387.

Fortner, V. L. (1986). Generalization of creative productive-thinking training to LD students' written expression. *Learning Disability Quarterly, 9,* 274–284.

Glover, J. A., & Sautter, F. (1977). Procedures for increasing four behaviorally defined components of creativity within formal written assignments among high school students. *School Applications of Learning Theory, 9,* 3–22.

Graham, S., & Harris K. R. (1987). Improving composition skills of inefficient learners with self-instructional strategy training. *Topics in Language Disorders, 7,* 66–77.

Graham, S., & Harris. K. R. (1988a). Instructional recommendations for teaching writing to exceptional students. *Exceptional Children, 54,* 506–512.

Graham, S., & Harris. K. R. (1988b). Research and instruction in written language: Introduction to the special issue. *Exceptional Children, 54,* 495–496.

Graham, S., & Harris, K. R. (1989a). Cognitive training: Implications for written language. In J. Hughes & R. Hall (Eds.), *Cognitive behavioral and psychology in the schools: A comprehensive handbook* (pp. 247–279). New York: Guilford.

Graham, S., & Harris, K. R. (1989b). A components analysis of cognitive strategy instruction: Effects on learning disabled students' compositions and self-efficacy. *Journal of Educational Psychology, 81,* 353–361.

Graham, S., Harris, K. R., MacArthur, C., & Schwartz, S. (1991). Writing and writing instruction for students with learning disabilities: Review of a research program. *Learning Disability Quarterly, 14,* 89–114.

Graham, S., Harris, K. R., & Sawyer, R. (1987). Composition instruction with learning disabled students: Self-instructional strategy training. *Focus on Exceptional Children, 20,* 1–11.

Graham, S., Schwartz, S., & MacArthur, C. (1990). [Learning disabled and normally achieving students' knowledge of the writing process]. Unpublished raw data.

Graves, A., Semmel, M., & Gerber, M. N. (1994). The effects of story prompts on the narrative production of students with and without learning disabilities. *Learning Disability Quarterly, 17*(2), 154–164.

Graves, D. (1975). An examination of the writing process of seven-year-old children. *Research in the Teaching of English, 9,* 231–236.

Hall, J. K. (1988). *Evaluating and improving written expression* (2nd ed.). Boston: Allyn & Bacon.

Harris, K. R., & Graham, S. (1985). Improving learning disabled students' composition skills: Self-control strategy training. *Learning Disability Quarterly, 8,* 27–36.

Hayward, L. R., & LeBuffe, J. R. (1985). Self-correction: A positive method for improving writing skills. *Teaching Exceptional Children, 18,* 68–72.

Kraetsch, G. (1981). The effects of oral instructions and training on the expansion of written language. *Learning Disability Quarterly, 4,* 82–90.

MacArthur, C., & Graham, S. (1987). Learning disabled students' composing under three methods of text production: Handwriting, word processing, and dictation. *Journal of Special Education, 21,* 22–42.

McGhee, R., Bryant, B. R., Larsen, S. C., & Rivera, D. M. (1995). *Test of written expression.* Austin, TX: PRO-ED.

Meyer, B. J. F., Brandt, D. H., & Bluth, G. J. (1980). Use of author's textual schema. Key for ninth-graders' comprehension. *Reading Research Quarterly, 16,* 72–103.

Montague, M., Graves, A., & Leavell, A. (1991). Planning, procedural facilitation, and narrative composition of junior high students with learning disabilities. *Learning Disabilities Research and Practice, 6,* 191–200.

Morocco, C., & Nelson, A. (1990). *Writers at work.* Chicago: Science Research Associates.

Phelps-Terasaki, D., & Phelps-Gunn, T. (1988). *Teaching competence in written language.* Austin, TX: PRO-ED.

Poplin, M. S., Gray, R., Larsen, S., Banikowski, A., & Mehring, T. (1980). A comparison of components of written expression abilities in learning disabled and non-learning disabled students at three grade levels. *Learning Disability Quarterly, 3,* 46–53.

Ray, R. (1986). *The eleven-sentence paragraph.* Unpublished paper. University of New Mexico at Albuquerque, Department of Special Education.

Schumaker, J. B., Nolan, S. M., & Deshler, D. D. (1985). *The error monitoring strategy.* Lawrence: University of Kansas Press.

Schumaker, J. B., & Sheldon, J. (1985). *The sentence writing strategy.* Lawrence: University of Kansas Press.

Stevens, D. D., & Englert, C. S. (1993). Making strategies work. *Teaching Exceptional Children, 26*(1), 34–43.

Stoddard, E. P., & Renzulli, J. S. (1983). Improved writing skills of talent pool students. *Gifted Child Quarterly, 27*(1), 21–27.

Thomas, C. C., Englert, C. S., & Gregg, S. (1987). An analysis of errors and strategies in the expository writing of learning disabled students. *Remedial and Special Education, 8*(1), 21–30, 46.

Towle, M. (1978). Assessment and remediation of handwriting deficits for children with learning disabilities. *Journal of Learning Disabilities, 11,* 370–377.

Warden, R., Allen, J., Hipp, K., Schmitz, J., & Collett, L. (1988). *Written expression.* San Antonio, TX: Psychological Corporation.

Welch, M. (1992). The PLEASE strategy: A metacognitive learning strategy for improving the paragraph writing of students with mild learning disabilities. *Learning Disability Quarterly, 15,* 119–128.

Wong, B., Wong, R., & Blenkisop, J. (1989). Cognitive and metacognitive aspects of learning disabled adolescents' composing problems. *Learning Disability Quarterly, 12,* 300–322.

Zipprich, M. A. (1995). Teaching web making as a guided planning tool to improve student narrative writing. *Remedial and Special Education, 16*(1), 3–15, 52.

Technology

Behrmann, M. M. (1994). Assistive technology for students with mild disabilities. *Intervention in School and Clinic, 30*(2), 70–83.

Edyburn, D. L. (1992, April). *Classroom implications of research on computer-based and hand-held spelling correction systems.* Paper presented at the meeting of the Council for Exceptional Children, Baltimore, MD.

Kerchner, L., & Kistinger, B. (1984). Language processing/word processing: Written expression, computers, and learning disabled students. *Learning Disability Quarterly, 7,* 329–335.

MacArthur, C. (1988). The impact of computers on the writing process. *Exceptional Children, 54,* 536–542.

MacArthur, C., & DeLaPaz, S. (1993). [Comparison of the performance of eight common spelling checkers on words misspelled by students with learning disabilities]. Unpublished raw data.

MacArthur, C., & Graham, S. (1987). Learning disabled students' composing under three methods of text production: Handwriting, word processing, and dictation. *Journal of Special Education, 21,* 22–42.

MacArthur, C., & Schneiderman, B. (1986). Learning disabled students' difficulties in learning to use a word processor: Implications for instruction and software evaluation. *Journal of Learning Disabilities, 19,* 248–253.

MacArthur, C., Schwartz, S. S., & Graham, S. (1991). Effects of a reciprocal peer revision strategy in special education classrooms. *LD Research and Practice, 6,* 201–210.

Raskind, M. (1993). Assistive technology and adults with learning disabilities: A blueprint for exploration and advancement. *Learning Disability Quarterly, 16,* 185–195.

Vacc, N. N. (1987). Word processor handwriting: A comparative study of writing samples produced by mildly mentally handicapped students. *Exceptional Children, 54*(2), 156–165.

Chapter 12
Mathematics

Although reading instruction is often emphasized with students with learning and behavior problems, mathematics is an important topic of instruction that must be stressed. Mathematical difficulties are persistent across elementary and secondary levels and into adulthood for many of these individuals. Research shows that students with mathematical learning problems experience developmental cognitive lags, which may impede their ability to perform mathematical skills as successfully as their same-age peers. Moreover, students with mathematical learning problems tend to plateau in mathematical knowledge, which limits their exposure to and retention of the curriculum presented at various grade levels. For instance, if students have a limited mastery of basic facts, they may have difficulties solving more advanced problems. Clearly, these data are disconcerting because the implication is that students with learning and behavior problems do not possess those mathematics skills necessary for successful adult adjustment. Thus, appropriate emphasis must be placed on mathematics instruction.

In this chapter, we focus on mathematics curriculum and instruction at the elementary and secondary levels. We provide suggestions for adapting mathematics instruction in the general education setting and for infusing technology applications into classroom lessons. Of particular interest is a list of suggestions for teaching youngsters from culturally and linguistically diverse backgrounds. The chapter is divided into three major sections: "Nature of Mathematics Instruction," "Skills for Instruction," and "Instructional Methods and Techniques."

Making Connections

Before you read, return to chapter 4 and identify those mathematics skills for which proficiency is important. Consider specific mathematics skills that might be part of the various curricular models. Relate the design of mathematics lessons to the different instructional arrangements. Review the instructional approaches in chapter 5 and think about how these approaches might be used to teach mathematics lessons; include evaluation procedures in chapters 3 and 6. Using information from chapter 2, identify ways in which you would work with the general education teacher to adapt mathematics instruction in the general education setting. Finally, review the generic interventions discussed in chapter 9 to determine which ones could be used to teach mathematics skills.

Objectives
After studying this chapter, the reader will be able to

1. Describe the nature of mathematics instruction.
2. Identify and explain components of mathematics instruction.
3. Explain instruction for components of mathematics.

● ●

Nature of Mathematics Instruction

As you read, think about...
1. Describing what constitutes mathematics instruction.
2. Providing a definition of mathematics literacy.
3. Identifying issues pertinent to mathematics education.
4. Explaining mathematics instruction according to the instructional approaches described in chapter 5.

In this section, we describe some of the qualities of mathematics instruction. We begin by offering a definition of mathematical literacy and explaining how that relates to mathematics instruction. We briefly discuss some of the issues and reform efforts in mathematics education and curricular and instructional design features inherent in mathematics instruction. Finally, we provide information about mathematics instructional approaches.

Definition of Mathematical Literacy

Mathematical literacy is the ability to use skills and concepts to reason, solve problems, and communicate about mathematical problems (National Council of Teachers of Mathematics [NCTM], 1989). Thus, mathematics instruction should involve activities, approaches, and interventions that assist students in meeting instructional objectives that are relevant to the development of mathematical literacy and that appear on students' IEPs.

Issues and Reform in Mathematics Education

The field of mathematics education has undergone many reform efforts (e.g., NCTM, 1989; National Research Council, 1989) because of current educational and sociological issues, including the recurring poor performance of America's youth on national mathematics tests (e.g., Lindquist, Carpenter, Silver, & Mathews, 1983; McKnight et al., 1987; NCTM, 1988), changing social forces (e.g., technological advancements, educational diversity), mathematical expectations for employment and life skill needs of adulthood, and interest in alternative assessment approaches to traditional, standardized testing (Rivera, Taylor, & Bryant, 1994–1995). Specifically, reform efforts have been aimed at redefining mathematics curriculum and instruction in relation to mathematical literacy, instructional goals and objectives, and teaching techniques.

In 1989, NCTM published *The Curriculum and Evaluation Standards for School Mathematics* (see Table 12.1 for a list of math skills from three sources). The intent of the *Standards* is to provide a holistic/constructivist foundation for mathematics instruction in all classrooms that broadens the scope of mathematics curriculum and instructional approaches. In particular, the authors of the *Standards* promote a

Table 12.1
Organizational
Schemes for
Mathematics
Curricula

NCTM standards	National institute of education: 10 basic skills	Key math areas
Math as problem solving	Problem solving	Content
Math as communication	Applying math to everyday situations	Numeration
Math as reasoning	Alertness to reasonableness of results	Fractions
Math connections	Estimations and approximations	Geometry and symbols
Estimation	Appropriate computational skills	Operations
Number sense and numeration	Geometry	Addition
Concepts of whole number operations	Measurement	Multiplication
Whole number computation	Reading, interpreting, and constructing	Division
Geometry and spatial sense	tables, charts, and graphs	Mental computation
Measurement	Using mathematics to predict	Numerical reasoning
Statistics and probability	Computer literacy	Applications
Fractions and decimals		Word problems
Patterns and relationships		Missing elements
Numbers and number relationships		Money
Number systems and number theory		Measurement
Patterns and functions		Time
Algebra		
Measurement		
Geometry from a synthetic perspective		
Geometry from an algebraic perspective		
Trigonometry		
Discrete mathematics		
Conceptual underpinnings of calculus		
Mathematical structure		

problem-solving approach to mathematics instruction and a curriculum that emphasizes diverse mathematical concepts and skills. As such, the role of computational
instruction is no longer overemphasized as in traditional mathematics curriculum.
Rather, computation is part of a total mathematics program and should be taught in
conjunction with other mathematical skills.

Although the *Standards* have been greeted with controversy (e.g., vagueness of
mathematics goals, lack of testable performance objectives, lack of explicit research
base, emphasis on "discovery" methodology) in the special education literature (see
Hofmeister, 1993; Hutchinson, 1993; Mercer, Harris, & Miller, 1993; Rivera, 1993),
they provide recommendations for mathematics curriculum, instruction, and assessment for kindergarten through high school and have been embraced nationally by
school districts, researchers, and textbook publishers. Thus, it is important for educators to be familiar with the *Standards* and to ensure that they ground their attempts
to use them in student performance data and proven methodology when teaching students with learning and behavior problems who are at risk for school failure.

Curricular and Instructional Design Features

In special education, researchers have spent years focusing on how students with learning problems acquire mathematical knowledge and skills and what curricular and instructional design features promote effective learning (Carnine, Jones, & Dixon, 1994; Mercer & Miller, 1992; Montague & Applegate, 1993; Rivera & Smith, 1988). Research results have shown that the characteristics (e.g., memory, language, attention, metacognitive difficulties) of students with learning and behavior problems are not amenable to the curricular and instructional design features commonly found in mathematics instruction (Carnine, in press).

Specifically, design features such as rapid presentation of unrelated math concepts and skills ("I have to finish teaching the textbook content by the end of the year" syndrome), limited explanations and examples, inadequate strategies (e.g., "draw a picture" strategy for problem solving), insufficient practice and review opportunities, overreliance on "paper-and-pencil" exercises, little use of manipulatives, and use of the "discovery" approach to instruction invite limited mastery and generalization of mathematical knowledge for students who have learning problems and who are at risk (Cawley & Parmar, 1992; Rivera & Bryant, 1992). The good news is that curricular and instructional design features that promote effective mathematics instruction have been identified; the authors present some of these features below.

Teach the Language of Mathematics

Wiig and Semel (1984) refer to mathematics as "conceptually dense"; that is, students must understand the meaning of each mathematical symbol and word because, unlike reading, contextual clues are limited or nonexistent. Take for example $4 < 9$. The student must understand each symbol to decide if the number statement is true or false. The language of story problems is another potential trouble spot for students. Two studies (Larsen, Parker, & Trenholme, 1978; Wheeler & McNutt, 1983) found that story problems' syntactic complexity affected students' ability to solve problems successfully. The studies suggested teaching students strategies to break difficult sentences into shorter, easier to read structures.

The language and symbolism of mathematics must be taught directly as part of a math lesson (Capps & Cox, 1991). This is especially true for secondary-level students who are often faced with abstract mathematical concepts, such as algebra and geometry, that require a solid foundation of mathematical skills (e.g., computation, math properties) and language. When teaching mathematical ideas, instructors must: (1) determine prerequisite symbolic and syntactic language for math skills, (2) determine current student understanding of this language system, (3) provide direct instruction to teach the language, and (4) include sufficient practice and review experiences that could involve different instructional arrangements.

Students who are from culturally and linguistically diverse backgrounds and who have learning problems may especially find the language of mathematics problematic. Scott and Raborn (in press) identified the linguistic and symbolic features of mathematics as "tricky spots" because words (e.g., odd and even) may be used in unfamiliar ways, structural relationships between words and syntax must be discerned (e.g., relationship of adjectives and nouns in sentence structure), and algorithmic formats (e.g., reading from left-to-right, up-and-down) may be contrary to cultural procedures. Therefore, teachers must be sure that all students have the necessary semantic, linguistic, and symbolic understanding of the mathematical concepts and skills presented for instruction. Spotlight on Diversity features ideas for addressing the mathematical needs of all students.

Ideas for Teaching Mathematics to Students from Culturally and Linguistically Diverse Backgrounds

- Provide math instruction in the native language if the student is stronger in math than in English.
- Identify words most frequently used in math instruction. Help the student learn these words in English or in the student's native language.
- Use different ways (e.g., gesturing, pictures, rewording) to communicate.
- Provide activities that allow practice in English as well as in the language of math.
- Create story problems that are relevant to the student's personal cultural identity.
- Share examples of the math heritage of various cultural groups.
- Use manipulatives to teach new vocabulary.
- Have students develop picture files of new vocabulary.

Teach "Big Ideas"

"Big ideas," such as volume, proportion, and subtraction with and without renaming (borrowing), are central concepts that consist of smaller "subordinate" concepts (Carnine, in press). Students are taught the big idea and introduced to related concepts, rather than learning independent discrete skills that lack instructional interrelatedness. Teaching big ideas is important for all school-age students whether they are learning subtraction algorithms or geometrical principles. For instance in teaching volume, Carnine have reduced the number of formulas from seven to three. Students are introduced to the big idea, volume, and learn that volume essentially refers to the area of the base times the height. Naturally, there are slight variations on this formula, but if students learn the big idea, then they can learn the few formulas for calculation purposes in relation to the big idea. Figure 12.1 illustrates volume as a big idea.

Use Math Basals and Manipulatives Judiciously

Math textbooks, supporting materials (e.g., worksheets, workbooks), and manipulatives (e.g., blocks, rods) can be used to teach instructional objectives. However, teachers should use these materials carefully as they plan and implement math instruction.

When using textbooks, teachers should avoid overrelying on them to dictate scope and sequence. Rather than moving through the textbook cover to cover with the content of a page dictating that day's instructional objective, teachers may want to select their instructional objectives based on the IEP and the textbook's curriculum chart, plan a sequence of instruction, and use the textbook's and supporting material's content to supplement instruction. For teachers who are required to use the school district's textbook sequentially, certain cautions apply. First, provide additional practice for skills presented; one page of practice probably won't be sufficient to ensure mastery before learning the next skill. Second, help students make connec-

Figure 12.1
Volume as a
"big idea"

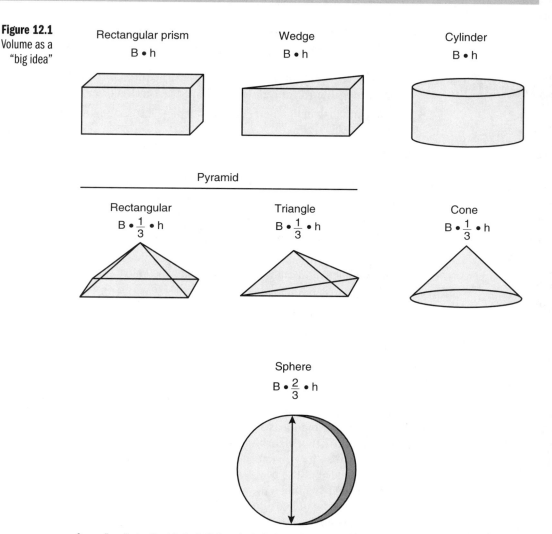

Rectangular prism
B • h

Wedge
B • h

Cylinder
B • h

Pyramid

Rectangular
$B • \frac{1}{3} • h$

Triangle
$B • \frac{1}{3} • h$

Cone
$B • \frac{1}{3} • h$

Sphere
$B • \frac{2}{3} • h$

Source: From "Instructional Design in Mathematics for Students with Learning Disabilities," by D. Carnine, in press, *Journal of Learning Disabilities.* Copyright by PRO-ED. Reprinted with permission.

tions between skills and concepts presented in the textbook; textbooks often lack sufficient interrelated activities to help students see connections between the many skills presented. Third, be aware of strategies presented in textbooks that may be too vague (too broad or too narrow) (see the section "Instructional Methods and Techniques" below). Teach specific strategies that can be used across skill learning (e.g., the number family strategy can be used to solve story problems).

Manipulatives can be an excellent instructional material to represent mathematical concepts and skills concretely. Manipulatives are appropriate for elementary- and secondary-level students; the type of manipulative will vary, depending on the student's age. Again, this material must be used cautiously to ensure accurate representation of the mathematical concept or skill. Research results have varied regarding the efficacy of manipulatives to promote mathematical understanding (e.g.,

Evans, 1990; Miller, Mercer, & Dillon, 1992). Yet, research findings also suggest that students should be given meaningful, experiential opportunities with math concepts before moving to the abstract level (Baroody, 1989). Therefore, teachers are advised to use manipulatives, but to do so carefully by ensuring that the material accurately represents the skill being taught. Tips for Teachers provides information about using textbooks and manipulatives to support math instruction.

Guidelines for Using Instructional Materials

Textbooks

1. Determine if lessons and activities are presented in a step-by-step format.
2. Make sure the directions are clear.
3. Identify the strategies used to correct student errors and to teach specific skills.
4. Examine the scope and sequence of the textbook to see if modifications are necessary.
5. Determine whether additional support materials and activities are necessary as supplemental practice.
6. Check for the adequacy of guided and independent practice opportunities.
7. Ascertain the degree to which the textbook covers the *Standards.*

Manipulatives

1. Select manipulatives that support the instructional objective.
2. Be sure the manipulative accurately portrays the skill.
3. Use a variety of manipulatives that are age-appropriate at the elementary and secondary levels.
4. Teach students how to use the manipulatives.
5. Move from the concrete (manipulatives) to the pictorial (semi-concrete; pictures, tallies) to the abstract (symbolic; numbers, symbols).
6. Have paper and pencil activities to correspond to manipulative representations. ■

Source: Adapted from "Mathematics Textbooks, Materials and Manipulatives," by M. Lambert, in press, *LD Forum.* Copyright 1996 by the Council for Learning Disabilities. Reprinted with permission.

Teach Strategies

Research findings document the effectiveness of teaching cognitive strategies (see chapter 5 for a review of cognitive strategies) to elementary- and secondary-level students with learning and behavior problems (Mercer & Miller, 1992; Montague & Applegate, 1993; Rivera & Smith, 1988). Examples of effective strategies appear in the "Instructional Methods and Techniques" section of this chapter. According to Carnine (in press), strategies should not be so narrow that they do not generalize to other, similar problems, or so general that they are merely guidelines; strategies need to be "just right." For example, a cognitive strategy for story problem solving that can be applied to different types of problems (e.g., one- and two-step story problems, problems with and without extraneous information) would fit the "just right" category. On the other hand, the "key word" strategy for solving story problems (i.e., having students read the question being asked as the only strategy for solving the story problem) is too general and ineffective for many types of problems.

Cognitive strategies should be: (1) taught using direct instruction, (2) practiced, and (3) reviewed. Strategy steps can be noted on a chart in the classroom, on cards that students use in small-group work, or in students' notebooks for use in other classrooms and at home. Students should learn how strategies can be linked to new skills and concepts across math instruction. For example, when solving a story problem involving linear measurement, students may draw on three strategies: one for recalling measurement formulas, another for solving computational problems with linear measurements, and a third for solving story problems. Over the course of several school days, students could review the three strategies with specific practice examples and link them to solve the new story problem with linear measurement. In this way, strategic knowledge can become more relevant, rather than being a string of unrelated strategies with little generalization to other problems.

Include Practice and Review Experiences

All school-age students with learning and behavior problems require more practice and review of mathematical concepts and skills than is typically offered in textbooks and classroom instruction. Practice and review opportunities should be relevant to the instructional objective, rather than mixing numerous skills and concepts together. Additional time and practice opportunities could be provided so students can move through the stages of learning (i.e., proficiency, mastery, maintenance, generalization). Practice and review can be accomplished in a number of ways. For instance, teachers can use different instructional arrangements (e.g., peer tutoring, learning centers, cooperative learning) to offer more practice opportunities. Instructional materials such as math software, audiotapes, videodiscs, and manipulatives can be used to promote relevant practice and review. Students need not practice 30 computational problems to "prove" that they have mastered the skill. Practice should be relevant to the skill and reasonable in quantity of items. Review activities can be offered periodically to promote maintenance.

Promote Automaticity

It is important for students to perform lower-level, cognitive skills (e.g., computing math facts, reading numerals, telling time, counting money) proficiently (automatically) and accurately so that they can acquire higher-level, cognitive math skills (Pellegrino & Goldman, 1987; Samuels, 1987). Direct instruction can be used to teach these lower-level skills, and tactics can be used to promote acquisition and proficiency (see chapter 9 and the "Instructional Methods and Techniques" section of this chapter). Periodic, timed drills, distributed practice (over several days or across weeks), and data analysis of student performance can be used to monitor automaticity abilities on lower-level, cognitive skills. Developing automaticity with these skills is particularly important at the elementary level. At the secondary level, automaticity development must continue in life skill areas (e.g., money, time); however, if a strong proficiency program existed at the elementary level and was unsuccessful, such development in basic facts may be questionable and should be discussed in light of the student's educational goals, transitional needs, and curricular program. For some students with more severe learning problems, automaticity in basic facts might be limited. In these cases, calculator instruction is the obvious choice. Table 12.2 provides suggested criteria rates for addition, subtraction, multiplication, and division facts.

Table 12.2
Criteria Rates for
Arithmetic Fact
Proficiency

Problem type	Sample		Grade	Correct rate	Error rate
Addition facts		2 + 3 5	1 6	19.8 82.0	0.2 0.8
Addition carry facts		9 + 9 18	1 6	3.1 45.3	1.5 0.2
Mixed addition facts	4 + 6 10	5 + 1 6	1 6	8.4 55.5	1.1 1.2
Subtraction facts		8 − 2 6	1 6	12.9 51.5	0.5 0
Subtraction borrowing facts		17 − 9 8	1 6	2.5 33.8	0.8 0.8
Mixed subtraction facts	16 − 8 8	5 − 3 2	1 6	4.8 44.8	0.8 0.3
Multiplication facts		3 × 3 9	3 6	43.4 68.2	0.8 5.0
Multiplication carry facts		7 × 6 42	3 6	21.3 40.0	0.3 0
Mixed multiplication facts	4 × 2 8	9 × 8 72	3 6	31.3 52.7	0.5 2.0
Division facts	8 ÷ 1 = 8		3 6	12.6 47.0	1.7 3.3
Division facts	14 ÷ 2 = 7		3 6	8.3 39.3	0.7 0
Mixed division facts	6 ÷ 2 = 5 64 ÷ 8 = 8		3 6	11.4 45.0	0.7 0.7

Source: Adapted from *The Computational Arithmetic Program*, by D. D. Smith and T. C. Lovitt, 1982, Austin, TX: PRO-ED.

Emphasize Problem Solving

Problem solving is an essential component of a total mathematics program because it is a major life skill and enables other skills (e.g., computation, estimation, reasoning) to be taught and reinforced (Cawley & Parmar, 1992; NCTM, 1989). Specific strategies for teaching problem solving appear in the "Instructional Methods and Techniques" section of this chapter; we now present general guidelines for instruction in problem solving. Students can (1) use manipulatives to depict problems, (2) use charts and tables to organize information, (3) solve problems with more than one "right" answer, (4) devise their own story problems, (5) solve "real" problems (e.g., classroom or current event situations), and (6) focus on the "language" of the story problem by paraphrasing problems with linguistic and symbolic variance and extraneous information.

Of particular importance in story problem solving is the reading level of the problems and the students. In some cases, students with very limited reading abilities may have great difficulty solving story problems simply because they are unable to read the words in the problem. Adapting instruction might be the answer to this type of problem. For instance, story problems could be presented on paper as well as on audiotape; in this way, difficult words are read aloud to the students. Another possibility for dealing with the reading level issue is to have students work in cooperative learning or peer tutoring arrangements. A student with a more advanced reading level could be the designated "reader" for the other student or students. A third possibility is to have students work individually or in small groups with the teacher, a family member volunteer, or a paraprofessional. This individualized attention could easily address the reading level problem and provide additional support in solving story problems. A fourth option could include selecting words in word problems to match the students' reading level more closely. The caution for secondary students with severe reading disabilities is to avoid designing story problems that may not be "age-appropriate." In this situation, an audiotape, a student-mediated instructional arrangement, or paraprofessional intervention might be a better choice.

Use Varying Combinations of Teacher and Student Interactions

Cawley, Fitzmaurice, Sedlak, and Althaus (1976) developed a model called the Interactive Unit (IU). The IU consists of 16 types of instructional interactions that could occur between teachers and students. The student's role is "output" consisting of manipulating, identifying, saying, or writing. The teacher's role is "input" consisting of manipulating, displaying (showing), saying, or writing. For instance, the teacher could manipulate base 10 blocks to illustrate regrouping in addition, and could instruct the student to watch, then imitate. The student could imitate the modeled instruction by manipulating a set of base 10 blocks. In another example, the teacher could display a pattern and ask the student to select the matching pattern from three choices. Thus, there are 16 possible interactive formats that allow teachers and students options in how information is presented and how students demonstrate mathematical understanding.

Instructional Approaches

Approaches to mathematics instruction are similar to those described in chapter 10 for reading; that is, mathematics instruction can be viewed behaviorally as a "bottom-up" approach (individual skills are taught), holistically as a "top-down" approach (students are presented with mathematical problems to solve using a variety of techniques and guided by teacher's questioning), and interactively as a combination of the two (see chapter 5 for a review of instructional approaches). In addition, the strategic instructional approach relies on teaching specific strategies to solve algorithms and problems. Examples of how these mathematics approaches are implemented appear later in the "Instructional Methods and Techniques" section of this chapter.

Skills for Instruction

As you read, think about...

1. Designing a mathematics curriculum that prepares students adequately for adult living.
2. Summarizing the role of computation in mathematics instruction.
3. Comparing recommended math skills on IEPs to the curriculum you designed.
4. Explaining the rationale for teaching (or not teaching) complex fraction computations.
5. Discussing the role of skills such as approximation, estimation, probability, and statistics in math instruction.
6. Designing a scope and sequence of math instruction for a grade level of your choice.
7. Describing ways in which math instruction can be made more motivating for secondary-level students.
8. Describing your philosophy on the use of calculators in the classroom.

Mathematics curriculum consists of a number of components for instruction. Different professional organizations and individual researchers have identified various skills that they think should comprise the mathematics curriculum. Table 12.1 (presented earlier in this chapter) lists skills used by the National Institute of Education (NIE), the National Council of Teachers of Mathematics (NCTM), and the Key Math test. These lists indicate what a federal agency, a professional organization, and test developers feel are the essential elements of mathematics. In this section, we describe some components of mathematics instruction.

Special education teachers must use their training and skills to plan the most appropriate instructional mathematics sequences for each student. To assist teachers in conceptualizing instructional programs for their individual students, we provide a list (see Figure 12.2) highlighting skills that might constitute students' mathematics programs throughout the school years. Many of the skills found on the list should be taught concurrently with other skills. For example, each year, basic consumer skills should be reintroduced as practical examples and applications of computation and problem solving. The importance of this list is to illustrate that numeration and computation are only components of the mathematics curriculum; they should not be considered a total mathematics program. Unfortunately, for many students with special needs, they are the only skills addressed during the school years.

Students whose disabilities do not preclude success with mathematics should be placed in the general mathematics classes (algebra, geometry, trigonometry) with their typical peers. For others, instructional time should be spent on mastering skills needed in adult life. In the following sections, discussion focuses on numeration, computation, measurement, problem solving, and consumer mathematics.

Numeration

There are a number of skills children should master before they begin to use numbers to calculate or solve problems. For example, they must understand that objects and things in their environment are related to each other. Many children master numerical concepts before they come to school. Others, however, need direct instruction concerning one-to-one correspondence, counting, quantitative relationships, and other topics. Because these concepts are difficult for many students with special needs to learn, we provide some discussion in the following sections.

Figure 12.2
Topics for
mathematics
instruction

Mathematics

- Numeration
  - Number concepts
  - Language vocabulary
  - One-to-one correspondence
  - Sets
  - Number usage
  - Place value
  - Relationships
  - Counting

- Computation
  - Calculator usage
  - Mental
  - $\boxed{+}\boxed{-}\boxed{\times}\boxed{\div}$ Facts
  - $\boxed{+}\boxed{-}\boxed{\times}\boxed{\div}$ Process
  - $\boxed{+}\boxed{-}\boxed{\times}\boxed{\div}$ Fractions
  - Associated calculating skills
    - Decimals
    - Estimates
    - Rounding off

- Measurement
  - Metric
  - English
    - Linear
    - Liquid
    - Time

- Problem solving
  - Real-life problems
  - Word problems

- Computer applications
  - Logo (a software program)

- Study skills
  - Graphs
  - Charts
  - Statistics
  - Maps

- Advanced skills
  - Algebra
  - Geometry
  - Proportions
  - Statistics

- Consumer skills
  - Salary
  - Net pay
  - Benefits
  - Taxes
  - Budgeting
  - Home
  - Auto
  - Leisure
  - Purchases
  - Cash
  - Checks
  - Credit cards
  - Loans

Number Concepts

Very young children seem almost naturally interested in number concepts (how many, how old). Because the concept of numbers is based on an abstraction related to quantity, however, some children with disabilities have difficulty with it from the outset.

Classification and grouping of objects is an early requisite skill. The notion of sets or clusters should come early in the instructional sequence. To be able to group things together requires an ability to discriminate and comprehend the properties of objects. Because shapes are rather easy to discriminate, they are usually taught during this initial period. Circles, for example, can become a set separate from triangles and squares. Size is another discriminating feature used in instruction about sets. Once children have learned to discriminate objects with several variables (shape, size, color), instruction about one-to-one correspondence can begin.

Other number concepts are important in students' early contact with mathematics. Students should develop a numerical vocabulary early. Words such as most, few, many, big, little, heavy, long, short, top, and bottom must become part of young children's active vocabulary. Such word knowledge and usage allows them to understand more difficult numerical concepts. When one-to-one correspondence is taught, for instance, the phrases "one too many" and "one more than" should also be taught, for later concepts are related to the notion of "greater than." Once these foundation skills are mastered, students move easily to the use of numbers in their environment.

Number Usage

As with many numerical concepts, many students come to school already able to use simple numbers. A standard instructional sequence is often used to teach number usage. It usually starts with rote counting by ones (to 10 or 20), recognition of simple (one-digit) numbers, and number writing (if the students possess the necessary prerequisite writing skills—see chapter 11). Whether the student matches, says, or writes numbers, the student then learns to count how many objects are within a set.

Once students can count objects, they are taught to compare. Relationships between sets (greater than, less than, and equal to) become the topic of instruction. Many teachers have found that the concrete representation of sets and their composition is a prerequisite to paper-and-pencil worksheet activities.

Other general number usage skills must be mastered before computational instruction begins. Whether these miscellaneous skills are taught concurrent with or subsequent to the skills listed above is up to the teacher and the performance of the students. Regardless, at some time early in the mathematics curriculum, students should be able to count by ones, twos, fives, and tens, and should also master ordinal numbers (first, second, third).

The exact and precise sequence of these precomputational skills is not definite. Clearly, however, these skills should be mastered before computation is presented in any concentrated way. Many youngsters possess "spotty" skills. Teachers of students who have difficulty with computation and other mathematical skills should assess their students' abilities in numeration to be certain that these prerequisite skills are definitely part of their repertoires.

Computation

Computation has received considerable attention from teachers and researchers. In fact, most of this attention has centered on addition and subtraction. Unfortunately, the only mathematics instruction many students with disabilities receive during their entire school career is in computational arithmetic.

The overemphasis on computation can be observed through the following example. Ron is a high school student who receives help from the special education teacher. Thirty minutes each day are devoted to mathematics. He spends ten minutes putting cards with multiplication facts written on them through a Language Master machine and twenty minutes computing problems on a worksheet. Sometimes these problems are only multiplication; other days the processes are mixed. Day in and day out, for the eleven years he has spent in school, mathematics instruction has been composed of similar activities. This is a travesty for all parties involved; Ron is still not proficient in computational skills, and the teacher is not providing an appropriate educational program. This overemphasis on computational arithmetic leaves a student with no usable mathematics skills.

Today, with our knowledge of well-researched interventions that can make computational instruction more efficient (see the "Instructional Methods and Techniques" section later in this chapter), and the availability of the handheld calculator, such situations should not occur. Instruction in computational arithmetic should not be eliminated, for computation is the basic tool in all mathematics. For those who cannot master it within a reasonable time, however—even when efficient, researched procedures are applied—supplemental aids or compensating devices such as calculators or computers should be provided. In any case, more emphasis must be placed on problem solving and life skills.

Computational Facts and Processes

There are four computational areas: addition, subtraction, multiplication, and division. Each can be further divided into two general types of problems: facts and process problems. The facts (7×8, $5 + 2$, $7 - 4$), consisting of 100 problems per operation, are those problems to be committed to memory. The process problems ($74 - 27$, 68×84) are solved by utilizing the facts and following operational rules. Usually, the first computational area taught is addition. Once addition is mastered, subtraction is taught, then multiplication, followed by division. For each area, the facts are taught first, followed by the larger process problems, or facts and process problems are presented together.

Fractions

Fractions often present a problem to both students and teachers. Many youngsters have great difficulty understanding and using fractions. Most seem to develop the concept of simple fractions and are able to divide circles and other geometric figures into halves, thirds, fourths, and even eighths. Using fractions in computations, however, can become an insurmountable task for many students with special needs. Adding and subtracting fractions with uncommon denominators, for example, is laborious for many youngsters. Some also find this function incomprehensible.

Fraction instruction presents two problems to teachers. First, a substantial amount of instructional time is often spent on fractions, but with little success. Second, teachers debate about whether to spend more instructional time after students learn simple fractions needed in cooking. If decimals are introduced earlier and students are taught to round off to the hundredth place (which correlates to our currency system), instruction on complicated fractional computations seems unnecessary.

Calculators

Computation is complicated, so it receives the majority of time allotted for mathematics instruction in most elementary and middle school classes. For students who are academically delayed, computational arithmetic has taken the place of all mathematics instruction, even in high school.

If more emphasis is to be placed on developing mathematical skills needed in daily life, less time must be spent on computation. Apportioning instructional time to adapt to this new emphasis presents a problem. Computation cannot be ignored; students must be able to add, subtract, multiply, and divide. The calculator provides a solution. Rather than struggling to acquire computational skills, which require continual practice, students could learn the simple computational functions of a pocket calculator. No longer would they waste their time on complicated, laborious computations; instead, they would spend their limited class time solving mathematical problems encountered in real life. These problems, such as developing a personal budget, calculating monthly wages from hourly wages, comparing unit pricing, computing gasoline mileage, and figuring tips and shared costs for a dinner, include computations that are often difficult and time consuming. If students first master computational functions on their calculators, they can achieve greater success in solving problems they will face every day of their lives. Even students in early grades can benefit from instruction in how to use handheld calculators and how to solve story problems. When the tediousness of computation is removed and real-life problems are presented, students should come to understand the importance of mathematics and be more motivated to learn it.

Teachers must provide basic instruction such as how to enter problems into the calculator and how to clear those problems after each calculation. For example, they must teach students which number to enter first in a subtraction problem and which to enter second. Students cannot be expected to develop calculator skills by chance.

The introduction of calculators into classrooms could cause some important curriculum changes. Students must become familiar with a calculator's basic functions. They must learn to recognize decimals and know their meaning. And, since many calculators conclude answers with more than two decimal numbers, they must learn to round off. They also must learn to estimate the results of their computations so that they can be reasonably confident about the accuracy of the answers they later obtain. Exposing students to a variety of mathematical problems would help them gain experience needed to judge when solutions indicated on the answer display are reasonable.

Measurement

With the move to a more practical mathematics curriculum, measurement becomes a vital component of the instructional sequence. Rather than being relegated to the back of mathematics textbooks, linear and liquid measurement should become integral parts of the instructional sequence. So, too, should the measurement of time. Students with special needs, in particular, require direct instruction on these topics. Results from standardized tests show that many of these students cannot measure or tell time; these skills are needed in most jobs and in many aspects of daily adult life.

Continuous measurement (variables represented on an uninterrupted scale) include time, height, weight, temperature, volume, and distance. Although things can be measured differently (hands, fathoms, meters), standard units of measurement are used for uniform communication. Students need to use instruments such as rulers, clocks, and thermometers to obtain standard measurements and to develop a concept of measurement.

Linear and Liquid Measurement

Measurement topics of practical importance are (1) converting and comparing units of measure, (2) estimating and measuring length, (3) determining perimeter, area, and volume, and (4) using measurement instruments. Students need to learn how to use various linear and liquid measurement devices, such as rulers, thermometers, and measuring cups. Since measuring length is the easiest skill, it should be presented first, followed by determining volume and area.

Measurement skills are difficult for many students with special needs to master. For those who have trouble conceptualizing, instructional units should be carefully planned and sequenced. Instruction should contain many redundant experiences to permit opportunities for youngsters to manipulate and experiment. For example, students might first visually compare the size of objects, estimating length and height. Students can build block towers, compare heights, learn to make them equivalent, and use primitive measurements (three blocks high, two blocks high). A sense of height and length can be developed gradually using these kinds of teaching procedures. Others might seek to develop these concepts through continued practice in games and other independent and group activities. Exposure, contact, and instruction in measurement are vital.

Time

Many special education teachers find that their students do not tell or understand time as well as their typical counterparts. Many students with special needs perform at least three grade levels below typical children on time-related items on standardized tests. When asked simple questions such as "How long does it take you to brush your teeth?" "How long does it take to send a letter from one town to another?" "How long does it take for a broken bone to mend?" answers from many students with disabilities at all ages are unrealistic. Often, these students respond that it takes anywhere from twenty seconds to an hour to brush their teeth, from ten minutes to a year to get a letter from one town to the next, and from five minutes to nine hours to ski downhill.

Before students can understand time (beyond the gross distinctions of morning, afternoon, night, lunchtime, and dinnertime), they must be able to tell time. Many supplemental aids are available that teachers can use in their instruction on telling time. Matching digital clockfaces with traditional clocks, for example, can facilitate mastery. Students must be able to tell time and use time wisely if they are to live independently. To help students achieve mastery and later independence, teachers should make digital clocks available to those who have great difficulty understanding standard clockfaces.

Throughout the school years, teachers should stress concepts about telling time and budgeting time because these concepts have been shown to be highly correlated to job success. As youngsters grow older and become more independent, they should be allowed to decide for themselves how to spend part of their day. With teacher guidance, students may gradually take more responsibility for scheduling their time. Eventually, routine self-management of daily schedules will foster students' better understanding and use of time.

Problem Solving

As emphasized throughout this text, more time and attention should be spent in developing instructional programs that address problem solving. Members of the NCTM have reached the same conclusion. In fact, in their recommendations for the focus of mathematics education, they list problem solving first. Problem solving is particularly important for students with special needs. These students need problem solving skills not only to solve word problems, but also to deal effectively with nonroutine functions in daily life. In many instances, problem solving involves applying mathematics to problems encountered in the real world. Students who learn to solve mathematical problems may find that they can solve other kinds of problems as well.

Problem solving requires a wide variety of skills and knowledge. Individuals must generalize knowledge to new situations; find relationships between skills, concepts, and principles; make decisions; be flexible; identify irrelevancies; seek similarities; estimate; and determine the reasonableness of their answers. They need to formulate questions, analyze and conceptualize problems, define problems, discover patterns and similarities, experiment, and transfer skills and strategies to new situations.

For youngsters to learn how to solve problems, they must have practice. Throughout the school years, many opportunities to solve problems arise. These opportunities, which include routine events (dividing the class into teams during physical education period), can be used to teach mathematics. Rather than the adults always handling difficult or novel situations, students should become involved in their solutions. For example, problems such as dividing a construction paper order among the fourth-grade teachers could be left to the children to solve. Using real situations at the children's level of understanding is meaningful and serves to illustrate problems for instructional purposes. Certainly, such problems are more interesting for groups of youngsters than determining the price of four different kinds of vegetables when they are mixed together.

Computer Applications

As noted in chapter 11, computers have become pervasive in American classrooms and homes. The use of computers in mathematics instruction is extensive due to the diversity of software programs for teaching math skills. Appropriate types of software including tutorials, drill and practice, educational games, and problem solving can be used to supplement mathematics instruction within a variety of instructional arrangements (see chapter 5 for general software information). An emphasis solely on drill-and-practice software is not recognized as "best practice"; rather, students should be exposed to a variety of software that emphasizes the curriculum set forth by the NCTM *Standards*. Software programs can be used after direct instruction of skills, in cooperative groups or teams, or individually for practice or review.

Study Skills

Study skills involve the use of information organizers to present materials. Graphs, charts, and tables are examples of organizers used in a wide variety of reading material found both inside and outside school. Many students with special needs do not become familiar with these information formats and therefore cannot function as well in the general curriculum. All students need to use some of these devices, particularly maps. Students who are mainstreamed for mathematics classes must become competent in using many of these organizers. The acquisition of these study skills has been too often ignored and now needs attention from both students and teachers.

Students who graph their academic improvement (see chapter 6 for review) learn important study skills. Small groups of youngsters can work together to interpret charts and tables found in newspapers or sports magazines. With the advent of easy-to-use computer software programs that create graphs and charts, students can collect data from their school environments to organize in one of these concise formats. Study skills are important tools that facilitate problem solving. Many experts believe that making tables, charts, and diagrams of problems helps students find solutions. Therefore, time spent teaching students to read, interpret, and create these information organizers is justified and could lead them to develop better problem-solving abilities.

Advanced Mathematics

Most students with special needs are not exposed to this section of the mathematics curriculum. Students whose disabilities do not preclude learning mathematics, however, should participate in standard algebra and geometry classes. If they need extra assistance to understand and master these more advanced classes, peer tutors, special education teachers, or others can help them.

Consumer Skills

All individuals living in our society must be able to select, evaluate, and use information relevant to purchasing. They need to spend money wisely and within their individual budgetary limitations. Americans face almost unlimited choices of goods to buy. These range from items and activities required for simple survival to those that bring pleasure. Most children's experience in making monetary choices begins early. If given a set amount of money to spend, children need to decide if one expensive toy is preferable to two cheaper toys. Adults' choices become more complex. They make most of their decisions with basic mathematical knowledge. Therefore, children must be prepared for independent adult living. This curriculum strand should be incorporated into children's educational programs throughout the school years. Unfortunately, consumerism has received little attention from researchers, instructional materials writers, or curriculum developers.

The mathematics list (Figure 12.2) indicates some general consumer skills that students could learn in preparation for adulthood. Units on money use, banking skills, making major purchases (cars, houses), and setting up a household could become practical exercises to teach problem solving and applications of computation. For example, in a unit on buying a car, groups of students could discuss such questions as, What is the purpose of owning a car? What is the cost of the car you want? How much can you afford to pay? How will you pay for it? What if you want a new car? What if you want a used car? How much does it cost you to operate a car? Because money skills are necessary for the more complex consumer decision-making abilities, we discuss those skills in the following section.

Money

As with telling time and other measurement skills, making change and money management are often neglected yet vital areas that should be topics of instruction for students with special needs. A number of different skills are required for proficiency in the use of money. At least the following skills should be incorporated into the mathematics curriculum: coin value and identification, counting money, making change, using money to make purchases, interpreting a budget, and having knowledge and understanding of checks and checking accounts. In today's society it is also important for students to understand the use of credit cards and to develop a concept of credit.

At present, no comprehensive money management program is available. Splinter skills are usually taught in isolated units. Making change, for example, is commonly presented in arithmetic texts. Interestingly, that skill is often taught through subtraction (the amount given to the clerk minus the price of the item). In real-life situations, however, change is obtained through a counting process (counting up from the price of the item to the amount given to the clerk). Therefore, students do not need to know how to subtract to make change, and change making and other simple money usage activities can be introduced early in the student's educational career.

Teachers who include a token economy facet in their classrooms have an excellent opportunity to teach such money-related skills as comparing the amount of money (or points) one has with the cost of an item (or privilege). Some teachers of middle and secondary school students even capitalize on this situation by setting up banking procedures, in which students make deposits into their accounts and write checks to purchase items or privileges they have earned through good work.

Money management should include information about such topics as budgeting, consumer awareness, and comparison shopping. Although these topics normally are not part of the elementary or middle school curriculum, teachers should at least be aware of their importance and begin to include related topics in their instructional day. By the high school years, money management should become an emphasized topic of instruction.

Instructional Methods and Techniques

As you read, think about . . .

1. Applying some of the interventions described in chapter 9 to mathematics instruction.
2. Developing a lesson plan for teaching basic math facts through the acquisition, proficiency, and maintenance stages of learning.
3. Developing real-life word problems that contain computational processes.
4. Explaining how to infuse instructional technology into the lesson plan you developed.
5. Discussing how to develop a "problem-solving" classroom environment.
6. Describing how various instructional arrangements can be used to promote math skills.
7. Developing a thematic unit, specifying math skills.

A wide variety of teaching approaches, methods, and tactics are available for mathematics instruction. Sometimes, an initially scheduled tactic is insufficient to bring about the learning necessary to master the skill. In this case, different instructional methods or approaches are necessary, depending on student performance data analysis. In this section, we discuss instructional methods and interventions for various components of mathematics instruction. In Adapting Instruction, we suggest ideas for adapting mathematics instruction to the general education setting. In Table 12.3, we present a summary of instructional interventions that have proven successful in both research and practice at the elementary and secondary levels for the different stages of learning; narratives are provided to give more detail on selected interventions. Finally, we feature technology that can help students with special needs learn mathematics.

Table 12.3
Mathematics
Teaching Tactics

Instructional target	Stage of learning	Possible tactics
Numeration		
Number concepts	Acquisition	Manipulatives
		Demonstration
		Guided practice
	Proficiency	Drill and practice
		Rewards
Number usage	Acquisition	Manipulatives
	Proficiency	Drill and practice
		Rewards
Basic facts	Initial acquisition	Manipulatives
		Abacus
		Rods
		Counting devices
		Hatch marks
		Number lines
		Time delay
		Audiotapes
		Tutoring
		Cue sheets
		Count Ons
		Doubles
		Near doubles
		Counting down
		Counting up
		Count by
		9s patterns
		Related facts
		Card reader
		Number families
		SOLVE
		DRAW
		Flow sheets
		Self-correction
		With calculator
		With answer keys
		Self-talk
		Verbalizing problem
		Drill
		Flashcards
		Card reader
		Computer games
		Rewarding for accuracy
		Individual
		Group contingencies

Table 12.3
Continued

Basic facts *(continued)*	Initial acquisition *(continued)*	Tutoring
		    Study groups
		    Drill

	Advanced acquisition	Error drill
		Telling
		Rewards
		Praise
		Fines

		Self-correction
		    With calculators
		    With answer keys

		Tutoring
		    Peer drill
		    Peer correction
		    Study groups

	Proficiency	Telling
		    "Work faster"
		    Goal

		Pacers Metronome
		Curricular slice
		Benchmark

		Feedback
		    Today's score compared to goal
		    Today's score compared to yesterday's

		Circle goal problem
		Computer games

		Competition
		    Team
		    Class
		    Self

		Drill
		Tutoring
		Rewards
		Praise
Processes whole numbers, fractions, decimals	Initial acquisition	Demonstration plus permanent model
		Problem solving
		Need to trade
		Are there enough?
		Manipulatives
		Key questions
		Expanded notation
		Sequence of instruction
		Facts and fractions
		Fractions are equal to or greater than 1

continued

Table 12.3
Continued

Processes whole numbers, fractions, decimals (continued)	Initial acquisition (continued)	Defining the whole
		Comparisons
		Cooking with fractions
		Money and decimals
		Decimals and fractions
	Advanced acquisition	Redemonstration of errors
		Telling
		"Be more careful"
		Add cues
	Proficiency	Fluency on facts
	Generalization	Sequence of instruction
		Telling
Calculator usage	Acquisition	Jigsaw technique
		Tutoring
		Study groups
		Peer
		Demonstration
Problem solving	Acquisition	Demonstration
		Manipulatives
		Blocks
		Physical model
		Student-made visuals
		Models
		Charts
		Diagrams
		Tables
		Pictures
		Graphs
		Write number sentences
		Personalize the problem
		Six-step problem-solving strategy
		Cognitive and metacognitive problem-solving strategy
		Fast draw
		Questions and actions
		Use problems that are experimentally based
		Restate problems with smaller numbers
		Study (solution) groups
		Guess and verify
		Discovery approach
		Self-talk
Estimation		Estimation language
		Is an estimate appropriate?
		Computation estimates
		Front-end strategy
		Clustering strategy

Adapting...

Adapting Mathematics Instruction for the General Education Setting

1. Reduce number of problems on worksheets.
2. Provide additional practice time.
3. Use graph paper to keep computational problems properly aligned.
4. Color-code signs.
5. Use directional arrows to signal algorithmic procedures.
6. Teach strategies to achieve mastery.
7. Use the Interactive Unit to tap math knowledge in a variety of formats. ■

Basic Facts Acquisition

Many interventions are used to teach students the 400 facts (100 each for addition, subtraction, multiplication, and division) that are the smaller components of larger computations. Both accuracy and fluency are important to develop as basic fact knowledge. A number of tactics for teaching facts in the acquisition and proficiency stage appear in Table 12.3. In Table 12.4, a list of rules and relationships for the four operations is presented; this information should be taught to all students using direct instruction. Other tactics for the four operations are described in further detail below.

Addition

Cue Sheets   The teacher needs to prepare or have available two sets of worksheets. One set is composed of facts for the students to solve; the other set provides the student with the problems and their solutions. It is advisable to have at least three different versions of each set so the students cannot memorize the location of specific problems. While answering facts on their worksheets, the students are encouraged to find those problems for which they do not know the answers. After using this search-and-find method for several days, the students are then rewarded for completing their pages more and more quickly, thereby discouraging them from looking for each problem and its solution. When instructed to answer problems from memory and to look only for those they cannot remember, students become less dependent on the cue sheet and complete their assignments more quickly.

Count Ons   When given addition fact problems, students are instructed to "start big" by selecting the larger of the two numerals and then to count on by the amount of the second number (Bley & Thornton, 1995). For example, $9 + 3 =$ is worked by saying 9 to "start big" and then counting on three more numerals, 10, 11, 12, to arrive at 12 as the answer. Students can verbalize this process to ensure accuracy in using the "counting-on" procedure, then use the strategy independently to complete their assignments.

Doubles   Doubles is a fairly easy strategy to teach students, and works well as one of the first strategies students should develop (Bley & Thornton, 1995). Doubles are addition fact problems with the same number, such as $6 + 6 =$, $7 + 7 =$, $1 + 1 =$. Doubles can be paired with the cue sheet strategy to promote learning and reward students for memorizing the answers. Students also can be given problems, doubles mixed with other types of problems, and be asked to circle the doubles. This technique can be used as a small-group or guided practice activity to be sure that students understand the concept.

Table 12.4
Mathematical Rules
and Relationships

Rules

Addition

1. Any number plus zero is the number.
2. Any number plus 1 is the next largest number.
3. The order of numbers in an addition problem doesn't change the answer.

Subtraction

1. Any number take away zero is the number.
2. Any number take away the same number is zero.
3. Any number take away 1 is the next smallest number.
4. In subtraction, when the bottom number in the ones column is bigger than the top number in the ones column, the ten is traded.

Multiplication

1. Any number times 0 equals 0.
2. Any number times 1 equals the original number.
3. Two times any number equals the number added to itself.
4. Changing the order of the numbers in multiplication does not change the answer.

Division

1. Zero divided by any number equals 0.
2. Any number divided by 1 equals the number.
3. Any number divided by the same number equals 1.

Relationships

Addition and Subtraction

1. Addition and subtraction facts have the same numbers, but in a different order.

$$\begin{array}{r} 9 \\ + 4 \\ \hline 13 \end{array} \qquad \begin{array}{r} 13 \\ - 9 \\ \hline 4 \end{array} \qquad \begin{array}{r} 13 \\ - 4 \\ \hline 9 \end{array}$$

2. Because addition and subtraction are related, you always can state a subtraction problem as an addition problem.

$$\begin{array}{r} 14 \\ - 8 \\ \hline ? \end{array} \qquad \begin{array}{r} ? \\ + 8 \\ \hline 14 \end{array}$$

3. To check a subtraction answer, add your answer to the number that is being subtracted. If the sum of these two numbers equals the top number in the subtraction problem, your answer is correct.

$$\begin{array}{r} 13 \\ - 5 \\ \hline 8 \end{array} \qquad \begin{array}{r} 8 \\ + 5 \\ \hline 13 \end{array}$$

Multiplication and Division

1. Multiplication and division facts have the same numbers, just in a different order.

$$7 \times 6 = 42$$
$$42 \div 6 = 7$$
$$42 \div 7 = 6$$

2. Because multiplication and division are related, you can always state a division problem as a multiplication problem.

$$56 \div 7 = ?$$
$$? \times 7 = 56$$

Table 12.4
Continued

3. To check a division answer, multiply your answer by the number by which the total is being divided. If the answer to this multiplication problem equals the total, your answer is correct.

$$24 \div 8 = 3$$
$$3 \times 8 = 24$$

Source: From "Promoting Strategic Math Performance among Students with Learning Disabilities," by S. P. Miller, S. Strawser, & C. D. Mercer, in press, *LD Forum*. Copyright 1996 by the Council for Learning Disabilities. Reprinted with permission.

Near Doubles   Near doubles can be taught once students have mastered doubles. Near doubles are addition fact problems in which one numeral is close to a double. For example, 6 + 7 = is close to 7 + 7 =; students should read the problem, identify the related double, solve the double problem, then determine if the original problem is one more or one less than the double. During direct instruction, students could be asked to name the double that is closest to the given problem; in pairs, students could verbalize the strategy and check each other's understanding of the procedure.

Subtraction

Counting Down   Students need to be able to count backward to be successful with this strategy (Bley & Thornton, 1995). A good warm-up might be to have students count backwards in unison from 10; proficiency in counting backward is recommended. Then given a subtraction problem, 9 – 3 =, students say the first numeral, 9, then count down or backward three numerals, 8, 7, 6 to find the answer, 6.

Counting Up   This strategy is similar to counting down; instead of counting backward, students count up, beginning with the smaller numeral. For instance, 9 – 3 =, students begin with 3 and then count up until they reach 9. They could keep a tally count of how many numbers were counted up before reaching the designated number; in this case, six tally marks would have been made to arrive at the answer. Students should understand one-to-one correspondence (for making tally marks) and be able to count forward proficiently to use this strategy successfully.

Multiplication

Count By   The count-by strategy can be used to teach multiplication facts. Students should be able to count by twos, threes, fours, fives, sixes, sevens, eights, nines, tens, elevens, and twelves proficiently. Count-bys can be taught using modeling, choral counting, and filling in charts. For instance, in Figure 12.3, three charts are presented to teach counting by nines; the charts have prompts, partial prompts, and no prompts. Students should demonstrate proficiency with each chart; practice can occur in a variety of instructional arrangements with answer keys available for the partial and no prompts charts. Once students have mastered the sequences, they can be taught the strategy shown in Tables 12.5 and 12.6 for multiplication and division.

Patterns   Students love patterns, and mathematics is a good instructional source for patterns (Bley & Thornton, 1995). The nines table is an excellent example of a math pattern. First, the sum of the digits of a multiple of 9 (up to 10) equals 9 (e.g., 9 × 6 = 54 — 5 + 4 = 9); this serves as a good check for accuracy. Second, the nines times table is lined up vertically, as shown below:

$$9 \times 1 = 9$$
$$9 \times 2 = 18$$
$$9 \times 3 = 27$$

The numbers can be counted sequentially in the answer column: in the ones column, the numbers count down by one, and in the tens column they increase by one. Again, this pattern strategy can serve as a good check for accuracy.

Division

Related Facts   Students should learn the relation between division facts to solve similar types of problems (Bley & Thornton, 1995). For example, given $35 \div 7 = 5$, teach students that $35 \div 5 = 7$.

All Facts

Card Reader   A strategy that can be individualized and is self-checking involves a card reader machine (e.g., Language Master) and a notched card. As seen in Figure 12.4, a fact is written and recorded on a card with a notch. When inserted into the

Figure 12.3
Count-by charts

1. Chart with Prompts

	0	1	2	3	4	5	6	7	8	9
9×	0	9	18	27	36	45	54	63	72	81

2. Chart with Partial Prompts

	0	1	2	3	4	5	6	7	8	9
9×		9		27	36		54		72	81

3. Chart with No Prompts

	0	1	2	3	4	5	6	7	8	9
9×										

Source: From "Teaching Mathematics Using Direct Instruction and Cooperative Learning," by D. P. Rivera, April, 1994, paper presented at the Council for Learning Disabilities International Conference, San Diego, CA.

Table 12.5
Attack Strategy for Multiplication Facts

Attack Strategy: Count by one number the number of times indicated by the other number.

Steps in Attack Strategy:	Example:
1. Read the problem.	$2 \times 5 = \underline{}$
2. Point to a number that you know how to count by.	student points to 2
3. Make the number of marks indicated by the other number.	$2 \times 5 = \underline{}$ /////
4. Begin counting by the number you know how to count by and count up once for each mark, touching each mark.	"2, 4 …"
5. Stop counting when you've touched the last mark.	"… 6, 8, 10"
6. Write the last number you said in the answer space.	$2 \times 5 = \underline{10}$ /////

Source: From "Strategy Training: A Structured Approach to Arithmetic Instruction," by D. Cullinan, J. Lloyd, and M. H. Epstein, 1981, *Exceptional Education Quarterly, 2*(1), p. 44. Copyright 1981 by PRO-ED. Reprinted with permission.

Table 12.6
Division Fact
Strategy

1. Look at the problem.
2. Find the number to divide by.
3. Count by that number.
4. Make a hatch mark or use a counting device for each number counted.
5. Stop at the other number in the problem.
6. Write the answer.

machine, the card stops at the notch, allowing the student time to answer the problem. Then, the card can be pushed through the machine to reveal the prerecorded answer.

Number Families   Facts can be taught in number families so that students learn the relationship of facts. For example, students could learn addition facts to 10 and the corresponding subtraction facts at the same time—3 + 4 =, 7 − 4 =, 7 − 3 =. Students can also practice the commutative property.

SOLVE   The SOLVE strategy is a mnemonic device (Miller & Mercer, 1993a). The steps of the mnemonic are: S = See the sign, O = Observe and answer (if unable to answer, keep going), L = Look and draw, V = Verify your answer, and E = Enter your answer. Students should learn the steps of the SOLVE strategy to mastery (see the strategic approach to instruction in chapter 5) and then be given problems to which the strategy can be applied.

DRAW   The DRAW strategy is another mnemonic device that can be used to help students acquire basic facts (Miller & Mercer, 1991). The steps include: D = Discover the sign, R = Read the problem, A = Answer, or draw and check, and W = Write the answer. As with other strategies, the steps should be taught to automaticity before students are expected to apply the strategy to problems.

Basic Facts Proficiency

Students must become proficient in their knowledge and use of basic arithmetic facts (see Table 12.2 for criteria rates). If they are not fluent in solving these problems, the

Figure 12.4
Card reader
notched card
example

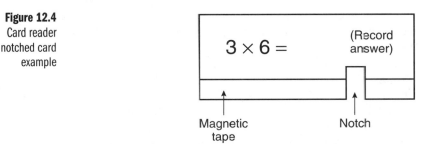

task of mastering larger computations is much more difficult and time consuming. Once youngsters who are proficient in the use of facts master a more complex process, such as regrouping in subtraction, they quickly reach proficiency in that area as well.

To promote basic fact proficiency, teachers can apply many of the same interventions to all four operations. Before making intervention changes, teachers should observe student response habits; sometimes proficient responding is impeded due to poor work habits (e.g., attending to distractions, focusing on the timing device rather than the facts, counting on fingers, moving the pencil away from the worksheet between problems). Inefficient work habits can impact proficiency and can be corrected easily. Thus, teachers can observe and remediate poor work habits, leading to more proficient responding. We now present examples of interventions in addition to those found in Table 12.3.

All Facts

Pacing   The pacing strategy is extremely motivating for those students who are ready to move from the acquisition to proficiency stage (Rivera, in press; Ryberg & Sebastian, 1983). Students should have some knowledge and accuracy with basic facts before implementing this strategy. Pacing devices (e.g., prerecorded audiotapes, metronomes), which make a sound at adjustable intervals (e.g., 25 beeps per minute, 40 beeps per minute), have facilitated fact proficiency. The interval can be set at the desired criterion rate for mastery or as part of a changing criterion design. The students are instructed to work from left to right and to write an answer at each sound on their assigned fact worksheets; they are to skip problems they don't know when the sound occurs. Skipped problems become "learning opportunities" rather than errors, and can be taught through error drill procedures, including the card reader machine, peer tutoring, flashcard practice, and curricular slices (see below).

Curricular Slice   Curricular slices are problems from a larger instructional objective that are particularly problematic for students. For example, if the instructional objective is "write multiplication facts ×0 to 5 with 40 correct problems per minute and no more than 2 errors per minute" and students require additional work with ×4 facts, then the ×4 facts would be practiced before the one-minute timing of the other facts. Thus, the ×4 facts become a curricular slice for practice purposes.

Another type of curricular slice is to identify learning opportunities from a pacing activity. The skipped problems are practiced before the one-minute timing of the other problems on the pacing worksheet. In this case, the skipped problems may vary and, returning to the ×0 to 5 facts example, could include several ×3, ×4, and ×5 problems. Curricular slices can be practiced in different instructional arrangements, with the card reader machine, and in warm-up one-minute timings.

Benchmark   With the benchmark strategy, a student receives a worksheet of facts and works in a left-to-right progression. A fact (benchmark) is designated as the target to reach by the end of the one-minute timing. Students can star, circle, or identify the designated fact in any manner. Rewards can be distributed for students who reach their benchmark. The benchmark fact can be determined by the teacher (1) identifying the number of correct problems previously answered in a one-minute timing, and (2) multiplying that number by 1.25 percent; this new number becomes the benchmark for the next one-minute timing. For example, if a student computed 20 problems correctly in one minute on Monday, then the benchmark figure is 25. The benchmark strategy is very motivating as it promotes self-competition.

Processes

Solving problems containing whole numbers, fractions, and decimals requires an understanding of the relationship between numbers and place value, and skill in estimating, determining reasonableness of answers, using a calculator, and using appropriate algorithms. Instruction in whole numbers fractions, and decimals should occur throughout the K–12 curriculum. It is not necessary for students to master addition before being introduced to subtraction, to learn whole number computations before computing fractions, or to know basic facts proficiently before being introduced to process problems. In this section, we highlight specific tactics for teaching whole numbers, fractions, and decimals.

Whole Numbers

Problem Solving   Present whole number computation within the context of story problems. Story problems can be based on life skills—shopping, money, checking account—or classroom situations. Reinforcing whole number computation in a problem-solving context is strongly recommended as a "best practice" in mathematics education.

Need to Trade   Need to trade, a prerequisite to renaming (carrying) in addition, can be introduced once students have practiced adding with no renaming (Bley & Thornton, 1995). Students are presented with a variety of addition problems with and without renaming. They are to identify those problems in which renaming is required or in which they need to trade 10 ones for one bundle of 10.

Are There Enough?   Are there enough? is used for subtraction problems with and without renaming (borrowing) (Bley & Thornton, 1995). Students are given different subtraction problems and must decide if the top number in the ones place is a large enough number from which to subtract the bottom number. This activity focuses students' attention on the ones place, number discrimination, and place value.

Manipulatives   A variety of manipulatives can be used to teach place value and the concept of whole number computation with and without regrouping. For example, teachers can use Stern Blocks, Cuisenaire rods, base 10 blocks, and bean sticks to teach whole number computation at the concrete level. These manipulatives have been field-tested and proven effective in denoting place value concepts and whole number computations. Figure 12.5 illustrates how bean sticks can be used to represent a math problem presented at the symbolic or abstract (i.e., numbers) level.

Demonstration Plus Permanent Model   Time after time, the *demonstration plus permanent model technique* (Smith & Lovitt, 1975; Rivera & Smith, 1987, 1988) has proven exceptionally effective in teaching students how to solve problems that include addition, subtraction, or multiplication. This technique takes approximately forty-five seconds of instructional time, is best applied individually, and can greatly

Figure 12.5
Using bean sticks
to solve
computational
problems

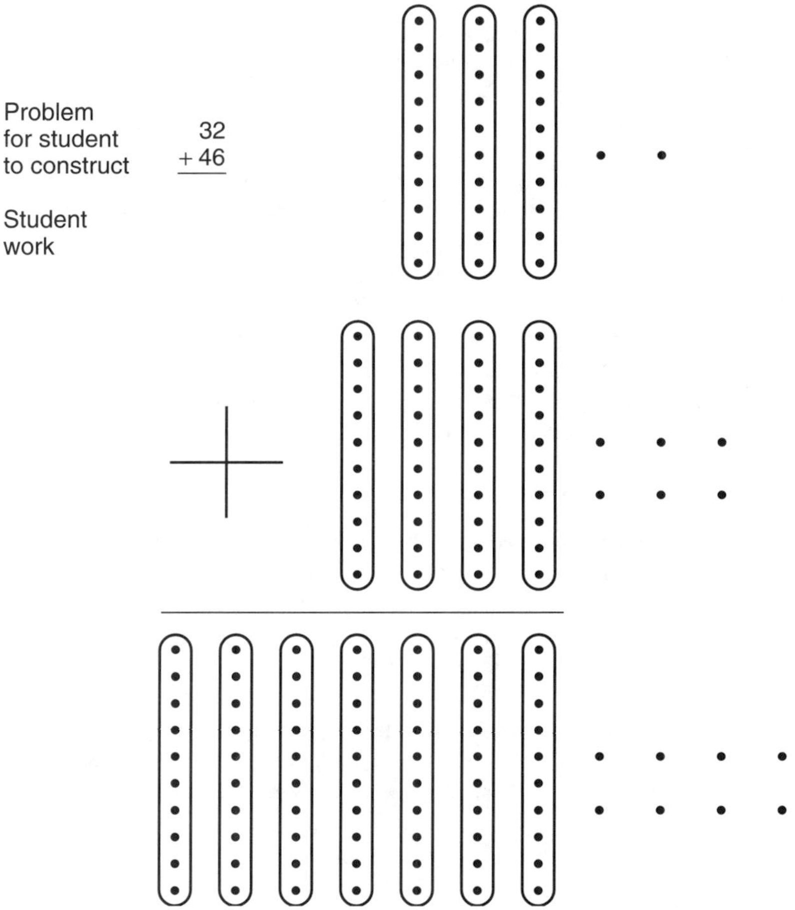

Problem
for student
to construct

Student
work

$$\begin{array}{r} 32 \\ + 46 \\ \hline \end{array}$$

Source: From "Mathematics Instruction for Students with Special Needs," by D. Rivera and B. R. Bryant, 1992, *Intervention in School and Clinic*, *28*(2), p. 79. Copyright 1992 by PRO-ED. Reprinted with permission.

facilitate mastery of computation. Teachers using this procedure often report that students have mastered an entire operation (subtraction) in only one month.

When using this tactic, the teacher instructs and demonstrates before the student completes the arithmetic assignment for the day. For example, the student is given a worksheet containing subtraction problems from the same response class (all three-digit problems in which the top number is a multiple of 100). Before the student solves the problems on the page, the teacher comes to the student's desk or chalkboard and computes a sample problem. Throughout this demonstration, the teacher verbalizes the steps used to arrive at the correct solution. The teacher then has the student solve another problem on the page to be certain that he or she can do so accurately. If that problem is correctly computed, the student completes the worksheet independently. This routine is followed for a minimum of three days or until the student reaches the criterion (three scores above 90 percent).

For long division, this procedure needs to be adapted slightly. Because of the complexity of long division problems and the number of steps involved in their solutions, some students need more than a single demonstration. The script to follow when demonstrating long division to students is found in Table 12.7.

Key Questions Some students become confused while solving multistep whole number computation (e.g., division, multiplication) (Rivera & Smith, 1988). The teacher can ask the following key questions to help students get back on track:

1. What is the problem?
2. What are the steps?
3. What did you just do?
4. What do you do next?

Furthermore, students can be taught to ask themselves these questions or to refer to a chart or cue card with the questions, thus promoting more self-directed learning.

Expanded Notation Expanded notation can be used as an alternative algorithm to traditional instructional procedures for whole number computation (Cawley & Parmar, 1992). For instance, a subtraction problem and its expanded notation are shown below:

Table 12.7
Daily Procedures and Script to Teach Long Division

Step 1

Teacher: Shows student how to use fact table.

Step 2

Teacher: Shows graphs to each student. Points our changes on graph.

Step 3

Teacher: Implements intervention on demonstration problem (e.g., 5)1240).
"Does 5 go into 1? Does 5 go into 12?"
"Place dot. 5)1240. How many numbers are in the answer?" (Student counts numerals in dividend from the dot.)
"Divide. How many times does 5 go into 12?" (Student says and writes answer.)
"Multiply."
"Subtract."
"Check. Is the subtraction answer smaller than divisor? Yes, continue. No, check work."
"Bring down." (Student brings down the next number.)
"Repeat."
"Put up remainder, even if zero."

Step 4

Student: Solves a sample problem and verbalizes steps.
If student completes problem correctly, student then completes worksheet independently.
If problem is computed incorrectly, steps 3 and 4 are repeated with different problems.

Note: Underlined words are key words emphasized by data collector.
Source: From "Using a Demonstration Strategy to Teach Midschool Students with Learning Disabilities How to Compute Long Division," by D. M. Rivera and D. D. Smith, 1988, *Journal of Learning Disabilities, 21*(2). Copyright 1988 by PRO-ED. Reprinted with permission.

$$
\begin{array}{r}
457 \\
-\ 35 \\
\hline
\end{array}
\qquad
\begin{array}{r}
400 + 50 + 7 \\
-\quad\ \ 30 + 5 \\
\hline
400 + 20 + 2 = 422
\end{array}
$$

This algorithm gives students a chance to show place value representations of numerals and to calculate the answer. Students could be asked to verbalize the steps in this problem, use manipulatives to represent the expanded notation, or work with a partner to solve problems.

Sequence of Instruction   Traditionally, special education teachers present information to students in a task-analyzed, sequenced format (Rivera & Smith, 1987, 1988). Students are taught the easiest skill in the sequence first. Once they master that skill, they learn the next one, and so on. Research has revealed that students do not have to be taught whole number computational skills in an easy-to-difficult sequence for learning to occur. Rather, the most difficult skill within a group can be taught; in general, students tend to generalize the algorithmic process understanding to the easier problems.

Here are some guidelines for teaching a difficult-to-easy sequence in which the difficult problems are taught and practiced and the easier problems are only practiced.

1. Develop a task analysis of whole number computation (e.g., two digits + one digit, two digits + two digits, three digits + two digits, three digits + three digits—all with no regrouping; two digits + one digit, two digits + two digits, three digits + two digits, three digits + three digits—all with renaming).
2. Test students to determine which skills they have mastered within the sequence and which skills require instruction.
3. Group skills by no renaming and renaming.
4. Select the most difficult skill within a group as the instructional target (e.g., three digits + three digits with no renaming; three digits + three digits with renaming).
5. Teach this most difficult skill using the demonstration plus permanent model intervention, for example.
6. Present practice problems representing all of the skills within a group (e.g., two digits + one digit, two digits + two digits, three digits + two digits, three digits + three digits—all with renaming).
7. Collect student performance data on all of the skills on the practice sheet.

Fractions

Demonstration Plus Permanent Model   This technique is just as effective with fractions as with whole numbers (see above).

Facts and Fractions   Combine instruction of basic facts with simple fraction problems (Atkinson, 1983). Build fluency in math fact responding. Then, present fractions containing the facts students have been practicing. For example, if the targeted multiplication facts are the ×8 table, then fraction problems might include

$$
\frac{8}{9} \times \frac{6}{8} = \frac{48}{72} = \frac{2}{3}
$$

This technique could help students make the connection between learning multiplication facts and multiplying fractions.

Fractions as Equal To or Greater Than 1 Teach students a range of fractional representations when first introducing the concept of a fraction (Kelly, Gersten, & Carnine, 1990). Rather than limiting instruction to 1/2, 1/4, and 1/3 initially, include fractions (concrete and pictorial representations) such as 5/5, 3/1, and 12/4. This way, students learn from the beginning of fraction instruction that fractions represent relationships and not specific amounts.

Defining the Whole Provide experiences with a variety of manipulatives so students learn that many different shapes can be partitioned (Baroody & Hume, 1991). Use Cuisenaire rods, fraction strips, fraction tiles, and pattern blocks to provide activities with quantities in different forms and shapes. Children need to see that fractions involve more than pies and pizza.

Comparisons Comparisons help students see comparative sizes of fractions and the relationship between the sizes (Baroody & Hume, 1991). For example, younger children might state that 1/3 is greater than 1/2 because 3 is greater than 2. Comparisons using manipulatives can help students develop an understanding of relative sizes. Students must know the identity of the whole (e.g., a cake, a stick of butter) to discern accurately that 1/2 is indeed greater than 1/3.

Cooking with Fractions Probably one of the best ways to teach and reinforce the concept of fractions is through cooking experiences. Reading and following recipes provide an excellent opportunity for students to measure specific fractional units, to discuss why certain amounts are specified, and to make comparisons between fractional units. Teaching older students how to double or halve a recipe adds another dimension of fraction instruction to the cooking experience. Cooking is an appropriate activity for all ages. It can be treated as a "life skills" class for older students, a language experience class for younger students, or a class activity in which family members are invited to reap the benefits of the experience.

Decimals

Demonstration Plus Permanent Model As with whole numbers and fractions (see above), decimals can be taught effectively with this technique.

Money and Decimals Teach money, decimals, and computational skills together. Money and decimals have a natural connection, are a life skill, and may have more relevance for students if taught together. These skills can be taught during a community-based shopping field trip or in a "store" operated in the classroom. Most authorities would recommend that students be taught money skills using real as opposed to "play" money, because some students with learning problems may have difficulty generalizing their knowledge of coin and bill recognition from "play" to real money. Some teachers use the newspaper to teach and reinforce money, decimals, and computational skills. Asking students to compute prices of items, to spend a designated amount of money by computing sale prices and to compare prices between different ads are all activities that require students to use money, decimals, and computational skills.

Decimals and Fractions   Teach decimals and fractions together. Decimals such as .25, .50, and .75 can be translated easily into fractions (and money) so that students can see connections between these skills (Bley & Thornton, 1995).

Solving Word Problems

Solving word problems is a basic life skill and is recommended as a major component of the mathematics curriculum (NCTM, 1989). Problem solving is a method of inquiry and application of mathematical content across diverse situations. Teachers can foster problem-solving abilities by emphasizing real-world story problems, turning classroom situations into story problems, having large as well as small numbers, and containing too little or too much information.

In solving word problems, many students have more success if they are allowed to use manipulatives, such as blocks, to count out the problem's solution. For some youngsters, being able to verbalize the problem as they either count up (to add) or down (to subtract) helps them find the solution. For others, being able to use a calculator removes the difficulty of having to compute the answer and allows the student to focus on the problem's demands. Some teachers have found that the questions cited in Tables 12.8 and 12.9 aid some children in solving word problems.

When teaching problem solving, teachers should keep in mind some general notions. To become good problem solvers, students need to have many opportunities to solve problems. They need sufficient time to think, plan, discuss, and test their solutions. Problem solving requires a great deal of thinking and decision making.

It is important for students to have considerable practice in solving math-related problems. Groups of youngsters could be given many different problems throughout the school year that match their interests and experience. They could find all possible

Table 12.8 Strategy for Approaching Word Problems	Are there words I do not know?
	Restate the problem.
	What's the problem's question?
	What's the important information?
	What are the key words?
	Is there unnecessary information?
	What numbers do I use?
	Choose the operation to perform.
	Do it!

Table 12.9 Areas to Consider When Solving Word Problems	What information is needed?
	Highlight the information that is needed.
	List needed, missing information.
	What operation will solve the problem?
	Mentally picture the problem.
	Is the answer reasonable?
	Estimate before computing.

ways to arrange five square blocks, or write the numbers from 1 to 25 as the sums of consecutive numbers. Have a group of three children share a banana. A group could be asked to divide a package of flower seeds equally among six pots or decide how many students would be in a group if there are only five microscopes to share. The number of practical problem-solving activities available in school settings is almost unlimited. Students need to develop these skills through instruction and practice.

Instructional guidelines for promoting successful story problem solving appear in Tips for Teachers (Bley & Thornton, 1995; Cawley, Miller, & School, 1987).

Tips for Teachers

Solving Word Problems

Techniques to use:

1. Diagnosing reasons for problem-solving difficulty (e.g., language, numbers too big, reading problem, extraneous information, linguistic structure) and rewriting problems accordingly.
2. Having students write story problems for peers to solve.
3. Monitoring student performance regularly.
4. Teaching explicit strategies.
5. Including problems with too little or too much information; ask students to tell what is needed or what is extraneous.
6. Having students substitute small numbers for large numbers that may be troublesome.
7. Encouraging the use of calculators.

Techniques to avoid:

1. Teaching key words to signal the use of specific operations.
2. Using problem-solving activities as an occasional wrap-up or filler activity.
3. Marking a child wrong if the computation is incorrect. ■

Students with learning and behavior difficulties need to be taught specific cognitive and metacognitive strategies to help them solve word problems. Table 12.10 shows field-tested strategies to teach story problem solving to students with special needs.

Estimation

Estimation is a life skill, yet receives little emphasis in daily mathematics instruction. Estimation can be part of a total school curriculum, being taught throughout the school day relative to school and life activities. We now present ideas for promoting estimation abilities.

Estimation Language   Teach students estimation language (about how much, close to, somewhere between, in the neighborhood of) (Trafton, 1986). Give students problem situations and have them listen to the language to determine whether or not an estimated answer is appropriate. Sample problem situations might include: About how long will it take to drive 650 miles? How much is the monthly rent? About how much is the shopping bill?

Table 12.10
Story Problem-
Solving Strategies

1. Six-step problem-solving strategy (Marzola, 1987)

    a. State the question.

    b. Identify the operation.

    c. Eliminate extraneous information.

    d. State how many steps are involved.

    e. Solve the problem.

    f. Check your work.

2. Cognitive and metacognitive problem-solving strategy (Montague & Bos, 1986)

    a. Read the problem.

    b. Paraphrase the information.

    c. Visualize the information.

    d. Identify the problem.

    e. Develop a hypothesis.

    f. Estimate the answer.

    g. Compute the problem.

    h. Check your work.

3. FAST DRAW (Mercer & Miller, 1992)

    a. **F**ind what you're solving for.

    b. **A**sk yourself, what the parts of the problem are.

    c. **S**et up the numbers.

    d. **T**ie down the sign.

    (See the section called "Basic Facts Acquisition" for the DRAW steps.)

4. Questions and actions (Rivera, 1994)

Step	Questions	Actions
a. Read the problem.	Are there words I don't know?	Underline words.
	Do I know what each word means?	Find out definitions.
	Do I need to reread the problem?	Reread.
	Are there number words?	Underline.
b. Restate the problem.	What information is important?	Underline.
	What information isn't needed?	Cross out.
	What is the question asking?	Put in own words.
	What are the facts?	Make a list.
c. Develop a plan.	How can the facts be organized?	Develop chart.
	How many steps are there?	Use manipulatives.
	What operations will I use?	Use smaller numbers.
		Select an operation.
d. Compute the problem.	Did I get the correct answer?	Estimate.
		Check with partner.
		Verify with calculator.
e. Examine the results.	Have I answered the question?	Reread question.
	Does my answer seem reasonable?	Check question and answer.
	Can I restate question or answer?	Write a number sentence.

Is an Estimate Appropriate?   Provide situations to students or have them work in teams to create situations that require an exact answer or an estimate. Have students decide whether the situations warrant an exact answer or an estimate. Ask students to describe reasons for their answers.

Computation Estimates   Give students problems (whole numbers, fractions, decimals) and have them estimate the answer after examining the numbers. Discuss rounding as a strategy to assist with this task. Students can compute the answer or use a calculator to verify how accurate their estimates were.

Front-End Strategy   The front-end strategy is useful for computing column addition (Reys, 1986). Provide students with a list of numbers to be added, such as 376 + 87 + 432 + 11. Tell the students to add the numbers in "front" first (i.e., 300 + 400 = 700). Then, show them how to adjust the numbers in the tens and ones column to form 100 (i.e., 87 + 11 is about 100 and 76 + 32 is about 100, which makes 200). Third, add the "front" number (700) to the adjusted number (200). Finally, estimate the answer (900 in this case). This strategy can be applied to adding money as well.

Clustering Strategy   The clustering strategy is appropriate to use when all of the numbers have about the same numerical value. For instance, the number of people who attend a football game during one month might be 15,833, 17,021, and 16,682. All of the numbers cluster around 16,000, so 16,000 × 3 = 48,000 people for three games.

Technology

Instructional technology can support instruction and mastery of instructional objectives in mathematics programs. Assistive technology devices can be used to help youngsters access mathematics instruction and curriculum (see chapter 5 for a discussion of assistive technology). Suggestions for infusing instructional and assistive technology into mathematics programs appear in Focus on Technology.

Focus on Technology

Technology that Aids in Mathematics

- **Assistive technology**

  1. Calculators
     Use large-key calculators for younger students or students with dexterity problems. This type of calculator makes it easier for some students to input numerals and operation symbols. Use talking calculators for students who might benefit from verbal feedback regarding numeral and symbol selection.

  2. Tape recorders
     Use audiotapes of basic math facts or other math skills with accompanying worksheets for students who might benefit from instructional practice activities presented both in writing and orally.

- **Instructional technology**

  1. Evaluate software carefully to determine presentation format of math skills. Be sure that the algorithms presented in the software match those presented during direct instruction.

2. Select a variety of instructional software; avoid strictly drill-and-practice formats.

3. Infuse math software into different instructional arrangements (e.g., peer tutoring, cooperative learning, learning center, individualized). ●

Software for readiness; computation; time, money, and measurement; algebra; and story problem solving is widely available and is the most common type of software programming (Lewis, 1993). Most programs are of a drill-and-practice nature and include a gamelike feature (see chapter 5 for a discussion of software). Software features should include data collection systems to monitor student performance, positive feedback systems, branching opportunities for additional practice, and adjustable responding rates to promote proficiency. We provide a brief listing of software and publishers for seven math areas. It is beyond the scope of this book to offer extensive descriptions of these software programs; readers are left to their own discretion to select software that fits their hardware options and meets their students' instructional needs. Furthermore, we do not endorse any publisher. We merely list examples of software and companies that were popular when we wrote this book.

Readiness software programs typically focus on counting, numeral recognition, and matching (Lewis, 1993). Examples of readiness programs include Stickybear Numbers (Weekly Reader Software), Counting Critters (Minnesota Educational Computing Corporation [MECC]), and Math and Me (Davidson).

Computation (process problems and basic facts) software is the most common type of mathematics software. Computer games can turn monotonous drill and practice into a fun and novel way for students to practice arithmetic facts. Some of the computational software available includes The New Math Blaster Plus! (Davidson & Associates), Conquering Math Series (MECC), Speedway Math (MECC), and Talking Math and Me (Davidson).

Time, money, and measurement are essential life skills and can be practiced with good instructional software. These life skills typically receive less instructional time than they deserve; thus, software programs in this area can greatly enhance instructional emphasis and time. Clock (Hartley), Clock Works (MECC), and Timekeeper (Edmark) are useful programs for instruction on time. Measurement skills can be practiced using Measure Works (MECC). Money! Money! (Hartley) and Money Works (MECC) are examples of programs to promote money skills.

Algebra is an area sorely neglected in math instruction for youngsters with learning and behavior problems. As noted earlier in this chapter, more advanced math skills, including algebra, might be better taught by teachers with secondary-level content preparation. Special education teachers could support such instruction; one way would be through computer-assisted instruction. Alge-Blaster Plus! (Davidson) is an example of software specifically targeting algebra skills. Math Blaster Mystery (Davidson) also includes pre-algebra and critical-thinking skills.

Story problem solving is strongly endorsed as an area requiring more intensive classroom instructional time. Although not as common as computation software, problem-solving software is becoming more popular in the classroom. Software selection should be based on strategies presented for solving story problems, level of problem difficulty (e.g., one- or two-step problems), presence of extraneous information, and language of the problems. Software for word problem solving includes Math Blaster Mystery (Davidson), Math Word Problems (Weekly Reader), Stickybear Word Problems (Weekly Reader), and Survival Math (Wings for Learning/Sunburst).

Summary

Mathematics is an important curricular area for all students—mathematics skills are important to independent adult living as well as to academic success. As teachers plan instruction, they must remember that mathematics is a complex area made up of several diverse skills. Although many students with special needs receive instruction predominantly in arithmetic computation, instructional balance should be sought. All students should be exposed to a wide variety of topics, such as consumer skills, measurement, problem solving, numeration, and computation. They should also be taught to use calculators and computers, which might facilitate reasoning skills.

A variety of curricular and design features are available to help students with special needs master mathematical skills and concepts more readily. For instance, teaching students the language of mathematics can promote a better understanding of symbols. Presenting skills as "big ideas" may help students make better connections across skills. Using textbooks and manipulatives wisely to support math instruction is recommended.

Research provides considerable information about many instructional tactics that help students master mathematical concepts and skills (see Table 12.3 for a review). These procedures include modeling, drill and practice, computer-assisted instruction, and problem-solving strategies. Teachers must remember, however, to apply the stages of learning theory as they help children master mathematics. Unless students have acquired skills in mathematics and can maintain their proficient use, they will be unable to think through situations requiring mathematics, which they will routinely encounter in daily life.

Technology can play a significant role in mathematics instruction. Numerous software programs are currently available that provide drill, practice, simulations, and problem-solving exercises in mathematical skills and concepts. Software can be used to supplement direct instruction and practiced in different student-mediated instructional arrangements. Furthermore, assistive technology devices can be useful for students who must find ways to compensate for their disabilities and gain access to the curriculum. Certainly, some students can use alternative keyboards and large-key calculators to facilitate computer use, problem solving, and self-correcting.

Mathematics instruction is receiving more attention by special education researchers and educators as it is now well recognized that many students with learning problems have difficulty mastering skills and concepts. More emphasis needs to be placed on the teaching components of an entire mathematics curriculum (not just computation) to prepare students better for the mathematical life skills of adulthood.

Study and Discussion Questions

1. Describe the nature of mathematics instruction.
2. Identify and explain components of mathematics instruction.
3. Provide explanations of instruction for components of mathematics.
4. Provide reasons to change the traditional mathematics curriculum for students with special needs.
5. Discuss how much emphasis should be placed on teaching computation to specific youngsters. Develop a case study.
6. Design a lesson that integrates calculators and technology into the instructional program.

7. Design a lesson with a general education teacher to adapt mathematics instruction in the classroom.

8. Prepare a list of activities for families to do at home with their children to reinforce mathematics instruction.

9. Develop a K–12 mathematics life skills curriculum. Design an elementary and secondary lesson plan to teach a skill from your curriculum.

10. Teach a student using one of the strategies described in the "Instructional Methods and Techniques" section; collect data using a measurement system in chapter 6 and include a technique to promote generalization.

• •

References and Suggested Readings

Cawley, J. F., Baker-Kroczynski, S., & Urban, A. (1992). Seeking excellence in mathematics education for students with mild disabilities. *Teaching Exceptional Children, 24,* 40–43.

Cawley, J. F., & Miller, J. H. (1989). Cross-sectional comparisons of the mathematical performance of children with learning disabilities: Are we on the right track toward comprehensive programming? *Journal of Learning Disabilities, 24,* 250–254, 259.

Garnett, K. (1987). Math learning disabilities: Teaching and learners. *Reading, Writing, and Learning Disabilities, 3,* 1–8.

Warner, M., Alley, G., Schumaker, J., Deshler, D., & Clark, F. (1980). *An epidemiological study of learning disabled adolescents in secondary schools: Achievement and ability, socioeconomic status, and school experiences.* Lawrence: Kansas University, Institute for Research in Learning Disabilities.

Nature of Mathematics Instruction
Definition of Mathematical Literacy
National Council of Teachers of Mathematics. (1989). *Curriculum and evaluation standards for school mathematics.* Reston, VA: Author.

Issues and Reform in Mathematics Education
Fleischner, J. E., Garnett, K., & Shepard, M. (1982). Proficiency in arithmetic basic fact computation by learning disabled and nondisabled children. *Focus on Learning Problems in Mathematics, 4,* 47–55.

Hofmeister, A. M. (1993). Elitism and reform in school mathematics. *Remedial and Special Education, 14*(6), 8–13.

Hutchinson, N. L. (1993). Students with disabilities and mathematics education reform—Let the dialogue begin. *Remedial and Special Education, 14*(6), 20–23.

Lindquist, M., Carpenter, T. P., Silver, E., & Mathews, W. (1983). The third national mathematics assessment: Results and implications for elementary and middle schools. *The Arithmetic Teacher, 31*(4), 14–19.

McKnight, C., Crosswhite, F., Dossey, J., Kifer, E., Swafford, J., Travers, K., & Cooney, T. (1987). *The underachieving curriculum: Assessing U.S. school mathematics from an international perspective.* Champaign, IL: Stipes.

Mercer, C. D., Harris, C. A., & Miller, S. P. (1993). Reforming reforms in mathematics. *Remedial and Special Education, 14*(6), 14–19.

National Council of Teachers of Mathematics. (1988). NAEP: Results of the fourth mathematics assessment. *Education Week, 7*(38), 28–29.

National Council of Teachers of Mathematics. (1989). *Curriculum and evaluation standards for school mathematics.* Reston, VA: Author.

National Research Council. (1989). *Everybody counts—A report to the nation on the future of mathematics education.* Washington, DC: National Academy Press.

Rivera, D. (1993). Examining mathematics reform and the implications for students with mathematical disabilities. *Remedial and Special Education, 14*(6), 24–27.

Rivera, D. P., Taylor, R. L., & Bryant, B. R. (1994–1995). A review of current trends in mathematics assessment for students with mild disabilities. *Diagnostique, 20,* 143–174.

Curricular and Instructional Design Features
Baroody, A. J. (1989). Manipulatives don't come with guarantees. *Arithmetic Teacher, 37*(2), 4–5.

Capps, L. R., & Cox, L. S. (1991). Improving the learning of mathematics in our schools. *Focus on Exceptional Children, 23*(9), 1–8.

Carnine, D. (in press). Instructional design in mathematics for students with learning disabilities. *Journal of Learning Disabilities.*

Carnine, D., Jones, E., & Dixon, R. (1994). Mathematics: Educational tools for diverse learners. *School Psychology Review, 23,* 406–427.

Carnine, D., & Kameeui, E. (1992). *Higher order thinking: Designing curriculum for mainstreamed students.* Austin, TX: PRO-ED.

Cawley, J. F., Fitzmaurice, A. M., Sedlak, R., & Althaus, V. (1976). *Project math.* Tulsa, OK: Educational Progress.

Cawley, J. F., & Parmar, R. S. (1992). Arithmetic programming for students with disabilities: An alternative. *Remedial and Special Education, 13*(3), 6–18.

Evans, D. G. (1990). *Comparison of three instructional strategies for teaching borrowing in subtraction.* Unpublished doctoral dissertation, University of Oregon, Eugene.

Lambert, M. (in press). Mathematics textbooks, materials, and manipulatives. *LD Forum.*

Larsen, S. C., Parker, R. M., & Trenholme, B. (1978). The effects of syntactic complexity upon arithmetic performance. *Learning Disability Quarterly, 1,* 80–85.

Mercer, C. D., & Miller, S. P. (1992). Teaching students with learning problems in math to acquire, understand, and apply basic math facts. *Remedial and Special Education, 13*(3), 19–35, 61.

Miller, S. P., Mercer, C. D., & Dillon, A. (1992). CSA: Acquiring and retaining math skills. *Intervention in School and Clinic, 28,* 105–110.

Montague, M., & Applegate, B. (1993). Middle school students' mathematical problem solving: An analysis of think-aloud protocols. *Learning Disability Quarterly, 16,* 19–30.

National Council of Teachers of Mathematics. (1989). *Curriculum and evaluation standards for school mathematics.* Reston, VA: Author.

Pellegrino, J. W., & Goldman, S. R. (1987). Information processing and elementary mathematics. *Journal of Learning Disabilities, 20*(1), 22–32, 57.

Rivera, D. M., & Bryant, B. R. (1992). Mathematics instruction for students with special needs. *Intervention in School and Clinic, 28*(2), 71–86.

Rivera, D. M., & Smith, D. D. (1988). Using a demonstration strategy to teach midschool students with learning disabilities how to compute long division. *Journal of Learning Disabilities, 21*(2), 77–81.

Samuels, S. J. (1987). Information processing abilities and reading. *Journal of Learning Disabilities, 20*(1), 18–22.

Scott, P. B., & Raborn, D. T. (in press). Realizing the gifts of diversity among students with learning disabilities. *LD Forum.*

Smith, D. D., & Lovitt, T. C. (1982). The computational arithmetic program. Austin, TX: PRO-ED.

Wheeler, L. J., & McNutt, G. (1983). The effect of syntax on low-achieving students' abilities to solve mathematical word problems. *The Journal of Special Education, 17*(3), 309–315.

Wiig, E. H., & Semel, E. M. (1984). *Language assessment and intervention for the learning disabled* (2nd ed.). New York: Macmillan.

Instructional Approaches

Brown, V. L. (1985). Direction mathematics: A framework for instructional accountability. *Remedial and Special Education, 6*(1), 53–58.

Carpenter, R. L. (1985). Mathematics instruction in resource rooms: Instruction time and teacher competency. *Learning Disability Quarterly, 8,* 95–100.

Cawley, J. F., & Parmar, R. S. (in press). Instructional practices in mathematics for students with learning disabilities. *Journal of Learning Disabilities.*

Engelmann, S., Carnine, D., Kelly, B., & Engelmann, O. (1991–1995). *Connecting math concepts.* Chicago: Science Research Associates.

Gersten, R., Woodward, J., & Darch, C. (1986). Direct instruction: A research-based approach to curriculum design and teaching. *Exceptional Children, 53*(1), 17–31.

Goldman, S. R. (1989). Strategy instruction in mathematics. *Learning Disability Quarterly, 12,* 43–55.

Goldman, S. R., Pellegrino, J. W., & Mertz, D. L. (1988). Extended practice of basic addition facts: Strategy changes in learning disabled students. *Cognition & Instruction, 5,* 223–265.

Jones, E. D., Wilson, R., & Bhojwani, S. (in press). Mathematics instruction for secondary students with LD. *Journal of Learning Disabilities.*

Pressley, M. (1986). The relevance of the good strategy user model to the teaching of mathematics. *Educational Psychology, 21,* 139–161.

Silbert, J., Carnine, D., & Stein, M. (1990). *Direct instruction mathematics* (2nd ed.). New York: Merrill.

Thornton, C., Langrall, C., & Jones, G. (in press). Mathematics instruction for elementary students with LD. *Journal of Learning Disabilities.*

Skills for Instruction and Instructional Methods and Techniques

Connolly, A. J., Nachtman, W., & Pritchett, E. M. (1988). *KeyMath revised: A diagnostic inventory of essential mathematics.* Circle Pines, MN: American Guidance Service.

National Council of Teachers of Mathematics. (1988). NAEP: Results of the fourth mathematics assessment. *Education Week, 7*(38), 28–29.

National Council of Teachers of Mathematics. (1989). *Curriculum and evaluation standards for school mathematics.* Reston, VA: Author.

National Research Council. (1989). *Everybody counts—A report to the nation on the future of mathematics education.* Washington, DC: National Academy Press.

Basic Facts Acquisition and Proficiency

Bley, N. S., & Thornton, C. A. (1995). *Teaching mathematics to students with learning disabilities.* Austin, TX: PRO-ED.

Brulle, A. R., & Brulle, C. G. (1982). Programming generalization of computational skills. *Learning Disability Quarterly, 4,* 203–216.

Cullinan, D., Lloyd, J., & Epstein, M. H. (1981). Strategy training: A structured approach to arithmetic instruction. *Exceptional Education Quarterly, 2,*(1), 41–49.

Garnett, K., & Fleischner, J. E. (1983). Automatization and basic fact performance of normal and learning disabled children. *Learning Disability Quarterly, 6,* 223–230.

Lloyd, J., Saltzman, N. J., & Kauffman, J. M. (1981). Predictable generalization in academic learning as a result of preskills and strategy training. *Learning Disability Quarterly, 4,* 203–216.

Lombardo, T. W., & Drabman, R. S. (1985). Teaching LD children multiplication tables. *Academic Therapy, 20*(4), 437–442.

Lovitt, T. C. (1995). *Tactics for teaching* (2nd ed.). Columbus, OH: Merrill.

Mattingly, J. C., & Bott, D. A. (1990). Teaching multiplication facts to students with learning problems. *Exceptional Children, 56*(5), 438–449.

Mercer, C. D., & Miller, S. P. (1992a). Teaching students with learning problems in math to acquire, understand, and apply basic math facts. *Remedial and Special Education, 13*(3), 19–35, 61.

Mercer, C. D., & Miller, S. P. (1992b). *Multiplication facts 0 to 81.* Lawrence, KS: Edge Enterprises.

Miller, S. P., & Mercer, C. D. (1991). *Addition facts 0 to 9.* Lawrence, KS: Edge Enterprises.

Miller, S. P., & Mercer, C. D. (1993a). Mnemonics: Enhancing the math performance of students with learning difficulties. *Intervention in School and Clinic, 29,* 78–82.

Miller, S. P., Strawser, S., & Mercer, C. D. (in press). Promoting strategic math performance among students with learning disabilities. *LD Forum.*

Rivera, D. P. (1994, April). *Teaching mathematics using direct instruction and cooperative learning.* Paper presented at the International Conference of the Council for Learning Disabilities, San Diego, CA.

Rivera, D. P. (In press). Using cooperative learning to teach mathematics to students with learning disabilities. *LD Forum.*

Ryberg, S., & Sebastian, J. (1983, April). *What to do if your chart goes flat: Pacing.* Paper presented at the International Conference of the Council for Exceptional Children, Detroit, MI.

Processes

Baroody, A. J., & Hume, J. (1991). Meaningful mathematics instruction: The case for fractions. *Remedial and Special Education, 12*(3), 54–68.

Blankenship, C. S., & Baumgartner, M. D. (1982). Programming generalization of computational skills. *Learning Disability Quarterly, 5,* 152–162.

Bley, N. S., & Thornton, C. A. (1995). *Teaching mathematics to students with learning disabilities.* Austin, TX: PRO-ED.

Cawley, J. F., & Parmar, R. S. (1992). Arithmetic programming for students with disabilities: An alternative. *Remedial and Special Education, 13*(3), 6–18.

Kelly, B., Gersten, R., & Carnine, D. (1990). Student error patterns as a function of curricular design: Teaching fractions to remedial high school students and high school students with learning disabilities. *Journal of Learning Disabilities, 23,* 78–79.

Marzola, E. S. (1987). Using manipulatives in math instruction. *Reading, Writing, and Learning Disabilities, 3,* 9–20.

Miller, S. P., & Mercer C. D. (1993b). Using data to learn about concrete-semi-concrete-abstract instruction for students with math disabilities. *Learning Disabilities Research & Practice, 8*(2), 89–96.

Rivera, D. M., & Bryant, B. R. (1992). Mathematics instruction for students with special needs. *Intervention in School and Clinic, 28*(2), 71–86.

Rivera, D. M., & Smith, D. D. (1987). Influence of modeling on acquisition and generalization of computational skills: A summary of research findings from three sites. *Learning Disability Quarterly, 10,* 69–80.

Rivera, D. M., & Smith, D. D. (1988). Using a demonstration strategy to teach midschool students with learning disabilities how to compute long division. *Journal of Learning Disabilities, 21,*(2), 77–81.

Smith, D. D., & Lovitt, T. C. (1975). The use of modeling techniques to influence the acquisition of computational arithmetic skills in learning-disabled children. In E. Ramp & G. Semb (Eds.), *Behavior analysis: Areas of research and application.* Englewood Cliffs, NJ: Prentice-Hall.

Smith, D. D., & Lovitt, T. C. (1976). The differential effects of reinforcement contingencies on arithmetic performance. *Journal of Learning Disabilities, 9,* 32–40.

Smith, D. D., & Lovitt, T. C. (1982). *The computational arithmetic program.* Austin, TX: PRO-ED.

Stern, M. (1987). Using the Stern blocks. *Reading, Writing, and Learning Disabilities, 3,* 21–30.

Solving Word Problems

Bley, N. S., & Thornton, C. A. (1995). *Teaching mathematics to students with learning disabilities.* Austin, TX: PRO-ED.

Bruni, J. V. (1982). Problem solving for the primary grades. *Arithmetic Teacher, 29*(6), 10–15.

Burns, M. (1982). How to teach problem solving. *Arithmetic Teacher, 29*(6), 46–49.

Carlson, J., Gruenewald, L. J., & Nyberg, B. (1980). Everyday math is a story problem: The language of the curriculum. *Language Disorders and Learning Disabilities, 1,* 59–70.

Case, L. P., Harris, K. R., & Graham, S. (1992). Improving the mathematical problem-solving skills of students with learning disabilities: Self-regulated strategy development. *The Journal of Special Education, 26*(1), 1–19.

Cawley, J. F., & Miller, J. H. (1986). Selected views on metacognition, arithmetic problem solving, and learning disabilities. *Learning Disabilities Focus, 2*(1), 36–48.

Cawley, J. F., Miller, J. H., & School, B. A. (1987). A brief inquiry of arithmetic word-problem-solving among learning disabled secondary students. *Learning Disabilities Focus, 2,* 87–93.

Enright, B. E., & Beattie, J. (1989). Problem solving step by step in math. *Teaching Exceptional Children, 22*(1), 58–59.

Fleischner, J. E., Nuzum, M. B., & Marzola, E. S. (1987). Devising an instructional program to teach arithmetic problem-solving skills to students with learning disabilities. *Journal of Learning Disabilities, 20,* 214–217.

Hutchinson, N. L. (1992). The challenges of componential analysis: Cognitive and metacognitive instruction in mathematical problem solving. *Journal of Learning Disabilities, 25*(4), 249–252, 257.

Kelly, B., & Carnine, D. (in press). Teaching problem-solving strategies for word problems to students with learning disabilities. *LD Forum.*

Larsen, S. C., Parker, R. M., & Trenholme, B. (1978). The effects of syntactic complexity upon arithmetic performance. *Learning Disability Quarterly, 1,* 80–85.

Maletsky, E. M. (1982). Problem solving for the junior high school. *Arithmetic Teacher, 27,* 18–21.

Marzola, E. (1987). *An arithmetic problem solving model based on a plan for sets to solution, mastery learning, and calculator use in a resource room setting for learning disabled students.* New York: Teachers College Press.

Mercer, C. D., & Miller, S. P. (1992). Teaching students with learning problems in math to acquire, understand, and apply basic math facts. *Remedial and Special Education, 13*(3), 19–35, 61.

Montague, M. (1992). The effects of cognitive and metacognitive strategy instruction on the mathematical problem solving of middle school students with learning disabilities. *Journal of Learning Disabilities, 25,* 230–248.

Montague, M., & Bos, C. S. (1986). The effect of cognitive strategy training on verbal math problem solving performance of learning disabled adolescents. *Journal of Learning Disabilities, 19,* 26–33.

Moser, J. M., & Carpenter, T. P. (1982). Young children are good problem solvers. *Arithmetic Teacher, 30*(3), 24–26.

Moyer, J. C., Moyer, S. B., Sowder, L., & Threadgill-Sowder, J. (1984). Story problems formats: Verbal versus telegraphic. *Journal for Research in Mathematics Education, 15*(1), 64–68.

National Council of Teachers of Mathematics. (1989). *Curriculum and evaluation standards for school mathematics.* Reston, VA: Author.

Riley, J. G., Greeno, J. G., & Heller, J. I. (1983). Development of children's problem solving ability in arithmetic. In H. P. Ginsburg (Ed.), *The development of mathematical thinking.* New York: Academic Press.

Rivera, D. M., & Denault, K. (1991). Assessing story problem solving abilities of students with learning disabilities, *LD Forum, 16*(2), 14–15.

Rivera, D. P. (1994, April). *Teaching mathematics using direct instruction and cooperative learning.* Paper presented at the International Conference of the Council for Learning Disabilities, San Diego, CA.

Suydam. M. N. (1982). Update on research on problem solving: Implications for classroom teaching. *Arithmetic Teacher, 29*(6), 56–60.

Szubinski, G., & Enright, B. (1992). Problem solving: Organize the facts. *Teaching Exceptional Children, 24*(3), 58–59.

Thornton, C. A., & Bley, N. S. (1982). Problem solving: Help in the right direction for LD students. *Arithmetic Teacher, 29*(6), 26–27, 38–41.

Tobin, A. (1982). Scope and sequence for a problem solving curriculum. *Arithmetic Teacher, 29*(6), 62–65.

Wilson, C. L., & Sindelar, P. T. (1991). Direct instruction in math word problems: Students with learning disabilities. *Exceptional Children, 57*(6), 512–519.

Worth, J. (1982). Problem solving in the intermediate grades: Helping your students learn to solve problems. *Arithmetic Teacher, 29*(6), 16–19.

Estimation

Reys, B. J. (1986). Teaching computational estimation: Concepts and strategies. In H. L. Schoen & M. J. Zweng (Eds.), *Estimation and mental computation: 1986 yearbook* (pp. 31–44). Reston, VA: National Council of Teachers of Mathematics.

Schoen, H. L., & Zweng, M. J. (Eds.). (1986). *Estimation and mental computation: 1986 yearbook.* Reston, VA: National Council for Teachers of Mathematics.

Trafton, P. R. (1986). Teaching computational estimation: Establishing an estimation mind-set. In H. L. Schoen & M. J. Zweng (Eds.), *Estimation and mental computation: 1986 yearbook* (pp. 16–30). Reston, VA: National Council of Teachers of Mathematics.

Technology

Beardslee, E. C. (1978). Teaching computational skills with a calculator. In M. Suydam & R. Reys (Eds.), *Developing computational skills: 1978 yearbook.* Reston, VA: National Council of Teachers of Mathematics.

Carpenter, T. P., Corbitt, M. K., Kepner, H. S., Lindquist, M. M., & Reys, R. E. (1981). Calculators in testing situations: Results and implications from national assessment. *Arithmetic Teacher, 28*(5), 34–37.

Chiang, B. (1986). Initial learning and transfer effects of microcomputer drills on LD students' multiplication skills. *Learning Disability Quarterly, 9,* 118–123.

Koscinski, S. T., & Gast, D. L. (1993). Computer-assisted instruction with constant time delay to teach multiplication facts to students with learning disabilities. *Learning Disabilities Research & Practice, 8*(3), 157–168.

Lewis, R. B. (1993). *Special education technology: Classroom application.* Pacific Grove, CA: Brooks/Cole.

Miller, D. (1982). *Motivational activities for low (and higher) achievers.* Columbus, OH: Calculator Information Center.

Morris, J. (1981). *How to develop problem solving using a calculator.* Reston, VA: National Council of Teachers of Mathematics.

O'Neil, D. R., & Jensen, R. (1982). Let's do it: Let's use calculators. *Arithmetic Teacher, 29,* 6–9.

Reys, R. E. (1980). Calculators in the elementary classroom: How can we go wrong? *Arithmetic Teacher, 29,* 38–40.

Trifiletti, J. J., Frith, G. H., & Armstrong, S. (1984). Microcomputers versus resource rooms for LD students: A preliminary investigation of the effects on math skills. *Learning Disability Quarterly, 7,* 69–76.

Chapter 13
Study Skills

Being able to study independently is an important skill, particularly for those students who try to compete successfully in general education classes at the middle and high school levels. The setting demands (discussed in chapters 1 and 5) of general education's content subject courses are difficult for many students with special needs. Most middle and high school teachers expect students to gain information from textbooks that are often beyond their reading abilities and from lectures that surpass their auditory comprehension abilities. If students with special needs are to pass classes in history, social studies, and science, they need to develop skills that allow them to organize and remember vast amounts of information. Students also must demonstrate their knowledge by writing reports, taking tests, and participating in class discussions.

Objectives

After studying this chapter, the reader will be able to

1. Define study skills.
2. Describe the components of a study skills curriculum.
3. Explain instruction for these components.

Many special education teachers of middle and high school students engage in "crisis teaching." They help students complete homework assignments. They tutor youngsters so they have a better chance of passing upcoming tests in their general education classes. This approach is not highly successful for most students with special needs; at best, it is only a temporary solution to academic difficulties. For such students to be more successful in general education classes, they must learn strategies that they can use to meet more advanced curricular demands. They need to develop study, test-taking, and theme-writing skills. As researchers develop more and more strategies for these skill areas, the content of many middle and secondary special education classes should change. For those students who remain in general education content courses, the teaching approach of special education classes should shift away from crisis teaching or tutoring to a learning strategies approach.

As students progress through the grades, the demands of teachers and the curriculum increase. Students are expected to become independent, responsible learners who are capable of obtaining, organizing, and expressing knowledge and information effectively. As students move from elementary to secondary schools (see chapter 14 for a discussion about transitions), they must adjust to instructional and curricular changes. At the secondary level, instructional formats focus primarily on lectures, seatwork, and homework, and test taking is the major source of grades (Putnam, Deshler, & Schumaker, 1992). The curriculum centers on textbook content; thus, students must possess effective reading comprehension, memorizing, and studying strategies. Unfortunately, for many students with learning and behavior problems, consistent reading problems (see chapter 10) impede their ability to comprehend subject area textbooks that contain difficult vocabulary and, in many cases, a reading level well beyond their frustration level.

In this chapter, the authors present recent innovations from researchers, curriculum developers, and teachers. We begin by describing study skills and instructional tips for "best practice." We discuss topics for study skills instruction and provide suggestions for teaching some of these skills.

The intervention strategies described here reflect only a sampling of tactics aimed to improve students' abilities to cope with general education classes and content subject information presented in the later years of school. Although most of these strategies were developed for students who have achieved at least a fourth-grade reading level, some of these concepts can be adapted for younger children as well. Students should begin learning how to study and learn independently early in their school careers. These skills will help students cope successfully with the academic demands of least restrictive environments.

Study Skills

As you read, think about . . .

1. Defining and providing examples of study skills.
2. Summarizing ways teachers can help students develop effective study skills.
3. Describing some of your efficient study habits.

Study skills are associated with acquiring, recording, organizing, synthesizing, memorizing, retrieving, and using information taught in school (Devine, 1987). Effective study skills are necessary across all subject areas at the elementary and secondary levels. Through study skills, students obtain new information and ideas by reading curricular materials and listening to the teacher and their peers. Very often, students must record information by taking notes, summarizing, or developing an outline. Students must then determine the most effective and coherent way to synthesize and organize this information to aid in the learning and retention process.

Students must understand that learning how to study can be difficult and time consuming. Teachers need to prepare students to learn study skills. They must indicate to their students that considerable work is required to master study skills and to persist in using them so their performance will be more successful. It is often helpful to provide students with rationales for expending energy to learn and apply these skills. Teachers should give these rationales as students acquire and begin to generalize their application of study skills. Some teachers have found that once students have mastered a particular study technique, cueing them to use that strategy helps with generalization. These reminders should be given by the special educator who taught the student the strategy and by the general educator who can help the student remember to use the technique in that setting. Possessing skills and applying them in the proper situations are two different aspects of learning. Teachers must be vigilant and continually monitor students' application of study skills to ensure that they are used to advantage.

Many of the strategies discussed throughout this book can be considered techniques to foster effective study habits. Study skills instruction should be nurtured across all subject areas. The reader can review other chapters in this book to find ideas for incorporating study skills instruction into everyday assignments, in addition to those ideas presented in this chapter. Tips for Teachers provides suggestions of "best practice" for teaching study skills.

Tips for Teachers

"Best Practice" for Study Skills Instruction

1. Conduct a study skills inventory to determine how students perceive their study habits.
2. Provide a rationale for study skills instruction; a one-semester course that focuses on developing effective study skills might be beneficial for many students.
3. Collaborate with other teachers to develop a study skills curriculum that cuts across all subject areas.
4. Teach study skills and effective studying habits at both the elementary and secondary levels. Invite a representative from a postsecondary institution to speak to secondary students about setting demands and the need for study skills.

5. Work collaboratively with parents to develop effective study skill habits at home (see the homework section of chapter 5).
6. Teach youngsters stress management techniques. ■

Skills for Instruction

As you read, think about . . .

1. Developing a study skills curriculum for the elementary and secondary levels.
2. Writing IEP goals and objectives for study skills at the secondary level.
3. Examining study skills needed to be successful at the postsecondary level and thinking about how to make those skills part of the secondary-level curriculum.
4. Developing a study skills curriculum to be infused into all subject areas.

For students to learn from textbooks, teachers' lectures, and class discussions, they must develop a number of skills. They must learn to organize information so it is useful, discriminate important from irrelevant information, gain knowledge, and remember it. They must demonstrate their mastery of content by taking objective tests, writing themes and reports, and answering short answer essays on tests. In this section, we discuss some aspects of these study skills (see chapters 10 and 11 for information about improved reading, comprehension, and writing skills). In Figure 13.1 we present a list of important topics for study skills instruction. Developing these skills throughout the school years will help students learn appropriate ways to manage and organize themselves and the instructional content.

Time Management

Organizational skills may be difficult for some students with learning problems; managing and organizing time is one component of the bigger self-management picture. Time management requires students to (1) identify what they must accomplish,

Figure 13.1
Topics for study
skills instruction

Study Skills

Time management	Listening	Note taking	Research skills
Schedules	Attending	Writing means	Dictionary
Tasks	Filtering out distraction	Listening	Alphabetizing
	Applying meaning	Main ideas and details	Definitions
		Organizational framework	Syllabication

Thinking, learning, remembering	Reading rate	Test taking	References
Memory	Four types	Memory skills	Charts and maps
Classification		Organizational skills	Footnotes
Association		Test format	Directories
Sequence			Glossaries

Library
  Indexes
  Card Catalogue
  On-line resources

(2) understand how long each task will take to complete, and (3) schedule blocks of time to do the job efficiently. Time management entails making judgments and estimations about the time requirements of various tasks. For students who lack good estimation skills and conceptual understanding of time, time management may be problematic. The youngster who does not begin a research paper until three days before the due date has not demonstrated sufficient time-management skills to complete a task by the deadline.

Teachers can help youngsters with time-management skills by teaching them to (1) designate a specific time each day for studying, (2) set a reasonable "stopping time" for studying in the evening, (3) tackle difficult or boring tasks first, (4) use consistent blocks of time for studying with built-in breaks, (5) study in the same place, one that should be comfortable and free of distractions, (6) be prepared by bringing all materials at the beginning of the study period, (7) break large tasks down into manageable components to tackle each day, and (8) use the cognitive and metacognitive strategies taught in class (Bassett, 1995). Bragstad and Stumpf (1987) provide 12 ideas to teach students for managing their time more efficiently (see Table 13.1). Teachers can teach, modify, and post these ideas for students' reference throughout the year.

Table 13.1
Twelve Tips for Studying and Managing Your Time

1. Plan a definite time for studying each day. This will discourage procrastination and prevent that pile-up of work.
2. Shorten your study time by knowing the purpose of each assignment, what to do, and how to do it before you leave class. Keep a record of all assignments in a special section of your notebook.
3. Predicting the amount of time needed for each assignment causes you to work harder so that you save time. By timing your assignments, you are more likely to concentrate and less likely to become bored.
4. Time yourself to see how long it takes you to read five pages of your textbook or a paperback. This will help you estimate the time needed to complete a reading assignment. Because a textbook is loaded with information, you may have to read some sections more than once. Even teachers have to reread material. Allow time for reflecting on what you read, too.
5. Pay attention to charts and diagrams. They can be shortcuts to understanding.
6. When you are assigned reading, you can expect to have a discussion of the material or a quiz in class. Take a little time to review just before class so that you are ready to participate.
7. Every time you study, spend ten minutes reviewing previous assignments. These "refresher shots" are the secret for long-term retention of material. Frequent review also makes you need to spend less time studying for a major test.
8. Use daytime for study if possible. At night, you are likely to be less efficient.
9. After studying about forty minutes, take a five-minute break. This refreshes your mind so that you can concentrate better and finish faster.
10. Setting a "stopping time" at night will encourage hard work in anticipation of being through by ten o'clock or whatever time you set. Sometimes you may even beat the clock. The increased impetus helps you concentrate.
11. Don't cram for hours the night before a test. Instead, distribute your study in half-hour segments over a period of days.
12. Since learning is cumulative, new ideas must be incorporated with previous learning from lectures, readings, and lab experiments. You have to keep making connections and associations. Putting it all together is easier if you schedule time daily to read, think, reflect, and review. Improved learning is the natural result of this approach to using your time.

Source: From *A Guidebook for Teaching Study Skills and Motivation* (2nd ed., p. 237), by B. J. Bragstad and S. M. Stumpf, 1987, Boston: Allyn & Bacon. Copyright 1987 by Allyn & Bacon. Reprinted with permission.

Learning and Remembering

A prerequisite to efficient studying is being able to organize information into usable units and knowing when and how to use that information. Several skills are particularly relevant to organizing and relating information: classifying, associating, and sequencing. Students can learn these skills through direct instruction, drill, and practice. Classifying, categorizing, and grouping items and information together by relevant characteristics allows individuals to "chunk" information so they can remember it more easily. Being able to associate items by some common denominator helps individuals to see the relationships that exist between different knowledge bases. Sequencing allows individuals to put items and concepts into an order that may be rather concrete (size, volume) or abstract (symbolic). These skills could be viewed as prerequisites to advanced learning, complex memorization, and study skills.

These cognitive skills are related to academic success. **Categorization** of, or "chunking" information into usable units, helps people to remember large amounts of information that they otherwise could not remember. For example, knowing that a list of forty items belongs to five common categories (fruits, vegetables, meats, types of cars, kinds of dogs) facilitates remembering long lists. Associating items along various dimensions also facilitates memory but, more importantly, allows information to be used in meaningful ways. Through associations, students find the connections or common elements between units of information. They are able to recognize common attributes that facilitate memory and problem solving. For example, relating items or things that are fast, cold, hard, tall, or sharp allows people to relate information on different dimensions. Sequencing allows people to put things into an order or hierarchy as another way to organize information.

These thinking skills are often not taught directly in school. Students do not have the opportunity to experiment in classifying, finding relationships, sequencing, determining the common attributes of items and information, clustering information, or identifying a category and its elements. With practice and guided instruction, they can develop these cognitive skills.

Memorization is an important skill that fosters learning and retention of information. Students must memorize a great deal of information in various subject areas and produce that information on tests and in class discussions. Therefore, abilities to store and retrieve information are vital. Research studies have shown that students with learning difficulties tend to exhibit problems with short-term and working memory resulting from ineffective information processing abilities (Swanson, Cochran, & Ewers, 1990; Torgesen & Goldman, 1977). Problems stem from lack of efficient memory strategies (e.g., chunking, organizing), lack of automaticity with basic knowledge (e.g., computational facts, sight words), and inefficient self-regulation (metamemory) strategies.

The following techniques can be used to help students improve their memory skills: (1) teach students how to create mnemonic devices to assist them in memorizing and recalling content such as lists of information, important people, steps in a procedure; (2) discuss how they can recall some information by creating mental images—have students provide specific examples of images they create; (3) teach students to "chunk" related information for easier memorization and recall—this necessitates discussing the concepts of comparing and contrasting and explaining that students must attend to specific categorical features in order to state how information is similar and different; and (4) give students opportunities to recite information through verbal rehearsal—this can be done in student-mediated groups or in a whole-group arrangement (Devine, 1987). Clearly, if students with special needs are to acquire, retain, and recall content information they must possess strategies to facilitate these cognitive processes.

Teachers can facilitate learning and memory through their mode of presentation. Darch and Carnine (1986) found that teachers can help students remember content information by using particular instructional formats. In their study, the group of students whose teachers used visual aids that categorized and organized information surpassed another group who studied the material from a textbook. As discussed earlier (see chapter 5), when teachers use advance organizers by introducing lessons and instructional topics well, it facilitates comprehension and memory. The ways in which teachers present content information to students influences how well students learn.

Regardless of how the material is presented, students need opportunities to think about and use information that exists in the world around them. These experiences can and should be planned for students throughout the school years. Developing these skills helps them process, organize, and learn the content presented in school.

Listening

Students use listening to obtain meaning from spoken language, to promote more efficient study habits, and to foster communication in general. Listening is not synonymous with paying attention. It is a skill that must be developed, yet research studies show that little time is devoted to listening instruction (Devine, 1987). Early research documented the deemphasis of instructional time allocated to listening. Rankin's study (as cited in Devine) showed that people generally spend about 45 percent of their daily verbal communication listening to someone talk about something. In the school setting, the percentage was higher; Wilt's research (as cited in Devine) showed that about 60 percent of time was devoted to listening. More recently, Putnam et al. (1992) reported that at the secondary level, lecturing (which necessitates listening) was the major form of instructional delivery in English, science, social studies, and mathematics classes. Only a small percentage of time was devoted to peer interactions.

According to Hoover (1988), listening requires (1) attending, (2) applying meaning to messages, and (3) filtering out distractions. Devine (1987) suggests that listening skills applied to school involve determining a purpose, noting transitional words (e.g., next, first, finally), recognizing the speaker's main points, noting the details, predicting possible test questions, and drawing conclusions. Thus, students must learn how to listen effectively to obtain the information for which they will be held accountable.

Teachers can help students develop better listening skills by (1) asking questions and then calling on a student—this heightens the "level of concern" (discussed in chapter 5), (2) using a variety of media (e.g., overhead projector, chalkboard, computer and projection panel, manipulatives) to keep lessons interesting and presentations diverse, (3) providing a short amount of information followed by a check for understanding (discussed in chapter 5), (4) asking students to summarize newly presented content on paper or with a neighbor (i.e., have students think about the information, summarize the information, pair with a partner, and share the information that was just presented), (5) using transitional words (e.g., "I am going to provide three important points. First, . . ."), (6) telling students there will be a quiz following the activity, and (7) providing an outline of the information presented and having students fill in the blanks.

Reading Rate

Reading rate, as a study skill, refers to how individuals pace themselves given specific reading material and a purpose for reading. Determining an appropriate reading rate depends on the topic, what the reader hopes to learn from the reading material, the reader's existing knowledge about the topic, and amount of time it will take to read the material (Vance, 1987). For instance, with a textbook assignment, the reader should probably choose a moderate reading rate to allow time for underlining main ideas and details, summarizing paragraphs, and answering questions. Someone might select a faster reading rate for reading a newspaper, which would permit him or her to scan headlines and examine pictures before choosing a story of interest for slower reading and processing.

Vance (1987) discusses the following four "gears of reading":

- First gear (study rate) is for studying new material while fostering comprehension, deciphering technical vocabulary, and identifying main ideas and details.
- Second gear (moderate rate) is typical pacing used for some assignments, enjoyment reading, and magazine/newspaper reading.
- Third gear (rapid rate) is for material (e.g., easy material, reviewing material, notes, magazines, newspapers) for which one seeks a general understanding.
- Fourth gear (reference rate) is used when one wants an overview of the material; skimming and scanning are typical reading behaviors for this gear.

Students may be unaware that different reading paces (gears) exist depending on the reading material and purpose. They may lack effective comprehension strategies that facilitate appropriate study abilities. Additionally, students may exhibit certain behavior patterns (e.g., lacking a purpose, concentration, and motivation, or reading every word) that contribute to inappropriate reading paces (Vance, 1987). Therefore, as part of study skills instruction, reading paces should be discussed and practiced relative to the material being read. Students can practice selecting reading paces by examining sample reading material and stating which gear would be most appropriate. Students could also be given material and instructions on which reading gear to use; after this activity, students could discuss their ability to comprehend the material and the appropriateness of the gear for the material.

Taking Notes

Note taking requires abilities in listening, recognizing important points and supporting details, utilizing an organizational framework, knowing some method for abbreviating information, and writing quickly. When listening to a lecture, students must implement listening skills and use some means for recording pertinent information. Teachers give students many subtle cues (both verbal and nonverbal) to indicate important information that will be on tests. For example, one teacher might underline important points written on the chalkboard or an overhead projector. Another might tell students, "This is important information to remember. It will be on the test."

Research has demonstrated a relationship between how thoroughly students take notes and how well they do on exams (Devine, 1987). Therefore, students need to learn how to apply their listening skills when taking many notes. Bragstad and Stumpf (1987) recommend that note-taking skills can be improved by using five steps.

- Step 1 is *Note take*, which involves taking notes on important facts during the lecture.
- Step 2 is *Note shrink*, in which students survey their notes, identify important points and "thought chunks," and record chunks in a quiz box.
- Step 3 is *Note talk*, which involves paraphrasing the content.
- Step 4, called *Note think*, entails linking the new information to previous knowledge and experiences.
- Step 5 is *Note review*, which involves going over the notes 10 minutes a day.

Research Skills

Research skills include conceptualizing a topic, locating reference materials, organizing ideas, writing the paper, and editing. Hoover (1988) notes that writing reports also involves including essential information, using proper mechanics, documenting clear introductory and concluding sentences, and proofreading. Certainly, some of the strategies for promoting written communication skills (see chapter 11) can be used to teach research skills.

Students with learning difficulties need careful instruction and teacher guidance when writing a research paper. Students should use organizational frameworks (see chapter 11) to plan and organize the paper's content. Students will need assistance in conducting research; they should receive instruction in using reference materials, online resources, and community resources. They will require guidance in selecting a writing structure (see chapter 11), depending on the purpose for writing. Students may benefit from access to a word processing program (see chapter 11) to facilitate writing and editing. Finally, students will require instruction in developing a reference list and citing references in their papers. For those students wishing to pursue postsecondary education, such skill development is critical. Instruction in this area should begin no later than middle school and should be emphasized throughout the high school years.

Taking Tests

Testing (e.g., multiple choice, true-false, fill-in-the-blanks, short answers) is one of the major ways secondary-level teachers determine the degree to which students have mastered instruction. Previous study skills, such as listening, note taking, organizing and memorizing material, contribute significantly to students' being able to pass tests. However, possessing knowledge in an organized format is only the first step toward successful test taking. Students must learn efficient and effective ways to retrieve their knowledge, read and understand test questions, monitor their test time, and make educated guesses.

Bassett (1995) offers guidelines for students to consider when taking tests. These guidelines include (1) read the entire test first, including the instructions, (2) complete the easier questions first, (3) use strategies to tackle multiple choice questions (avoid answers with absolute words, eliminate answers, look for the detailed answer), (4) review responses, and (5) have a positive attitude. Students with learning problems can learn specific test-taking strategies. Several strategies are discussed in the "Instructional Methods and Techniques" section of this chapter.

Instructional Methods and Techniques

As you read, think about . . .

1. Developing a lesson plan for teaching a study skill.
2. Developing a collaborative plan with a general education teacher for promoting generalization of study skills instruction from a special education setting to the general education setting.
3. Adapting study skills instruction to meet the needs of students with learning difficulties in the general education setting.
4. Modifying a test to make the format easier for some students.
5. Preparing organizational frameworks for instruction on taking notes.

In this section, we discuss interventions for managing time, learning information, listening, improving a reading rate, taking notes, doing research, and taking tests. We cover several specific strategies and procedures to teach students study skills; a more extensive list of interventions appears in Table 13.2. We also provide ideas for adapting study skills instruction in the general education classroom (see Adapting Instruction) and using technology to promote the development of effective study skills (see Focus on Technology). As interest in the area of study skills gathers momentum, more interventions will be developed and verified through research.

Focus on Technology

Technology that Aids in Study Skills

* **Assistive technology**

  1. Provide carbonless copying paper to a study partner for note taking.
  2. Provide a copy of the lecture's notes to a student who has great difficulty with the many skills involved in note taking.
  3. Permit students to tape record lectures rather than having to take extensive notes.
  4. Allow students to take tests using word processing or speech synthesis or both.

* **Instructional technology**

  1. Timeliner (Tom Snyder Productions, Inc.)
  2. Mastering Library Skills (Educational Publishing Concepts)
  3. Building Memory Skills (MCE, Inc.)
  4. Story Maker (Scholastic, Inc.)
  5. Story Tree (Scholastic, Inc.)
  6. How to Prepare for and Take Tests (Science Research Associates, Inc.)
  7. The Test Taker's Edge (Sunburst Communications) ●

Table 13.2 Study Skills Teaching Tactics	Instructional target	Stage of learning	Possible tactic
	Time management	Acquisition	Prompts
			Advance organizers
			Reward for accuracy
			Self-management
			Schedules
		Maintenance and generalization	Intermittent and social reinforcement
			Cooperative planning
	Thinking, learning, and remembering	Acquisition	Prompting
			Modeling
			Time delay
			Advance organizers
			Feedback
			Reward for accuracy
			Mnemonics
			Keyword mnemonics
			Visual displays
		Proficiency	Error drill
			Computer games
		Maintenance	Overlearning
			Intermittent reinforcement
		Generalization	Cooperative planning
			Social reinforcement
	Listening	Acquisition	Prompting
			Advance organizers
			Feedback
			Self-management
			Transitional words
			Checks for understanding
			Guided notes
			LINKS strategy
	Reading rate	Acquisition	Modeling
			Prompting
			Feedback
			Gears of reading
		Generalization	Social reinforcement
			Cooperative planning
			Self-management
	Research skills	Acquisition	Modeling
			Feedback
			Reward for accuracy
			Peer tutoring
			Self-management
			Computer games

continued

Table 13.2
Continued

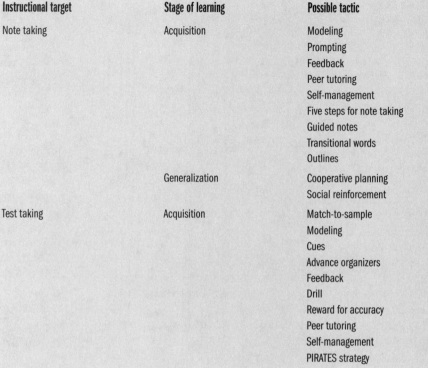

Instructional target	Stage of learning	Possible tactic
Note taking	Acquisition	Modeling
		Prompting
		Feedback
		Peer tutoring
		Self-management
		Five steps for note taking
		Guided notes
		Transitional words
		Outlines
	Generalization	Cooperative planning
		Social reinforcement
Test taking	Acquisition	Match-to-sample
		Modeling
		Cues
		Advance organizers
		Feedback
		Drill
		Reward for accuracy
		Peer tutoring
		Self-management
		PIRATES strategy

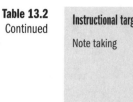

Adapting Study Skills Instruction for the General Education Setting

Time management

1. Provide a calendar for students to record assignment due dates.
2. Help students task-analyze components of assignments and designate blocks of time to complete each component by the due date.
3. Teach students to set a timer at home with a designated amount of time for task completion.
4. Have students estimate length of time to accomplish daily tasks.
5. Teach students to identify specific times of the day for accomplishing tasks.

Listening

1. Check for understanding of directions by asking students to repeat directions.
2. Give students purposes for listening.
3. Teach students transitional words to signal important information and new ideas.
4. Conduct listening exercises related to subject area content, such as practicing mental math problems, giving oral instructions for completing a task, and summarizing paragraph material.

Learning and remembering

1. Provide cue sheets to help students remember strategies and mnemonics.
2. Promote generalization of strategies instruction to general education settings.

3. Work closely with general education teachers to ensure that students use strategies, mnemonics, and cue sheets.
4. Present study guides, outlines, schematic webs and mnemonics to facilitate the learning process.
5. Have students work in cooperative learning and peer tutoring groups to practice instructional content.

Reading rate

1. Post a chart with the four gears for reading as a reminder of how various rates depend on reading purposes.
2. Ask students which reading rate is appropriate for various tasks at home and school.

Taking notes

1. Use assistive technology ideas listed in Focus on Technology.
2. Provide lecture outlines for students to complete; briefly review students' notes on the outline after the lecture.
3. Provide study guides.

Taking tests

1. Modify test questions to control for sentence structure complexity.
2. Provide practice sessions in test taking formats (e.g., multiple choice, short answers).
3. Review memorizing strategies; do practice warm-ups of content to check for understanding.
4. Include review sessions as part of daily instruction and test preparation.
5. Assign study partners.
6. Teach students to read directions, underline signal words, and break sentences into parts to promote comprehension.
7. Teach stress management techniques.
8. Help students plan studying time on their calendars as part of test preparation. ■

Time Management

Time Evaluation   Have students keep a daily log of how they spend their time (Bragstad & Stumpf, 1987). They can complete a chart containing days of the week and blocks of time. They can designate specific activities and the amount of time it takes to complete each activity. At the end of the week, teachers can work with students to examine daily logs, categorize activities that occur, and record amounts of time taken to complete various tasks. Students and teachers then can examine the logs for "time leaks," that is, time used inefficiently, mismanaged, or wasted. For example, it might be determined that the student spent too much time talking on the telephone during the designated study time. Or, perhaps activities were not well organized, requiring extra time to reorganize tasks or search for materials.

Schedules   Based on results from the time-evaluation exercise, students can develop schedules to manage their time more efficiently and to promote better organizational skills. Students can learn how to develop a realistic and manageable "Things to do today" list. They could sequence tasks from difficult to easy and jot down the estimated amount of time to complete each task. They can develop daily or weekly schedules that reflect designated time slots for accomplishing activities on the "Things to do today" list and for completing the "givens" (going to school, taking out the trash, practicing a musical instrument). Schedules can help students develop routines that, if used wisely, can facilitate the use of appropriate study skills at school and home. Parents and teachers can work together to ensure that schedules are followed and that children are reinforced for better time-management skills.

Learning and Remembering

FIRST Letter Mnemonic Strategy   The FIRST letter mnemonic strategy (known to students as FIRST) helps students learn and relate content information (Nagel, Schumaker, & Deshler, 1986). The steps used in this strategy are shown below.

Steps for designing a mnemonic device

Step 1: **F**orm a word.
Step 2: **I**nsert a letter(s).
Step 3: **R**earrange the letters.
Step 4: **S**hape a sentence.
Step 5: **T**ry combinations.

To learn and use the FIRST strategy, students must be able to discriminate main ideas from details. They must be able to identify a topic (deserts) and find the details (Mohave, Arabian, Thar, and Sahara). To help them remember the information, students develop mnemonic devices (in this case, MATS) for each group or cluster of information. Then to help remember which mnemonic device relates to specific information, students learn to associate their mnemonic with a picture they can visualize in their minds (mats on the desert). Some students who have mastered the FIRST strategy have improved their grades in general education classes from Fs to Bs.

Visual Displays   Content area textbook information that students read and organize varies depending on the subject. For example, students may have to compare and contrast concepts or locate main ideas and supporting details. Students may have to determine relationships between ideas or influences of one concept on another. Therefore, using visual displays can help students organize content information and comprehend the reading information.

Visual displays illustrate interrelated, hierarchical, comparative, and directional relationships between information. Visual displays can be (1) presented to students to complete as they read, (2) completed with students in group instruction, or (3) assigned as homework with a science or social studies chapter and corrected by the teacher. Examples of visual displays appear in Figure 13.2.

Keyword Mnemonics   The key word mnemonic technique is used to help students learn and remember vocabulary words in subject area material (Mastropieri, Scruggs, & Fulk, 1990). This is an effective technique to teach definitions of words

Figure 13.2
Visual displays

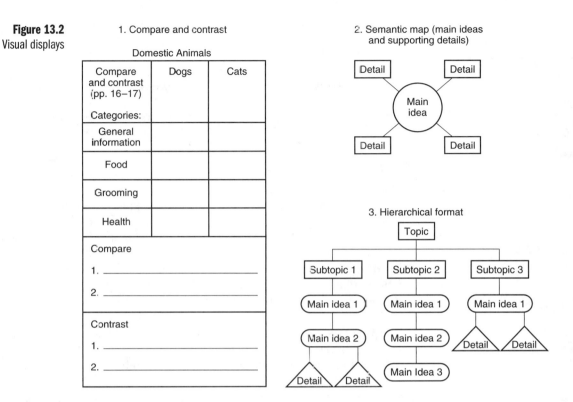

and to promote vocabulary development. There are three steps for designing key word mnemonics: recoding, relating, and retrieving.

Recoding involves changing part of an unknown word into a familiar sounding word (key word). For example, part of the vocabulary word "grapnel" could be recoded to the key word "grab." The key word is familiar to students and sounds similar to part of the vocabulary word.

Relating requires students to associate the key word with the definition of the vocabulary word. Usually, the student illustrates the relation between the key word and definition to provide a visual cue of the vocabulary word's definition. In this example, "grapnel" means "a small anchor with several flukes." Thus, a picture of a person grabbing at boxes with a small anchor and flukes could be drawn.

In *retrieving,* students activate their knowledge about the vocabulary words and related key words with pictures. According to Levin (1988), the link between the vocabulary word, the key word, and the picture helps the student's ability to define the vocabulary word. Hughes (1996) notes three steps to facilitate the retrieval process: (1) the teacher instructs students to define their vocabulary words by remembering the key words, (2) the students visualize the key word illustration and the related definition, and (3) the students define their vocabulary words.

Hughes (1996) and Mastropieri and Scruggs (1991) recommend using direct instruction steps (see chapter 5) to teach the three steps of designing key word mnemonics for vocabulary words. Specifically, Mastropieri and Scruggs suggest using a practice sheet similar to the one shown in Figure 13.3 for a guided practice activity. Teachers could provide information in different boxes about each vocabulary word and students would fill in the remaining boxes from the given clues.

Figure 13.3
Keyword
mnemonics chart

Vocabulary Word	Keyword (recode)	Definition (relate)	Picture (relate)
1. grapnel	grab		person grabbing boxes with a small anchor
2.	fan		
3.		moves quickly	

Source: Adapted from *Teaching Students Ways to Remember: Strategies for Learning Mnemonically,* by M. A. Mastropieri and T. E. Scruggs, 1991, Cambridge, MA: Brookline.

Listening and Taking Notes

Guided Notes   Provide an outline of the lecture, including a list of main ideas with sufficient space between each one (Lazarus, 1991). As students listen to the lecture, they should note specific details for each main idea. Teachers could model this procedure by (1) distributing a copy of a lecture for students to read, (2) locating the main ideas and details in the lecture notes, and (3) providing a completed outline of the lecture for students to review. Next, teachers could deliver a lecture while students complete the outline. Finally, teachers could share a completed outline for the lecture and allow students to compare their outlines with the completed one.

Transitional Words   Teach students words that signal important information and idea transitions. Bragstad and Stumpf (1987) list several categories and examples (see below) of transitional words that can facilitate listening and note-taking skills.

Developing lists	Cause-effect	Time order	Comparison	Contrast	Conclusions
I, II, III . . .	Because	After	Similarly	On the other hand	To summarize
First, second	Consequently	Next	As well as	Instead	To sum up
Finally	Resulting in	Before	Both	In contrast	Finally
		Later			

Students can learn the categories and examples of words that signal the different transitions. A chart could be posted for students' reference and to assist in their learning the words. Sample lectures could be distributed for students to locate the transition words and decide in which category the words belong. This technique should be one of the first listening and note-taking strategies taught to students, as other strategies may assume an understanding of transition words.

LINKS Strategy   LINKS is a mnemonic strategy that fosters listening and note-taking skills (Deshler, Schumaker, Alley, Clark, & Warner, 1981). The abilities to identify transitional words, main ideas, and supporting details are helpful prerequisite skills for using this strategy. The LINKS steps are listed below.

LINKS

1. **L**isten to the lecture
2. **I**dentify verbal cues
3. **N**ote
4. **K**ey words
5. **S**tack information into outline form

The LINKS strategy is used for taking notes during a lecture. Students use a two-column format as seen in Figure 13.4. Students listen to the lecture and identify verbal cues (words that teachers provide to signal that upcoming information is important). When students hear a cue word, they draw a circle in the left column. The circle signals that important information is going to be stated and that students should take notes; thus, the circle is a "link" between the verbal cue and the important information worthy of notes. After students make the circle, they write the main idea in the left column and record the details in the right column. In place of the column format, an outline format can be used that shows the main ideas and supporting details (see Figure 13.5).

Taking Tests

PIRATES Strategy   PIRATES does not help children memorize or learn the content found on tests (Hughes, Schumaker, Deshler, & Mercer, 1988). It does help students learn how to handle the testing situation, particularly for social studies and science. Students who cannot successfully answer short answer questions because they cannot write coherent paragraphs should learn the writing strategies discussed in chapter 11. Students can practice PIRATES test-taking skills on such questions as: Guyems who live in the Land of Ponch are this tall: (1) one foot, (2) about two and a half feet, (3) twelve inches, (4) ninety-two inches. Through a process of elimination,

Figure 13.4
Notes organized by main ideas and details

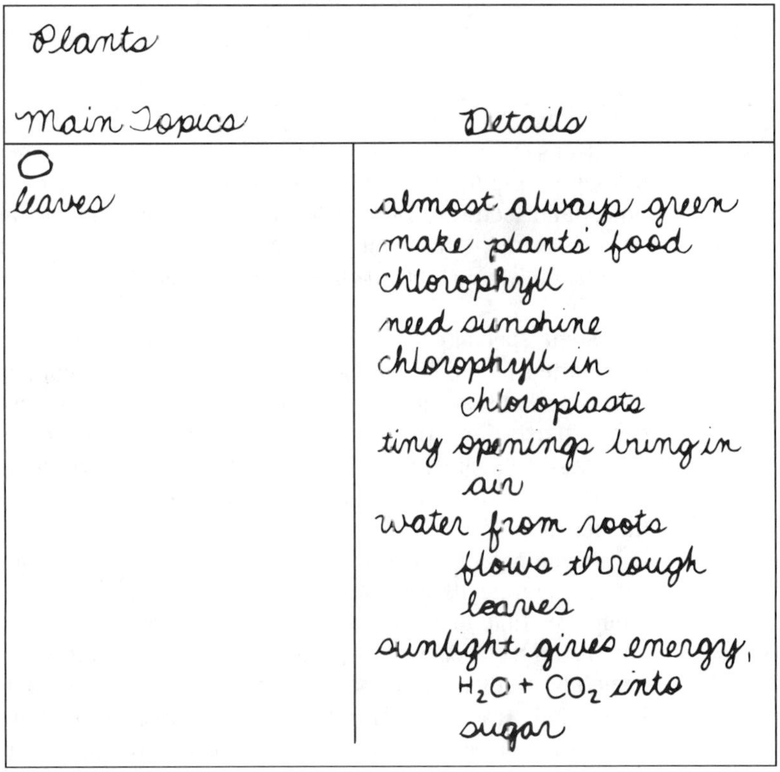

Plants

Main Topics   Details

○
leaves   almost always green
                                     make plants' food
                                     chlorophyll
                                     need sunshine
                                     chlorophyll in
                                          chloroplasts
                                     tiny openings bring in
                                          air
                                     water from roots
                                          flows through
                                          leaves
                                     sunlight gives energy,
                                          $H_2O + CO_2$ into
                                          sugar

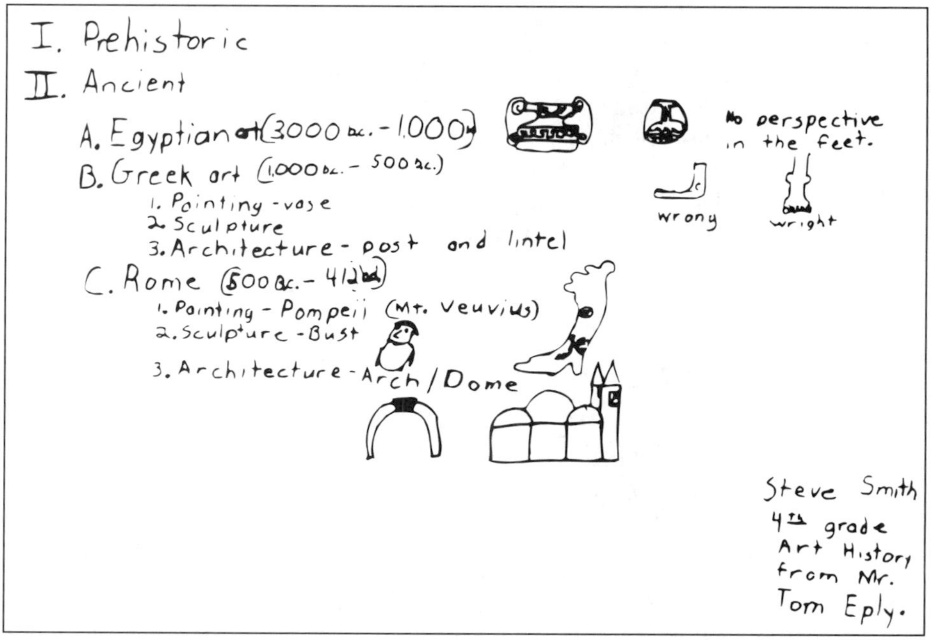

Figure 13.5
A fourth grader's art history notes using the traditional outlining method

students should select item (2) as their choice for these reasons: items (1) and (3) are the same answer, and item (4) is too exact to describe the height of a group of people. The strategy steps for PIRATES are listed in Figure 13.6.

Summary

As discussed in chapter 1, the demands of settings in middle schools and high schools are quite substantial. Students are expected to gain information from textbooks and lectures. They need to organize, remember, and use that information to pass tests and write themes and reports. Although study skills are not always taught directly at school, students need them in order to cope with the secondary school curriculum.

Some special educators would argue that not all students with mild or moderate disabilities should be retained in the general education curriculum. They believe that other, perhaps several, alternative curriculum tracks should be available for students, particularly those with special needs. However, students who are able to or who wish to compete with their typical counterparts in traditional history, English, and literature courses must develop the abilities to take notes and tests and write themes and reports.

A number of interventions and strategies for teaching study skills to students with special needs were presented in this chapter. We discussed instructional techniques for time management; learning and remembering; listening and taking notes; and taking tests. As with any skill, students are at different stages of learning when it comes to study skills instruction; thus, interventions must be selected accordingly. Direct and strategic instruction are important instructional approaches to use when teaching study skills; students should also have opportunities to practice their skills

Figure 13.6
Strategy steps
for PIRATES

Step 1: Prepare to succeed.

Put "PIRATES" and name on the test.
Allot time and order to sections.
Say something positive.
Start within two minutes.

Step 2: Inspect the instructions.

Read the instructions carefully.
Underline how and where to respond.
Notice special requirements.

Step 3: Read, remember, reduce.

Read the whole question.
Remember with memory strategies.
Reduce choices.

Step 4: Answer or abandon.

Answer the question.
Abandon the question if you're not sure.

Step 5: Turn back.

Turn back to abandoned questions when you get to the end of the test.
Tell yourself to earn more points.

Step 6: Estimate.

Estimate unknown answers using the "ACE" guessing techniques:
   Avoid absolutes.
   Choose the longest or most detailed choice.
   Eliminate identical choices.

Step 7: Survey.

Survey to ensure that all questions are answered.
Switch an answer only if you're sure.

Source: From *The Test-Taking Strategy: PIRATES*, by J. Hughes, J. Schumaker, D. D. Deshler, and C. Mercer, 1988, Lawrence: University of Kansas, Institute for Research in Learning Disabilities. Copyright 1987 by Edge Enterprises. Reprinted with permission.

in a variety of settings to promote generalization and transfer. Study skills are an important component of a total curriculum for students with learning and behavior problems. These skills foster academic success in elementary and secondary school instruction as well as in postsecondary settings.

Study and Discussion Questions

1. Define study skills.
2. Describe the components of a study skills curriculum.
3. Provide explanations of instruction for components of study skills.
4. Develop a practice test for students to use when learning the test-taking strategy PIRATES.
5. In your opinion, should there be different curricular options for students with special needs? If so, what should they be and how should students be selected for these options? If not, provide your reasons.

6. Plan at least one lesson to teach association, categorization, or sequencing skills.
7. Create a test to use in a lesson to teach students how to answer true-false, matching, and multiple choice questions.
8. Using a chapter from a social studies or history text, create mnemonics to help students remember the content.

References and Suggested Readings

Putnam, M. L., Deshler, D. D., & Schumaker, J. B. (1992). The investigation of setting demands: A missing link in learning strategy instruction. In L. Meltzer (Ed.), *Strategy assessment and instruction for students with learning disabilities: From theory to practice* (pp. 325–353). Austin, TX: PRO-ED.

Study Skills

Deshler, D. D., Warner, M. M., Schumaker, J. B., & Alley, G. R. (1983). Learning strategies intervention model: Key components and current status. In J. D. McKinney & F. Feagans (Eds.), *Current topics in learning disabilities,* (Vol. 1). Norwood, NJ: Ablex.

Devine, T. G. (1987). *Teaching study skills* (2nd ed.). Boston: Allyn & Bacon.

Schumaker, J. B., Deshler, D. D., Alley, G. R., & Warner, M. M. (1983). Toward the development of an intervention model for learning disabled adolescents. *Exceptional Education Quarterly, 4,* 45–74.

Wallace, G., & Kauffman, J. M. (1986). *Teaching students with learning and behavior problems.* Columbus, OH: Merrill.

Skills for Instruction and Instructional Methods and Techniques
Time Management

Bassett, D. S. (1995). A guide to the study units in this workbook. In D. D. Smith, *Study guide for introduction to special education* (2nd ed., pp. 1–10). Boston: Allyn & Bacon.

Bragstad, B. J., & Stumpf, S. M. (1987). *A guidebook for teaching study skills and motivation* (2nd ed.). Boston: Allyn & Bacon.

Learning and Remembering

Bragstad, B. J., & Stumpf, S. M. (1987). *A guidebook for teaching study skills and motivation* (2nd ed.). Boston: Allyn & Bacon.

Darch, C., & Carnine, D. (1986). Teaching content area material to learning disabled students. *Exceptional Children, 53,* 240–246.

Deshler, D. D., Schumaker, J. B., Alley, G. R., Clark, F. L., & Warner, M. M. (1981). *LINKS: A listening/notetaking strategy.* Lawrence: University of Kansas Institute for Research in Learning Disabilities.

Devine, T. G. (1987). *Teaching study skills* (2nd ed.). Boston: Allyn & Bacon.

Hughes, C. A. (1996). Memory and test-taking strategies. In D. D. Deshler, E. S. Ellis, & B. K. Lenz (Eds.), *Teaching adolescents with learning disabilities* (2nd ed., pp. 209–266). Denver, CO: Love.

Lazarus, B. D. (1991). Guided notes, review, and achievement of secondary students with learning disabilities in mainstream content courses. *Education and Treatment of Children, 14,* 112–127.

Levin, J. R. (1988). Elaboration-based learning strategies: Powerful theory=powerful application. *Contemporary Educational Psychology, 13,* 191–205.

Mastropieri, M. A., & Scruggs, T. E. (1991). *Teaching students ways to remember: Strategies for learning mnemonically.* Cambridge, MA: Brookline.

Mastropieri, M. A., Scruggs, T. E., & Fulk, B. J. M. (1990). Teaching abstract vocabulary to LD students with the keyword method: Effects on comprehension and recall. *Journal of Learning Disabilities, 23,* 92–107.

Mastropieri, M. A., Scruggs, T. E., & Levin, J. R. (1985). Maximizing what exceptional students can learn: A review of research on the keyword method and related mnemonic techniques. *Remedial and Special Education, 6*(2), 39–45.

Nagel, D. R., Schumaker, J. B., & Deshler, D. D. (1986). *Learning strategies curriculum: The FIRST-letter mnemonic strategy.* Lawrence, KS: Excel Enterprises.

Smith, D. D., Smith, J. O., Maxwell, B., Thompson, B., & Chaffin, J. (1985a). *MicroSoc Thinking Games: SocMatch.* Circle Pines, MN: American Guidance Service.

Smith, D. D., Smith, J. O., Maxwell, B., Thompson, B., & Chaffin, J. (1985b). *MicroSoc Thinking Games: SocMate.* Circle Pines, MN: American Guidance Service.

Smith, D. D., Smith, J. O., Maxwell, B., Thompson, B., & Chaffin, J. (1985c). *MicroSoc Thinking Games: SocSort.* Circle Pines, MN: American Guidance Service.

Swanson, H. L., Cochran, K. F., & Ewers, C. A. (1990). Can learning disabilities be determined from working memory performance? *Journal of Learning Disabilities, 23,* 59–68.

Torgesen, J. K., & Goldman, T. (1977). Rehearsal and short-term memory in reading disabled children. *Child Development, 48,* 56–60.

Listening

Devine, T. G. (1987). *Teaching study skills* (2nd ed.). Boston: Allyn & Bacon.

Hoover, J. (1988). *Teaching handicapped students study skills* (2nd ed.). Boulder, CO: Hamilton Publications.

Putnam, M. L., Deshler, D. D., & Schumaker, J. B. (1992). The investigation of setting demands: A missing link in learning strategy instruction. In L. Meltzer (Ed.), *Strategy assessment and instruction for students with learning disabilities: From theory to practice* (pp. 325–353). Austin, TX: PRO-ED.

Reading Rate

Vance, D. (1987). Strategic reading: Relating rate to purpose. In B. J. Bragstad & S. M. Stumpf, *A guidebook for teaching study skills and motivation* (2nd ed., pp. 141–152). Boston: Allyn & Bacon.

Taking Notes

Bragstad, B. J., & Stumpf, S. M. (1987). *A guidebook for teaching study skills and motivation* (2nd ed.). Boston: Allyn & Bacon.

Devine, T. G. (1987). *Teaching study skills* (2nd ed.). Boston: Allyn & Bacon

Research Skills

Hoover, J. (1988). *Teaching handicapped students study skills* (2nd ed.). Boulder, CO: Hamilton Publications.

Taking Tests

Bassett, D. S. (1995). A guide to the study units in this workbook. In D. D. Smith, *Study guide for introduction to special education* (2nd ed., pp. 1–10). Boston: Allyn & Bacon.

Hughes, J., Schumaker, J., Deshler, D. D., & Mercer, C. (1988). *The test-taking strategy: PIRATES.* Lawrence: University of Kansas, Institute for Research in Learning Disabilities.

Chapter 14
Transition Education

In recent years, students, parents, and professionals have recognized and addressed the continued presence of challenges for secondary and postsecondary students with learning and behavior problems. Efforts to modify curricula, instruction, and evaluation techniques to match learner characteristics better have demonstrated that some people can fully benefit from their instructional programs with the right kinds of supports or accommodations. The passage of P.L. 101–476, the Individuals with Disabilities Education Act (IDEA), has illustrated the potential achievements of persons with disabilities when given such support (Weicker, 1987). Concentrated efforts to establish individualized services for adolescents and young adults with special needs began during the late 1970s. These endeavors continue to increase today as educational programs at the middle school, high school, and postsecondary levels expand to address more aspects required for successful postschool adjustments.

Making Connections

Before you read this chapter, review the strategies for collaborative partnerships that were presented in chapter 2; those approaches will be critical for engaging essential partners in the transition process. Chapters 4, 5, and 6 include methods for designing, implementing, and evaluating instruction that are also important for the career development area. As you think about the student's instructional needs, review social skills in chapter 8 and identify other areas that might indicate a need for intervention.

This chapter was written by Dr. Ginger Blalock, University of New Mexico.

Objectives
After studying this chapter, the reader will be able to

1. Describe the varied types of transitions that all individuals typically make throughout life and the potential impact of learning and behavior problems on the nature of those transitions.

2. Describe a range of instructional and curricular models and strategies that support successful transitions throughout one's school life.

3. Describe essential partners in the transition process and strategies for engaging them.

The indications that students need to be prepared for adult life, work, and independence (White, 1987) have caused the orientation of students' instructional programs to change. For example, a study of the educational needs of people with mild and moderate learning disabilities revealed that many are likely to aspire to college at some point in their lives (Vocational Committee Survey, 1982; White et al., 1982). Those individuals for whom postsecondary education (particularly a two- or four-year degree program) is an appropriate goal appear to handle traditional secondary core curricula well, with minor instructional accommodations and some outcome-oriented transition planning at various stages. This group comprises more than half of all individuals with learning and behavior problems. However, another significant portion of secondary students requires a separate curriculum, during at least a portion of their educational experiences to help them gain independence during adulthood.

Over the past thirty years, several service delivery systems have emerged to prepare people for transition to employment (few have addressed other adult outcomes, such as social networks and residential living). Vocational education has offered training in job skills at secondary and postsecondary levels to some mainstreamed students who attended general education classes with some special education support; students with learning disabilities are included in this curriculum more often than any other group. Special education has provided prevocational skills classes, community-based instruction, and work-study experiences, originally intended for those with more complex situations but increasingly available for students with milder levels of disabilities. Vocational rehabilitation agencies have served many young adults through vocational assessment, job readiness training, counseling, on-the-job training, and job placement. In addition, many young adults with learning and behavior problems have used generic adult services, such as two-year colleges, military training, and job corps programs.

However, professionals from these systems have infrequently coordinated their efforts, until the transition initiatives propelled by the U.S. Department of Education ten years ago. A consistent, comprehensive continuum of services has not evolved in most local communities. State and national follow-up studies of special education graduates showed that students with mild disabilities often have great difficulty with competitive employment and independent living, even though their needs for supportive services may be minimal (Hasazi, Gordon, & Roe, 1985; Mithaug, Horiuchi, & Fanning, 1985). Many of the relatively dismal profiles of adult outcomes have indicated that traditional secondary curricula have not prepared many individuals with mild disabilities for adult life (Sitlington, Frank, & Carson, 1990).

The intent of this chapter is to offer a conceptual framework and several approaches, methods, and strategies that will help children and youth prepare for the challenges of next stages. To avoid excessive overlap with discussions of instruction at the elementary and middle school levels, most of the ideas will focus on preparing students for the transition from high school to adulthood's arenas (postsecondary education, employment, independent living). In addition, the author will discuss specific strategies for making transitions at each major school passage (eg., elementary to middle school, middle school to high school) to enable educators, students, and family members to make the most of each move to the next level.

Types of Transitions

As you read, think about . . .

1. Describing the developmental stages you and your peers have undergone.
2. Summarizing the typical or frequent traits of adolescents and adults with learning and behavior problems that indicate a need for support.
3. Explaining how diversity (cultural, linguistic, socioeconomic) affects one's aspirations, motivation, choice of options, and success.

A discussion of contemporary transition education approaches requires a brief conceptual perspective. This section summarizes the developmental stages that people face in school and life, the characteristics of adolescents and adults that require interventions, a discussion of the role that diversity plays in people's plans for the future, and the options that these groups traditionally need and have.

School and Life Stages

Transitions are passages from one life stage to the next. Students with special needs have many critical school transitions through which to move: (1) preschool to kindergarten, (2) elementary to middle school, (3) middle school to high school, and (4) high school to the adult world. In addition, childhood, adolescence, and adulthood can involve many other possible school and life transitions, such as moving from self-contained classes (or even schools) to more general settings, leaving special education, moving between correctional facilities and public schools, starting one's first job, beginning postsecondary education, or just plain moving, as in moving to a new school, city, state, or country. The same basic needs and principles apply to all situations: (1) sound preparation in the current program, (2) careful planning among all key parties, and (3) a range of options available at the next stage.

Child development has been studied extensively and will not be discussed in this chapter. However, a word about adolescent and adult development will lay the foundation for the remainder of the recommendations we make. Adolescence has long been studied as a period of complex and unique development, described as a "state of dynamic limbo" (Cullinan & Epstein, 1979). Developmental tasks during this stage include establishing one's identity and interaction style, setting goals, developing mental and physical coping strategies, defining one's points of view on social and moral issues, and planning for vocational activities (D'Alonzo, Arnold, & Yuen, 1986).

In contrast, adulthood has only recently achieved a status of its own as a "qualitatively distinct" developmental period (Bova, 1979). Several theories about development at various stages of life are suggested by work completed in the past twenty-five years. These theories seek to explain the roles and responsibilities that most individuals share as they mature (Knowles, 1979; Levinson, 1978).

Most adolescents and adults live their lives in patterns that alternate between stable periods and times of change. The former allow solidification and enjoyment of competence in some form; the latter periods bring new challenges and new directions (Aslanian & Brickell, 1980). Havighurst's "developmental task" schema (1972) is widely used to explain the reasons underlying these alternating stages. Table 14.1 outlines his three major stages of adulthood and their developmental tasks. While not exhaustive, this framework suggests the principal demands upon adults at various stages of their lives. The demands themselves illustrate the importance of striving for intellectual and social or emotional independence as well as occupational integrity.

Vocational concerns are critical during late adolescence and adulthood and should be addressed informally during early and middle adolescence. Super (1953) originally based his stages of vocational development on Ginzberg's occupational choice and life-stage theory and Havighurst's developmental tasks. Super proposed that one's self-concept is developed through each stage of childhood and drives one toward particular occupational decisions (see Table 14.2). Super's model depends heavily upon the idea of individual differences (abilities, interests, and personalities)

Table 14.1
Havighurst's
Developmental
Tasks

Stage/Age range	Developmental task
Early adulthood (Ages 18–30)	Selecting a mate
	Learning to live with a marriage partner
	Starting a family
	Rearing children
	Managing a home
	Getting started in an occupation
	Taking civic responsibility
	Finding a congenial social group
Middle age (Ages 30–60)	Assisting teenaged children to become responsible and happy
	Achieving adult social and civic responsibility
	Reaching and maintaining satisfactory performance in one's occupation or career
	Developing adult leisure time activities
	Relating to one's spouse as a person
	Accepting and adjusting to physiological changes of middle age
	Adjusting to aging parents
Late maturity (Age 60+)	Adjusting to decreasing physical strength and health
	Adjusting to retirement and reduced income
	Adjusting to death of spouse
	Establishing an explicit affiliation with one's age group
	Adopting and adapting social roles in a flexible way
	Establishing satisfactory physical arrangements

Source: From *Developmental Tasks and Education* (3rd ed.), by R. J. Havighurst, 1972, New York: McKay. Copyright 1972 by Longman. Reprinted with permission.

Table 14.2
Super's Stages of
Vocational
Development

Stage/Substage	Age	Major tasks or activities
Growth stage	Birth–14	Self-concept developed
a. Fantasy	4–10	Needs dominate; role playing
b. Interest	11–12	Likes are major determinants of aspirations, activities
c. Capacities	13–14	Abilities given more weight; job requirements considered
Exploration	15–24	Self-examination, role tryouts, occupational exploration in school, leisure activities, part-time work
a. Tentative	15–24	Tentative choices made and tried out in fantasy, talk, courses, and work
b. Transition	18–21	Implement self-concept via training or work; more thought given to reality
c. Uncommitted trial	22–24	First job tried
Establishment	25–44	Permanence sought
a. Committed trial and stabilizing	25–30	May undergo 1–2 changes before establishment
b. Consolidation and advancement	31–44	Efforts to solidify, usually most creative years
Maintenance	45–64	Concern about holding on, continuation of established lines, some innovation
Decline stage	65+	Work activity changes with declines in mental and physical power, new roles
a. Deceleration	65–70	
b. Retirement	71+	

Source: Adapted from "A Theory of Vocational Development," by D. E. Super, 1953, *American Psychologist 8*, pp. 185–190.

and therefore readily accommodates individuals with disabilities. He stressed that a range of occupations suits each person and conversely that many variations are seen among people in any given occupation.

Adolescents and Adults with Learning or Behavior Problems

Studies of adolescents and adults with learning and behavior problems have high-lighted specific areas of concern (see Table 14.3) that can guide educators in their decisions about curricula, modifications, and other areas (Gerber & Reiff, 1994; Masters, Mori, & Mori, 1993; Polloway, Schewel, & Patton, 1992). The list reflects that

Table 14.3
Problem Areas
Among Adolescents
and Adults with
Special Needs

Academic domain	Emotional and social domain	Vocational domain
Academic achievement	Emotional stability	Career attitudes
Intellectual functioning/ learning rate	Self-esteem/expectations for success	Career/vocational information
Oral language	Self-trust	Realistic goal setting
Thinking/reasoning skills	Personal maturity	Choosing satisfying vocations
Organization and study skills	Social experience	Long-range preparation
Memory and attention	Social perception	
	Making/keeping friends	
	Recreation/leisure lifestyles	
	Independent living skills	

these groups need help in developing the following skills: academic, self-advocacy, social and emotional, independent living, and vocational. Johnson and Blalock (1987) identified academic and vocational skills that require attention from both professionals and the students themselves (see Table 14.4).

Data from follow-up studies of students with disabilities indicate that many do not fare well as adults. Far too many end up unemployed or underemployed. Many describe their lack of satisfaction with work, interpersonal relationships, and recreation or leisure activities. A large number remain at home with family members in dependent arrangements. Many of today's adults with disabilities were not served adequately when they were children. Their disorders were often undisclosed or even unknown. For these reasons, they have received inadequate provisions. Assistance for difficulties in the educational arena is increasingly available for adults at postsecondary institutions in the United States. However, support in the social and interpersonal, independent living, and occupational realms is rarely available for persons with mild and moderate disabilities, and from few sources. Vocational rehabilitation agencies and advocacy organizations have created some options, described in the "Partnerships in Transition" section of this chapter. However, variables other than a disability may have a greater impact on someone's school and life experiences, and thus, should also be considered potential supports or barriers for adult adjustment. Ethnicity and language are two such factors discussed in the next section.

Table 14.4
Characteristics of
93 Adults with
Learning
Disabilities

Characteristic	No. reporting
Academic problems reported	
Written language	72
Reading	62
Oral language	26
Organization/planning	15
Mathematics	12
Attention	7
Nonverbal abilities	6
Conceptual thinking	4
Vocational achievements reported	
Students	26
Unemployed	18
Clerical/sales workers	13
Professional/technical workers	12
Laborers	8
Service workers	6
Craftsmen/foremen	4
Operatives	3
Managers/officials	3

Source: Adapted from *Adults with Learning Disabilities: Clinical Studies.* by D. J. Johnson & J. W. Blalock (Eds.), 1987, Orlando, FL: Grune & Stratton. Copyright 1987 by Grune & Stratton.

Focus on Diversity

Adolescents and adults with learning or behavior problems have an enormously heterogeneous span of abilities, interests, and personalities. No two individuals with special needs are alike; we have seen that age stages can make a big difference as well. The other traits that individuals carry with them to school and life also vary significantly. For example, culture, ethnicity, primary language(s), socioeconomic level, nuclear and extended family compositions, geographic locations, range of leisure and travel experiences, sexual preferences, school experiences, life experiences, and work experiences or skills acquired can distinguish two humans from one another and have significant impact on their experiences.

Rightfully or not, large numbers of culturally and linguistically diverse students tend to be diagnosed with certain categories of disabilities. Many researchers have found that non-white groups (especially African American, Hispanic, and Native American students) are often misidentified with learning problems, when in fact language and cultural differences are the major barriers to school success (Artiles & Trent, 1994; Lara, 1994). Biased or misused test instruments and procedures, as well as referring teachers who are ill-equipped to deal with students' language differences, are often the culprits in this situation. Teachers can help avoid this trap by observing students' abilities in a variety of situations and using interpreters when necessary to assess and instruct.

An additional situation offers unique challenges to students, families, and educators. A student's parents may be monolingually fluent in their native languages, and their children may be able to comprehend the family discourse orally but have few or no written language skills in the home language. As a result, the student may have poor academic skills in English. Thus, a significant body of students may find it very difficult to acquire English to an academically proficient level.

> Baca and Cervantes (1986) caution that one must consider a child's background when undertaking transition planning:...Development of culturally relevant IEPs requires an understanding of the characteristics of the child's reference group, including an understanding of language, customs, traditions, religion, family, diet, home, medical practice, and attitudes. The more information one has about the reference group, the easier and more accurate are the interpretations of individual behavior. (p. 195)

Smith and Luckasson (1995) cite a critical reason for responding to the specific concerns of ethnically diverse adolescents and young adults. Smith and Luckasson note that Hispanic and African American students continue to drop out at rates far greater than white students. Various sources have reported differing rates, depending on the method of counting, but all display a large gap not accounted for by proportion in the population. Table 14.5 compares some of the available data, all portraying a similar phenomenon.

Also noteworthy is that these ethnic groups comprise a disproportionately large portion of the imprisoned population in comparison to nonminority individuals. For example, among 444,584 total adult inmates profiled in the 1992 *Statistical Abstracts,* 191,362 (43.0 percent) were white, while 195,156 (43.9 percent) were Hispanic (although Hispanics comprise a much smaller proportion of U.S. residents). The number of inmates who also have disabilities remains unclear, with overall estimates ranging from 40 percent to 70 percent.

Table 14.5
High School
Dropout Rates by
Ethnicity

	Annual rates of dropout	No longer enrolled—not finished h.s.
Total	4.3%	12.7%
White	4.1%	12.2%
African American	4.9%	16.3%
Hispanic	7.9%	33.9%

Source: From U.S. Bureau of Census. (1992). *Current Population Reports Series P-20* (No. 413 & 474). Washington, DC: Author.

Districts and communities are beginning to address the needs of today's very diverse youth in schools. Cegelka, MacDonald, and Gaeta (1987) described an exemplary high school in San Diego where all general education classes were offered in three formats (or more), including English, a **bilingual transitional program,** and Spanish. Special education offered bilingual concept development, instruction in Spanish and English, personal and social development, and acculturation. A few states such as California now require bilingual education or ESL certification or training for all teachers, regardless of their specialization. More specific to career development, the Institute on Rehabilitation Issues (1992) provided recommendations for culturally responsive rehabilitation services and offered a wealth of ideas for evaluating and revamping programs to serve their diverse constituents better; the Spotlight on Diversity offers strategies that can be used to address diversity issues.

Strategies to Address Issues of Diversity

- Teachers, job coaches, paraprofessionals, or administrators can make home visits early in each school year or during the summer to learn about the home supports and factors that may affect the student's success in school, work, and the community. Establishing a one-to-one relationship with family members can make all the difference in their level of support for the student's studies, career development, or other activities.

- Educators can ask family or community members to teach them or their classes about certain aspects of the local culture or language to avoid violating cultural taboos out of ignorance.

- Because paraprofessionals are typically from the local community and often know the students' families (or may be related to them), they can serve as a source of information and offer valuable insights about cultural practices, expectations, attitudes, and other variables. They are often able to identify possible supports for and barriers to students' transitions from school to adult services. ●

Outcome Options

Educators must ask themselves two questions as they design curricula to address all of their students' needs:

1. What am I preparing my students for?
2. Will my current instruction truly help my students reach these aims?

Schloss, Smith, and Schloss (1995) summarize goals of secondary special education from a variety of sources, with the following broad maxims:

1. Students need opportunities to maximize their potentials, regardless of ability levels.
2. Students should participate in education in close proximity to their peers.
3. Students need independent learning and thinking skills that help them gain information in new environments.
4. Students need satisfactory employment and community living skills.

The range of more specific options available to youth and young adults appears in Figure 14.1. These options include the variety described in IDEA's definition of transition:

> Transition services means a coordinated set of activities for a student, designed within an outcome-oriented process, which promotes movement from school to postschool activities, including post-secondary education, vocational training, integrated employment (including supported employment), continuing and adult education, adult services, independent living or community participation. The coordinated set of activities shall be based upon the individual student's needs taking into account the student's preferences and interests and shall include instruction, community experiences, development of employment and other postschool adult living objectives, and when appropriate acquisition of daily living skills and functional vocational evaluation. [IDEA, 1990, Sec. 1401(a)(19)]

Transition Models

Ianacone offers a life span–oriented definition of transition:

> Transition is conceptualized as a process of movement through life phases or a methodology associated with the life development process of persons as they move from one service delivery system to another. This process encompasses the compendium of those activities which lead to independent living, employment, and other productive life situations. (1987, p. 1)

The Division on Career Development and Transition (DCDT) of the Council for Exceptional Children (CEC) also addresses transition from a life span perspective:

> Transition refers to a change in status from behaving primarily as a student to assuming emergent adult roles in the community. These roles include seeking employment, participating in post-secondary education, maintaining a home, becoming appropriately involved in the community, and experiencing satisfactory personal and social relationships. The process of enhancing transition involves the participation and coordination of school programs, adult agency services, and natural supports within the community. The foundations for transition should be laid during the elementary and middle school years, guided by the broad concept of career development. Transition planning should begin no later than age 14, and

Figure 14.1
Outcome options
for young adults

Vocational/Educational options

University (B.A. or graduate degree)
Community college (certificate or degree)
Vocational-technical school
Military
Apprenticeships
Independent employment
Family employment
Transitional employment (time-limited support)
Supported employment
Docent programs
Volunteer work
Family helper
Sheltered workshop
Day activity program
Day treatment program
Other

Residential options

Independent living, alone
Independent living, with roommate
Military
Dorm or college apartment
Independent living with personal care support
Supervised apartment
Parent/guardian's home
Other family member's home
Supervised living (boarding, foster home, apartment, group home)
Other

Transportation options

Own, drive vehicle
Drive family car or another
Public transportation (bus, subway, trolley, etc.)
Specialized transportation (cabs, etc.)
Family transports
Carpools
Bicycle, roller blades, skateboard
Walk

Social/Interpersonal networks

Extended family
Nuclear family
Friends (neighborhood, school, work, social clubs, organizations, recreation, etc.)
Acquaintances (support groups, social agencies, churches, volunteer agencies)

Community/Leisure options

Consumer initiation of events, participation
Consumer participation in events, program
Church attendance, participation
Participation in local government
Personal hobbies (card games, videos, hot air balloons)
Fine arts (art, music, dance, drama) events and instruction
Recreation/leisure activities—alone, with family and friends (travel, sports, leagues, block parties, etc.)
Organized sports and activities: government-operated, private, military, social service club

Financial/Income options

Earned wages (competitive, self-employed or supported)
Paid internship, grants, scholarships
Peace Corps/AmeriCorps
Professional sports with sponsor
Social Security
Supplemental Security Income (SSI)
Social Security Disability Income (SSDI)
Food stamps
Housing assistance
General or other assistance
Financial planning: checking/savings, wills and trusts, investments

Health options

Group insurance policy (e.g., Medicaid, HMO)
City/county health clinics
School health center
Research programs for serious rare illnesses
Veterans Administration, Lion's Club, etc.
Planned Parenthood
Local pharmacist
Mental/physical wellness activities:
    Support groups
    Advocacy groups
    Gyms, sports, recreation, hobbies
    Homeopathy, local folk medicine
    Hygiene maintenance

students should be encouraged, to the full extent of their capabilities, to assume a maximum amount of responsibility for such planning. (Halpern, 1994, p. 117)

Transition planning allows students, family members, and professionals from a wide range of disciplines to address all the life needs of the individual, rather than just focusing on academic instruction. Several models for transition from school to adulthood are currently used throughout the United States. Four approaches have been selected for discussion here. People devised these approaches in response to the national transition initiatives beginning in the early 1980s.

Halpern's (1985) Transition Model

Halpern suggests that successful transition depends on the secondary school, with the desired outcome being community adjustment. According to him, adult adjustment includes three broad areas: employment, social and interpersonal networks, and residential environments. His data-based rationale asserts that successful interventions in one life arena do not necessarily yield satisfactory outcomes in the other dimensions. Without direct programming, generalization does not occur for many individuals with disabilities; also, for many types of adult demands, entirely different skills are needed than might have been learned for different situations.

Clark and Kolstoe's (1995) Career Development and Transition Education Model

Clark and Kolstoe (1995) view individualized career preparation as the optimal mechanism for enhancing adult adjustment for all students. Three major phases form the framework of their life span model (see Figure 14.2). Initially, four components receive varying degrees of emphasis as students progress from preschool through eighth grade:

1. Identification of one's values, attitudes, and habits, and the relationships between these personal characteristics
2. Human relationships and the roles that communication and acceptance play in these relationships
3. Occupational information (work roles, job-specific language, employment alternatives, and basic "realities" about the work world)
4. Acquisition of critical skills for daily living related to work (e.g., transportation)

The second phase, spanning the high school years, builds upon and extends the first stage. Options in this phase should help students develop career skills. These options include four "levels" as portrayed in Figure 14.2. The third phase, the postsecondary years, portrays the range of choices for further training or preparation, as well as options for employment levels.

Career Education Model

In this author's opinion, the **career education** model promoted by Sidney Marland of the U.S. Office of Education in 1971 offers the most comprehensive and potentially fulfilling educational promise for all students that our educational system has seen. The goal of career education is the development of general career competencies

Figure 14.2
Career development
and transition
education

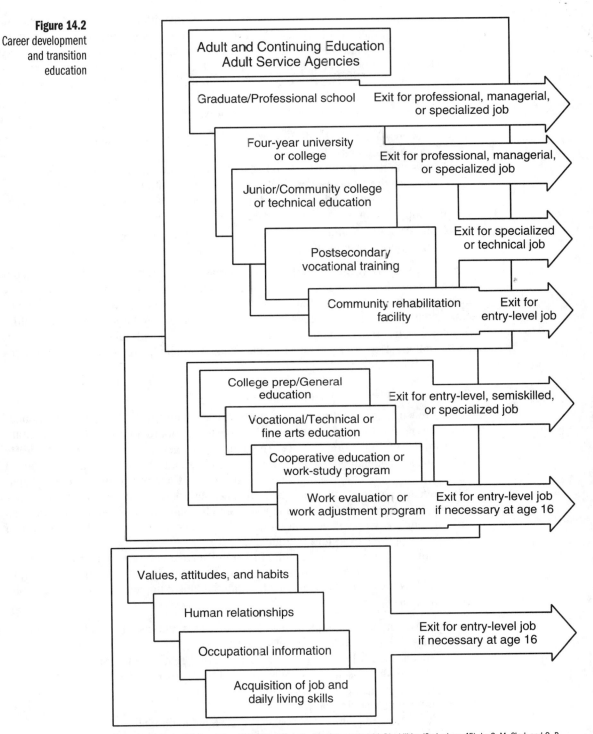

Adult and Continuing Education
Adult Service Agencies

Graduate/Professional school → Exit for professional, managerial, or specialized job

Four-year university or college → Exit for professional, managerial, or specialized job

Junior/Community college or technical education

Postsecondary vocational training → Exit for specialized or technical job

Community rehabilitation facility → Exit for entry-level job

College prep/General education

Vocational/Technical or fine arts education → Exit for entry-level, semiskilled, or specialized job

Cooperative education or work-study program

Work evaluation or work adjustment program → Exit for entry-level job if necessary at age 16

Values, attitudes, and habits

Human relationships

Occupational information → Exit for entry-level job if necessary at age 16

Acquisition of job and daily living skills

Source: From *Career Development and Transition Education for Adolescents with Disabilities* (2nd ed., p. 45), by G. M. Clark and O. P. Kolstoe, 1995, Boston: Allyn & Bacon. Copyright 1990 by Allyn & Bacon. Reprinted by permission.

(knowledge, skills, aptitudes, attitudes) that are useful within any vocational area and enhance individuals' overall growth. These skills therefore prepare students to become workers, family members, citizens, and consumers. This model reflects many of the tenets of Super's vocational development theory (1953), exemplifying how success in each age stage can be enhanced through the right kinds of activities, such as reality testing, role playing, and work on one's self-concept. Specific features of the career education model (Rusch, Mithaug, & Flexer, 1986) are:

1. Purposeful, systemwide (integrated into all curricula) sequence of planned educational activities
2. Systematic coordination of all school, family, and community components toward the student's personal, social, and occupational development
3. Focus on both paid and unpaid (volunteer, internship) work
4. Emphasis on a broad scope of abilities
5. Instruction at all age levels
6. Instruction by educators from all areas

According to White (1987), content areas within career education curricula include generic work behaviors sought by most employers: emergency and safety skills, awareness of work and job choices, appropriate behavior, social and communication skills, prevocational skills, awareness of aptitudes and abilities, and an ability to follow instructions. Community input about skills students need to be successful on the job must be solicited for more specialized areas of instruction to ensure relevancy for the local area.

Education System for Employability

A more recent interpretation of the career education model is reflected in the Education System for Employability (New Mexico State Board of Education and State Department of Education, 1992). The model engages learners in **employability skills,** basic academic skills, and **career awareness** all the way from kindergarten through postsecondary education (see Figure 14.3). **Career exploration** and preparation occur in middle and high school, respectively, and skill development and proficiency fall into place during the junior year and beyond. Within such a framework, as with the earlier career education model, all students are served to their potentials; appropriate options exist for all students.

Endorsed by the State Board and the State Department of Education, the Educational System for Employability aims to support students in achieving the state's standards for excellence. Eight strategies for state and local implementation of the model were outlined:

1. Development and implementation of curricula and instructional techniques
2. Professional development for all educators
3. Discussions with various institutions, parent groups, and programs
4. Partnerships between schools and businesses or industries
5. Career guidance and counseling
6. Informing the general public
7. Access to and support for critical programs and policies
8. Integrating quality education concepts into total school curricula

Figure 14.3
New Mexico's
Education System
for Employability

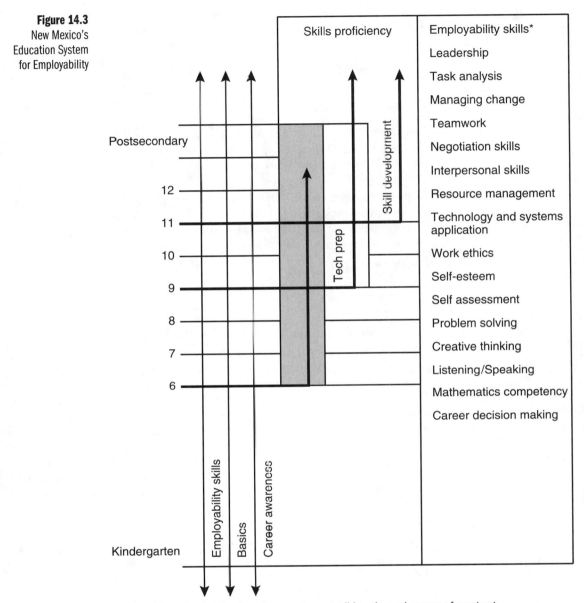

*Infused into the total education system at all levels and areas of content.

Source: From *New Mexico's Education System for Employability,* by the New Mexico State Board of Education and State Department of Education, 1992, Santa Fe: Author.

● ●

Instructional and Curricular Models and Strategies

As you read, think about . . .

1. Comparing and contrasting transition and career education curricula.
2. Designing a plan to foster more effective transitions between preschool and kindergarten, elementary and middle school, and middle and high school.
3. Developing a plan with families to promote effective transitions to adulthood.
4. Examining career options within your community for adults with disabilities.
5. Designing a transition curriculum for a student who will attend a local community college after high school.
6. Developing a transition program with community agencies, service providers, and postsecondary staff in offices for students with disabilities.
7. Writing a transition plan for a student who will attend a vocational training school following high school.
8. Designing a self-determination curriculum and lesson plan to teach one skill.
9. Designing a lesson to teach community skills in a community setting.

K–12 Curricula

Brolin's Life-Centered Career Education (LCCE) Model

Brolin's approach (1991) prepares students in four major areas of adult productivity: occupational, domestic, vocational, and preparation for volunteer work. Within these areas, critical steps begin with developing a "work personality" (unique abilities, work ethics, work motivation, work values, work goals, and work habits and behaviors). These facets are similar to Super's work-related self-concept (1953). From these, Brolin developed 22 major competencies and 102 subcompetencies that interface on two critical dimensions: (1) school, family, and community experiences, and (2) the four stages of career development (awareness; exploration; preparation; and placement, follow-up, or continuing education). The LCCE prepares students at the elementary, middle, and high school levels in personal, social, and occupational competence.

Project CERES

The community of Ceres, California, supported their local district in revamping their curricula to combat high dropout, low employment, and high incarceration rates among their students and graduates (Ceres Unified School District, 1988). This K–12 curriculum is designed within a career education framework for all students. The curriculum teaches (1) work-related identity and values, (2) career awareness, exploration, and education, (3) citizenship, (4) relationship skills, (5) consumer skills, (6) leisure or recreation skills, and (7) basic economics. Prepared lessons are easily infused into existing content area curricula, with the exception of a few separate activities that integrate multiple areas of instruction.

Transitions to Kindergarten and Elementary Programs: Basic Guidelines

IDEA authorizes early intervention services for eligible children from birth through age five with the intent of providing continuity of services as infants move to toddler stages (supported by Part H of IDEA, Sec. 303.344) and then to preschool levels (supported by Part B). This segment of the law specifies the Individualized Family Service Plan (IFSP) as the document to provide for the child's (and the family's) education-related needs. The IFSP (introduced in chapters 1 and 3) must include the steps to be taken to support the child's movement from birth-to-3 services to the preschool services under Part B of the Act, if appropriate, or other services that may be available. In other words, the law states that (1) discussions with the family (and training as needed) must occur regarding future placements and other matters related to the child's transition; (2) procedures to prepare the child for changes in service delivery must be planned and implemented, including steps to help the child adjust to and function in a new setting; and (3) with parental consent, information about the child must be sent to the local educational agency to ensure continuity of services. Training must be provided to service providers as needed to support the smooth movement from one system to another. In addition, Section 136 of the Head Start Transition Project Act states that each Head Start agency must develop family service coordinators to ensure the smooth transition to elementary schools by children served under the Head Start Act, Part B of Chapter I (Even Start), IDEA Part B, and comparable early childhood programs. A similar philosophy and comparable guidelines should be used in the transition from early childhood special education services to categorical special education services at the elementary level (Blalock et al., 1994). Planning and providing needed training for all parties well in advance of the student's passage will make an enormous difference in the child's adjustment in new settings.

Transitions to Middle School: Preparing the Base and Moving On Up

Two of the transition models presented earlier broadly describe the critical content of an elementary program needed to prepare students for their next stage. The major components of an elementary program for students with learning and behavior problems should be:

1. Basic academic skills, maximizing each student's potential
2. Social, interpersonal, and communication skills
3. Work- and family-centered values, attitudes, and habits (eg., work ethic, punctuality, task completion, initiative, cooperation)
4. Self-determination basics (knowing self, self-esteem)
5. Self-care skills
6. Career awareness

Special educators, even more than general educators, have long recognized that smooth passages from elementary to middle school require some preparation. Students with exceptionalities will especially need time to digest basic information about what to expect in middle school. York, Doyle, and Kronberg (1992) outline a sample planning tool to help general and special educators, as well as students, prepare for the transition. The activities listed in Figure 14.4 could be covered throughout the year preceding middle or junior high school, so that students attain adequate knowledge and skills.

Husted (1992) offers guidelines for preparing elementary students with cognitive disabilities for their next stage. His ideas include postorganizers (discussing the next

Figure 14.4
Sample planning tool for transition from elementary to middle school

When	What	Who	By

Step 1: Initial information from school sending information

General and special elementary educators complete "Student General Information Sheet" and copy log notes.

Both sending and receiving teachers share general information about student.

Middle school team member follows up if forms not received by (spring date).

Step 2: Middle school class placement

New students are assigned to classes, teachers, homerooms, and advisors through input by all key teams' members.

Individual support needs and student combinations within each classroom and family or grade are considered.

Middle school principal is contacted about new student placements for inclusion in computerized scheduling.

Letter informs parents of assignments and of upcoming transition planning meeting. Short parent questionnaire accompanies the letter.

Step 3: Teachers' and students' contact across settings

Middle school teachers visit elementary sites to observe.

Students are assigned middle school buddies and visit middle school, meeting with buddies in advisory group and having lunch.

Staff members welcome students in transition.

Step 4: Student-centered transition team meetings

Individual student teams meet in May to: review information on student's move, develop initial transition plan using existing tools, identify IEP meeting or periodic review for fall.

Step 5: Grade-level team meetings for further planning

Step 6: Setting dates for IEPs and periodic reviews

Source: Adapted from "A Curriculum Development Process for Inclusive Classrooms," by J. York, M. B. Doyle, and R. Kronberg, 1992, *Focus on Exceptional Children, 25*(4), pp. 1–16.

day's activities or a homework assignment), analogies, and rationales, such as the following:

1. Provide a sense of time—e.g., "Going to Grandma's takes about two hours, but planting the garden takes about a week."
2. Provide a sense of closure—e.g., "You've just finished the science project on nutrition. It took you about four weeks to do it, and you did a thorough job."
3. Provide a reason for doing a task—e.g., "If you hang up your coat, it will stay clean and you will look great when you go to the movies after school."
4. Provide natural opportunities, logic, and realism. For example, when planning field trips, link visits to students' interests. Discuss the realities of the setting and students' perceptions of the setting prior to going.
5. Ensure that the location of the activity is reasonable and not artificial. For instance, shopping should occur in real stores (whether on or off campus), not in token systems.

Figure 14.5 offers two additional components to support transitions to middle school. The first section lists topics about which students need to learn, while the second segment outlines strategies with which to teach those topics.

Figure 14.5
Issues and strategies to support transition from elementary to middle school

Content for preparing for middle school transitions

- Departmentalization
- Extracurricular activities
- Homework demands
- Credits needed to pass to next grade
- Population change from elementary level

- Peer pressure
- Expectations for self-accountability
- Demands for self-management, organization
- More teacher- and subject-centeredness

Strategies to prepare students for the transition

- Videotape of the receiving school program and its characteristics
- Visit middle school in advance
- Meet teachers, coaches, principal in advance
- Letter writing by sixth graders to fifth graders about middle school
- Flow chart or web about middle school
- Student-initiated student-teacher conferences
- Role plays of social skills for middle school
- Checklists of things to think about, prepare for
- Checklists for contents of locker, backpack, etc.
- Teaching rules and expectations of receiving setting

- Having middle school teachers or counselors visit the elementary school and answer questions, bring textbooks for display, bring sixth graders to answer questions
- Teaching map reading for buildings (symbols, signs)
- Discussing extracurricular activities
- Discussing electives
- Teaching study skills
- Teaching self-organization skills (e.g., assignment sheets punctuality, etc.)
- Jump Start Day (before seventh and eighth graders arrive)

Source: From University of New Mexico Special Education 542, Teaching Persons with Learning Disabilities, Spring 1995.

Transitions to High School: Career Exploration and Informal Transition Planning

Students in middle school are at the stage called *career exploration,* during which they need opportunities to check out a broad array of work options. Almost every middle school or junior high school in the United States offers at least basic offerings through which all students (should) rotate. At minimum, these include typing and computer keyboarding, home economics classes, and industrial arts. In addition, as depicted in Clark's and New Mexico's models (Figures 14.2 and 14.3, respectively), refinement of academic skills and employability skills should be a major outcome. For some students, **community-based instruction** may be an important way to help students understand the roles that school, work, home, and community play in one's life. Mentorships for gifted students (many of whom have learning or behavior problems) should certainly start at the middle school level to help combat leanings toward dropping out and apathy about school. Some districts have found that rotated monthly job-shadowing experiences work well for seventh and eighth graders with and without disabilities.

A package of activities during the last year of middle school or junior high has been found to engage learners more actively in their educational programs. Examples of activities that actively engage learners in the transition process are found in Scenario 14.1.

Scenario **14.1**

How One Local District Helped Middle Schoolers Prepare for High School

Several years ago, the Albuquerque Public Schools Special Education Department began preparing eighth graders with moderate and severe disabilities for the ninth grade. Over a period of several days, groups of students learned about the differences that high school would bring, in areas such as attendance policies, Carnegie units and their implications for passing, dress codes (if applicable), graduation requirements, high school competency exams, practical arts (vocational) and fine arts classes, ROTC, work/study programs, and general expectations about behavior and scholarship. Eighth graders learned through a true-false question format that was delivered with humor and active participation. A game of chance helped students explore future options related to jobs (or lack thereof), wage ranges, future schooling, social services, and other outcomes. The COPS II Interest Inventory (Knapp & Knapp, 1981) was administered orally in groups to help students assess their own interests and perceptions about their academic strengths and weaknesses; three to six occupational clusters were then targeted for each student for future exploration and for use in planning initial high school electives. Students carried out two homework assignments: a parent goal inventory (see Figure 14.6) and a worker interview (see Figure 14.7). An individual interview was held with each student to review the COPS II results and develop the four-year plan, as required in state educational standards prior to ninth grade. Finally, an exit IEP meeting was held at the high school in late spring so that sending and receiving teachers, the student, and parents could discuss the best options for the next year. Students who participated in the transition preparation understood the reason for the IEP meeting and that their decisions at that point would affect their long-range outcomes; as a result, they were much more articulate about their choices and more motivated to speak up than they would otherwise have been. ■

Figure 14.6
Career/Life Skills
Prep. Class—Spring
1990

Parent Goal Inventory

Student name _____   Date _____

Parent name _____   Relationship _____

1. What is your educational goal for your child? (Please check one.)

    _____ Not graduate from high school

    _____ Graduate from high school

    _____ Vocational training/trade school

    _____ Apprenticeship

    _____ A.A. degree/two-year college

    _____ Four-year college

    _____ Beyond four years of college

2. What is your vocational or work goal for your child after school?

3. Can you think of ways you can help your child reach these goals? If so, what are some ways?

4. What do you expect the high school program to do for your child?

Source: From University of New Mexico Special Education 593, Career/Life Skills Preparation of Special Needs Learners, Spring 1990.

Figure 14.7
Career/Life Skills
Prep. Class–Spring
1990

Worker Interview Assignment

Name _____   Worker s name _____

Date _____   Location _____

Select a person who has a job to conduct the interview. Ask each of the following questions. Use whatever help you need to record the worker's response.

1. What is your job called? _____

2. What do you do (job duties)? _____

3. What are your work hours? _____

4. What qualifications did you need to get your job? _____

5. What do you like about your job?

6. What do you dislike about your job?

7. What is your salary? _____

8. What is the starting pay for your job? _____

9. What kind of benefits do you get from this job?

10. Where can you go in this field?

11. How long have you worked in this job? _____

12. How long do you plan to be here? _____

Source: From University of New Mexico Special Education 593, Career/Life Skills Preparation of Special Needs Learners, Spring 1990.

Toliver (1995) drafted a thoughtful compilation of critical interventions to support transitions from middle school to high school. Toliver based his findings on interviews with school personnel, an article by Marshall (1992), and a report by Rossi and Stokes (1991). A synopsis of his paper appears in Figure 14.8.

Transitions to Adulthood: Skills Development and Individualized Transition Planning

Major Instructional Approaches

Since the early 1970s, professionals as a whole have addressed the education of some youth and adults with learning or behavior problems in a reactionary or "catch-up" manner, often taking their cues from the education of younger students, rather than creating new approaches specifically designed for the outcome needs of older students. In recent years, however, researchers have generated a variety of instructional programs specifically designed for older students with special needs. In 1979, Deshler, Lowrey, and Alley identified four major approaches being used with low-achieving adolescents, including **basic skills remediation** (which they found most prevalent), **study skills instruction,** the **tutorial approach,** and the **compensatory or content-equivalent approach.** They offered an alternative, the Strategic Intervention Model (SIM), of which the major instructional component was learning strategies.

Figure 14.8
Transition to high school—summary of topics and activities

I. Major curriculum essential areas
   A. Reading
   B. Writing
   C. Mathematics
   D. Speech
   E. Computers
II. Major skill areas
   A. Organizational skills
   B. Study skills
   C. Intrapersonal skills
   D. Interpersonal skills
III. Extracurricular activities
IV. High school support transition areas
   A. High school personnel visit middle school (two different events)
   B. Middle school personnel and families visit high school (two different events)
   C. Support programs once at high school
V. School/Work program for special education students (continuum of options)

Source: Adapted from *Transition to high school,* by L. T. Toliver, 1995, paper presented to Secondary Special Education Methods and Materials Class, University of New Mexico.

This model is used widely among educators serving students with mild disability levels. It is described in more detail in chapter 5. Increasing demands for approaches that teach students how to learn signal a recognition that content, although important, changes in some fields so rapidly that what one learns becomes obsolete in five or ten years. Finally, in recent years, there has also been a renewed interest in the **functional approach** (e.g., survival academics, vocational education, and community-based experiences).

When a full spectrum of these options are available within a school or program, adolescents' needs stand a good chance of being met. Problems arise when only one or two curricular options are available; they may or may not address each student's educational difficulties. At least three distinct options should be offered by every setting to truly address individuals' needs and goals. A continuum of options that begins at the preschool level and flows through postsecondary opportunities, branching off into many directions along the way, is clearly required for students with diverse needs (Blalock, 1988; Brolin, 1985).

Decisions about the most appropriate educational aims, approaches, settings, and materials for each adolescent or adult with special needs must be made continually. At the secondary level, major changes in educational programs warrant careful examination. Both parents and teachers need to wrestle with the decision about switching from an academics-only emphasis to a more functional emphasis, recognizing that a balance of both is possible and may be the most desirable. Variables to consider include:

1. The student's steady and solid progress in present coursework
2. The student's and parents' expressed aims and interests regarding future vocational and life activities
3. The instructional program's relevance to those future aims
4. Input about future options from all persons involved

An additional set of guidelines comes from the National Joint Committee on Learning Disabilities (1987) regarding placement decisions. The most important suggestions include individualized attention to both short- and long-term needs, as well as utilizing the individuals themselves as primary resources for ideas.

Major Assessment Approaches

Gathering information about students and their situations must precede the collaborative decision making that drives programs and settings. School personnel may find it important to conduct a formal or an informal **needs assessment** to identify what family members, students, other school personnel, adult agency or postsecondary education staff, and employers perceive as educational priorities. Area Department of Labor offices can help with employer mailing lists, and parent organizations can identify ways to solicit parent ideas. By gathering information from the broad range of parties in transition, school staff can have a much better idea of the best directions for program planning and implementation.

Functional assessment of students (often called *vocational assessment*) allows parents and educators to make much more informed decisions about program directions. Figure 14.9 portrays stages in which formal vocational evaluation is indicated and when updates are important. At minimum, interest inventories should be administered each year, since adolescents' interests naturally change frequently. Measurement of students' aptitudes or vocationally related skills may be obtained from tests, observations, simulated work tasks or situational assessments on the job. Work-related values may be assessed through inventories designed for that purpose, or from asking focused questions about preferred work conditions and qualifications. This information can be combined with what is already known about the student (cognitive and academic functioning, social and behavioral functioning, physical and motor performance) to afford more efficient and effective decisions about what to explore for the future. Most of these basic assessment strategies can be done readily by a teacher and are appropriate for the vast majority of students. Occasionally, a student's situation may call for a more thorough vocational evaluation by a certified or licensed vocational evaluator.

Figure 14.9
Formal transition planning process and time lines

9th grade	Formal vocational/functional assessment (basic interest, aptitudes/skills, values for most; more in-depth for a few)
	Completion of transition planning guide with student and family
	ITP development as part of annual IEP meeting
10th–11th grades	Implementation of education program as identified in ITP/IEP
	Update interest inventory, other assessments as needed
	Update ITP/IEP annually and implement annual follow-along procedures
	• Increase adult agencies' involvement during 11th and 12th grades (if applicable)
	• Provide ITP/IEP copies to all key parties
12th grade	Informal transition review in fall
	Exit transition meeting in spring, with movement to adult agency, higher education, employment, or other major life activity or support

Source: Adapted from "Transition of Youth with Learning Disabilities to Early Adulthood," by G. Blalock, 1996, in J. R. Patton and E. A. Polloway (Eds.), *Learning Disabilities: The Challenges of Adulthood* (pp. 25–44), Austin, TX: PRO-ED.

Self-Determination Models

Families and special educators have increasingly realized that learners must actively participate in their own education and lives, rather than having others learn and live for them. As a result, federal initiatives for **self-determination** instruction have generated very effective and important programs to assist youth with disabilities in learning about and requesting their desired goals. Most of these programs share common elements of helping students (1) know themselves, their values, and their goals; (2) understand their rights and responsibilities under the law; and (3) communicate their interests and goals effectively.

Field (1996) describes the Steps to Self-Determination 18-session curriculum that targets five major components: Know Yourself, Value Yourself, Plan, Act, and Experience Outcomes and Learn. Designed for integrated environments, this program includes all students, welcomes teachers and parents as co-learners and supports, incorporates experiential and cooperative learning, uses interdisciplinary teaching, emphasizes modeling and humor, and capitalizes on "teachable moments."

Serna and Lau-Smith (1995) recently completed a self-determination curriculum for students who are at risk for failure for a variety of reasons, particularly students with learning disabilities. Learning with PURPOSE builds, but is not dependent upon, prerequisite social skills that are directly taught within the social skills curricula. These curricula have been developed by the Kansas University Center for Research on Learning ASSETS and Social Skills for Daily Living. The program teaches a comprehensive range of skills that focus on students and others and that prepare students to meet their daily challenges with success (see Figure 14.10).

Functional or Life Skills Curricula

The Life-Centered Career Education and CERES curricula described in the "K–12 curricula" section earlier are excellent examples of **life skills curricula,** particularly the LCCE. In addition, Cronin and Patton (1993) have developed a program for developing and integrating real-life knowledge and skills into existing academic subjects. This model approaches planning from a backward or top-down perspective (see Figure 14.11), allowing targeted future outcomes to drive the instructional process. The process begins with six adult domains: (1) home and family, (2) employment and education, (3) community involvement, (4) physical and emotional health, (5) personal responsibility and relationships, and (6) leisure pursuits. Organizing for instruction, the last major step in the approach, depends on the existing instructional program, allowing specific life skills instruction to be incorporated into subjects such as psychology, health, history, or mathematics. Their materials lists, field experience procedures and tools, and other resource lists are invaluable aids for educators.

Special Education Work-Study Model

The goals of work-study programs include more than the acquisition of job skills and work-related behaviors. They also seek to enhance individuals' awareness of different jobs available in the community. Rusch et al. (1986) describe several components inherent in most secondary school work-study programs for special students:

1. Simultaneous classroom instruction in prevocational skills and survival skills related to jobs and daily living.

Figure 14.10
Learning with
PURPOSE: Program
content

Prerequisite social skills

Giving positive feedback (better thanks)

Giving criticism (better resolve)

Accepting criticism (better advice)

Resisting peer pressure (better resist)

Negotiation (better win/win)

Following instructions (better do it)

Conversation (better talking)

Problem solving (better answers)

Self-evaluation skills

Prerequisite skills: giving positive feedback, giving criticism, accepting criticism, and problem solving

Evaluating present skills

Evaluating skills needed for future goals

Self-direction skills

Action planning for accomplishing life achievements

Goal setting

Goal planning

Self-management to achieve goals

Evaluating outcomes

Networking

Informal networking

Prerequisite skills: conversation and rules for keeping friends

Seeking information

Seeking advice

Initiating activities

Dealing with rejection

Keeping friends (guidelines)

Formal networking

Seeking information from a qualified professional

Seeking advice from a qualified professional

Seeking a mentor

Seeking peer support

Proposing collaborations

Collaboration

Prerequisite skills: negotiation, problem solving, action planning, goal setting, and evaluating outcomes

Determining team needs (facilitator and team member skills)

Teaming to develop goals (facilitator and team member skills)

Planning strategies for goal achievement (facilitator and team member skills)

Implementing strategies (facilitator and team member skills)

Group problem solving (facilitator and team member skills)

Persistence and risk taking

Prerequisite skills: problem solving (answers)

Persistence through problem solving

Risk taking through decision making

Dealing with stress

Recognizing feelings

Expressing feelings appropriately (*all prerequisite skills are required for this skill*)

Stress reduction guidelines

Anger management guidelines

Time management guidelines

Health-related guidelines

Source: From *Learning with PURPOSE: An Instructor's Manual for Teaching Self-Determination Skills to Students Who Are At-Risk for Failure* (pp. xii–xiii), by L. A. Serna and J. Lau-Smith, 1995, Honolulu: University of Hawaii Department of Special Education and Hawaii University Affiliated Programs. Reprinted with permission of the authors and Brookes Publishing Co.

2. Placement and supervision by the special education teacher [or work-study or transition coordinator] (typically untrained and inexperienced in the work world).

3. Part-time (half-day) worksite placement, usually beginning in junior year; sometimes full-day placement in senior year in unusual circumstances.

4. Placement either on campus or in community (typically whatever is available; a common practice is to use on-campus sites in earlier years and off-campus sites later).

5. Vocational assessment procedures conducted by school, vocational rehabilitation personnel, or both.

Figure 14.11
Life skills instruction for all students with special needs

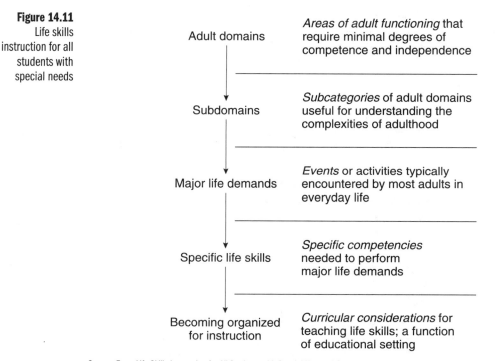

Adult domains	*Areas of adult functioning* that require minimal degrees of competence and independence
Subdomains	*Subcategories* of adult domains useful for understanding the complexities of adulthood
Major life demands	*Events* or activities typically encountered by most adults in everyday life
Specific life skills	*Specific competencies* needed to perform major life demands
Becoming organized for instruction	*Curricular considerations* for teaching life skills; a function of educational setting

Source: From *Life Skills Instruction for All Students with Special Needs: A Practical Guide for Integrating Real-Life Content into the Curriculum* (p. 10), by M. E. Cronin & J. R. Patton, 1993, Austin, TX: PRO-ED. Copyright 1993 by PRO-ED. Reprinted with permission.

6. Jobs usually unskilled or semiskilled; often "terminal" placements in the past (i.e., no exposure to other jobs).
7. Linkages to aid transition to rehabilitation services in many communities.

Brolin (1985) asserts that academic and work-study experiences planned years ago fell short of preparing special students for successful adult adjustment. Dangers to guard against include the following:

1. Students' training and employment opportunities may be limited because work-study teachers typically have few experiences working outside schools and little training in career development.
2. Even students with mild disabilities are at risk of working only in "food, filth, and flowers" positions, with little thought to long-term outcomes, due to the availability of such jobs.
3. The focus is generally on employment only, excluding daily living and social skills instruction.

Work-study programs, or vocational education cooperative programs, can be extremely powerful ways to prepare students for jobs; paid employment during school is the most important indicator of postschool employment success. Creating effective work-study programs depends on a few key elements:

- Rotated experiences that increase in duration over a few (or several) years, possibly building upon previous community-based instruction (CBI)

- Focused objectives for each experience, with data (outcomes) driving decisions to continue or to change
- Employers' paying commensurate wages, rather than schools or agencies providing a work-study stipend
- Long-range planning that prepares students for real careers and advancements

Siegel and colleagues (1993) describe a program that very effectively engaged employers as partners in the education of students with learning and behavior problems. Actual community classrooms, employment skills training, and linkages to postsecondary services were described in detail to employers for easy replication. Siegel's rationales and recommendations for changing work-study programs offer real hope for better postsecondary employment opportunities for students and families.

Vocational Education/Tech Prep Model

In **vocational** (formerly occupational) **education,** students select and acquire marketable skills in a career field that leads toward successful employment (Renzaglia, Bates, & Hutchins, 1981). It begins with broad exposure to a variety of occupations in middle or junior high school (the career exploration phase) and narrows to more selective, in-depth training in specific fields during high school and possibly at postsecondary levels. Vocational education offers many important opportunities for students with special needs. First, it embodies the application of academic skills within hands-on and community experiences. Classes include academic work (particularly vocabulary, procedures, components, relationship between the job and the broader economic scene), safety certification, and laboratory experiences taught by experts in the vocation. Second, links to the local employment scene are inherent within vocational programs' required advisory boards, which ensures that employment opportunities are likely upon graduation and that classes are offered in more than one occupational cluster. At the middle school level, home economics, industrial arts, and typing or keyboarding skills are the typical fare; the possible range is almost endless at the high school and college level. Third, cooperative work programs (not found in every school or district) provide training and experience in actual job sites that truly allow students to understand the full demands of work. Finally, the jobs (for which students will have support in seeking) are challenging and pay moderate to better-than-average wages (Rusch et al., 1986). Drawbacks to this model include the instructors' lack of training in accommodating the needs of students with disabilities, and the possible short-term life of a particular occupation.

Recently offered within vocational education, Tech Prep is a program designed to assure that high school students gain more technologically oriented knowledge and skills. Authorized by the Carl D. Perkins Vocational and Applied Technology Education Act (reauthorized in 1990), this program coordinates the last two years of secondary school with two (or more) subsequent years of higher education (typically linked with a community college vocational program). The program focuses on sequential, sophisticated skill development in mathematics, science, communications, and technology and should lead to a certificate, an associate degree, or even possibly a bachelor's degree in specific fields.

Tech Prep can be implemented in a variety of ways and may be called by different names (e.g., 2 + 2 program, or 2 + 2 + 2 program). Tech Prep agreements are typically developed between local high schools, a local or regional community college or vocational school, and other key entities, such as a nearby four-year college, trades associations, employers, or others. Through such agreements, students can undertake **concurrent enrollment,** earning simultaneous credit at both the secondary and the postsecondary institutions. A second common feature among tech prep programs is **applied academics,** whereby districts request approval for basic academic credits (such as communication skills, science, or mathematics) within applied courses (e.g., child development lab, foods and nutrition, automotive repair, graphic arts), thus providing a meaningful context within which to acquire or refine basic academic skills.

An additional facet related to Tech Prep may be **apprenticeship programs,** which have received increased attention through recent governmental emphases on the education-labor partnership, particularly the School to Work Opportunities Act. Apprenticeships are structured training opportunities in occupations that require a diverse range of specific skills and knowledge, as well as maturity and problem-solving skills. Apprenticeships involve planned, daily, on-the-job training under approved supervision, combined with related technical instruction. As modern industry currently practices it, apprenticeship is designed to provide workers entering an industry with comprehensive training through introduction to both the practical and the theoretical aspects of the work required in a highly skilled occupation. Trades organizations in the particular fields, schools, trade or technical schools, and others are close partners in apprenticeship programs. Internships and pre-apprenticeship programs appear increasingly in schools. These programs are often ideal options for many young adults with special needs who are interested in highly technical fields.

Transition Planning and the IEP

In general terms, several events should happen between 9th and 12th grade to plan for postschool outcomes. Each local education agency and each family will have particular twists to this process that make it work well in their respective situations. The questions in Figure 14.12 could be used to promise a fairly smooth passage into postschool life if carried out thoughtfully.

IDEA requires that planning for transition services occurs no later than age 14, and, as noted in the definition by the Division on Career Development and Transition,

Figure 14.12
Transition plan review questions

These questions are to be used as a guide when reviewing transition plans. It is imperative that the student and parent be present at the meeting.

Questions to student:

1. Are your goals still the same? (Refer to the transition planning guide or ask student his or her goals.)

2. What else do you think needs to be done to help reach your goals?

Questions when reviewing the transition plan document:

1. Were the goals accomplished? If not, do we need to reassign, reanalyze, or redefine?

2. Are there objectives that still need to be accomplished?

3. Do we need additional objectives?

4. What barriers are cropping up? How can we address these barriers?

5. Is the student's program developed in a cohesive fashion that makes sense?

Source: Adapted from Gallup-McKinley County (New Mexico) Schools Special Education Department (no date, no page).

many believe age 14 is the latest it should happen. This requirement means (1) that transition goals should be identified in any of the life domains relevant for the student, and (2) that the transition services needed for him or her to reach those goals should be identified and planned. Examples of transition goals are: "T will explore independent living options to move from the family home three years after graduation," and "R will attend a two-year college in a field of his choice." Transition services or activities might include, in the first case, teaching T how to manage a household budget or how to secure utilities in a timely fashion. Services in the second case might include helping R search for colleges that offer his chosen major and write letters of inquiry.

Transition planning guides have proven very helpful for students, teachers, and families to read prior to the typically rushed, formal IEP meeting, so that the student's and family's true desires can be discussed. The guides may have blanks next to the life domain categories (see Figure 14.11), requiring the group to fill in possible goals and activities. They may be a copy of the IEP form. Alternatively, they may ask specific questions about specific aspects of each domain.

Once transition goals have been identified, activities should be specified that will help achieve each goal, listing the responsible parties and time lines. The group will then need to translate those transition goals into annual IEP goals, then subsequently into instructional objectives through which to accomplish each goal. Again, responsibilities and time lines are identified. In T's case, an appropriate IEP annual goal driven by her transition goal could be "T will develop a complete home budget and manage it through simulated life activities." One of R's annual IEP goals could be "R will gather information about admissions, costs, programs, and special services from five colleges within a given geographic area, match their offerings to his identified priorities, and select at least one college to visit." By proceeding in this backward or top-down manner, transition planning becomes an integral part of the IEP process and keeps the instructional program very outcome-oriented.

The *Self-Advocacy Strategy for Education and Transition Planning* by Van Reusen, Bos, Schumaker, and Deshler (1994), formerly the *Education Planning Strategy,* is a motivation strategy intended to encourage students to be active participants and even leaders in their IEP-ITP meetings and their instructional programs. Students learn how to identify their learning strengths, the areas in which they can improve, and their choices for learning. In addition, they inventory their interests and needs related to all adult life domains (i.e., vocation, living, community, and leisure or recreation activities). They also set goals for learning and for preparing themselves for transitions from school to the adult world. To put all this together, participants acquire the necessary communication skills to convey their goals, interests, and needs in meetings and to participate actively in the decision making at those meetings. Educators who have used the Strategic Intervention Model's learning strategies or social skills strategies (Van Reusen et al., 1994) will find the following stages of instruction very familiar and equally useful:

Stage 1:   Orient and make commitments
Stage 2:   Describe
Stage 3A: Model and prepare for education planning conferences
Stage 3B: Model and prepare for transition planning conferences
Stage 4:   Verbal practice
Stage 5:   Group practice and feedback

Stage 6:   Individual practice and feedback

Stage 7:   Generalization

One of the common fears about setting transition goals is that students will then be trapped in a direction that may prove unsatisfactory later. For this reason, IDEA requires that transition plans (as part of the IEP) be reviewed annually to insure their continued appropriateness. A few pointed questions, such as those listed in Figure 14.12, can help the IEP team (including the student) accomplish the intended outcomes.

Partnerships in Transition

As you read, think about . . .

1. Designing components of an interagency agreement that you would like to address with service providers.
2. Developing a list of questions to ask community agency service providers about the levels of their support and services for their clients.
3. Designing an Individual Transition Plan with a family member and student.
4. Designing a lesson plan to teach students about the Americans with Disabilities Act.
5. Designing your own life skills curriculum.
6. Conducting a search for available housing and transportation services in your community for people with disabilities.

Interagency Agreements

Some communities and states have found that cooperative agreements between participating agencies are crucial for communication, planning, and accountability. Other localities have found them burdensome and unnecessary. If these agreements are developed, important elements include: (1) basic values and assumptions shared by the group to serve as guidelines for all planning and service provision activities, (2) defining the roles and responsibilities of each participant, (3) clarifying the overall scope of activities, and (4) establishing a common language and data base (Stodden & Boone, 1987). Simultaneous development of both state-level and local-level agreements seems to be very effective.

Family Involvement

Numerous authorities (Johnson, Bruininks, & Thurlow, 1987) have documented how important it is for parents and students to have maximum involvement in planning transition programs. Other data suggest that many parents think little about their child's even having a career and are unaware of the home activities that could enhance students' independence (Kokaska & Hughes, 1985).

Some states have advocated placing families at the agency level to facilitate communication and authority (Blalock et al., 1994). Parents can contribute a great deal to the transition process, including (1) exploring their values, (2) modeling employability and maintaining a job, (3) modeling living skills and maintaining relationships, (4) contributing specialized expertise about the student, and (5) sharing knowledge of the community and local culture. Parents' roles should include:

- Assisting in the local transition planning process as part of the community transition team (if one exists)
- Participating in the student's IEP team
- Working with the school to implement the IEP and to provide services as needed
- Providing support between school and adult life, as well as lifelong support
- Lobbying state and federal legislators for additional revenue and programs as needed

Getting parents to come to transition planning meetings may be difficult at first, because all parents want to let go of some school responsibilities when their children reach high school and because systems do not typically embrace family members as real partners in the educational process. Parents can play a more active role if they have been encouraged to do so from the time their child entered special education services. The very focused direction of transition planning can energize families and thus motivate greater participation in the future. Husted (1992) shares the following tips for enhancing parent involvement:

1. Start the transition plan in middle school.
2. Use the IEP as a report card to monitor progress toward goals (as it should be used).
3. Ask specifically for what you need from parents.
4. Share positive comments about the student as well as negative; focus on present levels of performance (i.e., abilities) rather than deficits.
5. Discuss the transition plan and IEP with the parents and student before the formal meeting.

Postsecondary Education and Training Options

Several resources for postsecondary education exist in the U.S., ranging from short-term vocational-technical training opportunities to graduate degrees (see Figure 14.1). Community colleges in particular offer comprehensive training programs as well as support services for a diverse body of learners. Most two-year colleges and many four-year colleges offer well-developed programs for students with learning or behavior problems. A number of reference guides to college programs for special populations (e.g., those with learning disabilities) can be found in the public and university libraries.

The Americans with Disabilities Act of 1990 prohibits discrimination against persons with disabilities in admissions, advising, assessment, and access to educational programs. The Act also protects the privacy of students, requiring only that the appropriate office verify entitlement to specific accommodations, not proof of a disability. Students themselves are responsible to request the particular accommodations they need.

Postsecondary versions of the work-study model are found in several community college programs. Two well-known programs in New York, Adelphi University and the City University of New York, offer self-contained experiences for adults with moderate and severe learning disabilities that are paralleled in few other places. Their highly structured training immerses students in vocationally oriented remedial classes, specific vocational training, supervised field placements, tutoring, and weekly group counseling (Barbaro, 1982: Blalock & Dixon, 1982).

Employment Options

Individuals with learning or behavior problems theoretically have a full spectrum of possible job opportunities available to them. However, their employment status in follow-up studies shows far too much unemployment and underemployment. Support services that may help to create more appropriate and satisfying work situations include programs within community colleges' and universities' job placement services, the Division of Vocational Rehabilitation for time-limited support (typically 18 months to 2 years), and the Department of Labor's generic programs that subsidize training and on-the-job training for many nontraditional candidates. In addition, some urban areas have community employment agencies that serve persons with learning and behavior problems, among others, and that can help with job readiness training, job placement, and follow-along support.

The Americans with Disabilities Act (ADA) of 1990 requires that employers not discriminate in the hiring process based on a disability and that they provide reasonable accommodations to an employee with a disability (if needed). The applicant or worker must show that he or she is otherwise qualified to do the job (i.e., that he or she can perform the essence of the job with accommodations if needed). The ADA's employment provisions apply to private employers, state and local governments, employment agencies, and labor unions; they do not apply to employers with fewer than 15 workers, the U.S. government (which is covered by the Rehabilitation Act of 1973), Native American tribes, or private membership clubs. ADA covers all aspects of employment: recruiting, advertising, compensation, fringe benefits, tenure and leave, promotion and advancement, hiring, training, transfers and layoffs, firing, and other activities (Goldberg & Goldberg, 1993).

Community Living Options

Little attention has been given to community living for adolescents and young adults with disabilities. Figure 14.1 describes what might be available for individuals with all types of disabilities, but large gaps remain; few community agencies support life skill development of adults with mild and moderate levels of disabilities. Sitlington (1996) decries the neglect of this area by education and human services agencies and urges several changes. Those recommendations include:

1. Continuing to study the efficacy of life skills instruction and transition planning
2. Including all adult life domains in follow-up studies
3. Examining students' competence and experiences while still in school, as well as after
4. Integrating life skills instruction and transition into general education programs
5. Knowing what drives secondary education and using it
6. Developing assessment models for the life skills areas
7. Counteracting the myth that adults with mild or moderate disabilities do not need life skills instruction and transition planning

8. Infusing transition education into teacher preparation programs that range from early childhood through adulthood in emphasis
9. Working more efficiently and not giving up

Summary

School instruction is meant to prepare students to embrace the responsibilities and privileges of adulthood fully and in an informed manner. Providing a comprehensive curriculum with instructional procedures that promote independent learning and performance should accomplish this goal. By the time students reach adolescence, teachers' selection of the most important content and strategies becomes even more critical. Opportunities for learning are rapidly disappearing, and the time in which the student remains in school should be spent on the most relevant skills possible. This is particularly true for students with exceptionalities who may require more time and different procedures to develop some skills. Follow-up studies of special education graduates indicate that our efforts have been inadequate to date. These students, whose needs are quite diverse, are not fully prepared to make transitions into adult life. Consequently, a carefully planned continuum of meaningful offerings is crucial at the secondary level.

Teachers must begin to shift their thinking from strictly a year-to-year, classroom perspective to a longer-term, broader community scope. Careful matching of required outcome-based competencies with the particular strengths and limitations of one's students helps to pinpoint specific areas for intervention. In addition, the teacher must consider all domains that research findings say are pertinent to school preparation: career and vocational development, personal and social skills, academic skills, independent living competencies, and community integration skills, including leisure pursuits. Curricular models described in this chapter offer an array of options for pertinent content related to these domains.

Guidelines for planning strategies to help students move from each stage to the next have been outlined. Time lines for functional assessment and transition planning have been suggested, serving as the critical foundation for all subsequent instruction. Finally, the reader is provided with a number of ideas for engaging partners in the transition education process and for utilizing outside resources. Although not directly instructional in nature, the latter opportunities facilitate the team-building and community involvement that must occur if secondary instruction of special students is to achieve the desired outcomes.

Study and Discussion Questions

1. Describe the varied types of transitions that all individuals typically make throughout life and the potential impact of learning and behavior problems on the nature of those transitions.
2. Describe a range of instructional and curricular models and strategies that support successful transitions throughout a student's school life.
3. Describe critical partners in the transition process and strategies for engaging them.
4. Interview an older friend or relative to determine the progression of his or her life tasks. Which transitions were most problematic during school? After school? What kinds of supports were available and helpful, if any?

5. Apply your own vocational development to Super's theory. Outline specific events and activities in your life for each of the substages. How closely did you follow the same progression? What differences have you experienced from Super's model? What differences might exist for those with learning or behavior problems?

6. Describe the in-school resources required to serve students with learning and behavior problems at the middle or high school you attended. What do you remember as being available? Where would you need to go to get the necessary supports?

7. Describe at least two instructional strategies and two curricular models that would be important to include in a comprehensive transition education program at each level (elementary moving to middle school, middle school to high school, high school to adulthood.)

8. Give five examples of community resources that would be critical in a transition education program in a high school or adult setting (eg., people, things, events, etc.). Describe your plan for getting those resources involved.

9. Generate an approach for getting several of your secondary students' parents committed to your transitional program. What do you see as your biggest hurdle? What are possible solutions to that barrier?

10. Imagine that your superintendent has just given you the task of improving collaboration between vocational and special educators in your district. What would you do?

References and Suggested Readings

Hasazi, S. B., Gordon, L. R., & Roe, C. A. (1985). Factors associated with the employment status of handicapped youth exiting high school. *Exceptional Children, 51,* 455–469.

Mithaug, D. E., Horiuchi, C. N., & Fanning, P. N. (1985). A report of the Colorado follow-up survey of special education students. *Exceptional Children, 51,* 397–404.

Sitlington, P., Frank, A., & Carson, R. (1990). *Iowa statewide follow-up study: Adult adjustment of individuals with mild disabilities one year after leaving school.* Des Moines: Iowa Department of Education.

Vocational Committee Survey. (1982). *Association for Children and Adults with Learning Disabilities Newsbriefs* (pp. 20–23).

Weicker, L. P., Jr. (1987). A look at policy and its effect on special education and vocational rehabilitation services. *Career Development for Exceptional Individuals, 10,* 6–9.

White, S. (1987). Least restrictive environment: The challenge to special education. *Career Development for Exceptional Individuals, 10,* 33–41.

White, W. J., Alley, G. R., Deshler, D. D., Schumaker, J. B., Warner, M. M., & Clark, F. L. (1982). Are there learning disabilities after high school? *Exceptional Children, 49,* 273–274.

Types of Transitions
School and Life Stages
Aslanian, C. B., & Brickell, H. M. (1980). *Americans in transition: Life changes as reasons for learning.* New York: College Entrance Examination Board.

Blalock, G., & Dixon, N. (1982). Improving prospects for the college-bound learning disabled. *Topics in Learning and Learning Disabilities, 2,* 69–78.

Bova, B. (1979). *Motivational orientation of adult learners in credit and non-credit classes at the University of New Mexico and Albuquerque Technical-Vocational Institute.* Unpublished doctoral dissertation, University of New Mexico.

Clark, G. M., & Kolstoe, O. P. (1995). *Career development and transition education for adolescents with disabilities* (2nd ed.). Boston: Allyn & Bacon.

Cronin, M. E., & Gerber, P. J. (1982). Preparing the learning disabled adolescent for adulthood. *Topics in Learning and Learning Disabilities, 2,* 55–68.

Cullinan, D., & Epstein, M. H. (1979). *Special education for adolescents: Issues and perspectives.* Columbus, OH: Merrill.

D'Alonzo, B. J., Arnold, B. J., & Yuen, P. C. (1986). Teaching adolescents with learning and behavioral differences. In L. F. Masters & A. A. Mori (Eds.), *Teaching secondary students with mild learning and behavior problems: Methods, materials, strategies.* Rockville, MD: Aspen.

Gerber, P. J., & Reiff, H. B. (1994). *Learning disabilities in adulthood: Persisting problems and evolving issues.* Boston: Andover.

Ginzberg, E. (1952). Toward a theory of occupational choice. *Personnel and Guidance Journal, 30,* 491–494.

Hasazi, S. B., Gordon, L. R., & Roe, C. A. (1985). Factors associated with the employment status of handicapped youth exiting high school. *Exceptional Children, 51,* 455–469.

Havighurst, R. J. (1972). *Development tasks and education* (3rd. ed.). New York: McKay.

Johnson, D. J., & Blalock, J. W. (Eds.). (1987). *Adults with learning disabilities: Clinical studies.* Orlando, FL: Grune and Stratton.

Knowles, M. (1979). *The adult learner: The neglected species* (2nd ed.). Houston: Gulf.

Levinson, D. J. (1978). *The seasons of a man's life.* New York: Knopf.

Masters, L. F., Mori, B. A., & Mori, A. A. (1993). *Teaching secondary students with mild learning and behavior problems: Methods, materials, strategies* (2nd ed.). Austin, TX: PRO-ED.

Mithaug, D. E., Horiuchi, C. N., & Fanning, P. N. (1985). A report of the Colorado follow-up survey of special education students. *Exceptional Children, 51,* 397–404.

Polloway, E. A., Schewel, R., & Patton, J. R. (1992). Learning disabilities in adulthood: Personal perspectives. *Journal of Learning Disabilities, 25,* 520–522.

Sitlington, P., Frank, A., & Carson, R. (1990). *Iowa statewide follow-up study: Adult adjustment of individuals with mild disabilities one year after leaving school.* Des Moines: Iowa Department of Education.

Super, D. E. (1953). A theory of vocational development. *American Psychologist, 8,* 185–190.

Vocational Committee Survey. (1982). *Association for Children and Adults with Learning Disabilities Newsbriefs* (pp. 20–23).

White, W. J., Alley, G. R., Deshler, D. D., Schumaker, J. B., Warner, M. M., & Clark, F. L. (1982). Are there learning disabilities after high school? *Exceptional Children, 49,* 273–274.

York, J., Doyle, M. B., & Kronberg, R. (1992). A curriculum development process for inclusive classrooms. *Focus on Exceptional Children, 25*(4), 1–16.

Adolescents and Adults with Learning or Behavior Problems

Gerber, P. J., & Reiff, H. B. (1994). *Learning disabilities in adulthood: Persisting problems and evolving issues.* Boston: Andover.

Johnson, D. J., & Blalock, J. W. (Eds.). (1987). *Adults with learning disabilities: Clinical studies.* Orlando, FL: Grune and Stratton.

Masters, L. F., Mori, B. A., & Mori, A. A. (1993). *Teaching secondary students with mild learning and behavior problems: Methods, materials, strategies* (2nd ed.). Austin, TX: PRO-ED.

Polloway, E. A., Schewel, R., & Patton, J. R. (1992). Learning disabilities in adulthood: Personal perspectives. *Journal of Learning Disabilities, 25,* 520–522.

Focus on Diversity

Artiles, A., & Trent, S. (1994). Overrepresentation of minority students in special education: A continuing debate. *The Journal of Special Education, 27*(4), 410–437.

Baca, L. M., & Cervantes, H. T. (1986). *The bilingual special education interface.* Columbus, OH: Merrill.

Cegelka, P. T., MacDonald, M., & Gaeta, R. (1987). Promising programs: Bilingual special education. *Teaching Exceptional Children, 20,* 48–50.

Chinn, P. C., & Hughes, S. (1987). Representation of minority students in special education classes. *Remedial and Special Education, 8*(4), 41–46.

Gonzales, E. (1989). Issues in the assessment of minorities. In H. L. Swanson and B. Watson (Eds.), *Educational and psychological assessment of exceptional children: Theories, strategies, and applications* (pp. 383–402). Columbus, OH: Merrill.

Institute on Rehabilitation Issues. (1992, October). *Report from the Study Group on Cultural Diversity in Rehabilitation.* Proceedings of the 19th Institute on Rehabilitation Issues. Fayetteville: University of Arkansas and Arkansas Rehabilitation Services, Arkansas Research & Training Center in Vocational Rehabilitation.

Lara, J. (1994). *State data collection and monitoring procedures regarding overrepresentation of minority students in special education. Project FORUM* (Contract No. HS92015001). Alexandria, VA: National Association of State Directors of Special Education.

Smith, D. D., & Luckasson, R. (1995). *Introduction to special education—Teaching in an age of challenge (2nd ed.).* Boston: Allyn & Bacon.

U.S. Bureau of Census. (1992). *Current Population Reports* Series P-20 (Nos. 13 & 474). Washington, DC: Author.

U.S. Bureau of Justice. (1992). Statistical abstracts. Washington, DC: Author.

Outcome Options

Schloss, P. J., Smith. M. A., & Schloss, C. N. (1995). *Instructional methods for adolescents with learning and behavior problems* (2nd ed.). Boston: Allyn & Bacon.

Transition Models

Clark, G. M., & Kolstoe, O. P. (1995). *Career development and transition education for adolescents with disabilities* (2nd ed.). Boston: Allyn & Bacon.

Halpern, A. S. (1985). Transition: A look at the foundations. *Exceptional Children, 51,* 479–485.

Halpern, A. S. (1994). The transition of youth with disabilities to adult life: A position statement of the Division on Career Development and Transition, Council for Exceptional Children. *Career Development for Exceptional Individuals, 17*(2), 115–124.

Ianacone, R. N. (1937, April). Introduction: Expanding the definition of transition. In R. N. Ianacone (Chair), *Next steps: A continuum of transitional training and service.* Paper presented at the International Conference of the Council for Exceptional Children, Chicago.

New Mexico State Board of Education and State Department of Education. (1992). *New Mexico's education system for employability.* Sante Fe: Author.

Rusch, F. R., Mithaug, D. E., & Flexer, R. W. (1986). Obstacles to competitive employment and traditional program options for overcoming them. In F. R. Rusch (Ed.), *Competitive employment issues and strategies.* Baltimore: Brookes.

Super, D. E. (1953). A theory of vocational development. *American Psychologist, 8,* 185–190.

White, S. (1987). Least restrictive environment: The challenge to special education. *Career Development for Exceptional Individuals, 10,* 33–41.

Instructional and Curricular Models and Strategies

Blalock, G. (1988). Transitions across the life cycle. In B. Ludlow, R. Luckasson, & A. Turnbull (Eds.), *Transitions to adult life for persons with mental retardation: Principles and practices.* Baltimore: Brookes.

Blalock, G. (1996). Transition of youth with learning disabilities to early adulthood. In J. R. Patton & E. A. Polloway (Eds.), *Learning Disabilities: The challenges of adulthood* (pp. 25–44). Austin, TX: PRO-ED.

Blalock, G., Brito, C., Chenault, B., Detwiler, B., Hessmiller, R., Husted, D., Oney, D., Putnam, P., & Van Dyke, R. (1994). *Life span transition planning in New Mexico: A technical assistance document.* Sante Fe: New Mexico State Department of Education.

Brolin, D. E. (1985). Preparing handicapped students to be productive adults. *Techniques, 1,* 447–454.

Brolin, D. E. (1991). *Life-centered career education model.* Reston, VA: Council for Exceptional Children.

Ceres Unified School District (1988). *Career education responsive to every student (CERES) curriculum.* Ceres, CA: Author.

Clark, G. M., & Kolstoe, O. P. (1995). *Career development and transition education for adolescents with disabilities* (2nd ed.). Boston: Allyn & Bacon.

Cronin, M. E. (in press). Life skills curriculum for students with learning disabilities: A review of the literature. *Journal of Learning Disabilities.*

Cronin, M. E., & Patton, J. R. (1993). *Life skills instruction for all students with special needs: A practical guide for integrating real-life content into the curriculum.* Austin, TX: PRO-ED.

Deshler, D. D., Lowrey, N., & Alley, G. R. (1979). Programming alternatives for learning disabled adolescents: A nationwide study. *Academic Therapy, 14,* 54–63.

Field, S. (1996). Self-determination instructional strategies for youth with learning disabilities. *Journal of Learning Disabilities, 29*(1), 40–52.

Greenan, J. P. (1982). Problems and issues in delivering vocational education instruction and support services to students with learning disabilities. *Journal of Learning Disabilities, 15,* 231–235.

Halpern, A. S. (1985). Transition: A look at the foundations. *Exceptional Children, 51,* 479–485.

Halpern, A. S. (1994). The transition of youth with disabilities to adult life: A position statement of the Division on Career Development and Transition, The Council for Exceptional Children. *Career Development for Exceptional Individuals, 17*(2), 115–124.

Hunt, P. (1995, Summer). Collaboration: What does it take? *What's Working: Transition in Minnesota.* Minneapolis: University of Minnesota Institute on Community Integration.

Husted, D. (1992). *Parent involvement in the transition process.* Paper presented at the University of New Mexico, Albuquerque.

Ianacone, R. N. (1987, April). Introduction: Expanding the definition of transition. In R. N. Ianacone (Chair), *Next steps: A continuum of transitional training and services.* Paper presented at the International Conference of the Council for Exceptional Children, Chicago.

Knapp, R. R., & Knapp, L. (1981). *COPS II Interest Inventory.* San Diego, CA: EDITS Corp.

Marshall, D. (1992). Making a smooth transition to high school. *Middle School Journal, 24,* 27–28.

National Joint Committee on Learning Disabilities. (1987). Adults with learning disabilities: A call to action. *Journal of Learning Disabilities, 20,* 172–175.

New Mexico State Board of Education and State Department of Education. (1992). *New Mexico's education system for employability.* Sante Fe: Author.

Renzaglia, A., Bates, P., & Hutchins, M. (1981). Vocational skills instruction for handicapped adolescents and adults. *Exceptional Education Quarterly, 3*(3), 61–73.

Rossi, K. D., & Stokes, D. A. (1991). *Easing the transition from the middle level to the high school.* Report to the National Association of Secondary Principals, Reston, VA.

Rusch, F. R., Mithaug, D. E., & Flexer, R. W. (1986). Obstacles to competitive employment and traditional program options for overcoming them. In F. R. Rusch (Ed.), *Competitive employment issues and strategies.* Baltimore: Brookes.

Schloss, P. J., Smith, M. A., & Schloss, C. N. (1995). *Instructional methods for adolescents with learning and behavior problems* (2nd ed.). Boston: Allyn & Bacon.

Serna, L. A., & Lau-Smith, J. (1995). *Learning with PURPOSE: An instructor's manual for teaching self-determination skills to students who are at-risk for failure.* Honolulu: University of Hawaii Department of Special Education and Hawaii University Affiliated Programs.

Siegel, S., Robert, M., Greener, K., Meyer, G., Halloran, W., & Gaylord-Ross, R. (1993). *Career ladders for challenged youths in transition from school to adult life.* Austin, TX: PRO-ED.

Super, D. E. (1953). A theory of vocational development. *American Psychologist, 8,* 185–190.

Toliver, L. T. (1995). *Transition to high school.* Paper presented to Secondary Special Education Methods and Materials class, University of New Mexico.

Van Reusen, A. K., Bos, C. S., Schumaker, J. B., & Deshler, D. D. (1994). *The self-advocacy strategy for education and transition planning: Preparing students to advocate at education and transition conferences.* Lawrence, KS: Edge Enterprises.

University of New Mexico Special Education 542, Teaching Persons with Learning Disabilities, Spring 1995.

University of New Mexico Special Education 593, Career/Life Skills Preparation of Special Needs Learners, Spring 1990.

Weicker, L. P., Jr. (1987). A look at policy and its effect on special education and vocational rehabilitation services. *Career Development for Exceptional Individuals, 10,* 6–9.

White, S. (1987). Least restrictive environment: The challenge to special education. *Career Development for Exceptional Individuals, 10,* 33–41.

York, J., Doyle, M. B., & Kronberg, R. (1992). A curriculum development process for inclusive classrooms. *Focus on Exceptional Children, 25*(4), 1–16.

Partnerships in Transition

Barbaro, F. (1982). The learning disabled college student: Some considerations . . . setting objectives. *Journal of Learning Disabilities, 15,* 599–603.

Blalock, G., Brito, C., Chenault, B., Detwiler, B., Hessmiller, R., Husted, D., Oney, D., Putnam, P., & Van Dyke, R. (1994). *Life span transition planning in New Mexico: A technical assistance document.* Sante Fe: New Mexico State Department of Education.

Blalock, G., & Dixon, N. (1982). Improving prospects for the college-bound learning disabled. *Topics in Learning and Learning Disabilities, 2,* 69–78.

Goldberg, D., & Goldberg, M. (1993). *The Americans with Disabilities Act: A guide for people with disabilities, their families, and advocates.* Minneapolis, MN: PACER Center.

Husted, D. (1992). *Parent involvement in the transition process.* Paper presented at the University of New Mexico, Albuquerque.

Johnson, D. R., Bruininks, R. H., & Thurlow, M. L. (1987). Meeting the challenge of transition service planning through improved interagency cooperation. *Exceptional Children, 53,* 522–530.

Kokaska, C. J., & Hughes, C. M. (1985). Perspectives: Position statement on career development. *Career Development for Exceptional Individuals, 8,* 125–129.

Sitlington, P. L. (1996). Transition to living: The neglected component of transition programming for individuals with learning disabilities. *Journal of Learning Disabilities, 29*(1), 31–39, 52.

Stodden, R. A., & Boone, R. (1987). Assessing transition services for handicapped youth: A cooperative interagency approach. *Exceptional Children, 53,* 537–545.

Glossary

academic learning time   the amount of time students are on-task in a learning situation

academic skills   skills that relate to the school's curriculum, involving reading, mathematics, and written communication

accommodation   changes in schemata to extend or modify current assimilated understandings resulting from an inability to make sense of current situations

active engagement   having students be highly involved in learning, by writing or speaking, as opposed to receiving knowledge passively by listening or reading

active listening   demonstrating verbal and nonverbal behaviors that tell the speaker his or her message is being received by the listener

acuity evaluations   testing of vision or hearing to determine how well an individual sees at various distances or hears at various levels

adaptive instruction   changes made to instructional procedures, curriculum, management, materials, or the physical environment to foster successful learning

advance organizer   the opening step of the lesson in which teachers tell students the purpose and objective of the lesson and provide a short review of previously presented material

aim scores   criterion levels or performance standards

allocated time   the amount of time scheduled during the school day or year for various content areas and types of instruction

Americans with Disabilities Act (ADA)   federal disability antidiscrimination legislation passed in 1990

analysis of services step   the step in the IEP process in which the special services committee decides, based on assessment information, which related services best serve the needs of students identified as having a disability

anchoring   strategy training based on specific domains or content areas

anecdotal logs   regularly kept notes of a student's academic, social, or behavior progress

annual goals   broad academic, social, or behavioral statements documenting general areas in need of instruction as designated on the IEP, IFSP, or ITP

antecedent behavior consequence (ABC) analysis   a log in which behaviors of concern are documented, including the events that occur before and after them

antecedent event   something that occurs prior to the target behavior that may influence the behavior

applied academics   awarding academic credits to applied coursework, often vocational education courses

applied behavioral analysis   the study of observable problems in how individuals interact with their environments in natural settings

apprenticeship programs   formal training programs, traditionally at the post–high school level, approved through the State Department of Labor, that allow trainees to study under master tradespersons to learn a particular trade; often requires a few years to advance through all the stages

array of services   a constellation of services, personnel, and educational placements from which a program of services can be developed

assertive behaviors   letting individuals know about one's wants and needs to accomplish tasks; stating one's needs directly and using nonverbal behavior to reinforce one's messages

assessment step   the step of the IEP process in which formal testing occurs to determine the presence of a disability, current levels of performance, and strengths and weaknesses

assimilation   the process of interpreting and reconstructing experiences and information in relation to present knowledge

assistive technology devices   devices that help students with disabilities in their daily lives; they include tape recorders, computers, pencil grips, wheelchairs, and a wide array of equipment

assistive technology services   assistance provided to individuals with disabilities to secure the appropriate types of assistive technology devices needed to compensate for their disabilities; services might include funding resources, assessment, and counseling

attention   the act of concentrating on a task or the features of a task for an appropriate amount of time

attribution   internal justification that individuals devise to explain their success or failure at a task

authentic assessment   informal assessment that tests students' progress by using a variety of measures, such as videotapes, drawings, speeches, and verbal explanations

automaticity   being able to perform a skill fluently

basal textbooks   books adopted by school districts to serve as a primary source of curricular content for subject areas

baseline   the phase in which data are collected for at least three days on the targeted instructional objective with no teaching occurring

basic skills remediation   instructional approach that aims to teach basic reading, writing, and mathematical skills through direct instruction, often without natural or applied contexts

behavioral instructional approach   an approach to teaching that is based on the principles of applied behavior analysis and that involves the manipulation of antecedent and consequent events to modify behaviors

behavioral management   the implementation of procedures that are designed to increase appropriate and to decrease inappropriate student behaviors

behavioral manager   one whose classroom behavior is usually appropriate and who has earned the privilege of dispensing praise and rewards to a peer

big ideas   central concepts that consist of smaller, subordinate concepts

bilingual transitional program instructional programs taught in the native language and in English to continue academic development of the first language and allow easier acquisition of English

career awareness the initial stage of career development, usually covering the elementary years; signifies a planned program over time that allows students to learn about the world of work, its relationship to learning and school, and a broad range of occupations

career education the final stage of career development, at the high school and postsecondary levels, when specific occupational skills are developed through vocational-technical coursework and work experiences

career exploration the middle stage of career development, typically the middle school or junior high years; involves systematic opportunities for students to learn more about expectations for employment in general and in specific occupations through field trips, vocational education classes, guest speakers, job shadowing, and other experiences

career skills tasks that students need to be successful in various employment positions

categorization a cognitive strategy to organize information into meaningful clusters to assist in memorization, retention, and retrieval

central tendency average score for a set of data

check for understanding techniques used during instruction to determine if students comprehend the skill being taught

closure the instructional step at the end of each lesson in which students or teachers review the lesson's content, summarize, and discuss the following day's related lesson

coaching working with a peer to teach new skills and to support the implementation of the skills

code emphasis direct instruction in phonological processing

cognitive strategies behaviors that influence how information is processed

collaboration professionals, family members, and paraprofessionals working cooperatively to provide educational services

collaborative consultation an interactive process that enables groups of people with diverse experience to generate solutions to mutually defined problems

community-based instruction (CBI) a service delivery model in which skills are initially taught in the classroom, but are practiced and refined in natural settings to enhance generalization of learned skills

compensatory instruction techniques taught to students to enable them to circumvent their disability and access their environments more readily

compensatory or content-equivalent approach instructional approach through which targeted concepts and skills taught to all students are acquired through nontraditional means (e.g., audiovisual materials, hands-on projects, technology)

computer-assisted instruction (CAI) using the computer or software to supplement the teaching of an instructional objective; CAI can be used in various teacher- or student-mediated instructional arrangements

concurrent enrollment a common element of Tech Prep agreements between a college and a high school whereby students can earn simultaneous credit at both levels

conflict a disagreement of interests or ideas

consequent events something that occurs after the target behavior that may influence the behavior

contingent instructions after an occurrence of the behavior, the teacher quietly and on a one-to-one basis tells the student not to engage in that behavior

contingent observation removing a disruptive student from a group activity, but still allowing the student to observe the proceedings

continuum of services a graduated range of educational services; one level of services leads directly to the next one

cooperative consultation a collaborative process between special and general education teachers that involves examining instructional expectations, identifying problems, generating alternative interventions, and monitoring process

cooperative learning an instructional arrangement consisting of heterogeneous groups of students who work together to complete tasks (student-mediated instructional arrangement)

corrective feedback contingent on student incorrect response, teacher may prompt or tell student correct response; student then repeats correct response

criterion-referenced tests informal assessment that measures student performance on specific skills in relation to a set level of mastery

criterion-specific rewards the student earns a special privilege only for reaching the desired performance standard for the instructional objective

cueing movement (teacher points to correct response), position (the correct response is closest to the student), and redundancy (the correct response is obvious) hints to help a student make the correct response

cumulative review review of skills taught

current levels of performance statements of a student's academic, social, and behavioral strengths and weaknesses

curriculum a school's program of studies

curriculum-based assessment (CBA) a method of evaluating and monitoring students' performance by regularly collecting data on their progress

curriculum guide a resource containing a scope and sequence of skills and concepts to be taught for a content area (reading, language arts, mathematics, science)

data calculations and analyses   mean scores and trends used to analyze student performance on a regular basis and to decide if progress is occurring

data collection systems   measurements that can be used to assess student performance

data displays   graphic illustrations of student data

decision-making abilities   knowing how to perceive situations, consider possible actions with their consequences, and make a decision based on available information, knowledge, and experiences

decoding skills   the ability to convert letter combinations into words

dependent group contingency   when a student earns privileges or rewards for peers by behaving appropriately

desired rates   aim scores or levels of mastery of learning tasks

direct instruction   a systematic approach to instructional and curricular design and classroom management

distributed practice   opportunities to practice a mastered or nearly mastered skill along with other skills

drill   practice on skills to foster mastery

due process hearings   a noncourt proceeding before an impartial hearing officer that can be used if parents and school personnel disagree on a special education issue

educational software   computer programs that present information to foster learning

employability skills   work-related behaviors, such as dependability, following instruction, social skills, initiative, asking for help, punctuality, task completion, critical thinking

environmental restructuring   when the class is reinforced for encouraging a classmate's appropriate behavior

error analysis   careful examination of a student's errors in academic, social, and behavioral skills to determine the source of errors for remedial purposes

error correction   providing the correct answer when the student's response is incorrect

evaluation   the instructional step in which teachers monitor student performance and make decisions about the lesson's effectiveness

exclusion   removing a student from class as a punishment for undesirable behavior

exclusion time-out   when the student is excused from class upon substantial disruption

explicit strategies   techniques to solve problems that can be used across domains

expulsion exclusion   removal of a student from school either permanently or for an indefinite time, usually exceeding 10 school days

feedback   informing students about the accuracy of their responses and providing corrections if necessary

fines   when the student loses privileges for engaging in the target behavior

fixed interval reinforcement schedule   regularly scheduled reinforcement for a selected period of appropriate behavior

fixed ratio schedule of reinforcement   regularly scheduled reinforcement for a specified number of occurrences of the behavior

flow lists   a continuous list of items to be learned that involves adding new items as items on the list are mastered, dropped, and targeted for later maintenance checks

formal assessment   the administration of standardized, norm-referenced tests that yield information about student performance

free appropriate public education (FAPE)   one of the provisions of IDEA that ensures that children and youth with disabilities receive necessary education and services without cost to the family

functional academics   academic skills, such as telling time and counting money, that are necessary in daily living and relate directly to the school's curriculum and the student's IEP

functional approach   an instructional approach or curricular focus, usually aimed at adolescents or at students with more severe disabilities, in which life skills are taught

functional life skills   those skills that individuals must possess to achieve success in daily living activities

functional (vocational) assessment   assessment approach that measures the whole student's functioning, including development in academic/cognitive, social/behavioral, independent living, vocational, and physical/motor areas; vocational and overall life interests are a critical part of functional assessment

generalization   occurrence of a behavior with different people, settings, or materials

general vocabulary   words that are used on a regular basis during conversation

group contingencies   presentation or loss of a reinforcer contingent on the behavior of an individual, a small group, or the whole group

guided practice   the instructional step in which teachers provide students with opportunities to practice the skill or concept under teacher supervision

high-interest/low vocabulary materials   instructional materials that are appropriate for older students in terms of content and graphics but that have lower reading levels so that students with reading disabilities can read the content

holistic/constructivist instructional approach   an approach that emphasizes students' interactive learning to develop meaning based on their knowledge and experiences

hyperactivity   nonpurposeful excessive movement and inability to sustain meaningful attention

identification step   the step in the IEP process in which the special services committee examines all assessment information to reach a decision about the presence or absence of a disability

IEP   *see* Individualized Education Program

IFSP   *see* Individualized Family Service Plan

ignoring   systematically and consistently not paying attention to each occurrence of the target behavior

imagery   a cognitive strategy that involves visualizing information in meaningful pictures to assist in retention, memorization, and retrieval

imitate   having students repeat teacher response as it was modeled

inactive learning   an approach to learning that lacks planning and strategies to engage the learner in the task

inclusion   assuring that all students with disabilities participate with other students in all aspects of school

independent group contingency   when students earn reinforcement for achieving a goal established for the group

independent practice   the instructional step in which students practice a previously taught skill to foster mastery, maintenance, generalization, or adaption

Individualized Education Program (IEP)   a requirement of IDEA that guarantees a specifically tailored program to meet the individual needs of each student with disabilities

Individualized Family Service Plan (IFSP)   a written plan that identifies and organizes services and resources for children under age 3 with special needs and for their families

Individual Transition Plan (ITP)   a statement of the transition services required for coordination and delivery of services as the student moves to adulthood

information processing theory   a theory that emphasizes an understanding of the cognitive and metacognitive strategies used to receive, transform, store, and retrieve information

in-school supervision exclusion   removal of a student from one or more classes while requiring him or her to spend the time in a designated school area

instructional arrangements   teacher- and student-mediated arrangements (such as whole or small-group instruction and peer tutoring or cooperative learning) by which instruction is presented

instructional decision making   the step in the IEP process in which the special services committee determines current levels of academic, social, and behavioral strengths and weaknesses and writes the IEP

instructional language   the language of the curriculum, teacher, and student, which is incorporated into a lesson

instructional management procedures   those procedures that must be infused into a lesson, including managing student behavior, providing effective directions, using attention signals, managing teacher behavior, and making transitions

instructional materials   supplemental aids, such as textbooks, kits, software, and manipulatives, that are used to teach instructional objectives

instructional objectives   specific academic, social, or behavioral statements related to annual goals that detail skills to be taught

instructional plans   lesson plans or units that specify objectives, activities, materials, and time lines

instructional steps   the steps teachers use to teach a lesson, including an advance organizer, presentation of subject matter, guided practice, closure, independent practice, and evaluation

instructional technology   scientific devices that facilitate instruction by offering a means of extending, augmenting, individualizing, and enriching learning

interdependent group contingency   when a class or group earns a special reward because the entire class has met an established goal

intervention conditions   when an intervention is instituted to foster learning and when data are collected regularly using probes

intrinsic reinforcement   the desire to achieve success based on self-satisfaction and internal drive

isolated skills   discrete skills (e.g., specific phonetic sounds, basic facts) that are taught to mastery separate from other skills

ITP   *see* Individual Transition Plan

lead   working with students to generate the correct response by using verbal cues, descriptions, and prompts

learned helplessness   lack of belief in one's abilities that leads to lack of effort

learning centers   a collection of activity-based tasks that reinforce skills; they may be set up in various classroom locations to permit students to work at the centers independently or with peers (student-mediated instructional arrangement)

learning strategies   cognitive strategies or techniques that individuals use to organize, store, and retrieve information

least restrictive environment   one of the principles of IDEA that must be balanced when considering the best educational placement for an individual student with disabilities

level of concern   the students' amount of interest in and motivation for learning the topic being discussed

life skills curricula   curricula and approaches that teach the skills needed to survive in today's world, including basic literacy, employment, community living, social, consumer, citizenship, personal well-being, and leisure or recreation skills

mainstreaming   including students with disabilities in general education classrooms for some or all of their school day

maintenance   the phase of instruction in which the intervention is withdrawn to determine if the student is capable of performing the targeted skill independently

maintenance checks   periodic reviews of previously mastered skills

manipulatives   concrete objects that are used to represent a skill and to provide hands-on instruction

massed practice   opportunities to practice the skill being taught

mastery learning   achieving the designated criterion for success for a skill

match-to-sample   when the correct response is provided with other responses from which the student can choose

meaning vocabulary   words that the reader understands

mechanical skills   written communication skills, including capitalization, punctuation, grammar, and spelling

metacognition   the ability to think about the strategies needed to complete tasks that involve self-regulatory skills

metacognitive strategies   self-regulatory behaviors that help people select, monitor, and revise their approaches to tasks

mnemonics   a memory trick, usually a word in which each letter stands for a specific step and set of instructions for a strategy

modeling   demonstrating the correct response; may involve "think-aloud" procedures to describe thinking processes to generate responses

modem   a computer peripheral that accesses telephone lines to send information from one computer to another

multimedia technology   interactive software that may involve sound, graphics, text, and video and that can be programmed to give learners access to different levels of instruction based on their individual needs

needs assessment   identification of a student's needs through formal or informal measurements or both, for the purposes of planning and evaluation; comprehensive approaches to needs assessment that collect data from all key sources are advocated

nonexample   an example that shows the student what is not desired

noninstructional tasks   classroom routines or activities that are not of an instructional nature but that address management concerns

nonverbal behavior   physical cues or indicators that have communicative meaning

observational measurement systems   systems designed to assess behavior through observation

one-to-one instruction   instruction that the teacher or paraprofessional delivers to one student in need of extra assistance (teacher-mediated instructional arrangement)

operant conditioning theory   a technique that changes behavior through the manipulation of consequent events

overcorrection   a procedure that reduces inappropriate behavior through the use of restitution or positive practices

overlearning   sufficient presentation of a skill beyond mastery

pacing   moving the lesson at an appropriate "speed" so that students remain engaged but do not get lost in instruction

paraprofessionals   individuals who work with teachers in a supportive role

parent action   parents' involvement in the design, implementation, or evaluation of their child's progress

peer management   using peers to promote the occurrence of a targeted behavior

peer tutoring   pairs or small groups of students working together to practice a skill; usually one student is more familiar with the skill and helps the other student(s) with practice and feedback (student-mediated instructional arrangement)

performance standard   a criterion established for skill mastery

phase   a period of time during which data are collected and all factors remain constant

phase change line   a vertical line drawn on a graph between the day of the last phase and the day of the new phase

phonological awareness   the ability to recognize speech sounds and blend them into meaningful units

physical guidance   physically moving the student through the appropriate motions to achieve the target behavior

placement   the step in the IEP process in which the special services committee uses assessment information and knowledge of the disabling condition to decide the most appropriate special education service in the least restrictive environment; parental written permission must be obtained before any special education placement is initiated

portfolio assessment   a compilation of informal (and some formal) assessment measures that document students' progress across a period of time

positive practice overcorrection   extreme practice of the desired forms of the target behavior

posttest   weekly tests administered to determine whether or not the student is maintaining the mastered skill

prebaseline   the assessment phase of instruction when instructional objectives are established for teaching

prereferral step   the step in the IEP process before the referral step; during prereferral, general education teachers provide adapted instruction to determine if student progress is possible

prerequisite skills   knowledge required to do a new task successfully

presentation of subject matter   the instructional step in which teachers define concepts and terms, model correct responses, provide examples and nonexamples, and check for student understanding

primary reinforcer   a reinforcer that is a daily necessity (food, sleep, water)

probes   written or verbal samples of students' abilities on instructional target behaviors

problem solving   identifying, implementing, and evaluating a plan to solve a mutually agreed-upon problem

procedural safeguards   specific legal procedures guaranteed by IDEA to ensure protection of the child and family during the IEP process

program evaluation   the step in the IEP process in which evaluation of student progress, annual review and update of the

IEP goals and objectives, or reevaluation of the student occurs

prompting providing verbal, physical, or written cues to assist students in generating correct responses

punishment applying an aversive event after an undesired behavior occurs

questioning a technique used to tap lower-order (e.g., recall, comprehension) and higher-order (e.g., analysis, synthesis, evaluation) thinking; can be used to check for understanding and to generate discussion

rationales providing reasons for learning specific information

reading comprehension the ability to understand what is read

referral step the step in the IEP process that occurs before assessment; during referral, parents are asked to provide written approval for a comprehensive evaluation of their child to determine reasons for school problems

rehearsal a cognitive strategy that involves the review of steps or information to mastery; may be done verbally

reinforcement techniques that increase the probability that a behavior will recur

reinforcer anything that is desirable to students and that increases the likelihood that they will perform a desired behavior

related services services that the student requires in order to meet his or her individual needs, including speech and language therapy, adapted physical education, special transportation, counseling, physical therapy, and so forth

remedial instruction instruction that focuses on interventions or methods different from those commonly used in the general education setting to teach skills that have been previously introduced but not mastered

requisite abilities skills needed concurrently to perform a difficult skill

response cost *see* fines

restitutional overcorrection when the student destroys or alters environment and must restore it to an improved state as punishment

role taking the ability to take another person's perspective

rules a code of conduct determined by the entire class (teacher and pupils) for all to follow

scaffolded instruction teacher support and guidance that promotes an understanding and completion of tasks; the metaphor of a "scaffold" can be used to explain this concept

scope and sequence the instructional objectives and skills found in a curriculum

seclusion time-out when the pupil is placed in an isolation room for severe, out-of-control behavior

secondary reinforcer a reinforcer whose value students must come to learn

self-checking/self-correction a metacognitive strategy in which individuals monitor their own performance to ensure comprehension of a task

self-determination the ability to identify and act upon one's own life goals

self-evaluation when students correct their own performances, recording the frequency, and graphing the resulting data

self-graphing when students graph their own data

self-management skills such as self-evaluating, self-questioning, and self-regulating that prompt an individual to take a more active role in the learning process and that thereby promote successful learning

self-monitoring a metacognitive strategy in which students regulate their own behavior by using checking and questioning progress

self-questioning a metacognitive strategy in which individuals ask themselves specific questions to see if they have understood a task

self-recording *see* self-monitoring

self-regulation when individuals monitor their own behavior, seeking to avoid those situations that precipitate inappropriate behavior, and stopping that behavior if it is initiated

self-reinforcement when students reward themselves for correct behavior

self-reporting when students report their progress to the teacher

setting demands the characteristics of the learning environment and teachers' expectations for student behavior and performance

shaping reinforcing successive approximations of the desired behavior

signals visual, auditory, or verbal cues to gain students' attention before beginning a lesson or giving directions

small-group instruction instruction that the teacher or paraprofessional delivers to groups of students who usually perform at a similar academic level (teacher-mediated instructional arrangement)

social cognition the ability to gather information from the social setting, process the information, and plan a course of action

social competence knowledge about and appropriate application of social cognition, social interaction, social effectiveness, and decision-making skills

social comprehension understanding social situations and being able to initiate appropriate, positive actions

social constructivist learning theory a theory of learning that views the student's social interactions as crucial for developing an understanding of their environment; focuses on teacher guidance, support, and questioning to promote assimilation of new information

social effectiveness the student's ability to be accepted by peers and others

social interaction the ability to perceive social situations correctly and to initiate appropriate verbal and nonverbal communication skills

social reinforcement   reinforcement from peers and adults

social skills   skills individuals need to promote effective interpersonal, behavioral, and nonverbal relationships

specialized vocabulary   words that have multiple meanings depending on the context

special services committee   a group of professionals (counselor, nurse, principal, teachers, speech and language pathologist) who collaboratively problem-solve the specific needs of individual students

specific praise   stating and describing the behavior that has been performed appropriately, rather than saying "good job" or "well done"

speech and language pathologist   a professional with expertise in the areas of speech and language development who works with students in clinical settings and in classrooms

speech synthesizers   computer hardware devices that convert words on the computer monitor to speech that is heard by the user

spiral curriculum   skills and concepts presented in basal textbooks in increasingly more depth with each grade level

stages of learning   levels of learning through which learners pass, leading to skill mastery and application; the stages include acquisition, proficiency, maintenance, generalization, and adaption

strategic instructional approach   an approach that emphasizes teaching specific cognitive and metacognitive strategies to students

study skills instruction   an instructional approach that teaches study skills that apply across content areas, such as outlining, note taking, test taking, or organizational skills

suspension exclusion   the removal of an individual from school for a specified number of days, usually not longer than 10 school days

target behavior   specific instructional objective to be taught

task analysis   a sequenced set of instructional objectives for a specific skill

task structure   in cooperative learning, ways that task responsibilities are presented to foster interdependent group learning

teacher proximity   teachers standing near a student or in a specific location to decrease the likelihood of behavioral problems

teacher-scripted instructions   lessons that contain specific instructional scripts for content presentation

technical vocabulary   words used in a particular content area

telling   stating to the student what behavior is desired

theme-based integrated curriculum   a unit of study based on a topic in which skills from various curricular areas are taught together

thinking aloud   saying aloud the specific steps used to solve any problem

time delay   presenting a question or problem to the student and allowing a specified amount of time to pass for the student to respond, if there is no response the teacher gives the answer

time-out   removing a student from an escalating situation to allow time to "cool off"

transition (activity)   passage from one life stage to the next; a coordinated educational program leading to a desired outcome; movement from one service system to another; taking on adult roles

transition (life)   movement from preschool to kindergarten, elementary to middle school, middle school to high school, and high school to adulthood

trend lines   slope lines that demonstrate the direction of the data set

tutorial approach   an instructional approach involving one-on-one support that helps students acquire mainstream concepts and skills or complete general education assignments or exams

tutorial instruction   short-term instruction on a specific skill to assist the student in achieving mastery

variable interval schedule   variably scheduled reinforcement contingent on the passage of variable time periods

variable ratio schedule of reinforcement   variably scheduled reinforcement for a variable number of occurrences of a behavior

varying stimulus conditions   providing different instructional factors in which students must apply their learning

verbal rehearsal   a cognitive strategy that involves repeating information orally to achieve mastery

vocational education   a major category of instructional programming at the secondary and postsecondary levels that offers broad career exploration and education experiences as well as specific skill development in an array of occupations

wait time   the period that elapses after the teacher asks a question or calls on a student to answer a question and before the teacher requests a response; usually three to four seconds

whole-group instruction   instruction that the teacher delivers to the entire class (teacher-mediated instructional arrangement)

with-it-ness   teachers' ability to be aware of all activity in their classrooms at all times

word recognition   the ability to say a word when it is presented in isolation or in context

Author Index

Forness, S. R., 21
Forsberg, H., 269
Fortner, V. L., 324, 347
Foss, G., 240
Foster, K., 346
Fowler, L., 90, 113
Fowler, S. A., 218
Fox, R., 216
Foxx, R. M., 219, 241
Fradd, S., 48
Frame, R. E., 59, 71
Frank, A. R., 84, 112, 415, 446
Freeman, T. J., 290
Friend, M., 25, 27, 47
Friend, P., 85, 112, 207, 218
Frith, G. H., 392
Fry, E. B., 283
Fuchs, D., 3, 19, 47, 71, 94, 113, 131, 155, 187
Fuchs, L. S., 3, 19, 47, 59, 71, 88, 94, 113, 131, 155, 187
Fulk, B. J. M., 332, 346, 406
Fulton, R., 59, 71

Gable, R. A., 216
Gaeta, R., 421, 447
Gallagher, P. A., 217
Garcia, S. B., 47
Garnett, K., 11, 21, 85, 111, 112, 154, 349, 388, 390
Gast, D. L., 117, 118, 154, 198, 213, 217, 219, 391
Gatlin, D., 239
Gaylord-Ross, R., 439, 448
Gerber, M. M., 218, 318, 323, 336, 346, 347
Gerber, P. J., 418, 446
Gersten, R., 91, 113, 119, 126, 130, 154, 155, 292, 381, 389, 390
Gettinger, M., 346
Gilman, S., 187
Gilstrap, R., 333, 346
Ginzberg, E., 417, 446
Glover, J. A., 347
Goin, L. I., 79, 111, 154
Goldberg, D., 444, 449
Goldberg, J., 444, 449
Golden, N., 112, 224, 228, 239, 240
Goldman, S. R., 356, 389
Goldman, T., 398
Goldsmith, L., 216
Goldstein, P., 88, 89, 112
Goodman, K. S., 273
Goodman, Y. M., 273
Gordon, B., 217
Gordon, J., 332, 346
Gordon, L. R., 415, 446
Gordon, T., 42, 48

Graden, J., 16, 21, 24, 47
Graham, S., 89, 113, 310, 311, 312, 313, 322, 324, 331, 333, 337, 342, 344, 345, 346, 347, 348, 390
Graves, A. W., 11, 21, 310, 323, 336, 345, 346, 347, 348
Graves, D., 323, 347
Greener, J., 16, 21, 216
Greener, K., 439, 448
Greeno, J. G., 391
Greenwood, C. R., 94, 113
Gregg, S. L., 310, 322, 345, 347, 348
Gresham, F. M., 222, 232, 233, 238, 240, 241
Grimes, L., 6, 20
Gromoll, E. W., 90, 112
Gruenewald, L. J., 137, 139, 155
Gunn, B., 291
Guralnik, D. B., 44, 48
Guzak, F., 284

Haager, D., 10, 20, 221, 222, 224, 225, 238, 239
Hale, R. L., 141, 156
Hall, J. K., 348
Hall, R. J., 318, 346
Hall, R. V., 94, 95, 113, 205, 208, 216, 217, 218, 346
Hallahan, D. P., 61, 72, 208, 218, 346
Halloran, W., 439, 448
Halpern, A. S., 424, 447
Hamblin, R. L., 9, 20
Hamlett, C. L., 71, 131, 155, 187
Hammill, D. D., 57, 282
Hanley, T. V., 156
Hansen, C. L., 330, 331, 346
Harriman, N. E., 141, 156
Harris, A. J., 272
Harris, C. A., 351, 388
Harris, C. D., 156
Harris, F. R., 216
Harris, K. C., 43, 44, 45, 46, 47, 48, 311, 312, 322, 324, 337, 345, 346, 347, 348, 390
Harry, B., 48
Hart, B. M., 196, 216
Hart-Hester, S., 12, 21
Harter, S., 239
Hartman, D. K., 90, 112
Hasazi, J. E., 318, 346
Hasazi, S. B., 415, 446
Hasazi, S. E., 318, 346
Hass, K., 346
Hasselbring, T. S., 79, 111, 154
Hathaway, R., 347
Haussman, S., 219
Havertape, J. F., 259

Havighurst, R. J., 417, 447
Hayes, J. R., 323, 347
Hayward, L. R., 348
Hazel, J. S., 4, 84, 112, 220, 225, 226, 228, 234, 238, 239, 240, 241
Heller, H. W., 3, 19, 21, 141, 156
Heller, J. I., 391
Henderson, L. M., 347
Hendrickson, J. M., 129, 155, 216
Herman, J. L., 185, 187
Heron, T. E., 43, 44, 45, 47, 48, 92, 94, 113
Herzog, A., 20
Hessmiller, R., 429, 442, 448, 449
Heward, W. L., 94, 113
Hildreth, G. H., 317, 346
Hill, D. S., 94, 113
Hinshelwood, J., 276
Hipp, K., 348
Hoffman, A., 228, 239, 240
Hoffman, P., 34, 48
Hofmeister, A. M., 351, 388
Hogan, A., 239
Hollinger, J. D., 238
Hollingsworth, M., 154
Holmes, D. L., 112, 224, 228, 239, 240
Holubec, E., 95, 113
Honsaker, M. S., 217
Hoover, J. J., 124, 155, 399, 401
Hopkins, B. L., 78, 111
Horiuchi, C. N., 415, 446
Horn, E., 333, 346
Horton, S., 302
Horvath, M., 11, 21
Hourcade, J. J., 27, 47
Houser, J. E., 205, 218
Hudson, F., 24
Hudson, P. J., 21, 48, 308
Huey, E. B., 268
Hughes, C., 269
Hughes, C. A., 5, 19, 207, 218, 346, 407
Hughes, J., 409, 411
Huhn, R. H., 285
Hume, J., 387, 390
Husterd, D., 429, 442, 443, 448, 449
Hutchins, M., 439, 448
Hutchinson, N. L., 351, 388, 391
Hutchinson, R. M., 271

Ianacone, R. N., 72, 221, 238, 422, 447
Idol, L., 22, 24, 25, 42, 43, 45, 47, 48, 53, 71, 78, 111, 293, 294, 295
Irvin, L. K., 240
Ivancic, M. T., 217, 219

Jackson, S. C., 239
Jacobs, J. E., 247

Subject Index